Cisco CallManager Best Practices

Salvatore Collora, CCIE No. 4321
Ed Leonhardt, CCIE No. 3264
Anne Smith

Contributing authors: Dave Corley

Stefano Giorcelli

Scott Keagy

Jeff Knight

Michael Purcell

Cisco Press

Cisco Press
800 East 96th Street
Indianapolis, IN 46240 USA

Cisco CallManager Best Practices

Salvatore Collora

Ed Leonhardt

Anne Smith

Copyright©2004 Cisco Systems, Inc.

Published by:
Cisco Press
800 East 96th Street
Indianapolis, IN 46240 USA

Printed in the United States of America 1 2 3 4 5 6 7 8 9 0

First Printing June 2004

Library of Congress Cataloging-in-Publication Number: 2003101620

ISBN: 1-58705-139-7

Warning and Disclaimer

This book is designed to provide best practices for Cisco CallManager and related Cisco IP Telephony components. Every effort has been made to make this book as complete and accurate as possible, but no warranty or fitness is implied.

The information is provided on an "as is" basis. The authors, Cisco Press, and Cisco Systems, Inc. shall have neither liability nor responsibility to any person or entity with respect to any loss or damages arising from the information contained in this book or from the use of the discs or programs that may accompany it or are referenced by it.

The opinions expressed in this book belong to the authors and are not necessarily those of Cisco Systems, Inc.

Trademark Acknowledgments

All terms mentioned in this book that are known to be trademarks or service marks have been appropriately capitalized. Cisco Press or Cisco Systems, Inc., cannot attest to the accuracy of this information. Use of a term in this book should not be regarded as affecting the validity of any trademark or service mark.

Corporate and Government Sales

Cisco Press offers excellent discounts on this book when ordered in quantity for bulk purchases or special sales.

For more information, please contact:

U.S. Corporate and Government Sales 1-800-382-3419 corpsales@pearsontechgroup.com

For sales outside of the U.S. please contact:

International Sales 1-317-581-3793 international@pearsontechgroup.com

Feedback Information

At Cisco Press, our goal is to create in-depth technical books of the highest quality and value. Each book is crafted with care and precision, undergoing rigorous development that involves the unique expertise of members of the professional technical community.

Reader feedback is a natural continuation of this process. If you have any comments about how we could improve the quality of this book, or otherwise alter it to better suit your needs, you can contact us through e-mail at feedback@ciscopress.com. Please be sure to include the book title and ISBN in your message.

You can also reach the authors directly by sending e-mail to ccmbestpractices@external.cisco.com.

We greatly appreciate your assistance.

Publisher	John Wait
Editor-in-Chief	John Kane
Cisco Representative	Anthony Wolfenden
Cisco Press Program Manager	Nannette M. Noble
Executive Editor	Jim Schachterle
Production Manager	Patrick Kanouse
Development Editor	Betsey Henkels
Copy Editor	Gayle Johnson
Technical Reviewers	Bob Bell, Sumita Biswas, Luc Bouchard, Mick Buchanan, Erick Burgess, John Cameron, Jim Cardon, Tej Chadha, Bae-Sik Chon, CT Chou, Dave Cronberger, Abhijit Dey, Richard Dodsworth, Margaret Doty, Joe Duffy, Clayton Eddings, Abid Fazal, Roger Forehand, Bill Forsythe, Juhee Garg, Paul Giralt, Dave Goodwin, Graham Gudgin, Manish Gupta, Mike Howell, Steven Hunter, Ketil Johansen, Ramkumar Kaleeswaran, Subbiah Kandasamy, Ramesh Kaza, Suresh Kumar, Jackie Lee, Rex McAnally, Kevin McMenamy, Priya Mollyn, Abderrahmane Mounir, David Neustedter, Keith O'Brien, Alex Oldham, Suresh Padmanabhan, Chris Pearce, Joe Pinkus, Akanksha Puri, Jan-Willem Ruys, Jayaram Sankaranarayanan, Herb Sayre, Troy Sherman, Sanjay Sheth, Wes Sisk, Rohit Srivastava, Alan Treece, Amit Tripathi, Gert Vanderstraeten, Ganesan Venkataraman, Xi Zhao
Team Coordinator	Tammi Barnett
Cover Designer	Louisa Adair
Compositor	Tolman Creek Design
Indexer	Tim Wright

iv

Corporate Headquarters
Cisco Systems, Inc.
170 West Tasman Drive
San Jose, CA 95134-1706
USA
www.cisco.com
Tel: 408 526-4000
    800 553-NETS (6387)
Fax: 408 526-4100

European Headquarters
Cisco Systems International BV
Haarlerbergpark
Haarlerbergweg 13-19
1101 CH Amsterdam
The Netherlands
www-europe.cisco.com
Tel: 31 0 20 357 1000
Fax: 31 0 20 357 1100

Americas Headquarters
Cisco Systems, Inc.
170 West Tasman Drive
San Jose, CA 95134-1706
USA
www.cisco.com
Tel: 408 526-7660
Fax: 408 527-0883

Asia Pacific Headquarters
Cisco Systems, Inc.
Capital Tower
168 Robinson Road
#22-01 to #29-01
Singapore 068912
www.cisco.com
Tel: +65 6317 7777
Fax: +65 6317 7799

Cisco Systems has more than 200 offices in the following countries and regions. Addresses, phone numbers, and fax numbers are listed on the
Cisco.com Web site at www.cisco.com/go/offices.

Argentina • Australia • Austria • Belgium • Brazil • Bulgaria • Canada • Chile • China PRC • Colombia • Costa Rica • Croatia • Czech Republic
Denmark • Dubai, UAE • Finland • France • Germany • Greece • Hong Kong SAR • Hungary • India • Indonesia • Ireland • Israel • Italy
Japan • Korea • Luxembourg • Malaysia • Mexico • The Netherlands • New Zealand • Norway • Peru • Philippines • Poland • Portugal
Puerto Rico • Romania • Russia • Saudi Arabia • Scotland • Singapore • Slovakia • Slovenia • South Africa • Spain • Sweden
Switzerland • Taiwan • Thailand • Turkey • Ukraine • United Kingdom • United States • Venezuela • Vietnam • Zimbabwe

About the Authors

Salvatore Collora, CCIE No. 4321, is a network consulting engineer for Cisco Systems Advanced Services, who specializes in implementing IP telephony and security in large customer networks. He has deployed many large CallManager-based IP telephony networks and often works in emergency situations to fix improper installation and configuration of CallManager. He is the author of *Cisco: A Beginner's Guide* (ISBN: 0-07219-385-9) and is the coauthor of *Using Microsoft Exchange Server* (ISBN: 0-78970-687-3). He was a technical editor on *CCNA 2.0 All-in-One Exam Guide* (ISBN: 0-07212-998-0), and has written numerous articles on technology for publications such as *PCWeek* (now *eWeek*). He lives in Los Angeles with his wife and two children.

Ed Leonhardt, CCIE No. 3264, is a consulting systems engineer and serves as a full-time technical lead in the Enterprise/Service Provider Technology Leadership Program at Cisco Systems. He joined Cisco Systems in 1996 and currently drives new product requirements to the individual product teams, helps with messaging from the product teams to the Cisco field teams, and guides overall system engineer (SE) development in the IPT space. Ed has been a long-term advocate of IP telephony since the Selsius Systems acquisition in 1998 and now helps guide the evolving voice product set across Cisco. He has designed and installed networks on airplanes, Humvees, ships, and land, built from anything ranging from arc-net over broadband to Gigabit Ethernet for customers such as the Department of Defense and the single home office user.

Anne Smith is a technical writer in the CallManager engineering group at Cisco Systems. She joined Cisco in 1998 as part of the Selsius Systems acquisition, and writes internal and external documents for CallManager, IP phones, and other Cisco IP Telephony products. She holds a bachelor's degree in language and literature. Anne is a coauthor of *Cisco CallManager Fundamentals* (ISBN: 1-58705-008-0), *Developing Cisco IP Phone Services* (ISBN: 1-58705-060-9), and *Troubleshooting Cisco IP Telephony* (ISBN: 1-58705-075-7), all in the Cisco AVVID Solution series of books from Cisco Press.

About the Contributing Authors

Dave Corley is an engineer in the Internet Protocol Communications Business Unit at Cisco Systems. He was the senior product line manager for CallManager for seven years, responsible for defining and marketing CallManager. Previously he served in technical and marketing positions with Selsius Systems and its predecessor organization, Incite. He is a former nuclear-trained submariner; he served on three nuclear-powered fast-attack submarines for 12 years. Dave holds a master's degree in mechanical engineering from the U.S. Naval Postgraduate School. With several colleagues, he holds a patent on distributed call processing.

Stefano Giorcelli is a technical marketing engineer in the Voice Technology Group at Cisco Systems. He works closely with engineering and product management and focuses on assisting Cisco technical salespeople, partners, and customers to design IP telephony networks. He has contributed to numerous design guides, application notes, and technical white papers on various topics related to IP telephony, and he regularly gives technical presentations at public conferences and internal training events. Stefano holds a master's degree in telecommunications engineering from the Politecnico di Torino, Italy.

Scott Keagy, CCIE No. 3985, is the author of *Integrating Voice and Data Networks*. He has three VoIP patents pending. Formerly he was the senior product manager at Cisco Systems responsible for security, extension mobility, and emergency services across IP communications products. He is the founder and CEO of Emergicom, which makes IP communications products for the public safety industry. He cochairs the VoIP Operations Committee of the National Emergency Number Association (NENA), responsible for documenting VoIP and IP best practices and requirements for the E-9-1-1 industry in North America.

Jeff Knight is a consulting engineer for Cisco Systems in EMEA. He works in the Voice Consulting group, specializing in unified communications, messaging and directory services, and has several years' experience designing and deploying such systems for large enterprise customers.

Michael Purcell, CCIE No. 4110, is a consulting systems engineer in Worldwide Channels, specializing in IP telephony. En route to becoming the world's first sextuple CCIE, Michael obtained CCIEs in Routing/Switching, ISP-Dial, SNA/IP, Security, Communications & Services, and Voice. Before joining Cisco in 1997, he earned a BSEE from North Carolina State University and an MSEE from Georgia Tech.

About the Technical Reviewers

Bob Bell is a technical leader in the CallManager engineering group at Cisco Systems, focusing on security architecture. He is also the chair of the TIA TR41.4 IP Telephony Infrastructure and Endpoints Subcommittee. He has been involved in the development of telephony standards since 1985 and IP telephony since 1990.

Sumita Biswas is a programmer analyst with Infosys Technologies, Ltd, in Bangalore, India. She has worked on Java applications since 2001. She has been involved in the development of the CDR Analysis and Reporting (CAR) tool for CallManager since 2002.

Luc Bouchard is a technical marketing engineer in the Voice Systems Engineering group at Cisco Systems. He holds a bachelor's degree in electrical engineering from Université Laval, Quebec, Canada. He has been integrating voice and data technologies for the last 13 years, and he has been a Cisco employee since June 2000.

Mick Buchanan, CCNA, CCDA, CIPT, MCP, CNE, began working with CallManager in 1998 as one of the original Selsius Systems customer support engineers. He currently works as a technical resource and consultant to large named accounts using the Cisco AVVID solution.

Erick Burgess is a software developer at Cisco Systems working with Microsoft Windows Server operating system installation, upgrades, and security. He has worked with operating systems installation and support for more than nine years.

John Cameron, CCIE No. 12180, is a networking consulting engineer with the Advanced Services group at Cisco Systems. He holds an undergraduate degree from Case Western Reserve University and has worked for Cisco Systems since 1997.

Jim Cardon is a consulting engineer with the Advanced Services group at Cisco Systems, focusing on voice technologies and IP telephony for the past five years. He holds a master's degree in computer science from New York University and has worked for Cisco Systems since 1996.

Tej Chadha is a software engineer with Cisco Systems, working on the CallManager productivity applications. He has worked in the telephony industry for more than eight years, of which the past five years have been focused on IP Telephony.

Bae-Sik Chon is a technical leader in the software development group at Cisco Systems and has worked for Cisco Systems since 1998.

CT Chou is a technical leader in the Cisco CallManager Serviceability team. He holds a master's degree in computer science from the University of Iowa and has worked for Cisco Systems since 1998.

Dave Cronberger, a systems engineer with Cisco Systems, works with large named accounts to architect IP telephony and unified messaging deployments with up to 30,000 seats. He is intimately involved in securing CallManager with role-based security integrated with Active Directory. He has been with Cisco for more than five years and has been in networking for 15 years.

Abhijit Dey is a software engineer at Cisco Systems, focusing on the development of JTAPI applications such as Cisco CallManager Attendant Console. He has been with Cisco for five years and started working on IP telephony applications in 2000. He holds a master's degree in computer science.

Richard Dodsworth, CCIE No. 1466, is a consulting engineer in the Voice Technology Group at Cisco Systems, based in Singapore. He holds a bachelor's degree in organic chemistry from Adelaide University and has worked for Cisco Systems since 1997.

Margaret Doty is a project manager with the Advanced Services group at Cisco Systems. She earned her PMP certificate in 2002 and has worked for Cisco Systems since 1997.

Joe Duffy is a software engineer with Cisco Systems and has worked with telecommunications technologies for more than 25 years. He holds a master's degree in electrical engineering and was part of the Cisco acquisition of Selsius Systems in 1998.

Clayton Eddings is a manager in the CallManager development group, focusing on CallManager installation, backup and restore software, and MCS platform OS installations. He has worked for Cisco Systems since 1999. Clay has worked in software support, software development, and networking technologies for more than 20 years.

Abid Fazal is a system integration engineer with Cisco Systems. He has worked as a system and network engineer for more than 10 years. For the last three years, he has been focusing on system integration of IP telephony technologies.

Roger Forehand is a network engineer with Cisco Systems, supporting internal AVVID deployments in the Americas. He has been in the IT field for more than 15 years and has been with Cisco for more than seven years. The last three years he has focused on IP telephony technologies.

Bill Forsythe is a manager in the software development group at Cisco Systems. He holds a master's degree in computer science from Texas A&M and has worked for Cisco Systems since 1995. He is the author of four patents.

Juhee Garg is a software engineer at Cisco Systems, currently working on rich media collaboration products. She holds a bachelor's degree in computer science from Indian Institute of Technology, Delhi.

Paul Giralt, CCIE No. 4793 (Voice and Routing & Switching), is an escalation engineer at the Cisco Systems Technical Assistance Center (TAC). He has been working with the complete line of Cisco IP Telephony products since 1999. He has worked on many of the largest Cisco IP Telephony deployments and has provided training for TAC teams around the globe. Paul holds a bachelor's degree in computer engineering from the University of Miami and is the coauthor of *Troubleshooting Cisco IP Telephony: A Cisco AVVID Solution* (ISBN: 1-58705-075-7).

Dave Goodwin, CCIE No. 4992 (Voice and Routing & Switching), is a customer support engineer for the Cisco TAC. He is responsible for providing escalation support to the Cisco TAC voice teams worldwide, as well as discovering and resolving issues in new and emerging Cisco IP Telephony products. He also works closely with the Cisco engineering teams and is actively involved in field trials of new products. Dave has been with Cisco for six years and has worked as a network engineer for nine years.

Graham Gudgin, CCIE No. 2370, is a member of the Voice Systems Engineering group at Cisco Systems. His responsibilities include producing the IP Communications Solutions Reference Network Design. He has worked as a field service and TAC engineer based in Europe, where he specialized in the design and development of packet, cell, and voice-based systems.

Manish Gupta is a software development manager at Cisco Systems. He holds a master's degree in computer science from the University of Kentucky and has worked for Cisco Systems since 1999. His interests include networking, distributed systems, and directories/databases. Manish has worked in the field of IP telephony for the past five years.

Mike Howell is a customer support engineer at Cisco Systems.

Steven Hunter, CCIE No. 12670 (Voice), is an engineer with Cisco Systems Information Technology group. He is the AVVID technical lead for IT in the Asia Pacific region. He has been deploying and supporting CallManager since release 2.2. Steven has more than 10 years of experience with large enterprise IT teams and holds postgraduate qualifications in networking from the University of Technology, Sydney. He has worked at Cisco for four years and plans to complete his master's degree in 2004.

Ketil Johansen, CCIE No. 1145, is a business development manager with Cisco Systems, working with companies integrating their applications with CallManager. He has worked with networking technologies for more than 20 years and has been a CCIE since 1994. The last five years he has focused on IP telephony technologies.

Ramkumar Kaleeswaran has been a software engineer with Cisco Systems for the past three years, working on the design and development of Computer Telephony Interface for CallManager. He holds a master's degree in software systems from BITS, Pilani.

Subbiah Kandasamy is a software development manager with Cisco Systems, working on building security infrastructure for CallManager. He has worked for Cisco since 1998 in network management, VoIP, and VoIP applications. He has worked on operating systems and networking technologies for more than 20 years.

Ramesh Kaza, CCIE No. 6207, is a technical leader with the Advanced Services group at Cisco Systems. He has provided design and implementation support in building the IP telephony networks for Fortune 500 companies, presented topics at Cisco Networkers, and worked with networking technologies for more than 10 years. He holds a bachelor's degree in electronics and communications.

Suresh Kumar is a manager in the software development group at Cisco Systems. He holds a master's degree in electrical engineering from Clemson University, South Carolina, and has worked for Cisco Systems since 1998.

Jackie Lee is a manager in the CallManager software development group at Cisco Systems. She holds a master's degree in EECS from the University of California and has worked for Cisco Systems since 1999.

Rex McAnally is a software developer in the CallManager software engineering group at Cisco Systems. He has more than 12 years of experience in telephony software development. The last three years he has focused on software-based conferencing and music on hold applications for Cisco Systems.

Kevin McMenamy is a technical marketing engineer at Cisco Systems. He is a core member of the team responsible for integrating video technologies into CallManager and related products. He specializes in call signaling protocols, call routing/call control theories, and networking best practices for deploying large-scale voice and video networks. Kevin has been with Cisco since February 2000.

Priya Mollyn is a software engineer at Cisco Systems, working on the CallManager Serviceability features. She has worked for Cisco Systems since 2001.

Abderrahmane Mounir, CCIE No. 4312 (Voice and Routing & Switching), is a network consulting engineer with the Advanced Services group at Cisco Systems. He has assisted large-scale Cisco IP Telephony customers with CallManager deployments since release 2.3, and he contributed to the creation and design of the CCIE voice track. He holds a master's degree in electrical and computer engineering.

David Neustedter is an IT engineer with Cisco Systems, working on the design and architecture of the internal Cisco AVVID technology deployments. He holds a bachelor's degree in information systems from the University of Phoenix and has been working with information systems and support for more than 17 years.

Keith O'Brien, CCIE No. 2591, is a distinguished systems engineer with Cisco Systems. He holds a master's degree in telecommunications management from Stevens Institute of Technology. Keith has been with Cisco since 1996, focusing on IP telephony technologies for the past five years.

Alex Oldham, CCIE No. 4652, is a network consulting engineer with the Advanced Services group at Cisco Systems. He is responsible for implementation and technical design of IP telephony products across various customer environments. He has worked for Cisco since 1999.

Suresh Padmanabhan is a software engineer at Cisco Systems. He has worked for Cisco Systems since 1997, and has been developing software applications for IP telephony since 2000.

Chris Pearce is a distinguished engineer, coauthor of *Cisco CallManager Fundamentals: A Cisco AVVID Solution,* and one of the creators of CallManager. He continues to work on improving CallManager.

Joe Pinkus is a diagnostic engineer for the Advanced Engineering Services group at Cisco Systems. He is responsible for helping customers design, implement, and troubleshoot IP telephony solutions in their environment. He has been working at Cisco as a TAC engineer for more than five years.

Akanksha Puri is a programmer analyst with Infosys Technologies, Ltd., working as a consultant for Cisco Systems. She has more than four years of experience in Cisco VoIP solutions and currently specializes in CallManager system configuration and backup technologies. She holds a bachelor's degree in computer science from I.E.T., India.

Jan-Willem Ruys, CCIE No. 1207, is a consulting engineer in the EMEA Voice Technical Consulting group at Cisco Systems. He has spoken Dialtone since 1986 and Packet since 1990. He combined them by joining Cisco in 1998 and focusing on IP telephony technologies.

Jayaram Sankaranarayanan is a programmer analyst with Infosys Technologies, Ltd. He holds a bachelor's degree in electrical and electronics engineering from National Institute of Technology, Calicut, India. He has worked as a consultant for Cisco Systems at the Infosys Offshore Development Centre for the past three years.

Herb Sayre, MCSE No. 1332518, is a software engineer with Cisco Systems. He has worked in the software industry for 13 years while focusing on telecommunications for the past eight years. The last four years he has focused on IP telephony and the software design and development of CallManager.

Troy Sherman, JAG 1024, is a technical marketing engineer at Cisco Systems. He has a background in IP telephony and is currently focused on security. He has worked for Cisco since 1997.

Sanjay Sheth is a software engineer working on IP telephony technologies at Cisco Systems. He holds a master's degree in computer science and has worked for Cisco Systems since 1999.

Wes Sisk, CCIE No. 12455, is a Cisco TAC engineer supporting AVVID since 2000. He holds a bachelor's degree in computer engineering from Georgia Tech.

Rohit Srivastava is a consultant from Infosys Technologies, Ltd, and has worked with Cisco Systems since 1999. He has more than four years of experience in Cisco VoIP solutions and specializes in bulk system configuration. He holds a bachelor's degree in electronics and power from REC, Maharashtra, India.

Alan Treece is a technical leader in the CallManager database group. He has been issued one patent. He has worked with embedded phone software for 10 years and embedded printer controllers for six years. For the last five years he has focused on database installation, replication, and provisioning for CallManager.

Amit Tripathi is a software engineer in the software development group at Cisco Systems. He holds a bachelor's degree in electronics and telecommunications. He has worked for Cisco Systems since 1999.

Gert Vanderstraeten has been a member of technical staff with Cisco IT since September 2002. He is currently responsible for designing and testing the architecture of the Cisco internal voice and video deployment. He has worked as a telecom/datacom engineer for companies such as Alcatel, Bell, and Lucent Technologies since 1993. From 1998 to 2002, he worked as an independent consultant for the Cisco Systems IT department, focusing on the design, implementation, and maintenance of VoIP, IP telephony, and voice and video applications, and the integration of AVVID technologies into large-scale solutions.

Ganesan Venkataraman is a technical leader in the VoIP software development group at Cisco Systems. He has been working in the areas of network management tools, IP telephony, CallManager, and productivity applications. His prior experience was in UNIX kernel development. He holds a master's degree in computer science from Indian Institute of Science, Bangalore, India.

Xi Zhao is a network engineer and software programmer at Cisco Systems. He has years of experience in software development and network design. His primary focus is on emerging network technologies, including distributed objects, design patterns, and generic programming. He holds master's degrees in computer science and electrical engineering and likes to write clean, elegant code.

Dedications

Salvatore Collora

This book is dedicated to the loving memory of my mother, Joann Collora, who passed away during the writing of this book. She lives on through those she touched. She will always be in the hearts of my family.

Ed Leonhardt

I dedicate this book to my mom, who has encouraged me to attempt new things at every opportunity, no matter the challenge. To my faithful four-legged friend, Tasha, for being there through it all.

Anne Smith

For Herb and Vaughn.

Dave Corley

To ADM Hyman Rickover, USN, the ultimate personal motivator.

Stefano Giorcelli

To Lisa, for being the center of my life and for always being patient and understanding. To my parents, for teaching me the value of work and for encouraging me to study and work abroad.

Scott Keagy

I dedicate my contributions to my growing family.

Jeff Knight

For Elaine, and my daughters Danielle and Renée.

Michael Purcell

To all the special ladies in my life—namely, my mom, June, for encouraging me to "just get it on paper"; my sisters, Lindsay, Allison, and Ashley, for keeping me young; and the Cool Girl Crew, Andrea, Eileen, and Sarah, for the many weekend writing breaks on Jordan Lake. To the crew at Cisco—namely, Shays, Gordon, Duce, Mason, Tyler, Dodson, Chad, Bill, Steve, DZ, and BG—for making life at Cisco much more than a job. Finally, to this man's best friend, Brinks, who had to settle for many "short walks" during the writing process.

Acknowledgments

Salvatore Collora

I want to thank my darling wife Amy, my two beautiful children Joseph and Salvatore, my mother, Joann, my father, Joseph, and my brother Sandy for all their love and support throughout this process.

I also extend my thanks to my manager, Greg Rosell, and most of all to Anne Smith, without whom I couldn't have succeeded. Her passion for excellence is inspiring.

Ed Leonhardt

I thank Sal Collora for the invite to join in on the opportunity to write a book that is drawn from field experiences and recommendations.

Without Anne Smith we all would still be lost in getting this thing assembled. Thank you for your patience with this new guy.

Special thanks go to Joe Andres for being there to bounce ideas off of and to teach me some proper English skills along the way.

Thanks to Abid Fazal for answering the beta e-mail no matter if it was us or the code that was at fault.

Thanks to Christina Hattingh, the singular knowledge receptacle of all things gateway. Thanks for your encouragement, dedicated work, and open chat window.

Thanks to deployment guru Graham Gudgin for lending a helping hand and producing incredible material to reference.

Thanks to Craig Cotton for the MCS platform information, along with providing the subject to write about.

Thanks to all the mystery TAC CallManager Tech Note writers: Your work is always good reading and timely.

Thanks to all the reviewers who contributed to this book. Without your input, it would only be half the book it is.

Anne Smith

My thanks go to Scott Veibell and Richard Platt, as always. Scott is the guiding light behind the books in the Cisco AVVID Solution series.

My thanks go to Paul Giralt for always being a valued sounding board and voice of wisdom with wisdom in voice. Thanks for making me laugh, consistently going above and beyond, and working so hard on a book that isn't even one of your own.

Thanks to Brian Sedgley for always making time to answer every question I can think of about IP telephony, and for developing the services recommendations in Chapter 8 (Tables 8-2 through 8-6).

Thanks to Mick Buchanan, one of the all-time best content shredders, for his knowledge and willingness to help, even after he swore he would never work on another Cisco Press book again.

Thanks to Chandra Mulpuri for the IPMA best practices that appear in Chapter 7.

My thanks and deep appreciation to the folks who took time out of their busy schedules to help out in a pinch: Paul Giralt—thank you for never closing your IM window; Conrad Zgliczynski, Mick Buchanan, Joe Pinkus, and John Cameron on Chapter 1; Sanjay Sheth and Sumita Biswas on

Chapter 12; and Greg Moore, Clay Eddings, Erick Burgess, and Keith O'Brien on Chapter 6. Special thanks go to Greg and Clay for their detailed work on that chapter. In particular, I thank Clay for rewriting the "CallManager Account/Password Policies" section on very short notice. Clay, your dedication to accuracy and customer success is admirable.

My thanks and respect to the many engineers who contributed their knowledge: Tripti Agarwal, Marc Ayres, Luc Bouchard, Mick Buchanan, Sumita Biswas, Erick Burgess, Ed Chen, Lijun Chen, Vicky Chen, Stephen Cheng, Darrick Deel, Abhijit Dey, David Doherty, Joe Duffy, Paul Giralt, Moises Gonzalez, Dave Goodwin, Mark Hendrickson, Mike Howell, Dinesh Kallam, Madhava Kidambi, Cheryl Li, Man Loh, Rex McAnally, Kevin McMenamy, Charlie Munro, Thang Nguyen, Thu Nguyen, Sanjay Pawar, Chris Pearce, Therese Phuong, John Restrick, Herb Sayre, Brian Sedgley, Sanjay Sheth, Rohit Srivastava, Alan Treece, Amit Tripathi, Satyam Tyagi, Jamie Zhuang.

Special thanks go to Stefano Giorcelli for writing the text and creating the figures for the best practice, "Use Line-Based Calling Search Spaces in Addition to Phone-Based Calling Search Spaces (with Caveats)," which appears in Chapter 7. Be sure to read the IP Telephony SRND, created by Voice Systems Engineering Technical Marketing Engineering Team, of which Stefano is a part, at the following link:

http://www.cisco.com/go/srnd

Special thanks go to Jim Schachterle, Chris Cleveland, Patrick Kanouse, and John Kane at Cisco Press for all your hard work and dedication to this book and the other books in the Cisco AVVID Solution series.

And finally, thanks to all the dedicated technical reviewers we relied on to provide their specific areas of expertise on the material we wrote, and Sal and Ed for making the book possible.

Stefano Giorcelli and Jeff Knight

Our thanks to Manish Gupta and Sandeep Kapur in the Voice Engineering team for their availability and their patience in explaining the technical details of the CallManager directory architecture. We would also like to thank our managers, Bob Kelly and Owen Bridle, for their support of this effort.

Dave Corley

My thanks to the entire CallManager engineering team for their diligence in creating a world-shaking product.

Scott Keagy

I am grateful to Bob Bell, Paul Giralt, Manish Gupta, Keith O'Brien, and Ketil Johansen for reviewing sections of Chapter 6 and for providing insightful comments. Special thanks go to Erick Burgess, Clay Eddings, and Troy Sherman for insightful reviews and for providing input while I was writing. Chapter 6 reflects countless conversations I had with folks in the Cisco sales force, customers, product developers, and other security experts sprinkled throughout Cisco.

Michael Purcell

Thanks to Addis Hallmark and David G. Wirths for their application notes.

Contents at a Glance

Contents

Command Syntax Conventions

The conventions used to present command syntax in this book are the same conventions used in the Cisco IOS Software Command Reference. The Command Reference describes these conventions as follows:

- **Bold** indicates commands and keywords that are entered literally as shown. In actual configuration examples and output (not general command syntax), bold indicates commands that the user inputs (such as a **show** command).

- *Italic* indicates arguments for which you supply actual values.

- Vertical bars (|) separate alternative, mutually exclusive elements.

- Square brackets ([ ]) indicate an optional element.

- Braces ({ }) indicate a required choice.

- Braces within brackets ([{ }]) indicate a required choice within an optional element.

Foreword

When I was a telecom manager in the 1980s and early 1990s, deploying a high-availability voice system was simple: You ordered a box and had your vendor bolt it down in the wiring closet. What could be easier? But those systems were expensive to acquire and maintain. You needed one in every site, and the key system you bought for a small office was completely different from the PBX you bought for a large office. The data network in those days was just a convenience for file and print sharing, not a necessity. And the pace of innovation for voice systems was incredibly slow. I still remember how thrilled my colleagues were the first time they saw the message waiting indicator on their phones light up!

Today, businesses around the world are moving more and more mission-critical services to their data network. Whether it is an enterprise financial application, a help desk program, an IP-based contact center, IP telephony services, or networked storage, these services must provide the same or better availability than the legacy systems they replace. This trend calls for a new approach to designing, implementing, and managing mission-critical converged networks—one that is based on the 3Ps principle: predictive, preventative, and proactive.

The trend toward converged systems also calls for a new kind of communications professional. It is no longer sufficient to be an expert in data only or voice only. Today, telecom and data network managers must have expertise in both data systems and voice systems. For example, data network managers must understand how to manage delay, jitter, and loss budgets for voice services on the IP network. Voice system managers must understand the importance of QoS, security, and availability on the data network. Whether you are a data professional or a voice professional, this book is designed to guide you in the best practices for building a high-quality, secure, reliable converged IP telephony solution.

With the introduction of Cisco CallManager release 4.0, we have reached an important milestone in the evolution of IP telephony solutions. Incorporating the traditional calling features businesses have come to expect in legacy PBXs, standards-based protocols such as SIP and Q.SIG and innovative new features like integrated videoconferencing and media encryption, CallManager 4.0 represents a new benchmark for both employee productivity and ease of migration from existing TDM systems to new IP-based systems.

As of May 2004, Cisco has sold 3 million IP phones—more than all the IP phones sold by all other vendors combined—and we have 15,000 IP customers using our IP Telephony, unified messaging, rich-media conferencing, and customer contact solutions, including more than half of the Fortune 500.

The privileged position of Cisco in the IP telephony market means that we have learned more about what it takes to design, implement, and manage mission-critical converged networks than anyone else in the industry. *Cisco CallManager Best Practices* brings the benefit of that experience to you. The authors have spent the last five years in the trenches building IP-based voice networks, from the bleeding edge solutions of several years ago to the reliable and robust systems being used by all kinds of businesses around the world today. This book is an invaluable resource in helping communications professionals successfully manage the fundamental transition in the voice business we are experiencing today.

Donald R. Proctor
Vice President and General Manager
Voice Technology Group
Cisco Systems, Inc.

Introduction

This book describes best practices for CallManager and related IP Telephony components, such as IP phones, gateways, and applications. Detailed coverage of other elements of the Cisco IP Telephony solution is provided, including planning an implementation, installing, backing up and restoring, using services and parameters, call detail records, and much more. You will get the most from this book if you are already familiar with CallManager and the Cisco IP Telephony solution, but even if you haven't yet deployed the solution or you're just planning the deployment, you can glean valuable information. Be aware that concepts and components are not explained in detail; you can learn this information from other books in the Cisco AVVID Solution published by Cisco Press or through the Cisco IP Telephony documentation.

NOTE	Not all best practices should be deployed for every installation, so we have tried to provide an array of best practices. You should carefully consider which best practices make sense for your deployment.

The inspiration for this book was fueled by customers, who time after time would ask the same questions: How do I track things? How do I know what's going on? How do I configure intercom? How do I know when a gateway is down? The management, monitoring, provisioning, and operations capabilities of CallManager release 4.0 are a direct result of customer feedback. This book's goal is to document the best ways of taking advantage of all the capabilities CallManager offers.

The information contained in these chapters is the result of painstaking experience in the field, working with real customers, combined with time spent in the lab on a new product. Although we've tried to cover everything, there will invariably be things you don't find as you read. The reason is that every environment is different, and all customers need different things. We cast a wide net within Cisco, asking for input, and we received many suggestions. We polled systems engineers, Cisco partners, and customers. Hopefully, our experiences, put on paper in this book, will enable you to run a top-notch system and provide you with ideas you wouldn't have considered.

Target CallManager Release

This book is written to CallManager release 4.0(1). Updates to this book might be provided after publication. You should periodically check the Cisco Press website for updates and free downloads. Go to

http://www.ciscopress.com/1587051397

Goals and Methods

The goal of this book is to provide you with best practices in the form of small, digestible nuggets of information that make a real difference when you're running a CallManager installation. The writing style is meant to be "bursty" rather than providing long narratives and lots of screen captures. In some cases, references are made to other books in the Cisco AVVID Solution series from Cisco Press and the various release notes, tech notes, application notes, white papers, design guides, and configuration guides that are posted on Cisco.com. Rather than repeat the information you can find on Cisco.com, we reference those documents and provide links so that you can find that valuable information yourself.

Using Links

This book provides many links to Cisco.com and other websites. Over time, documents might get moved, so it's possible that some of the links referenced in this book may no longer work. You can use the search engine at Cisco.com to try to find the document. For Cisco.com documentation links (which have /univercd/cc/td/doc/ in the path), you can investigate to try to find the referenced document or a newer document that might provide the same information.

Take the following link, for example:

http://www.cisco.com/univercd/cc/td/doc/product/lan/cat6000/sw_8_1/confg_gd/vtp.htm

If you try that link and find it broken, you can start removing pieces of the address from the end of the link until you find the root and perhaps a newer document. For example, this link points to a document called "Configuring VTP." Remove the **vtp.htm** portion and retry the link. You'll find the main page of links for the Catalyst 6500 Series Software Configuration Guide, version 8.1. Look for a document that might be related to VTP in that list of links.

If removing that portion of the address doesn't return a hit, try removing the next portion, **confg_gd/**. The link http://www.cisco.com/univercd/cc/td/doc/product/lan/cat6000/sw_8_1 brings you to the Catalyst 6500 Series Software Documentation for version 8.1. If you are using a newer version, you might want to remove the version-specific portion of the address to see if relevant documentation for your version exists. In that case, remove **sw_8_1/** and try http://www.cisco.com/univercd/cc/td/doc/product/lan/cat6000/, which brings you to the root of the Catalyst 6500 Series Switches documentation.

Who Should Read This Book?

This book is intended for voice and data networking professionals who either have CallManager installed or are considering installing it. Some experience with CallManager and other Cisco IP Telephony components will result in the best understanding of all the material presented here. This book is written to be understood by the person with moderate skill levels in either voice or data networking.

Some of the concepts introduced in this book have background material associated with them, but many do not. The purpose of this book is to offer best practices, not repeat much of the basic conceptual and configuration information you can easily find in other resources. References throughout the book point you to various websites or other resources for more information. We also encourage you to read the books listed in the "Further Reading" section.

How This Book Is Organized

This book is organized as a useful guide in running a CallManager system. It should be read cover-to-cover in a linear fashion if you currently don't run CallManager. If you have a running system, feel free to jump to individual chapters of interest.

- **Chapter 1, "Planning the CallManager Implementation,"** details planning considerations such as assessing the current infrastructure and voice environment, choosing the right equipment, establishing the rollout plan, and providing training.

- **Chapter 2, "Planning Centralized Call Processing Deployments,"** addresses the best practices to follow when you initially deploy CallManager. This chapter focuses on wide-area network deployments, optimizing voice quality, and surviving outages with minimal user disruption.

- **Chapter 3, "Installing CallManager,"** describes preinstallation, installation, and post-installation best practices to ensure the smoothest possible installation and the maximum amount of uptime after the software is installed.

- **Chapter 4, "Backing Up and Restoring the Environment,"** helps you plan a backup strategy, back up the environment, restore the environment, and troubleshoot typical backup problems.

- **Chapter 5, "Upgrading and Patching CallManager,"** continues where Chapter 3 left off. This chapter addresses the best way of upgrading and patching the system so that you experience the least downtime, yet stay current.

- **Chapter 6, "Securing the Environment,"** describes a set of best practices to mitigate security threats, including account and password management, OS hardening, security considerations for remote administration, secure endpoint provisioning, and a variety of infrastructure prevention and detection mechanisms that operate at layers 2 through 7.

- **Chapter 7, "Configuring CallManager and IP Telephony Components,"** provides best practices and configuration tips for the CallManager system and features such as music on hold, extension mobility, intercom, video, system and group speed dials, IP phones, gateways, dial plan components, toll fraud prevention, tools, and applications such as IPMA, SoftPhone/Communicator, BAT, and Attendant Console.

- **Chapter 8, "Managing Services and Parameters,"** describes best practices for CallManager-related services and highlights some of the pertinent service and enterprise parameters. It also provides several recommendations for which services should be activated on each server in a cluster, based on the size of your deployment.

- **Chapter 9, "Using Multilevel Administration,"** details best practices associated with the MLA feature in CallManager, including monitoring the Access log, creating custom groups, and maintaining security.

- **Chapter 10, "Mastering Directory Integration,"** addresses the main design principles for integrating CallManager with a corporate LDAP directory, and summarizes design considerations for providing IP phones with access to a corporate LDAP directory.

- **Chapter 11, "Administering Call Detail Records,"** details best practices associated with the use of call detail records and call management records in CallManager, including troubleshooting, using CAR, and using third-party CDR applications.

- **Chapter 12, "Managing and Monitoring the System,"** provides best practices for the various facilities available within the CallManager environment for management and monitoring. These include things such as authentication, authorization, and accounting, Simple Network Management Protocol (SNMP), Microsoft Performance, and syslog.

- **Chapter 13, "Using Real-Time Monitoring Tool,"** details the most important aspects of running RTMT. This chapter addresses how to set alerts and provides points of focus.

- The **Appendix, "CallManager 4.0 New Feature Description,"** briefly describes the new features in CallManager release 4.0. It is not a substitute for formal product documentation, but it can help you understand the basics of the new features.

- The **Glossary** defines terms and acronyms used in this book.

Comments for the Authors

The authors are interested in your comments and suggestions about this book. Please send feedback to

ccmbestpractices@external.cisco.com

Updates and Free Downloads

Check the Cisco Press website for updates to chapters and free downloads, such as a starter spreadsheet for interviewing users to develop user classes (FeatureInventory.xls, as discussed in Chapter 1), and a sample dial plan document in Visio format (Sample-Dial-Plan.vsd, as discussed in Chapter 1). Check the following link regularly

http://www.ciscopress.com/1587051397

Further Reading

The authors recommend the following resources for more information. You can find the books mentioned here at a technical bookseller near you or at an online bookseller.

Cisco Documentation

You should be familiar with and regularly using the documentation that is provided with the Cisco IP Telephony system to supplement the information in this book.

You can find Cisco IP Telephony documentation by searching for a specific product on Cisco.com or by starting at the following link

http://www.cisco.com/univercd/cc/td/doc/product/voice/index.htm

Cisco CallManager Fundamentals: A Cisco AVVID Solution

You'll find detailed information about CallManager's inner workings in the book *Cisco CallManager Fundamentals* (ISBN 1-58705-008-0). You can examine this book at a technical bookseller near you or at an online bookseller.

Troubleshooting Cisco IP Telephony: A Cisco AVVID Solution

You can find extensive troubleshooting information and methodology in the book *Troubleshooting Cisco IP Telephony* (ISBN 1-58705-075-7). You can examine this book at a technical bookseller near you or at an online bookseller.

Developing Cisco IP Phone Services: A Cisco AVVID Solution

You can find instructions and tools for creating custom phone services and directories for Cisco IP Phones in the book *Developing Cisco IP Phone Services* (ISBN 1-58705-060-9). You can examine this book at a technical bookseller near you or at an online bookseller.

Cisco IP Telephony

You can find installation, configuration, and maintenance information for Cisco IP Telephony networks in the book *Cisco IP Telephony* (ISBN 1-58705-050-1). You can examine this book at a technical bookseller near you or at an online bookseller.

Integrating Voice and Data Networks

You can find information on how to integrate and configure packetized voice networks in the book *Integrating Voice and Data Networks* (ISBN 1-57870-196-1). You can examine this book at a technical bookseller near you or at an online bookseller.

Icons Used in This Book

Throughout this book, you will see a number of icons used to designate Cisco-specific and general networking devices, peripherals, and other items. The following icon legend explains what these icons represent.

Network Device Icons

CallManager

IP Phone

Stations

SRST Router

Used for:
Application Server
DHCP
DNS
MOH Server
MTP
SW Conference Bridge
Voice Mail Server

Router

Switch

Layer 3 switch

PIX Firewall

Gateway or 3rd-Party H.323 Server

Used for:
HW Conference Bridge
Transcoder
Voice-Enabled Switch

Access Server

ATM Switch

Used for:
Analog Gateway
H.323 Gateway
Gatekeeper
Gateway
Transcoder

PBX/PSTN Switch

PBX (small)

Cisco Directory Server

Local Director

PC

Laptop

Server

PC w/software

Modem

POTS Phone

Relational Database

Fax machine

DAT Tape

Cisco VT Advantage

Media/Building Icons

Network Cloud

Ethernet connection

Serial connection

Telecommuter

Building

Branch Office

## CHAPTER 1

Planning the CallManager Implementation

Cisco IP Telephony operates at a system level by interacting with many different IP Telephony components: CallManager, IP phones, gateways, applications, and much more. The system as a whole must be properly configured and maintained to ensure a smooth, successful deployment. This book highlights those best practices that aid in a successful deployment, and this chapter helps you ensure that all aspects of the IP Telephony solution work together seamlessly to meet business objectives and fulfill user expectations.

You'll notice a strong focus on PBX migration in this chapter because this type of installation is becoming the most prevalent. However, successful implementations of any telephony solution depend on careful planning. Most steps covered in this chapter apply equally well to green field deployments (new installations with no prior IP telephony) because most users have experienced phone systems before and have a standard set of expectations. A good plan ensures a smooth, methodical, documented deployment of the complete Cisco CallManager solution. This chapter focuses first on the current environment as it covers these topics:

- Assessing and documenting the current network infrastructure to ensure proper quality of service (QoS), availability, and security

- Documenting the existing and desired dial plan, classes of service, analog requirements, recording needs, and the call detail record (CDR) method to ensure transparency of operation

- Talking with existing users to determine the current applications in use, phone usage patterns, and most-used features

- Understanding the various add-on hardware in use by end users, including headsets, conference room microphones, amplifiers, wallboards (used in call centers for displaying real-time queue statistics), and recording equipment

- Choosing Cisco equipment

Then the focus of the chapter progresses to the actual implementation of the solution, with topics such as:

- Creating various templates for phone creation
- Selecting training topics

- Establishing a rollout plan
- Developing a second-day support plan
- Creating a problem reporting and escalation plan
- Establishing operations procedures

Read the Solution Reference Network Designs

This book is not meant to be a design guide. Cisco Solution Reference Network Designs (SRND), shown in Figure 1-1, provide guidelines for designing network infrastructures. The SRNDs are based on the experiences of many Cisco customers and engineers and give you information that outlines the best deployments. The SRNDs supply design guidance to implement an overall network architecture. There's no reason to repeat that information here, because all the SRNDs can be found on Cisco.com at either of the following links:

http://www.cisco.com/go/srnd
http://www.cisco.com/warp/public/779/largeent/it/ese/srnd.html

Figure 1-1 *SRNDs on Cisco.com*

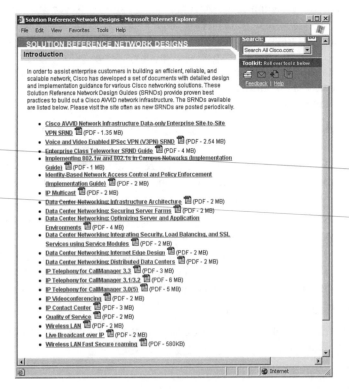

Check the Compatibility Matrix

Cisco posts a compatibility matrix on Cisco.com (see Figure 1-2) that helps you determine whether the parts of the IP telephony system you want to deploy are compatible with other parts. You need to be certain that all upgrades, firmware loads, applications, gateways, and other hardware devices are compatible with the version of CallManager you plan to deploy. Access the compatibility matrix at the following link or search Cisco.com for "CallManager compatibility matrix" (when you get the search results, look for the Cisco recommendation to the right of the results screen):

> http://www.cisco.com/univercd/cc/td/doc/product/voice/c_callmg/ccmcomp.htm

Figure 1-2   *CallManager Compatibility Matrix on Cisco.com*

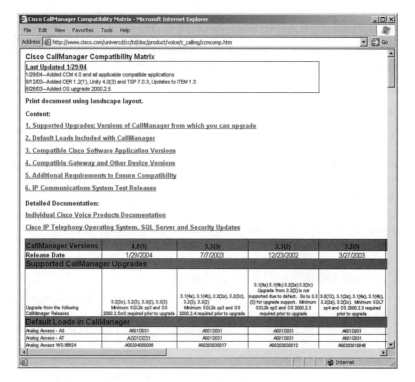

Assess the Current Data Infrastructure

The most important aspect of a successful implementation is ensuring that your data infrastructure is stable before you attempt to deploy voice applications. There are many factors to consider. QoS, availability, and security are the top three. The following sections help you determine whether the network can support the level of service to which telephony users are accustomed.

Implement Quality of Service

Voice is a delay-sensitive application. You have to ensure that the network components can support consistent delay characteristics to keep voice sounding natural and smooth. You have to configure the network devices to provide a priority queue for voice packets in case network congestion occurs. For a complete guide to implementing QoS, read "Cisco AVVID Network Infrastructure Enterprise Quality of Service Design," available at the following link or search Cisco.com for "Quality of Service Solutions Reference Network Design" or "Cisco AVVID Network Infrastructure."

http://www.cisco.com/application/pdf/en/us/guest/netsol/ns17/c649/ ccmigration_09186a00800d67ed.pdf

Maintain the Highest Availability Possible

Network availability has many facets. To maintain the highest level of availability, focus on power and network design, as discussed in the following sections.

Make Sure You Have an Uninterruptible Power Supply

To maintain service in the event of a power failure, you should provide uninterruptible power for all network devices, such as servers, switches, and routers. Whether you rack-mount uninterruptible power supplies (UPS) in each closet or provide a centralized UPS for the entire building, redundant power is crucial. When putting UPSs in your closets, the most important decisions are how long the battery backup must last and what receptacles your switches should use. In addition, it's important to use a UPS that conditions power so that you can protect your switching equipment from power spikes.

Ensure an Optimum Operational Environment

All network devices should be placed in locations with stable environmental characteristics such as adequate heat dissipation, ventilation, and air conditioning. Excessive heat has a large impact on mean time between failures (MTBF). Although it is surprising, some deployments actually store servers and switches in broom closets and under desks. Improper care of your equipment contributes to environmental and security hazards that can disable or degrade your voice deployment. Security is discussed in detail in Chapter 6, "Securing the Environment."

For exact specifications on operating temperatures, see the data sheets posted on Cisco.com at the following link. You also can search Cisco.com for the phrase "data sheet" coupled with the product name (for example, "CallManager Attendant Console data sheet" or "Cisco CallManager version data sheet").

http://www.cisco.com/en/US/products/sw/voicesw/ps556/ products_data_sheets_list.html

Build Redundancy into Your Network Design

Your network design should have a redundant core (central site) and distribution layer switching. Network designs that employ a single switch in the distribution layer with two supervisor modules do not provide the desired level of redundancy. Should you incur a software bug that causes the switch to reset spontaneously, an entire building could be adversely affected. For more information on network designs, see the "Cisco IP Telephony Solution Reference Network Design" document at the following link, or search Cisco.com for "CallManager SRND."

http://www.cisco.com/application/pdf/en/us/guest/netsol/ns268/c649/ ccmigration_09186a008017bb4a.pdf

---

NOTE   In traditional PBX deployments, one best practice is the wiring of user ports in a given area to different line cards on the PBX. In this case, a line card outage would not result in an entire area or department being without phone service. This technique can be replicated on the data network, but if you have an existing network, it takes a significant amount of labor to recable each wiring closet. You must weigh the cost versus the benefit in your environment.

A separate server farm layer in your network, connected in a redundant fashion to the core, is highly recommended. This lets you keep servers off the core and distribution switches, which is critical to running a network that can be upgraded and maintained without service interruption. When servers are attached to core and distribution layer switches, performing upgrades and maintenance is more difficult, because rebooting a switch after an upgrade causes a server outage. If you are a voice support person, be sure to work with your data networking team to follow the network design recommendations outlined in the SRND.

Security

It's critical to ensure that the data network is as secure as possible before adding voice. When planning for IP telephony, you should take many security facets into account:

- **Physical security**—First and foremost, physical security is important. At a bare minimum, do not leave any network devices, including servers, routers, and switches, in open areas that do not have locked doors. Keep access limited to key individuals, and, if possible, use electronic door locks that provide an access log.

- **Virus/worm mitigation**—Mitigating the effect of viruses and worms is important at both the network and server level. At the network level, viruses and worms consume bandwidth resources that can adversely affect communications between the various devices. At the server level, they can attack the various IP telephony servers and render them unusable.

At a bare minimum, you should run Cisco Security Agent (CSA) on all IP telephony servers. CSA is provided in a headless version free of charge from Cisco. To download it, go to the following link or search Cisco.com for "Cisco Security Agent":

http://www.cisco.com/en/US/products/sw/secursw/ps5057/index.html

- **Layer 2 security**—Unprotected IP networks are vulnerable to various man-in-the-middle attacks, Dynamic Host Configuration Protocol (DHCP) rogue server attacks, DHCP starvation, and Address Resolution Protocol (ARP) spoofing/poisoning attacks. Cisco has enabled IOS and CatOS software to defeat these attacks. Features such as port security, DHCP snooping, dynamic ARP inspection, and IP SourceGuard mitigate these attacks and keep the network available for IP telephony use. See Chapter 6 for more information.

- **Routing protocol security**—Use neighbor authentication when configuring your routing protocols. Without it, hackers can form neighbor adjacencies with your routers and inject invalid routes into the network. Cisco's RIPv2, EIGRP, OSPF, and BGP implementations all support authenticated neighbors.

- **Firewall policy**—If you have a firewall between the IP voice network subnets and the traditional data subnets, be sure your firewall policy allows the passing of all necessary protocols to ensure functionality. Be ready to approach your network security group to make changes to the firewalls if applicable. For more information about security, see Chapter 6.

The key message is this: plan for security to ensure availability. Making sure your network is protected is critical to ongoing success and uptime.

For more in-depth information on security, see Chapter 6. Also refer to the white paper "SAFE: IP Telephony Security in Depth," located at the following link or search Cisco.com for "SAFE IP telephony security."

http://www.cisco.com/en/US/netsol/ns340/ns394/ns171/ns128/networking_solutions_white_paper09186a00801b7a50.shtml

Document the Current Data Infrastructure

The importance of up-to-date documentation cannot be overstated. Be sure to have both physical and logical representations of the network to assist in troubleshooting. It's also essential to have copies of the topological diagrams saved in a portable format such as PNG, JPG, or GIF to give technical support personnel easy access to data. Not everyone will have identical network diagramming packages, so having documentation in a usable format speeds up the troubleshooting process.

Assess the Current Voice Environment

Organizations profit from the unique expertise and skills of their employees and partners. A properly configured, flexible telephone system can help you take advantage of these unique skills by providing customized features at users' desktops. But deploying these customized features requires that the installer understand the skills required of each individual in the organization. Deploying appropriate phone features and eliminating unused features makes the most effective use of the system. You should inventory user requirements and skills and then categorize users into user classes. User classes are an effective method of distributing the right features and capabilities to the right users. Planning this activity before the initial installation and configuration avoids customer frustration and change orders and saves you time and money.

Creating user classes has an ongoing advantage. As new users are added to an organization or existing users are moved from one part of the organization to another, they inherit phone feature requirements associated with their new positions. Applying an existing feature template that efficiently serves users with similar job descriptions consumes less time than creating a customized template for each new user. Over the system lifetime, it is this concept of user and feature templates that saves system administrators configuration time. CallManager provides softkey templates, phone button templates, device profiles, and device pools to aid in developing user class-based configurations. In addition, Cisco provides several different phone models designed for different types of employees. For example, phones models differ in the number of line/feature buttons they provide, because some employees, such as executives or their assistants, might need more buttons than other employees.

Conduct a Feature Inventory and Create User Classes

If you're migrating from an existing phone system, the simplest path to efficient inventory and classification is to use what is already at hand. In many cases, an enterprise's voice team already maintains separate spreadsheets or databases of users and the phone features associated with their jobs. Frequently, these databases associate a named user class to each user. This user class represents a set of users with equivalent requirements and skills. Common phone features are normally assigned to each phone in a given user class. In the absence of an existing spreadsheet or database, some PBXs have tools to create such databases or spreadsheets based on the existing PBX configuration. Use these tools when available to provide a good starting point. Third-party data extraction tools such as those from Unimax (http://www.unimax.com/home.php) can aid in the transition as well. You can find a list of all certified partners at the following link or search Cisco.com for "AVVID find a partner":

http://www.cisco.com/pcgi-bin/ecoa/Search

Data extraction tools can form the basis of CallManager softkey and button templates. Without these tools or existing data, you would need to create the database from scratch. The accuracy and time required for this inventory are a direct function of the scope of the inventory: The broader the database, the longer it takes to create it.

The approach of gathering the inventory has two extremes—representative sample and exhaustive sample. The *representative sample* is composed of a sample of the user population that represents a reasonable percentage of each user class in the organization. The *exhaustive sample* approach requires an interview with every user in the organization. An advantage of the representative sample approach is that the time required to complete the interviews and inventory is considerably shorter than with the exhaustive sample approach. The primary disadvantage of the representative sample approach is the likelihood that one or more special user classes will fall through the cracks, necessitating follow-up interviews and inventories.

The recommended approach includes a combination of representative sample and exhaustive sample. Conduct random sample interviews of up to 10 percent of the total organization's population. Conduct a 50 percent sampling of users identified as having critical positions within the organization. When an organization has fewer than five critical users, interview and inventory all of them. In addition, consider a baseline of users across all job functions that might require special features or services. For example, users with hearing impairments have special requirements such as amplified handsets. Finally, event-specific features associated with an event or brief task normally are not assigned as common features to a user class. An example is a malicious call trace, which might be applied to an individual's phone during a brief interval.

The first step in creating the feature inventory database from scratch is to construct a list of all users to be interviewed. List all user features and capabilities in rows, and list all the interviewees in columns. As users in the listing are interviewed, query them for the features they have used in the past and the job responsibilities they have not been able to fulfill as a result of existing phone feature deficiencies. The goal of the interview is to identify requirements as well as deficiencies in previous phone configurations that have prevented or hindered users from accomplishing their jobs. Table 1-1 is a sample interview form.

You can complete the form by devising a legend for interviewee responses, such as **R** for a required feature, **D** for a desired feature, **X** for an unused feature, and so on, and marking the interviewees' responses in the row associated with each feature. Be sure to have a second page listing all the interviewees' names so that you have a place to make notes during the interviews. You can photocopy Table 1-1 or download it (FeatureInventory.pdf) from the Cisco Press website (go to http://www.ciscopress.com/1587051397). If Table 1-1 doesn't satisfy your needs, use it as an example for the tables you design. Be sure your tables include all the features and custom IP phone services your deployment offers.

Table 1-1   *Sample Interview Form*

Cisco IP Telephony Feature Inventory User Group (for example, general population or executive users)																
	Interviewees															
Features	User Name Here															
Number of lines																
Maximum number of calls at one time																
Number of speed dials																
Hold																
Redial																
Conference																
Meet-Me Conference																
Transfer																
Call park																
Call pickup																
Group call pickup																
Auto-answer																
Barge/cBarge																
Call back																
Privacy																
Call join																
Method of MWI indication (**A**udible/**V**isual/**B**oth)																

continues

Table 1-1 *Sample Interview Form (Continued)*

Cisco IP Telephony Feature Inventory User Group (for example, general population or executive users)	Interviewees												
	User Name Here												
Disable speakerphone													
Disable headset													
Extension mobility													
Malicious call trace													
Cisco IPMA													
Preferred locale													
MLPP													
SoftPhone/ Communicator													
Personal Fast Dials													
Personal Address Book													
Corporate directory dial from web (WebDialer)													
Personal Assistant													

TIP   You might prefer to record your interview feedback in an application such as Microsoft Excel, which would provide greater flexibility than handwritten documents.

Check the Cisco Press website for a free starter spreadsheet that you can use or customize for your deployment (go to http://www.ciscopress.com/1587051397). Check the site regularly for updates to the spreadsheet or the book chapters. Figure 1-3 shows the FeatureInventory.xls file that is available for download.

For future releases of CallManager, the form you use, whether Table 1-1 or the downloadable file shown in Figure 1-3, should be updated to include new features.

Figure 1-3   *Exec Admin Tab on FeatureInventory.xls*

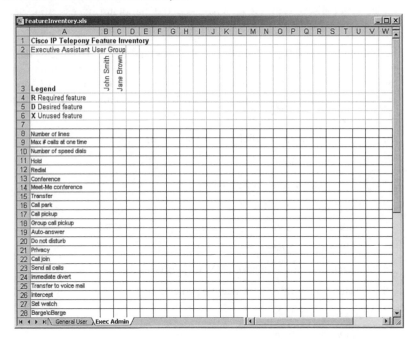

The interviewing sessions with members of the various user groups in your organization are also opportunities to educate users about new features, services, and capabilities that could help them work more effectively. For example, Cisco provides a broad range of mobility solutions that give mobile users choices for staying connected while on the road or moving around the organization's campus. Exposing these new capabilities to users allows you to provide a solution to a user's problem that might not have been solvable with a previous phone system. The interview also serves as an opportunity to set user expectations about phone system operation, planned training, and installation and configuration plans.

After the feature inventory is collected, create a set of user classes that represent a common set of user features and capabilities identified during the interviews. Although CallManager can store hundreds of button template configurations, you should try to limit the number of user classes to a reasonably manageable quantity—10 or fewer—to most efficiently manage subsequent personnel moves, adds, and changes.

Document the Existing and Desired Dial Plan

During every installation, whether new or existing, you should document the dial plan in fine detail—down to the last known number. Whether you are integrating with a PBX, replacing a PBX, or bringing up a new site, the dial plan is an essential element you must master.

If you don't know the numbers in use in your system, you are completely in the dark. In some cases, you might be neglecting certain populations of users without knowing it. When the cutover to Cisco IP Telephony occurs, those users will not have 100 percent service. At the worst, you might be assigning numbers to IP phones that are already in use in other parts of the network, which can cause serious havoc.

The most common uses of dial plan numbers are

- Internal extensions
- Rollover extensions (if line 1 is busy)
- Emergency numbers
- Trunk-access codes
- Tie-line access codes
- Message waiting indicator (MWI) on/off numbers
- Application numbers (call center, voice mail)
- System speed dials
- Route/hunt patterns
- Translation patterns

You must meticulously document the existing dial plan and determine where the IP phones and applications will fit. The best way to do this is by using a spreadsheet that details the number ranges in use, groups of devices to which the number ranges are assigned, and any number translations in use. For an example of a dial plan document, check the Cisco Press website (http://www.ciscopress.com/1587051397) for a downloadable dial plan document in Visio format called Sample-Dial-Plan.vsd. You can modify this sample document and use it for your deployment.

Document Classes of Service

It's important to understand any existing restrictions and to whom they apply. By understanding the current environment, you can provision CallManager to meet the same level of restriction. Many times, only the simplest forms of restriction are implemented. Some of the most common classes of numbers in the U.S. are

- Internal-only
- Local
- National
- International
- Intra-LATA (Local Access and Transport Area)
- Local toll
- 900
- 976

Non-North American Numbering Plan dial plans might use classes such as

- Internal-only
- National
- Mobile and pager
- Emergency
- Premium rate numbers
- Free-call

Normally, partitions are designed around some of these classes of service. They are classes of numbers that represent route patterns that can be assigned to partitions, which are then assigned to calling search spaces (CSS), which in turn are applied to phones. You can use any combination of these classes to create calling search spaces that result in classes of restriction for users. Restricting calls by using calling search spaces is discussed in more detail in Chapter 7, "Configuring CallManager and IP Telephony Components."

How the classes actually get implemented depends on your company culture. Some companies like to restrict long distance calls for certain employees. Generally, all premium-rate services (such as 976 and 900 numbers in the U.S.) are blocked. Publicly accessible phones generally offer local calling only. These are just guidelines; every organization is different.

Document the CDR Method

If you're migrating from an existing phone system, you should document the method you're currently using to gather call details. It's important to understand the existing system, if any, and to choose the right CDR package to meet your billing and call accounting needs. If you are not using any CDR method currently, Cisco provides a solution. The CDR Analysis and Reporting (CAR) tool offers some CDR functionality. However, in most cases, and especially for deployments with existing CDR systems, a third-party tool may be required.

In most PBX environments, transfer of CDR data is achieved via serial interface to the PBX using a printer, PC, or spooling server. One improvement that IP telephony brings, especially in a centralized call processing environment, is that a single CDR management system can service many sites. Traditional PBXs require a PC at every PBX location.

See Chapter 11, "Administering Call Detail Records," for more information on CDRs.

Talk with Existing Users

A critical component of any successful deployment is learning from the various user communities how people actually interact with their phones. Without direct input from the end users, it's impossible to determine the proper softkey templates and training topics. If you have an existing PBX, you have to pay close attention to the difference in feature access methods and address these differences in your training sessions.

Talking to manager/assistant (boss/admin) users and to console operators or receptionists is essential. You'll find that many boss/admin interactions differ. Not everyone uses the functions in the same way. For some users, IP Manager Assistant (IPMA) is the right application, but for others a simple shared-line scenario suffices. Depending on the type of business or organization, other user types might include the following:

- General worker (individual contributor)
- Mobile workers/telecommuters
- Sales or marketing
- Dorm residents
- Teachers/professors in a classroom

Get a representative sample of users from all these types and other types that are applicable to your organization or business. See the earlier section "Conduct a Feature Inventory and Create User Classes" for more information.

It's also critical to understand how end users interact with callers and how their customers are used to being handled. Do not make any assumptions. During the planning process, be sure to sit with some end users and watch them work using the current system. Try to map what they're doing to possible CallManager configurations, but at the same time, try to build a better mousetrap using CallManager's advanced functionality. Perhaps you can improve their call-handling iterations. A good example is how PBXs handle music on hold (MOH). Generally, a single music source is attached to a CD player. With CallManager, up to 50 different groups or departments can stream different, specially recorded messages to callers on hold. Rather than meaningless music, you can play a unique message that can positively impact your clients or customers.

Categorize users into various groups based on how they use their phones. You will surely find that the majority of users use hold, transfer, and conference. You also might find a group that uses park and group pickup.

The user features get implemented using different CallManager components such as button templates, calling search spaces, partitions, and more. So, after you talk to the users and build a matrix of user classes and features, you can use it to define each of the required components. If you are not yet familiar with components such as calling search spaces, partitions, and softkey templates, read through the documentation and other Cisco Press books in the Cisco AVVID Solutions series and get a little hands-on experience. The following list provides some examples of user features.

- **Calling restrictions required by different user types**—These allow you to start scoping the different calling search spaces, such as Internal/Emergency, Local, National, and International. You'll read more about calling restrictions in Chapter 7.

- **Line appearance requirements**—You can define different phone button templates, such as Standard (Cisco IP Phone 7960 with one line appearance), Manager (7960 with two line appearances and a privacy button), Receptionist (7960 with a 7914 line expansion module to have 10 line appearances), and so on.

- **Feature requirements**—You can define the different softkey templates, such as Standard, Manager (iDivert), Receptionist (CallBack, Quality Reporting Tool [QRT], Malicious call trace), and so on.

- **MOH requirements**—You can define multiple MOH audio sources, with names like Silence, Standard, Department Specific, and so on.

With these components created, plus the other device-specific features defined within the matrix, the specific user classes can be accurately described in a way that anyone can implement. Table 1-2 provides an example.

Table 1-2 *Sample User Classes and Configurations*

Component	User Class and Related Configuration			
	Public	**Standard**	**Manager**	**Standard-Dept0001**
Calling search space	Internal/ Emergency	Internal/ Emergency + Long Distance	Internal/ Emergency + Long Distance + International	Internal/ Emergency + Long Distance
Phone button template	Standard	Standard	Manager	Standard
Softkey template	Standard	Standard	Manager	Standard
MOH source	Standard	Standard	Standard	Dept0001
Extension mobility	Disabled	Disabled	Enabled	Disabled
Voice mail profile	None	Standard	Standard	Standard
Maximum number of calls	2	4	6	4
Busy trigger	2	2	4	2

Determine the Current Applications

Determine all the voice applications that are currently running on the voice network. These may include but are not limited to those listed in Table 1-3, which are provided either natively in CallManager, via an optional Cisco solution, or optional third-party solution. Table 1-3 does not provide a comprehensive list of partner solutions. You should check the Cisco AVVID Find a Partner page on Cisco.com at the following link for the complete list of third-party solutions, or search Cisco.com for "AVVID find a partner":

http://www.cisco.com/pcgi-bin/ecoa/Search

Table 1-3   *List of Features and Cisco Equivalents*

PBX Application	Cisco and Third-Party Equivalent
Automatic Call Distributor (ACD)	Cisco IP Contact Center (IPCC) Express
Interactive Voice Response (IVR)	Cisco IP IVR
Call center	Cisco IPCC
Call recording	Third-party systemwide applications from NICE, Witness, MIND CTI, and more (**http://www.cisco.com/pcgi-bin/ecoa/Search > IP Telephony > IP Voice Endpoints > Search**) Third-party single phone from JK Audio THAT-1
Remote monitoring	CallManager Serviceability's Real-Time Monitoring Tool (**Application > Cisco CallManager Serviceability > Tools > Real-Time Monitoring Tool**) Third-party applications from Integrated Research Prognosis, NetIQ, Vivinet, and more (**http://www.cisco.com/pcgi-bin/ecoa/Search > IP Telephony > Operations, Administration & Maintenance (OAM) > Search**)
Modem	Cisco VG248 Cisco VG224 Cisco IOS gateways
Fax	Cisco VG248 Cisco VG224 Cisco IOS gateways
ISDN	Cisco IOS gateways
Tie-lines	Centralized call processing Intercluster trunks
Ringdown lines	Use of NULL translation pattern (see Chapter 7)
Elevator phones	Cisco VG248 Cisco VG224 Cisco IOS gateways
Overhead paging	Third-party applications from Bogen Communications (Bogen units generally are connected to CallManager via a standard Foreign Exchange Station [FXS] interface)

continues

Table 1-3 *List of Features and Cisco Equivalents (Continued)*

PBX Application	Cisco and Third-Party Equivalent
Zone paging	Third-party products available from Norstan
Emergency phones	Direct to Central Office
Encryption devices	Cisco IP Phone model 7970 Third-party phones that connect inline with a phone handset
Forced account codes	CallManager releases 3.3(4), 4.1, and beyond (**Feature > Client Matter Code**) Third-party solutions from Berbee, Circle 24, and more (**http://www.cisco.com/pcgi-bin/ecoa/Search > IP Telephony > IP Phone Applications > Search**)
Client matter codes	CallManager releases 3.3(4), 4.1, and beyond (**Feature > Client Matter Code**) Third-party solutions from Berbee, Circle 24, and more (**http://www.cisco.com/pcgi-bin/ecoa/Search > IP Telephony > IP Phone Applications > Search**)
Hoteling	Extension mobility (Cisco Extension Mobility service)
Call coverage paths	Hunt list logic (**Route Plan > Route/Hunt > Route/Hunt List**) Third-party solutions from Berbee and more (**http://www.cisco.com/pcgi-bin/ecoa/Search > IP Telephony > IP Phone Applications > Search**)

You should have a migration plan for each of these applications, all of which can be developed either natively with CallManager or Cisco products or with third-party solutions. The point is to avoid overlooking anything and to address all needed applications at the beginning of the project. Nothing puts a project off schedule like missing applications. You also want to avoid having to explain why an application doesn't work as expected.

Document All Existing Hardware

Various types of nonphone hardware are in use at most companies or organizations. These include devices such as

- Headsets
- Amtel units (user-to-user text messaging)
- Recording equipment
- Dictaphones
- Attendant consoles
- Conference room speakerphones

- Remote microphones
- Wallboards (used in call centers for displaying real-time queue statistics)
- CD players
- Muzak units (piped-in ambient music, also known as *elevator music*)
- Wireless phones such as Cisco Wireless IP Phone 7920 or other third-party wireless (DECT) phones

Check and fully test the compatibility of each of these devices with CallManager. In some cases, you can phase out the existing equipment and use native CallManager functionality. A good example of this is CD players used for MOH. Given the prevalence of the MP3 file format, you might decide to stream hold music directly from a server rather than worrying about connectivity to a CD player or Muzak box.

Choose the Right Equipment

In general, it's good to use switches with redundant power and redundant supervisor modules such as the Catalyst 4507R and Catalyst 6500 series. Making your access layer switches as redundant as possible results in greater network availability should something fail.

Choose a Server Hardware Vendor

First, use the Cisco IP Telephony SRND to determine the desired number of each type of server in the cluster, the redundancy strategy the cluster uses, and the physical server placement. (For the SRND, go to http://www.cisco.com/warp/public/779/largeent/it/ese/srnd.html, or search Cisco.com for "IP Telephony Solutions Reference Network Design.") Then you must decide whether to use the Cisco-branded Media Convergence Servers (MCS) or the private-label servers from Compaq and IBM. In addition to the design guidelines provided in the SRND, you must consider other important ramifications when choosing a server hardware vendor.

In general, it's difficult to make a blanket recommendation, because there are so many variables to consider. Surely the easiest and most hassle-free option is to choose all Cisco MCS. These servers are specially built, thoroughly tested, and easily ordered, and they provide a single-vendor solution. However, the decision is not always so simple.

You must consider other factors when deciding whether to purchase Cisco MCS or Cisco-certified hardware from Compaq or IBM:

- **Relationship with the server vendors**—Perhaps you have a great relationship with your Cisco account team and support structure, and you prefer all Cisco hardware to get a single point of support for the CallManager software, hardware, and network infrastructure. On the other hand, maybe you have a large server farm that is all IBM, and you prefer to keep your environment all-IBM hardware.

- **Pricing and discounts**—You might have an aggressive pricing structure with a particular server vendor that you want to leverage when purchasing servers for your CallManager implementation.

- **Service and support**—Purchasing non-Cisco branded hardware causes your solution to be implemented using equipment from multiple vendors, potentially adding a layer of complexity when you're trying to determine whether a problem's cause is hardware or software. If the problem is the hardware, you must contact a different support organization to troubleshoot or replace the non-Cisco branded hardware.

- **Hardware availability**—Both Compaq and IBM frequently release new hardware. Cisco does not certify every platform available from every vendor, so only certain models are tested and approved for use with CallManager. It's quite possible that Cisco will not support new hardware at the time of its release, and older models might not be available except through Cisco. Any hardware used must be approved by Cisco. For a list of supported platforms, check the Cisco 7800 Series Media Convergence Servers brochure at http://www.cisco.com/go/swonly.

Server Memory Requirements

You should also consider another server specification: the amount of memory required by the various applications. You should have at least 1 GB of RAM in your server, but additional memory is advisable. The general rule is that you can never have too much memory. However, no matter how much memory is present in a server running Windows 2000 Server, no more than 2 GB of memory can be allocated to a particular process. For example, the CallManager service controls call processing on all CallManager servers. If you have a server with 3 GB of memory, CallManager can use all the memory it can get and leave the rest for other processes. Cisco MCS 7845 servers use Windows 2000 Advanced Server, which can address 3 GB of RAM per process, the amount of RAM that is recommended for large clusters with tens of thousands of phones.

If you want a server with less than 2 GB of RAM, you must consider the number of device weights and dial plan weights supported by the server when determining the minimum amount of RAM required for each CallManager server. For the latest information on device weights and their effect on memory requirements, refer to the SRNDs on Cisco.com (see the earlier section "Read the Solution Reference Network Designs").

Adding Hard Drives to a Server

The CallManager redundant array of independent disks (RAID) configuration uses two mirrored disks. Each drive is partitioned into a C:\ partition containing the operating system and program files and a D:\ or E:\ partition containing some operating system installation files.

Adding a disk to the system might be a good idea for these reasons:

- **Storing log files**—When troubleshooting CallManager, the trace facility can produce numerous log files. Rather than limit the number of log files you can keep, using an extra disk to store log files might be the best way of keeping the install drive from running out of space.

  In addition, you can send the extra drive to the Cisco Technical Assistance Center (TAC) when the log files contain so much data that they cannot easily be sent over the Internet. A good example of this is SDL trace files.

- **Storing downloads and patches**—The size of the various CallManager upgrade files and operating system (OS) patches has been growing since CallManager was released. Often, administrators download the images from the Voice Software Center on Cisco.com (http://www.cisco.com/kobayashi/sw-center/sw-voice.shtml) and place them on the CallManager server's C:\ drive. The result is excessive clutter and the potential to overload the drive, which usually causes CallManager failures. Instead, as a best practice, use a spare drive or a network share to store these files.

Choosing Phone Types

Company policy often dictates the right phone for the various user classes. In the absence of established policy, common Cisco IP Phone-to-user pairs are shown in Table 1-4.

The choice of the standard employee phone often depends on company culture. Some organizations believe that everyone should have headset capability, speakerphones, and speed dials. Other organizations have policies that oppose the use of speakerphones in cubicles and other unenclosed areas.

Table 1-4   *User Type and Phone Model Pairings*

User Type	Cisco IP Phone Model
Call center employee	Cisco 7940G (XML is required for phone agent)
Standard employee	Cisco 7912G, 7940G, 7960G, Cisco IP Communicator
Executive assistant	Cisco 7960G with Cisco IP Phone 7914 Expansion Module(s)
Executive	Cisco 7970G Cisco 7960G Cisco 7936G
Attendant operator	Cisco 7960G with Cisco IP Phone 7914 Expansion Module(s)

continues

Table 1-4 *User Type and Phone Model Pairings (Continued)*

User Type	Cisco IP Phone Model
Conference rooms	Cisco 7936G
Warehouse employee	Cisco 7920
Telecommuter	Cisco 7902G, 7905G, Cisco IP Communicator
Common/public area phones	Cisco 7902G

NOTE One option that is often discussed but almost never implemented is an "all-SoftPhone" solution, in which Cisco IP SoftPhone or Cisco IP Communicator is deployed with no physical phones placed at users' desks. Although this is an economically appealing option, the idea often gets declined. Many companies want the phone to be separate or don't consider users' PCs to be "always-on" devices, which makes management and tracking a bit more difficult with software-based phones.

As discussed earlier, using an inventory of the existing system (in the case of a PBX migration) is the best way to achieve parity. Many customers make a matrix of the existing phones in use and then map Cisco devices to those of the existing vendor. This works extremely well and is recommended because it keeps the amount of change for users to a minimum.

Create a Training Curriculum for Users and Administrators

Training is an important part of any implementation. Your users need training on the most-used functions of their phones and user-accessible web pages. Administrators must understand all aspects of the system so that they can perform daily management and monitoring, as well as moves, adds, and changes.

You should also consider appointing employees in each department to undergo training before the cutover or initial deployment. That way, on the first and second day that the new system is deployed, employees can ask knowledgeable peers for help.

User Training Techniques

How you perform user training is entirely up to you. It usually depends on your time and resource allocations. However, it's important to perform your training before you actually place the phones on users' desks. Training gives users exposure to the new system before they have to use the phones in production. The recommended approach is to use a large conference room to stage up to 24 phones for user training sessions.

Invite 24 students per class, and have them pair off to follow the different lessons by calling each other and testing the features. If more than two people must be involved, such as for conference-related functions, student pairs can call other student pairs.

Training for the Cisco CallManager User Options web page is best conducted in electronic format. Tools such as Camtasia from TechSmith (http://www.techsmith.com) can be used to record the instructor's interactions. You can then add voice-overs and post the finished file on your company intranet in a variety of formats. Live training of anything PC-based is difficult because of the large number of PCs that must be dedicated to the task. Offering web-based training is much better, because students can follow along with the training at their own pace and even rewind and fast-forward.

TIP   In general, users have the most difficulty with transfer and conference operations features because of their consultative nature. Invoking the feature with a single softkey press and then completing the operation by pressing the softkey again is an operation you should plan to repeat multiple times to ensure that trainees fully understand how to perform transfer and conference.

The most important topics to cover during user training are

- Managing multiple calls per line
- Alternating between the speaker, handset, and headset modes
- Using hold
- Using transfer
- Using conference
- Using call join
- Using barge/cBarge
- Using call park
- Using the drop any party softkey
- Using malicious call trace
- Using immediate divert
- Blocking caller ID on a per-call basis

In addition to all the feature-related training, you should train users on how to seek support. When calling the Help Desk for support, the user should provide the following information:

- The time as displayed on the phone at the time of the problem
- The line appearance on which the problem occurred
- The called party number if applicable
- A specific description of the problem

Having this information lets Help Desk personnel troubleshoot the problem much more effectively. The most important thing is the time. Without that, it's harder to find the exact information in the trace files. It's important to get the time that is displayed on the phone because phones are synched with CallManager, making the correlation between phone time and times listed in CCM trace files more precise.

NOTE The QRT softkey can be used in conjunction with or in lieu of making a call to the Help Desk. It really depends on the company culture. Some companies like the perception of increased customer service that comes from the human interaction.

Be sure to read the sections on user training in Chapter 7 for additional information.

Administrator Training

You should plan on providing formal training for your administrators. Many options are available. Cisco has a standard curriculum, as shown in Figure 1-4, which is offered by various Cisco Certified training partners. Use the following link and click **IP Telephony Training**, or search Cisco.com for "IP Telephony training":

> http://www.cisco.com/en/US/learning/le31/le29/learning_training_from_cisco_learning_partners.html

How you provide the administrator training is up to you. Options include customized training, in-house training, and the standard five-day CIPT classes. The key is to determine exactly what your administrators need. For example, if you are having Cisco Advanced Services or a Cisco Certified Partner install your systems, do you really need to cover installation in the training, or can that be part of the knowledge transfer from the installation team?

In addition to formal training, there's train-the-trainer. This style of training can be even more valuable, because it is one-on-one and more concentrated. Your staff member can take the learning class(es), filter out the information that's pertinent to your deployment, and then train all the administrators on what they really need to know.

Figure 1-4   *IP Telephony Training for System Administrators*

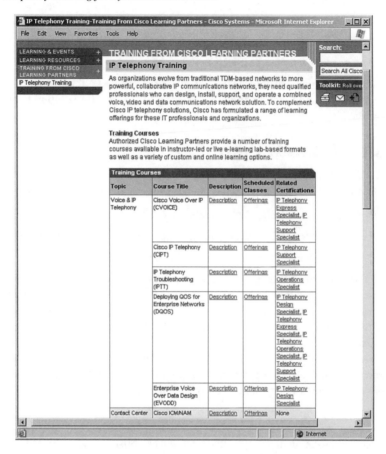

If a Cisco reseller is installing the system for you, it's important (if possible) to watch and learn what the implementation team does and to absorb the subtleties of the installation from the people actually installing the system.

The key things to watch for are

- Dial plan configuration
- Enterprise parameters configuration
- Gateway configuration
- IP Phone services configuration
- Media resource configuration
- Phone configuration

Also, you should consider adding the following books to your library:

- *Cisco CallManager Fundamentals: A Cisco AVVID Solution* (ISBN: 1-58705-008-0)
- *Troubleshooting Cisco IP Telephony: A Cisco AVVID Solution* (ISBN: 1-58705-075-7)
- *Cisco IP Telephony* (ISBN: 1-58705-050-1)

Be sure to search ciscopress.com periodically for new IP Telephony- or CallManager-related titles and second editions of existing Cisco AVVID Solution books.

Establish a Rollout Plan

A *rollout plan* represents the method you will use to enter phones into the CallManager database and distribute the actual phones to users' desks. A rollout plan should include

- Time of day of phone placement
- How users will be notified of the technician's visit to their offices
- How phones will be connected to the network

The rollout plan is critical to the success of any installation. Without a solid plan, your visits to users' desks will be haphazard, you might forget some users, or you might place the wrong phone models on the wrong desks. Without a plan to keep you on track, you might not finish the rollout on time, which is probably one of the worst things that can happen, especially for a large cutover. On top of that, without the plan, you could find yourself running around the building at 3 A.M. on a Sunday morning looking for someone's office because you didn't have the right floor plan, didn't know that a user moved his or her desk, or couldn't get security personnel to open the necessary doors.

TIP   Consider investing in a project manager and establish a process for the rollout that includes company engineers working alongside implementation engineers. By doing so, the people who will ultimately be charged with maintaining the system can see how the system was initially configured.

Determine How to Add Phones to the System

Depending on the size of your rollout, the most labor-intensive job might be placing the phones on users' desks. There are two basic approaches: Use BAT in concert with the Tool for Auto-Registered Phones Support (TAPS) with dummy MAC addresses generated by BAT, or configure all the phones in the system with the actual MAC address and extensions.

To decide between these two approaches, you have to consider the following factors:

- Number of phones

- Amount of time to cutover
- Quality of end-user logistics

Consideration: Number of Phones

If you are rolling out a large number of phones (more than 200 to 300), it's probably best to use TAPS. With TAPS, you can add the phones to CallManager using dummy MAC addresses, which means you don't have to enter every MAC address for all the phones and associate them with a directory number. Instead, TAPS assigns dummy addresses that are later updated with the phone's actual MAC address when a user dials a specific directory number to download the phone's configuration. Using TAPS means that technicians can simply place the phones and an instruction sheet on users' desks. The instructions should explain how to plug in the phone (if the technicians do not install the phones), dial a specific directory number, and follow the steps to use TAPS. By the time the user hangs up, the phone will have downloaded its specific configuration and will be ready to use.

The TAPS method is relatively low-risk and works well. The downside is that the users must perform some actions to make the phones work; they don't just arrive at work on Monday and find a working phone. TAPS is deployed as part of an IVR through Cisco Extended Services. Extended Services Customer Response Solution (CRS) ships with two ports only, so the maximum number of simultaneous calls that TAPS can accept is two. On a full CRS deployment, the number of simultaneous calls into TAPS depends on the number of licenses you purchase and the number of computer telephony integration (CTI) ports you configure for TAPS. Consult the CRS and TAPS documentation on Cisco.com for installation and configuration information.

- TAPS is documented as part of the Bulk Administration Tool documentation at http://www.cisco.com/univercd/cc/td/doc/product/voice/sw_ap_to/admin/bulk_adm/index.htm.
- CRS documentation is available at http://www.cisco.com/en/US/products/sw/custcosw/ps1846/prod_software_versions_home.html.

TAPS is a great tool when used in combination with a single, standard phone model for all users because you don't have to spend a lot of time on the logistics of where specific users sit. When you're installing a system, location is by far the hardest information to gather accurately, especially in a green field installation. The information almost always changes, resulting in people having the wrong phone models.

WARNING   Users with special add-ons such as Cisco IP Phone 7914 Expansion Modules, text telephone (TTY) devices, external encryptors, and external recording devices have to be identified so that the specialized equipment can be delivered to the correct location.

A middle-ground approach involves gathering as much user information as possible and having the installer do the TAPS login at install time. The issue with this approach is the uncertainty involved with getting the correct user information.

If you are a Cisco Certified AVVID partner, be sure to have several company employees available on site to help you locate users' offices and cubicles and to open doors. It's also critical to have the support of the security officers at the site. Ask for additional security officers to be on hand to help unlock doors.

Consideration: Amount of Time to Cutover

When you're working on a tight schedule, you might not have time to unbox all the phones, enter their MAC addresses in CallManager Administration, and rebox the phones for placement on desks. Using TAPS means you can simply dispatch the phones to the proper locations for placement and have end users dial TAPS to configure their phones. When you have more time during the cutover, you have the luxury of adding the phones' actual MAC addresses into CallManager Administration.

Consideration: Quality of End-User Logistics

When you are working in an environment in which you don't have good floor plans for the buildings, you have almost no idea where specific users sit. For that reason, using TAPS in combination with a single, standard phone model for all users (such as Cisco IP Phone 7960) allows you to put phones in every occupied cubicle or office, and people can dial the TAPS number and enter their extensions to download the phone configuration. In addition, there are delicate situations in which getting information about extension numbers can be challenging. Again TAPS helps, because users can enter their own information. If you encounter such a situation during the planning process, it's generally a good idea to make the rollout easier by using a standard phone model for most or all users.

If you have up-to-date floor plans with up-to-date usernames, adding the phones using the real MAC addresses is quite feasible, because you know where people sit, you can count on security to open the doors, and you can plan certain floors for certain nights.

Migrating from PBX or Green Field

TAPS is generally very good for green field deployments, because no existing information needs to be converted on a user-by-user basis. However, in certain PBX migration scenarios, especially when direct inward dial (DID) numbers are changed or when phone migrations are happening in small groups (rather than in large batches), using the Bulk Administration Tool (BAT) or manually entering the phones in CallManager Administration is probably a better method.

Determine the Cutover Method

When planning the system's rollout, you must decide how to migrate from the existing system (if applicable) to the new system. If you're working in a new environment or green field, no cutover choice needs to be made, so you can skip this section.

The following sections discuss the three different ways to migrate a system:

- Flash cut
- PBX migration
- Dual phone

Flash Cut

A *flash cut* is a clean break from one system to the other. It often occurs over a weekend. Users go home on Friday and come in on Monday to a new phone system. All original phones are removed, and users begin using the new system immediately.

Flash cuts are best for small organizations and for small remote sites attaching to a larger cluster in a centralized CallManager deployment.

One of the most significant factors in a flash cut is user training and second-day support, which was discussed earlier in this chapter. Without good training before the cutover, there's no way for users to become familiar with the phone until it is on their desks in full production.

Testing the system is critical when doing a flash cut. After the system is installed and configured, it must be thoroughly tested in what is generally a short time frame. Flash cuts require a great deal of precision in the planning phase to ensure readiness.

Most often, the servers are preinstalled and configured in a staging environment before being brought onsite, which makes a flash cut a little more manageable. Instead of a staging environment, you might have had the system running in pilot mode with select users for a few weeks (known as an *alpha cluster*). Even with either of these pre-deployment testing phases in place, second-day support is critical because there are always unforeseen configuration tasks that get missed with high-pressure flash cuts. Users have no alternative phone system after the new system is installed, so having good user support in the first week after the cutover is highly recommended.

For more information about installation, refer to Chapter 3, "Installing CallManager."

PBX Migration

PBX migration is the type of cutover that involves connecting tie-lines between CallManager and the existing PBX. *Tie-lines* are simply lines that connect CallManager and the PBX. This method is often used in larger deployments because there is simply no other way.

In general terms, these kinds of cutovers are used especially when new buildings are put up or remote sites are added to the network. There are groups of users using CallManager, and groups of users using the PBX, and they need to talk to each other.

This method is quite viable, but there are some key best practices you should adhere to:

- **Use Primary Rate Interface (PRI) or Q.SIG when integrating**—These protocols provide the most functionality between the two systems. Things such as calling and called party name display are supported.

- **Have enough tie-line trunks available**—It's better to overprovision the trunking between systems than have too few channels between systems. When integrating systems, you must choose whether the CallManager phones will have their own Public Switched Telephone Network (PSTN) trunks. If the CallManager phones are on a campus, it's recommended that you have them act as extensions off the PBX and use the PBX for inbound and outbound PSTN connectivity. Because of cost and PBX space constraints, you might not be able to overprovision trunks. You might have to migrate tie-lines one at a time, which requires some level of accuracy. One way to get an idea of how many trunks you need between systems is to do a traffic study on the PBX for the groups of users you intend to migrate. For example, say you intend to migrate Building A. If you have the capability, check the call detail records on the PBX to see how much calling the users of Building A actually do. Using this information ensures that you have enough trunks between CallManager and the PBX when you migrate the users. If the CallManager phones are at a remote site, it's best to provision PSTN connectivity directly on CallManager.

  For more information about traffic analysis, refer to the "Traffic Analysis for Voice over IP" document at the following link or search Cisco.com for "traffic analysis for VoIP."

    http://www.cisco.com/en/US/tech/tk652/tk701/technologies_white_paper09186 a00800d6b74.shtml

- **Understand the impact on the attendant operator**—During your migration, you will have some users on the PBX and some on CallManager, which means that any attendant operators need visibility into the busy status of all the phones on the system. If maintaining visibility status of all phones is important to you during the migration, you have to use a console application that supports both platforms. It's impossible to give a recommendation because of the number of variables involved, such as PBX type and supported features. Check with your PBX vendor for supported third-party console applications, and cross-reference them with Cisco's Find a Partner list at http://www.cisco.com/pcgi-bin/ecoa/Search.

- **Establish the voice mail integration method early on, and test**—A difficult and critical decision involves voice mail integration. There are many options. If you decide to use your existing PBX voice mail, you can use a Cisco VG248 gateway and Simplified Message Desk Interface (SMDI) to integrate CallManager. If you have an Octel system with digital interfaces, you can use a Cisco Digital Phone Adapter (DPA).

If you decide to use Cisco Unity with CallManager and integrate Unity with your existing voice mail system, you can use either the VPIM or AMIS-A protocols. If your PBX voice mail system is an Octel system, you can integrate using Analog Octelnet with the Cisco Unity Bridge. Refer to the "Cisco Unity Interoperability Features and Functionality Comparison" document at the following link or search Cisco.com for "Cisco Unity Interoperability."

http://www.cisco.com/en/US/products/sw/voicesw/ps2237/products_data_ sheet09186a00800e9c23.html

Migrating your existing PBX voice mail to Unity is supported by Unity's dual-switch integration feature. For PBX compatibility with Unity, check the *Cisco Unity Bridge System Requirements, and Supported Hardware and Software* documentation at the following link or check the "Supported Phone System Integrations" section of the "Cisco Unity System Requirements and Supported Hardware and Software" document.

http://www.cisco.com/en/US/products/sw/voicesw/ps2237/prod_pre_ installation_guide09186a0080117617.html#31803

Dual Phone and Then Flash Cut

Some people managing deployments migrating from a PBX decide to place both CallManager and PBX phones on the users' desks but do not integrate the systems at all. This lets you configure and test CallManager completely and then flash cut the system in one evening.

This approach provides the greatest amount of time to actually roll out the phones, perform the training, complete all the needed testing, and answer all the users' questions and concerns before cutting over to the new system.

At the time of cutover, you have to move the components that CallManager will use from the PBX to CallManager. These components include PSTN trunks, analog stations, and voice mail connections. You also need to power off the PBX.

In addition, this approach provides a degree of safety in that you can simply power on the PBX and move the components back over if a catastrophic event occurs.

The dual phone and then flash cut option is recommended for large campus installations that leave their PBX behind and do not call for integration of CallManager. The sheer number of phones that have to be placed means that a simple flash cut won't work. In some cases you don't want to integrate with the PBX because of a lack of tie-line trunk ports on the PBX or a lack of license for the PRI and/or Q.SIG protocols.

Create User Information Packets

A best practice that is too frequently ignored is providing information to the user. Without a list of instructions, second-day support is made much harder because the Help Desk gets overwhelmed with calls.

Be sure to distribute user information packets (leave-behind materials) that give the user the following information:

- Extension (for example, 1000)
- Full DID number (for example, 214-555-1000)
- Voice mail number (internal access number, such as 5000, and external access number, such as 214-555-5000)
- Voice mail password
- Voice mail quick reference
- Phone PIN
- Help Desk number
- Phone user guide
- Name of installation technician
- Date, time, and contact information for phone training

One often-used technique is to print simple business cards with the name of the installer and the Help Desk number. These can be left on the users' chairs or stuck in their keyboards, where they will not be missed.

Without this information, users roam the halls looking for information and are generally not in a good mood on the first day of production. Users who can't acquire the information they need feel that the change from the previous phone system to the new one is a bad idea and that the new system is much harder to use. This significantly reduces satisfaction with the deployment and makes training the users on the new system more difficult.

Establish a Second-Day Support Plan

Most second-day support centers around the following items:

- **Moves, adds, and changes**—Be sure to have a plan to cover the inevitable changes that must occur during the first and second days of production. Have a handful of CallManager configuration people at the ready. The most common changes are the addition of shared lines, fixing incorrect extension numbers, and configuring intercom groups.
- **Additional training**—Users invariably need one-on-one training for certain features and functions. Some of this happens informally within workgroups, but it's important to be ready to do some handholding.

TIP Appoint certain department members who were trained before the cutover to help fellow team members when they forget how to do certain tasks.

- **Establish a "war room"**—Reserve a dedicated conference room (sometimes called a "war room" during IP telephony deployments) where support staff can all work together to field questions as they arise and make any needed modifications to the system. Having the support team close to each other gives a sense of camaraderie and provides a way for everyone to learn from the problems and solutions that invariably occur during the first week of an installation.

- **Addressing complaints about the process**—This is one of those touchy subjects that always causes consternation among users. Sometimes users just need to vent their frustration with the process and the differences with the new phone system. Be sure to have a sympathetic ear, and be ready to help the user adjust.

- **Broken or missing items in offices**—Installing phones in people's offices sometimes results in damage. Be sure that you have some kind of formal grievance process for users to lodge their complaints and concerns. Sometimes personal items are misplaced or damaged as a result of installing the phone. In general, the network cable from the user's PC is plugged into the back of the phone, and a cable from the back of the phone is plugged back into the computer. This means that the technician installing the phone needs to get at the back of the PC. People have a habit of burying their PCs under lots of personal effects or in hard-to-reach corners of their desks. Be sure to instruct your installation technicians to report any damage. Institute a policy that allows for direct communication with the affected user, and replace damaged items. Being candid about any damage is always the best policy.

Institute a Problem Reporting and Escalation Plan

During the rollout period, it's important for the system administrator to understand how to get help. In addition, it's important to have the proper staff to address issues in a timely fashion.

The best approach if you need extra help is to use Cisco Advanced Services (shown in Figure 1-5; search Cisco.com for "advanced services"). You also can arrange for a Cisco Certified Partner to supply onsite resources up to two weeks after implementation to handle the influx of issues any new phone system can bring.

Figure 1-5 *Cisco Advanced Services Page on Cisco.com*

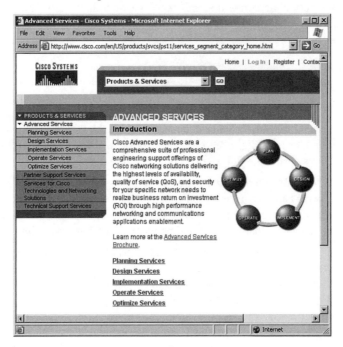

Companies often are caught short of resources, and customer service levels suffer. Regardless of resource constraints, be sure to set the right expectation with your users during training sessions so that they are not caught by surprise, waiting for problem resolution.

It's also important to have an escalation plan for employees who have critical needs. Be sure to have all Cisco Technical Support contracts and support numbers handy, and be ready to prioritize your users' needs. Again, increasing the size of your staff is highly recommended in the first two weeks of implementation.

Establish Operations Procedures

It's extremely important to synchronize the network operations team with the telephony operations team to ensure that network connectivity is not spontaneously interrupted. One of the biggest problems you'll face is that your phones are up and working, but you don't have an operations and management infrastructure in place. One of the first things you should do is create an e-mail/voice mail distribution list that includes either the heads of all departments or all users so that you can keep the relevant personnel informed when changes will occur.

Operations tasks include the following:

- **Scheduled network upgrades**—One of the biggest issues you could face is that random network engineer who constantly reboots switches and routers in the middle of the day because there's a problem or because a switch needs to be upgraded. Each time this happens, phone service or supplementary services such as conferencing might go down for some or all of your users.

  It's critical to establish a regular outage window in which to perform upgrades. In addition, it's important to establish an e-mail or voice mail distribution list to alert all involved parties to any planned or unplanned outages.

  Voice is one of the most critical applications you can put on a network. You need to ensure that the telephony operations personnel are aware of any network maintenance activity. Many unplanned phone outages are caused by simple lack of communication.

NOTE   Check the section "Subscribe to the CallManager Notification Tool to be Advised of New Fixes, OS Updates, and Product Patches" in Chapter 6 to learn how to be automatically notified each time Cisco approves a CallManager fix, OS update, or product patch.

- **Scheduled application server upgrades**—It's important that you avoid taking down your voice systems every time a new patch or software version is released. You need to have a schedule and a procedure that alerts people that an upgrade is taking place. Be sure to document and send e-mail to your users if any changes in phone behavior occur. No one likes to be surprised when something as seemingly simple and basic as phone operation suddenly changes without warning.

- **Scheduled dial plan changes**—Sometimes making changes to the dial plan necessitates the restarting of CallManager services. Do not make major changes to the dial plan in the middle of the day and start resetting services, which causes calls to terminate without warning. Bring up new circuits and connect to other systems during a scheduled maintenance window using a standard change control procedure, not during regular production hours when a large number of users are affected.

- **Scheduled new application deployment**—When bringing new applications online, whether call center applications, Emergency Responder, Cisco MeetingPlace, and so on, it's important to use a scheduled outage window to perform these installations. Even with proper testing before deployment, you can't be 100 percent certain of the impact the application will have on the network until you deploy it, and it's best to not affect production users.

- **Scheduled media resource moves, adds, and changes**—If you intend to change conference, MOH, or media termination point (MTP) configurations, do so during a standard change control window, not during production hours.

- **Scheduled gateway moves, adds, and changes**—If you need to make changes to gateways, do so during a scheduled change control window. In almost every case, gateways need to be reset for the changes to take effect. Resetting a gateway during production hours most likely results in dropped calls, so it's best to make necessary changes when they least affect users (nonproduction hours).

- **Established change management procedures**—This is where some companies fall flat: They let their staff make fundamental changes to the system without following a change management procedure. In one real-life example, a company changed the name of its gateway routers during business hours, causing a major outage, but no one on the voice team knew anything about the changes. Because the voice team didn't know about the change, they didn't change the Media Gateway Control Protocol (MGCP) name in CallManager Administration. Therefore, the company suffered an outage while troubleshooting the issue. Establishing a change management and control procedure that includes everyone involved is important. See the "Change Management: Best Practices White Paper" at the following link or search Cisco.com for "Document ID 22852."

  http://www.cisco.com/en/US/tech/tk869/tk769/technologies_white_paper 09186a008014f932.shtml

Summary

Planning, designing, and implementing a Cisco IP Telephony solution is a much more manageable task if you carefully consider each step before moving on to each subsequent step. Efficient installation starts with a good plan that ensures a smooth, methodical, and successful deployment of the complete CallManager solution.

In addition to the resources discussed in this chapter (Cisco certified training, Cisco partners, Cisco Advanced Services, other Cisco Press books), periodically check the Technical Support website (http://www.cisco.com/en/US/support/index.html > *click the link to* **Technology Support** > *choose the* **Voice** *category*). This website provides articles on all aspects of voice technology, as shown in Figure 1-6.

Figure 1-6   *Voice Technical Support on Cisco.com*

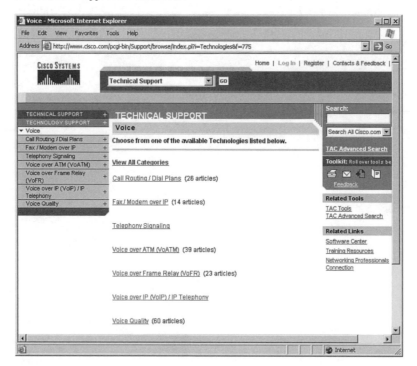

## CHAPTER 2

Planning Centralized Call Processing Deployments

Centralized deployments characteristically employ low- to medium-speed WANs to interconnect geographically distinct locations to a headquarters site. Typically labeled hub-and-spoke reference design, this type of WAN links the remote spokes or offices to the hub or main site. Because most resources and related traffic originate or terminate at the center, and only minimal remote site-to-site conversations occur, this model suits many organizations. The hub-and-spoke reference model is a good base to build on when employing any WAN connectivity. It can be readily expanded to form regional centers of communication.

Typically, the following WAN technologies are used for IP data:

- Leased lines
- Frame Relay
- Asynchronous Transfer Mode (ATM)
- Multiprotocol Label Switching (MPLS)
- Virtual private network (VPN) overlays

These same technologies can be used to interconnect remote voice and data communications, all over IP. Figure 2-1 illustrates a generalized Cisco CallManager centralized deployment. With the addition of voice over IP (VoIP), the key advantages of centralizing the data equipment, staff, and expenses are further enhanced. Managing call processing centrally provides the same benefits as centralizing servers in data networks. In addition, you can gain the same benefits by centrally managing voice mail, automated attendant, Interactive Voice Response (IVR), and conferencing. As a result of centralization, all call control occurs at the central site, which is the hub of administration for every phone within the deployment. Each regional center can scale to 30,000 IP phones and can be managed by a single CallManager Administration console. Connectivity to the locations through the central site router, or a dual-purpose routing and IP voice gateway, may take the form of a single link or multiple links, depending on the chosen WAN architecture.

The centralized CallManager model exemplifies a typical regional enterprise scenario and is the most frequently implemented CallManager deployment, but it is only one of two deployment models. Distributed CallManager scenarios place CallManager servers and their associated call processing in multiple locations on the network instead of one centralized location, and then tie those locations together via links typically greater in size and smaller in quantity than those found in the centralized model. Distributed deployments manage each location individually, and each location can be as complex as the centralized model covered within this chapter. From a simplified point of view, the distributed call processing model ties together multiple centralized CallManager deployments.

Figure 2-1 *Centralized CallManager Deployment*

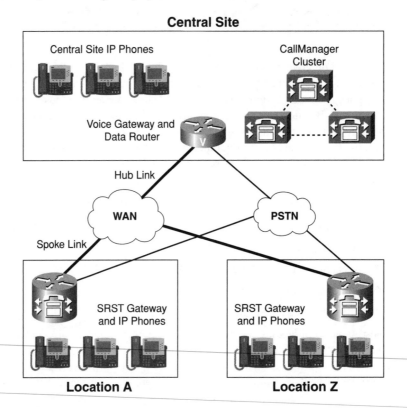

WAN failures must be planned for, because voice transport across sites is dependent on an operating link between the central site and remote locations. Survivable Remote Site Telephony (SRST) can be added to the gateways at each location to provide local call processing service during a WAN outage. SRST automatically takes over during a failure scenario and then restores normal operation when WAN service returns. SRST not only protects against WAN failures, it's a major component of the centralized CallManager solution.

This chapter discusses the various aspects of planning and deploying CallManager on either a new or existing centralized deployment. It walks you through the basic functionality and best practices, starting with the lowest link layer of basic connectivity. From there you move through the tasks of tuning those links for optimal voice quality, routing calls over busy links, and selecting gateways. The chapter finishes with remote site survivability in case of a WAN failure. This chapter is not meant to be an exhaustive study of each of these areas. It's meant to provide the best practices in implementing a typical centralized CallManager deployment scenario. For additional information, refer to the Solution Reference Network Design guides on Cisco.com at the following links:

> http://www.cisco.com/go/srnd or
> http://www.cisco.com/warp/public/779/largeent/it/ese/srnd.html

The following sections can be summarized as follows:

- **WAN connectivity architectures**—Establishing basic connectivity: basic leased lines, Frame Relay, ATM, MPLS, and voice and video VPN scenarios

- **Quality of service (QoS) for the WAN**—Tuning the links that carry VoIP: queuing and latency, fragmentation and jitter, compression, and bandwidth

- **Locations-based connection admission control (CAC)**—Preventing too many calls from using one link: codec selection and regions, accounting for call bandwidth and locations

- **Automated alternate routing (AAR)**—Using the Public Switched Telephone Network (PSTN) to route calls around a congested WAN link

- **SRST**—Surviving a complete WAN outage for VoIP: providing short-term call processing, PSTN connectivity, and voice mail services

- **Choosing gateways for centralized call processing**—Picking the right gateways for central and remote sites, depending on location and desired functionality

Establishing Basic WAN Connectivity

This section provides a brief overview of the most common WAN deployment architectures used to connect multiple remote locations to a central or regional site. These five deployment scenarios are the most frequently deployed topologies for transporting data. They are not meant to be an exhaustive listing of all carrier and technology offerings, and combinations of technologies can be used to gain cost or technology advantages. The scenarios given here are meant to illustrate the basic topologies for which we will explore the QoS and CAC issues that commonly arise.

Deployment Using Leased Lines

Leased-line deployments are perhaps the simplest WAN connectivity model architecturally. Each location has a link to the central site. This means that for 20 locations, 20 interfaces are needed on the central site router. Links are typically $n * 64$ kbps, up to a 1.544 Mbps

(T1) or 2.048 Mbps (E1) maximum link rate. These links can vary from a switched ISDN line to a dedicated T1 or E1. Some carriers might offer the ability to aggregate multiple locations into a T1 or E1 and reduce the number of physical hub links. The leased-line model is not the most economical when considering the cost of original equipment purchase or monthly line charges.

Figure 2-2 depicts a central site and two remote location sites tied to the central site via leased lines. Two remote locations mean that two links come to the central site from the carrier.

Figure 2-2 *Centralized Deployment Using Leased Lines*

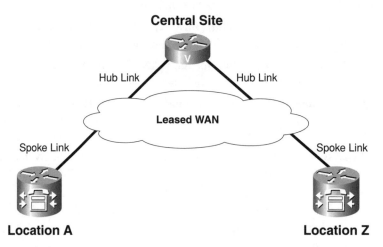

Centralized deployment using leased lines has the following advantages over other deployment scenarios:

- Diverse paths can be mandated from the carrier to prevent all locations from riding across a common hub link as they do in other deployment models. Dependence on a common hub link creates a potential catastrophic failure point.

- Leased lines are typically more reliable than other forms of transport because they do not require a higher level of signaling to establish connectivity.

- The leased-line path through the carrier's network is dedicated to a single customer. Therefore, traffic traversing the path is never intermixed with data from other companies, which typically enhances security and reduces the potential for congestion issues.

- Bandwidth and latency are guaranteed to remain the same all the time. This consistency makes leased lines a good model for any deployment, and certainly for VoIP.

- Leased lines might be the only choice for locations that do not have any other service offering available to them because of a limited number of carriers, remoteness, or cable plant infrastructure.

Deployment Using Frame Relay

Frame Relay deployments typically offer the lowest cost for initial equipment purchase as well as monthly outlay. Frame Relay is an attractive and popular WAN transport where it is available. The location sites again are $n * 64$ kbps, up to a 1.544 Mbps or 2.048 Mbps maximum link rate. This has a direct effect on the number of links at the central site. The central site link is an aggregation of one or more spoke links. For example, a single T1 hub link can support up to six locations with a 256-kbps link at each location. These are virtual links that exist on the one physical link.

Figure 2-3 shows a general overview of a Frame Relay deployment. The central site and two location sites all have a single connection into the carrier's network. Depending on the number of locations and the speed of each connection, the number of links between the central site and the carrier may need to grow.

Figure 2-3   *Centralized Deployment Using Frame Relay*

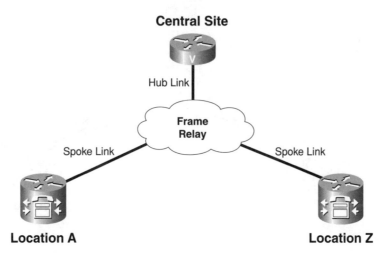

The most unique feature introduced with Frame Relay is the ability to burst beyond the rate at which the bandwidth is guaranteed or subscribed. This allows locations to send more than the guaranteed rate, perhaps up to the maximum link rate of 1.544 Mbps for a short time. Frame Relay poses some hurdles when applying VoIP, because the amount of true bandwidth available at an instant can vary, and the delay between packets or jitter can also fluctuate. You can overcome these challenges by using newer Frame Relay protocols and IOS features, which are covered later in this chapter.

Deployment Using Asynchronous Transfer Mode

Asynchronous Transfer Mode (ATM) deployments break the maximum available local link size barrier by employing inverse multiplexing (also known as *muxing*). Inverse multiplexing, which allows the multiple physical links to operate as a single pipe, can have significant advantages when you need more bandwidth than a single T1 or E1 can provide. Inverse multiplexing not only allows remote locations to gain more bandwidth to the carrier, but it also allows a bigger hub link from the carrier to the central site.

Availability of larger ATM links running at 45 Mbps or greater can be used to interconnect the carrier to the central site, allowing a larger number or higher-speed locations support over a single connection. Use of inverse multiplexing or larger links via ATM combined with the Frame Relay model allows greater bandwidth between the carrier and the central site. This is called ATM to Frame Relay service interworking.

Figure 2-4 shows an inverse multiplexed scenario. Notice that all connections to the carrier have multiple physical connections but are logically treated as a single connection.

Figure 2-4 *Centralized Deployment Using Asynchronous Transfer Mode*

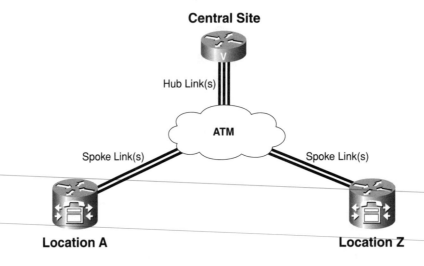

Although never the cheapest layer 2 option, ATM offers not only increased bandwidth but also flexibility in service guarantees. Much like leased lines, constant bit rate (CBR) connections have a rigid loss ratio and information rates. CBR is generally best for voice connectivity because voice has very regular sample sizes. On the other hand, available bit rate (ABR) connections have a minimum information rate but allow bursting up to the available rate, much like a Frame Relay link. ABR is generally best suited for data traffic only, which is bursty and tolerant of jitter and loss. Variable bit rate (VBR) is a combination of the two: It provides a rigid loss ratio with a variable burst size. VBR connectivity is generally best for a video, voice, and data mix, because it requires a low loss ratio but the sample sizes are variable. Service type availability varies greatly by geography and local carrier choices.

TIP   See the sidebar "A Word About Layers" in Chapter 6, "Securing the Environment," to learn more about the OSI model and the various network layers.

Deployment Using Multiprotocol Label Switching (MPLS)

Multiprotocol Label Switching (MPLS) can be carried over any of the other transport technologies that have been described—leased lines, Frame Relay, and ATM. MPLS can also be carried over newer technologies such as cable and DSL. MPLS is not a traditional layer 2 technology. It's actually a higher-level carrier-managed service that can take advantage of any underlying infrastructure. Typical layer 2 services necessitate that all traffic originating or terminating at a location pass through the central site. This normally flows well, because all services are hosted at the central site. When location-to-location data needs grow, congestion at the central site can grow as well, which can affect the entire deployment. MPLS can solve this.

Figure 2-5 shows a logical overview of MPLS-provided service from a carrier. The data flows represent connectivity through the carrier's network. Notice that the location-to-location data flow does not depend on central site connectivity.

Figure 2-5   *Centralized Deployment Using MPLS*

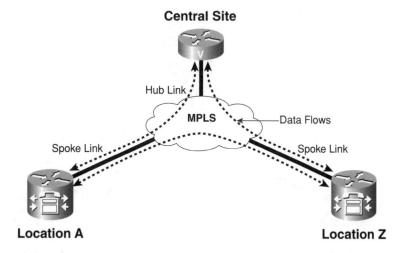

QoS is built into MPLS. QoS is a driving factor in the adoption of MPLS and makes it suitable for VoIP. MPLS can be provisioned to operate in traditional layer 2 mode, or at layer 3 because of the unique tagging that occurs at each endpoint. The endpoint tagging allows the service to behave as if it were native to either layer, and it can tag voice flows separate from data. Equipment in the carrier's network can treat the uniquely identified tags differently as they flow through the network. The service essentially operates like a leased line or routed network. Latency and jitter through the network can be variable and should be used to compare service offerings from multiple service providers. Which transport technology underlies the service and which layer options exist greatly depend on the carrier and location.

Deployment Using Voice and Video Virtual Private Networks

Much like the MPLS networks, voice and video virtual private network (V3PN) architectures can take advantage of any form of connectivity or even be overlaid onto existing network architectures. Potentially anything from a dialup connection through a 622-Mbps OC-12/STM-4 can be used as the V3PN's transport. V3PN architectures can be either a managed service or a completely self-managed operation. Endpoints are authenticated, and all traffic is IPSec-encrypted before it goes onto the exterior network, ensuring a secure channel. This is a flexible, cost-efficient way of interconnecting sites and enabling extranets to suppliers or temporary locations.

Figure 2-6 shows an overview very similar to the MPLS example. Note how easy it is to add extranets or temporary locations in the V3PN architecture. If connectivity between two points exists, a V3PN can provide secure communications.

Figure 2-6   *Centralized Deployment Using V3PN*

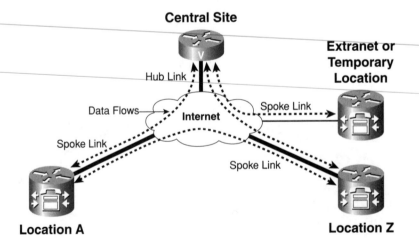

Organizations using traditional WAN architectures often focus on per-mile charges. With V3PN, budgets can instead focus on obtaining fast, reliable connectivity to an Internet service provider (ISP) that has the ability to interconnect all the sites. The enterprise, however, becomes dependent on the ISP's reliability and its ability to deliver packets with minimal delay, jitter, and loss. When moving to V3PN, organizations should choose a single provider to service all network locations—preferably one that recognizes QoS settings in each packet. Organizations should do everything possible to obtain a service level agreement (SLA) from the carrier to ensure compliance with expectations.

Tuning Quality of Service on the WAN

In centralized deployments, the individual spoke links typically run at speeds less than a T1 or E1 because of the number of locations and telecommunication costs associated with connecting them to your central site. Because every mile and every location has an associated cost, telecommunications budgets force the most efficient use of bandwidth possible. In this situation, a well-implemented QoS strategy not only enhances the average throughput but also allows a sensitive application such as VoIP to operate well.

End-to-end delay (*latency*) between two VoIP endpoints and changing time intervals between VoIP packets (*jitter*) are the two variables that most affect the audio quality in a VoIP conversation. When a network path is optimized using the QoS features found in Cisco IOS software, it can be near capacity and still maintain good voice quality by minimizing latency along with jitter and still guarantee consistent delivery of VoIP packets ahead of data packets.

Minimizing Latency

Latency is the measurement of how long it takes a packet to traverse the entire network from end to end. It can also be measured on a per-hop basis with respect to how much latency a particular segment (or *hop*) contains. The International Telecommunication Union (ITU) defines toll quality voice as being less than 150 ms end-to-end latency. You can minimize per-hop latency by ensuring that voice packets get sent out an interface ahead of packets that are not time sensitive.

For any link in a network, WAN or LAN, setting up some form of priority handling of voice packets is a must. Priority queuing is particularly necessary for WAN links because of the inherent delays caused by moving packets from high-speed interfaces such as 100-MB Ethernet to low-speed serial interfaces such as a 128-kbps serial WAN link. Priority queuing for voice is a basic building block for every complex queuing scenario. Both IP Real-Time Transport Protocol (RTP) priority and low latency queuing (LLQ) achieve the same goal of putting delay-sensitive packets such as voice ahead of other traffic.

All routers and switches provide a basic queuing method—appropriately named first-in, first-out (FIFO) queuing—by default. FIFO does not provide any form of QoS and does not prioritize one traffic type over another, making it unsuitable for network links that carry

VoIP traffic. Therefore, for every link in the network, both WAN and LAN, you must configure some form of prioritized queuing rather than relying on the default FIFO queuing scheme.

This section focuses on reducing latency on the WAN. Three ways of achieving this are illustrated, but only one is a best practice. The other two take into account smaller scenarios and products that do not explicitly mark their packets for QoS differentiation.

- The best practice is to establish a trust boundary or logical edge of the network where QoS marking on packets is trusted and to use LLQ to forward the marked packets with preference over the WAN. Devices such as IP phones may mark the packets and be trusted, or intermediary devices such as Ethernet switches or routers may be used to mark or remark QoS parameters. Any device that sources or terminates a call needs this capability or needs to have it done on the edge of the trust boundary.

- In environments where packets can be implicitly trusted, it might be an option to accept packets as they come in because of their protocol port number and/or QoS markings. After the incoming packet is identified, it can be marked and forwarded via LLQ, ensuring minimal latency. With IP SoftPhones and third-party devices that do not explicitly mark packets, matching protocols or port numbers is the only option. As soon as the matching is complete, the packet is placed in the priority queue and is preferentially sent. Matching can be used both to identify voice and signaling packets for queuing and to mark or remark QoS parameters.

- Last, as an absolute minimum, as well as providing a comparison to the two LLQ techniques, the IP RTP priority method (discussed in the following section) can be used. Although this isn't recommended, it does provide some level of preferential service to RTP packets. This method requires minimal configuration and provides minimal latency protection and minimal applicability to anything other than a simple scenario.

These three methods are covered in the following sections in reverse order of the preceding list to demonstrate the mechanisms and the need to implement a full LLQ technique.

TIP   When choosing between IP RTP and LLQ, always deploy LLQ. It allows for much greater long-term flexibility and functionality for existing applications. As additional services are added to the network, the need for LLQ only becomes greater.

Use IP RTP Priority Queuing if You Cannot Use LLQ

IP RTP priority provides a combination of a priority queue (PQ) for voice packets and a weighted fair queue (WFQ) for all other data. The classification of voice packets is achieved through the use of an access control list (ACL) to match the UDP port range used by voice RTP packets. The major drawback is that this puts any UDP packet within the range specified in the priority queue. Applications such as video compete for the same priority queue on the same interface as voice, potentially causing no true preference for either. In addition, because IP RTP priority cannot be coupled with link fragmentation and interleaving (LFI), it only helps reduce latency, not jitter. IP precedence is followed to provide WFQ treatment for all other packets that are not within the given UDP range.

Figure 2-7 diagrams a mix of incoming packets to an interface with IP RTP queue logic enabled. In this case, voice packets are output before any other traffic, and the other traffic follows the voice based on its IP precedence value markings.

Figure 2-7   *Simple Queuing with IP RTP Priority*

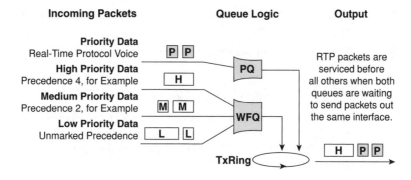

Enable IP RTP priority by issuing the following command. Replace the italicized information (for example, *starting-rtp-port-number*) with the appropriate values.

```
Router(config-if)#ip rtp priority starting-rtp-port-number port-number-range
bandwidth
```

Only three variables need to be identified. The RTP port information for a CallManager deployment is listed in the following steps. The bandwidth to be used for the priority queue should be set to less than the link's maximum bandwidth to allow voice signaling, routing protocols, and other critical applications to operate.

The following steps detail the IP RTP priority configuration:

Step 1   Choose the RTP port number to start with (16384 for all Cisco voice applications); this is the *starting-rtp-port-number.*

Step 2   Choose the ending RTP port number (32768 for all Cisco voice applications) or the last RTP port used.

Step 3   Calculate the range of ports between the start and end values; this is the *port-number-range.*

Step 4   Calculate the number of RTP streams multiplied by the codec rate with IP overhead in Table 2-1; the result is the PQ *bandwidth.*

Step 5   Apply the command with the derived values to the interface.

Table 2-1   *Codec Plus Transport Bandwidth Usage on the WAN*

20-ms Data Packets (Default)	G.729	G.711	Wideband
Codec Raw Bit Rate	8 kbps	64 kbps	256 kbps
Rate with IP Overhead[*], No RTP Header Compression	26.8 kbps	82.8 kbps	274.8 kbps
Rate with IP Overhead[*], RTP Header Compression Enabled	11.6 kbps	67.6 kbps	259.6 kbps

[*]Includes IP overhead as well as PPP or FRF.12

The following IP RTP priority sample interface command allows three G.729 calls to be serviced by the priority queue:

```
Router(config-if)#ip rtp priority 16384 16383 81
```

At a Minimum, Use LLQ for Marked or Unmarked Packets

LLQ is a more flexible and dynamic alternative to IP RTP priority but is also more complex to implement. LLQ provides a PQ for select packets based on multiple parameters and a class-based weighted fair queue (CBWFQ) that can further differentiate all other packets, based again on multiple parameters. LLQ is the best-practice method of queuing for voice. It not only prioritizes the RTP packets that carry the audio, but it also prioritizes the call setup signaling and can be further configured to prioritize other applications, such as video.

Endpoints that do not mark the Differentiated Services Code Point (DSCP) QoS values need an intermediary device to do the marking, as covered in the following steps. Match criteria of incoming packets for the best-practice configuration use DSCP code values from trusted endpoints such as Cisco IP Phones, transcoding and conferencing resources, and gateways or devices that remark QoS settings of all packets on the edge of an established trust boundary. The marked packet configuration is shown in the following section and is the best practice.

When used in combination with lower-speed links, large packets that pass through the CBWFQ can be fragmented to interleave voice PQ packets, as shown in Figure 2-8. Fragmentation is important to any link running at 768 kbps or less, as you will read a bit later. When using both LLQ and LFI, both latency and jitter are reduced.

The steps for LLQ configuration for marked, unmarked, trusted, or untrusted packet QoS parameters with packet remarking are as follows:

Step 1   Create a class map to match voice payload traffic, along with an access control list to achieve desired granularity.

Step 2   Create a class map to match call signaling, along with an access control list to achieve desired granularity.

Figure 2-8 *Granular Queuing and LFI with LLQ*

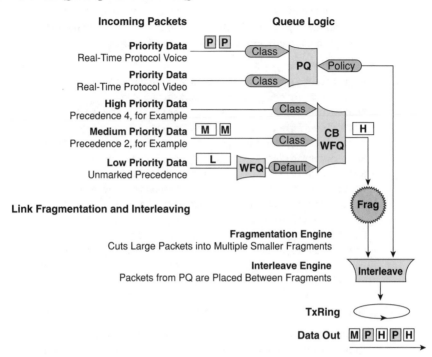

Step 3 Create a policy map to enforce the class maps and associate bandwidth.

Step 4 Apply the policy map to the interface servicing the WAN.

The following steps show an implementation of the LLQ configuration with unmarked incoming packets:

Step 1 Create the class map to match the voice payload traffic with an associated access control list that captures the UDP port range; this works well with Cisco and third-party devices:

```
Router(config)#class-map match-all voice-payload
Router(config-cmap)#match access-group 101
Router(config)#access-list 101 permit udp any any range 16384 32767
```

As an alternative for greater voice payload matching accuracy, use the following access control list in an all-Cisco 7900 implementation:

```
Router(config)#access-list 101 permit udp any any precedence critical
```

Step 2 Create the class map to match the voice signaling traffic with the associated access control list that captures H.323/H.225/H.245/RAS (TCP 1720, UDP 1718), Skinny (TCP 2000-2002), and Media Gateway

Control Protocol [MGCP] (TCP 2428, UDP 2427). Executing these commands allows these specified signaling protocols to be processed through the PQ to speed call setup and help eliminate any lost audio or clipping at the beginning of the conversation because of signaling being delayed.

```
Router(config)#class-map match-all voice-signaling
Router(config-cmap)#match access-group 102
Router(config)#access-list 102 permit tcp any eq 1720 any
Router(config)#access-list 102 permit tcp any any eq 1720
Router(config)#access-list 102 permit udp any eq 1718 any
Router(config)#access-list 102 permit udp any any eq 1718
Router(config)#access-list 102 permit tcp any eq 2000 any
Router(config)#access-list 102 permit tcp any any eq 2000
Router(config)#access-list 102 permit tcp any eq 2001 any
Router(config)#access-list 102 permit tcp any any eq 2001
Router(config)#access-list 102 permit tcp any eq 2002 any
Router(config)#access-list 102 permit tcp any any eq 2002
Router(config)#access-list 102 permit tcp any eq 2428 any
Router(config)#access-list 102 permit tcp any any eq 2428
Router(config)#access-list 102 permit udp any eq 2427 any
Router(config)#access-list 102 permit udp any any eq 2427
```

Step 3 Create a policy map to enforce the class maps and associate bandwidth. In this example, three 24 kbps calls or 72 kbps of voice payload, 8 kbps of voice signaling, and all other bandwidth during a time of congestion are given fairly to the rest of the traffic. Packets are remarked as well to the proper DSCP values:

```
Router(config)#policy-map VOIPPOLICY
Router(config-pmap)#class voice-payload
Router(config-pmap-c)#priority 72
Router(config-pmap-c)#set ip dscp EF
Router(config-pmap)#class voice-signaling
Router(config-pmap-c)#bandwidth 8
Router(config-pmap-c)#set ip dscp AF31
Router(config-pmap)#class class-default
Router(config-pmap-c)#fair-queue
```

Step 4 Apply the policy map to the interface servicing the WAN. In this case, the interface is a multilink PPP connection that allows fragmentation and interleaving. Be assured that any standard interface will work. Links of 56 kbps may allow up to 80 percent of this interface to be consumed by the policy map.

```
Router(config)#interface multilink 1
Router(config-if)#max-reserved-bandwidth 80
Router(config-if)#service-policy output VOIPPOLICY
```

Be careful not to unintentionally starve critical data or routing protocols for voice. You may optionally provide a class map and policy map for those applications. Make sure that the physical interface has the correct bandwidth setting; otherwise, the LLQ settings will not have the desired effect.

Best Practice: Use LLQ with Marked and Trusted Incoming Packets

The following steps show an implementation similar to the LLQ configuration described in the preceding section, this time as a best-practice configuration with marked and trusted incoming packets. The sections build on themselves, so be sure to read the preceding section to get some additional information that may be useful when you follow these steps.

Step 1   Create the class map to match the voice payload traffic with an associated DSCP **match** command:

```
Router(config)#class-map match-all voice-payload
Router(config-cmap)#match ip dscp EF
```

Step 2   Create the class map to match the voice signaling traffic with the associated DSCP **match** commands:

```
Router(config)#class-map match-any voice-signaling
Router(config-cmap)#match ip dscp CS3
Router(config-cmap)#match ip dscp AF31
```

Step 3   Create a policy map to enforce the class maps and associate bandwidth. In this example, 72 kbps of voice payload, 8 kbps of voice signaling, and all other bandwidth during a time of congestion are given fairly to the rest of the traffic:

```
Router(config)#policy-map VOIPPOLICY
Router(config-pmap)#class voice-payload
Router(config-pmap-c)#priority 72
Router(config-pmap)#class voice-signaling
Router(config-pmap-c)#bandwidth 8
Router(config-pmap)#class class-default
Router(config-pmap-c)#fair-queue
```

Step 4   Apply the policy map to the interface servicing the WAN. Again, the sample interface is a multilink PPP connection that allows fragmentation and interleaving:

```
Router(config)#interface multilink 1
Router(config-if)#service-policy output VOIPPOLICY
```

Always be careful not to unintentionally starve critical data or routing protocols for voice. You may optionally provide a class map and policy map for additional applications such as video with a **match ip dscp AF41** for trusted video endpoints on WAN links that have available bandwidth greater than 384 kbps.

Reducing Jitter

So far this chapter has discussed using LLQ techniques or IP RTP priority to address the latency problems of having voice payload and signaling packets wait in a common buffer that is backlogged with other traffic that is not time sensitive. This still leaves the problem of jitter, or having small voice packets wait for single large packets that beat them to the interface. It takes 214 ms for a 1500-byte packet to be sent down a 56-kbps link. A single voice payload packet contains 20 ms of audio, so a great many voice packets might get stalled while waiting for the single data packet to finish serializing down the link. This interrupts audio in a voice stream. The solution is LFI; LFI helps control the variable amount of time that packets may take to cross the network because of other traffic sharing the links. Table 2-2 breaks down the serialization delay for a given packet size and link speed.

Table 2-2   *Serialization Delay for Various Packet Sizes and Link Speeds*

Link Bandwidth	64-Byte Packet Delay in ms	256-Byte Packet Delay in ms	512-Byte Packet Delay in ms	1024-Byte Packet Delay in ms	1500-Byte Packet Delay in ms
64 kbps	8.00	32.00	64.00	128.00	187.50
128 kbps	4.00	16.00	32.00	64.00	93.75
256 kbps	2.00	8.00	16.00	32.00	46.88
384 kbps	1.33	5.33	10.66	21.33	31.25
512 kbps	1.00	4.00	8.00	16.00	23.44
768 kbps	0.667	2.67	5.33	10.67	15.63
1536 kbps	0.333	1.33	2.67	5.33	7.81

Use LFI for Point-to-Point Links Slower than 768 kbps to Reduce Jitter

LFI takes large packets, breaks them into smaller pieces, and places PQ traffic such as voice among those pieces. With LFI, big packets attempting to use the same network path do not affect small packets. Running multilink PPP on both ends of a link enables the use of LFI and therefore reduces jitter for voice packets. LFI is not recommended on links faster than 768 kbps, because a serialization delay of less than 10 ms does not warrant fragmentation (see Table 2-2).

Be sure to set the bandwidth to the speed the data is running at in kbps on the WAN interface so that the fragment delay can be made correctly. In Example 2-1, the fragmentation occurs every 10 ms to allow PQ packets to mix among the fragments. As a best practice, fragment every 10 ms to provide many opportunities for interleaving voice with other traffic, as depicted in Figure 2-8.

Example 2-1 *Enabling Multilink PPP on a 256-kbps Link*

```
Router(config)#interface multilink 1
Router(config-if)#bandwidth 256
Router(config-if)#ppp multilink fragment-delay 10
Router(config-if)#ppp multilink interleave
```

Use LFI with Traffic Shaping for Frame Relay

Frame Relay poses a unique scenario based on the ability to burst beyond the subscribed rate and operate up to the rate of the clocking being received on the interface. There's also the potential for the one-to-many spoke links shown in Figure 2-3 to produce more traffic than the hub link can service, causing congestion and dropped packets that affect voice quality. Ensure that each location is configured not only to keep from bursting over the link's local committed information rate (CIR), but also to keep from overwhelming the link to the central site when all the locations are taken into consideration. Frame Relay Fragmentation (FRF.12) is the standards-based method of implementing LFI on a Frame Relay network. The configuration differs from Example 2-1, which is a simple PPP link.

Use Table 2-3 as a guideline to obtain fragment size values for LFI with traffic shaping.

Table 2-3 *Recommended Frame Relay Fragment Sizing with 10-ms Fragmentation Values*

Link Bandwidth	Fragment Size in Bytes	CIR Value in bps	Bc Value in Bits Per Tc
64 kbps	80	60952	610
128 kbps	160	124872	1250
256 kbps	320	252832	2530
384 kbps	480	382978	3830
512 kbps	640	508816	5090
768 kbps	960	764940	7560
1536 kbps	—	—	—

The only parameter you need from your provider in order to use from Table 2-3 is the CIR of your link. The CIR is the link's true sustaining bandwidth. You never want to burst beyond what the Frame Relay network can guarantee; otherwise, voice packet loss can occur. The committed burst rate (Bc) is optimally set as the CIR divided by 100, and the table rounds to the nearest whole number. The excess burst rate (Be) must be set to 0 to keep from creating buffering delays. The minimum CIR (MINCIR) is set to the same value as the CIR because you never want to burst and potentially lose packets and affect audio quality. Adaptive shaping is also undesirable. Last, the fragment size is set to fragment the packets for 10-ms interleaving of PQ voice packets.

To configure LFI with the shaping just described, follow these steps:

Step 1   Create a map class for Frame Relay to let IOS know the link's characteristics.

Step 2   Apply the map class to the subinterface, and enable fragmentation.

Step 3   Enable traffic shaping on the major interface servicing the WAN.

The following list shows an implementation of the LFI with the shaping configuration steps that were outlined in the preceding list:

Step 1   Create a map class to establish the link's characteristics (384 kbps in this example):

```
Router(config)#map-class frame-relay frts384k
Router(config-map-class)#frame-relay cir 382978
Router(config-map-class)#frame-relay bc 3830
Router(config-map-class)#frame-relay be 0
Router(config-map-class)#frame-relay mincir 382978
Router(config-map-class)#no frame-relay adaptive-shaping
Router(config-map-class)#frame-relay fragment 480
```

Step 2   Apply the map class to the subinterface:

```
Router(config)#interface Serial0/0.1 point-to-point
Router(config-subif)#frame-relay class frts384k
```

Step 3   Enable traffic shaping on the major interface servicing the WAN:

```
Router(config)#interface Serial0/0
Router(config-if)#frame-relay traffic-shaping
```

Adjusting Bandwidth Consumption

The codec that is chosen for the WAN and the optional compression of the audio stream are major factors in the number of conversations that can be carried by the link servicing the location. CallManager Release 4.0 has the option of encrypting the RTP audio streams, which adds overhead because of the 4-to-7-byte authentication tag on each packet. Examples and tables in this chapter depict unencrypted audio streams. Encrypted audio consumes 2 to 4 percent more bandwidth for each G.711 stream and 6 to 24 percent more bandwidth for a G.729 stream on the WAN, depending on security and compression settings. Decisions made on the RTP codec, compression, and encryption all affect bandwidth consumption and need to be planned before the deployment.

Use Compressed Real-Time Transport Protocol in Some Cases

Using Compressed Real-Time Transport Protocol (cRTP) is optional and is recommended only for deployments with gateways that can support the extra CPU load that cRTP requires. CPU loading is minimal at each location, but the central site can be become significantly burdened given enough RTP flows. (Table 2-7, shown later, lists the number of cRTP flows per Cisco router model.) You should enable cRTP as soon as the deployment has been successfully tested to ensure that no other applications improperly load the gateway and start to affect voice and application quality. Even with these disclaimers, cRTP can compress the IP+UDP+RTP packet header from 40 bytes to 2 or 4 bytes, which can be significant on a 56-kbps or 64-kbps link. Enabling cRTP is quite simple. On each end of the link, put this configuration on the WAN interface:

```
Router(config-if)#ip rtp header-compression iphc-format
```

Compressed RTP is a hop-by-hop compression technique, which means that the header is compressed and then decompressed across each link. Packets going from location to location through the central site might have to go through the compression-decompression cycle twice, depending on the platform and IOS version. Remove the command if CPU utilization on the gateway peaks at 75 percent or consistently runs at more than 65 percent. Use the **show process cpu** command via the command line interface (CLI), or use a management package such as CiscoWorks for monitoring. The companion command **ip tcp header-compression iphc-format** appears in the gateway configuration automatically if it wasn't previously enabled. cRTP does add a small amount of jitter to the stream. When CPU utilization is more than 75 percent on the gateway, cRTP adds latency as well.

Choosing the Codec

When choosing to deploy across the WAN with CallManager, you really have only two reasonable choices, G.711 or G.729. With slower-speed links, the choice is even easier. Implementing G.729 uses minimal bandwidth and has excellent fidelity given the low bit rate. Using the 256-kbps wideband codec between a location and a central site is rarely an option for a centralized deployment model. Table 2-1, shown earlier, lists the raw codec bit rates and associated overhead with and without cRTP enabled.

The values used in Table 2-1 are based on a 20-ms sample size, which is the preferred and default CallManager setting for the WAN. The Rate with IP Overhead values include not only the IP overhead but also the WAN overhead associated with multilink PPP for point-to-point networks, or FRF.12 for Frame Relay networks. Values given in Table 2-1 allow for accurate gauging of the true link bandwidth requirement. The PQ calculations for latency tuning are just slightly larger than maximum queue needs but are right on target for the true WAN requirement. ATM and Frame Relay interworking calculations are more complex and much more bandwidth-intensive. See the Technical Assistance Center's (TAC) Voice Codec Bandwidth Calculator at http://tools.cisco.com/Support/VBC/do/CodecCalc1.do (a login is required) for more information and for help in calculating ATM scenarios.

Preventing WAN Oversubscription by Using Locations-Based Call Admission Control (CAC)

CallManager employs locations to control how many phone conversations can be placed between two ends of a link. It also employs regions to determine which codec to use when calls are placed within or between a pair of locations. These two concepts go hand in hand when you're designing and deploying the centralized call processing model. CAC and the chosen codec have implications for any originating or terminating audio stream involving gateways, voice mail, and conferencing, as well as phones in codec negotiation and calculating numbers of calls between locations.

Configure Regions for Central and Remote Locations

You can configure a codec for the WAN that differs from the local LAN via CallManager Administration (**System > Region**). Doing so allows calls within a location that has little or no related charge and plenty of bandwidth on the LAN to enjoy higher fidelity than a call placed across the relatively expensive and bandwidth-constrained WAN. For this to work, all devices must be able to support any requested codec to the Region setting.

Cisco IP Phone series 7900 supports wideband, G.711, and G.729 audio codecs. As you read in the section "Choosing the Codec," codec choice determines how many calls can be placed on a link. Using more than one codec achieves a balance between audio fidelity and bandwidth frugality. When devices do not support the required codec type, transcoding from one codec to another can be done with the aid of additional hardware such as the Catalyst 6000 WS-X6608 blade. However, transcoding can be costly to deploy in a centralized CallManager environment because of the number of locations involved. When possible, plan the deployment without using transcoding resources, for cost reasons and because they add a certain amount of delay to the audio stream. Figure 2-9 shows a scenario in which both locations and the central site use the G.711 codec for on-site calls but use the bandwidth-friendly G.729 codec for calls between locations or to the central site.

Figure 2-10 illustrates the configuration of the deployment shown in Figure 2-9 for Location Z. All devices are placed in a device pool that is tied to a region. Often, the Default region becomes the name for the central site. The audio codec selected between Location Z (RegLoc_Z), Location A (RegLoc_A), and the central site (Default) is set at G.729. Calls within Location Z use G.711.

New to CallManager Release 4.0 is the Video Call Bandwidth setting on the Region Configuration page (**System > Region**). This setting refers to CallManager-based video call control between endpoints. Setting Video Call Bandwidth as shown in Figure 2-10 to **None** disables video calls from this region to all others. If this were a 128-kbps link, it would be very important to specify None for the Video Call Bandwidth, because the default setting is 384 kbps—a setting that could potentially allow a single video call to consume more bandwidth than is available.

Figure 2-9 *Logical View of Centralized Region Deployment*

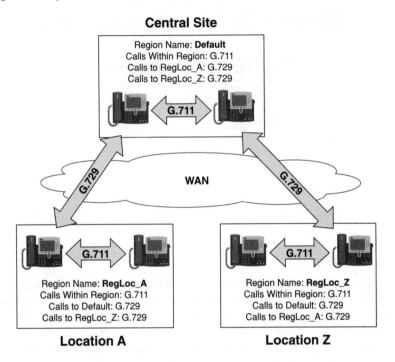

The values shown in Figure 2-10 should be the combination of the IP overhead plus the video codec bit rate. As you saw earlier in Table 2-1, the IP overhead for voice codecs affects the total amount of bandwidth used. Video streams have both a video and audio codec component, and there are numerous combinations of the two. Transporting a video stream over IP carries an approximate 13 to 15 percent overhead of IP header information. This means that a 384-kbps video call can consume 442 kbps of WAN bandwidth. If the WAN is ATM, an approximate increase of 17 percent must be added because of the ATM cell overhead, making the 384-kbps video call consume about 500 kbps of bandwidth on the ATM WAN. Compressed RTP is not recommended for video.

Figure 2-10 *Region Configuration in CallManager Administration*

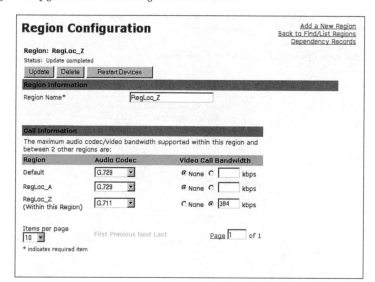

Configure Locations

Locations are the heart of the centralized hub-and-spoke deployment model. A single CallManager cluster can support up to 500 locations. To keep the terminology from becoming overwhelming and to demonstrate the importance of the concept, each remote site is called a *location*. Each CallManager device exists within a location and is associated with a device pool. The region and the location information determines which codec to use, the total amount of bandwidth available to communicate between locations, and the bandwidth to be deducted from the total available for each call. When the device pool no longer has sufficient bandwidth, the call is not placed, the caller hears a reorder tone, and the message "Not Enough Bandwidth" appears on the phone. This locations-based CAC ensures that no more audio streams are allowed than the link can support, ensuring audio quality for the existing calls.

WAN architectures that follow the hub-and-spoke model account for each call through the location's allowed bandwidth, as represented by the Audio Bandwidth setting shown in Figure 2-11. When links are built between locations, or if a layer 3 MPLS WAN architecture is deployed, there must be accounting of not only the bandwidth used between the central site and the location, but also from location to location. In these two cases, the central site must also become a location, and all devices must also be configured to reside within that location.

Figure 2-11   *Logical View of Centralized Locations Deployment*

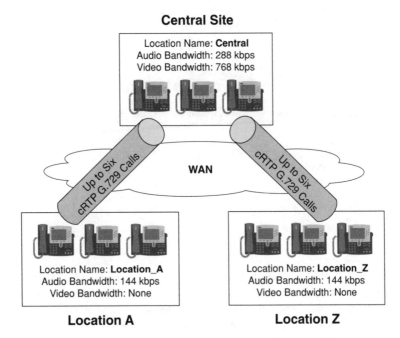

The CallManager configuration of location bandwidth is not as straightforward as it might seem because CallManager doesn't have exact knowledge of network specifics. As you saw in Table 2-1, enabling cRTP effectively halves the amount of bandwidth needed for a G.729 call. This creates unique configuration scenarios. Calculating bandwidth needs between locations is based on the number of calls and the amount of available bandwidth. Table 2-4 lists the amount CallManager deducts from the available bandwidth for each call versus the codec bit rate, and Figure 2-12 shows a low-bandwidth example.

Table 2-4   *CallManager Codec Values for Locations*

	G.729	G.711	Wideband
Codec raw bit rate	8 kbps	64 kbps	256 kbps
CallManager locations rate	24 kbps	80 kbps	272 kbps

Figure 2-12 *Location Configuration in CallManager Administration*

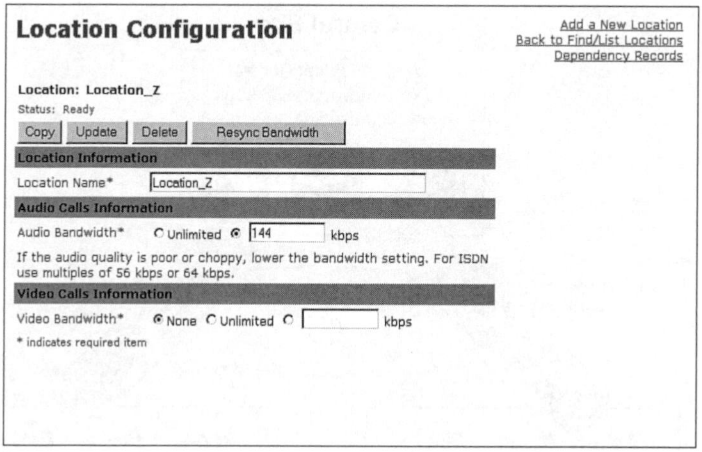

Figure 2-12 shows a sample Location Configuration page in CallManager Administration (**System > Location**) that is potentially valid for a 128-kbps Frame Relay link even though the Audio Bandwidth setting is 144 kbps. Because CallManager does not know if cRTP is enabled on the network, it deducts the G.729 value listed in Table 2-4. This causes CallManager to overstate the true used bandwidth when cRTP is running on both ends of the link.

TIP   CAC that is based on CallManager locations does not have exact knowledge of any network. Because of this, it is highly recommended that you plan the value placed in the audio bandwidth configuration. Knowing the true bandwidth needs, number of calls, and CallManager behavior, enter a calculated value rather than the link's true speed. This must also correlate to the priority queue bandwidth allocated for the site.

To explain the 144-kbps setting in Figure 2-12, six G.729 cRTP calls are to be allowed across the 128 kbps link at 11.6 kbps each with 69.6 kbps total, leaving enough room for data needs. You know that CallManager effectively deducts double the true bandwidth needed, which is 24 kbps for each call, and does not allow any more calls after the fifth call. This is because the sum at that point is 120 kbps, and a sixth call exceeds the 128-kbps allotment. To understand how much bandwidth to configure, work the desired result backwards. The end goal is to busy out this location's link after six calls are active. Every call costs 24 kbps from the available bandwidth; multiplying that by 6 equals 144 kbps. You should enter this value in the Audio Bandwidth field, because CallManager doesn't know the actual bandwidth used.

Moving equipment between locations sounds unlikely at first, but it is indeed quite common in unexpected ways. Cisco or third-party SoftPhones, Cisco IP Communicator, and the Cisco 7920 wireless phones are examples of roaming devices that frequently change physical location but still refer to the logical location for which they were originally configured. When roaming devices are deployed, they must be accounted for, blocked, or left in the default queue to keep from disrupting all other calls on the link. Reserve the appropriate amount of bandwidth across the WAN to account for roaming endpoints, or block endpoint movement entirely from the WAN via an access control list for a unique DHCP scope. Leaving roaming device voice traffic in the default queue is the least-desirable option, but you can accomplish this by using tighter matching in the class map of the LLQ configuration for the stationary endpoints.

Roaming endpoints can cause CAC and bandwidth calculation problems, interfere with the dial plan and local gateway choice, and most importantly potentially cause emergency personnel to arrive at the wrong location. You should thoroughly consider all movement of equipment before supporting roaming endpoints.

NOTE   Currently, no automated tools exist to dynamically change the location setting based on device movement. This can have serious consequences with service. Therefore, Cisco does not recommend using software-based phones or wireless phones for emergency services at this time.

Figure 2-10 showed the Region Name setting for video calls. Figure 2-12 shows the corresponding Location Name setting for specifying the total available bandwidth for video between the central site and one of the locations. The location setting works exactly as it does for audio calls: every time a video call is set up between locations, the call value is deducted from the available video bandwidth. The numeric value in Figure 2-12 must include IP header overhead and be a calculated value versus a sum of plain codec bit rates for the number of streams desired. When you add IP overhead and WAN overhead to a single 384-kbps call, this can add up to approximately 500 kbps, as described earlier in the "Configure Regions for Central and Remote Locations" section. It's not recommended that you have LFI enabled on lines that carry video traffic, but with the bandwidth requirements, any line carrying video would likely be faster than 768 kbps, making LFI unnecessary (as explained in the "Reducing Jitter" section). Anything other than a centralized call processing model presents challenges for CallManager-based video across the WAN.

Dynamically Rerouting Calls Using Automated Alternate Routing

Automated alternate routing (AAR) is particularly useful in centralized deployments because it allows CallManager to dynamically reroute a call through the PSTN if the WAN has insufficient bandwidth to place the call. This lets CallManager use the PSTN for additional on-demand call capacity when the need arises. No additional user action is required, and AAR can be configured to work location-to-location or central site-to-location.

As a best practice, correctly configure the external phone number mask along with the directory number for all endpoints (**Device > Phone >** *find and select a phone* **> Directory Number**). To send the call out the PSTN, AAR retrieves this destination information along with a dialing prefix. Without the destination information, there's not enough information to place the call. Having adequate local gateway ports to the PSTN at each location as well as the central site greatly enhances a remote site's ability to conduct business as usual during WAN congestion.

The call flow using AAR is as follows:

1 A user dials an extension.

2 CallManager attempts to place the call on the WAN, but bandwidth is unavailable for the call.

3 A message appears on the phone's display; by default the message is "Network Congestion, Rerouting."

4 After retrieving the external phone number mask and directory number of the destination extension to create a complete PSTN digit string, CallManager sends the call out the appropriate gateway based on the associated AAR group.

5 A new destination string appears on the phone.

6 The call is placed from a local gateway using the AAR calling search space.

7 The call is received on the destination gateway, which completes the call to the destination.

Figure 2-13 shows the call flow of a call that has been redirected via AAR over the PSTN because of congestion on the WAN. Notice that the user dials only four digits; AAR takes care of the rest automatically.

NOTE   AAR is to be used only for directory numbers associated with lines or voice mail ports on CallManager. Computer telephony integration (CTI) route points and legacy gateway voice mail systems are not supported as of CallManager release 4.0(1). Calls to voice mail ports do not contain supplementary information, and because of this the user is sent to the main voice mail greeting.

Figure 2-13 *AAR in Action*

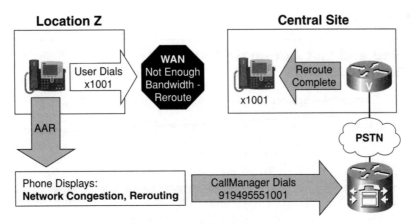

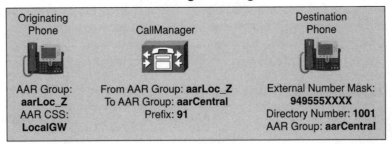

Follow these steps to configure AAR:

Step 1 Set the clusterwide CallManager service parameter Automated Alternate Routing Enable to **True** (**Service Service Parameters** > *select a server* > **Cisco CallManager**).

Step 2 Configure an AAR group (**Route Plan > AAR Group**). Note that the From and To fields do not appear until more than one group exists. Configure **Prefix Digits** for location to central site, between locations, and central site to location. Prefix digits within the site are not applicable to this scenario. Prefix digits cover routing within internally congested sites in a distributed or campus deployment type scenario.

Figure 2-14 and Table 2-5 show the settings shown in Figure 2-13.

Figure 2-14 *Settings Shown in Figure 2-13*

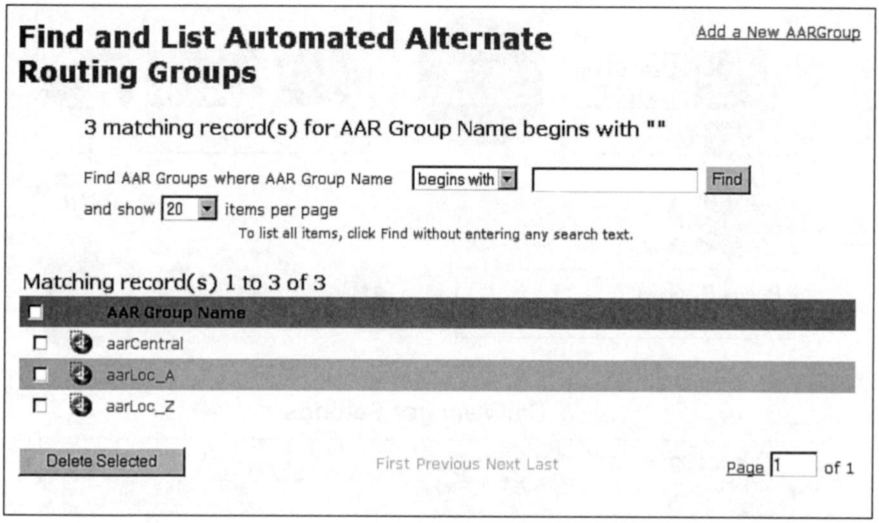

Table 2-5 *AAR Prefix Examples*

From AAR Group	To AAR Group	Prefix Digits
aarCentral	aarLoc_A	9
aarCentral	aarLoc_Z	91
aarLoc_A	arCentral	9
aarLoc_A	aarLoc_Z	91
aarLoc_Z	aarCentral	91
aarLoc_Z	aarLoc_A	91

Step 3 Check the settings on the local gateway (**Device > Gateway**). Ensure that the Device Pool and Location reflect a remote location or a central site locality. The AAR Group and AAR Calling Search Space settings are not applicable to this scenario. These fields are for routing within internally congested sites in a distributed or campus deployment-type scenario.

Step 4 Configure the AAR Calling Search Space for a device (**Device > Phone >** *find and select a phone*). Set the AAR Calling Search Space as needed to reach the local gateway.

Step 5   Configure the AAR Group for a line or voice mail port. (**Device >
Phone >** *find and select a phone* > *select a line* or **Feature >
Voice Mail > Cisco Voice Mail Port >** *find and select a port*). Select the
corresponding AAR Group to enable AAR functionality for that line or
port. Ensure that the External Phone Number Mask and Directory
Number show the correct values.

In this example, calls between Location A and the Central site are within the same area code
but require 10-digit dialing. Location Z is in a different area code altogether. Sending the
PSTN a full 10-digit string even for local dialing is permitted. The 9 prefix, a steering digit,
is stripped at the gateway. Extension mobility, laptop-based Cisco IP SoftPhones, and
Cisco Wireless 7920 phones cause problems for AAR when the roaming devices change
locations.

Survive WAN Outages by Using SRST

The SRST IOS feature license provides a layer of redundancy to the centralized
deployment. It encompasses a subset of CallManager functionality in the local gateway that
can take over call processing duties when all CallManager servers are unreachable. WAN
outages sometimes occur; a phone system outage for any time period is unacceptable.
Enabling SRST at each location provides failover functionality so that phone service stays
up despite WAN outages, planned or otherwise.

Calls in progress locally phone-to-phone are not affected by the failover to SRST. Calls in
progress that use local gateway resources either to the PSTN or across the WAN are
dropped as a result of the failover. Users are notified on newer phone models such as the
7960, 7940, and 7970 with the message "CM Fallback Service Operating" and users might
never notice the switchover aside from the message. Figure 2-15 illustrates SRST running
at the two locations to allow call processing to continue even though the WAN is
unavailable.

NOTE   Although they might be supported by CallManager, not all phone types are supported in
SRST mode—in particular, legacy IP phones such as the VIP30+ and SP12+. SRST
Release 3.0 supports most of the 7900 series phones, along with the VG248, the ATA series,
and the Cisco IP Phone 7914 Expansion Module. The latest phones, such as the 7970 and
beyond, are to be supported in SRST versions greater than 3.0. Check the IOS release notes
for SRST version information and the SRST release notes for device support. Cisco also
provides a CallManager compatibility matrix; see Chapter 1, "Planning the CallManager
Implementation" for details.

Figure 2-15 *SRST Gateway Functionality*

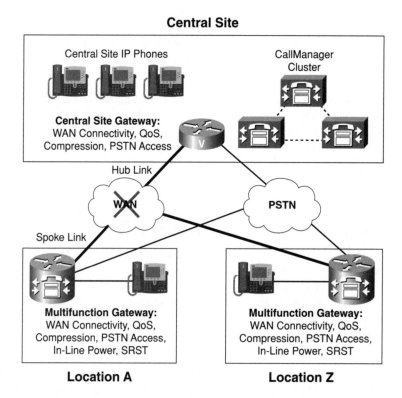

Understanding SRST User Functionality

Users typically notice some change in functionality when in SRST operation. Just after discovering the "CM Fallback Service Operating" text on their display, they may also notice that many supplemental services are unavailable, including

- Call park
- Group pickup
- Cisco CallManager Attendant Console
- Local voice mail through VG248 or DPA gateway
- IP phone services that call URLs through the WAN
- IP Manager Assistant
- Cisco Conference Connection

The main goal of SRST is to be a temporary fallback service run during a WAN outage, not to be a hot standby CallManager. This is one major differentiator between centralized call processing and distributed call processing. When complete CallManager functionality is required during a WAN failure, the distributed model with a CallManager platform at each location is the solution. The centralized call processing model leverages both SRST and the fact that most WAN outages are typically short-lived.

Training the users at the location on SRST behavior before an outage occurs benefits everyone and introduces users to the "CM Fallback Service Operating" message. Core functionality virtually remains the same: IP phone-to-IP phone dialing, IP phone-to-PSTN, Ad Hoc conferencing, consultative and direct transfer, music on hold, and more. Voice mail and complete PSTN connectivity require additional configuration steps, but they too can be set to emulate CallManager functionality during a WAN outage.

Understanding SRST at the Central Site

Planning for WAN failure starts at the central site. When a remote location is severed from communicating over the WAN, it's forced to send voice traffic over the PSTN to reach the desired destinations. Having adequate or standby PSTN connectivity to service these internal calls over the PSTN from the many locations is the key to the SRST deployment's success. This differs greatly for each organization, because all call traffic patterns do not necessarily flow to the central site. Patterns instead might need to be serviced by adequate PSTN connectivity at each of the remote locations because of increased location-to-location calling necessitating more PSTN connectivity at each location.

Complex CallManager dial plans at the central site are not mirrored during SRST operation. A single calling search space and partition exist virtually when SRST is operating. Because of their smaller size, locations typically have a simple set of dialing rules as compared to the central site, but this is not always the case. The dialing rules must be taken into consideration during the planning stage. Restrictions can be placed on outgoing calls, incoming calls, and transferred calls, and specific phones can be disabled during SRST operation.

Configuring CallManager to support SRST is a simple affair. First you identify the SRST gateways, and then you use those identifications in the device pool settings so that the phones can use SRST. The phone by default uses the default gateway entry without any CallManager configuration. The identified SRST gateway in CallManager speeds failover time and ensures that the phone uses the appropriate gateway for SRST service. The real power of the device pool setting is to use the **Disable** option in a second device pool for the same location, as shown in Figure 2-16. This allows nonessential phones to be masked out of participating in SRST, thus freeing up licenses and enhancing security by shutting down phones in untrusted physical locations. The setting is contained in the configuration file that the phone downloads when it registers with CallManager.

Figure 2-16 *Device Pool Settings*

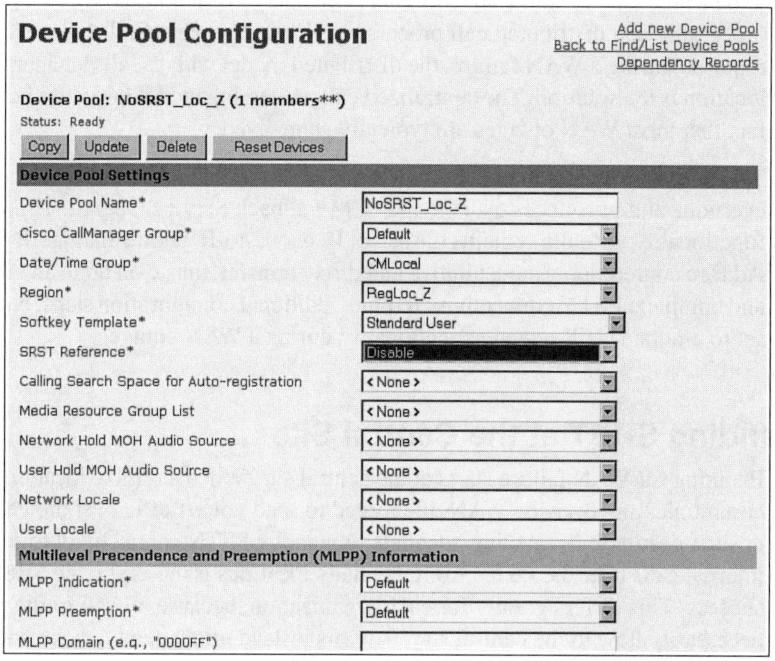

TIP   Using the dual device pool approach lets you reduce the number of SRST licenses, enhance security, and minimize fraud. However, it can also cause confusion, because not all phones are operational while SRST is operating. Tell users beforehand which phones will be functional during a WAN failure.

The following steps describe how to configure CallManager to support SRST:

Step 1   Add a new SRST gateway reference (**System > SRST**).

Step 2   Configure or add one device pool (**System > Device Pool**) for the location with the SRST Reference set to either the new SRST reference or **Use Default Gateway** when the SRST gateway is also the default gateway for the location.

Optionally, add a second device pool for the location, depending on the need to disable phones during SRST operation, and set the SRST Reference to **None**.

Step 3   On the phone, select the device pool (**Device > Phone >** *find and select a phone*). To permit or deny SRST operation, set the device pool for the phone to either of the device pools from Step 2 for the location.

Deploying SRST at the Location

Deploying SRST at the location is a straightforward process. It essentially auto-configures after four specific IOS commands are made to the local gateway. Preparing the SRST location takes more effort than enabling it. Follow these steps:

Step 1   Purchase an SRST license.

Step 2   Load an SRST-capable image onto the gateway.

Step 3   Deploy inline power (optional).

Step 4   Build a separate voice virtual LAN (VLAN).

Step 5   Configure the local Dynamic Host Configuration Protocol (DHCP) server.

Step 6   Configure SRST.

SRST is an optional feature license to the IOS base licensing. Use the Feature Navigator Tool on Cisco.com (you must be a registered user and logged in to access the tool) at http://www.cisco.com/go/fn. To locate an IOS image that includes the SRST feature set, search by feature for SRST. The IOS Software Center displays the requirements by platform that are needed to support the image found within the Feature Navigator. Ensure that the gateway contains at least the minimum requirements for RAM and Flash memory before loading the image onto the platform. Preferably, configure the gateway to meet the RAM and Flash recommendations that are listed in Table 2-8, shown later, to gain the maximum performance.

Inline power for the phones can be obtained from the switching infrastructure or through a switching module within the gateway itself. When the switching infrastructure is accompanied by an uninterruptible power supply (UPS), the phones can keep operating even during a power outage. Depending on the PSTN interface and the outage's severity, the phones can make outside calls. Individual power cubes do not readily lend themselves to power redundancy.

TIP   Depending on the size of the location and the available budget, you can provide UPS to service the IP phones along with the Ethernet switching and gateway infrastructure. Having a secondary means of powering the equipment can provide emergency phone services.

Employing a separate VLAN for voice and data enhances the location's manageability and stability. This allows devices that might currently reside at each location to continue with their current scenario and allows a new DHCP address range to be deployed for the phones. It also enhances network security by keeping voice completely separate from data. The separation allows access control lists on interfaces specific to either voice or data and restricts denial of service attacks or other problems to the data network.

DHCP is the preferred choice to deploy IP addresses to IP phones. Providing DHCP services at the location for the IP phones allows uninterrupted lease serving along with lease renewals. Centralized DHCP service cannot operate when a server is across a down WAN link. Providing DHCP from the gateway at the location is the preferred option and is easily configured.

The configuration shown in Example 2-2 configures the gateway to serve DHCP addresses between 172.27.101 and 199 for the interface on the 172.27.27.0 network. It also sets the primary CallManager address to 10.0.0.1 and the secondary to 10.0.0.2. Multiple CallManager entries cause delays when going into SRST mode as the phones attempt to contact all entries listed at the rate of approximately 1 minute per entry. The default router entry is the IP interface on the gateway facing the phones, or the first hop router to reach the gateway from other places on the network.

Example 2-2 *DHCP Service from an IOS Gateway*

```
Router(config)#ip dhcp excluded-address 172.27.27.1 172.27.27.100
Router(config)#ip dhcp excluded-address 172.27.27.200 172.27.27.254
Router(config)#ip dhcp pool location-z
Router(config-dhcp)#ip network 172.27.27.0 255.255.255.0
Router(config-dhcp)#option 150 ip 10.0.0.1 10.0.0.2
Router(config-dhcp)#default-router 172.27.27.254
Router(config-dhcp)#dns-server 10.0.0.200 66.51.205.100
```

Only four commands are required to deploy SRST, as shown in Example 2-3: enable the service, specify the interface that connects to the phones, set the maximum number of directory numbers to be serviced, and set the maximum number of phones to be serviced. The maximum number of directory numbers and phones depend on the gateway platform (see Table 2-8 later in this chapter). The SRST licensing comes in multiples of 24 phones. Ensure that the number of licenses you have matches the entry for **max-ephones**.

Example 2-3 *Enabling SRST Operation*

```
Router(config)#call-manager-fallback
Router(config-cm-fallback)#ip source-address 172.27.27.254
Router(config-cm-fallback)#max-dn 96 dual-line
Router(config-cm-fallback)#max-ephones 24
```

Limit the Number of Lines on Particular Phone Types

The maximum directory number value from Table 2-8 along with the number of phones deployed at the site determine the need for limiting the number of lines for a particular phone type. When CallManager has six line appearances configured for a phone, that phone requests six lines from SRST. Potentially it could consume more directory numbers than the platform can support, thereby not allowing all phones at a location to operate in SRST mode. For example, each 7960 can support up to six lines. Each line can be put into dual-line mode to allow all call waiting, call transfer, and conferencing for those lines while SRST is in operation. A total of 12 directory numbers are used for each 7960 in a maximum configuration. This becomes more important depending on the device. A 7960 with a 7914 Expansion Module can use 40 licenses, and a VG248 can potentially consume 96 licenses.

By setting a maximum line appearance count with the **limit-dn** command, you can allow a smaller set of line appearances on the phone during SRST operation. This causes only the number of specified lines to appear. Appearances start with the first line appearance and continue to the second, third, and so on until the maximum value has been reached. This is a global setting. The following configuration gives an example for the 7960 and 7940 phone types. Using these commands, the 7960 is limited to four directory numbers, and the 7940 to two.

```
Router(config-cm-fallback)#limit-dn 7960 4
Router(config-cm-fallback)#limit-dn 7940 2
```

Maximize Three-Party Ad Hoc Conferencing

From Table 2-8, use the maximum number of three-party G.711 Ad Hoc conferences that can be established. Without connectivity to CallManager, no conferencing resources exist, and the gateway provides the Ad Hoc functionality while SRST is operating. The gateway typically defaults to fewer conferences than your platform can support.

The following command adjusts the maximum number of conferences to match what the platform can support:

```
Router(config-cm-fallback)#max-conference-numbers 16
```

Enable Consultative Transfers

Many organizations rely on speaking with the destination before finishing the transfer, known as a *consultation transfer*. Blind transfers are the default setting. The following command enables consultative transfer:

```
Router(config-cm-fallback)#transfer-system local-consult
```

Enable G.711 Music on Hold Sourcing at the Location

Deploying multicast music on hold (MOH) at a location can yield two major benefits. The first is having MOH available while SRST is in operation, and the second is having MOH sourced at the branch during normal CallManager operation. This second benefit allows the gateway to source an MOH stream and save the WAN from being burdened by carrying an audio stream from the central site.

The file **music-on-hold.au** is included in the download of SRST in the voice software download area (available to registered Cisco.com users on the Software Download page at http://www.cisco.com/pcgi-bin/tablebuild.pl/ip-key). However, you can use any mono 8-bit 8-kHz .wav or .au file after placing it in the router's Flash memory. This allows the remote site audio to be the same as or different from the central site and other locations.

The first step is to identify the MOH file to be played. The second step is to exactly mirror the CallManager settings for the MOH source on the gateway. Each phone listens only to the MOH multicast address that CallManager has placed in the phone's configuration file based on the media resource group list setting. The source of the multicast becomes the gateway using the same multicast configuration, and the source audio comes from the Flash file on the gateway. You can set these multicast settings on the Music On Hold (MOH) Server Configuration page in CallManager Administration (**Service > Media Resource > Music On Hold Server**), as shown in Figure 2-17. Audio source number 1 has the same multicast values shown in Figure 2-17. Audio source number 2 increments either the port number or the IP address, depending on the Increment Multicast **on** setting. Table 2-6 lists the IP address and port number incremental values. As a best practice, use the **Increment Multicast on IP Address** setting, which makes for easier troubleshooting and debugging as well as access control list matching. To configure the location's gateway, use the following command sequence:

```
Router(config-cm-fallback)#moh music-on-hold.au
Router(config-cm-fallback)#multicast moh 239.1.1.1 port 16384
```

As a best practice, use IP addresses instead of port numbers when configuring MOH sources in CallManager (both are listed here for completeness). The values in Table 2-6 are based on the base Multicast IP address of 239.1.1.1 and base Multicast port number of 16384. Values continue to increment in the same fashion for additional source values.

Multicast packets do not traverse layer 3 or router boundaries unless Multicast routing is enabled. When Multicast routing is configured between the central site and the locations, ensure that the Max Hops field in the Selected Multicast Audio Sources area is set appropriately, or use access control lists on the gateways to ensure that Multicast MOH packets do not inadvertently cross the WAN from either the central site or the remote location.

Figure 2-17   *CallManager Music on Hold Settings*

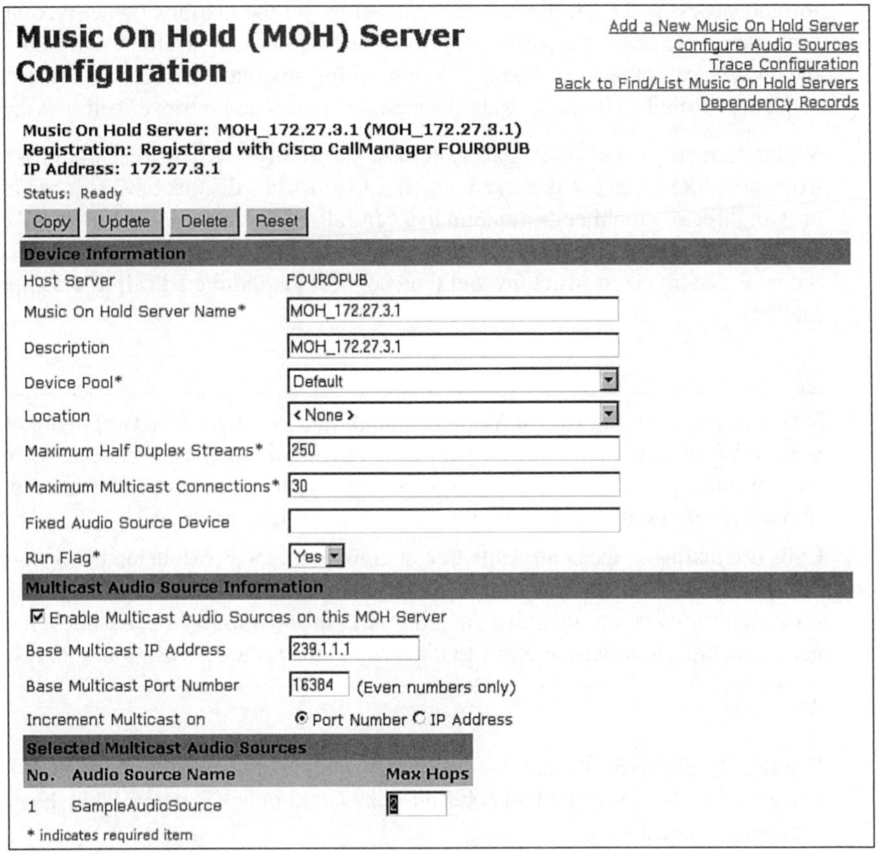

Music On Hold (MOH) Server Configuration

Add a New Music On Hold Server
Configure Audio Sources
Trace Configuration
Back to Find/List Music On Hold Servers
Dependency Records

Music On Hold Server: MOH_172.27.3.1 (MOH_172.27.3.1)
Registration: Registered with Cisco CallManager FOUROPUB
IP Address: 172.27.3.1
Status: Ready

| Copy | Update | Delete | Reset |

Device Information

Host Server	FOUROPUB
Music On Hold Server Name*	MOH_172.27.3.1
Description	MOH_172.27.3.1
Device Pool*	Default
Location	< None >
Maximum Half Duplex Streams*	250
Maximum Multicast Connections*	30
Fixed Audio Source Device	
Run Flag*	Yes

Multicast Audio Source Information

☑ Enable Multicast Audio Sources on this MOH Server

Base Multicast IP Address	239.1.1.1
Base Multicast Port Number	16384 (Even numbers only)
Increment Multicast on	⦿ Port Number ○ IP Address

Selected Multicast Audio Sources

No.	Audio Source Name	Max Hops
1	SampleAudioSource	2

* indicates required item

Table 2-6   *Multicast IP Address and Port Increment Values*

Source	G.711μ-law	G.711a	G.729	Wideband	IP Address or Port Number
1	293.1.1.1	293.1.1.2	293.1.1.3	293.1.1.4	IP address
	16384	16385	16386	16387	Port number
2	293.1.1.5	293.1.1.6	293.1.1.7	293.1.1.8	IP address
	16388	16389	16390	16391	Port number
3	293.1.1.9	293.1.1.10	293.1.1.11	293.1.1.12	IP address
	16392	16393	16394	16395	Port number

Voice Mail During SRST Fallback

Remote access to a centralized voice mail server for the mailbox owner typically is not a problem during WAN failure, because most users know how to check their mailboxes from payphones, cell phones, or home. When reaching any outside line, they know the proper sequence of digits to enter to walk through the menus and retrieve their messages.

Within those menus in voice mail systems is the ability to leave voice mail for a particular extension. SRST can use these same menus to redirect calls that have reached a busy or no answer directory number destination to a centralized voice mail system. SRST can dial the voice mail system pilot number, send DTMF tones to emulate the button presses to navigate the mail system menu structure, and then connect the redirected call to the appropriate mailbox.

NOTE	Message waiting indicator (MWI) is not supported in a centralized deployment via SRST voice mail integration. MWI on each phone potentially might not indicate the mailbox's current status after a WAN failure. The failure to indicate current status is because of lack of reachability immediately following message storage or retrieval.
	Calls originating at the central site that attempt to reach an extension being supported by SRST immediately divert to voice mail if the voice mail number is configured as the call forward no answer setting. Callers at the central site attempting to reach the remote location need to add the appropriate digits to dial around the failure by using the PSTN.

Figure 2-18 illustrates the call flows of an inside and outside caller being redirected to a voice mail system over the PSTN because the target phone is unavailable, busy, or is retrieving messages.

Three variables are used to hold state information:

- Calling number information (CGN)
- Called number information (CDN)
- Forwarding number (FDN)

TIP	Calling Line ID (CLID) is also needed for this mechanism to operate as described. CLID is not always available, especially internationally. Outside call interaction varies depending on CLID information availability.

Figure 2-18   *SRST Voice Mail Integration over the PSTN*

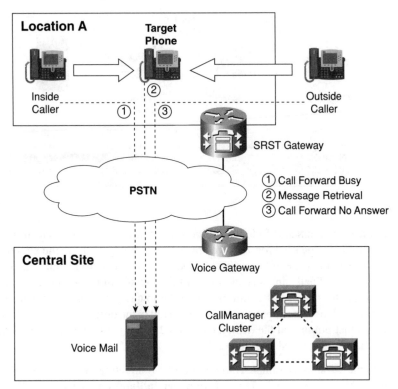

Three events can cause call routing to a voice mail server in SRST:

- The user presses the **messages** button on the phone.

- The call is not answered before being routed to voice mail as a result of the call forward no answer setting.

- The called destination is busy, and the call is routed to voice mail as a result of the call forward busy setting.

Figure 2-19 shows an example of a complex call redirection flow and resulting variables being filled.

The voice mail setting is the dial string that reaches the voice mail system via the **messages** button. Call forward busy and no answer settings are likely to be the same voice mail server, but they can differ if sent to a general mailbox. With the CGN, CDN, and FDN strings, it becomes a task of getting the **pattern** command to match the voice mail system menu structure.

Figure 2-19 *SRST Voice Mail Variables*

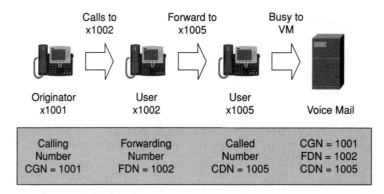

All **pattern** commands follow a similar format: first, a keyword to identify what the command is to be used for, followed by a digit to navigate the menu structure of the voice mail server, then one of the strings (CGN, CDN, or FDN) to identify the original target or mailbox, and finally an * to end this set of digit instructions. Multiple digit instructions are supported for one **pattern** command in order to navigate complex menu structures, and would continue to be appended to the command in the order just described. For a voice mail system that prompts at the main menu for a 2 as the subscriber login, the corresponding command is displayed in Figure 2-20.

Example 2-4 shows a sample configuration for redirecting calls over the PSTN via plain old telephone service (POTS). The **call-manager-fallback** commands establish the voice mail, call forward busy, and call forward no answer redirection numbers. Next, the **vm-integration** pattern commands send the appropriate DTMF digits along with the CGN, CDN, and FDN strings to reach the correct mailbox for extension and trunk calling combinations.

TIP   Redirecting calls over the PSTN is recommended only for ISDN because of the inherent capability of Q.931 and other trunks that can provide quick call setup times. Foreign Exchange Office (FXO) connectivity can be challenging because of the variable timing involved in call setup, which in turn affects the **pattern** command and is not recommended. Use the **timing digit** and **timing inter-digit** commands on POTS dial peers to slow dual-tone multifrequency (DTMF) tone sending.

Figure 2-20   *Sample* **pattern** *Command*

SRST Gateway   Voice Mail

Voice Mail Menu:
2 to Retrieve Your Messages
5 to Leave a New Message
...

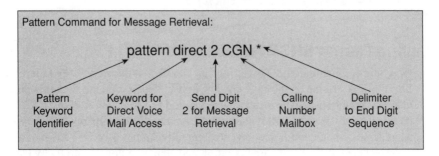

Pattern Command for Message Retrieval:

pattern direct 2 CGN *

| Pattern Keyword Identifier | Keyword for Direct Voice Mail Access | Send Digit 2 for Message Retrieval | Calling Number Mailbox | Delimiter to End Digit Sequence |

Example 2-4   *POTS Voice Mail Routing Sample Configuration*

```
all-manager-fallback
 voicemail 9999
 call-forward busy 9999
 call-forward noan 9999 timeout 3
!
vm-integration
 pattern direct 2 CGN *
 pattern ext-to-ext no-answer 5 FDN * CGN *
 pattern ext-to-ext busy 7 FDN * CGN *
 pattern trunk-to-ext no-answer 4 FDN * CGN *
 pattern trunk-to-ext busy 6 FDN * CGN *
```

ISDN lines can carry redirect within the call Q.931 setup information and require no special SRST DTMF sequence configuration. Redirected dial number ID service (RDNIS), the outgoing option in the settings of the central site gateway, must be enabled.

TIP   RDNIS information is not always supported by the carrier, especially internationally. Check to ensure that RDNIS information is indeed transported by your carrier if you're attempting to use this functionality.

Example 2-5 shows a sample configuration for redirecting calls over ISDN via RDNIS.

Example 2-5 *ISDN RDNIS Voice Mail Routing Sample Configuration*

```
transfer-pattern 91714T
voicemail 917145551212
call-forward busy 917145551212
call-forward noan 917145551212 timeout 3
```

PSTN Calling During SRST Fallback

Outgoing and incoming PSTN calling can be affected during a WAN failure even though SRST is in operation on the gateway. The impact depends on the signaling protocol chosen to signal VoIP between the location gateway and CallManager. Either MGCP or H.323 can be employed to provide call signaling functionality. Both protocols have their strengths and weaknesses. MGCP configurations are generally simpler to configure and have less overhead per call, with all administration and signaling done centrally by CallManager. H.323-controlled gateways can operate without any other processing components because they house their own dial plan, though they require more configuration steps. When the WAN is down in a centralized call processing scenario, H.323-controlled gateways can still place or take calls, whereas MGCP-controlled gateways cannot do either.

MGCP fallback allows for some middle ground, allowing MGCP signaling during normal CallManager operation and then falling back into H.323 mode when CallManager is unreachable. Much like SRST, this allows call processing to continue during a WAN outage.

Example 2-6 shows a sample configuration for a POTS dial peer controlled by MGCP. For IOS Releases 12.2(15)ZJ and later, the dial peer **application** command is unnecessary and can potentially cause unwanted interaction.

Example 2-6 *Sample Configuration with a POTS Dial Peer Controlled by MGCP*

```
mgcp call-agent 172.27.3.1
mgcp dtmf-relay codec all mode cisco
ccm-manager mgcp
ccm-manager config
!
dial-peer voice 1 pots
 application mgcpapp
 port 3/0/0
```

Example 2-7 shows a sample configuration for a POTS dial peer controlled by H.323. This is common configuration allowing inbound calling with DID and outbound calling when the number is prefixed with a 9.

Example 2-7 *Sample POTS Dial Peer Controlled by H.323*

```
dial-peer voice 1 pots
 incoming called-number .
 destination-pattern 9T
 direct-inward-dial
 port 3/0/0
```

Example 2-8 shows a sample configuration for MGCP POTS configuration with H.323 fallback. Notice it is very similar to the two previous individual examples with the additional **ccm-manager fallback** and call application commands.

Example 2-8 *Sample MGCP POTS Configuration with H.323 Fallback*

```
mgcp
mgcp call-agent 172.27.3.1
mgcp dtmf-relay codec all mode cisco
ccm-manager mgcp
ccm-manager config
ccm-manager fallback-mgcp
call application alternate DEFAULT
!
dial-peer voice 1 pots
 application mgcpapp
 incoming called-number .
 destination-pattern 9T
 direct-inward-dial
 port 3/0/0
```

Lines capable of direct inward dial (DID) frequently provide digit information that does not match the directory numbers during SRST fallback. The second line in Example 2-9 uses the last four digits of an incoming string beginning with 444 as the directory number. The third line uses only the last three digits of the incoming 333 string and adds a leading 5. Location DID ranges and extension assignments affect the number of entries—only five are permitted.

Example 2-9 *Setting DID Strings to Match Dial Plan Patterns*

```
Router(config)#call-manager-fallback
Router(config-cm-fallback)#dialplan-pattern 1 444.... extension-length 4
Router(config-cm-fallback)#dialplan-pattern 2 333.... extension-length 3
  extension-pattern 5...
```

You can reroute incoming calls destined for unregistered IP phones during SRST operation via the alias feature. Because of the use of the SRST disable option in the device pool, select phones might purposefully fail to register, and the following command allows redirecting those calls to another number, internal or external. Example 2-10 sends all calls for directory numbers 1000 to 1099 that fail to register to SRST to extension 1102.

Example 2-10 *Setting up an Extension Range Alias to Forward Calls*

```
Router(config)#call-manager-fallback
Router(config-cm-fallback)#alias 1 10.. to 1102
```

Restrict calls from dialing to or from specific numbers via the Class of Restriction (COR) feature, which is available to all dial-peers whether SRST is in operation or not. SRST can use COR lists during operation and block ranges of directory numbers from dialing specific numbers. What differs during SRST operation is that the sourcing dial-peer or ephone-dn is virtual and temporary. SRST addresses the directory numbers given by CallManager to the line appearances on the phones instead of having permanent dial-peer or ephone-dn entries. Example 2-11 attaches **corList** as the first list to directory numbers 1000 through 1099.

Example 2-11 *Correlating a COR List to an Extension Range*

```
Router(config)#call-manager-fallback
Router(config-cm-fallback)#cor outgoing corList 1 1000 - 1099
```

Call transfer patterns can be used to limit the transfer of calls during SRST operation. This can be used to allow only certain dial strings to be transfer targets. By default, only SRST phones can be transfer targets. If outside PSTN transfer targets need to be included, they must be specified. Example 2-12 allows an outside 800 number transfer target with a leading 9 to match a dial peer.

Example 2-12 *Enabling Transfers to Outside Numbers*

```
Router(config)#call-manager-fallback
Router(config-cm-fallback)#transfer-pattern 91800T
```

To keep parity with the CallManager behavior if enabled, provide secondary dial tone during SRST operation, and keep user confusion to a minimum. In Example 2-13, secondary dial tone is provided after a single 9.

Example 2-13   *Providing Secondary Dial Tone*

```
Router(config)#call-manager-fallback
Router(config-cm-fallback)#secondary-dialtone 9
```

Choosing Gateways to Support Centralized Call Processing Functionality

You must balance a set of complex variables to ensure that the gateway at each remote location can handle the required load, has the necessary support for the number and type of interfaces, supports SRST, and fits within your organization's budget. Several factors discussed in this chapter help narrow the choices in the Cisco portfolio. The choices depend on what features you are planning to deploy in your centralized CallManager architecture:

- cRTP support and scaling
- PSTN interface type, count, and speed
- SRST support and number of IP phones supported
- WAN interface type, count, and speed
- LAN and inline power support

The first three features are the most important criteria in the decision-making process. Tables 2-7 and 2-8 provide a snapshot of the platforms and testing data available as of February 2004. Check the URLs in the table footnotes for further details and updates.

TIP   Standardizing on common gateways in all or most locations allows a common set of spares to be used between sites, reducing the number of parts on hand needed to quickly restore a site should failure occur. Configuring the physical interfaces to exactly match site to site makes remote configuration less error-prone. Manageability should be a key concern during all phases of network design.

Table 2-7   *Cisco Gateway Testing as of IOS Release 12.2(8)T Not Exceding 75 Percent Utilization*

Cisco Gateway Feature/ Function	261x-XM	262x-XM	265x-XM	3640	2691	3725	3660	3745
Simultaneous G.729 Calls								
Voice gateway only[*]	60[1]	70[1]	90	96[1]	90	120	300[1]	240
WAN gateway[**]	30[1]	35[1]	60[1]	50[1]	90	120	200[1]	240
WAN gateway + cRTP[***]	22[1]	25[1]	42[1]	30[1]	90	120	160[1]	240
Maximum Calls Per Second								
Call setups per second	0.5	1	2	2	4	15	4	20
Maximum Physical DS0 Connectivity								
FXS	12	12	12	36	12	24	72	48
FXO	8	8	8	24	8	16	48	32
E&M	4	4	4	12	4	8	24	16
Analog DID	4	4	4	12	4	8	24	16
BRI	4	4	4	12	4	8	24	16
T1/E1 physical ports	3	3	3	6	2/3	4/6	12	8/10
T1 channels	72	72	72	144	72[2]	120[2]	288	240[2]
E1 channels	90	90	90	180	90	180	360	300

[*]Fast Ethernet interface; no QoS features; no data, only voice traffic

[**]T1/E1 serial interface, LLQ, LFI, TS, voice (approximately 50 percent of bandwidth) + data (approximately 25 percent of bandwidth)

[***]T1/E1 serial interface, LLQ, LFI, TS, cRTP voice (approximately 50 percent of bandwidth) + data (approximately 25 percent of bandwidth)

[1]75 percent platform CPU utilization reached for this number of voice channels with a moderate amount of data flow

[2]Physical port DS0 connectivity limit reached for this configuration; not all channels can be used

For further platform information, see the Cisco 2600, 3600, and 3700 Voice Gateway Router Interoperability with Cisco CallManager data sheet at the following link:

http://www.cisco.com/warp/public/cc/pd/rt/2600/prodlit/imgcp_ds.htm

Table 2-8   *SRST 3.0 Gateway Support and Scaling Parameters in IOS Release 12.2(15)ZJ2*

Cisco Gateway Model	Maximum Number of IP Phones	Maximum Number of Directory Numbers	Maximum Number of Three-Party Conferences	Recommended RAM	Recommended Flash
1751, 1751V	24	120	8	96 MB	32 MB
1760	24	120	8	96 MB	32 MB
261x-XM	24	96	8	128 MB	32 MB
262x-XM	24	96	8	128 MB	32 MB
265x-XM	48	192	8	128 MB	32 MB
2691	72	288	8	128 MB	32 MB
3640/A	72	288	8	128 MB	32 MB
3660	240	960	16	128 MB	32 MB
3725	144	576	16	128 MB	32 MB
3745	240	960	16	128 MB	32 MB
Catalyst 4500 Access Gateway Module (AGM)	240	480	16	128 MB	32 MB

For further details and updates, see the Cisco SRS Telephony website at the following link:

http://www.cisco.com/en/US/products/sw/voicesw/ps2169/index.html

For the gateway at the central site, the parameters for selection are similar, but the real focus is the cRTP scaling along with the proper WAN interfaces to support the number of locations. Product series such as the 7200VXR and Catalyst 6500 offer a multitude of interfaces along with scaleable cRTP performance. Depending on your needs and future scalability requirements, the gateways listed in Tables 2-7 and 2-8 can service the central site as well. No matter the deployment's size, aggregating central site connections across multiple gateways minimizes the impact of having a central site gateway failure.

Summary

This chapter explored the various strategies and technologies that enable centralized call processing deployments, which included basic link layer connectivity, QoS, CAC, and SRST. The chapter illustrated the best practices and considerations involved with each technology. Although this chapter was singularly focused on centralized CallManager deployments, many variables exist in such a deployment, with a greater number of options available to help solve them. Centralized call processing models are the basis of the next larger deployment scenario: distributed call processing. Although distributed call processing deployments can look complicated, they are essentially composed of several centralized call processing centers as discussed in this chapter.

## CHAPTER 3

Installing CallManager

This chapter discusses the best practices for Cisco CallManager installation. Fortunately, the installation routine is automated, but a few possible pitfalls still must be avoided.

The purpose of this chapter is to ensure the smoothest possible installation and the maximum amount of uptime after the software is installed. At first glance, some of the advice given in this chapter could be perceived as dictatorial; however, the instructions are based on lessons learned the hard way by many engineers over the course of many CallManager installations. The authors consulted the Cisco Technical Assistance Center (TAC) teams that support CallManager for their view of the most common causes of failed installations. In addition, the authors consolidated the experiences of several integrators.

Following the recommendations in this chapter will support the success of your installations.

Before the Installation

Chapter 1, "Planning the CallManager Implementation," explored the planning necessary before installing CallManager. Before you turn on the Media Convergence Server (MCS) or the Cisco-certified server to install CallManager, you should consider the following steps, which smooth out the installation process:

- Determining the installation logistics
- Preparing the installation checklist
- Preparing the installation media
- Verifying network connectivity
- Verifying power, basic input/output system (BIOS) settings, and hardware compatibility
- Using only supported third-party hardware
- Using dual network interface cards (NICs)
- Having your Cisco SmartNet contract number or system serial number on hand
- Reading the release notes

Determine the Installation Logistics

Before performing any kind of installation, be sure you thoroughly organize all the installation logistics. The checklist shown in Table 3-1 highlights some of the most important items. Use it to track completion of the necessary tasks and place a check mark in the first column when you have completed the task.

Table 3-1   *Partial Installation Checklist for Logistics*

Logistics Installation Checklist

	Task	Comments
☐	Rack space available	
☐	Rack-mounting hardware available	
☐	Power outlets sufficient	
☐	Uninterruptible power supply (UPS) available	
☐	Network connectivity in place	
☐	Date and time of installation communicated to interested parties	
☐	Network drop available in the correct VLAN	

In general, it's best to perform CallManager installations in a test environment that is configured to mimic the production network topology. Working first in a test environment affords the time needed to perform all installation, testing, and documentation tasks without the time pressure of an outage window. It also provides time for the logistics mentioned in Table 3-1 to be addressed.

NOTE   CallManager is so flexible that it really does not need to be installed on site. Often, network integrators who are certified in IP Telephony perform most, if not all, of the phases of the installation and configuration off-premises. They often arrive on the day of installation with a fully configured server. This is normal and to be expected. Be sure to ask for full installation documentation if you are the customer, and be sure to provide it if you are the integrator. If issues arise, proper documentation eases interactions with TAC. Table 3-2 provides a means for you to document the current server characteristics.

If you follow the best practices described in this chapter, such as recommendations against joining Windows domains, CallManager servers do not interfere with any other network components. Therefore, if you cannot perform the installation in a lab environment, you can safely do it on the production network, subject to your company's policy on new server introduction.

Check with your server administrators for their checklists of steps necessary to add servers to the production network.

Prepare the Installation Checklist

Before beginning an installation, you should document the characteristics of each server by using a document similar to that shown in Table 3-2. This table supplies the minimal information necessary for troubleshooting. Use it to document the servers prior to installation and place a check mark in the first column when you have documented the information.

Table 3-2   *Pre-Installation Server Characteristics*

Pre-Installation Server Characteristics

	Item	Description
☐	Host name	
☐	Windows operating system (OS) version	
☐	Windows OS patch level	
☐	CallManager version	
☐	CallManager patch level	
☐	Workgroup name	
☐	IP address	
☐	IP subnet mask	
☐	IP default gateway	
☐	IP DNS servers	
☐	Publisher or Subscriber	
☐	sa password (CallManager 3.3 and below)	
☐	Password key (CallManager 4.0 and above)	
☐	DC Directory Manager password	

continues

Table 3-2   *Pre-Installation Server Characteristics (Continued)*

Pre-Installation Server Characteristics

Item	Description
☐	Administrator password
☐	Backup server or target
☐	Location of backup
☐	LMHOSTS file entries
☐	NIC speed and duplex

Be sure to place the information in Table 3-2 where the operations team can find it. You would be surprised how much useful documentation often remains inaccessible in locked desks just when needed. If you keep the documentation in printed form, be sure to either black out password information or store passwords in accordance with your company's policy on documents that contain sensitive information. In addition to the server information, it's important that an updated network topology diagram be kept in the folder for aid in troubleshooting. If the documentation is kept in electronic form, it's best to password-protect it.

TIP   Whenever you make changes on the server, be sure to update your documentation.

Prepare the Installation Media

This might seem obvious, but it's important to have all the media available at the time of installation. Depending on the server you are using, you will use CD or DVD media for the installation.

The CD/DVD pack from the factory has Windows OS CD/DVDs and CallManager application software CDs. Depending on the type of server you use, Hewlett-Packard (HP) might include SmartStart CDs in the package. CallManager definitely does not use these HP CDs, although HP provides them in the standard server package.

NOTE   In rare cases, the media shipped with your server are incorrect for your system. Be sure to read the release notes to ensure that the labels on your media match the supported versions of the hardware. If you find that your media are incorrect, contact the Cisco Technical Assistance Center at 1-800-553-2447 or http://www.cisco.com/tac.

Verify Network Connectivity

Before performing an installation, be sure the system is connected to a network. Even if the system is not connected to the production network at the time of installation, ensuring Ethernet connectivity with the correct speed and duplex settings speeds up the boot sequences during installation.

If the network is unavailable, the CallManager service fails to start, causing errors on the screen that could result in confusion. In addition, the timeout values for the various services make the machine slow and unresponsive.

Verify That Both Power Plugs Are Connected

CallManager 4.0 still supports several older MCS platforms that have dual power supplies, such as the MCS-7835-1266. By default, if both power supplies are not connected, the system does not boot unless you press the F1 key. The default can be changed through the BIOS, but this is not recommended, because it's possible that future upgrades will disable it. See the next section for BIOS information.

The point of the boot interruption is to remind you to replace a bad power supply so that you'll have a way of knowing something is wrong.

Do Not Modify the Original BIOS Settings

Do not change any of the BIOS settings before installation. It's important to leave the computer in the pristine state in which it arrived from the factory. Changing settings without approval from Cisco TAC only makes troubleshooting more difficult should you encounter a problem.

In addition, changing the BIOS settings might cause the installation to fail or cause Windows to behave abnormally. Cisco strongly recommends that you leave the factory default settings as they are. Although many savvy server technicians might be able to make perceived performance improvements by changing the BIOS settings, all the testing of CallManager and the underlying Windows OS is done with the BIOS settings shipped from the factory.

Do Not Add Unsupported Third-Party Hardware

Do not under any circumstances add any third-party hardware that is not supported. Unsupported hardware includes

- Unsupported sound cards
- RAID controllers

- Fibre Channel host/bus adapters
- Tape drives
- Unsupported hard disks
- USB devices
- Memory

These devices are not recognized by the installation routine and therefore can potentially cause the installation to fail. In addition, if an unsupported third-party device is installed in the machine, TAC asks you to remove it before troubleshooting.

Use Dual Network Interface Cards (Adapter Teaming)

Several MCS platforms have two NICs onboard. Adapter teaming is supported starting with CallManager 3.2 and Windows OS 2000.2.4. *Adapter teaming* provides a way for an MCS server to have two connections to the network to provide continuous connectivity in the event of network switch failure.

The following servers currently support the adapter teaming driver:

- Cisco MCS-7825H-2.2-EVV1
- Cisco MCS-7835H-2.4-EVV1
- Cisco MCS-7845H-2.4-EVV1
- Cisco MCS-7835-1266
- Cisco-verified, customer-provided HP DL380 G2 server
- Cisco-verified, customer-provided HP DL380 G3 server, including single and dual processors
- Cisco-verified, customer-provided HP DL320 G2 server

Before you install the adapter teaming driver, Cisco requires that you have installed the Cisco-provided OS version 2000.2.4 or later.

To install the driver, it's crucial that you follow the Installing the Cisco Media Convergence Server Network Teaming Driver instructions on Cisco.com at

> http://www.cisco.com/en/US/products/hw/voiceapp/ps378 prod_installation_guide 09186a008015a131.html

Using adapter teaming is not a requirement for fault tolerance. Fault tolerance is also achieved using CallManager SQL-based clustering. It's important that you connect your CallManager Publisher and Subscriber servers to different switches in the network to provide fault tolerance in the event of a switch outage.

Locate Your Cisco SmartNet Contract Number or System Serial Number

Before starting any installation or upgrade, it's a good idea to have your contract number in hand. When you call TAC, the operator first requests your contract number. If you have a new machine and have not received your contract number, the serial number of the MCS server will work.

Read the Release Notes

It's absolutely critical to read the release notes for the version of CallManager and the Windows OS you will install. The Achilles' heel of most installations is the failure of the installer to read the release notes thoroughly, which causes him or her to miss something during the setup.

Windows OS Version

As mentioned, you should not assume that you should use the Windows OS CDs that shipped with your product. Which Windows OS you should install depends on the version of CallManager you are installing. Read the section "Check the Compatibility Matrix" in Chapter 1, "Planning the CallManager Implementation" for more information. The release notes list the various OS versions and patch levels that have been tested with each version of CallManager. Install the OS that correlates to the version of CallManager you are installing. If your server did not ship with the proper OS, open a case with TAC to obtain the proper installation media.

CallManager Version

Do not assume that the CallManager CDs that shipped with your server are the most recent or those you should actually install. As the software changes, the various Cisco distribution channels are populated with servers and CDs. It's quite possible that the server you ordered came from a warehouse that had not yet been refreshed.

It's key to determine the version of CallManager you want to run. After you do this, be sure to check Cisco.com to find the latest patches available. Patches generally contain bug fixes that keep your system running smoothly.

Read the release notes for the main CallManager version as well as the patches. The release notes generally list all the bugs that the patch fixes.

For the latest CallManager release and service releases, check the Software Center at http://www.cisco.com/kobayashi/sw-center/. You need a Cisco.com login ID and password to access the Software Center. To ensure smooth installation, read the release notes for the version you will install. For example, you might think that the latest Windows OS version posted on Cisco.com would be the right OS to use in every case. This is not true. In every set of release notes, whether they are for CallManager or the Windows OS, a matrix lists what has been tested and what is recommended. It's essential to the success of your installation that you follow the guidelines in the release notes.

Hardware Compatibility

CallManager 4.0 does not support MCS-7820, MCS-7822, MCS-7830, IBM X330, or IBMX340 servers. Be sure to check the release notes for hardware compatibility.

During the Installation

Whereas the preceding section focused on what you should do before starting the installation process, this section discusses the best practices to use during the installation itself by covering the following topics:

- Locating key directories and files
- Avoiding Windows domain participation
- Updating the LMHOSTS file
- Using consistent passwords across servers

The installation process has two stages—the Windows OS installation and the CallManager installation. The Hardware Detection CD/DVD is used during the Windows OS phase.

Locate Key Directories and Files

After the Windows OS installation is completed, you are prompted for the CallManager installation media. The CallManager media contains Microsoft SQL Server 2000, DC Directory, and CallManager.

When installing CallManager, it's useful to know the key directories and files and their locations, as shown in Table 3-3. Knowing where these files are located makes troubleshooting easier and contributes to better overall knowledge of the environment.

Table 3-3 *Important File Locations*

Directory	Files that the Directory Contains
C:\CiscoPlugins	CallManager plugins listed under **Applications > Install Plug-Ins** in Cisco CallManager Administration
C:\CiscoWebs	CallManager Administration web pages

Table 3-3 *Important File Locations (Continued)*

Directory	Files that the Directory Contains
C:\program files\cisco\bin	CallManager application binary files and tools such as CCM.EXE
C:\program files\cisco\CallDetail	Call detail record (CDR) files
C:\program files\cisco\CallManagerAttendant	Cisco CallManager Attendant Console files
C:\program files\cisco\common	Files common to many CallManager services
C:\program files\cisco\EM	Cisco Extension Mobility service
C:\program files\cisco\JRE	Java Runtime Engine
C:\program files\cisco\MA	Cisco IP Manager/Assistant application
C:\program files\cisco\MOH	Music on Hold service
C:\program files\cisco\QRT	Quality Reporting Tool
C:\program files\cisco\TFTPPath	Path from which IP phones and gateways get their configuration files
C:\program files\cisco\trace	CallManager trace files
C:\program files\cisco\users	CallManager Attendant Console that users share
C:\program files\cisco\xntp	XTNP Time Server, used to keep CallManager server clocks synchronized
C:\utils\	Windows 2000 utilities such as KILL and SHUTDOWN
C:\utils\vnc	Virtual Network Computing, which can be used instead of Terminal Services; upgrades can be made using VNC
C:\dcdsrvr	DC Directory
C:\program files\common files\cisco\logs	Common installation log folder for OS and CallManager installation and upgrades
C:\utils\DualNIC	HP adapter teaming driver

Avoid Windows Domain Participation

One question often asked is, "Should I have CallManager servers participate in our Windows domain?" The best practice is to create a workgroup instead of using the Windows domain structure. Although it's true that adding a CallManager server to the Windows domain allows for the use of existing groups and passwords, issues with domain participation arise during installations or upgrades.

Most of the issues revolve around domain policies, such as password aging and system access policies. For example, if the domain policy is to change passwords every 30 days, and in this cycle the administrator password is changed, it's very possible that the CallManager services will not start on a reboot.

Although it's possible to have CallManager in a domain, having it there is a potential detriment that can cause difficulties.

Update the LMHOSTS File

The installation routine gives you the option of adding hosts and IP addresses to an LMHOSTS file. It's critical that you add the host names and IP addresses of all the servers in your cluster to the LMHOSTS file on every server. Microsoft SQL replication depends on NetBIOS name resolution, which is accomplished by the LMHOSTS file. If you do not add the servers to the LMHOSTS file, Subscriber installations might experience problems with database replication, which causes CallManager to be nonfunctional.

Sometimes the installation routine does not prompt you to add the servers, so you must manually edit the file. All CallManager systems come with two files on the system:

    C:\winnt\system32\drivers\etc\hosts
    C:\winnt\system32\drivers\etc\lmhosts.sam

The latter is a sample LMHOSTS file provided by Microsoft as an example of the file's syntax. If the installation routine fails to prompt you, rather than editing that file, use the following procedure to manually create a valid LMHOSTS file. Perform this procedure after the OS installation and before CallManager installation.

Step 1 Click **Start > Run**.

Step 2 Enter **notepad c:\winnt\system32\drivers\etc\lmhosts**. (Be sure to include the period.)

Step 3 After Notepad is loaded, enter your information as shown in Figure 3-1.

Figure 3-1   *LMHOSTS File Syntax Using Notepad*

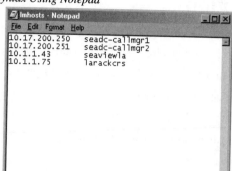

Use Consistent Passwords Across Servers

Before CallManager 4.0, you had to specify passwords for the Directory Manager, the SQL Server 2000 sa, and CallManager Administrator.

CallManager 4.0 forces SQL 2000 to use Windows Authentication mode. This mode has no internal SQL Server 2000 usernames and passwords to be specified. For security reasons, however, the CallManager 4.0 installation still prompts for and sets the sa account password.

Although it's not mandatory that all three passwords be the same, it is important that all the passwords be the same across servers. In other words, the Publisher and all Subscribers must use the same Directory Manager, sa, and Administrator passwords. If these passwords are not the same, synchronization does not occur, and you are forced to use the CCM Password Changer tool. To access the CCM Password Changer tool, open a DOS window (**Start > Run >** *type* **cmd**), enter **CCMPwdChanger**, and press **Enter**.

Many installations complete unsuccessfully because of password issues. You will save yourself much grief by making the passwords consistent.

TIP   Many keyboard, video, and mouse (KVM) switches inadvertently change the Caps Lock status when switching between systems. Be sure to double-check that the Caps Lock is OFF before entering any passwords.

After the Installation

This section describes tasks to perform after the installation of CallManager is completed:

- Double-check the items from your pre-installation checklists in Tables 3-1 and 3-2.
- Do not add unauthorized software to CallManager servers.
- Do not change OS parameters.
- Do not create other accounts on the system.
- Do not add Microsoft software updates.
- Verify database synchronization.
- Ensure that the NIC is set to 100/Full.
- Add the Cisco Security Agent.
- Add approved virus protection software.

Double-Check Your Pre-Installation Checklist

Whether you print the installation guide and check off the steps one by one, or you use the checklist provided at the beginning of this chapter, be sure that your installation routine is documented.

There are two main reasons for documentation: to verify that the appropriate steps were taken, and to enable the replication of the procedure by other teams.

TIP   If possible, perform a dry run through the CallManager installation in a lab environment to make sure your processes and procedures are sound.

Dry runs are useful for troubleshooting. If you encounter a problem during the installation, TAC can review your procedure to ensure its validity.

Do Not Add Unsupported Software to CallManager Servers

Under no circumstances should any unapproved software be added to any CallManager system. Unapproved software includes items such as backup utilities and unsupported antivirus programs. CallManager is tested and supported by Cisco "as is" without any unapproved modifications to the OS or hardware.

Adding unapproved software can expose issues in the underlying OS and can adversely affect CallManager operation. Utilities such as backup and virus protection can severely affect a server's CPU load, which can cause performance degradation that negatively affects phone service. In addition, TAC cannot support any system on which unsupported applications have been installed.

WARNING	Your CallManager installation will not be supported by TAC if it has unapproved software installed. This cannot be overemphasized. Cisco thoroughly tests the system's performance and cannot support any unauthorized software. Third-party software vendors must go through a rigorous testing procedure to gain approval for the use of their products on a CallManager server.

Backing up the system is always a concern, and that is addressed in Chapter 4, "Backing Up and Restoring the Environment." In addition, security and management are concerns. Table 3-4 lists the various third-party applications that are supported on CallManager.

Table 3-4   *Supported Third-Party Applications*

Application	Category	Vendor
Prognosis	Management	Integrated Research
Vivinet	Management	NetIQ
Norton AntiVirus	Security	Symantec
McAfee Netshield	Security	Network Associates
Cisco Security Agent	Security	Cisco Systems

Do Not Change OS Parameters

Many customers have an information technology (IT) checklist that must be completed before a Windows 2000 system is allowed to be on the network. Although these policies exist for good reason, sometimes one or more steps on the checklist should be skipped. If you are challenged for skipping a step on the checklist, explain that this system should be treated as a closed system even though it uses Windows 2000 as the OS, Microsoft SQL Server 2000 as the database, and Internet Information Server (IIS) as the web server.

Cisco has gone to great lengths to harden the OS, thus obviating the need for further lockdown. In addition, Cisco includes Cisco Security Agent (CSA) free with each CallManager license. CSA protects the system from many types of network attacks. See Chapter 6, "Securing the Environment," for more information on security.

In addition, any and all OS and IIS changes are wiped out during some types of upgrades because the upgrades use a standard image. For example, the upgrade to version 3.3 from versions 3.1 and 3.2 requires a complete server rebuild, and no OS changes are preserved. It's not practical to be required to repeat the changes for each server after each upgrade.

Do Not Create Other Accounts on the System

Several customers have a policy by which the local "administrator" account is disabled, and other accounts with administrative privilege are created and used in day-to-day system operation. This kind of policy is analogous to the types of post-installation tasks covered in the preceding section.

You should avoid modifying or disabling the local administrator account at all costs. CallManager upgrades use this account for various installation tasks, and the password change prompt is presented at the end of every installation. Creating other accounts with administrator privileges is not a problem, but disabling the local administrator account causes many problems during upgrades.

Use Only Microsoft Patches and Updates That You Download from Cisco.com

Under no circumstances should you ever install any Microsoft update or patch directly from the Microsoft website. Do not enable the Windows 2000 Auto Update feature either, because doing so would result in a system that is unstable and unsupported by TAC.

Patches and updates are supplied by Cisco at the Software Center on Cisco.com at http://www.cisco.com/kobayashi/sw-center/. You must be logged in with a valid Cisco.com account to access CallManager software. You must install only patches approved by Cisco. Cisco performs regression testing on all patches, which ensures compatibility with all applications.

In addition, various tools such as C:\utils\mcsver.exe and the Details button on CallManager Administration (**Help > About Cisco CallManager**) use the information contained in the Cisco-packaged updates to maintain the integrity of that data. If you install a Microsoft patch and then you need assistance from TAC, the version of software that you give the customer support engineer could easily be incorrect, which could lead to unplanned downtime.

More information about patching and updates is provided in Chapter 5, "Upgrading and Patching CallManager."

Verify Database Synchronization

When you install a Subscriber server, the Microsoft SQL 2000 Database Pull Subscriptions are created automatically. However, it's important to double-check the subscription's integrity.

To double-check subscriptions, follow this procedure on the Subscriber:

Step 1   Click **Start > Programs > Microsoft SQL Server > Enterprise Manager**.

Step 2   Double-click **Microsoft SQL Servers**.

Step 3   Double-click **SQL Server Group**.

Step 4   Double-click the Subscriber server.

Step 5   Double-click **Databases**.

Step 6   Double-click the CCM*XXXX* database with the highest value of *XXXX*.

Step 7   Click **Pull Subscriptions**.

Be sure the status of the subscription is set to Running. If the database status is not Running, follow the procedure outlined in "Using DBLHelper to Reestablish a Broken Cisco CallManager Cluster SQL Subscription," Document ID 46082 at the following link:

> http://www.cisco.com/en/US/products/sw/voicesw/ps556/products_tech_note 09186a00801e7ddf.shtml

Set the NIC to the Highest Link Speed and Full Duplex

Set the NIC to the highest speed supported by both the server and the switch. Also, be sure to set the duplex to Full. A sample is shown in Figure 3-2. If this is left on auto-detect, which is the default, problems can occur, such as signaling delays, voice cut-through, poor Music on Hold quality, and poor quality on software-based conferences. The NIC is often the last thing you check, but setting the NIC speed and duplex immediately after installation helps you avoid problems related to speed and duplex mismatches.

Do not leave the switch port to which CallManager is connected in auto-negotiate mode. Leaving the port in auto-negotiate mode creates speed and duplex mismatches. Instead, set the port to match the server's speed and duplex.

Follow these steps to change the switch port settings:

Step 1   Click **Start > Settings > Network and Dialup Connections**.

Step 2   Double-click **Local Area Connection**.

Figure 3-2 *Setting the NIC Settings to 100/Full*

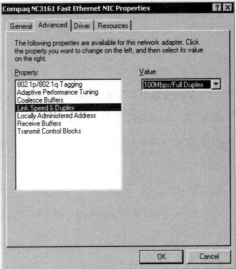

Step 3 Click **Properties**.

Step 4 Click **Configure**.

Step 5 Click the **Advanced** tab.

At this point, each server provides a different way to set the speed and duplex. As soon as you are at the screen described in Step 5, it should be an intuitive operation to set the speed and duplex. If you have trouble finding the right settings, contact your server support team.

On CatOS-based Cisco switches, run these commands:

```
set port speed x/y 100
set port duplex x/y full
```

On Cisco IOS software-based Cisco switches, the commands to apply at the interface level are

```
speed 100
duplex full
```

NOTE When you perform an upgrade to CallManager or the OS, checking speed and duplex should be part of the post-installation procedure, because the installation routine could reset these settings.

Use the Cisco Security Agent

Cisco Security Agent (CSA) provides protection against many kinds of malicious code, including Trojan horses, worms, denial of service attacks, and buffer overflows.

CSA software is provided free with each license of CallManager. Download it from: http://www.cisco.com/cgi-bin/tablebuild.pl/cmva-3des. You must be logged in with a valid Cisco.com account to access CSA software.

Add Cisco-Supported Virus Protection Software

Although Cisco provides a headless license of Cisco Security Agent free of charge, you may still want to install approved virus protection software on CallManager servers. Search Cisco.com using keywords such as "virus protection CallManager" and check for Cisco CallManager Bulletins at the following link for virus protection software that has been approved by Cisco. Do not, under any circumstances, install a product that is not specifically supported by Cisco. You may impair the operation of CallManager by doing so.

http://www.cisco.com/en/US/products/sw/voicesw/ps556/prod_bulletins_list.html

Summary

The best practices for installation, which are detailed in this chapter, ensure that you have a clean CallManager system ready to be configured. The system documentation you have prepared as part of performing the installation will be useful when you upgrade the system.

The major steps for installation include the following:

- Before installation
    - Determine the installation logistics.
    - Prepare the installation checklist.
    - Prepare the installation media.
    - Verify network connectivity.
    - Verify that both power plugs are connected.
    - Do not modify the original BIOS settings.
    - Do not add unsupported third-party hardware.
    - Use dual NICs (adapter teaming).
    - Locate your Cisco Smartnet contract number or system serial number.
    - Read the release notes.

- During the installation
  - Locate key directories and files.
  - Avoid Windows domain participation.
  - Update the LMHOSTS file.
  - Use consistent passwords across servers.
- After the installation
  - Double-check your preinstallation checklist.
  - Do not add unsupported software to CallManager servers.
  - Do not change OS parameters.
  - Do not create other accounts on the system.
  - Use only Microsoft patches and updates that you download from Cisco.com.
  - Verify database synchronization.
  - Set the NIC to the highest link speed and full duplex.
  - Use the Cisco Security Agent.
  - Add Cisco-supported virus protection software.

## CHAPTER 4

Backing Up and Restoring the Environment

As nearly everyone has experienced, failures occur at the most inconvenient time possible. Unless you have saved backups in a location that is remote from the affected system, you could waste many hours or days rebuilding your database because restoration involves so many aspects: extensions, users, calling search spaces, partitions, and more. Some say Murphy of Murphy's Law fame was an optimist, so we all must be ready for the worst.

This chapter presents the best practices for preparing for unexpected events:

- Consider the deployment as a whole
- Prepare for recovery
- Become familiar with backup and tools
- Understand how to restore and recover
- Gain the ability to troubleshoot typical issues

Cisco Media Convergence Servers (MCS) provide redundant hard drives. These drives not only eliminate the chance that a single disk failure will take out an MCS, but they also enhance Cisco CallManager upgrade options. However, redundant disks do not provide recovery and redundancy for botched upgrades and common disasters such as lightning strikes, floods, fire, and earthquakes. Employing redundant media in a single chassis does not solve as many failure scenarios as having redundant media in multiple locations. You should keep copies of a working configuration in one or more offsite locations; when human error or natural disasters strike, access to such a backup is worth its weight in gold.

Clustering servers allows you to add geography between individual servers and designates a single server in the cluster as the master Publisher (see Figure 4-1). Because all other servers read from this master copy, backing up the Publisher is not only recommended but obviously necessary.

Figure 4-1 *Publisher and Subscriber Relationships*

Backing up Subscriber servers can be very important. Even though a server is designated as a Subscriber, it might be doing several things in addition to copying to disk the master database from the Publisher. Other duties might include diagnostic logging, storing Music on Hold (MOH) audio sources, and storing call detail records (CDR) locally when the Publisher fails. As a minimum backup practice, when CDRs are used in your organization's billing, you should be backing up individual Subscriber servers in a cluster.

Although it doesn't operate with a true copy of the CallManager configuration, Survivable Remote Site Telephony (SRST) does offer a mechanism to keep select IP phones in operation during a WAN outage or even a local CallManager outage. Chapter 2, "Planning Centralized Call Processing Deployments," covers SRST and centralized CallManager deployments in detail. If your CallManager deployment is remote from a centralized CallManager, or just plain small, you might want to think about adding SRST to your gateway routers. SRST potentially adds another layer of dial tone protection to the Cisco IP Telephony service.

Consider the Whole Deployment

Although this chapter mainly focuses on CallManager and related aspects of backing up and restoring applications, it's just as critical to have both redundancy and backup strategies for the multitude of other components in your IP Telephony deployment. Everything between an IP phone and an outside line must have some form of failure plan to recover from a power outage, equipment failure, or other disaster.

Be sure that your backup strategy does not overlook small files in remote areas of the network which, when lost, can cause a great deal of pain. Examples of such files include custom scripts and audio prompts that might be difficult or costly to reconstruct when no secondary storage locations exist. Gateways that use custom scripting and prompting are particularly unpleasant to rebuild by hand. All the applications that enhance the core CallManager functionality need a backup strategy as well—Unity, Conference Connection, Emergency Responder, and Personal Assistant, to name just a few.

IP Telephony solutions are built from many individual components: servers, software, Ethernet equipment, and IP phones. To tie together some functionality and perhaps some departmental responsibility, all the components that make up the solution can be viewed as functional elements of a complete system. To operate, each element depends on the other elements, much like departments within an organization, so they all should share a consistent backup methodology to ensure reliable recovery for the entire organization.

A backup plan should take the following elements into consideration:

- CallManager
- Call detail records (CDR) and call management records (CMR)

- MOH sources
- CallManager log files
- Other files
- Unity messaging repository
- Additional CallManager applications
- Gateway connectivity
- Ethernet switching and routing
- Frequency of backups

Back Up All Important Data on the CallManager Server

CallManager keeps all servers updated with a copy of the CallManager database, which might make you question the need to back up any of the Subscriber servers in a cluster, since all members of the cluster share a copy of the same database found on the Publisher.

Files not installed as part of the CallManager release or shared databases that reside on individual servers can often be overlooked. By design, the Cisco Backup and Restore System (BARS), included with CallManager, does not back up every file on the server. Settings within BARS also affect what is and is not backed up. Depending on the overall architecture of the CallManager deployment, the following files might be lost in a catastrophic server failure, regardless of the BARS settings and whether the CallManager server is designated as a Publisher or Subscriber:

- CDRs and CMRs (known collectively as CDR data)
- Custom files placed on the server for MOH
- CallManager log files
- Tool for Auto-Registered Phones Support (TAPS) data
- Third-party directories using Lightweight Directory Access Protocol (LDAP)
- Third-party files and files not installed as part of CallManager

Back Up Subscriber Databases to Ensure CDR and CMR Survivability When the Publisher Is Down

As mentioned earlier, when the Subscribers cannot reach the Publisher, the Subscribers can no longer post CDR data (CDRs and CMRs) to the common cluster CDR database. This potentially makes the CDR data on each Subscriber unique during the time the Publisher is unreachable. If it's not possible to recover a Publisher, you need to have backups of all Subscriber CDR data. This is critical for any organization employing CDR data for billing or accounting.

Back Up All Music on Hold Audio Sources

The Cisco IP Voice Media Streaming App service provides sample audio source files, but you may use custom-developed audio files. Individual servers in the cluster frequently source unique greetings, advertisements, jingles, and the like. The Cisco IP Voice Media Streaming App service moves the converted audio files between servers as needed. (The Cisco MOH Audio Translator service places the master audio files in the C:\Program Files\Cisco\TFTPPath\MOH directory of the server that is running the Cisco TFTP service.) However, the original source file (*.wav, *.mp3, and so on) is not moved. This leaves open the possibility of losing the master audio file on a single server that is damaged by a random lightning strike or other disaster. Be sure to back up your custom audio source files.

Consider Backing Up CallManager Log Files

Backing up the log files is normally the last thing you want to do—or is it? If you're in the middle of debugging something that led to a failure or was minimally a contributor, you just might want to back up the log files for a certain amount of time. Trace files essentially come in two flavors: CCM (also known as SDI) and SDL. You should consider whether your backup plan should include CCM and SDL trace files, which are stored in C:\Program Files\Cisco\Trace.

Caring for Other Files

As the CallManager cluster grows, invariably (and perhaps inevitably) other unique and irreplaceable files are placed on specific servers without regard for their care, feeding, and backup schedule. BARS becomes more inclusive as the CallManager software evolves, but site-unique files and placement of those files must be considered. Types of files that are frequently stored and sourced on CallManager servers outside Cisco guidelines include small files such as custom phone ring and image files, XML applications, and the like. If you store such files on the CallManager servers, ensure that there is no loss of critical data by storing the files in directories that BARS backs up.

TAPS data is not captured with BARS as of CallManager Release 4.0(1). TAPS data is likely to be either unnecessary, because all registered phones are accounted for, or already duplicated, because the configuration file was created and edited on another system.

Back Up the Cisco Unity Messaging Repository

Don't overlook Cisco Unity in your backup strategy. Preferably the Unity deployment employs a separate message store in Microsoft Exchange or LotusNotes Domino that facilitates failure recovery, but that alone does not provide a recovery mechanism for the Unity server. Individual configurations for each user housed in the Unity server itself correlate the mailbox number to the message store, along with a host of other settings. If you have a small deployment in which the message store lives on the same server as Unity, you need a working backup strategy. For more information, navigate to the Cisco Unity System Administration Guide from the following link. Look at the chapter titled "Maintaining a Cisco Unity System," and the section "Backing Up and Restoring a Cisco Unity System."

http://www.cisco.com/univercd/cc/td/doc/product/voice/c_unity/index.htm

Back Up Extended CallManager Functionality

The Cisco Customer Response Solutions (CRS) engine allows you to develop scripts that can manipulate and queue calls and provide interactive voice response (IVR), database searches, and a host of other features. The automated attendant (AA) CRS script bundled with CallManager has become the most frequently used CRS application.

BARS, which backs up the bundled CRS engine, also backs up the standalone CRS engine. BARS, which is discussed in depth later in this chapter, supports the Cisco Emergency Responder (CER) and CDR Analysis and Reporting (CAR) tools as well.

IP phone services and custom XML applications used to enhance interaction with IP phone endpoints also need to be backed up. CallManager features such as extension mobility and call back are included as part of the CallManager backup, but third-party and custom-developed applications are not included. Be sure files relating to your extended CallManager functionality are backed up or stored in directories that BARS routinely backs up.

Back Up CallManager-Based Gateways and IOS-Based Gateways

Like CallManager and Unity, gateways can house complex configurations. Gateways can either be nearly completely configured by CallManager, such as voice cards for the Catalyst 6000 series, or be virtually independent, like the Cisco 3700 series. When the CallManager database is backed up, the CallManager-configured gateways are backed up as well. Independent gateway configurations that are not stored in the CallManager database, such as the IOS-based Cisco 3700 series, must be backed up separately.

IOS-based gateways can provide a multitude of features and functionality in a single box. WAN and/or LAN interfaces along with some form of legacy voice connectivity such as a Foreign Exchange Office (FXO) or a Primary Rate Interface (PRI) connection typically identify an IOS gateway. When deployed at remote sites, gateways frequently have more software features enabled than their local counterparts. These features run the gamut of Cisco technologies: frame fragmentation and interleaving, traffic shaping and advanced queuing, frame filtering and marking, multiple voice dial peers, and complex interface signaling. Select IOS-based gateways can also support voice scripts for automatic attendant, calling card, and prompting functionality with recorded audio samples. As you have surmised by now, the configurations in a router might be complex, but a device that is acting as both a router and a voice gateway might have an exponentially more complex configuration than the average LAN-to-WAN router. Many options exist for saving a copy of the IOS configuration off the gateway. The simple command **copy running-config** or a full network management application can be used to safeguard against configuration loss and gateway downtime.

Back Up Ethernet Switches and Router Configurations

With the deployment of IP phones, the network infrastructure probably has received an update to accommodate new virtual LAN (VLAN) and quality of service (QoS) requirements. These new parameters affect settings from the port that has an IP phone attached to it, to the end destination of any voice traffic that phone might generate. As the complexity of individual port settings increases, so does the need to back up the configurations of these devices. As soon as separate voice and data VLANs become deployed network wide, every Ethernet switch may have a unique configuration. As with the gateways described in the preceding section, make sure your backup plan accommodates saving the Ethernet switches and router configurations.

Five Steps to a Solid Backup

During subsequent installations and deployments it's critical that you have a good backup to depend on in case of a catastrophic misconfiguration of the system. Misconfiguration typically happens when major changes are made to accommodate large rollouts or when importing data into CallManager. The number of major changes typically drops off quickly after the base functionality has been completed, thereby making backups a mundane yet critical task. Follow these recommendations for a solid backup strategy:

- Tailor the strategy to the environment. If local network shares exist and are dependably backed up, use them. Use local tape backups as a second choice, or primarily for remote site backups.

- Keep your mass storage media fresh. Replace tapes every 3 months or as frequently as the tape manufacturer recommends.

- Label the storage media with the exact server name and IP address of the backup target, the complete CallManager version (for example, 4.0(2)) and patch information, the date of the backup, and the date the storage medium was first used.

- Use one tape for every day of the week for daily backups during deployment or major CallManager changes. When the number of configuration changes lessens, move to one tape for each week of the month for weekly backups thereafter.

- At an off-site location, store tapes that will not be used for that given week.

Keep your mass storage media fresh and well-documented. A tape without a label indicating what version of CallManager it contains can be disastrous during a recovery or upgrade scenario. A tape that does not indicate what date it was first used might have been reused so many times that there might be no hope of pulling data from it when you need to. Keeping a set of tapes, each with a dedicated day for use, allows recovery in time and is especially useful when applying software upgrades. Having all your backup tapes on-site can leave you with no backups at all if the room or building where your backups are stored is destroyed by flood, fire, or another catastrophic event.

NOTE   The length of time you should keep your backups varies widely by company. Refer to your company's data retention policy to determine how long you should store your backups.

Planning Your Backup Strategy

When planning your backup strategy, you should consider the following tasks:

- Select the appropriate backup server
- Determine backup schedules
- Become familiar with and make use of BARS

Select the Appropriate Backup Server

Not all CallManager servers are best suited to be backup servers. When considering the use of a server for backup, consider the following: processor type and speed, hard drive space, and the availability of an optional digital audio tape (DAT) drive.

Designate the Publisher server to be the backup server; doing so is not just a best practice but is also a Cisco recommendation. The Publisher holds the master configuration database that is shared with all members of the CallManager cluster. The CDR database for the entire cluster also resides on the Publisher. Most importantly, the Publisher server offers few external dependencies that could interrupt the backup process, since the source databases are stored there potentially along with the backup media. The Publisher optimally has few or no phones homed to it, making it the server in the cluster with the most resources available. Given adequate hard disk space in the backup server's staging directory, BARS runs with minimal administrative interaction.

NOTE   The Cisco BARS nomenclature of backup server and backup target might be confusing at first, especially during the installation of the first server. A *backup server* frequently has a DAT drive, or some other form of removable or remote mass storage media, and performs the actual copying of information from servers targeted for backup to the medium used for backing up, such as a DAT drive. A typical scenario has only one backup server per cluster. The *backup target* is the server containing the data to be backed up, or the server to which backed-up data is restored. When the backup server is the Publisher, all Subscribers are backup targets. Simply put, if a server is not the backup sever, it's a backup target.

Determine Backup Schedules

By default, BARS schedules the backup server to write to the mass storage media once at 2 a.m. Tuesday through Saturday, as shown in Figure 4-2. Because the backup process consumes considerable CPU time and could affect all processes running on the backup server (preferably the Publisher), backups should be run only during off-peak hours. CAR report generation or CDR cleanup activities (triggered by the Cisco Database Layer Monitor service parameters Maintenance Time and Maintenance Window) may also be scheduled to run during off-peak hours. Therefore, set start times appropriately to avoid resource constraints. You would not want the CDR cleanup to occur at the same time as a backup operation. Instead, configure the start times for each task to run consecutively.

It might seem that the BARS default backup schedule (**BARS > Backup > Scheduler**) does not back up any changes made on Monday. However, all of Monday's changes throughout the workday, which are typically made after 2:00 a.m., are saved on Tuesday's backup at 2:00 a.m., and so on through the week, ending with a save of Friday's changes early Saturday morning. The default schedule does not back up any changes made over the weekend, but those changes are captured on the next regular backup, which occurs Tuesday at 2 a.m. by default.

If your organization does not follow the typical 8:00 a.m. to 5:00 p.m. Monday through Friday work schedule, you should change the default backup schedule so that it reflects the times and days you need backups. For example, an organization that runs around the clock with multiple administrators might be better suited to run backups during a shift change. If constant configuration changes are expected throughout the week, you should configure BARS to run every day of the week at a time when the least activity is occurring on your IP Telephony network.

Use BARS to Back Up the Environment

Use BARS to perform backups. Doing so is not just a best practice but also is a Cisco recommendation. BARS functionality has been tested and proven. If you choose to employ your own backup method or software, you should be aware that doing so is unsupported by Cisco.

Figure 4-2   *Backup Schedule Settings*

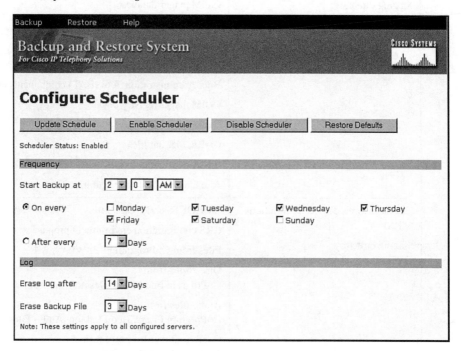

BARS can be used to back up the following:

- CallManager Publisher (usually designated as the backup server)
- CallManager Subscribers (known as backup targets)
- TFTP servers that are configured as Subscribers (known as backup targets)
- CDR Analysis and Reporting (CAR)
- Cisco Customer Response Solutions (CRS)
- Cisco Emergency Responder (CER)

Table 4-1 lists the files that BARS captures by default.

Table 4-1 *Files and Directories Captured by BARS*

Backup Target	Files and Directories Copied to the Backup Server
CallManager Staging directory: C:\STI\Backup\CM\MachineName	LMHOSTS and HOSTS files CallManager database CDR database (optional) DC Directory database TFTP subdirectories and files Bulk Administration Tool (BAT) components and files CallManager registry keys CallManager DSN CDR/CMR flat files IPMA configuration files Attendant Console configuration files
Cisco Customer Response Solutions (CRS) Staging directory: C:\STI\Backup\Apps\Machine_Name	LMHOSTS and HOSTS files CRS configuration environment properties Files from C:\Program Files\Wfavvid\ Directories from C:\Program Files\Cisco\Desktop_config\ Audio files from C:\Program Files\Cisco\Desktop_Audio Files\ Configuration files (.cfg) from C:\Program Files\Cisco\Desktop\ Alarm service file from C:\Program Files\Cisco\AlarmService.ini Files referenced in C:\Program Files\Wfavvid\sysparams.properties User and system grammar files (.GSL and .DIGIT) User and system prompt files (.wav) Databases and remote databases (DB_CRA, DB_CRA_CCDR, SCHEDULERDB, FCRasSvr)
CDR Analysis and Reporting (CAR) Staging directory: C:\STI\Backup\ART\Machine_Name	CAR database[*] CAR pregenerated reports Registry keys

Table 4-1   *Files and Directories Captured by BARS (Continued)*

Backup Target	Files and Directories Copied to the Backup Server
Cisco Emergency Responder (CER) Staging directory: C:\STI\Backup\CER\Machine_Name	LMHOSTS and HOSTS files CER database Directories from C:\Program Files\ Cisco Systems\CiscoER\ Individual .jar and .ini files Registry keys

* CAR was formerly called ART (Administrative Reporting Tool). Some directory and other structures still refer to ART.

The use of a third-party backup utility does not restore replication between Publisher and Subscriber servers for the SQL database and LDAP; therefore, the replication must be reestablished manually. Restoring SQL replication is a complex task that most people find quite difficult unless they have extensive SQL administration knowledge. Also, the system user accounts cannot be restored correctly when using third-party tools, because such tools are not configured to work specifically with CallManager. The best way to ensure that CallManager is backed up in a way that can be reliably restored is to use BARS. To back up data files that aren't explicitly backed up by BARS, you may choose to implement a third-party backup tool in addition to BARS, but not as a replacement for BARS.

WARNING   Third-party applications, including backup tools, running on the same platform as CallManager are not supported by Cisco.

Become Familiar with BARS

BARS can be configured to back up CallManager, CRS, CAR, and CER. BARS is supplied on a separate CD-ROM with the CallManager CD-ROM set, but it is not part of the base CallManager installation. It needs to be individually installed on every server that contains data you want backed up (Subscribers) and on the Publisher (which is the backup server). If you are certain that a Subscriber contains no unique information—such as CDR data, coresident applications such as CRS, or other configuration files—there is no need to install BARS on that server.

Table 4-1 summarizes the files and directories that BARS backs up. Always read the BARS release notes on Cisco.com for the latest information on what files are included in a BARS backup. As shown in Figure 4-3, databases go through a dump process that extracts the information from the database to a flat file that is placed in the staging directory before the contents are archived.

Figure 4-3 *Backup Target Through the Backup Destination*

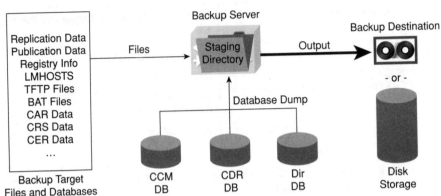

Check the Log Files for Errors During Backup

BARS saves the log data displayed during a backup or restore operation in the
C:\Program Files\Common Files\Cisco\Logs\BARS\ directory on the backup server. Files
on the backup server contain the date within the filename, such as Restore04-01-04.log or
Backup1-30-04.log. The existing log file is appended with additional information about
each subsequent backup or restore operation if more than one backup or restore operation
is performed on the same date. You should periodically check the log files for recent backup
operations by opening the log file and searching for "failed" or "fatal." It's important to
check the log file regularly, because your future recovery from disaster depends on BARS
working as expected.

Move Backup Files if You Perform Multiple Backups in a Single Day

Like the log files, the backup file that contains the actual backed-up data includes the date
information within the filename. The directory location or tape device that contains the
backup file is specified in BARS. But unlike log files, the backup files, which have a .tar
(tape archive) extension, are not appended. So if a backup occurs on June 30, resulting in
the file Backup6-30-2004.tar, and another backup is run later in the day, the second backup
overwrites the data contained in the Backup6-30-2004.tar file. To prevent the tar file from
being overwritten during multiple backup operations on the same day, rename the file or
move it from the directory before subsequent backups are performed. In the case of a tape
device, remove the tape and insert another blank tape cartridge.

Access BARS via the Web Browser

Before CallManager Release 4.0, the Virtual Network Computing (VNC) remote console
package was the preferred tool to use when accessing CallManager and remotely installing
software. Windows Terminal Services is not recommended and is disabled during a default

installation. After BARS is installed it can be reached though the web much as the CallManager Administration pages are. The base URL is http://*hostname*/BARS/ BARSmain.asp. Accessing BARS via a web browser completely eliminates the need for VNC to control backup and restore actions.

Make Sure You Have Enough Free Disk Space on the Backup Server and the Backup Target

BARS displays warnings if the free disk space on the backup server is less than 1.5 times the space needed for the last backup. At least 400 MB of space must exist for a backup to succeed. Each backup target needs enough free disk space for local database dumps plus the files. Therefore, even if sufficient free space is available on the backup server but less than 400 MB of free space is on the backup target, the backup on the target machine is likely to fail.

As soon as all the backup data has been gathered (the action of gathering data at this point is called *staging*) from the backup server and target machines, it is written to the backup storage location. This location can be one of the following:

- **A network share location**—The best practice option when the network share is dependable and backed up
- **A local tape drive**—The recommended option when a reliable network share location is not available
- **The local hard drive**—Not recommended

Use Consistent Private Password Phrases

During the BARS installation, you are prompted to input a private password phrase that will be used to create a local system user account called BackAdmin, as shown in Figure 4-4. The BackAdmin account is given Administrator privileges into the local system and database. The private password phrase is used as the seed to create a complex password that conforms to Microsoft guidelines; it is not the actual password generated. The private password phrase entered during backup target installation should be exactly the same password phrase that was entered during backup server installation.

NOTE   For more information on Microsoft password guidelines, see http://www.microsoft.com/ntworkstation/technicalresources/pwdguidelines.asp.

For the backup server to access a target and initiate a backup process via the BackAdmin account, an administrative account on the backup target needs to be defined in BARS (**BARS > Backup > Data Source Servers**). The backup server remotely executes backup functions on servers designated as backup targets and pulls the files to the backup server. Therefore, it's unnecessary for backup targets to have a tape drive installed. Use the local Administrator account and password unless your security policy requires the establishment of a separate account.

Figure 4-4 *Password Phrase for BARS Installation*

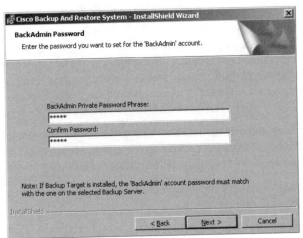

<table>
<tr><td colspan="2">Cisco Backup And Restore System - InstallShield Wizard   ✕</td></tr>
</table>

BackAdmin Password
Enter the password you want to set for the 'BackAdmin' account.

BackAdmin Private Password Phrase:

`*****`

Confirm Password:

`*****`

Note: If Backup Target is installed, the 'BackAdmin' account password must match with the one on the selected Backup Server.

InstallShield

     < Back   Next >   Cancel

NOTE   Before CallManager release 4.0, the password phrase defaulted to the computer name of the backup server as the seed for the BackAdmin account and went unnoticed during the installation. Because the password phrase is now manually entered during the installation, you should make a note of the phrase designated during installation so that it can be reused for subsequent BARS installations on servers designated as backup targets.

After you install new backup target servers, the backup targets must be added to the backup server configuration. The list of targets within BARS does not automatically populate with new servers that are added to the CallManager cluster. The new backup targets must be added manually to the BARS configuration on the backup server.

NOTE   To be properly backed up, the backup server must be listed and enabled for backup within BARS just like backup targets.

Things to Be Aware of When Restoring from a BARS Backup

All the preparation that goes into the backup process is evident during the restoration process. Exact tracking of machine names, software versions, and media make rebuilding a server a breeze. Haphazard tracking or lack of tracking makes for a difficult restoration. Take the time to label the backup storage media with complete software version numbers (for example, CallManager 4.0(2)) and installed patches, as mentioned earlier.

The server names and IP addresses are contained within the CallManager SQL database, along with many other parameters. BARS captures the SQL database. Each machine must have a unique computer name; this is a critical fact in CallManager clusters. When you restore the servers, you must give them exactly the same computer name and exactly the same IP address as they had at the time of the backup. The process of restoring other supported applications has similar dependencies on keeping the computer name and IP address exactly as they were when BARS backed up the data.

BARS backs up only data and configuration information. It does not back up system or application files that were placed on the system at installation time. Therefore, the restoration process restores only the configuration and data of the applications that were selected in BARS at the time of the backup, not the applications themselves. The applications need to be reinstalled before the restoration process occurs.

BARS performs only one task at a time. It cannot both back up and restore data at the same time. Be aware that a restore operation might conflict with the automatic backup schedule. Also, BARS restores only a single sever at a time, and user interaction is required; BARS does not automatically restore a server.

Restoring a server is straightforward. The key is to install the operating system and related updates along with the application (CallManager, CAR, CRS, or CER) and application updates first, and then start the restore operation. An overview of the steps follows:

Step 1   Rebuild the server. Start by booting from CallManager installation CD number 1.

Step 2   Apply operating system updates if needed.

Step 3   Reinstall BARS.

Step 4   Reinstall the appropriate applications.

Step 5   Apply application updates if needed.

Step 6   Start the BARS Restore Wizard.

The Big Decision: Reinstall, Restore, or Recover?

You have three options when deciding how to bring a failed server back into working order. Your choice depends on your situation:

- Reinstalling a server involves starting from the first CallManager installation CD and completely erasing the hard disk as though it were a brand new installation.

- Restoring a server starts from the first CallManager installation CD and completely erases the hard disk but then pulls the application configuration from a backup tape or network location.

- Same-server recovery is an option when you boot from the first CallManager installation CD. You should use this option only during upgrades to recover the working system configuration from data contained in the STI_Data partition of the hard drive.

When CallManager is the only application installed on the Subscriber and there is no risk of data loss (such as unique files stored on the Subscriber), you should reinstall Subscribers in their entirety rather than restoring from a backup. This is recommended because a complete install of a Subscriber executes more easily than a server restoration. Use the following criteria to determine whether reinstallation is preferred over restoring from a backup:

- Reinstall the server completely if a failed Subscriber had no unique files on it and did not have CDR collection enabled.

- Reinstall the server completely if the Subscriber had CDR collection enabled, if the Publisher was available at the time of Subscriber failure, and if no unique files were on the Subscriber.

- Always be aware of the potential for losing unique files. (Unique files are described earlier in this chapter in the sections under "Consider the Whole Deployment.")

NOTE Duplicating a Subscriber from a backup of a different server has no constructive purpose. Duplicating in this fashion also corrupts the CallManager cluster database because of the duplicate data.

When you are restoring data to the Subscriber, make sure that during the restoration operation you manually disable any intrusion detection software from Cisco or third parties.

The Restore Wizard Makes Restoring a Server Less Painful

The BARS Restore Wizard, shown in Figure 4-5, gathers the necessary information and account permissions needed by the restoration operation. The restore process is performed from the backup server, not the backup target.

When you complete all the Wizard steps, a summary appears, and the restore process begins. Here is an overview of the Wizard steps:

Step 1   Identify the backup file location.

Figure 4-5   *Step 1 of the Restore Wizard Backup*

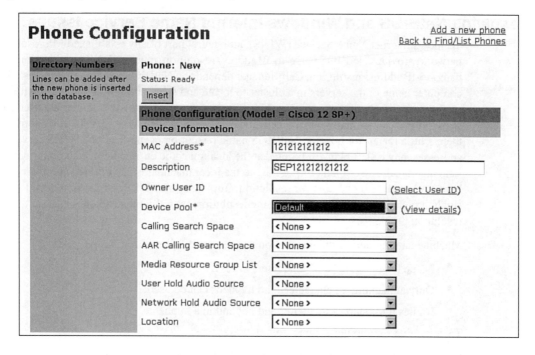

Step 2   Choose the server and application to be restored.

Step 3   Enter the administrative account information.

Step 4   Verify the settings and start the restore process.

After the restore process successfully completes, you need to reboot the restored server when prompted by the Wizard.

Troubleshooting Typical Backup Problems

Two of the most common problems with new and old deployments revolve around computer name resolution and password issues. The third and fourth most common problems involve the Microsoft SQL passwords and database replication. These issues affect BARS' ability to accurately capture backup data.

BARS is no longer tied to NetBIOS name resolution, but it does require either DNS resolution or IP address information to reach all backup targets. Network shares that are configured in BARS may use NetBIOS names and therefore are potentially prone to name resolution problems.

Resolving NetBIOS and Windows Internet Name Service Issues

Windows Internet Name Service (WINS), an integral part of any established Microsoft network, provides NetBIOS name-to-IP address resolution, much as DNS provides domain name-to-IP address resolution. CallManager depends on NetBIOS to uniquely establish the computer name of the servers in a cluster to locate and share configuration data. BARS might depend on both the naming and locating aspects when NetBIOS names are used for share points. Occasionally when a new network is established to support IP Telephony, there's little regard for how the NetBIOS name resolution occurs, and the WINS server addresses may be left blank or pointed at the local machine during the installation process. Leaving the addresses blank or pointing to the local machine is usually not a problem, because NetBIOS broadcasts for resolution. But in any network configuration outside a single broadcast domain, NetBIOS name resolution naturally fails and causes basic resolution problems.

Machine naming during the installation process must follow a few simple rules:

- Name length must be 15 characters or less.
- Only alphanumeric characters and hyphens can be used.
- Names must start with a letter and not end in a hyphen.

To determine a computer's name, follow these steps:

Step 1   Right-click **My Computer** on the Desktop and select **Properties**.

Step 2   Click the **Network Identification** tab.

Step 3   Click **Properties**.

Step 4   Click **More** and wait for the new window.

Step 5   The **NetBIOS Computer Name** field displays the current name.

Use the **NBTSTAT -c** command from a command window to verify that a NetBIOS name cache entry exists for the device you are attempting to reach. To force a NetBIOS lookup for a particular name and to put it into the cache as well, in a command window enter **NET VIEW **_SERVER_ (where _SERVER_ is the computer name). Then use the **NBTSTAT -c** command to view the cache.

Two approaches help you deal with NetBIOS name resolution problems:

- Configure the necessary devices so that they locate WINS.
- Enable the local machine to resolve a specific NetBIOS name or names.

If WINS has already been established on the network with a primary and backup WINS server, make use of those services. The computer name resolution process looks first in the cache, second at the LMHOSTS file, third to a properly configured WINS entry, and last at a local broadcast on the local broadcast domain.

To configure the WINS addresses on a machine, follow these steps:

Step 1 Click **Start > Settings > Network and Dial-up Connections**. Then double-click the Ethernet interface being used.

Step 2 Click **Properties**, and in the new window, double-click **Internet Protocol (TCP/IP)**.

Step 3 In the Advanced TCP/IP Settings window, click **Advanced**.

Step 4 Click the **WINS** tab, and then click **Add/Edit/Remove** and enter the appropriate WINS server addresses.

Step 5 Repeat this procedure on every server in the CallManager cluster.

TIP Use a local LMHOSTS file that lists all backup and target servers in conjunction with a WINS environment as an additional means of computer name resolution.

If you have little or no need for WINS, if you want WINS isolation, or if administrative domain issues prevail, you can edit the LMHOSTS file to support local NetBIOS name lookups. The file lmhosts.sam, located in the C:\WINNT\system32\drivers\etc directory, is a flat text file that can be opened with Notepad and edited as shown in Example 4-1.

Example 4-1 *Sample LMHOSTS File with Edits*

```
# Copyright (c) 1993-1999 Microsoft Corp.
#
# This is a sample LMHOSTS file used by the Microsoft TCP/IP for Windows.
#
# This file contains the mappings of IP addresses to computernames
# (NetBIOS) names.  Each entry should be kept on an individual line.
# The IP address should be placed in the first column followed by the
# corresponding computername. The address and the computername
# should be separated by at least one space or tab. The "#" character
```

continues

Example 4-1   *Sample LMHOSTS File with Edits (Continued)*

```
# is generally used to denote the start of a comment (see the exceptions
# below).
#
# This file is compatible with Microsoft LAN Manager 2.x TCP/IP lmhosts
# files and offers the following extensions:
#
#      #PRE
#      #DOM:<domain>
#      #INCLUDE <filename>
#      #BEGIN_ALTERNATE
#      #END_ALTERNATE
#      \0xnn (non-printing character support)
#
# Following any entry in the file with the characters "#PRE" causes
# the entry to be preloaded into the name cache. By default, entries are
# not preloaded, but are parsed only after dynamic name resolution fails.
#
# Following an entry with the "#DOM:<domain>" tag associates the
# entry with the domain specified by <domain>. This affects how the
# browser and logon services behave in TCP/IP environments. To preload
# the host name associated with #DOM entry, it is necessary to also add a
# #PRE to the line. The <domain> is always preloaded although it is not
# shown when the name cache is viewed.
#
# Specifying "#INCLUDE <filename>" forces the RFC NetBIOS (NBT)
# software to seek the specified <filename> and parse it as if it were
# local. <filename> is generally a UNC-based name, allowing a
# centralized lmhosts file to be maintained on a server.
# It is ALWAYS necessary to provide a mapping for the IP address of the
# server before the #INCLUDE. This mapping must use the #PRE directive.
# In addition the share "public" in the example that follows must be in the
# LanManServer list of "NullSessionShares" in order for client machines to
# be able to read the lmhosts file successfully. This key is under
# \machine\system\currentcontrolset\services\lanmanserver\parameters\
```

Example 4-1 *Sample LMHOSTS File with Edits (Continued)*

```
# nullsessionshares in the registry. Simply add "public" to the list found there.
#
# The #BEGIN_and #END_ALTERNATE keywords allow multiple #INCLUDE
# statements to be grouped together. Any single successful include
# causes the group to succeed.
#
# Finally, non-printing characters can be embedded in mappings by
# first surrounding the NetBIOS name in quotations, then using the
# \0xnn notation to specify a hex value for a non-printing character.
#
# The following example illustrates all of these extensions:
#
# 102.54.94.97      rhino          #PRE #DOM:networking  #net group's DC
# 102.54.94.102     "appname  \0x14"                     #special app server
# 102.54.94.123     popular        #PRE                  #source server
# 102.54.94.117     localsrv       #PRE                  #needed for the include
#
# #BEGIN_ALTERNATE
# #INCLUDE \\localsrv\public\lmhosts
# #INCLUDE \\rhino\public\lmhosts
# #END_ALTERNATE
#
# In the preceding example, the "appname" server contains a special
# character in its name, the "popular" and "localsrv" server names are
# preloaded, and the "rhino" server name is specified so it can be used
# to later #INCLUDE a centrally maintained lmhosts file if the "localsrv"
# system is unavailable.
#
# Note that the whole file is parsed including comments on each lookup,
# so keeping the number of comments to a minimum improves
# performance.
# Therefore it is not advisable to simply add lmhosts file entries onto the
# end of this file.
10.10.10.10    justatest       #PRE       #just a test
```

The lmhosts.sam file shown in Example 4-1 was edited by adding the last line to the file. It was saved in the same directory under the name LMHOSTS (all uppercase with no .txt extension). Performing a simple **File > Save** operation does not add a file extension, but a **File > Save As** operation does, so be careful. In addition, use Windows Explorer to ensure the correct filename. (Be sure Explorer displays file extensions. If they do not appear, click **Tools > Folder Options**, and click the **View** tab, uncheck the **Hide file extensions for known file types** box.) For changes to this file to take effect, you need to reload the cache. Do so by executing the command with a capital R, **NBTSTAT -R**. Example 4-2 shows the NBTSTAT display after the file has been edited and the cache updated.

Example 4-2 *NBTSTAT Output*

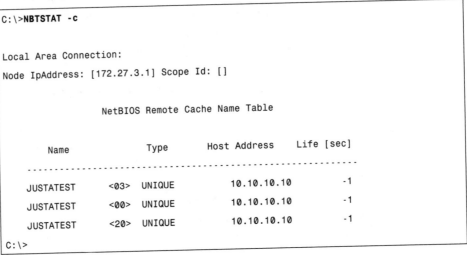

```
C:\>NBTSTAT -c


Local Area Connection:
Node IpAddress: [172.27.3.1] Scope Id: []


              NetBIOS Remote Cache Name Table


      Name              Type      Host Address    Life [sec]
  -----------------------------------------------------------

   JUSTATEST     <03>  UNIQUE       10.10.10.10       -1
   JUSTATEST     <00>  UNIQUE       10.10.10.10       -1
   JUSTATEST     <20>  UNIQUE       10.10.10.10       -1
C:\>
```

If you rely on this file method of resolving NetBIOS names, you can understand that adding servers and then updating all the other servers with a new LMHOSTS entry or file can be time-consuming and leaves room for errors (such as forgetting to update the file when a new server is added). It's a good idea to get WINS running if you have more than a few servers in your cluster. Save a master copy of the LMHOSTS file on a floppy disk or a common network share, and then use the Import feature to eliminate manual editing of all servers. Perform the following steps to import the master file:

Step 1 Click **Start > Settings > Network and Dial-up Connections**, and choose the Ethernet interface being used.

Step 2 Click **Properties**. In the new window, double-click **Internet Protocol (TCP/IP)**.

Step 3 In the Advanced TCP/IP Settings window, click **Advanced**.

Step 4 Click the **WINS** tab, and then click **Import LMHOSTS**. Browse to the location where the master LMHOSTS file is stored.

Step 5 In a command window, execute **NBTSTAT -R** to refresh the cache.

Identifying SQL Password and Replication Problems

Identifying SQL replication problems is straightforward: Configuration changes made to the Publisher are not replicated to the Subscribers. At least three major factors can cause replication to break down:

- Loss of network connectivity
- SQLSvc password mismatch
- Broken subscription between the Publisher and Subscriber

You can test replication by inserting a new device on the Publisher, such as the fictitious test phone shown in Figure 4-6.

Figure 4-6   *Fictitious Phone Creation*

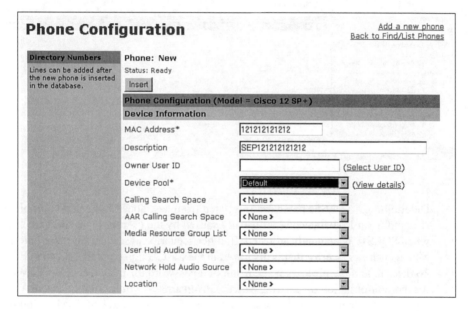

The new device you added should appear in CallManager Administration on the Subscribers. You can also check replication status by using the SQL Server Enterprise Manager to look at the status of the database subscription, as shown in Figure 4-7:

Step 1   Launch the SQL Server Enterprise Manager by clicking **Start > Programs > Microsoft SQL Server > Enterprise Manager**.

Step 2   Open the SQL server by expanding the tree until you reach the local server (click the **+** next to Microsoft SQL Servers, SQL Server Group, and the local server).

Step 3 Click the + next to the Replication folder to expand it, and then highlight the **Subscriptions** folder. The Last Action column increments as changes from the Publisher deliver onto the Subscriber. Click **Action > Refresh** to update the window.

Step 4 Delete the test device you inserted on the Publisher while refreshing the Enterprise Manager window. By doing so, you can watch the Last Action column to see the change replicated to Subscribers.

Figure 4-7 *Good Status of SQL Subscription*

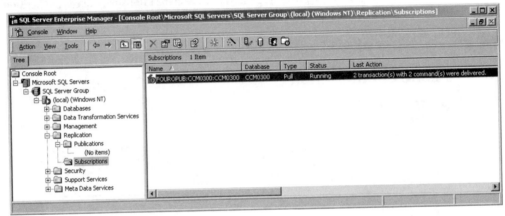

Determining a SQLSvc password mismatch from a database subscription problem is straightforward. Mismatches are usually caused by the user during a software upgrade or when SQLSvc is manually adjusted. If either scenario causes a failure, the Enterprise Manager shows an error that is displayed in the Last Action column (shown in Figure 4-7). To determine if the problem is the result of a password mismatch, check the Event Viewer for more information by clicking **Start > Programs > Admin Tools > Event Viewer**. Highlight **System Log**, and examine the errors from the Source of Service Control Manager. An error has a white X in a red circle next to it. If Figure 4-8 matches your error, the cause of the problem is a SQLSvc password mismatch.

You can search Cisco.com for documentation that further describes how to resolve replication and SQLSvc password mismatch issues.

Figure 4-8   *Event Viewer and Error Properties*

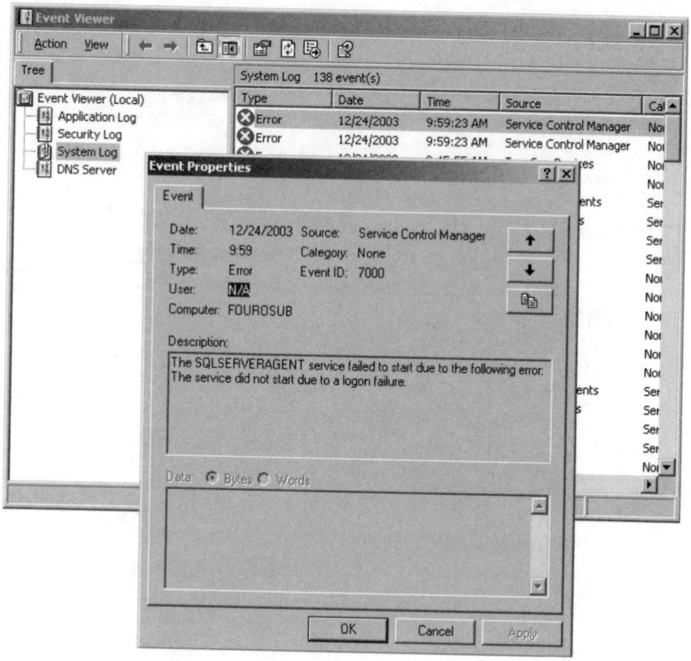

Summary

This chapter explains how BARS operates, how to tune it to your particular CallManager deployment, and how to repair common configuration problems. Always read the release notes for the version you're operating, and use the LMHOSTS file as described in the "Troubleshooting Typical Backup Problems" section.

Prepare for catastrophe by using BARS (available on the CallManager installation CDs) to ensure that you have a usable backup of CallManager data. Cisco provides BARS as part of the CallManager installation CDs, and it's up to you to make use of it.

Remember that many components make up an IP Telephony deployment, so you must pay careful attention to backing up the system as a whole.

## CHAPTER 5

Upgrading and Patching CallManager

This chapter discusses the best methods for upgrading and patching Cisco CallManager. These tasks generally require thorough planning and careful implementation. The information provided in this chapter is intended to bring you through the process smoothly and to point out the best methods for accomplishing an upgrade with the least amount of downtime.

Organizations cannot use these best practices in every situation. You might often have to compromise best practices to accommodate budgets, time constraints, and other circumstances. When you do so, keep in mind that cutting corners increases the risk of errors and downtime.

NOTE CallManager 4.0 leverages Windows 2000 and Microsoft SQL Server. As with all software-based systems, patches and fixes are required to keep the system functioning as effectively as possible. Given this reality, it's important to plan carefully to avoid downtime for patching. Patches generally take about 10 to 15 minutes per server, and it's best to plan on patching once or twice a quarter. Whether you actually have to apply patches or not, it's good to have the time set aside for a regularly scheduled maintenance window.

Preparing for an Upgrade or Patch

This section covers fundamental concepts you must understand and implement before you apply a patch or upgrade an existing CallManager system:

- Understand the difference between patching and upgrading
- Understand the importance of a staging environment
- Determine the version of CallManager you want to run
- Determine the version of the Windows operating system (OS) you want to run
- Read the release notes thoroughly
- Determine hardware compatibility

- Prepare an upgrade checklist
- Obtain the upgrade media
- Download minor upgrades
- Download Windows OS upgrades
- Burn the files to CD-ROM/DVD
- Run the CallManager Upgrade Assistant Utility

Understand the Difference Between Patching and Upgrading

It's important to understand the distinction between patching and upgrading. As discussed later in this chapter, *patching* is a quick, temporary, reversible process to fix a software bug. In contrast, *upgrading* is a more complex, more permanent process that fixes bugs and introduces new features or enhancements.

There are two kinds of upgrades: major and minor. Major upgrades generally contain numerous new features and functionality and increment the major release number. For example, the release number could change from 3.x to 4.x. Figure 5-1 breaks down a typical release number.

Figure 5-1   *CallManager Release Template*

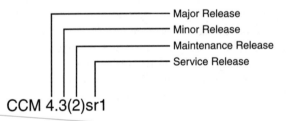

It's reasonable to expect that a certain amount of training might be necessary between major releases, such as moving from CallManager release 3.x to 4.x. For example, CallManager release 4.0 contains major new features that you must understand before implementing, such as the appearance of multiple calls per line and Multilevel Precedence and Preemption (MLPP). For complete information on new features, see the Appendix, "CallManager 4.0 New Feature Description."

Minor releases generally contain a few new small features and several bug fixes and enhancements. Minor releases increment the minor release number, such as 4.0(1) to 4.0(2).

Table 5-1 explains the timing of the release process for the various CallManager components.

Table 5-1   *CallManager Release Timelines*

File Type	Description	Release Frequency
Windows OS installation	Machine-specific CD/DVD media containing installable images for the various Cisco Media Convergence Server (MCS) platforms	Once or twice a year, depending on releases of new Cisco hardware. A new OS installation version must be created to support any new MCS released by Cisco.
Windows OS upgrade	Machine-independent, web-based upgrades containing Microsoft service packs, hotfixes, drivers/BIOS/ firmware, security enhancements, bug fixes	Two or three times a year, commensurate with Microsoft service pack releases
Windows OS service release	Machine-independent, web-based upgrades containing Microsoft hotfixes released after major Microsoft service packs	Once per month
Critical security hotfix	Machine-independent, web-based upgrades containing Microsoft security fixes deemed critical by Microsoft and Cisco	One day after Microsoft releases any critical security fix for IIS, SQL Server, or Windows 2000
CallManager major release	A new release of CallManager that brings major feature enhancements and platform capability	Once per year
CallManager maintenance release	Machine-independent, web-based upgrades that bring bug fixes and minor feature enhancements	Twice per year
CallManager service release	Machine-independent, web-based, bug-fix releases of CallManager	One per month or one every two months, depending on the criticality of the bug fixes

Use a Staging Environment (if Applicable)

When you upgrade CallManager, using a staging environment in which you can test the upgrade before putting it into your production environment can expedite the process and result in a safer upgrade. Performing an upgrade without worrying about the time constraints and pressure of an outage window results in a more successful and stable upgrade.

WARNING	Be aware that if you are pulling Redundant Array of Independent (or Inexpensive) Disks (RAID) drives for upgrades, you should minimize the time you take, because you have to freeze changes to maintain the integrity of the configuration database. This is explained in more detail later in this chapter.

Although not every user can afford the extra hardware necessary, it's highly recommended that you build a staging environment that replicates your existing production environment. At a bare minimum, a spare machine of the exact same model as the Publisher should be used in staging.

TIP	Using RAID-capable servers makes implementing a staging environment simpler. Rather than having to install CallManager from scratch and restore a backup, you can simply remove a mirrored drive and place it in your staging system. This is covered in detail later in this chapter.

Staging lets you document the upgrade procedure in great detail. This is especially useful if you have a large deployment with many clusters that require an upgrade, and also if you outsource the upgrades to a Cisco partner. You can be assured of a successful upgrade at every site, because everyone will be following the same procedure.

Although the minimum staging environment would be a replica of the cluster, the best method of staging is to replicate all the application servers and subscribers to ensure compatibility with the upgrade.

Create an Alpha Cluster

Many users employ an *Alpha cluster*—a complete, working CallManager environment that is used by a small group of people as the test bed for the rest of the company. Alpha clusters are most practical for large installations in which user-acceptance testing is important for a particular release of code. A cross section of users is selected to participate in the Alpha cluster to provide feedback on new features. At the same time, the support staff can gauge compatibility with the current applications and services and plan for new services that will be offered.

Cisco operates large Alpha cluster in Richardson, Texas. This small group of users employs CallManager code before it is released into the production environment of more than 20,000 users.

Select the Appropriate Upgrade Version of CallManager

The first step in any upgrade is to determine the versions of software to which you want to upgrade. Do not upgrade just because a new version is released. Also, do not assume that the latest release of software is the most stable or contains the newest features.

Some users wait for the "dot 1" release (for example, 4.1) of any version of software before upgrading. The reason is that a new major feature release of *any* software often contains bugs that many people cannot tolerate in their environment. On the other hand, users who have been waiting a long time for a certain feature might be compelled to take a chance to get the new feature. It's really a matter of planning and evaluating risk versus reward. This also demonstrates that having a staging server makes a big difference: You can test the features and stability in a nonproduction environment to ensure stability.

Be sure to check the compatibility of the CallManager release with your hardware and supported third-party applications. For example, if you use Cisco IP Telephony Environment Monitor (ITEM), be sure it's supported with the release of CallManager you intend to use. It might be that other applications such as billing software and monitoring applications are not supported without modification. It's essential to check with the individual software vendors for support of any particular CallManager release. All Cisco compatibility information is detailed in the release notes for a particular version of CallManager. You should also read the compatibility matrix, as discussed in the section, "Check the Compatibility Matrix" in Chapter 1, "Planning the CallManager Implementation."

Ensure Version Compatibility with the Windows OS

When determining the proper Windows OS version, it's important to read the release notes to determine CallManager's compatibility with a particular release. Major releases of the Windows OS are issued every 6 to 12 months.

Do not upgrade the Windows OS unless there is a reason to do so. The Windows OS service release process is generally the best way to ensure that the underlying Windows OS is kept up to date with the latest security fixes. This is discussed later in this chapter. Windows OS upgrades generally contain all patches released since the last Windows OS upgrade release. If you cannot bring the system down for an outage window to install the latest service releases of the Windows OS as they are released, using Windows OS upgrades is the best way to get all the applicable patches.

NOTE	CallManager release 4.0 requires a minimum of Windows OS 2000.2.4 or 2000.2.3 with the 2000.2.4 upgrade applied.

Read the Release Notes

After you have selected the release of CallManager and Windows OS to run, you must read the release notes. The importance of this documentation cannot be understated. In it, you find the list of open caveats, resolved caveats, hardware and software prerequisites, and installation instructions.

Failure to read, understand, and implement the procedures in the release notes ultimately leads to problems either at the time of upgrade or in the future. For example, if an open caveat in the software directly affects your environment, and you upgrade anyway, you are subjecting your users to potential downtime and loss of productivity.

Ensure Hardware Compatibility with CallManager and the Windows OS

It's critical that you determine whether the hardware you use is compatible with the releases of CallManager and Windows OS you intend to use. For example, CallManager 4.0 does not support the MCS-7830, MCS-7822, MCS-7820, IBM X330, and IBM X340 servers. Installing release 4.0 on an unsupported server results in an error message saying the server is not supported. Many of the procedures discussed previously, such as the use of a staging environment and reading the release notes, make compatibility (or lack thereof) apparent.

WARNING	Do not let CallManager's ease of use and Windows-centric nature keep you from following strict procedures when upgrading. You need to treat the system like any other Private Branch Exchange (PBX) and follow documented procedures.

Prepare the Upgrade Checklist

Before installing CallManager, you should prepare a checklist for each server that clearly defines each item that is involved in the installation. Table 5-2 is a sample checklist. Use this checklist before you perform an upgrade to document the existing configuration, and then use the checklist again to document the changes that occurred as a result of the upgrade. The checklist contains passwords, so you should keep it in a secure location. If you keep it in electronic form, give read permission to only appropriate support staff.

Table 5-2   *Upgrade Checklist*

Item	Pre-Upgrade Value	Post-Upgrade Value
Hostname		
Windows OS version		
IP address		
Windows OS patch level		
CallManager version		
CallManager patch level		
Publisher or Subscriber		
sa Password (CM 3.3 and below)		
Private password phrase (CM 3.3(3) and above)		
DC Directory Manager password		
Administrator password		
Last backup time and date		

NOTE   You should have your initial installation checklist available to transfer accurate information to the upgrade checklist. See the section "Prepare the Installation Checklist" in Chapter 3, "Installing CallManager," for more details.

Obtain Media Well in Advance of Upgrading by Using the Product Upgrade Tool

Obtaining major upgrades requires using the Product Upgrade Tool (PUT), which you can find at http://www.cisco.com/upgrade. You must enter your SmartNet contract number for entitlement to upgrades. Complete the appropriate information and the media for the upgrade will be sent to you.

To obtain the media for the upgrade, you must plan well in advance. Some major upgrades cannot simply be downloaded from Cisco.com. The PUT is the only way to obtain these major upgrades and have physical installation media.

Download Maintenance Releases

If you have determined that you want to run CallManager 4.0(2) or subsequent maintenance releases, you need to download the maintenance release after you install the major version. Maintenance releases are available for download from Cisco.com under **Technical Support > Software Center > Voice Software**. You need to log in using your Cisco.com name and password; if you do not log in, you will not have access to the appropriate software. You can also reach the Cisco CallManager Voice Software Download Center page at the following link:

http://www.cisco.com/kobayashi/sw-center/sw-voice.shtml

NOTE   If you do not have a login, register using your SmartNet contract number at the following link: http://tools.cisco.com/RPF/register/register.do.

Do not use CallManager servers to download any software and updates. Doing so could potentially expose CallManager to various security problems such as malicious HTTP code and viruses.

Download Windows OS Upgrades

OS upgrades are available for download from Cisco.com on the CallManager & Voice Apps Crypto Software page on Cisco.com at the following link. Log in first using your Cisco.com name and password or you will be unable to access the appropriate software.

http://www.cisco.com/cgi-bin/tablebuild.pl/cmva-3des

NOTE   The download area has a link at the top of the page labeled Cisco IP Telephony Operating System, SQL Server, Security Updates. This file contains the documentation necessary to determine the Windows OS service release you need to install and what files are included. Always check this file before downloading. It lists all the Microsoft patches that are included in any particular file offered by Cisco.

Burn Files to a CD

After you download the necessary upgrade files, it's best to burn them to a CD if possible. Installing from a CD eliminates the need to mount network shares or access files from external sources. This also facilitates installation in a staging environment and ultimately leads to a safer upgrade. Many things can happen on a network during an installation that can cause it fail. For example, the server or network can become unavailable because many other departments may be performing upgrades during a maintenance window. Using a local CD-ROM drive to perform the upgrade results in a clean upgrade every time and eliminates reliance on external sources for the upgrade.

Run the Upgrade Assistant Utility

Cisco created the Upgrade Assistant Utility to help users determine whether a given system is ready for an upgrade. The Upgrade Assistant is a non-intrusive tool that does not change the system's state. It detects the health of the servers in the CallManager cluster before you perform an upgrade to CallManager. This utility complements the checks done by the CallManager upgrade process.

The CallManager Upgrade Assistant Utility release corresponds to the CallManager release to which you plan to upgrade the server. For example, if you plan to upgrade to CallManager release 4.0(1), use CallManager Upgrade Assistant Utility release 4.0(1). The utility does not run if the server does not meet the minimum requirement for the CallManager 4.0(1) upgrade.

Documentation for CallManager can be found at http://www.cisco.com/univercd/cc/td/doc/product/voice/c_callmg/index.htm. Click the link to the release you're installing and then click **Installation Instructions**.

Before you perform an upgrade or re-image the system, the Upgrade Assistant Utility must be run on the Publisher and all Subscriber servers. The Utility performs the following information checks on the system.

Checks performed on a CallManager Publisher:

- Software version validation
- dBConnection0 setting validation
- DC Directory health check
- Security settings validation
- Backup file validation
- CallManager database replication status

Checks performed on a Subscriber:

- Software version validation
- dBConnection0 setting validation
- DC Directory health check
- Password validation
- Security settings validation
- Hostname resolution validation

Performing a CallManager Upgrade Using a Staging Server

This section focuses on using a staging server to perform the upgrade. The following topics are covered:

- Scheduling an outage window
- Scheduling a change freeze
- Pulling the drive from the production system
- Performing and documenting the necessary upgrades and patches
- Moving the hard drive back into the production system

WARNING   Many customers attempt to perform CallManager software upgrades using their production equipment. If you do not have a spare server, this is unavoidable. Two things are critical in this scenario. First, be sure to perform a backup of the system and place the backup files on another server. Second, pull a RAID drive from the system so that you can recover easily. It's strongly recommended that you purchase a spare server for staging purposes.

There are two ways of using a staging server. The first is to simply perform the upgrade, test it, and document it. The other is to perform the upgrade with the intention of moving the staging hard disk to the production servers.

The major differences between the two methods are the amount of time that can transpire and the types of change control that must be instituted. If you intend to use the upgraded drive in a production system, it's important to minimize the time between pulling and returning the drive to the production system because you have to freeze changes for the duration of the upgrade.

TIP   When performing the upgrade in a staging environment to simply document and test the procedure, make a note of the following:

- The amount of time that transpires during the upgrade
- Passwords required during the upgrade
- Step-by-step procedure

Documenting these things ensures the smoothest possible upgrade in the production environment.

Schedule an Outage Window

A short outage is required to shut down the Publisher and remove the hard disk in Slot 0. Although service should not be affected if you have redundant CallManager servers, having the outage window provides a margin of safety because removing a mirrored drive from a running system may result in file corruption.

Schedule a Change Freeze

Because the upgrade will be done in a staging environment, if you intend to use the upgraded drive in production, it's important to freeze all changes. If you intend to use the staging system just to document and test the upgrade procedure, freezing all changes is unnecessary. You're simply shutting down the server to pull out the drive.

WARNING   Pulling out a drive while the system is running can result in data loss. Be sure to shut down the system when pulling out a drive.

It's important to institute the change freeze for the amount of time you need to perform the upgrade on the staging system and test accordingly. Do not make the outage window too long, because this could affect production moves, adds, and changes.

The optimal change freeze time is during a weekend, when few users are making changes to their settings and few administrators are making changes to the configurations.

The following sections describe actions that cause changes to the Publisher's master database. These changes must be frozen to maintain the database's integrity during the upgrade procedure in the staging environment.

Stop the IIS Service to Freeze CallManager Administration Changes

You can use your company's change control process to suspend changes. *Change control* is the process by which companies implement changes such as patches, upgrades, service-impacting database or application changes, and more, on the network, desktops, and servers. It generally entails documenting the changes beforehand, freezing unrelated database updates, and implementing the controlled changes at a specific, pre-defined time. Because freezing database updates is an important part of the process, every person who might make such changes needs to be notified of the pending change control window. However, in many environments, it's difficult to reach every person who might have access. The easiest way to freeze changes is to completely disable web accessibility to the

Publisher server, which prevents changes to CallManager Administration and the Cisco CallManager User Options web page. You can do this using the following procedure:

Step 1   Click **Start > Programs > Administrative Tools > Internet Services Manager**.

Step 2   Click the server name.

Step 3   Click **Default Web Site**.

Step 4   Right-click **CCMAdmin**.

Step 5   Select **Stop**.

Step 6   Once your upgrades are complete, repeat Steps 1 to 4 and in Step 5, select **Start**.

This simple procedure renders CallManager Administration and the Cisco CallManager User Options website inaccessible, thereby effectively eliminating changes by system administrators and end users alike. Be sure to notify users of the timeframe when the website will be inaccessible so that you can avoid numerous complaints from users who cannot log in to set call forwarding or subscribe to phone services, and so on.

Freeze Call Forward All Setting from IP Phones

Users can set a call forward all directly on their IP phones by pressing the CFwdAll softkey. Preventing users from making this type of configuration change during a change freeze is by far the hardest thing to control. The best practice is to simply notify the user community by e-mail or voice mail, asking them not to use the CFwdAll softkey on their phones during the period of the change freeze. There will always be a user who does not receive the message and who performs this function, but that is the exception rather than the rule. The only impact of changing the setting during the change freeze is that after the upgraded drive is returned to the production system, the change made during the freeze is not saved. It returns to the value that was set before the change freeze. Users who made changes during the change freeze will need to set the CFwdAll function again after the change freeze is over.

Resynchronize the Voice Mail Message Waiting Indicator

The message waiting indicator (MWI) status is impossible to control during a change freeze. Users continue to leave and retrieve voice mail messages, and the MWI's status is kept in the database on the Publisher. When you pull a drive from the production system, the upgrade you perform is accomplished using the MWI status at the time the drive is removed.

If users check or receive voice mail messages during the upgrade window, the MWI status becomes inaccurate and causes user confusion and disruption. This is another good reason to choose a weekend or late evening for your upgrade and to notify users that an upgrade is occurring and that certain functions may not be available or may behave differently than expected.

If you are using Cisco Unity voice mail, it's relatively easy to fix unsynchronized MWI status. Cisco Unity can resynchronize the MWI based on the user's actual mailbox. This is done through the Unity Telephony Integration Monitor (UTIM) application. For resynchronization on any Unity server that services the particular cluster you are upgrading, perform the following procedure on the Unity server:

Step 1   Click **Start > Programs > Unity > Manage Integrations**.

Step 2   Double-click **Cisco CallManager**.

Step 3   Click **Properties**.

Step 4   Click the **Resynchronize Now** button (see Figure 5-2).

Figure 5-2   *Managing Unity Telephony Integrations*

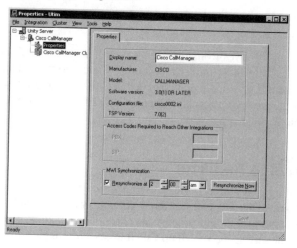

Performing these steps forces Unity to inspect every user's mailbox and signal CallManager to set the proper MWI state.

Unsynchronized MWI is much harder to fix if you're using a third-party voice mail system, because each type of voice mail system handles setting MWI differently. Check with your voice mail system provider for more information on how to resynchronize MWI status.

The difficulty in MWI resynchronization might be a reason to perform the upgrade on a staging server for documentation purposes only, as opposed to upgrading with the intention of drive reinsertion. As soon as you have a solid procedure that you can perform with confidence, your window of possible MWI mismatches is much smaller. Most users with third-party systems, particularly Octel 250 and 350 series, opt for in-production upgrades only after staging has been performed because of tedious MWI resynchronization issues.

Shut down the production CallManager Publisher at the scheduled time and pull the hard disk from Slot 0. Reboot the production server. When you do, an HP server (or MCS H-class server) prompts you to "Press F2 to start the system in interim recovery mode." On an IBM server (or MCS I-class server), you need to press **F5**. After you choose this option, the system boots normally. Do not simply press the power button on the production system to boot it and walk away. The system does not boot unless you select a boot option.

NOTE   Newer server models from HP delay for 10 seconds but boot into interim recovery mode by default.

Take the drive you removed from the production system, and with the staging system shut down, place it in Slot 0 of the staging system.

Remove all other drives from the staging system, and boot it. You receive the same boot message regarding "interim recovery mode." Choose to run in that mode. Be sure that the staging system is on a completely isolated network, because it boots with the same IP address as the production system. You now have two identical systems—one in production and one on the staging network.

Use a Spare Drive to Remirror

After the staging system is started, insert a spare drive of the same exact type and model into the server. This reestablishes the RAID mirror automatically and creates an exact duplicate of the system. The process can take up to an hour. When the process is complete, shut down the server, and keep it on a shelf in case the upgrade does not proceed as planned. You can always start the procedure over again with the mirror copy of the system.

Perform and Document the Necessary Upgrades

As soon as the staging system is booted and operational, you can follow the upgrade procedure in the release notes for your specific version of Windows OS and CallManager.

Upgrade to the version of Windows OS first and apply all mandatory patches as defined by the release notes. It is not recommended that you install any other patches at this point unless they are security related. The reason for this is that if the release notes for the version of CallManager you intend to run state minimum requirements, that specific version of CallManager has been thoroughly regression-tested to run with the recommended version of Windows OS.

WARNING	Although Cisco strives to ship software that is completely regression-tested, if Microsoft finds a security issue with any Windows component in use on CallManager, the Cisco policy for critical patches is to perform minimal compatibility testing and release the patch to Cisco.com within one business day. Those individual patches are then wrapped into Cisco-released Windows OS service releases and are more thoroughly tested.

As soon as the Windows OS is at the release-and-patch level specified in the release notes (plus any critical security fixes), you can install the CallManager upgrade. Follow the upgrade procedure outlined in the release notes and installation documentation.

When the upgrade is complete, the hard disk is ready to be swapped back into the production system. Be sure you have documented your upgrade using the checklist provided in Table 5-2.

Check the Event Log

After the upgrade is complete, check the Event Viewer for any System or Application Log messages of ERROR severity. Such errors alert you to problems in the installation before you move the drives back into production.

Perform Chkdsk and Defrag Operations

Running chkdsk after your upgrade ensures the disk's integrity and health before you move it back to the production system. You should run these operations during any upgrade or outage window. Follow these steps:

Step 1   Click **Start > Run**.

Step 2   Type **CMD** and press **Enter**.

Step 3   Enter **chkdsk /f** and press **Enter**.

Occasionally defragmenting the disk keeps it operating at maximum efficiency. Call processing is optimized to run from memory, so disk fragmentation does not directly affect it. However, depending on the trace level set, CallManager can be very disk I/O-bound. As the disk drive starts to get full, fragmentation can affect the speed at which trace files are written. Cleaning up temporary files and defragmenting can then improve performance. Follow these steps:

Step 1   Click **Start > Programs > Accessories > System Tools > Disk Defragmenter**.

Step 2   Select the **C:** drive and click the **Defragment** button.

Move the Hard Disk into the Production System in Careful Order

When moving the system back into the production system, you must carefully follow in order the steps outlined in this section. Performing these steps in the proper order results in a successful upgrade.

Step 1   Shut down the production system.

Step 2   Remove all drives.

Step 3   Insert the upgraded drive in Slot 0.

Step 4   Boot the system.

Step 5   Choose to boot in **Interim Recovery Mode**.

Step 6   After the system is booted, insert the redundant drive in Slot 1.

Installing Windows OS and CallManager Service Releases

Once a month Cisco releases patches (called *service releases*), for the underlying OS components. These releases generally contain the various Microsoft security patches for Microsoft Internet Information Server (IIS), Microsoft Internet Explorer, Windows Media Player, and Microsoft Windows 2000 that were released during that one-month period. In addition, Cisco releases patches for Microsoft SQL Server, BIOS updates for the various hardware platforms, and individual security updates that are deemed critical.

Read the Master File of Windows Updates

Cisco maintains a master file of all Windows component updates and the most recent files. The master file provides a road map for the Cisco-posted patches that have been rolled into single files. Figure 5-3 shows a snippet.

The master Cisco IP Telephony Operating System, SQL Server, Security Updates file can be found at the following link, which is updated whenever service releases and upgrades are released:

http://www.cisco.com/univercd/cc/td/doc/product/voice/c_callmg/osbios.htm

Read the README File

The README files contain information such as install time, minimum OS requirements, and the location of log files. They also list the Microsoft patches included in the service release, the corresponding Knowledge Base article, a description, and when the patch was first released by Cisco.

Figure 5-3   *Windows File Tracking Document*

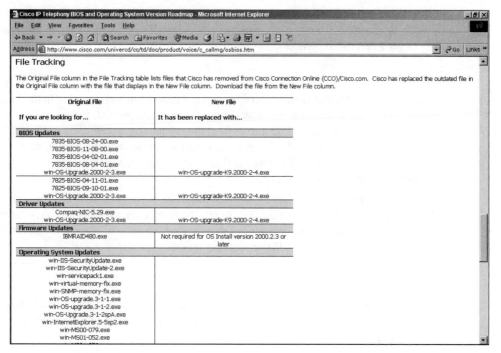

The README also contains installation instructions. It is important to closely follow these instructions. As with every other type of installation, you need to read the release notes completely before installing any patches on the system.

Service releases are available to registered Cicso.com users from the Software Center at the following link:

http://www.cisco.com/kobayashi/sw-center/sw-voice.shtml

Simply navigate to the proper major release of CallManager, and click the link for **Download Operating System, BIOS Updates and CallManager Cryptographic Software**.

Install the Service Release While Observing Precautions

When installing patches, you have a few options. Some users choose to install the patches directly on the production system, whereas others install patches in a staging environment first to get a feel for the process.

TIP   Many customers maintain a mirrored drive of their production environment in their staging environment, which is used to test new configurations, new phones, and so on. This mirror is best created by pulling a RAID mirror from the production system and installing it in the staging server. After it's installed, that drive is synchronized with the hard drive that's already in the staging server. When that is done, the original production mirror can be reinserted into the production server.

When the staging server finishes completing its RAID mirror, you have an exact duplicate of the production server. This allows you to test the service releases and patches effectively. As soon as you have a high degree of confidence that your patching procedure is correct, you can roll out the patches to the production servers.

However, because of the release cycle of service releases, if your intent is to install every service release as it is posted to Cisco.com, it may be impractical to use a staging environment.

NOTE   Not all users choose to install every service release of the Windows OS. Many users have a quarterly patching process in which all patches are installed at a fixed interval regardless of release date. Because the Cisco Security Agent software, which can be downloaded for free for use with CallManager, protects the OS from many security-related issues, some users believe that quarterly updates provide effective protection. The best practice is to follow your company's guidelines for server patching.

If you must install service releases directly onto production servers, take a few simple precautions:

- **Print the README file**—Whenever you perform any kind of upgrade, print the README file and place it in the documentation binder. That way, a record exists of what was installed and what issues were addressed in the patch.

- **Perform a backup before applying the patch**—It's important to back up the system before installing any software, whether you are installing the Windows OS or the CallManager service release. The backup gives you a way to maintain a valid copy of the database should something go wrong.

- **Download the service release from another system**—Not using the CallManager servers to download software from the Internet protects the system from being exposed to viruses, worms, and Trojan horses unnecessarily.

- **Burn the patch onto a CD**—Using CDs allows you to perform the installation irrespective of network access at the time of installation. Many users have change windows for their various systems that overlap. Using CDs avoids any possible issue. Also, it provides a way of archiving what was installed and when. Place the CDs in the documentation binder with the README file.

- **Pull a RAID drive**—Using RAID systems is absolutely the best way of providing a back-out strategy should something fail during an in-production upgrade. It's critical to shut down the server before pulling out the drive.

If you take these simple precautions, an in-production upgrade should go smoothly if you follow the instructions contained in the README file.

Summary

Upgrading and patching CallManager and the underlying Windows components can seem daunting at first glance. When you peel back the onion, however, this process can be made safer by following a few simple guidelines:

- Have a staging environment if possible.

- Read all documentation thoroughly.

- Use CDs to perform the upgrades.

- Pull a RAID drive for an easy back-out.

Following these simple steps allows you to upgrade and patch systems with minimal downtime and minimal impact to your users.

## CHAPTER 6

Securing the Environment

Traditional phone system engineers are likely to have very different thoughts about security than traditional data network engineers. People who have managed phone systems are likely to be concerned primarily with issues of unauthorized access and toll fraud, whereas people with a data networking background are likely to have a wide range of concerns. This chapter considers security more from a data networking perspective, as a critical foundation to implementing a secure IP communications system. Toll fraud mitigation techniques, which are generally familiar to veteran voice system engineers, are not covered in detail in this chapter. If you want additional background material on this topic, you can search for white papers and other documents on Cisco.com. You also can read the "SAFE: IP Telephony Security in Depth" white paper at the following link:

> http://www.cisco.com/en/US/netsol/ns340/ns394/ns171/ns128/
> networking_ solutions_white_paper09186a00801b7a50.shtml

The section "Use Dial Plan Features to Prevent Toll Fraud" in Chapter 7, "Configuring CallManager and IP Telephony Components," also provides best practices for avoiding toll fraud.

Security is not simply a feature that can be turned on or off in a system; rather, it is a holistic set of features, operational best practices, and considerations built into every other system feature. Cisco CallManager and the entire Cisco IP Communications solution fit into this holistic approach.

The high-level functions associated with securing a voice, video, data, or any type of information network are essentially similar. They follow the AAA ("triple A") model of authentication, authorization, and accounting:

- **Authentication**—Ensure the trusted identity of users and devices in a system, and validate the authenticity of information stored or in transit between users or devices.

- **Authorization**—Establish criteria for which users and devices have permission to access information, generate or modify information, or perform an action in relation to information (whether it is stored in servers or transiting a network).

- **Accounting**—Keep track of which users and devices have attempted to use, access, modify, or act on information, whether they are successful, and provide alerting to administrators who can respond to potential security incidents.

Auditing is an implicit part of accounting, the third "A" of the AAA model. For example, in the business world, people audit the accounting details of companies to make sure they are following established policies and practices. Enhanced policies and practices may be derived from this process. The information security world also requires people to audit the accounting details and review and test operations to make sure that information security policies and practices are being followed. Sometimes these security audits are called *penetration tests* or *pen-tests* in the world of security. Accounting can also be a simple review of user access logs that comprise the system accounting records. These processes may lead to updated information security policies and practices, and this cycle forms the essential model of a continuously improving security process.

NOTE   You might consider cryptography an extra branch of the AAA functional set, but in fact cryptography is a tool to deliver and enforce security functions. Cryptographic tools let you limit information access to only authenticated and authorized parties, to authenticate the origin of information, and so on.

Although a general security treatment of IP networks is outside the scope of this book, the following subjects are described in this chapter:

- Classes of voice security threats
- Creating a security policy to guide your efforts
- Avoiding single points of security policy failure
- Reviewing the infrastructure security feature checklist
- CallManager account and password policies
- OS hardening for CallManager and related voice applications
- IP Phone hardening features
- Secure remote administration of CallManager
- Secure endpoint provisioning
- Secure endpoint operation
- Secure inter-server communications
- Implementation considerations
- Administering CallManager security features

The Real Security Best Practice

The real best practice for a secure IP Telephony deployment is to thoroughly understand all the vulnerabilities. To that end, this chapter focuses more on concepts and less on specific step-by-step best practices than you'll find in the other chapters.

Classes of Voice Security Threats

Voice security threats can be categorized as follows:

- Unauthorized access
- Denial of service
- Violation of integrity
- Violation of privacy
- Violation of nonrepudiation

All of these threats can have undesirable consequences when exploited.

TIP   This chapter offers numerous links. If the link is broken, check the section "Using Links" in this book's Introduction for tips on how to find the document or a newer, related document.

Unauthorized Access

Unauthorized access can refer to many things in a networked system. In general, *access* is considered any viewing, creation, modification, or execution of information, whether it is stored or in transit. For example, access can mean any user profile or system configuration information stored on servers or endpoints, voice mails stored on a server, call signaling information or audio conversations transiting a network, and so on. *Unauthorized access* refers to any of these activities performed by a person or service that is not explicitly permitted to be engaged in that activity.

Denial of Service

In a voice security context, denial of service (DoS) basically means that you lose dial tone, specific voice features, access to outside phone lines for OffNet calling, access to voice mail, and so on. You identify potential DoS vulnerabilities by examining the chain of messages and events that must occur for users to obtain their service, and then look at ways any event in that chain can be blocked or disabled or have its capacity exceeded.

Violation of Integrity

Violation of integrity, in a voice security context, means that you cannot trust the identity of the device or user on the other end of your communication stream, and you cannot trust the content of what you receive from it. A violation can involve a variety of scenarios:

- A phone registering to a false CallManager run by a hacker
- CallManager receiving a false phone registration from a hacker
- A phone receiving funny (or disturbing) sound files for ringing sounds
- A phone call redirected to an unintended recipient
- Hackers logging into the Cisco CallManager User Options web page to forward your phone calls to their phones

To function in an organization, you and the rest of the users and devices in your network need to trust that the source and content of communications are as they appear to be. You can base this trust on faith, in which case you might be in for disillusionment. Or you can base this trust on confidence earned in security audits that validate the integrity properties designed into the system.

Violation of Privacy

Violation of privacy or *confidentiality* means that you cannot trust that the information you send, receive, or store has not been viewed, heard, or otherwise made known to unauthorized third parties. For example, this can mean that a voice conversation you are having is listened to or recorded by an unauthorized party, or the dual-tone multifrequency (DTMF) digits you enter for telephone banking or voice mail access are captured.

Violation of Nonrepudiation

Nonrepudiation means that you cannot deny that you did something or sent something. In other words, if nonrepudiation is effective in a system, a hacker cannot repudiate an accusation or assertion because proof of the hacker's actions exists. If nonrepudiation is violated in a system, you can blame the guy in the next office or cube, or whomever you want, but he can't be held accountable. Nonrepudiation is important to banks because they don't want you denying that you withdrew $1000 from your bank account. Nonrepudiation is important to telecom managers with billback operations because they don't want groups denying that they generated large phone bills. Nonrepudiation is important to IT InfoSec organizations because they don't want potential hackers denying their bad behavior. Using AAA terminology, nonrepudiation is another label for accountability. If you can't identify policy violators and hold them accountable for their actions, you will have a difficult time enforcing your security policies.

You can also remember these classifications with the acronym CIA—confidentiality, integrity, availability.

Create a Security Policy to Guide Your Efforts

If you don't know what you want, it is difficult to get it. A security policy provides a written set of principles tailored to your environment that guide all design and implementation decision-making related to security. Think of it as your mission, vision, and goals for security.

The following links provide references to help you create a site security policy that addresses the IP application and PBX nature of an IP communications system:

- RFC 2196, Site Security Handbook—http://www.ietf.org/rfc/rfc2196.txt
- SANS Security Policy Project—http://www.sans.org/resources/policies/
- InfoSysSec Security Policy References—http://www.infosyssec.org/infosyssec/secpol1.htm
- Computer Security Resource Center (CSRC) of the U.S. National Institute of Standards and Technology (NIST)—http://csrc.nist.gov/
- Cisco IOS Security Configuration Guide—http://www.cisco.com/univercd/cc/td/doc/product/software/ios122/122cgcr/fsecur_c/scfoverv.htm#1000988
- NIST Publication 800-24, "PBX Vulnerability Analysis," Appendixes B and C—http://csrc.nist.gov/publications/nistpubs/
- SAFE: IP Telephony Security in Depth—http://www.cisco.com/en/US/netsol/ns340/ns394/ns171/ns128/networking_solutions_white_paper09186a00801b7a50.shtml (or search Cisco.com for "SAFE IP telephony security")

If a security policy already exists and is owned by someone else in your organization, you can coordinate to ensure that voice-related considerations are represented in the security policy.

It's also important to note that a set of security configuration guidelines for a site is not quite the same thing as a security policy. To be clear, a security policy is the higher-level framework, the guiding principles that reflect management decisions in a given installation. In addition to these management guidelines, it's customary to have a set of security standards that capture how to implement the management guidelines. The security standards are a tangible manifestation of the security policy, such as firewall or access list configuration templates, lists of permitted and denied hosts for server configuration files, and so on.

Avoid Single Points of Security Policy Failure

You probably design a voice or data network to be resilient to connectivity failures (for example, by using redundant transmission paths and equipment). You should also implement your security policy using security features in layered and redundant ways so that a failure or breach in one security feature does not render the infrastructure or applications defenseless.

For example, to protect the CallManager database synchronization from curious or malicious end users, you might have a security policy that states the following: "CallManager SQL*net traffic is permitted only between CallManager servers. It is not permitted from client data VLANs to voice servers." In this case, you can implement the security policy item in several places in the infrastructure and applications to increase the likelihood that the policy remains in effect. Specifically, your site security standards might recommend the following configurations:

- Access control lists (ACLs) on the Ethernet interface where the client data virtual LANs (VLANs) connect (or the VLAN interface if you have a converged layer 2/layer 3 switch)

- ACLs on the egress interface that is upstream toward the CallManager servers

- ACLs on other routers in the path toward CallManager

- IPSec Filter Lists (a feature of the Microsoft Windows 2000 operating system) on the CallManager servers that are set to accept only SQL*net connections (identified as traffic to certain TCP/UDP ports) from certain IP addresses

- Strong passwords for SQL database synchronization between CallManager Publisher and Subscriber servers

Within the preceding sample security standard for implementing the policy of "protect voice servers from undesired network services," if you accidentally remove an access list from an edge router, you do not expose CallManager servers to a violation of this security policy because another router has an access list to block any attacks that now slip by the first line-of-defense access list you disabled. You might hear people in the security industry call this layered security approach *defense in depth*.

An extreme example of redundant security policy implementation is companies that implement two firewalls in serial. The idea is to avoid having the person configuring the firewall become a single point of failure in the implementation of the security policy. If that person becomes disgruntled, is incompetent, or for whatever reason fails to properly restrict traffic to implement the security policy, the next firewall in the chain will have appropriate filters that are configured by a different person. Sometimes companies even go so far as to use firewalls from different vendors in serial so that any bugs or product defects that affect one of the firewalls are less likely to affect the other firewall. This also reduces the likelihood of copy/paste collusion when configuring the two devices, so that a mistake in one configuration does not readily propagate to the configuration of the other firewall.

Your choice of how much security redundancy to build into the system is a trade-off between security requirements and cost, ease of use, and ease of maintenance.

A Word About Layers

Throughout this chapter, you'll notice references to layer 1 through layer 7. These layers refer to the protocol layers identified in the Open System Interconnection (OSI) seven-layer network reference model, developed by the International Organization for Standardization (ISO). For more details, do an Internet search for the preceding terms to produce numerous listings.

Layer 1 is the physical layer, comprising the electrical and mechanical definitions for moving information bits on a wire or through the air. An example is Category 5 unshielded twisted-pair cable, along with the appropriate impedance and electrical transmission specifications for transmitting an electrical current and voltage over the cable.

Layer 2 is the data link layer, comprising the encoding methods and protocols for exchanging information between two directly connected devices. An example is Ethernet (choose your favorite variant). In the telecom world, the Q.921 protocol is the link layer for the D-channel communications in ISDN circuits such as BRI and PRI.

Layer 3 is the network layer, comprising the intelligence for how to forward information to the appropriate destination machine via any number of intermediate machines that are directly connected at layer 2. The increasingly universal example is IP. In the telecom world, the Q.931 protocol is the network layer for the D-channel communications in ISDN circuits such as BRI and PRI.

Layer 4 is the transport layer, which distinguishes multiple information flows to the same machine and sometimes provides flow control and ordered delivery. Examples include TCP and User Datagram Protocol (UDP). TCP provides guaranteed and ordered delivery of messages to an appropriate application socket of a destination machine. UDP is a less cumbersome protocol that provides just gross error checking and delivery of messages to an appropriate application socket of a destination machine. Applications that use UDP need to either build in extra intelligence to check that all the information arrived and that it is properly ordered, or at least that it is robust enough to handle errors.

Layer 5 is the session layer, which manages separate "conversations" within the same application on host machines. It is this meaning of session that gave rise to Session Initiation Protocol (SIP).

Layer 6 is the presentation layer, which is usually part of the host operating system and manages the details of how to encode text symbols, whether or not there is a carriage return and line feed sequence or simply a newline character at the end of each line of text, and so on. This is not a layer you generally need to watch closely in practical network design, but it should be obvious that this layer is critical for allowing machines from different vendors to communicate with each other. You certainly wouldn't want the numbering order to be reversed when you deposit 1000 units of a monetary currency into your bank account.

Layer 7 is the application layer, where application-specific attributes such as user identifiers, security requirements, and quality of service requirements are negotiated and managed.

Review an Infrastructure Security Feature Checklist

The primary intent of this section is to increase your awareness of specific technologies that secure the foundation of your IP infrastructure. Although this section is called a checklist, the items in the checklist each require so much elaboration that it is easy to lose the thread of organization. The guiding structure is to first summarize the major types of security vulnerabilities and mitigation techniques in general, and then traverse the OSI communication reference model layers (just discussed) while discussing specific security considerations.

Consult the Cisco product documentation for additional information on each of these subjects because the details are outside the scope of this book. Check the *Cisco IOS Security Configuration Guide* at the following link for fairly comprehensive coverage of infrastructure security topics (although the amount of information available might be daunting):

> http://www.cisco.com/univercd/cc/td/doc/product/software/ios123/123cgcr/
> sec_ vcg.htm

In general, infrastructure security features are designed to thwart several types of threats:

- Unauthorized traffic types going where they should not go (unauthorized access and denial of service)
- Authorized traffic types using more bandwidth or other resources than they should (denial of service)
- Unauthorized devices mimicking authorized devices (violating integrity)
- Unauthorized devices intercepting communications intended for other devices (violating privacy)

At the infrastructure level, these threats are thwarted by

- Securing the routers and switches themselves so that they continue to perform their packet/frame forwarding and filtering functions.
- Keeping unauthorized devices from being in the communication path by using filters and security mitigation features at different layers of the protocol stack and protecting against frame forgery and spoofing attempts to bypass the filters.

Filters that operate at most layers of the protocol stack under various feature names are appropriate at the following points in the network:

- Ingress directly on hosts, servers, or endpoint devices (considered separately under host hardening, as opposed to infrastructure security features) (Note that this is distinct from filters that you can apply on Ethernet switches or other networking gear.)
- Ingress Ethernet ports in wiring closet switches, where traffic first enters a network
- IP subnet boundaries where traffic crosses between VLANs
- Boundaries between network segments that are in different administrative domains

The following protocols that form the core of IP network functionality are critical components to consider as candidates for spoofing attacks:

- Ethernet frame headers that contain source/destination link layer addresses

- IP packet headers that contain source/destination network layer addresses

- Address Resolution Protocol (ARP), which binds permanent Ethernet hardware addresses to configuration-specific IP logical addresses

- Dynamic Host Configuration Protocol (DHCP), which automatically assigns IP addresses to devices

- Domain Name Service (DNS), which maps human-readable names to IP addresses

- Hot Standby Router Protocol (HSRP), which provides a single virtual Ethernet hardware address and IP address for a group of routers that provide redundant default gateway services

- IEEE 802.1d Spanning Tree Protocol (STP), which controls the layer 2 Ethernet frame forwarding behavior in a switched Ethernet LAN or metropolitan area network (MAN)

- IEEE 802.1q Ethernet trunk interfaces, which let a single physical Ethernet port share multiple VLANs

- Virtual Trunking Protocol (VTP) and other control protocols, which switches use to exchange VLAN configuration information

- Routing protocols that control the layer 3 packet forwarding behavior in a network

Remember that a system is only as secure as its most vulnerable path, and it is difficult (if not impossible) to build a secure voice solution if the infrastructure foundation is insecure.

Harden Access to Routers and Switches

Security experts who are aware of the range of technologies that must interact to create a secure environment sometimes jokingly ask, "Do you have an *auto-secure* feature?" Well, there actually is an AutoSecure feature. It is described in the AutoSecure documentation at the following link, or you can search Cisco.com for "autosecure IOS":

> http://www.cisco.com/univercd/cc/td/doc/product/software/ios123/
> 123newft/123_1/ftatosec.htm

This is not a true feature, but rather a macro command in IOS to enable a variety of other features that you might or might not already be using. The AutoSecure documentation at Cisco.com provides a great summary of *some* of the security features to make a router more resilient to hack attempts.

WARNING   Do not indiscriminately apply the AutoSecure feature to your routers. Be sure to save a backup of your running configuration before applying the command because there is no way to selectively undo it. To return to an earlier configuration state, you need to reload the saved configuration from before you ran the auto-secure command.

You should definitely consult other sources of documentation at Cisco.com to increase router security:

- Infrastructure Protection Access Control Lists at the following link or search Cisco.com for "infrastructure protection access control lists":

  http://www.cisco.com/warp/public/707/iacl.html

- Check the following link or search Cisco.com for "improving security on Cisco routers":

  http://www.cisco.com/warp/public/707/21.html

For example, you can implement Network Time Protocol (NTP) with authentication options so that routers are not tricked into using false time sources. This is not an obviously significant security concern, but it can lead to toll fraud through a willful underreporting of call times on voice over IP (VoIP) gateways, or it can be a small part of larger attacks in which replaying of captured information is required. In any event, Cisco IOS supports authentication of NTP messages, and you should implement this feature. For more information, search Cisco.com for "NTP authenticate."

You should also be sure to manage the NTP server host in a secure fashion so that the NTP server itself is not compromised. Secure communications to the NTP server are worthless if the NTP server itself is insecure. This advice applies for every type of server with which secure communications are desired. If it's worth your time and attention to provide confidentiality, integrity, and availability for any communication stream, it's worth hardening the server on the other end of the communication.

Here are some other configuration/implementation suggestions:

- Use Simple Network Management Protocol (SNMP) version 2 or later to authenticate SNMP read/write messages.

- Use the "secret" option instead of the "password" option with local usernames configured in IOS.

- Display in a login banner a warning about unauthorized access and your intent to monitor activities. Doing so facilitates your ability to prosecute offenders.

- Use off-box logging to capture forensic evidence in case a hacker subverts a box and deletes local logging records. Consider routing this traffic via an IPSec connection to maintain the information's integrity and privacy.

- Disable Telnet and enable Secure Shell version 2 (SSHv2) for remote terminal access, or connect the console port to an asynchronous (async) line on a communications server with SSHv2 support.

- Use permit lists to restrict which source IP addresses are authorized to make connection attempts to the router or switch for given protocols. For example, SNMP, Secure Shell (SSH), and HTTP access might be authorized from only IP subnets in an out-of-band management network.

It's outside the scope of this book to provide additional details or examples for each of these suggestions, but it's within the scope to make you aware that these items are important. You can refer to Cisco IOS configuration manuals or read books dedicated to the topic of network security to learn more details. Or, if you're fortunate enough to have the assistance of personnel who are responsible for security in your network, you can mention these items to them. They should have enough information to follow up (and potentially ask you more questions to get the job done).

NOTE   An additional reference is *Hardening Cisco Routers* by Thomas Akin (O'Reilly and Associates), ISBN/ASIN 0596001665.

In addition to specific configuration issues, also think about these operational issues:

- How securely is syslog or other network management data stored?

- How securely are IOS configurations stored in TFTP servers or other locations? Do you have printed copies visible in insecure areas?

The following sections summarize additional considerations for secure remote management. (The AAA feature set in Cisco IOS software and CiscoSecure ACS is explored more fully in Chapter 12, "Managing and Monitoring the System.")

Out-of-Band Management for CatOS/IOS Devices

The primary reasons to implement an out-of-band (OOB) management system for routers and switches are

- To keep end users from seeing management traffic

- To block management traffic that originates from end users

- To have remote access to your network devices when there's a network failure, such as a spanning-tree loop or a routing protocol problem and in-band management is not possible

Some people refer to IPSec or SSL-enabled connections as out-of-band management. Others don't consider it out-of-band if the communication path reaches the router or switch via the same interfaces that forward production traffic. In other words, a true out-of-band management network would still enable remote management of all devices, even if routing protocols fail for production traffic. Examples of this type of out-of-band management include the following:

- Modem access to console or auxiliary ports

- Console servers connected via asynchronous serial links to the console ports of routers and switches

- Building an autonomous network with separate interfaces into the routers and switches on a totally non-routed VLAN. ACLs would limit management access on each piece of equipment on that interface only

- Enabling SSH access, instead of Telnet, only from an intermediate server that is carefully secured and logged

Encrypted Connections for Management Control Traffic

In theory, if you use a truly independent out-of-band management network, there is little opportunity for hackers located on production network VLANs to gain access to the bitstream of administrative traffic. In keeping with the principle of layered defenses, however, it's a good idea to encrypt management traffic to provide integrity and privacy of configuration and management operations. Integrity for this type of traffic ensures that configuration changes originate from sources that are trusted by the device being configured, and also that no changes to this control traffic occur in transit. Privacy for this type of traffic ensures that eavesdroppers cannot decipher administrative passwords or other configuration elements that might give clues to help hackers perform other attacks.

The basic methods to encrypt administrative control traffic include

- Connecting IPSec virtual private networks (VPNs) directly to the device or to the edge of an out-of-band management network from which the device can be managed

- Connecting Secure Socket Layer/Transport Layer Security (SSL/TLS) connections directly to the device or to the edge of an out-of-band management network from which the device can be managed (for example, SSHv2 for command-line access or HTTPS for web-enabled remote administration)

One-Time Passwords for Authentication

A key benefit of using TACACS+ or RADIUS for authentication is the flexibility to support a one-time password mechanism such as RSA SecurID tokens (see http://www.rsasecurity.com/products/securid/).

The idea is that even if a hacker sniffs a password sent via Telnet, or applies an offline dictionary attack to decrypt a password sent via SSHv2, or tries a simple replay attack to gain access, the password so obtained would not be of use for subsequent authentication attempts. In other words, the password that the server expects continually changes in parallel with a client software or hardware component that also changes.

Layer 2: Statically Restrict MAC Addresses on a Switch Port Using Port Security

The port security feature, which has been around for a long time, is an idea heading in the right direction, but it's difficult to manage. You don't want to keep track of what media access control (MAC) address is allowed on which switch port and then update this every time you move IP phones. Heck, one of the key benefits of IP telephony is reducing the cost of moves, additions, and changes. If you have to manually configure a change to port security, you are not availing yourself of this key benefit.

On the other hand, you might say to yourself, "I just take a snapshot of my current environment, and the switch automatically configures the Ethernet MAC assignments for me." This is fine if you have a static environment that starts in a known, trusted state and never changes. But every time you retake the snapshot following phone moves (you'll know about phone moves because people will call and complain that their phones don't work after they moved them), you are introducing the possibility for hackers on the network to be accepted as trusted endpoints. The whole point of port security is to keep out the bad guys, so anything you do to make it easier to manage also makes it easier to let the bad guys in.

In general, you can look to other features such as DHCP Snooping or 802.1x to provide a dynamic version of the functionality you expect from port security, but there are some cases in which port security is a complementary feature. For example, you can use the port security feature to enforce a policy of no phone movement. If you really don't want people moving the phones around, you can take a snapshot of the environment after you roll out the phones, and then the phones will work only when plugged into their present locations. The pitfall of this strategy is that someone can rearrange a wiring closet, and suddenly all the phones stop working because they are now connected to different switch ports.

For more details, check the Configuring Port Security documentation at the following link:

> http://www.cisco.com/univercd/cc/td/doc/product/lan/cat6000/sw_8_1/confg_gd/sec_port.htm

---

NOTE Requirements for E-9-1-1 in North America or requirements for knowing the physical location of endpoints are not a strong reason to lock phones to a single port. You can let phones move around in your network and then use products such as Cisco Emergency Responder to automatically locate phones and handle location-based call routing.

NOTE Keep the following restrictions in mind if you decide to use port security:

- A secure port cannot be a trunk port.

- A secure port cannot be a destination port for Switch Port Analyzer (SPAN).

- A secure port cannot belong to an EtherChannel port-channel interface.

- A secure port cannot be an 802.1x port. If you try to enable 802.1x on a secure port, an error message appears, and 802.1x is not enabled. If you try to change an 802.1x-enabled port to a secure port, an error message appears, and the security settings are not changed.

Layer 2: Dynamically Restrict Ethernet Port Access with 802.1x Ethernet Port Authentication

Ethernet port authentication protects against unauthorized access to a LAN segment via a physical Ethernet jack in a manner similar to how dialup modem, ISDN, or Internet-based VPN connections require authentication. In the past, it was assumed that people who gained physical access to an Ethernet jack were implicitly authorized as a function of getting past whatever physical security mechanisms restricted access to the areas where Ethernet jacks were located. With a greater focus on layered security mechanisms, and the reality that most network attacks are insider-based (probably because perimeter firewalls work pretty well!), LAN users are no longer assumed to have authorization to use the network.

Although an authorized person can still perform attacks after authenticating via 802.1x, a key difference is that LAN-based attacks can no longer be performed anonymously. It is possible, and even likely, that attacks can occur after end users' computers have been compromised via a virus, worm, or other mechanism that originates from an anonymous source, but the scope of damage resulting from these types of attacks can be greatly restricted. This is because secure identification of users and devices opens the possibility to dynamically apply quality of service (QoS), rate limiting, and security filtering policies to the Ethernet port that specifically limits the scope of authorization based on the needs and privileges of specific users or devices.

It's important to note that the IEEE 802.1x specification explicitly does not support VLAN trunk ports in which multiple Ethernet MAC addresses can be associated with a single port. This means that you cannot implement the pure IEEE standard for 802.1x if you want to enjoy the benefits of a single cable from the wiring closet to IP phones that have internal switches for downstream desktop computers. For this reason, Cisco created extensions to the 802.1x standard to support trunk ports with multiple Ethernet MAC addresses associated to the same wiring closet switch port.

As of February 2004, you can implement 802.1x on the data VLANs whenever you are ready, even for PCs that are connected to the wiring closet switches via Cisco IP Phones with internal switches. This is because Cisco switches support independent instances of 802.1x authentication for each MAC address on each VLAN, and Cisco IP Phones transparently pass 802.1x Ethernet frames from downstream PCs to the Ethernet switches in the wiring closet. A PC that authenticates to a data VLAN cannot automatically gain access to a voice VLAN just because the same physical Ethernet port also supports voice VLANs. Aside from the fact that the wiring closet switch does not allow this behavior, Cisco IP Phones include features to thwart these types of attacks (as discussed later in this chapter).

Although Cisco IP Phones can pass 802.1x from a connected PC to an 802.1x Authenticator in the upstream Ethernet switch, there is currently no mechanism for the IP phone to notify the Authenticator when the PC disconnects from the phone. This allows an intruder to replace the attached PC and enter the network. To mitigate this threat, the switch needs to be configured to automatically reauthenticate the PC periodically to make sure that the PC that authenticated is still the one attached to the phone.

TIP   As of February 2004, Cisco IP Phones cannot authenticate via 802.1x to a wiring closet Ethernet switch, but the back-end features to support integrated authentication databases are included in CallManager release 4.0. These features will be supported in the Cisco IP Phone 7970 model first and then will become available to additional phone models over time. For the latest information, consult the Cisco IP Phone documentation and release notes.

Some folks think that deployment of 802.1x for data VLANs is pointless if it's not also applied to voice VLANs, but this is not true. Deploying 802.1x on the data VLAN mitigates the threat of a large-scale automated attack in which every PC in an organization is subverted and is used as a drone to attack the voice VLAN. Such an attack could be plausibly triggered via an e-mail virus. If PCs connect behind an IP phone that drops 802.1q-tagged Ethernet frames (see the later section "Harden Access via IP Phones"), and the data VLAN employs 802.1x, and ACLs restrict access between voice and data VLANs, PCs cannot be remotely controlled to directly attack the voice VLAN.

Having 802.1x on both the data and voice VLANs protects against attacks in which a person unplugs his or her PC from the PC port behind the phone and plugs it into the jack to which the phone was previously connected. At this point, attackers could sniff the control traffic from the switch to learn which VLAN ID is associated with the voice VLAN and then send Ethernet frames tagged with the voice VLAN into the voice network. You can mitigate these threats by using rate limiting and traffic filters on the auxiliary or voice VLANs for these ports. These types of filters are called VLAN Access Control Lists (VACLs). They are discussed in more detail later in this chapter.

You have several design issues to consider when deploying 802.1x in your site(s):

- Which switch ports require authentication?
- What authentication mechanism should you use?
- Do all your clients support 802.1x?
- Does 802.1x have security vulnerabilities?

For more details, check the Configuring 802.1x Authentication documentation at the following link:

> http://www.cisco.com/univercd/cc/td/doc/product/lan/cat6000/sw_8_1/confg_gd/8021x.htm

Which Ethernet Ports Require 802.1x Authentication?

It's appropriate to enable 802.1x authentication on any and all Ethernet ports on which you do not explicitly trust the device connected to the port. Be aware that to really trust the device, you need to have a high level of confidence in the physical security of the Ethernet switch, the device connecting to it, and the Ethernet cable path connecting them. It's generally assumed that wireless connections are not secure in real-world deployments. People widely recognize the need for security such as 802.1x on wireless links. Wired Ethernet does not enjoy the same widespread recognition of the need for extra security measures, so the requirements are explicitly identified here.

Typically, the only places where you can be lax in deploying 802.1x are within data centers or wiring closets. For example, the connections from your servers, gateways, or other infrastructure devices such as routers and switches are not as susceptible to hackers unplugging the devices and trying to connect rogue devices. That being said, if you have a large organization in which numerous vendors come in and out of data centers with little accountability for who is doing what, you might consider deploying 802.1x even in these areas.

What 802.1x Authentication Mechanism Should You Use?

Although the common name for Ethernet port authentication is 802.1x, it might as well be called Extensible Authentication Protocol (EAP) for Ethernet ports. That's because the real authentication session is directly between the endpoints being authenticated and an access control server such as CiscoSecure ACS. This EAP exchange is carried over 802.1x Ethernet frames between the supplicant and the authenticating switch and over RADIUS between the switch and the authentication server.

As you might guess, EAP supports a variety of authentication mechanisms, and more methods can be added to this framework. The most common authentication choices include EAP-MD5 and EAP-TLS. The EAP-MD5 variant is similar to Challenge Handshake Authentication Protocol (CHAP), which traditionally has been used for dialup modem or

ISDN remote access. This mechanism relies on a username/password combination for the authentication credentials. The EAP-TLS variant is more closely related to e-commerce applications, in which an X.509v3 certificate represents the server's identity and the client's identity is provided through another X.509v3 client-side certificate or username/password combination.

In addition to the authentication protocol in use, you need to understand whether a user of a device or a device itself is being authenticated. This distinction is important because user and device authentication solve different problems. For example, at a conceptual level, a multiaccess IP phone might have a single credential that proves to the network that it's not a rogue piece of hardware touching the network. In this case, the individual user logins to the phone might trigger a user-based 802.1x authentication that lets a different set of QoS and security policies be applied to the switch port based on the individual user permissions.

Cisco IP Phones will support device-based 802.1x via EAP-TLS as part of a future release, with X.509v3 certificates in the phone serving as the credentials for the TLS handshake. The TLS handshake is discussed in more detail later as it applies to Skinny Client Control Protocol (SCCP or Skinny protocol) authentication.

Do All Your Clients Support 802.1x?

Before you embark on a plan to configure 802.1x support on your Ethernet switches, you need to make sure that you coordinate with the desktop PC administrators so that they are ready to enable 802.1x in the client machines. As long as you need clients on your network that do not support 802.1x, you cannot widely implement 802.1x. You might be able to start a pilot project that applies to a limited set of Ethernet jacks in your campus, but note that these jacks do not permit clients lacking 802.1x support to connect. Don't forget to consider workgroup printers and other Ethernet devices along with desktop PCs.

Does 802.1x Have Security Vulnerabilities?

Reaping the full security benefits of an 802.1x deployment involves important design considerations. Imagine that your network resources are a reservoir of water held back by a dam, and that dam is the security policy as implemented by access lists that filter traffic and authentication at the network's ingress points. Just as a dam must be watertight, all ports in an 802.1x deployment for ingress authentication must be part of the deployment. If you have any devices or users who cannot authenticate via 802.1x, or if you have Ethernet jacks with 802.1x not enabled, you have holes that need to be plugged. To gain access to the LAN segments that 802.1x is designed to protect, a hacker can simply use an Ethernet jack on which 802.1x is not enabled or masquerade as a user or device that does not support 802.1x.

Taking a more pragmatic approach, you can also prioritize the areas of physical access sensitivity. You should first roll out 802.1x support to the areas that are least regulated, such as lobbies and cafeterias with limited security checks. Next in order would be break rooms, temporary worker areas, or other areas with minimal restrictions. Finally, you can focus on the common office or cubicle areas. In general, work your way through from the least physically secure areas to the most physically secure.

Layer 2: Don't Trust Class of Service Settings from PCs Behind IP Phones

Users who decide they are more important than anyone else in your organization might inflate the prioritization of Ethernet frames they transmit into your LANs. If you have a different opinion about their prioritization (and your opinion wins if you administer the network elements), you can configure the Cisco Catalyst switches to limit this activity. You can configure the switches to tell the Cisco IP Phones to ignore the class of service (CoS) bit settings on Ethernet frames received through the PC interface on the phone and then reset these values to a predefined value. Of course, the CoS settings from the IP Phone itself remain intact.

This feature is important to limit the damage that can be done by DoS attacks against the voice VLAN. Client PCs can be subverted to send a large amount of traffic into the voice VLAN, although this is not easy to do because of other features that block 802.1q frames received from the PC port on the phones. If the PCs are subverted, the prioritization of voice frames over normal data frames ensures that voice traffic receives the desired quality of service while the rest of the network is congested.

For more information, check the section "Configuring a Trusted Boundary to Ensure Port Security" in the Configuring a VoIP Network documentation at the following link:

> http://www.cisco.com/univercd/cc/td/doc/product/lan/cat6000/sw_8_1/confg_gd/
> voicecfg.htm#1004498

Layer 2: Use Private VLANs to Restrict Layer 2 Connectivity

You can think of private VLANs (PVLANs) as sub-VLANs or VLANs within a VLAN. The idea is to reduce layer 2 adjacencies to the minimal point required to provide desired network connectivity and functionality. This keeps network connectivity on a need-to-know basis. In most corporate networks, for example, client computers typically access information from centralized application servers and the public Internet, with occasional use of workgroup servers or printers. In these types of deployment scenarios, there is no need for PCs to communicate with each other directly, so PVLANs deployed in the wiring closet ensure that different client PCs don't even have Ethernet connectivity to each other. Private VLANs complement layer 2 access lists by forming an independent layer of defense (that is, by blocking LAN connectivity).

As mentioned earlier, in terms of the basic voice security threats, private VLANs mitigate the threat of unauthorized access from other devices within the same IP subnet. However, it's important to remember that IP phones in a voice VLAN often need to communicate with each other, such as when you call your boss or someone else who sits in your vicinity. As such, it is impractical to break Ethernet connectivity between IP phones in the same voice VLAN. For this reason, PVLANs generally are inappropriate for voice client subnets.

There is value in using PVLANs for voice application servers, gateways, and other centralized voice network components. As part of building a layered security defense, you can protect these centralized voice components from potential weaknesses or exploitations of other data servers. In other words, you might have a breach in your data network in which some centralized data application servers are compromised in a wiring closet or data center. You can, however, mitigate the risk to your voice networks by not allowing Ethernet connectivity from these potentially compromised machines that have no business reason to interact with voice servers.

For more details on using the different types of private VLANs, check the "Configuring Private VLANs on the Switch" section in the Configuring VLANs documentation at the following link:

> http://www.cisco.com/univercd/cc/td/doc/product/lan/cat6000/sw_8_1/confg_gd/
> vlans.htm#1093407

Layer 2: DHCP Option 82 Stops Broadcast of DHCP Replies

One of the lesser security issues with DHCP is that everyone in a subnet receives responses from a DHCP server, so all devices can learn the information contained in those responses. Specifically, this includes the mapping of IP addresses to Ethernet MAC addresses, the IP address of the DNS servers and TFTP servers associated with IP phone provisioning, and so on. In practice, anyone who has access to your LAN can easily learn any of the server information contained in DHCP responses, so this is not a big issue. However, you may be more restrictive in sharing the Ethernet MAC address-to-IP address binding information. Realize that this is exactly the same information maintained by ARP in the client machines and routers. (See the later section "Layer 2: Turn on Dynamic ARP Inspection" for details.) Any policies that limit the distribution of ARP information should also consider limiting DHCP responses by using the Option 82 "circuit ID" feature.

When you configure DHCP Option 82 in the Ethernet switch, the switch adds the port identification as an option in the request to the DHCP server so that the server can provide a customized response that takes into account the actual switch port to which the device is attached. This feature is instrumental in associating a device's physical location based on the Ethernet switch association. A side effect of DHCP Option 82 is that when the switch receives a response from the DHCP server, the switch now knows exactly which Ethernet port to use to forward the response. The net effect is that other devices on the LAN no longer receive DHCP responses that are not intended for them.

For more details, search for "DHCP Option 82" on Cisco.com.

Layer 2: DHCP Snooping Protects Against DHCP Spoofing

A major security threat associated with DHCP is that unauthorized devices can respond to requests and effectively execute a man-in-the-middle attack. The way this happens is that the hacker can reply to DHCP requests with a valid IP address assignment and a bogus value for DNS servers, TFTP servers, default gateways, or other parameters. The bogus values are typically chosen in such a way that IP packets are steered to the hacker's machine. For voice VLANs with IP phones, you should prevent this because any of these tricks can cause IP phones to register with false CallManagers or send audio streams to unintended destinations.

It's not easy for endpoints to identify whether DHCP responses originate from a hacker or a valid DHCP server, although emerging standards will enable authentication of DHCP responses. DHCP authentication can be problematic if endpoints need to move between multiple administrative domains because some sort of pre-enrollment is necessary for the endpoint to know what DHCP servers it can trust.

The DHCP snooping feature is a nice solution to this problem because it allows you as the network administrator to regulate the security of DHCP in your environment without making any demands on the client support.

DHCP snooping provides security by blocking untrusted DHCP responses (in other words, responses received on switch ports that you haven't associated with DHCP servers) and by building and maintaining a DHCP snooping binding table. The DHCP snooping binding table contains the MAC address, IP address, lease time, binding type, VLAN number, and interface information that correspond to a switch's local untrusted interfaces (typically all the switch ports going out to client subnets). It does not contain information on hosts interconnected with a trusted interface (typically the switch ports connected to servers, gateways, or other devices in a data center or wiring closet).

As described in following sections, the DHCP snooping feature is a prerequisite to using the IP Source Guard and Dynamic ARP Inspection features, which greatly improve the security posture of your VLANs.

For more details, check the Configuring DHCP Snooping and IP Source Guard documentation at the following link:

http://www.cisco.com/univercd/cc/td/doc/product/lan/cat4000/12_1_19/config/dhcp.htm

Layer 2: Turn on Dynamic ARP Inspection

To understand how Dynamic ARP Inspection (DAI) works, you need a basic understanding of how ARP functions in an IP network and how hackers can exploit this function to redirect Ethernet frames to themselves or other false destinations. After you review the following sections, a discussion of DAI behavior will make more sense.

ARP and GARP Associate Layer 2 and Layer 3 Addresses

ARP maps logical IP addresses (that are administratively assigned to devices in a given deployment environment) to permanent Ethernet hardware MAC addresses burned into devices at the time of manufacture. In other words, ARP forms a link between layer 2 and layer 3 addressing within a given VLAN or broadcast domain. When you configure your PC with a default IP gateway (that is, the router interface for all IP traffic not destined for your local IP subnet), your PC still needs a way to know what layer 2 Ethernet address to use in the destination field of the Ethernet frame within the vLAN. When your PC (or any IP-enabled device) needs to send IP traffic to a destination, it broadcasts a query onto the subnet to ask which Ethernet MAC address it should use to reach that IP address. Every time a machine needs to send traffic to a new IP address within the same IP subnet, it must send an ARP request and get an ARP reply from a destination before it can forward traffic to the destination.

An extension to ARP is Gratuitous ARP (GARP), in which a machine can gratuitously send out a mapping of its own Ethernet MAC address to its IP address. This transmission is a courtesy to other devices on the IP subnet that saves them from making the ARP request in the first place. In theory, this would reduce the amount of ARP traffic on an Ethernet subnet because each device would need to send out only a single GARP message rather than a separate ARP message in response to every ARP reply. Well, that's the theory, anyway. Endpoints also use GARP to enable an early detection mechanism when multiple devices are using the same IP address in the broadcast domain. Regardless of the intended use, the problem is that none of these exchanges (ARP request, ARP reply, or GARP) has any type of authentication.

NOTE   If you got lost in the preceding discussion, you can review more-detailed coverage of this information in numerous TCP/IP introductory texts, including *TCP/IP Illustrated,* Volume 1, by W. Richard Stevens or *Internetworking with TCP/IP,* Volume 1, by Douglas Comer.

Hackers Can Exploit ARP and GARP

It's easy for a hacker to falsify ARP replies or GARPs so that machines on the IP subnet cache erroneous information about which Ethernet MAC addresses are used to reach given IP addresses. For example, a hacker can poison the ARP caches maintained in every machine in a subnet by using his or her own MAC address as the layer 2 destination for the IP default gateway. If that happens, all machines in the subnet start forwarding IP traffic destined for outside the local IP subnet to the hacker machine's Ethernet MAC address, which in effect gives total control of the traffic to the hacker. This is a basic form of man-in-the-middle attack.

It's important to note that this behavior is possible even with a layer 2 switch instead of an Ethernet hub. Some people think that switches are more secure because traffic destined for a given Ethernet MAC address is forwarded only out the appropriate switch port, as opposed to the flooding behavior of a hub. Broadcast frames such as ARP are still forwarded by default out all ports on a switch, as are the first unicast frames before the establishment of cached forwarding information. If someone passively sniffed the bits on an Ethernet cable, he or she would learn only about the traffic flows associated with devices on the same cable, not about all the rest of the established traffic flows in a switched VLAN. However, hackers don't have to be passive. The ARP attacks described here can divert all traffic to the hacker's machine regardless of the real Ethernet switch port for which traffic was originally intended. The Dynamic ARP Inspection feature mitigates these types of attacks.

If you think this discussion is merely esoteric and theoretical, know that it is not! Hacker tools such as Ettercap and Ethereal trivially exploit these security vulnerabilities. It's likely that other tools allow novice hackers with virtually no technical knowledge to perform these attacks.

DAI Blocks Inconsistent GARPs and ARP Replies

DAI intercepts all ARP requests and replies that are sent and received on untrusted ports. The network administrator specifies which ports are not to be trusted, such as all ports connecting to client workstations. Each intercepted packet is verified for valid IP address-to-MAC address bindings. The DHCP snooping feature maintains IP address-to-MAC address bindings. DAI helps prevent man-in-the-middle attacks by not relaying invalid ARP replies to other ports in the same VLAN. This solution requires no change to the end-user or host configurations. The switch logs denied ARP packets for auditing. Incoming ARP packets on the trusted ports or isolated PVLAN trunks are not inspected.

For more details, check the Understanding and Configuring Dynamic ARP Inspection documentation at the following link:

> http://www.cisco.com/univercd/cc/td/doc/product/lan/cat4000/12_1_19/config/
> dynarp.htm

You might be wondering how an IP address filter acts as a layer 2 security tool. Well, the line is getting fairly blurry these days between layer 2 and layer 3 technologies, and this one sits right on the edge. Because the mechanism to filter traffic based on layer 3 content is actually applied to each physical switch port and VLAN combination (that is, in a Port ACL [PACL]), it's called a layer 2 tool operating on layer 2 traffic flows (albeit with decisions being made on the layer 3 or higher contents).

Basically, the output of the DHCP snooping feature is used to create a dynamic PACL that blocks inbound traffic on a port if it contains a source IP address other than that learned through DHCP for the VLAN, or a MAC address other than that used to generate the DHCP request. In other words, whatever IP address a phone obtains via DHCP is the only address that is allowed to send IP packets through a switch port that is configured with IP Source Guard. In addition, the source MAC address must be the same as the one that first issued the DHCP request to get an IP address. Violations of the binding can result in the packets being dropped or the port being disabled at the administrator's request.

NOTE   If you enable the IP Source Guard feature with MAC address filtering too (not just IP address filtering), you have to allow DHCP Option 82 (circuit ID) traffic to be added from the switch to the DHCP server on the upstream request so that the response contains information on the port to which the DHCP response should be sent.

As of February 2004, the Cisco DHCP server (Cisco Network Registrar) supports DHCP Option 82 usage for circuit identification, but the Microsoft DHCP server does not.

The most important implication here is that you can't configure your phone endpoints in the voice or auxiliary VLANs to use static IP addresses. Most network administrators would cringe at using static IP addresses for more than 10 or 20 phones, so this becomes irrelevant. In other words, DHCP is your friend for assigning phone IP addresses. It is secured via the DHCP snoop feature on Catalyst switches, and it provides a dynamic layer 3 version of port security.

If you use Cisco IP Phone endpoints that support 802.1x to firm up the authentication and authorization of Ethernet MAC addresses on the switch port, you will have a fairly bulletproof multilayered set of security features. The final element in the utopian solution is per-frame Ethernet integrity checking for wired ports as it is provided in wireless Ethernet.

Layer 2: Lock Down Layer 2 Control Protocols

Hackers can attempt to divert bits to their machines in many ways. If you've been reading this chapter from the first page, you know that you can mitigate ARP spoofing attacks and DHCP attacks and limit authorization by source Ethernet MAC address (in static and dynamic ways). The following sections discuss all the protocols that switches use to exchange information with each other.

Layer 2: Use or Turn Off Cisco Discovery Protocol

Cisco Discovery Protocol (CDP) has evolved from a useful troubleshooting tool to a useful network management tool to an important protocol for the following:

- Certain functions of the Cisco Emergency Responder (ER) product
- Future location-based or presence-based applications
- Inline power negotiation to save power when it is not fully needed

The challenge in the realm of security is that you don't want to give out information that can be useful for hackers, such as voice VLAN assignments or IP addresses of switches and so on. Given the range of other security features that lock down layer 2, you might have some flexibility in deciding on the security risks associated with CDP. For example, because CDP enables fully automated phone location discovery for dynamic support of

E911 features, there is a fairly compelling argument to assume the risk of sharing a limited amount of information through CDP. However, if you choose not to take the risk and want to disable CDP, Cisco ER can still locate phones based on source IP address rather than source MAC address. Of course, you lose some location granularity, but these are the trade-offs you can make for your own environment.

A more serious trade-off when you disable CDP is that you lose dynamic assignment of the voice VLAN to IP phones. This means you give up the following:

- An easy mechanism to overlay a separate IP address space for IP phones
- A mechanism to create a layer 3 boundary between voice and data devices
- A mechanism to enforce quality of service requirements that prioritize Ethernet frames on the voice VLAN ahead of Ethernet frames on the data VLAN

In addition, it is likely that future Cisco products will leverage CDP for other application-specific features, so you are in an awkward position if you choose to disable CDP. The most pragmatic advice on this topic is to leave CDP turned on in spite of the risk of hackers finding a little extra network configuration information. The overall productivity benefits for network administrators likely outweigh the potential costs of a hacker learning a little more information to attempt another hack because you can bolster security in other parts of your network.

Layer 2: Stop VLAN Membership Policy Service Query Protocol to VLAN Membership Policy Server

Cisco Catalyst switches support a feature called VLAN Membership Policy Service (VMPS), whereby devices connecting to the switched infrastructure can be dynamically assigned to a VLAN based on the device's Ethernet MAC address. This feature was an early incarnation of what is now provided with 802.1x features. Although it is more flexible than static MAC address filtering with the port security feature, the way of the future is clearly 802.1x.

In the early VMPS feature set, one or more Cisco switches acted as VMPS servers and maintained a database to map Ethernet MAC addresses to VLANs. Client switches would then talk to the VMPS server using the VMPS Query Protocol (VQP) to obtain the VLAN assignments when new devices appeared on a client switch port. The problem with this protocol is that all traffic is passed in clear text and can be easily forged.

You are advised to disable VMPS features and VQP protocol exchanges and to look to 802.1x features to satisfy dynamic VLAN assignment requirements. However, there might be some cases in which VMPS features are a stopgap feature to enable IP phone mobility while still restricting the auxiliary VLANs to the known MAC addresses of phones in your network. This isn't scalable for a large number of phones, and even in a small network the amount of work it takes to manage this feature might not be worth the minimal security value it provides. It stops casual users from adding new phones to your network, but it won't stop a determined hacker.

For more details on disabling VMPS and not using VQP, check the Configuring Dynamic Port VLAN Membership with VMPS documentation at the following link:

http://www.cisco.com/univercd/cc/td/doc/product/lan/cat6000/sw_8_1/confg_gd/vmps.htm

Layer 2: Stop Bridge Protocol Data Unit Spanning-Tree Attacks with BPDU Guard

For the sake of high availability, you should have redundant physical connections between Ethernet switches to ensure that you have a connectivity path in the event of link or switch failures. However, an issue arises in this physical topology in which Ethernet broadcast frames that go from switch A to switch B on one link might be forwarded back to switch A on a different link. The Ethernet frames just cycle around using up bandwidth, and eventually all the links are saturated with old broadcast traffic spinning around the loop. If the Ethernet topology contains any type of physical loop like this, whether it's between just two switches or between tens or hundreds of switches in a complex topology, broadcast storms can occur. Spanning Tree Protocol (STP) selectively shuts down links to ensure a loop-free topology so that broadcast storms don't occur.

One issue with spanning tree was that the calculations could take a long time (up to 40 seconds) to determine a loop-free topology, and the switch ports had to remain in a blocking state until this calculation was complete. As desktop PCs with fast CPUs became prevalent, a PC could complete its boot sequence and be ready to ask for an IP address via DHCP (or make a variety of other network queries) before the switch port was finished with the calculation. Users became frustrated with the perceived sluggish response, and a new feature called PortFast was created for the switches. The idea is to configure end-user ports (that is, ports on which client devices are connected) in PortFast mode so that they remain in the forwarding state when a link is established but continue to perform the spanning-tree calculation in case the port needs to be shut down to prevent loops. The only way a loop can occur in this scenario is if someone connects a hub or another switch (or potentially a PC with dual network interface cards [NICs]) to the jacks on which client machines normally connect. Hackers could also be mean enough to connect a crossover Ethernet cable between jacks going to the switch. In these scenarios, the PortFast command places the port in a blocking state and removes the blocking state when the loop is no longer detected.

The updated feature to STP support in Cisco switches is called STP PortFast BPDU Guard. BPDU stands for bridge protocol data unit, which is part of STP. STP PortFast BPDU Guard provides a global switch command to behave in a stricter manner for ports configured in PortFast mode. There's no reason for client devices to transmit BPDU frames as part of an STP communication with an Ethernet switch. If a switch does receive a BPDU frame from a client, it is likely to be a hacker trying to use STP to change the layer 2 switching topology. One reason a hacker would make such an attempt is to alter the topology such that the hacker's device is a root switch through which all the traffic in the switching topology must traverse. This elaborate ploy is yet another way that a hacker can attempt to gain access to the stream of bits from all the devices in the LAN—even devices that are connected to different Ethernet switches. Having access to this stream of bits, the hacker can then violate the confidentiality of the communication flows by viewing the bits. Then he or she can violate the integrity of the communication stream by altering bits or can simply drop the bits to reduce the availability of the communication stream to the intended recipients. You don't want to leave any jack going to cubicles open to these sorts of attacks, so BPDU Guard puts the port in a down error state. You can configure it such that an administrator must re-enable the port, or you can have it automatically come out of the lockout period after some length of time.

For more details on the IOS implementation of this feature, check the Configuring Spanning Tree PortFast, UplinkFast, and BackboneFast documentation at the following link:

> http://www.cisco.com/univercd/cc/td/doc/product/lan/cat6000/ios127xe/config/stp_enha.htm

The Configuring Spanning Tree PortFast, UplinkFast, BackboneFast, and Loop Guard documentation at the following link contains information for the CatOS implementation of this feature:

> http://www.cisco.com/univercd/cc/td/doc/product/lan/cat6000/sw_8_1/confg_gd/stp_enha.htm

Layer 2: Enable STP on Client Ports if They Behave Well

Although the BPDU Guard feature just described is thorough in stopping spanning-tree attacks, it's a bit heavy-handed in its approach. You get spanning-tree security by not allowing it at all on client ports.

Let's say you want to connect an IP phone in a redundant way to two different Ethernet switches. In this case, spanning tree is required to arbitrate potential loops flowing through the phone. With the BPDU Guard feature enabled on the switch side, homing the phone in this manner disables the switch ports to which the phone is connected, and the phone loses connectivity. The right approach in this case is to use the STP Root Guard feature.

Root Guard for STP makes sure you can run spanning tree on a port, as long as the device on the other end does not get delusions of grandeur and try to become the root node of the spanning tree. For example, you would never want to have a hacker box become the root of the spanning tree and force all traffic to switch through the hacker box at 10 Mbps rather than the 1000 Mbps between core Ethernet switches.

In general, if you need to balance the features, Root Guard is the moderate choice for securing spanning tree, but BPDU Guard provides tighter security if you know you don't need to support anything other than client PCs, workstations, and phones with a single-homed Ethernet connection.

For more details, check the Spanning-Tree Protocol Root Guard Enhancement document at the following link or by searching Cisco.com for "Spanning-Tree Protocol root guard enhancement":

http://www.cisco.com/warp/public/473/74.html

Layer 2: Configure VTP Transparent Mode to Disable VLAN Trunking Protocol

One way that hackers can attempt to disrupt traffic on a voice VLAN or gain unauthorized entry is to trick the switch into thinking that the VLAN configurations have changed. Cisco Catalyst switches use VTP to simplify the distribution of VLAN configurations from a central switch to other switches. The idea is that you can configure VLANs on a single switch and have this information propagated automatically to all the other switches in the organization. Although VTP can be a great feature to simplify management, there are several reasons why it's not a good idea from a security perspective.

One long-standing issue with VTP is that an accidental misconfiguration (let alone a malicious attack) can remove all the VLAN configurations in the Ethernet switching infrastructure, effectively implementing a complete network denial of service (DoS) attack. This is possible because all the switches in a VTP domain can be automatically updated with VLAN configuration changes you make at any switch in the domain (if the switch is acting as a VTP server). A "configuration table version" is associated with the change updates that are sent out via VTP, and every other switch that has a lower configuration version adopts what is presumed to be the latest and greatest configuration. This time-saving feature was intended to save you from replicating the configuration to every other switch in a large infrastructure. The problem with this feature is that if you make a number of configuration changes on a given switch such that it has the highest configuration version number and then you decide to delete all the VLANs, the configuration with deleted VLANs is propagated to all the other switches in the VTP domain. This actually has occurred accidentally in large deployments with thousands of users, where the configurations had to be rebuilt and pushed out to all the switches. If somebody wanted to maliciously exploit VTP, you would have your hands full! Of course, your exposure is only as great as the number of switch ports where VTP is listening for VLAN updates.

To mitigate threats associated with VTP, you can configure the switches so that they do not receive VTP updates by setting the switch ports to VTP transparent mode, as described in the Configuring VTP documentation at the following link:

http://www.cisco.com/univercd/cc/td/doc/product/lan/cat6000/sw_8_1/confg_gd/vtp.htm

Layer 2: Change the Default Native VLAN to a Value Other Than VLAN 1

Hackers can launch a variety of attacks against the layer 2 infrastructure when you use the default native VLAN for control protocol traffic. For example, hackers can perform a VLAN hopping attack in which they hide an Ethernet frame with an access-restricted VLAN tag inside another allowed VLAN tag. This is similar to dressing a wolf in sheep's clothing. The switch would normally block any Ethernet frames that are destined for the protected VLAN, but the switch examines only the outermost VLAN tag, which the hacker purposefully creates with a trusted VLAN ID. The switch strips this outermost VLAN tag. A different part of the Ethernet switch forwards the frame with the access-restricted VLAN tag (because the frame has already bypassed the ingress filters in the switch). The frame is delivered to a downstream switch en route to the restricted destination. For all this to work, the hacker needs to match the native VLAN on his or her machine to the native VLAN on the switch port.

Because the default VLAN 1 is common knowledge, it's an easy point of access if you don't protect it. For this and other reasons, you should not use VLAN 1 for *anything,* and you should change the native VLAN of all switch ports to a different VLAN ID. For more information on changing the VLAN association of switch ports, check the Configuring Ethernet VLAN Trunks documentation at the following link:

> http://www.cisco.com/univercd/cc/td/doc/product/lan/cat6000/sw_8_1/confg_gd/
> e_trunk.htm#14340

Don't forget that ports configured as an 802.1q trunk still have a native VLAN, and by default, that native VLAN is 1. There is a documented VLAN hopping attack whereby the intruder can come into that port on the native VLAN and hop to any other VLAN that the trunk is configured to carry. This attack requires that the intruder know the VLAN ID of the native VLAN, and 1 is a pretty good guess. The simple remedy is to assign the native VLAN of all your 802.1q trunks to some arbitrary VLAN that's not so easy to guess.

Layer 2: Disable Dynamic Trunk Protocol and Limit VLANs on Trunk Ports

Cisco Catalyst switches can automatically negotiate ISL or 802.1q VLAN trunks. This can be a problem if you have endpoints negotiating to be trunk peers. The problem with this capability is that the endpoint can have access to all VLANs configured that are allowed access on the port.

You need to enable 802.1q trunking on ports with phones attached even though this can be a security concern, but you can at least limit which VLANs are accessible on that switch port. On IP phones the feature that blocks 802.1q frames from PC ports mitigates this same threat when the attack is remotely triggered and the PC is still physically connected behind the phone. When the hacker has physical access, he or she can connect a PC directly to the switch port. However, the hacker can bypass layer 3 ACLs to gain access to any VLAN directly—that is, if the hacker's machine can negotiate as a trunk peer via Dynamic Trunk Protocol (DTP). For this reason, you should disable DTP negotiation on all switch ports where you can.

If you cannot disable DTP without breaking the normal trunk behavior required for IP phone functionality, you should at least limit which VLANs the trunk peer can access. For example, you can limit the client-facing ports to the client voice and client data VLANs. In no case should the VLANs on which CallManager and other servers are located be accessible directly from the ports where clients can connect.

TIP   Make sure that VLANs for CallManager and other servers are not accessible for trunking on switch ports where end users have access. This includes all switch ports in common and lobby areas, as well as normal user offices and cubicles.

For more information on configuring DTP and other trunk port behavior, check the "Configuring an ISL/802.1q Negotiating Trunk Port" section in the Configuring Ethernet VLAN Trunks documentation at the following link:

> http://www.cisco.com/univercd/cc/td/doc/product/lan/cat6000/sw_8_1/confg_gd/
> e_trunk.htm#1021308

Layer 2: Beware of 802.1q Tunneling

The basic idea of 802.1q tunneling is to enable nested VLAN tags to traverse a service provider network. The only other reason you would want this feature is if you run such a large network that 4096 VLANs are insufficient for your switched campus infrastructure. If you don't fall into either of these categories, you can skip the rest of this section and just leave the default setting of 802.1q tunneling as disabled. If you don't know the answer, your VLANS are probably sufficient.

If you do have a valid reason to use 802.1q tunneling, you need to be concerned about how hackers can exploit this feature. Hackers might transmit Ethernet frames with nested VLAN tags in an attempt to get the switch to peel off the outer VLAN tag and leave the inner VLAN tag matching the voice VLAN. This lets them send traffic into voice VLANs even if you have access lists that block traffic apparently to voice VLANs.

For more details about 802.1q tunneling, check the Configuring IEEE 802.1Q Tunneling and Layer 2 Protocol Tunneling documentation on Cisco.com at the following link:

> http://www.cisco.com/univercd/cc/td/doc/product/lan/cat6000/sw_8_1/confg_gd/
> dot1qtnl.htm

Layer 2: Beware of Broadcast Storm Control

This feature protects networks from bandwidth consumption following broadcast storms. Broadcast storms can result from STP misconfigurations, unidirectional transmission errors, or hardware errors in Ethernet interface cards. Of course, malicious users can also purposefully trigger broadcast storms.

By default, as of IOS 12.1(19)EW in Catalyst 4000 series switches, the broadcast storm control feature is disabled. It's probably safest for ports with IP phones to leave this command disabled. However, it is worth exploring the SNMP trap alerting behavior when it becomes available—probably by the time you read this.

If you choose to enable broadcast storm control, and you select the shutdown action in response to the detection of broadcast storms, you are exposing phones to a DoS attack. A malicious e-mail virus or other compromise of a PC downstream from the IP phone can trigger a stream of broadcast frames from the PC, which triggers a response from the switch to disable the port until administrative action reenables the port. This would be unfortunate because all phones would lose network connectivity. It would be better to rely on rate-limiting configurations and QoS policies to keep the voice traffic protected from data VLAN bandwidth surges. However, be careful that attempts to improve data VLAN performance, such as broadcast storm control, do not jeopardize the resiliency of IP phones.

For more information on broadcast storm control features, consult the Configuring Port-Based Traffic Control documentation at the following link:

http://www.cisco.com/univercd/cc/td/doc/product/lan/cat4000/12_1_19/config/bcastsup.htm

Ensure QoS Settings That Prioritize Voice Traffic

Voice-related QoS issues are not covered in this chapter, but there is good coverage in *Integrating Voice and Data Networks* by Scott Keagy (Cisco Press, ISBN/ASIN 1-57870-196-1). That being said, it's important that you enable QoS features that are voice-friendly on both the low-bandwidth edge links and the core backbone links in your network. The core-side configurations typically relate to congestion avoidance technologies such as Weighted Random Early Detection (WRED). The edge bandwidth-constrained interfaces typically use link fragment interleaving (LFI), traffic shaping and policing, and queuing technologies.

From a security perspective, you need these QoS features to protect bandwidth for voice applications even in the presence of DoS attacks. DoS attacks that consume bandwidth might starve other applications and significantly affect the performance of your data network, but they will not adversely affect your voice applications except in the rare case that the routers or switches themselves are incapacitated and unable to forward any traffic. Strictly speaking, this would not be the result of a bandwidth consumption attack, but rather an exploitation of a bug in the router or switch software.

For more information on QoS-related issues, you can also check the Cisco IOS Quality of Service Solutions Configuration Guide for release 12.3 at the following link:

> http://www.cisco.com/univercd/cc/td/doc/product/software/ios123/123cgcr/
> qos_ vcg.htm

Although it is certainly important to make sure that voice traffic receives preferential treatment through routers, switches, and firewalls, it's even more imperative that control traffic between routers and switches receive the highest-priority treatment. Prioritizing voice traffic won't help you if the routers don't know how to route the IP packets. You need to make sure that under critical load conditions the routers still can exchange routing protocol updates and other control messages that let the infrastructure maintain its core functionality.

Cisco IOS provides a number of keywords for use with access list configurations that make it easier for you to associate OSPF, EIGRP, RIP, IS-IS, or BGP traffic with a higher-priority traffic group. However, you don't want a batch of router updates to cause poor voice quality because voice packets are waiting in the same queue as high-priority routing updates.

The best way to manage this is to use the Low Latency Queuing (LLQ) feature. It ensures that Real-Time Transport Protocol (RTP) traffic gets the highest priority for moving to the front of queues while routing control traffic is placed in a class-based weighted fair queue (CB-WFQ) that receives a guaranteed amount of bandwidth.

For more details on configuring LLQ and CB-WFQ, check the *Cisco IOS Quality of Service Solutions Configuration Guide for Release 12.3* at the following link:

> http://www.cisco.com/univercd/cc/td/doc/product/software/ios123/123cgcr/
> qos_ vcg.htm

Restrict Access by Filtering Network Traffic

ACLs restrict what types of traffic are allowed through a certain control point in the network based on a series of **permit** and **deny** statements that classify traffic types and assign a desired behavior. ACLs can classify traffic based on various criteria, and they can be applied at different physical points in the network. For an overview of access lists, consult the Configuring IP Access Lists document at the following link or by searching Cisco.com for "configuring IP access lists":

> http://www.cisco.com/warp/public/707/confaccesslists.html

The following technologies are discussed in this section:

- VACLs and PACLs
- Network-Based Application Recognition

VLAN and Port Access Control Lists

VACLs operate at VLAN boundaries similar to the operation of ACLs at layer 3 interfaces. There are two main differences: VLAN boundaries include only layer 3 boundaries when routing between VLANs (in other words, VLAN interfaces), and VLAN boundaries operate directly at Ethernet ports where traffic enters the network and is admitted to the VLAN. So VACLs are like a combination of router interface ACLs and port-based ACLs.

Aside from the best-practice use of ACLs for protecting your data network (which is outside the scope of this book), the main points in your network where you should consider the use of access lists to protect the voice network include

- Port ACLs on Ethernet ports to client workstations and IP phones
- Between client voice and data VLANs in wiring closet switches
- Between voice and data VLANs used for back-office servers (which implies that you have voice services on separate VLANs in the first place)

TIP Although it is outside the scope of this book to discuss firewalls between the enterprise and the public Internet, some people still run networks without implementing firewalls. This is truly negligent in any scenario. It's just plain irresponsible to have a production voice network without an external firewall. If you have a production voice network exposed to the public Internet without a firewall, put down this book, deal with that urgent issue, and then pick up where you left off in this chapter.

Consider the traffic that needs to be passed on the voice VLAN. Phones send RTP (UDP) to each other and send TCP to CallManager or other servers, presumably on another subnet. A simple two-line VACL can mitigate the majority of layer 2 attacks against IP phones. The first line permits UDP in the range 16384 to 32768 between a phone and any other device. The second line permits TCP to the subnet where the servers are.

How about this ACL at the egress to your CallManager servers? You don't need many ports open for basic telephony operation: DHCP (unless served somewhere else), TFTP, SCCP, and S-SCCP. Do you need port 80? That depends. Remote administration is web-based, necessitating that port 80 be opened. An alternative is to use VNC, which runs on ports 5800 and 5900. XML services on IP phones also require port 80. Because most XML applications have to go to the Internet to get data, you're better off moving XML onto a dedicated server in your DMZ and not opening port 80 to your active call processing servers. If you'll run CAPF to load digital certificates into IP phones (described later in this chapter), you need port 3805. You need UDP (using the same ports just defined) if you have media streaming apps, such as Music on Hold, or media termination apps, such as audio conferencing. Just make sure your ACL uses the Established parameter so that the UDP can be initiated only from the server subnet. Other ports are needed for extended applications, such as IPMA, MLPP, Auto Attendant, and Extension Mobility. Several more ports are needed for clustering over the WAN. You're better off tunneling that traffic through an IPSec VPN instead of opening all those ports.

For other guidelines on specific ACL configuration details, such as which TCP/UDP ports should be permitted or denied at different points in the network, check for the most recent documentation updates on the SAFE Blueprint and Solution Reference Network Design websites at the following URLs:

- Cisco SAFE Blueprint—http://www.cisco.com/go/safe
- Solution Reference Network Designs—http://www.cisco.com/go/srnd

Network-Based Application Recognition

You can think of Network-Based Application Recognition (NBAR) as an ACL that makes permit/deny decisions based on deep packet inspection. In other words, traditional access lists on Cisco routers make permit/deny decisions based on header fields in layers 3 and 4, whereas NBAR makes permit/deny decisions based on any arbitrary content up through layer 7. As you might expect, there are performance trade-offs when using this feature, so you need to weigh the available router CPU against the incremental security benefits of using NBAR.

A detailed overview of NBAR functionality and implementation is provided in the Network-Based Application Recognition and Distributed Network-Based Application Recognition documentation on Cisco.com at the following link:

> http://www.cisco.com/univercd/cc/td/doc/product/software/ios122/122newft/122t/122t8/dtnbarad.htm

It is judicious to use NBAR to complement the normal layer 3/layer 4 ACLs at the edge of a data center (in other words, at the router boundary where CallManager and other voice servers are located) with an NBAR policy that provides HTTP web traffic filtering.

The idea is that you might need to leave HTTP port 80 open in your access lists to allow clients to reach certain web applications, but you want to have granularity to filter the types of web content users can access. A specific example relevant to CallManager is to distinguish web URLs that include CCMAdmin (http://*CallManagerIPAddress*/CCMAdmin/) from URLs that include CCMUser (http://*CallManagerIPAddress*/CCMUser/). You might need to give all users access to the Cisco CallManager User Options web page (also known as CCMUser pages because of the URL) so that they can administer their own speed dials, call forwarding behavior, and other XML application settings. However, there is no reason for all users to have access to the CallManager Administration web pages (also known as CCMAdmin pages because of the URL) to make CallManager system configuration changes. There is already a layer of security in which clients need to authenticate as an administrator to make changes to CCMAdmin pages on CallManager.

However, you can limit the number of users who can even attempt to authenticate by dropping packets destined for these URLs except from predetermined acceptable management subnets.

The following configuration example for a router running Cisco IOS lets a filter match and block URLs that contain "CCMAdmin":

```
class-map foo
match protocol http url CCMAdmin*
```

This example barely scratches the surface of the potential to use NBAR for advanced filtering in your network. You can create nearly arbitrary filters using regular expressions to match on web page URLs and any other type of protocol you care to characterize with Packet Description Language Modules (PDLMs). Cisco has predefined a number of PDLMs that are useful to limit nonstandard protocol applications in a network. You can download information on these from the Determining the Traffic Not Recognized by NBAR tech note at the following link, you also can search Cisco.com for "determining traffic not recognized by NBAR":

http://www.cisco.com/warp/public/105/custompdlms.html

You have numerous opportunities to use this feature in a security context. The focus here is on how to supplement security for CallManager and related voice applications.

TIP   If you are daring and brave enough to experiment with NBAR features to filter Skinny (SCCP) or other call signaling or control traffic used by CallManager, keep in mind that these filters might break when you turn on the encrypted signaling features in CallManager release 4.0 and later. If you are the type of person who can figure out how to beneficially use NBAR in these situations, it is likely that you already have considered this.

Layer 3: Simplify ACLs by Smartly Allocating IP Addresses

There are at least two reasons to have a consistent plan for allocating IP addresses in your network. The main reason is to simplify access list definitions to classify groups of clients, servers, routers, and so on. The other reason is simply to make it easier to recognize the nature of devices by making them recognizable just by the IP addresses assigned to them.

The most basic and common conventions include

- Assigning the highest or lowest IP address in a subnet to the router interface

- Assigning a small range of every subnet for hosts with static IP addresses, whereas the remainder is assigned to a DHCP scope

- Consistently assigning certain network devices such as print servers or other servers to the same IP address within a subnet

These conventions can be extended with conventions such as

- Assigning a contiguous block of IP addresses for switch admin interfaces and router loopback interfaces, with each router loopback interface using a 255.255.255.255 subnet mask

- If CallManager servers for a given cluster are all in separate IP subnets, setting the final octet of the IP address for each CallManager server to the same value

The benefit of following these practices is reaped when you create access lists or need to troubleshoot them later. For example, you can disable ICMP traffic from client subnets to any router or switch in your network with a single access list line such as **deny icmp any** $x.y.z$**.0 0.0.0.255**. If you have carefully assigned IP addresses, you can also make policies such as "Allow only H.323 traffic on my voice gateways from CallManager servers" with a single access list line. Such an entry might look like **permit tcp 1720 10.0.0.**x **0.255.255.0 host 10.**$y.z.w$, where x specifies the last octet consistently used for CallManager servers and y, z, and w refer to a specific voice gateway.

Other policy examples in which smart IP address allocation can simplify your life include the following:

- Allow SNMP queries only to CallManager servers from dedicated network management stations.

- Allow the SQL*net protocol only between CallManager servers.

- Allow Media Gateway Control Protocol (MGCP) protocol traffic only between CallManager servers and voice gateways.

You get the idea.

Layer 3: Authenticate Routing Protocol Traffic

Routing protocols provide an easy target for hackers to execute man-in-the-middle attacks and DoS attacks. Simply by generating routing protocol traffic and communicating with routers, hackers can trick the network into diverting all traffic toward their own devices. You can mitigate this risk by allowing routers to check the integrity and authenticity of every routing-related packet they receive.

For example, both the OSPF and IS-IS routing protocols support clear-text passwords embedded in routing protocol traffic. The problem with allowing clear-text passwords is that anyone who can sniff the routing protocol traffic (for example, by starting a routing protocol process on a client workstation) learns the passwords. OSPF and IS-IS can also use a slightly stronger protection method involving message digest authentication. This is basically a mathematical blender that mixes the actual data stream with a secret password to create a hash value that is appended to the routing protocol packet contents. The intended recipient of the traffic can then use the secret value he or she shares to recalculate the hash value and make sure it matches.

With this basic form of message digest authentication, there is still a risk that hackers can learn the secret key used to encrypt the routing protocol traffic because the secret key used in the hash is static and is subject to an offline brute-force attack. In other words, a hacker can conceivably capture a stream of encrypted routing protocol traffic and try to guess many permutations of possible passwords to decrypt the traffic. Whenever a given key generates an expected sequence of bits from the routing protocol update format (which is simple, because routing protocol traffic has well-known formats and headers), hackers know they've guessed the right key. They can then use it to participate in authenticated routing protocol updates.

The best forms of routing protocol authentication can periodically rotate keys to reduce the likelihood of guessing a static message digest key through a brute-force attack. Cisco implements several routing protocols with a key rotation concept, including EIGRP and RIP version 2.

For more details on how to implement the best forms of authentication available for each of the main IP routing protocols, check the following resources:

- Enabling RIPv2 Authentication section (not supported on RIPv1) in the Configuring Routing Information Protocol RIP Configuration Task List documentation— http://www.cisco.com/univercd/cc/td/doc/product/software/ios122/122cgcr/fipr_c/ ipcprt2/1cfrip.htm#1001083

- IS-IS HMAC-MD5 Authentication and Enhanced Clear Text Authentication documentation—http://www.cisco.com/univercd/cc/td/doc/product/software/ ios122s/122snwft/release/122s14/ftismd5.htm

- Sample Configuration for Authentication in OSPF document at http://www.cisco.com/warp/public/104/25.shtml, or search Cisco.com for "sample configuration for authentication in OSPF."

- Configuring EIGRP Authentication section in the Configuring Enhanced IGRP documentation—http://www.cisco.com/univercd/cc/td/doc/product/software/ios122/ 122cgcr/fipr_c/ipcprt2/1cfeigrp.htm#1001087

- BGP authentication examples in the eBGP Peer Group Example section of the Configuring BGP documentation—http://www.cisco.com/univercd/cc/td/doc/ product/software/ios122/122cgcr/fipr_c/ipcprt2/1cfbgp.htm#1003113

Layer 3: Authenticate HSRP and VRRP

Hot Standby Router Protocol (HSRP) and Virtual Router Redundancy Protocol (VRRP) are important tools to maintain high operational uptime in a networking environment. Cisco first created HSRP, and VRRP followed as a similar standard protocol to provide the same function. The weakness of HSRP is that it's used mainly without authentication, so a hacker can easily join an HSRP group and become the default gateway to which endpoints send their traffic. HSRP does have a weak form of authentication—namely, a shared secret that is displayed in router configurations in plain text and is sent in HSRP messages in clear text.

VRRP improved the security of HSRP by including an MD5 authentication mechanism. The contents of the message are hashed along with the shared secret into a secure hash fingerprint of the message in one of the message fields. Cisco currently implements the clear-text password option for VRRP but does not support the MD5 option.

The following documents provide additional information on HSRP and VRRP:

- Learn more about configuring HSRP in Cisco IOS in the Hot Standby Router Protocol Features and Functionality tech note at http://www.cisco.com/warp/public/619/hsrpguidetoc.html or by searching Cisco.com for "HSRP features and functionality."

- RFC 2338, Virtual Router Redundancy Protocol (VRRP)—http://www.ietf.org/rfc/rfc2338.txt

- Learn more about configuring VRRP in Cisco IOS software in the Virtual Router Redundancy Protocol Feature Overview documentation—http://www.cisco.com/univercd/cc/td/doc/product/software/ios120/120newft/120limit/120st/120st18/st_vrrpx.htm

Layer 3: V3PNs Let Voice Traffic Traverse an Untrusted IP Network

There was a time when you could configure IPSec tunnels in Cisco IOS, and you could configure voice QoS features such as Low Latency Queuing or LFI on WAN interfaces, but you could not use both of these feature sets together. In other words, you could not apply QoS features to tunnel or crypto interfaces. These feature sets now work together. They are referenced under the marketing name V3PN, or Voice and Video Virtual Private Networking.

If you want to replace a WAN composed of dedicated WAN circuits (for example, Frame Relay, ATM, or leased lines) with VPN connections traversing the public Internet, you need to consider a strategy for voice as well. The V3PN feature set, combined with an ISP that provides service-level agreements that meet the latency and jitter requirements of voice, can be just the strategy you need.

In a more general case, you can configure IPSec tunnels to transport voice across a variety of untrusted networks.

V3PNs assume that you trust the network near the source and destination (that is, from the traffic origin to the ingress tunnel point and from the egress tunnel point to the destination) but that you do not trust some middle part of the network. If you are trying to protect the end-to-end privacy of communications, and insider attacks are part of the threat model, V3PNs might not be the best choice. For voice traffic, preferred methods to encrypt signaling and media include TLS and SRTP.

For non-RTP voice traffic that requires UDP (such as MGCP signaling between CallManager and an IOS voice gateway), IPSec functionality might be important, but it might not be strictly V3PN. The queuing features can be enforced only for traffic leaving the IOS gateway. The CallManager side of the link has no special queuing behavior (aside from first-in-first-out [FIFO]). LFI is not supported on links between CallManager and IOS gateways.

Excellent resources for deploying voice- and video-enabled IPSec VPN solutions are available at the Voice and Video Enabled IPSec VPN Solution website at the following link, or you also can search Cisco.com for "voice and video enabled IPSec VPN solution":

> http://www.cisco.com/en/US/netsol/ns340/ns394/ns171/ns241/
> networking_solutions_package.html

In summary, this long section has enumerated many cases of security considerations that relate to the TCP/IP family of protocols and the routing and switching infrastructure that supports these protocols. The remedies presented in this section have largely centered on configuration issues with routers and switches, which are often outside the range of expertise of typical CallManager administrators. The people traditionally responsible for implementing these configurations (such as the network administrator or perhaps a security analyst) might not have not been diligent in applying these security best practices. And they might not have encountered problems resulting from these lapses. As a quick aside, this doesn't mean there were no security breaches! The point is, you cannot count on these folks to apply the security best practices unless you point out the potential impact to voice services. What follows is a shift to the features that are more likely to be directly in your control as part of administering CallManager.

Harden Access via IP Phones

Beginning with CallManager release 3.3(3), several new IP Phone security features can be configured:

- ARP cache behavior following GARPs
- 802.1q Ethernet frame forwarding behavior
- PC port mirroring behavior

Layer 2: Configure IP Phones to Ignore GARP

You reviewed the functionality of ARP requests, ARP replies, and GARPs earlier in this chapter in the section "Layer 2: Turn on Dynamic ARP Inspection." Any introductory-level book or website on TCP/IP provides a more detailed explanation of ARP.

The lack of authentication and integrity in ARP replies and GARP messages presents an easily exploited security hole for hackers. Hacker tools such as Ethereal and Ettercap take advantage of GARP to implement man-in-the-middle attacks on a LAN segment. They simply send out spoofed GARPs with the source Ethernet MAC address of whatever device they want to intercept traffic for. Following these spoofed GARP messages, all devices that receive the broadcast typically update their ARP caches with this faulty information, which essentially poisons the ARP cache of all devices on the LAN segment.

By default, Cisco IP Phones act on GARP messages they receive unless you specifically disable GARP. This means that ARP caches in Cisco IP Phones can be poisoned by spoofed GARPs that hacker tools send, unless you specifically protect them by disabling Gratuitous ARP in the Product Specific Configuration area of the Phone Configuration page in CallManager Administration, shown in Figure 6-1. In the unlikely event that you have a network application that requires GARP (for example, an ancient device that sends GARPs during a boot sequence and then never replies to ARP requests), you need to leave the default, which allows the phones to update their ARP cache when GARPs are received.

Figure 6-1   *Product-Specific Configuration Area for Cisco IP Phone Model 7960*

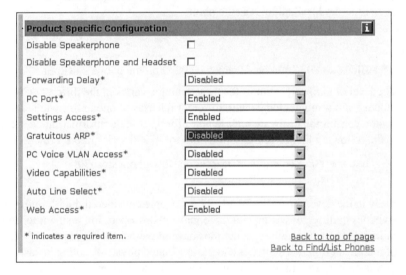

Product Specific Configuration		ℹ️
Disable Speakerphone	☐	
Disable Speakerphone and Headset	☐	
Forwarding Delay*	Disabled ▼	
PC Port*	Enabled ▼	
Settings Access*	Enabled ▼	
Gratuitous ARP*	Disabled ▼	
PC Voice VLAN Access*	Disabled ▼	
Video Capabilities*	Disabled ▼	
Auto Line Select*	Disabled ▼	
Web Access*	Enabled ▼	

* indicates a required item.   Back to top of page
                                                 Back to Find/List Phones

TIP   Use the Bulk Administration Tool (BAT) to bulk-update the Gratuitous ARP field on some or all phones. (**Configure > Phones > Update Phones**. Search for all or some phones and then update the **Gratuitous ARP** field.)

For more details on this feature, consult the section "Using the Gratuitous ARP Feature" in the CallManager 3.3(3) Release Notes at the following link:

http://www.cisco.com/en/US/products/hw/phones/ps379/
prod_release_note 09186a008019214f.html#94575

Layer 2: Drop 802.1q Frames Received via the PC Port on IP Phones

One potential point of entry into voice VLANs is through the PC port on IP phones. If hackers learn the voice VLAN ID and send 802.1q-tagged Ethernet frames using this VLAN ID, they can send traffic directly into the voice VLAN and bypass the access lists that protect voice VLANs from data client VLANs. Having 802.1x support on voice VLANs would mitigate this threat in general, but the PC port behind IP phones would still be a vulnerability. This is because downstream hacker machines would still be able to spoof the IP phone's source Ethernet MAC address, and the wiring closet switch would have no way of determining whether the Ethernet frames are actually from the IP phone or from a downstream hacker machine.

In theory, there are several potential fixes for this security exposure:

- Block Ethernet frames inbound on the phone's PC port that have the same source Ethernet MAC address as the phone

- Block 802.1q tagged frames inbound on the phone's PC port that use the voice VLAN ID

- Block all 802.1q tagged frames inbound on the phone's PC port

The level of hardware support for these features varies in the different Cisco IP Phone models, and it might change with different releases of phone firmware. Therefore, you should consult the firmware release notes for up-to-date information on these features. Go to the following link or search Cisco.com for "7900 series phones release notes":

http://www.cisco.com/en/US/products/hw/phones/ps379/
prod_release_notes_ list.html

Early in the development of IP telephony, people considered dual-homing IP phones to switches in different wiring closets to make phone operation resilient to Ethernet switch failures. In practice, few organizations have implemented this strategy because of the cost of redundant Ethernet switches and the associated physical cabling infrastructure. A legacy of this early design requirement is that all Ethernet frames to or from the phone on the network port were mirrored out the PC port so that it could be used as a redundant network port.

The security threat here is that someone can connect a PC with a sniffer application behind the phone and capture all the traffic. The incremental privacy risk for telephone conversations is minimal because this exposure enables only recording of or listening to conversations that involve the local telephone. However, the bigger risk is having all network transactions, including the Skinny protocol and other traffic, vulnerable to being captured and analyzed. In reality, this risk is already a given and is being exploited because a hacker can take a CallManager system and analyze the packets in a lab environment without needing to learn the protocols in your production environment.

As of CallManager 3.3(3), phone firmware images have had this port mirroring behavior enabled by default. It can be configured by CallManager (in the PC Voice VLAN Access field on the Phone Configuration page in CallManager Administration).

Harden CallManager and Voice Application Servers

The following sections describe the facets of hardening a CallManager server and related voice application servers:

- Cisco default OS hardening
- OS, BIOS, and SQL patch maintenance
- Reactive, signature-based virus/worm recognition and defenses
- Proactive attack prevention with Cisco Security Agent

Cisco-Provided OS Hardening

Cisco hardens the Windows 2000 operating system, just as an IT InfoSec organization would, using input from a variety of sources, including the National Security Agency guidelines for hardening the Windows 2000 OS (http://www.nsa.gov/snac/index.html).

To get a cumulative and detailed listing of specific tasks that Cisco performs as part of the OS customization, read the release notes associated with each of the OS upgrades and patches at the following link:

> http://www.cisco.com/cgi-bin/tablebuild.pl/cmva-3des

Maintain OS, SQL, and BIOS Security Patches and Updates

You must periodically maintain your servers by running various software patches and upgrades to gain the benefit of bug fixes that resolve security vulnerabilities. Consult the Cisco IP Telephony Operating System, SQL Server, and Security Updates at the following link:

> http://www.cisco.com/univercd/cc/td/doc/product/voice/c_callmg/osbios.htm

Download software updates from the Voice Software Center at the following link:

> http://www.cisco.com/kobayashi/sw-center/sw-voice.shtml

Subscribe to the CallManager Notification Tool to Be Advised of New Fixes, OS Updates, and Product Patches

Cisco provides automatic notification of new fixes, OS updates, and patches for CallManager and related components such as Attendant Console, IP Manager Assistant (IPMA), and BAT. To subscribe, send a blank e-mail to majordomo@cisco.com. The return address on your e-mail is the address that will be subscribed to the Tool alias. In the body of the message, enter the single line **subscribe customer-ccm-announce**. Do not place this text in the Subject line, and do not enter any other text in the body. Be sure to delete any automated text such as a signature. Figure 6-2 shows your subscribe message.

Figure 6-2   *Subscribing to the* **customer-ccm-announce** *Alias*

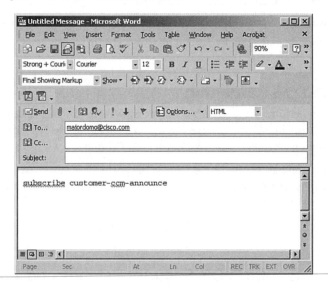

When you receive the confirmation e-mail to subscribe to **customer-ccm-announce**, open it and click **Reply**. In your reply e-mail, copy the authorization line and paste it so that it appears as the first line in the body of your confirmation e-mail. Click **Send**, and you're done. Figure 6-3 shows your confirmation message.

For more information, see the instructions at the following link:

http://www.cisco.com/warp/public/779/largeent/software_patch.html

Verify Security Patch Status with Microsoft Baseline Security Analyzer

If you want to verify that you have updated all the patches that are appropriate for your servers, you can use the Microsoft Baseline Security Analyzer (MBSA) tool. Note that this tool supersedes the HFNetChk.exe tool, with which you might be familiar.

Figure 6-3   *Confirming Your Subscription*

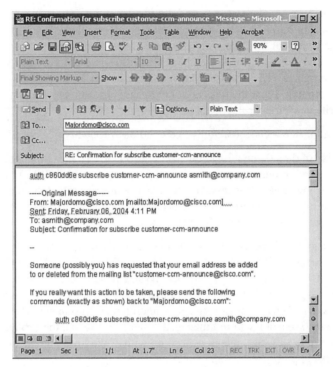

The MBSA tool reports missing patches, although some patches are false warnings if you disable the services associated with them. However, in case you or your staff accidentally enable a service that has not been patched and thereby create a vulnerability, it's a good idea to maintain all the patches as part of the periodic OS upgrades. The Readme file for the associated OS upgrade provides additional information on the use of the MBSA tool in conjunction with Cisco voice applications.

This information will most likely be available in more recent service pack updates for the Windows operating system used in conjunction with your voice application servers. The general URL for downloading the CallManager and Voice Apps Crypto Software service packs and other updates is at the following link, and you need a Cisco website login ID to access these resources:

http://www.cisco.com/cgi-bin/tablebuild.pl/cmva-3des

TIP   As an independent method of validating the security of your CallManager system, you can use various security scanner tools to check for insecure TCP/UDP port activity on the servers. Nessus is one such recommended tool.

Use McAfee or Norton/Symantec Virus Protection

To provide a degree of protection from viruses and worms that can infiltrate your organization and bypass existing containment mechanisms, it's a good idea to run antivirus software on your CallManager servers and related voice application servers. For the latest releases of Norton/Symantec and McAfee software that have been validated with Cisco voice products, check the CallManager Security and Virus Protection Guides at the following link. Click the link for your release (for example, 4.0), and then click the link to Security and Virus Protection.

http://www.cisco.com/univercd/cc/td/doc/product/voice/c_callmg/

The risk of directly enabling your voice servers to get antivirus signature updates downloaded through the Internet is that you are opening TCP/UDP ports for these servers to have direct Internet access. You can balance this risk of potential downtime in your voice network against the certainty of effort to manually maintain these patches through an intermediate server that has Internet access.

Be sure to disable heuristic scanning in your antivirus software, or it might block legitimate access to the CallManager Administration (CCMAdmin) or Cisco CallManager User Options (CCMUser) web pages. Also, be sure to schedule file scans to occur during times of low usage, such as the middle of the night because these processes consume system resources and cause performance degradation on CallManager. If you want your antivirus software to function within a managed system, ensure that the service account under which the antivirus software runs is an account with a Windows domain and that it has access to the other appropriate servers in your network.

Use Cisco Security Agent for Proactive Attack Prevention

Although it is great to recognize known virus signatures and to be able to block these types of attacks, a primary challenge today is that new viruses and worms are constantly emerging. It is a tough administrative chore to stay updated with virus signature definition files. In addition, viruses and worms can propagate so fast that your machines might become infected before you receive a page from a security alert service.

The strategic direction for combating viruses and worms is not toward reactive, signature-based mechanisms that recognize the specific incarnation or variation of malicious code. Rather, the solution is a proactive mechanism whereby systems are measured for a known baseline behavior, and then anomalous behavior is flagged as a likely security violation. These behavior characteristics can be measured in terms of which system files are accessed, which TCP/UDP ports are used, which Windows Registry keys are modified, and so on.

Cisco Security Agent (CSA) was created with this philosophy in mind—which highlights an important point about using CSA and similar products. It is not enough to get a generic, straight-out-of-the-box implementation that is a security cure-all for all your application servers. You need to have CSA and any other anomaly-detection software suites custom-tailored for the application servers or clients on which they reside. The challenge is that every software release or utility you add to a server changes the server's baseline behavior. So when you plan for rolling out Cisco Security Agent on your voice servers (which you should!), pay attention to how it has been customized (if at all).

Cisco has greatly simplified the process of rolling out CSA for many voice application servers by creating customized profiles based on the server's intended use (such as CallManager server, Unity server, and so on). The nice thing for you about these customized profiles is that Cisco has also tested all the third-party supported utilities that you want to run in the real world. Make sure that you are using only Cisco-approved utilities to get the most mileage out of this security testing. Of course, you can also create your own customized profiles from scratch using the Cisco Security Agent, but you are on your own in terms of protection assurance.

For more information on the customized profiles that Cisco provides in conjunction with Cisco Security Agent, consult the Cisco Security Agent documentation at the following link:

> http://www.cisco.com/univercd/cc/td/doc/product/voice/c_callmg/sec_vir/csa/

For more general background on the Cisco Security Agent product and other applications, check out the CiscoWorks Management Center for Cisco Security Agents at the following link, or search Cisco.com for "CiscoWorks Management Center for Cisco security agents":

> http://www.cisco.com/en/US/products/sw/cscowork/ps5212/index.html

Use CiscoWorks VPN/Security Management Solution to Manage Your Cisco Security Agent

The CiscoWorks VPN/Security Management Solution (VMS) for Cisco Security Agents enables central administration of CSA agents, including updates to CSA policies. For more information on CSA management, check the following link, or search Cisco.com for "CiscoWorks VPN/Security Management Solution":

> http://www.cisco.com/en/US/products/sw/cscowork/ps5212/index.html

A customized security policy for Cisco Security Agent has been available for CallManager since release 3.3(3). The release that ships with CallManager is a *headless agent*, which means that it performs its functions without external management interaction. This mode of operation is fine in small deployments if you have no interest in customizing the security functions, but if you want to update policies across a large number of servers or otherwise maintain centralized logging to enable some form of event correlation, you need a centralized management station that interacts with the CSAs distributed on each server.

The Cisco VMS manages the CSAs on CallManager and other servers, as well as the Network IDS appliances and other Cisco security products. For more information on configuring the CSA on CallManager to be managed by a VMS station, consult the Cisco CallManager Security and Virus Protection Guides at the following link:

http://www.cisco.com/univercd/cc/td/doc/product/voice/c_callmg/sec_vir/

Secure Remote Administration of CallManager

CallManager and related voice applications currently do not support secure HTTP or Secure Virtual Network Computing (VNC) for remote administration of CallManager Administration (CCMAdmin) web pages. What this means is that your administrator login credentials are passed across the network in clear text when you log in to a CallManager web page. This is also true of usernames and passwords for Cisco CallManager User Options (CCMUser) web pages. To avoid the risk of a hacker learning your administrator credentials and making arbitrary configuration changes to your whole voice system, you are advised to create network filters that block access to CCMAdmin web pages and administer CallManager only from a local interface.

Even if secure HTTP is supported by CallManager and other voice applications, you still need a method to securely administer file system changes, log viewing, utility installations, and myriad other tasks performed through the windows GUI console that cannot be done through CCMAdmin or other web pages.

If you require remote administration facilities, you can use IPSec VPN to a secure out-of-band network, in which an IP-based keyboard-video-mouse (KVM) switch provides remote access to voice servers. The IP-based KVM solution is an elegant solution that has zero impact on the voice network and thus requires no official testing or sanction by Cisco.

VNC over Secure Shell (SSH)

As of February 2004, the VNC over SSH solution had not been tested by Cisco and was not officially supported. However, you can always remove this setup in the process of obtaining help from the Cisco TAC.

CallManager officially supports VNC for remote administration. Official documentation for VNC is currently maintained at the RealVNC website at http://www.realvnc.com/.

You need to secure the normal VNC operation by tunneling it over SSH, a process that is summarized here at a high level. As a prerequisite, you need to install an SSH client on your administrator workstations that run the VNC client. You also need to install an SSH server on your machines that run the VNC server (this part is not officially supported by Cisco). You then build an SSH tunnel between the clients and servers in a manner that is conceptually similar to building IP tunnel interfaces on Cisco routers. On the client side, you configure all traffic normally bound for a remote VNC server (TCP port 5900 by default) to be redirected to a local loopback interface with a dummy port number. This is the ingress to the SSH tunnel. The egress point is defined by the original IP address destination that you use in the VNC configuration. At the server side, you make a similar configuration that accepts traffic from localhost (the loopback address 127.0.0.1) and maps the dummy TCP port to the real TCP port where the VNC application listens. In this scenario, both the VNC client and VNC server are unaware of the SSH tunnel, but you get the security benefits of the SSH tunnel for the application anyway. An excellent guide for setting up this functionality is available at http://www.shebeen.com/vnc_ssh/.

You can also use any other secure server to act as a bastion host sitting between the unsecured enterprise network (where the client workstations are attached) and a more trusted and isolated management network. In this scenario, clients forward SSH-tunneled traffic to the bastion host, which then forwards the clear-channel traffic within the trusted management network. This technique is slightly messier, involves extra servers, and has more opportunities for hackers to see the clear-channel part of the communication, so it's not the recommended approach. If you do decide to pursue this method (which is also fine), information is available in the VNC archive pages at the following link:

http://www.uk.research.att.com/archive/vnc/sshvnc.html

If you are having difficulty understanding how SSH tunneling works, check the link to the VNC archive information, which has an alternative description.

Use IPSec VPN to Reach an IP-Based KVM Switch

Using IPSec VPN to reach an IP-based KVM switch is purely a system integration effort. It doesn't affect the voice network in any way. As far as CallManager or other voice servers are concerned, they are sending and receiving information on the normal physical interfaces for keyboard, video, and mouse. However, the IP-based KVM switch can relay the information to a remote location. The novel approach here is to place the KVM switch in an isolated and protected part of the network that can be accessed only through an IPSec VPN, or maybe via an SSH tunnel as described in the preceding section.

Describing a full implementation of IPSec VPNs or SSH tunnels is outside the scope of this book. Your local InfoSec guru or security consultant can help you without your needing to understand anything about the particulars of the voice network.

Compartmentalize Services on Different Servers in Large Deployments

It is important to focus on preventing attacks to a server, but it is also important to consider how to handle situations when an attack is successful. Submarines have watertight chambers that can be isolated when damaged to prevent damage to adjacent compartments. The idea is to contain a security breach to the area that has been compromised and to allow the rest of the system to function as normally as possible. For CallManager systems, each service component is like a separate submarine chamber. You can make the overall system more resilient by distributing the service components in separate submarine chambers. In the event of an auxiliary service failure that can potentially cause a server crash, whether it relates to a system glitch or a malicious attack, you want to have this service on a machine separate from the call-processing function so that basic call routing continues to function. Candidates for offloading include DHCP, TFTP, XML, Music on Hold, and software conferencing. As noted earlier, XML especially should be offloaded to its own server and located in the DMZ because most XML apps routinely access the Internet for up-to-date information. You don't want your active call processors to be accessible from the Internet.

Spreading services across many different servers is appropriate if you have a deployment that is large enough to allow you to amortize the cost of additional servers across a large number of users. Otherwise, the cost of implementing this suggestion is potentially greater than the losses you might incur as a result of system downtime.

Turn off IIS on Subscribers

80 percent of the attacks against Windows are against IIS, which is the parent process for WWW, SMTP, and FTP. If all CallManager administration is done on the Publisher, as Cisco recommends, IIS can be turned off on all the subscribers. IIS must be available during upgrades. If IIS is set to Disabled, you must remember to set it back to Enabled when you do upgrades. If IIS is set to Manual/Stopped, the installer can start it during the upgrade and set it back to Stopped when it's finished. This easy task closes the door on four out of five attacks against your active call processors.

CallManager Account/Password Policies

The CallManager installation process assumes a "black-box" mentality in which the installer is prompted to provide only minimal configuration and password information to complete the installation process. The system must also be able to function without being joined to a Windows NT or Windows 2000 Active Directory domain. Therefore, all user accounts are created on the local computer regardless of its membership role in a domain. Each server in the CallManager cluster must be able to communicate (authenticate) with the Publisher. This is accomplished by using the Windows NT network authentication protocol, NT LAN Manager (NTLM), combined with identical system service accounts (local user accounts) on each system and stored in the local User Accounts Database (UAD) with identical passwords.

The installer is prompted for three passwords during a new installation of the CallManager server:

- Local administrator
- LDAP Directory Manager
- Microsoft SQL system administrator (sa) account

The installer also is prompted for a private password phrase during a new installation of the CallManager server. This phrase is an alphanumeric string of 1 to 15 characters.

At the present time, CallManager must be installed or updated using the local administrator account. Windows domain and/or local NT user accounts with Administrator privileges are not supported.

The local administrator password must be identical for every CallManager server in the cluster. During the software installation and upgrade process, this password is verified locally. Within a Subscriber installation, the password is also verified with the Publisher before the installation is allowed to proceed. If you need to change the local administrator password, you must perform this task on all systems in the cluster. Otherwise, problems will occur during the next software installation. Maintenance of the local administrator password should be performed via the standard Microsoft Windows 2000 Server Computer Management interfaces.

You are prompted for the LDAP Directory Manager password only during a fresh installation of a CallManager system—for both the Publisher and the Subscriber. During a software upgrade, you are not prompted for this password on either the Publisher or the Subscriber. If you need to change the Directory Manager password, use the CCM Password Changer utility, located at C:\DCDSRVR\BIN\CCMPWDChanger.exe. Launch the Password Changer utility from the Publisher server only. For the latest information about this utility and its function, refer to the appropriate documentation for the particular release of the CallManager you are using.

The Microsoft SQL sa account is a built-in account in the SQL system and cannot be removed. Just like the LDAP Directory Manager password, you are prompted for this password only during a fresh installation of a CallManager system, on both the Publisher and the Subscriber. You are not prompted for this password during a software upgrade. In CallManager release 4.0 and later, CallManager no longer uses this account. However, you should still input the same passwords for all systems in the cluster for legacy applications that might still need to access the databases via this account. Maintenance of this password should be performed via Microsoft SQL Server Enterprise Manager.

CallManager and its subcomponents are run as local NT system services of the operating system (OS). In CallManager release 4.0, a significant effort was undertaken to move from SQL mixed-mode authentication to NT authentication. The move to NT authentication enabled the removal of Named Pipes compatibility within the OS and closed several known potential security breach points in the system.

During the CallManager installation process, the passwords for these service accounts are automatically generated by a 128-bit algorithm based on the 1-to-15-character alphanumeric private password phrase as the seed and the NT service account as the constant. The passwords generated comply with the Windows NT complex password requirements in that they have at least 15 characters and contain lowercase and uppercase letters, numbers, and symbols (see the following sidebar). In the initial phase of the

CallManager installation, the installation process verifies that the internal service account and password between the Subscriber and Publisher are identical by connecting to the Publisher with these internal NT service account and password combinations. If the connection fails because the password is not in sync, the installation displays an error message and prompts you for the "correct" private password phrase.

NOTE

The Windows password guidelines can be found at http://www.microsoft.com/ntworkstation/technicalresources/PWDguidelines.asp.

- English uppercase letters (A, B, C, ... Z)
- English lowercase letters (a, b, c, ... z)
- Westernized Arabic numerals (0, 1, 2, ... 9)
- Nonalphanumeric "special characters" such as punctuation symbols ({}[],.<>;:'"?/|\`~!@#$%^&*()_-+=)

Guess Internal System Passwords? Not Likely!

The internal account passwords are auto-generated because there is no reason for someone to know the passwords and use them to emulate interprocess communication. Nobody, including you, sees any of these passwords unless he or she successfully guesses one. The odds against guessing one of these passwords are worse than 1 in 87 octillion (8.7354 * 1028). To put this in terms of time for a brute-force attack, if you could try 100 guesses per second, it would take you more than 100 quadrillion centuries. If you had every computer on the Internet making one million guesses per second, it would still take more than 13 centuries to guess. In other words, the weak link in the security chain is more likely to be that you chose a local administrator password that is easier to guess.

Even so, some information security personnel prefer to rotate these passwords periodically to comply with site security policies. One good reason is that the randomness of the pseudorandom algorithm, which is a key presumption in this password strength discussion, could someday be discovered to be not so random—and the time-to-crack estimates shrink to a matter of days or worse. To accommodate this possibility and feature requirement, Cisco provides the CallManager Admin utility. It is of little consequence, but it's interesting to note that the CallManager Admin utility has actually reduced the effective level of security for the internal system accounts to be dependent on the local administrator account protection. This is a moot point because protecting the internal system account passwords is worthless if the administrator account is compromised. A well-chosen administrator account password is just as difficult to guess as the internal account passwords.

The following are the system-generated local system accounts used to run as NT system services. These accounts do not have rights to log on locally or to interact with the desktop. They only have the right to run as a service:

- CCMServiceRW
- CCMService
- CCMCDR
- CCMUser
- SQLSvc

Unfortunately, because of the "black-box" paradigm in which the installation process was designed, adding a system to the cluster or recovering a system in the cluster after the local system account passwords have been manually changed presents a huge administration and troubleshooting problem (see the following warning). Therefore, an Admin utility is provided in C:\Program Files\Cisco\Bin\AdminUtility.exe. The Admin utility can be executed only from the Publisher. This utility allows you to maintain and synchronize these independent local system accounts, their passwords, and the NT services that comprise CallManager in case the system administrator wants to change these passwords. For the latest information about the Admin utility and its function, refer to the appropriate documentation for the CallManager release you are using.

WARNING   Although it is technically possible for you to discover all the NT services, COM, and other interdependencies necessary to change the passwords for these accounts manually, missing a single component can render CallManager partially or completely inoperable. For this reason, if you must change these passwords to comply with security policies in your organization, you have to use the Admin utility, as just described.

Secure Endpoint Provisioning

The process of provisioning endpoints for operation in a trusted secure network includes securely updating phone firmware images (loads) and securely enrolling endpoints into the trust domain (including the creation of locally validated X.509v3 phone certificates). These topics are considered in the following sections.

TIP   If you want to skip the theory and go straight to the configuration controls to implement device security, you can set the Device Security Mode and Cluster Security Mode enterprise parameters in CallManager Administration (**System > Enterprise Parameters**). Read the online help text for these parameters for more information.

The phones also allow you to override the security settings on a per-device basis in the Phone Configuration page in CallManager Administration (**Device > Phone**).

Endpoint Image Authentication

Beginning with the service release of CallManager 3.3(3), Cisco IP Phones authenticate newly downloaded firmware images (also known as *firmware loads*) before running them. These firmware load names begin with P00305 or P00405. The basic mechanism is that the current firmware image has embedded within it a verification key that can be used to validate the next firmware image that can overwrite the current image. One implication is that after you have upgraded to the first secure firmware image, you can't readily go back to an older image. If backward compatibility were preserved, the whole point of securely signing firmware images would be defeated. Hackers could just downgrade the firmware image to an old version that doesn't support image authentication and then load whatever nasty firmware images they create.

Each Cisco IP Phone model has a unique signature. Thanks to that, a phone will only accept the firmware image intended for it. Prior to signed images it was possible to load the firmware for the wrong model into a phone with the net effect of rendering it useless.

Cisco is committed to fixing bugs or defects associated with new secure firmware images, so you shouldn't find yourself in the awkward position of needing to downgrade to a firmware image that predates authentication to resolve a problem you are experiencing.

For more details on Cisco IP Phone firmware image authentication, check the Image Authentication and Signed Binary Files section of the release notes for Cisco IP Phone 7960, 7940, and 7910 Series Firmware Releases P00305000300 and P00405000300 document at the following link:

> http://www.cisco.com/univercd/cc/td/doc/product/voice/c_ipphon/english/ipp7960/relnotes/50_300rn.htm#1051808

Secure Enrollment of Endpoints

When you closely examine the protocols and technologies that underlie an IP communications system, perhaps the most complex and challenging concept is the secure enrollment of endpoints when physical security cannot be assumed. This includes migration of existing devices from an insecure mode to a secure mode, or bringing new IP phones, analog gateways such as the VG-248, or ATA devices to your network in common areas other than a locked wiring closet or data center. The basic conflict is between the need for a scalable and easy-to-administer process for enrolling a large number of endpoints and the need to perform this function in a secure way through an untrusted physical environment with virtually no pre-established trust credentials on which to build cryptographic operations. In other words, how do you start to trust an endpoint to be on your network when you first need to exchange information with it to establish this trust, and these very exchanges are subject to hack attempts? After you have established trust with an endpoint, it is relatively easy to apply cryptographic techniques to maintain secure communications, but initiating the trust, getting the cryptographic credentials into the device in the first place, is a nontrivial challenge.

The basic functions for securely enrolling Cisco IP Phones into a CallManager system are

- Generate a unique public/private key pair in each phone.

- Generate a locally significant X.509v3 certificate for each phone, in which the phone's public key is bound to the phone's identity (Ethernet MAC address). In addition, the phone's public key must be attested to by a locally significant certification authority (CA) acting as a trusted third party (either a local CA server or an outsourced service such as VeriSign or Entrust).

- Establish a site-wide list of certificates for trusted servers with which phones and servers can communicate. This is known as a Certificate Trust List (CTL).

- Get the CTL into each phone to enable future cryptographic operations.

Generate Unique Public/Private Key Pairs in Phones

The process of generating public/private key pairs in Cisco IP Phones is not unusual. A pseudorandom number generator is used as part of a Rivest Shamir Adelman (RSA) algorithm to generate 1024-bit or 2048-bit binary number sequences. This creation process is triggered in response to a request from the Certificate Authority Proxy Function (CAPF) server element that coresides on CallManager. For more information about the CAPF, consult the Cisco CallManager Security and Virus Protection Guides at the following link:

http://www.cisco.com/univercd/cc/td/doc/product/voice/c_callmg/sec_vir/index.htm

To get the Cisco IP Phone Authentication and Encryption for Cisco CallManager 4.0(1) documentation go to the following link:

http://www.cisco.com/univercd/cc/td/doc/product/voice/c_callmg/4_0/sec_vir/ae/auth_enc/index.htm

Certificates in Cisco IP Phones

An X.509v3 digital certificate is a document that a device shares with other devices on the network to submit its trusted identity. The certificate has several data elements, including a certificate ID, the device's public key, the issuing authority (CA), and a signature of the certificate from that authority. Among other things, the certificate is the device's way to share its public key in such a way that the recipient knows that it can trust it because it holds the certificate of the signing authority and can validate the signature on the certificate.

Certificates can get into Cisco IP Phones in one of two ways: in Cisco manufacturing or locally by the customer.

Phones with Manufacturing Installed Certificates

Some phones have certificates installed by Cisco in nonvolatile, nonerasable memory during installation. These are called Manufacturing Installed Certificates (MICs). These phones are capable of secure enrollment with a trusted CallManager upon delivery from Cisco. However, it is strongly recommended that customers supercede these certificates with their own certificates of local consequence, as described in the next section.

Generate Locally Significant Certificates in Phones

Other phones that don't have certificates installed by Cisco can use a customer-installed certificate, called a Locally Significant Certificate (LSC).

NOTE   Currently, the Cisco 7970 supports only MIC certificates, and the 7940 and 7960 support only LSC certificates. In the future, there will be a cross-pollination in which all three phone models will support both types of certificates. None of Cisco's low-end phones support either type of certificate.

Generating the locally significant certificates is the technical crux of the enrollment process. The tricky part is establishing a trust relationship between the phone and the CA while the local certificate is being generated.

In brief, you have several options:

- Accept some risk and make a leap of faith to mass-migrate all endpoints to a secure mode (in other words, an amnesty program for enrolling endpoints).

- Plan additional resources for a manually intensive and more secure enrollment process.

- Have initial trust in the Cisco manufacturing process, and achieve the best of both alternatives with a compromise solution.

On the more-secure-but-administratively-painful end of the spectrum, you can establish trust between the phones and the CA out of band from the untrusted physical environment, such as through a direct local interface on the phone. This direct-entry mechanism bypasses the untrusted network and removes the anonymity on which a hacker relies to intervene in the process. This means that an administrator walks up to every single phone and enters a sequence of digits provided out of band by CAPF. At best, this is a horribly tedious (albeit secure) process. The other end of the spectrum is to make a leap of faith (quite possibly unfounded) that no hackers are on the network, and a centralized automated process pushes out new certificates to all the phones and maybe a few hackers too. The obvious weakness of this approach, for all its convenience, is that you can easily give keys to the same entities you are trying to keep out of your network.

You can implement the compromise strategy of using a secure depot in which you feel comfortable that hackers are not present. In other words, you enroll new phones in a locked-room staging area in which administrators bring many phones at a time to be enrolled. Here, you are making a qualified leap of faith that no hackers are present between the entity that pushes out new certificates (CallManager) and the entities that receive the new certificates (IP phones) in the secure depot. As of CallManager 4.0, the qualified leap of faith method is not totally automated because an administrator must press the # key on each phone as part of the process. This is somewhat tedious, but it is significantly easier than finding a number sequence and carefully entering it in the phone display. You simply walk by a row of phones and press the # key on each one.

The process for enrolling new phones is included in the Cisco IP Phone Administration Guide for Cisco CallManager, available at the following link:

> http://www.cisco.com/univercd/cc/td/doc/product/voice/c_ipphon/english/ipp7960/admin/

Additional background information and server-side processes are included in the Cisco CallManager 4.0 Administration and Features and Services Guide at the following link:

> http://www.cisco.com/univercd/cc/td/doc/product/voice/c_callmg/

If you are not already familiar with public-key cryptography and X.509v3 terminology, and you want to understand more than what is required to blindly follow the list of steps provided in the administrator guides, you should spend some time becoming familiar with the new concepts. Detailed coverage of these concepts is beyond the scope of this book, but you can get started with the public-key infrastructure (PKI) overview provided by Microsoft at the following link:

> http://www.microsoft.com/windows2000/techinfo/howitworks/security/cryptpki.asp

After you have a solid overview, you can get the full details from the Public Key Cryptography Standards (PKCS) documents maintained by RSA Labs at the following link:

> http://www.rsasecurity.com/rsalabs/pkcs/

NOTE   A novelty of the PKCS implementations with Cisco IP Phones is that the client-side processing is split between the fundamental operations that must occur on the phone itself and other protocol formatting functions that occur in the CAPF that resides on a CallManager server. This separation facilitates a small firmware image size so that the essential security features can fit in the limited physical Flash memory of Cisco IP Phones that predated the security features.

Establish a CTL File

The CTL file is the critical linking structure that allows the endpoints to receive public key information on the servers and system administration identities that are relevant to the endpoint. The file is the security glue that holds the system together.

Traditionally, a PKI uses a set of trusted CAs and associated Certificate Revocation Lists (CRLs) to authenticate the identities presented to a consumer of that identity. For example, your web browser has a default list of CAs that are deemed acceptable because the CAs have paid the web browser manufacturer to have themselves installed as trusted roots. When you visit a secure website, the web server presents an identity and an associated certificate to your browser, and your browser validates the certificate through a certificate chain-chasing process. In this process, your browser checks whether the certificate's signing authority is in the trusted root list. If it isn't, your browser checks whether the signing authority of that CA is in the trusted root list, and so forth, until the chain terminates in one of the listed trust anchors.

If your browser can't relate the certificate chain to a trust anchor, the web browser asks you if you are willing to trust the server that presented the original certificate. If you agree, your browser installs the received certificate in its trust list, and it doesn't need to verify the certificate chain. If the chain is rooted to one of the trust anchors, each certificate in the chain is validated against the CRL of the issuing CA. The certificate in the chain is considered valid if these circumstances apply:

- The certificate has not been revoked (in other words, it's not in the CRL for that CA).
- The digital signature is valid.
- The usage is allowed and within the operationally valid dates.

The chain is then validated all the way back to the originally presented certificate. If all the checks are verified, the presented certificate is considered valid, and the browser is allowed to trust the server presenting the certificate.

NOTE   CRLs might be familiar to you in another form if you remember how credit card transactions were verified before the introduction of point-of-sale terminals. (This author had occasion to learn the process while working in the food-service industry during high school.) In the old days, when a customer presented a credit card to make a payment, the store clerk consulted a weekly or monthly printed magazine that contained a list of lost, stolen, or otherwise invalid credit card numbers. If the customer-provided credit card number was present in the printed list, the clerk refused card payment (and was supposed to confiscate the card in question). This printed magazine was just like a CRL, albeit with a painfully slow update interval that provided a long time for fraudulent users to succeed with transactions before the CRL was updated.

From the preceding description, you can see that the traditional approach for certificate validation is composed of many steps. It requires that the validating application have access to the CRLs of the issuing and intermediate CAs all the way to a root trusted CA. This normally means connecting to the Internet (in the case of public CA services) or potentially multiple CA servers in an enterprise data network. In addition, implementation challenges exist when these functions are part of automated transactions in simple appliances (such as registration events in IP phones) that don't typically involve end-user interaction.

The CTL was developed to help overcome the challenge of validating the various servers and systems administrator security tokens. The CTL is a file containing a list of identities that are attested to by a systems administrator using a security token. This token contains a certificate signed by a CA that is in the application's trust anchor list (in this case, the application is the Cisco IP Phone firmware). This allows the IP Phone firmware to validate the CTL's signature in a simple set of steps. It validates the system administrator's security token certificate and then validates the file signature using the public key contained in that certificate. After the signature on the CTL file is validated, all the identities contained in the CTL file may be installed as trusted systems elements by the phone firmware. This eliminates the chain chase for each individual element and solves the problem of how to extend trust to servers using self-signed certificates without having the user approve each individual server request. This places the responsibility for certificate approval in the hands of the security systems administrator, where it belongs, rather than with end users who predictably accept false certificates.

To provide for the scenario in which a security administrator's hardware token certificate must be removed from the CTL, you are required to have multiple security admin hardware tokens and associated certificates.

Consider what happens if you need to remove access from a security administrator. Because any of the included security administrator hardware tokens can be used to sign the CTL file, you simply use a valid hardware token to generate a new CTL file that excludes the recently departed or newly untrusted security administrator. If this is part of a handoff process from a consultant who installs the network for you, or during a friendly job termination, the process works well.

However, if a formerly-trusted-but-now-malicious security administrator wants to wreak havoc, he or she can generate a new CTL file that invalidates all other security administrators except himself and one other. It would seem that you have a chance to fight back because you still have one valid security administrator who can change the CTL file again to lock out the bad administrator and include another trusted administrator. The uglier side of this scenario could be that two security administrators are corrupt, or that the single corrupt administrator knows his or her job well and simply acquires another hardware security token to be a placeholder in the CTL file. In this case, the CTL file would be totally compromised. You would have to restore all phones to an initial factory-default state and rebuild the network.

To keep this worst-case scenario in perspective, if you have a security administrator who turns malicious and wants to cause damage to your organization, you are in bad shape and are exposed on countless fronts. In this situation, trying to protect against this scenario through technology is appropriate only in precious few environments that justify draconian practices to ensure high security. The real protection comes through operational practices and policies that limit single-person accountability for any aspect of a critical system. The problem of a security administrator who turns malicious is primarily a managerial problem, not a technical problem.

A more pragmatic application of the rule to have at least two security administrator hardware tokens in the CTL file is a case in which you lose a hardware token and don't want an unaccounted-for key to your secure network floating around. You can simply remove the key from the CTL file and not worry about it, other than the cost of acquiring a new one.

The details of generating a site-specific, locally significant CTL file are provided in the following links and are not echoed here:

- Cisco CallManager Security and Virus Protection Guides—http://www.cisco.com/univercd/cc/td/doc/product/voice/c_callmg/sec_vir/index.htm

- Cisco IP Phone Authentication and Encryption for Cisco CallManager 4.0(1)—http://www.cisco.com/univercd/cc/td/doc/product/voice/c_callmg/4_0/sec_vir/ae/auth_enc/index.htm

Get a CTL into Phones

An important ramification of the CTL implementation in Cisco IP Phones is that a phone blindly accepts the first CTL file it receives after it has been manufactured. This is because the phone is programmed to have no prior knowledge of and no way to validate the entity that signs the first CTL file.

An emerging expression to describe this initial leap of faith is *imprinting* because the process is analogous to a fabled newborn bird that associates as its trusted mother the first face it sees. This process is safe when you have a controlled environment for preparing the birth of an IP phone into your network because you have a high degree of certainty that a trusted administrator is facilitating the introduction. Consider an alternative case in which a hacker imprints an unsafe CTL file into a new phone. This threat is not a significant concern because an authorized administrator does not add the phone's device ID to the CallManager database, so the phone cannot register with the local CallManager.

Only one threat model you should watch out for relates to this discussion. A hacker imprints a new phone with a bogus CTL file, and the phone subsequently is added to the CallManager database unwittingly (or maliciously) by an authorized administrator. This sequence is conceivable only if there is a breakdown in the operational process of enrolling the phone. It highlights the importance of ensuring a safe enrollment environment that includes both the CTL file imprinting and including the phone in the CallManager database through the BAT or CallManager Administration. You should avoid an operational process that introduces a significant amount of time or distance between these two steps. If you are really concerned about security, this process should also involve multiple people who check each other's work so that a corrupt administrator cannot circumvent the security process.

Secure Endpoint Operation

You have X.509v3 certificates embedded in the phones after resolving the thorny issue of initial secure enrollment of endpoints and trusted identity establishment. These certificates are the anchors on which cryptographic functions rely to provide identity, integrity, and privacy services for all communications to and from the phones.

The following sections describe these methods of providing identity, integrity, and privacy services:

- Phone configuration file download
- SCCP signaling between phones and CallManager
- SRTP media streams to and from supported phones

Endpoint Configuration File Authentication

After Cisco IP Phones have acquired a CTL file (whether it is imprinted from the first download or validated during a subsequent update download), they can validate the authenticity of configuration files. Configuration files downloaded via the TFTP server are cryptographically signed by the CallManager Publisher server. Assuming that the CallManager Publisher server has a certificate and is included in the CTL file used by the phone, the phone validates the contents of the new configuration file and proceeds to use the configuration information contained therein.

Encrypt SCCP Signaling via SCCP/TLS

The Skinny Client Control Protocol (SCCP or Skinny protocol) provides messaging to enable phone registration, call control, media control, and call statistic reporting. Skinny messages are transmitted across a TCP session established between IP phone endpoints and CallManager servers. The process of securing these transactions with SSL/TLS is nearly identical to the process of securing HTTP web traffic in Internet e-commerce applications.

In a typical e-commerce application, the client first authenticates the web server by trusting a website X.509v3 certificate that is signed by a CA trusted by the client. The web server authenticates the client by accepting a username and password entry that might correspond with a static or dynamic password depending on the back-end web application architecture and authentication database source. The client protects the integrity and privacy of the username/password submission to the web server by encrypting this information with the website's public key. Only web servers that have the private key associated with the website's public key can decipher the username/password message. Note that the username/password combination authenticates the actual message in which the username/password combination is submitted, but subsequent transmissions from the client to the server are not explicitly authenticated. The legally binding authentication of the client to the server in e-commerce applications occurs when the client provides a credit card and related validating material that the server can validate through back-end connections to a credit card validation service.

The primary differences between this example and SSL/TLS as used by Cisco IP Telephony solutions is that Cisco uses a true mutual authentication mechanism that is based on server- and client-side certificates. Both sides of the transaction present their public keys, and Diffie-Hellman calculations allow a common shared secret to be derived unknown to third parties, who can observe only the public keys. The magic that lets this happen lies in the mathematical properties of the public and private key pairs. Specifically, each side of the transaction can calculate the same shared secret number as the remote side by using the remote party's public key along with its own private key. Both ends of the transaction possess private keys that are critical in the authentication process. Third parties observing the public keys in transit do not have access to the private keys.

For more information, consult the Cisco CallManager 4.0 System Administration and Features and Services Guide at the following link:

> http://www.cisco.com/univercd/cc/td/doc/product/voice/c_callmg/sec_vir/index.htm

---

WARNING Beware of voice applications you might be using in your network that capture packet streams by spanning ports on an Ethernet switch or by sniffing phone traffic on the phone's PC port. As soon as you encrypt this traffic, it no longer can be deciphered by the applications that rely on the information gathered by the sniffing application.

Encrypt RTP Media Streams via Secure RTP

Secure RTP (SRTP) is a standards-track protocol specified in a draft standard as of this Secure Real-Time Transport Protocol Internet-Draft:

> http://www.ietf.org/internet-drafts/draft-ietf-avt-srtp-09.txt

By the time you read this, the draft version might have incremented one or more times, or the draft might have advanced to an RFC. To learn the latest status of the SRTP standards-track protocol, search the list of deliverables from the IETF Audio-Visual Transport working group for "SRTP" at the following link:

> http://www.ietf.org/html.charters/avt-charter.html

The main goals of SRTP are to provide confidentiality (privacy) of RTP payloads, integrity for RTP and RTCP frames including the RTP and RTCP headers, and protection against replay attacks for RTP and RTCP frames without appreciable increases in packet size. The privacy and integrity features are by now familiar to you, but the importance of antireplay protection might not be immediately clear. Its importance becomes evident when you think about an IVR script in a banking application. Imagine that you are using your DTMF keypad to enter an amount of money to transfer for a payment. You would not want a third party to intercept your encrypted RTP stream containing a couple of DTMF tones and replay this encrypted sequence to make your original 10 appear as 1000.

Conceptually, SRTP sits in the protocol stack between RTP and the transport layer (most commonly UDP). It converts RTP frames into SRTP frames that have an encrypted RTP payload and a signed hash appended. The Cisco IP Phone implementation of SRTP uses AES-128 Counter Mode for the cipher suite, as described in the SRTP standards-track document. The predefined authentication mechanism for SRTP is HMAC-SHA1, as specified in RFC 2104 at the following link:

http://www.faqs.org/rfcs/rfc2104.html

CallManager computes an SRTP session key and transmits it to both endpoints via the respective signaling links. This is why secure signaling is a prerequisite to having secure media. In the case of IP Phones, the SRTP session key is sent as part of a Skinny message. In the case of MGCP gateways to be supported in a future CallManager release, the SRTP session key is passed as an attribute in the Session Description Protocol (SDP) body. Future Session Initiation Protocol (SIP) support for SRTP also uses the SDP delivery format unless another standards-track format is created and adopted.

Because DTMF tones might or might not be passed via the secure RTP channel (depending on the vendor implementation), it is important to separately consider the potential security assurance levels afforded to voice-band audio and signaling tones. According to RFC 2833, *RTP Payload for DTMF Digits, Telephony Tones, and Telephony Signals,* DTMF and other tones are passed in RTP frames out of band from the voice-band audio conversation. This feature enables excellent transmission quality for tones that don't process well through low bit rate codecs optimized for human speech. Cisco IP Phones, CallManager, and other voice application servers use another method to provide the same functionality. Instead of sending DTMF digits in-band in the audio path, they are transmitted in the signaling path (such as Skinny messages for Skinny-based IP phones). This is not a particularly important point, but it does underscore the importance of having an encrypted signaling link to protect DTMF tones that are part of the media privacy feature for IP phones.

WARNING   Beware of voice applications you might be using in your network that capture packet streams by spanning ports on an Ethernet switch or by sniffing phone traffic on the phone's PC port. As soon as you encrypt this traffic, it can no longer be deciphered by the applications that rely on the information gathered by the sniffing application. In addition, any stateful firewalls that rely on inspection of the call signaling to open UDP ports for the RTP streams stop allowing the media streams when you encrypt the signaling. The solution to this problem will be provided in a future CallManager release. Among other features, it will include the Simple Traversal of User Datagram (STUN) protocol through Network Address Translation (NAT).

SRTP Behavior with Call Features

In general, the initial implementation of SRTP in CallManager 4.0 supports point-to-point calls between supported endpoints. If you invoke features such as hold (with music on hold), transfer, park, Ad Hoc conference, or Meet-Me conference, the phone falls back in midcall to use RTP instead of SRTP. Following the completion of the feature invocation, the phone automatically reverts to SRTP if that type of connection can be resumed. For example, if you are on a secure call and you transfer it to another extension, the call temporarily reverts to RTP mode while the transfer operation is processed. As soon as the call is reestablished at the destination extension, it reverts to using SRTP if this can be negotiated by both endpoints. If you place a call on hold, the session falls back to using RTP between the remote party and the music on hold server. When you resume the call, the SRTP session is again established between the remote party and your phone.

Support for secure conference modes is unavailable in CallManager 4.0. This feature requires that you delegate authority for determining the call security status to the conferencing server instead of the CallManager server. This is because only the conferencing server can determine the signaling security status and SRTP capabilities of all conference participants.

User Notification of Call Security Status

When CallManager confirms that both ends of a call are using secure signaling links (only Skinny/TLS in the initial CallManager 4.0 release), and an SRTP session is successfully established between the endpoints, the Cisco IP Phone provides notification in the form of a padlock icon, similar to what is displayed in a web browser when you visit a secure website. If a call that is initially in a secure state reverts to an insecure state, the padlock icon disappears. It reappears when the call returns to a secure state. There is no audible indication of the call security status because there is no reliable way to provide this information. Any audio signal that could be assigned for such a function can easily be spoofed by a hacker on the remote end of the call by simply playing out the audio signal that indicates a secure call.

A potential feature that might be included in a release subsequent to CallManager 4.0 is the ability to administratively define the desired behavior of call establishment when SRTP communication fails. On a per-endpoint or global basis, you might be able to specify whether the call falls back to regular RTP and continues in an insecure mode (with an unlocked padlock icon displayed to the user) or whether the call simply fails. In general, you would not want to use this latter option except when high security is a strong requirement and you can accept call drops when remote parties don't support SRTP or unsupported call features are invoked.

Secure Interserver Communication for MGCP, SIP, H.323, and Java Telephony API Signaling via IPSec

For communication between voice application servers and gateways, you can use IPSec to authenticate and encrypt traffic. This is a general method that maintains integrity and privacy in traffic types that don't have application-specific support for these security features. The only downside of using IPSec is that it is somewhat complex for widespread use among client endpoints on a per-application basis to diverse destinations. As such, client-based Java Telephony API (JTAPI) applications are difficult to secure.

Also beware of end-to-end trust for SRTP media security. Although end-to-end trust is clearly absent when the signaling protocol on at least one leg of a call does not support the passing of SRTP session keys, other cases are not so clear. For example, you might have MGCP signaling that is passing the SRTP session key in the SDP exchange, but you might not be implementing IPSec to secure this signaling exchange. As a result, the IP phone side of the connection might perceive that the end-to-end connection is secure when in fact the session keys are passed in clear text across the MGCP portions of the link. When the MGCP links are terminated on the local CallManager cluster, CallManager has visibility to the security status of the MGCP signaling link and can update the IP phone (via a Skinny message) of the call session security state. This is important because the phone uses this information to present a locked or unlocked padlock icon to the phone user.

NOTE   MGCP support for SRTP is not included in the initial release of CallManager 4.0 but is scheduled for CallManager 4.1 and a corresponding IOS software release.

An additional feature that might be supported in a later maintenance release of CallManager 4.0 is the ability to administratively define the trust policy for a given voice signaling trunk. This is important for at least two common scenarios. In the first, you might be able to use IPSec to secure a voice trunk that otherwise uses an insecure protocol. In the second scenario, you might have a connection to a trusted remote CallManager cluster and have no method to signal the security status of phones associated with the remote cluster back to the local CallManager cluster. By configuring the administrative setting for trunk security status, you can expand the range of secure calling between endpoints in your extended network. Beware of this risk or potential vulnerability with this feature. End users might still perceive end-to-end calls to be secure, when in fact some signaling might be exposed in clear text if the IPSec association fails.

WARNING   Beware of voice applications you might be using in your network that capture packet streams by spanning ports on an Ethernet switch or by sniffing phone traffic on the phone's PC port. As soon as you encrypt this traffic, it can no longer be deciphered by the applications that rely on the information gathered by the sniffing application.

Implementation Considerations

The following sections summarize several issues that are important to consider when deploying the security features described in preceding sections.

Account for Higher Device Weights with Authenticated Endpoints

Don't forget to account for the increased CPU requirements placed on CallManager servers when Skinny signaling authentication and privacy are enabled. The impact of SRTP is minimal on CallManager because most media streams are terminated elsewhere, but the Skinny signaling from all endpoints registered to a CallManager is directly terminated on CallManager servers. These servers carry the burden of encrypting and decrypting all the TLS-wrapped signaling sessions.

Consult the CallManager 4.0 Release Notes for the latest information on device weights.

Don't Use NAT in the Path of Encrypted Voice Signaling

For NAT devices to support voice signaling traffic flows, they cannot simply replace the source and destination IP addresses. Because signaling streams typically have IP addresses buried in the data payload, NAT devices must inspect the payload contents and replace IP addresses in the payload to maintain consistency with the NAT policy.

When the voice signaling traffic is authenticated, NAT devices cannot modify IP addresses in the payload without invalidating the authentication checks at the destination. Furthermore, if the voice signaling traffic is encrypted, NAT devices cannot even inspect the payload to know where IP addresses are embedded.

Until this issue has a solution, you should avoid using NATs in the path of encrypted voice signaling traffic.

Summary

Exploiting most voice security threats requires access to voice application servers, the client voice VLANs, or the network path between them. Your first line of defense in all network security considerations is restricted physical access.

Wiring closets and data centers that house voice infrastructure elements must stay locked. It's a good idea to use card or badge readers rather than physical keys to provide individual accountability for physical access. With physical access restricted, infrastructure components can be logically shielded with multiple layers of authentication processes and network and host-based filtering that operate on source or destination addresses, protocol types, and in some cases payload content patterns.

For attacks that originate from commonly accessible areas, the six main attack points are

- Data client workstations that have been subverted
- IP phone instrument as the source of attack
- PC port on IP phones
- Ethernet jacks in offices or cubicles where an IP phone can connect
- Ethernet cable between an IP phone and a downstream device
- Ethernet cable between an IP phone and a wiring closet switch (including the cabling sections that run through an overhead plenum space)

Voice security issues associated with client workstations are the most serious because these can plausibly enable remote-controlled attacks. Remote-controlled attacks magnify a hacker's destructive power and reach and increase the pool of hackers who can exploit the vulnerability. In addition, it's more difficult to identify, capture, and prosecute the hacker following the attack. With remote-controlled attacks, resolving client workstation issues that lead to voice security vulnerabilities is a high priority. In addition to whatever host-based mechanisms you use to secure client workstations (which are outside the scope of this book), you should use network compartmentalization and containment to keep subverted workstations from wreaking further havoc on voice networks. This means

- Placing voice and data clients on separate VLANs with access lists between them
- 802.1x authentication for voice and data VLANs
- Blocking inbound frames on the IP phone's PC port that have the same source Ethernet MAC address as the phone or that are 802.1q tagged for the same voice VLAN

The other threats are less serious because they require local physical access to exploit the target. This means that a hacker has a much greater chance of getting caught and that the scope of attack is limited to the hacker's physical reach and manual efforts. Still, these threats are worth mitigating whenever it is reasonable to do so.

The IP phone itself is of limited value in implementing an attack, except that it may be used as part of a piggybacking attack to gain access to a voice VLAN protected by 802.1x. The solution to this narrow problem is per-frame Ethernet authentication (or encryption that provides privacy in addition to integrity) on wired links, as is currently done via 802.11i on wireless links. Note that this attack is relevant only when 802.1x is supported on voice VLANs, which currently is not the case. Other potential attacks using the IP phone tend to have more of a social engineering nature. A hacker spoofs the identity of a legitimate user (simply by using that person's phone) and tricks another party into revealing secret information or providing additional access.

As was briefly mentioned for mitigating threats of subverted workstations, the PC port on the IP phone can be a point of entry for attacks. Just as the damage done by a subverted workstation can be limited by filtering inbound traffic at the phone's PC port, this inbound filtering protects hackers who directly attach to the phone's PC port.

802.1x for voice VLANs mitigates the threat of hackers who attempt to enter the voice VLAN by directly attaching to the Ethernet port where IP phones normally connect.

The cable between the IP phone and the client workstation attached to the PC port is a point of vulnerability because a hacker can insert a simple Ethernet hub and collect all traffic to and from the client workstation and also insert traffic. This threat is significant for the client workstation, but it's a minimal threat to the voice network because of the IP phones' PC port filtering capability.

The cable between the IP phone and the upstream switch in the wiring closet is a potential point of vulnerability with risks similar to direct access to the Ethernet jack when the phone is unplugged. However, the threat is somewhat greater because future protection afforded by 802.1x on voice VLANs can be subverted. This is because a hacker machine inserted between the IP phone and the wiring closet switch can have full access to the voice VLAN even without knowing the 802.1x authentication credentials (whereas the IP phone continues to handle the authentication challenges by the wiring closet switch). The only restriction here is that the hacker machine must use the same source Ethernet MAC address and VLAN ID as the IP phone to pass the 802.1x filter in the wiring closet switch. Of course, to implement this type of attack, a hacker would need to cut and crimp cables, create custom hardware that can receive and supply Cisco inline power, have physical access to the plenum space above a cubicle area, and so on. Although all of this is not inconceivable, it is certainly difficult enough for a hacker to consider other more rudimentary means to achieve nefarious objectives.

In addition to protection methods out on the client-facing edges of your network, you can use various features in the wiring closet switches to limit access, such as dynamic ARP inspection, access lists, and rate limiting.

Application-based integrity and privacy features build on the secure network foundation described in the preceding paragraphs. The sum of all these features is a formidable defense against would-be hackers.

Securing the environment of a Cisco IP Communications network requires a patchwork quilt of technologies and operational processes that work in concert. The ultimate goals of all of these technologies and operational processes are to

- Authenticate users and devices
- Move bits around the network only when they need to be based on traffic types and authentication status
- Restrict access to the bits (both stored and in transit) by unauthorized entities
- Encrypt bits (both stored and in transit) so that unauthorized entities that gain access to them can't decrypt or modify them

If you implement the security precautions outlined in this chapter, you will have an IP communications network that is resilient to threats, and risks to your operational uptime will decrease. This lets you preserve the productivity benefits and cost savings associated with a converged network and increase your risk-adjusted return on investment.

## CHAPTER 7

Configuring CallManager and IP Telephony Components

This chapter presents best practices for Cisco CallManager, IP phones, gateways, features, and applications. The goal of this chapter is to make your life as a CallManager administrator easier by supplying you with detailed configuration best practices you can use to improve the scalability and manageability of your CallManager implementation. In addition, you will learn new features and methods to

- Help prevent toll fraud by correctly configuring your partitions and calling search spaces
- Make mass changes using the Bulk Administration Tool (BAT)
- Implement common telephony features such as intercom, which is not natively offered in CallManager, by combining other CallManager features

This chapter is organized into sections on best practices for the following:

- General CallManager system
- IP phone
- Gateway
- Dial plan
- Features
- Tools and applications

General CallManager System Best Practices

System best practices help you enhance the resiliency and manageability of your CallManager implementation. The best practices covered in this section are as follows:

- Read the documentation and the recommended reading list.
- Use IP addresses instead of server host names.
- Leave the CallManager name as is.
- Use descriptive names for all configuration items.
- Add all applicable time zones, and do not use CMLocal.

- Create detailed device pools with intuitive names.
- Use device pools to configure common parameters and bulk-reset devices.
- Design user-friendly softkey templates.
- Enable dependency records.
- Reduce the interdigit timeout default value.

Read the Documentation (Recommended Reading List)

Cisco provides extensive documentation that explains concepts and features and provides step-by-step configuration information. You can access targeted help online in CallManager Administration, CallManager Serviceability, BAT, and more by selecting **Help > For This Page**. Doing so takes you directly to the information for the page you're viewing. Selecting **Help > Contents and Index** displays the Cisco IP Telephony Solutions Help, where you can use index and search features to find what you're looking for. Best of all, the books in the Cisco IP Telephony system are linked, so searching results in an array of resources. You can also access the complete suite of Voice documentation on Cisco.com at

http://www.cisco.com/univercd/cc/td/doc/product/voice/index.htm

To supplement the information you get from documents published by Cisco, you should check out these other resources:

- *Cisco CallManager Fundamentals* — Often referred to as the CallManager bible, this book provides information about CallManager architecture and explains in detail the behavior of media resources, CDRs, stations, trunks, and, most importantly, the dial plan. Chapter 2 provides what is probably the most comprehensive treatment of dial plan issues in print. Tools to manage and monitor the system are also explained. Look for this book at local technology centers, online booksellers, and local bookstores (ISBN 1-58705-008-0).

- *Troubleshooting Cisco IP Telephony* — This book explains important components at the conceptual level, such as voice quality, faxes and modems, gateways, and much more. It has information that appeals to beginner through advanced administrators. Of course, detailed troubleshooting information is also provided, along with best practices to avoid getting into problems that require troubleshooting in the first place. Look for this book at local technology centers, online booksellers, and local bookstores (ISBN 1-58705-075-7).

- **http://www.answermonkey.net** — Hosted by Cisco Unity expert Jeff Lindborg, this website provides extensive information about Unity, including prerelease or non-Cisco-supported scripts and applications for debugging or administering Unity.

- **http://forums.cisco.com/** — Access the online voice and video discussion on Cisco.com. Click the link to **Join the discussions now at http://www.cisco.com/go/ netpro**, and then click the heading **Voice and Video** to access the voice-specific area of the networking forum, shown in Figure 7-1.

Figure 7-1   *Networking Professionals Connection: Voice and Video Forum*

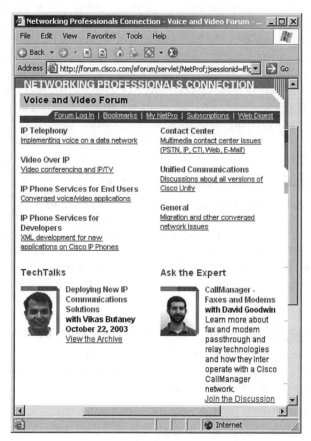

Use IP Addresses Instead of Server Host Names

As discussed in detail in Chapter 1, "Planning the CallManager Implementation," you should use IP addresses in all CallManager Administration pages instead of host names for CallManager servers so that your CallManager implementation does not depend on correct Domain Name System (DNS) configuration and operation. If you have already configured the system using host names, this means changing all the host names to IP addresses on the Server Configuration page (**System > Server**). You also must change the Publisher's host name to an IP address in all the URLs on the Enterprise Parameters Configuration page (**System > Enterprise Parameters**). Using IP addresses means that your IP telephony endpoints contact the CallManager servers directly using their IP addresses instead of resolving their host names via DNS. Do not change the host name of the machine itself (in Windows 2000) to the IP address.

NOTE	There is one case in which using host names instead of IP addresses is required. If you're running Skinny-based IP phones behind a Network Address Translation (NAT) boundary, the device outside the NAT boundary cannot connect to CallManager using its IP address. A specialized implementation such as this requires complex DNS/NAT configuration.
	Also, in cases where disaster recovery scenarios might require redeploying CallManager servers with new IP addresses (for example, in a different data center), you might want to rely on DNS name resolution, which allows the entire system to retain the existing naming conventions by relying on the DNS infrastructure to propagate the new IP addresses.

Leave the Default CallManager Name as Is

When you install CallManager, it creates an instance of the Cisco CallManager service, to which a name is assigned. This name takes the form CM_*ServerName,* as shown in the Cisco CallManager Configuration page in CallManager Administration (**System > Cisco CallManager**). You do not need to change this to an IP address because it doesn't matter what this is named. The CM_*ServerName* format also makes configuring CallManager groups easier because you can see the CallManager name.

Use Descriptive Names for All Configuration Items

For all items you configure in CallManager Administration, use descriptive names when possible or intelligent descriptions that let you determine at a glance what (or who) the item pertains to. Here are some examples:

- For voice mail ports, preface the device name with **VM_** or **voice mail**.
- For application ports, use **apps_**.
- For users' phones, use their e-mail ID, first name and last initial, first name and department, or some other naming strategy. Examples are **jsmith_**, **JohnS_**, and **John-Finance**.

Descriptive names let you identify the owner or the category of device at a glance. They also enhance your ability to search for and update those items in CallManager Administration or in BAT.

CAUTION	Partition names should balance the need to name configuration items descriptively with the 512-character limit in calling search spaces (CSS). In other words, for a given CSS, the sum of all characters of every member partition's name (plus one delimiter character for each partition) must be less than 512 characters. The longer the partition names, the fewer partitions that can fit within a single CSS.

Name CallManager Redundancy Groups Descriptively

The two common strategies used for CallManager server redundancy are 2:1 and 1:1 server redundancy. After choosing a redundancy strategy, implementing it is the easy part. Be careful to name each CallManager group accordingly (**System > Cisco CallManager Group**). Descriptive names ease CallManager's administrative burden by quickly and easily identifying the groups' order. For example, if you implement a 1:1 redundancy strategy and name the servers of your CallManager cluster CM-Pub, CM-TFTP, CM-A, CM-B, CM-C, and CM-D, using redundancy group names such as A-then-B, B-then-A, C-then-D, and D-then-C would be simple and descriptive. All that remains is to divide your endpoints equally among the various redundancy groups.

Include a Phone Number and Name in the Description Field When Adding Phones

Make the description field for phones you are adding to CallManager Administration contain the user's name, a space, a dash, a space, and the extension. For example, a description field could be **John Smith - 5100**. When you do this, the route plan report exports that information in the CSV, which helps if you ever need to recover a system. Also, having the number and name in the Description field lets you identify at a glance the person to whom the phone is assigned and its assigned number. Without this information, only the MAC address is available. In a system of 5000 MAC addresses, for example, it's difficult to update a setting on John Smith's phone without first going to the user's office to check the phone or requesting that the user supply the MAC address.

Never Use the Default Device Pool

Avoid using the default device pool because it's not descriptive and can cause confusion during troubleshooting. When you're presented with a list of tens or hundreds of device pools, using a descriptive name makes troubleshooting much easier.

Add All Applicable Time Zones and Do Not Use CMLocal

The default date/time group CMLocal gets configured upon installation of CallManager to synchronize to the date and time of the CallManager server's operating system. Although CMLocal might be suitable to use in cases in which all endpoints reside in the same time zone as the CallManager server, it's still best to define a date/time group for every applicable time zone in which an endpoint will reside (**System > Date/Time Group**). This is true even if all endpoints will share a single time zone because the name CMLocal is not as descriptive as names such as Eastern, Central, Mountain, and Pacific. Using descriptive names for every aspect of CallManager configuration allows you to see at a glance the details of the configuration item you are examining.

In addition, servers tend to move around as companies define new agreements with service providers. For example, for some customers, it makes more sense to house the CallManager servers in a collocation facility, and this might necessitate a time zone change for some or all devices in CMLocal. Acquisitions and expansion into new geographies can also expose naming problems. Creating and naming the time zones up front takes little time, and it's one less worry after the system is in production.

Use Standard Usernames

Use a consistent username logon convention across your voice and data network. For example, if users access company web pages using a specific username or ID, such as their phone extension or the user ID portion of their e-mail aliases, make sure your telephony system also recognizes users by their phone extension or user ID portion of their e-mail aliases when logging into the Cisco CallManager User Options web page. If you are adding telephony to an existing network that already employs a username standard, make sure the telephony system also uses the network standard already in place. Not employing a consistent convention across voice and data networks is a common mistake. In many instances, the telecom department has responsibility for the phone system and might not contact the Windows or UNIX administrators responsible for network logons. In the rush to get the system running, they might choose a different standard. Avoid this common mistake.

Create Detailed Device Pools with Intuitive Names

Device pools are a means of attributing common characteristics to a group of similar devices. Device pools can be used to help speed the configuration of devices such as IP phones, gateways, conference bridges, transcoders, media termination points, voice mail ports, computer telephony integration (CTI) route points, and so on. Devices can be configured more quickly because common parameters such as the following can be defined at the device pool level: CallManager group, date/time group, region, Survivable Remote Site Telephony (SRST) reference, media resource group list, MOH audio sources, user and network locales, calling search spaces (CSS) for auto-registration, and softkey template.

As with other CallManager parameters, it's best to use the most intuitive and descriptive names possible for your device pools. Device pool names can have up to 31 alphanumeric characters. Because some device pools have names similar to other configuration parameters such as regions, partitions, or CSS, it's a good idea to prepend **DP_** or append **_DP** to device pool names, such as DP_Atlanta_Branch_IPPhone or Atlanta_Branch_PSTN_Gateway_DP.

When deciding which devices to place in device pools, it's important to group them according to a common characteristic they all share. For example, if you have a campus environment with multiple buildings, it's a good idea to group phones by building or department. In many cases, departments share traits such as MOH audio source, which makes it advantageous to put a single department in a device pool. That way, as new on-hold messages are recorded, you can change the MOH source for all the phones at one time simply by updating the device pool used by all phones in that department. Another common device pool assignment technique is to group devices by CallManager group. In this fashion, it's easy to track the devices that should register to a particular server. In addition, the modular search and reset possibilities afforded by device pools make searching for phones in a specific building or department much easier.

Although there's no one-size-fits-all way to use device pools, many system administrators unfortunately place all phones in the Default device pool and then later regret it when the Default pool becomes too large to manage. Segmenting devices into unique device pools might require a little more configuration up front but results in greater efficiency for the future.

CAUTION   When defining a device pool, be careful to choose only a network locale that is already installed and supported by the associated devices. The network locale defines the ring cadence along with tones and is geographically specific. If a device is associated with a network locale it does not support in the firmware, the device will fail to register.

Use Device Pools to Configure Common Parameters and Bulk-Reset Devices

Use device pools over individual device configuration for quick changes to settings that are defined by a device pool, such as date/time group, region, softkey template, network locale, and more. For example, if you want to change the Music on Hold (MOH) server in use by a certain group of phones, you can select a different media resource group list (MRGL) and update the device pool. All devices belonging to that device pool are automatically updated to use the media resources defined by the newly selected MRGL. You can also easily reset a large group of devices at one time by resetting the device pool. Device pools also allow you to update the MOH audio source quickly and easily as new music or advertisements become available.

TIP   If you're looking for a way to reset every device in the system at one time and you don't mind writing a little code, see the later section *"Use the AXL SOAP API to Write Custom Scripts That Interact with the CallManager Database."*

Design User-Friendly Softkey Templates

When designing a softkey template, consider the features that your users use most. Focus on minimizing the number of times the user has to press the **more** softkey. Depending on the model, Cisco IP Phones support four or five softkeys. Users access additional softkeys by pressing the **more** softkey. If you have more softkeys than can display initially, user-friendly templates place those most-used features in the first, second, and third (and fourth, if applicable) softkey positions to minimize the number of times users have to press the **more** softkey to access the features they use frequently. For example, if you have a group of users who use Hold, Transfer, and Conference more than anything else, create a softkey template that has those functions in the first, second, and third softkey positions for the Connected state. Rely on your user class interviews (discussed in Chapter 1) to determine appropriate positioning for the EndCall softkey.

After you deploy softkey templates, try not to change them because users become accustomed to the templates. When softkeys begin moving to new positions, users quickly become confused and frustrated.

Enable Dependency Records

Use dependency records to determine which records in the database use other records. For example, you can determine which device types (CTI route points, phones, and so on) use a particular calling search space, or what types of devices or resources use a particular device pool, as shown in Figure 7-2. This information is useful if you need to delete a device pool or make a dial plan change, for example. You can determine what other actions need to take place first (such as assigning devices to different device pools and reassigning calling search spaces or partitions) to enable the delete operation.

Figure 7-2 *Dependency Records for the Device Pool*

Dependency records are disabled by default. Enable them by setting the enterprise parameter Enable Dependency Records to True (**System > Enterprise Parameter**).

Running a list of dependent records consumes server resources on the Publisher and can easily affect CallManager performance if you have a large database. Even for small databases, it's best to run dependency records during nonpeak hours. However, if phones are not registered to the Publisher, the service impact is minimal.

Reduce the Interdigit Timeout Default Value

CallManager employs an interdigit timer, the CallManager service parameter T302 Timer, which restarts each time the user presses a digit on the phone (except the first digit dialed— see the following note for more information). Do you ever start dialing a number while still looking it up? That's where this timer comes into play. It also comes into play when you dial any number in a variable-length dialing plan, such as international calls from the U.S.

When the timer expires, CallManager routes the call using the digits dialed up to the point when the timer expired, or it instructs the phone to play the reorder tone if the call cannot be routed based on the digits dialed (no route pattern matches the dialed digits). The default duration for the interdigit timer is 15 seconds, which is a generous amount of time to wait for a user to dial another digit. Consider reducing the T302 Timer to a shorter duration, such as 10 seconds. This is a long-enough time to allow the user to enter another digit, but not so long as to frustrate a user who has entered all the digits and is waiting for the call to route.

To change the interdigit timer to 10 seconds, go to the Service Parameter Configuration page (**Service > Service Parameters > Cisco CallManager**), scroll to the T302 Timer, and change it to 10000 milliseconds (10 seconds). If your users do a lot of international dialing, you can make this even lower to decrease the amount of time users must wait for digits to be matched.

NOTE   Another CallManager service parameter, Offhook to First Digit Timer, determines the timeout between going off-hook and dialing the first digit. The default for this timer is 15 seconds. You might want to change this to 10 seconds as well.

You can read more about these parameters, including behavior with overlap sending, in Chapter 8, "Managing Services and Parameters."

IP Phone Best Practices

This section provides the following best practices for IP phones:

- Teach users how to use IP phones.
- Teach users to use the Cisco CallManager User Options web page.

- Download the Cisco IP Phone Services Software Development Kit (SDK) to deploy free services on your phones.
- Configure IP phone services on line/feature buttons on the phone.
- Configure PLAR for emergency access.
- Use abbreviated dialing to provide more speed dials for users.
- Teach users to press the QRT softkey when they encounter audio problems or have trouble with their phones.

Teach Users How to Use IP Phones

Organize a training class that explains how to use the IP phone and highlights the various features available to your users. Although such training might be unpopular because of the costs of trainers and user participation, making sure your users understand how to use the features on their phones is important if end users are to be satisfied with the IP telephony solution and take full advantage of all the time-saving and useful benefits the phone system offers.

You also might consider separate training for managers or executives who want to learn about the specialized features for managers, such as IP Manager Assistant and group call pickup.

During training, be sure to address the following features (if they are implemented):

- The phone itself—softkey functions, accessing the full menu of softkeys, using the touchscreen (if applicable), using the **i** or **?** button help, plugging in a headset, adjusting the height of the footstand, changing the ringer type, adjusting the volume and LCD contrast, saving the volume/LCD adjustments, muting a call, and so on
- Transfer, hold, and resume
- Switching between calls when there are multiple calls per line (explain the maximum number of calls users can accept per line)
- Conferencing options (Meet-Me and Ad Hoc)
- Call park (explain the time limit for parking and what happens to the call when the timer expires)
- Call pickup and group call pickup
- Forwarding calls
- Configuring speed dials
- Extension mobility
- Per-call blocking of caller ID
- Call join, drop last party, and other features

- Personal Assistant, Personal Address Book, MyFastDials, and any other applications
- Directories (including checking for missed calls and dialing numbers from the Missed, Received, and Placed Calls directories)
- Subscribing to, unsubscribing to, and using IP phone services
- Using the Cisco CallManager User Options web page (see the following section)
- Accessing voice mail
- Reporting call problems (can't reach a dialed number, audio quality problems) — what information the user should collect and how to collect it (whether by pressing the **i** or **?** button twice in quick succession during an active call or by pressing the QRT softkey during an active call)
- Custom features or IP phone services

Instead of a training class, you could have basic training information created for your users. However, fewer users will voluntarily read the documentation than will attend a half-hour or hour-long training class (especially if compelled to attend by management). Cisco also offers eLearning tutorials for some of the older Cisco IP Phone models. Search Cisco.com for "Cisco IP Phone eLearning tutorial."

TIP   See the section "Create a Training Curriculum for Users and Administrators" in Chapter 1 for more information about training.

Teach Users to Use the Cisco CallManager User Options Web Page

Users can manage their IP phones through the Cisco CallManager User Options web page. You should publish the link to this web page and advertise it to users as a corporate-bookmarked link. You can design a menu page that lists other related IP telephony links such as WebDialer (described in this chapter). Encouraging users to manage their phones on the web reduces the number of questions you have to field on changing speed dials and subscribing to IP phone services — activities users can perform themselves if given access to the Cisco CallManager User Options web page.

Users log in to the Cisco CallManager User Options web page using the user ID/user password configured in the directory (the User Configuration page in CallManager Administration). Depending on the phone model, users can set a Call Forward All directive, configure speed dials, subscribe and unsubscribe to IP phone services, choose the language that is displayed on the phone, view help for the phone, and much more, as shown in Figure 7-3.

Figure 7-3   *Cisco CallManager User Options Logon Page for Cisco IP Phone Model 7960*

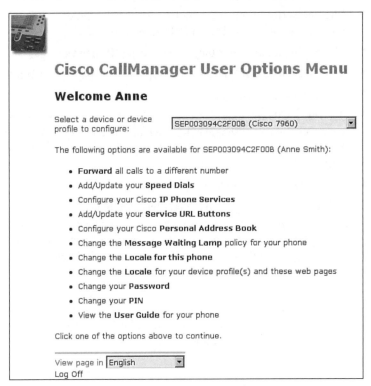

The URL is http://*CMName*/CCMUser/, where *CMName* refers to the Publisher server's IP address (or host name) in the cluster.

Download the Cisco IP Phone Services SDK to Deploy Free Services on Your Phones

Cisco offers several IP phone services when you download the free Cisco IP Phone Services SDK. You can get phone services such as a clock that displays a large time-of-day readout when the phone is not in use (shown in Figure 7-4). The clock service is useful for common areas and conference rooms. Also available is a photo directory service that displays pictures along with directory details such as user ID and department. Other features of the SDK include an onscreen keyboard service for the Cisco IP Phone 7970 touchscreen and a Customer Response Solutions (CRS) push step and subsystem for integrating IP phone services with CRS CTI applications.

Figure 7-4   *Free Clock Service*

You can acquire the IP Phone Services SDK through the Developer Support Central page at the following link:

http://www.cisco.com/pcgi-bin/dev_support/access_level/product_support

Click the **Log in now** link, log in, and then in the Voice Technology/AVVID list box select **CallManager—IP phone Services SDK**.

Write Your Own Custom Phone Services

You can write custom phone services specifically for your organization by following the instructions and information in the Cisco IP Phone Services SDK. You need some knowledge of Extensible Markup Language (XML), but many services are easy to write. Download the free SDK from the link in the preceding section, and think up custom services that would improve productivity or enhance the end user's experience with your phone system.

TIP   Cisco Press offers a book devoted to the subject of writing IP phone services: *Developing Cisco IP Phone Services: A Cisco AVVID Solution* by Darrick Deel et al (ISBN: 1-58705-060-9). You can read a chapter from the book at

http://www.amazon.com/exec/obidos/tg/detail/-/1587050609

Configure IP Phone Services on Line/Feature Buttons on the Phone

By updating the phone button template, you can apply a specific URL to a line/feature button on the IP phone (**Device > Device Settings > Phone Button Template**). Basically, you put the URL of an IP phone service on a line/feature button. This way, instead of requiring the user to press **services** and select the IP phone service, this feature lets the user simply press one line/feature button on the phone. The service displays in one button press. When you configure the line/feature buttons for Service URL, be sure to indicate the service name in the associated Label so that users know which button provides what functionality, as shown in Figure 7-5.

Figure 7-5 *Cisco IP Phone 7970 Button Template with Four Service URLs*

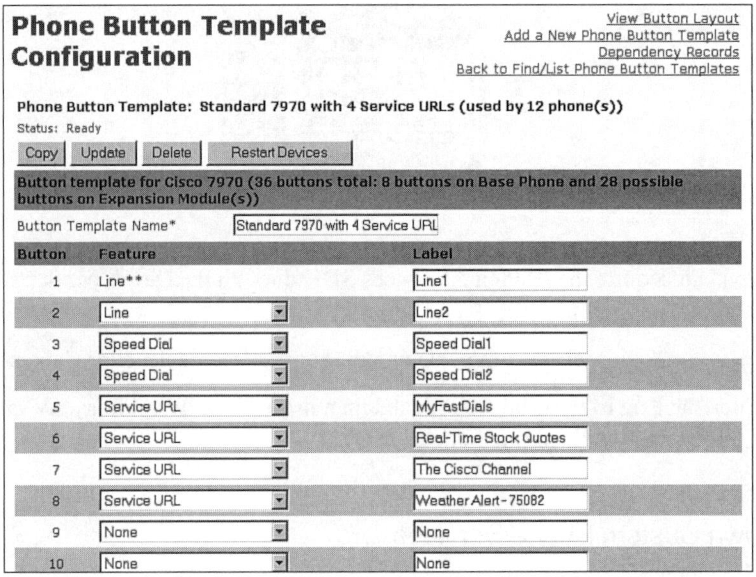

For example, the MyFastDials XML service can be configured as an IP phone service that is accessed from the Services menu after the **services** button is pressed. Alternatively, you can configure it on one of the user's line/feature buttons. The application is immediately invoked when the user presses the line/feature button assigned to the MyFastDials service.

Configure Private Line Automatic Ringdown for Emergency Access

Private line automatic ringdown (PLAR) is typically used to provide dedicated telephone service between two phones. When the PLAR-configured phone goes off-hook, it immediately dials a predetermined telephone number.

For example, some organizations require phones to have an EMERGENCY key that provides a hotline to a security desk staffed 24/7/365. You can achieve such an EMERGENCY button by using a speed dial, but configuring PLAR is the best way to ensure that users cannot modify their EMERGENCY button (there's no way to prevent user modification when a speed dial is used.)

A phone that has been configured with an automatic ringdown line is called a PLAR phone. This feature is often used for top officials or key personnel who need to have a direct private line to a particular destination (think of the red phone you see in American movies that provides a direct line to the President or the Bat Phone that Commissioner Gordon used to contact Batman).

Another common application is to place a PLAR phone outside a restricted or controlled area so that visitors may simply pick up the phone to request access. An even more important use of PLAR could be to establish an emergency line on your IP phones so that when the emergency line appearance is pressed, a call is automatically made to the onsite security personnel. You can implement PLAR in CallManager by using a combination of partitions, calling search spaces, and translation patterns.

CallManager can be configured to provide PLAR functionality on IP phones and analog phones connected to gateways. You accomplish this by assigning a unique CSS to the directory number of the IP phone or the Foreign Exchange Station (FXS) port of the gateway connected to an analog phone. This unique CSS can access only a unique partition that contains a blank translation pattern and nothing else. The translation pattern, in turn, translates the blank (no digits dialed) translation pattern into the PLAR call's destination using the called party transformation mask. This translation pattern must be assigned the necessary CSS to reach the desired destination.

If the desired destination of a PLAR call is a long distance phone number, the translation pattern's CSS must be able to access a partition containing a long distance route pattern. It's important to note that for every PLAR *destination* in your network, you have a corresponding partition, CSS, and translation pattern just for enabling the PLAR functionality to that destination. Be sure to include the PLAR destination in the name and description of each of these dial plan components. After configuration is complete, when the PLAR phone or directory number goes off-hook, the empty translation pattern is matched, and the called party transformation mask is applied, as shown in Figure 7-6. This allows CallManager to call the intended destination without any digits ever being dialed on the phone. This entire process is performed quickly. Within just a few seconds of going off-hook on the PLAR phone, the preconfigured destination starts ringing.

Figure 7-6 *PLAR IP Phone Functionality*

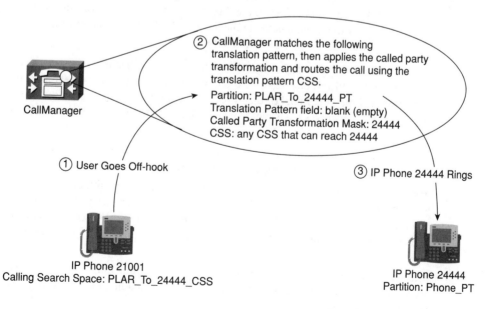

② CallManager matches the following translation pattern, then applies the called party transformation and routes the call using the translation pattern CSS.

Partition: PLAR_To_24444_PT
Translation Pattern field: blank (empty)
Called Party Transformation Mask: 24444
CSS: any CSS that can reach 24444

CallManager

① User Goes Off-hook

③ IP Phone 24444 Rings

IP Phone 21001
Calling Search Space: PLAR_To_24444_CSS

IP Phone 24444
Partition: Phone_PT

The following steps describe how to configure an IP phone (extension 21001) to automatically call extension 24444 when the phone goes off-hook:

Step 1 Create a new partition, such as PLAR_To_24444_PT.

Step 2 Create a new CSS, such as PLAR_To_24444_CSS, and add only the PLAR_To_24444_PT partition to it.

Step 3 Create a new translation pattern, and leave the Translation Pattern field blank. Select PLAR_To_24444_PT as the partition. Assign a CSS that has access to the partition that contains the destination the PLAR phone needs to reach (in this case, 24444), such as Phone_CSS, which contains the partition Phone_PT.

Caution   Do not leave the partition as <None> under any circumstances. Doing so results in every off-hook event being translated.

Step 4 Enter the destination number, 24444, in the Called Party Transformation Mask field of the translation pattern.

Step 5 Assign the calling search space PLAR_To_24444_CSS to the directory number 21001 on the IP phone, and reset the phone for the change to take effect. If you are using an analog phone, assign the calling search space PLAR_To_24444_CSS to the directory number of the FXS port on the gateway that is connected to the analog PLAR phone, and reset the gateway for the change to take effect.

When implementing PLAR for the sake of providing a dedicated emergency line, you should configure PLAR on a separate directory number (line appearance) on the phone and configure the Line Text Label of that directory number with a term such as "Emergency" or "Security." This gives users clear, one-touch access to emergency or security services.

Using Cisco Emergency Responder

You can augment this simple translation pattern configuration with the Cisco Emergency Responder (CER) application to allow direct emergency services calls from these emergency stations to a local Public Service Answering Point (PSAP), such as 911 in the United States. Configure CER to simultaneously alert your organization's security personnel.

Make certain that it is legal in your area to have a phone that dials 911 automatically. In some cases, local legislation prohibits this to avoid overloading the emergency center with accidental 911 calls.

You must statically configure CER to recognize the calling party phone number and assign that phone number to the appropriate emergency response location (ERL). As part of the ERL configuration, you assign whatever onsite notification mechanism you want, such as e-mail/pager or phone number. For more information about CER, consult the CER product tutorial or documentation.

Use Abbreviated Dialing to Provide More Speed Dials for Users

The Abbreviated Dialing feature allows users to gain more speed dial entries than the number of line buttons on their phones would otherwise permit. To use abbreviated dialing, users preconfigure abbreviated dialing phone numbers in the Cisco CallManager User Options web page. To activate it, they dial the index number associated with the phone number they configured and then press the AbbrDial softkey on the IP Phone. The phone then speed-dials the phone number configured as an abbreviated dial.

TIP   You can also implement a variant of so-called abbreviated dialing by assigning a URL to a line/feature button and combining it with MyFastDials, a free application packaged on the CallManager CD-ROM. See the earlier section "Configure IP Phone Services on Line/Feature Buttons on the Phone."

Teach Users to Press the QRT Softkey When They Encounter Audio Problems or Have Trouble with Their Phones

CallManager provides a Quality Reporting Tool (QRT) that allows users to create a log of quality problems that occur during an active call. It provides an easy way for users to communicate problems with their phones, such as phones rebooting or users being unable to make calls. Make sure that the QRT softkey is available on the softkey template for the various connected states, and teach users to press it when they encounter problems on the call. The web-based QRT Viewer allows you to view and filter the reports submitted by users.

When users press the QRT softkey to report audio problems during an active call, a log begins to capture streaming statistics for the duration specified in the Cisco Extended Functions service parameters Streaming Statistics Polling Duration and Streaming Statistics Polling Frequency. By default, the log files are kept at C:\Program Files\Cisco\QRT\QRT.xml so that you can view the calling statistics for troubleshooting purposes.

To make the process more user-friendly and to provide a bit of additional information about what the user experienced, enable the Display Extended QRT Menu Choices service parameter (**Service > Service Parameters > Cisco Extended Functions**). Doing so means that after the user presses the QRT softkey, a menu of common call problems is displayed, such as "I hear echo," "Can't hear other end," "Choppy sound," and more. The user selects the audio problem by pressing the number associated with the problem that is occurring.

When users are not active in a call, they can use the QRT softkey to report other problems associated with the phone, such as the phone recently rebooting or an inability to place calls, as shown in Figure 7-7.

Figure 7-7 *QRT Menu Choices When the Phone Is On-Hook*

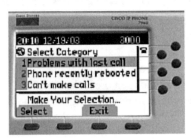

Gateway Best Practices

The following sections provide best practices for gateways:

- Choose Media Gateway Control Protocol (MGCP) over H.323 in most cases.

- Do not include other gateways in gateway calling search spaces.

- Override the sending of automatic number identification (ANI) out a gateway if desired.

Choose MGCP over H.323 in Most Cases

Most of the time, you'll want to use MGCP as the gateway signaling protocol because MGCP gateways are configured in CallManager Administration with little configuration on the device itself, making ease of configuration a benefit of MGCP. In addition, MGCP provides audio preservation on CallManager failure. Other signaling protocols such as H.323 do not offer a way to preserve active calls during a CallManager failure. A general rule of thumb is that if MGCP is available on a gateway, you should use it.

The exceptions include cases in which features that are needed on the gateway are not supported in CallManager. Some of these are T1-CAS Feature Group D and Network Facility Associated Signaling (NFAS). Also, if you need to terminate DS3 circuits, the AS5850 series of gateways is the only option; it supports only H.323 with CallManager.

That being said, the overwhelming majority of networks use MGCP, and it is the recommended protocol for standard use.

Do Not Include Other Gateways in Gateway Calling Search Spaces

The gateway's CSS determines what destinations that gateway can reach on an incoming call. If the CSS on a gateway includes route patterns in partitions that point to other gateways, a path exists for calls that are inbound to go outbound through another gateway, which could result in forwarding loops and the potential for toll fraud. The CSS for incoming calls should include only partitions that contain directory numbers for internal extensions, voice mail, and any externally reachable application.

This doesn't preclude you from allowing users to forward their phones to outside destinations because a completely separate CSS exists for call forward all (you configure this on the Directory Number page in CallManager Administration). If you intend to restrict call forward all to internal extensions, you should apply the same CSS you applied to the gateways to the Forward All CSS field on the Directory Number Configuration page (**Device > Phone >** *find and select a phone > click a line*).

Override ANI Display out a Gateway if Desired

If your organization has a policy against providing automatic number identification (ANI) down to the station level, set the Calling Line ID Presentation field on the Route Pattern/ Hunt Pilot Configuration page to Restricted (**Route Plan > Route Pattern/Hunt Pilot**). Through the gateway, you can also edit the Calling Line ID Presentation field on the Gateway Configuration page (**Device > Gateway**) to globally block ANI from being sent. The result is that when outbound calls are made, "Private" shows on the called party's display. This could cause problems when calling residential customers who block calls that have presentation restricted.

To avoid this, you can configure a main number on the gateway itself using the Caller ID DN field. This also might be useful for companies that do not have Direct Inward Dial (DID). The result is that the number you choose, which is generally the company's main number, shows up on the called party's display instead of the generic "Private" presentation. Replacing the caller ID with a generic main number means that emergency calls to Public Safety Answering Points (PSAP) will not include the caller's specific number. This is generally an undesirable result if you have DID numbers. To ensure that emergency calls are not affected, do not configure a main number at the gateway level on the Gateway Configuration page. Instead, to block station-specific ANI, you need to configure the main number as the calling party transformation mask in all route patterns except the emergency services pattern (for example, 911). For the emergency services route pattern, configure a mask that provides the complete phone number, such as 214-555-1234.

Dial Plan Best Practices

The backbone of any telephony system is the dial plan, which is a composition of rules you define to allow calls to reach the intended destinations. CallManager performs digit analysis in the call control layer of the CallManager software. CallManager's digit analysis component handles dial plan responsibilities such as analyzing the dialed digits, performing digit manipulation in conjunction with translation patterns if necessary, and routing the call to the destination. CallManager performs these functions using a combination of route patterns, route lists, route groups, and route group devices.

CallManager also incorporates the use of other parameters such as partitions and calling search spaces (CSS) as a means of enforcing calling restrictions, offering various classes of service and gateway selection, and preventing toll fraud. The dial plan can quickly become complex, so it's important to implement a dial plan that is as detailed and intuitive as possible.

Understanding the Important Role of Calling Search Spaces

Calling search spaces are most often used to create classes of restriction so that users cannot make unauthorized calls. But a CSS can serve many other purposes; you can think of it as a way of grouping sets within the dialing plan. This usage can extend the paradigm of simple restriction-based CSS. Imagine that a set of calling search spaces are defined, as shown in Table 7-1.

Table 7-1 *Common Calling Search Spaces*

CSS	Description
Internal	Internal extensions only
Local	Local partitions
National	Local + long distance partitions
International	Local + long distance + international partitions

For example, group speed-dial lists can be created using calling search spaces and translation patterns. Joe, a marketing manager, asks you to create 10 speed dials for his 20-person staff. You need to make the speed dials accessible only to his group, and each user has a Cisco IP Phone 7940 (which offers two line/speed dial buttons). None of Joe's employees has a Cisco 7914 Extension Module onto which you could place 10 speed-dial entries. This scenario is a perfect opportunity to create non-restriction-based calling search spaces. Create a partition called JOE_GRP_SPEED_PT and the calling search spaces shown in Table 7-2.

Table 7-2   *Specific Calling Search Spaces to Enable Group Speed Dial for Joe's Group*

CSS	Description
JOE-GRP-Internal	Internal Extensions Only + JOE_GRP_SPEED_PT
JOE-GRP-Local	Local Partitions + JOE_GRP_SPEED_PT
JOE-GRP-National	Local + Long Distance Partitions + JOE_GRP_SPEED_PT
JOE-GRP-International	Local + Long Distance + International Partitions + JOE_GRP_SPEED_PT

After these calling search spaces are created, you apply them to the phones used by the people in Joe's group. Finally, you create translation patterns for each speed dial and place them in the JOE_GRP_SPEED_PT partition. See Table 7-3 for an example.

Table 7-3   *Translation Patterns Used by Joe's Group*

Translation Pattern	Called Party Transformation Mask
*5301	914155553345
*5302	95555645
*5303	917145556452
*5304	912135550987

Using calling search spaces provides the security needed for Joe's group and also allows you to reuse the speed dials with other groups. Most often, using a speed dial access code such as *53 is the best way to provision group speed dials. To activate the group speed-dial, one of Joe's users dials *53 followed by the two-digit code (01 through 10) for each of the speed dial numbers designated by Joe.

The following sections describe dial plan best practices:

- Implement class of service restrictions by ordering your partitions in calling search spaces.
- Never use the <None> partition.
- Use well-named partitions and calling search spaces to effectively segment the dial plan.
- Create a partition for globally blocked numbers, and create specific partitions for exceptions to the globally blocked numbers.
- Use the 9.@ route pattern with great care.

- Use urgent route patterns when applicable.
- Use line-based calling search spaces in addition to phone-based calling search spaces (with caveats).
- Accommodate extension mobility in the dial plan.
- Use dial plan features to prevent toll fraud.
- Configure explicit external route patterns.
- Accommodate PBX requirements for prepended digits by using the prefix digits (outgoing calls) field.
- Use the Cisco Dialed Number Analyzer to test your configuration.

Implement Class of Service Restrictions by Ordering Your Partitions in Calling Search Spaces

Create separate partitions for the following:

- Applications (voice mail, interactive voice response [IVR], Personal Assistant [PA], and so on)
- Destinations for applications (internal, local, long distance, international, and so on)
- Departmental groups (intercom and speed dial)

Then create calling search spaces, which are ordered lists of those separate partitions. The order of partitions in a CSS matters only if there are two equal matches, at which point closest-match routing rules take precedence over partition order in a CSS. Essentially, CallManager uses the order of partitions in a CSS only to break ties.

Never Use the <None> Partition

CallManager provides a default <None> partition that can be accessed universally regardless of the CSS configuration. That means that any directory number or route pattern in the <None> partition can be matched by digit analysis at any point in the string. System administrators often mistakenly lump all internal directory numbers into the <None> partition. This makes it difficult to roll out future functionality such as intercom because intercom groups generally use overlapping directory numbers.

Using the <None> partition can also result in misrouted calls, inability to restrict outbound calls, and troubleshooting difficulties. When looking at CCM traces, the CSS does not include the <None> partition; remember that the <None> partition is in every CSS.

Use Well-Named Partitions and Calling Search Spaces to Effectively Segment the Dial Plan

Partitions are simply logical groups of directory numbers, route patterns, and translation patterns. It's critical to logically design your partitions to enable things such as toll-fraud prevention, call restrictions, and premium-rate number blocking (such as 900 numbers in the U.S.).

Each partition can include directory numbers, route patterns, and translation patterns. Design the dial plan so that only the desired directory numbers can reach certain route patterns and vice versa.

Consider the following practical example. Table 7-4 shows a subset of a common North American Numbering Plan (NANP) for a large company. The route patterns 4XXX through 7XXX represent DID extension numbers assigned to user phones. The **9.** patterns are OffNet locations that can be reached through gateways.

Table 7-4   *NANP Example*

Directory Number/Route Pattern	Partition
4XXX	ATL-Line1
5XXX	ATL-Line2
6XXX	HOU-Line1
7XXX	LAX-Line1
9.1XXXXXXXXXX	HOU-TOLL
9.[2-9][2-9]XXXXX	HOU-LOCAL
9.911	HOU-EMER
9.011	HOU-INTL
9.1XXXXXXXXXX	ATL-TOLL
9.[2-9][2-9]XXXXX	ATL-LOCAL
9.911	ATL-EMER
9.011	ATM-INTL
X	ATL-SCOLLORA-INTCM
X	ATL-ELEONHARDT-INTCM
X	ATL-ASMITH-INTCM
X	ATL-DVCORLEY-INTCM

As you can see, the dial plan is logically laid out: There are overlapping numbers, but they are in separate partitions. Notice the partitions for intercom. By not putting the primary line extensions in the <None> partition, you can use a single digit represented by X for the intercom extensions. In addition, the segmentation of OffNet patterns lets you establish classes of restriction in the future.

When creating your partitions and calling search spaces, it's important to consider the naming of each partition. As with other parameters in CallManager, it's always best to make the names as descriptive and intuitive as possible; however, partition naming has a catch. Although longer names would certainly be more descriptive, a length limit is imposed. Each combined CSS has a maximum length of 1024 characters, including the separator between each partition name. However, the real limit to be respected is 512 characters per CSS. For example, the string Atlanta_Phone:Atlanta_Local:Atlanta_LD contains 38 characters. The *combined calling search space* is the line's CSS concatenated with the device's CSS. Therefore, name your partitions carefully so that you do not exceed the maximum length for any combined CSS (which is 1024) or the limit for any single CSS, which is 512. For example, a single CSS of 513 characters is impossible, even though if it were combined with a 3-character CSS, the combined CSS would be less than 1024 characters. If you believe you might approach the 512 maximum per CSS, try to keep the names short and descriptive by using abbreviations where appropriate.

Create a Partition for Globally Blocked Numbers, and Create Specific Partitions for Exceptions to the Globally Blocked Numbers

Every network contains some numbers that are globally disallowed, such as 976 and 900 numbers in the NANP, and other premium-rate numbers in non-NANP countries. The easiest way to block any given pattern globally is to create a partition called Global_Block and place all route patterns to be blocked in that partition. In addition, make that partition the first partition of every CSS.

If a user needs to dial a specific premium rate number (many technical support lines use them), follow these steps:

Step 1 Create a specific pattern to the exact number—for example, a support number such as 900-555-1234.

Step 2 Place it in a separate partition specifically named for that number, such as 900WidgetTechSupport.

Step 3 Make a copy of the user's existing CSS and call it 900WidgetTechSupportAllow.

Step 4 Place the 900WidgetTechSupportAllow CSS on the user's line.

Use the 9.@ Route Pattern with Great Care

The 9.@ route pattern is a collection of route patterns that serves as a macro that represents the NANP by default. It's important to understand that if you want to establish classes of restriction based on items such as area codes a user can call or block the user's ability to dial outside his or her local area, you have to use route filters, which can become complex when a large number of filters are applied. For example, to block numbers that have international area codes, you must build a 9.@ route pattern with a filter that uses multiple AND clauses for AREA-CODE ==. Because of the 1024-character limit, you sometimes have to configure two 9.@ patterns with filters.

The easiest patterns to configure are the explicit digits for routing, such as 9.[2-9]XXXXXX for seven-digit dialing, 9.1[2-9]XX[2-9]XXXXXX for 10-digit dialing, and so on. This syntax is easier to troubleshoot and takes less time to configure. On the blocking side of things, it's true that you have to configure more patterns to block, but they are explicit and easy to read and troubleshoot. It's really a personal choice; the point is to know what you're getting into when you use the @ macro.

TIP   Device weights are used to manage the number of physical devices that can register with a CallManager server. The weight values are based on memory consumption and CPU resources. Dial plan weights manage the number of dial plan entries you can configure on a given server.

You can learn more about device weights and dial plan weights in Chapter 1 and in the Cisco IP Telephony Solution Reference Network Design (SRND) guide. To read the latest SRND, go to http://www.cisco.com/go/srnd.

Use Urgent Route Patterns When Applicable

CallManager routes calls based on the route patterns configured in CallManager Administration. If more than one pattern could feasibly match the digits dialed by a user, CallManager waits for additional digits or until the interdigit timer (T302 Timer service parameter) expires before routing the call. Sometimes you might want a dialed digit string to route immediately after the pattern match is made and not wait for additional dialed digits or the interdigit timer to expire. To accomplish immediate routing, you can create specific route patterns and mark them as Urgent Priority. Urgent route patterns cause CallManager to route the call as soon as the dialed digits match the urgent pattern.

For example, consider the following three patterns configured with either normal or urgent priority: 991 (normal), 9.911 (urgent), and 99112 (normal). The patterns 991 and 99112 are extensions for IP phones; 911 is the emergency services number in North America (represented by the 9.911 route pattern). If a user dials 991, CallManager recognizes a potential pattern match and waits for either of these occurrences:

- The entry of additional digits to confirm which pattern (991, 9.911, or 99112) to route the call through
- Expiration of the interdigit timer

If a user dials 9911, CallManager immediately routes the call to emergency services because pattern 9.911 is marked as urgent priority. If a user attempts to dial 99112, the call is routed to the emergency services number as soon as the user dials the second 1, which is not the desired behavior.

The key to successfully using urgent patterns is specificity. Configure only specific patterns as urgent, and be sure there are no patterns that use the same syntax and that are longer than the urgent pattern. In the preceding example, if you configured a user with the extension 99112, that user would never receive any internal calls because when someone tried to dial 99112 OnNet, CallManager would immediately route the call to emergency services. The exception is if the calling party uses a speed dial that sends all the digits at once, thus bypassing CallManager's digit-by-digit analysis.

TIP	To avoid this kind of problem, do not to use the same digit that you use for outbound PSTN access as the initial digit in your internal dial plan.

Use Line-Based Calling Search Spaces in Addition to Phone-Based Calling Search Spaces (with Caveats)

Traditionally, the phone CSS effectively creates classes of service by specifically allowing only certain numbers to be reached. Figure 7-8 shows a traditional dial plan layout for implementing classes of service for sites in San Jose (SJ) and New York (NY). However, in a deployment with a large number of remote sites, the traditional method can lead to the creation of many partitions and calling search spaces. For each site, you need a certain number of partitions for the various classes of routes (Local, National, International, Emergency, and so on). In addition, you need calling search spaces to assign the classes to users' phones.

However, when a CSS is assigned to the lines on a phone in addition to the phone itself, the resulting CSS is an ordered list of partitions, as shown in Figure 7-9.

Figure 7-8   *Traditional Dial Plan for Centralized Deployment*

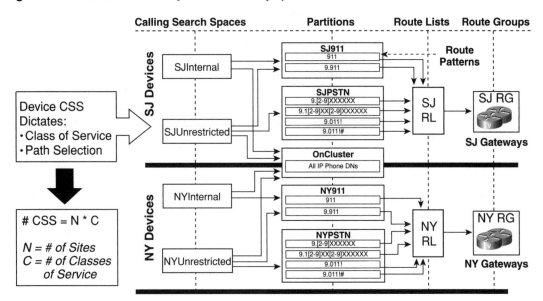

Figure 7-9   *Ordered List of Partitions for Line/Phone CSS Combination*

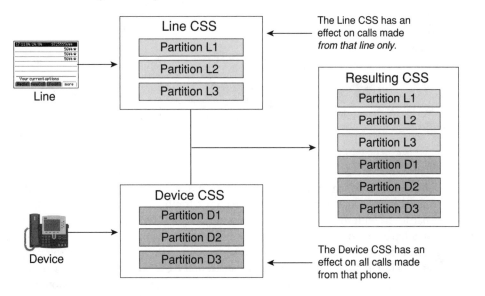

Assigning calling search spaces to the line leads to a better way of implementing classes of service when you have many sites, as shown in Figure 7-10. (It's also useful in large campus designs, but the real efficiency comes in ease of configuration when multiple WAN branches are involved.) The key is introducing *blocked* translation patterns (translation patterns that use the **Block this pattern** option) for patterns you want to restrict and then assigning that translation pattern to a partition that is included in a CSS assigned to the line. The phone CSS contains a single partition with all PSTN patterns for a given set of gateways. In other words, the phone CSS is used for path selection or gateway selection. The line CSS contains partitions with blocked translation patterns for the patterns you want to restrict.

Figure 7-10 *Using Blocked Translation Patterns*

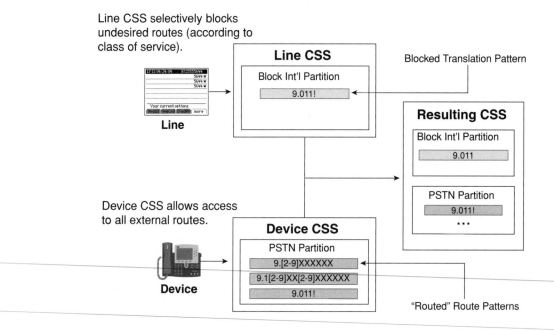

Because CallManager uses closest-match routing, the line CSS that contains the blocked patterns must match more closely. The reason for this is that the phone CSS should contain partitions with route patterns such as 9.@ or 9.[2-9]XXXXXX. You can simply put all available patterns in a single partition, assign it to a single CSS, and apply it to the phone. The blocked translation patterns will be more specific, such as 9.976!. You simply create a translation pattern with no digits discarded in the Called Party Transformations section, which results in the class of service you want, but with less administration. Figure 7-11 shows an example of a translation pattern that blocks international calls (**Route Plan > Translation Pattern**).

Figure 7-11 *Translation Pattern Configuration*

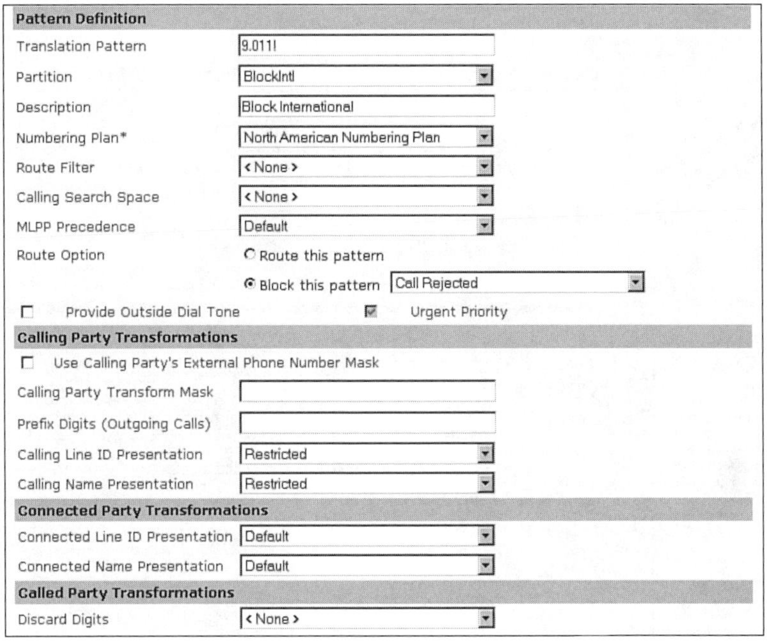

Pattern Definition	
Translation Pattern	9.011!
Partition	BlockIntl
Description	Block International
Numbering Plan*	North American Numbering Plan
Route Filter	< None >
Calling Search Space	< None >
MLPP Precedence	Default
Route Option	○ Route this pattern
	● Block this pattern Call Rejected
□ Provide Outside Dial Tone	☑ Urgent Priority
Calling Party Transformations	
□ Use Calling Party's External Phone Number Mask	
Calling Party Transform Mask	
Prefix Digits (Outgoing Calls)	
Calling Line ID Presentation	Restricted
Calling Name Presentation	Restricted
Connected Party Transformations	
Connected Line ID Presentation	Default
Connected Name Presentation	Default
Called Party Transformations	
Discard Digits	< None >

NOTE   It's critical that you specify explicit patterns to block. Use as many specific digits as possible. Also try to keep your permissive route patterns as general as possible to facilitate the approach. The exclamation point (!) is used to stop CallManager from accepting more digits when the pattern has been reached. For example, if you use 9.976XXXX as a blocked translation pattern, the user can dial the whole string before hearing the reorder tone. If you use 9.976!, users hear reorder tone when they press the 6. The reason for this is that the exclamation point means "any set of digits." When configuring a blocking translation pattern, using the exclamation point tells CallManager that it doesn't matter what digit comes after the 9976—the call must be blocked. It also has the positive effect of immediately informing the user via reorder tone that all numbers to 9976 are blocked. Using 9.976XXXX tells CallManager to wait until a complete string of eight digits is dialed before deciding whether to block the call and also potentially making the user think it is a single number block.

If you fail to follow the rule of specificity, you will have a lot of trouble getting the right classes of restriction implemented because calls you want to allow might get blocked and calls you want to block might be allowed.

Figure 7-12 shows the net effect of the dial plan.

Figure 7-12 *Best-Practice Dial Plan for Centralized Deployment*

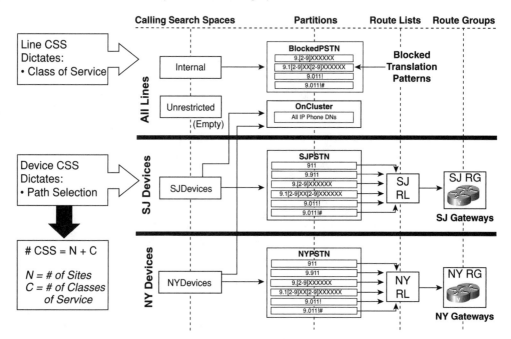

Figure 7-13 compares the traditional method and the best practice. At the bottom of the figure, you can see the resulting formulas for deriving the number of calling search spaces and partitions that are required for a given number of sites.

This best practice has some important caveats:

- Forwarded calls use the Forward All, Forward Busy, and Forward No Answer (*CallFwdxxx*) calling search spaces only. These values are not concatenated with the line CSS or device CSS.

- If forwarded calls must have unrestricted privileges, set the *CallFwdxxx* calling search spaces to the site-specific device CSS.

- If forwarded calls must be restricted to internal numbers only, set the *CallFwdxxx* calling search spaces to a single, global CSS with only internal partitions.

- If forwarded calls must have some intermediate restriction (for example, no international calls), the best-practice approach might become less efficient because additional calling search spaces are needed.

Figure 7-13 *Comparing the Traditional Dial Plan and the Best-Practice Dial Plan with Formulas*

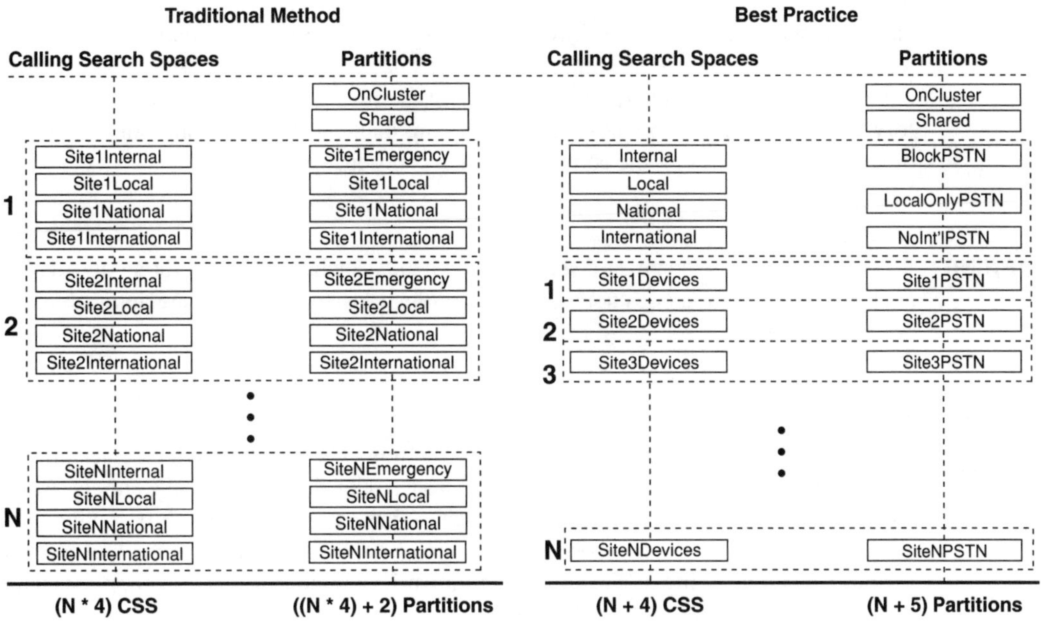

- Blocking translation patterns configured within the line CSS must be *at least as specific* as the route patterns configured within the device CSS (watch for the @ wildcard because its patterns are very specific).

- Automated alternate routing (AAR) uses a different CSS for rerouted calls. In most cases, the AAR CSS can be the same as the unrestricted site-specific device CSS.

- Some implications, described in the following section, exist for extension mobility users.

TIP	See the Solution Reference Network Designs at http://www.cisco.com/go/srnd for more information.

Accommodate Extension Mobility in the Dial Plan

When calling search spaces are defined to lines and phones using the best-practice method described in the preceding section, there are some implications for extension mobility users.

General Deployment Guidelines

When you use a standard set of blocked translation patterns across every site to determine class of service and use phone CSS for gateway selection, extension mobility works quite well when users log in at different sites. It works because the gateway selection is being done at the phone CSS level. Extension mobility profiles replace the line CSS and call forward CSS, but not the phone CSS, which means that under normal conditions, regardless of where the user logs in, the correct gateway is chosen.

WARNING   When you do not use a standard set of dialing habits, such as dialing 9 for an outside line at all sites, this method does not work because the translation patterns are applicable.

Call Forward Settings

It's important to understand that Call Forward settings are assigned on the device profile and that this has implications for the CSS approach. Consider a practical example: Amy, who normally works at her office in Los Angeles, has an extension mobility profile that allows her to log in at the San Jose office. When she arrives in San Jose, she logs in with her profile. Before going to a meeting, she forwards her phone to her cell phone, which is 310-555-4444. Her Forward All CSS is set to LA_Local.

If people in the Los Angeles office call her, the call goes out the local Los Angeles (LA) Public Switched Telephone Network (PSTN) gateway. When a call comes in from the PSTN to her Los Angeles office, the call hairpins back out the LA PSTN gateway attempting to reach her cell phone. All of this is fine. However, if someone in the San Jose office calls Amy, the call goes across the WAN that connects the San Jose and Los Angeles sites and goes out the LA PSTN gateway. This is something to consider for call admission control (CAC) purposes if you'll have many traveling users. Be sure to either instruct users not to forward their phones when traveling, or simply restrict Call Forward All to internal extensions only.

AAR Caveats

AAR simply doesn't work with extension mobility users moving across sites. When extension mobility users log in at their "home" sites, it works fine, but when they move, it doesn't work because the external phone number mask for a DID doesn't change.

Consider Amy again. Her external phone number mask on her extension mobility profile is 310555XXXX. She goes to San Jose and logs in (Call Forward All is off). Someone from LA calls her extension, and CAC denies a call because of the lack of available bandwidth on the WAN. AAR then tries to kick in and reroute the call out the LA gateway. Unfortunately, the call comes right back into the same gateway, and CAC denies the call again because Amy is across the WAN in San Jose. AAR doesn't know that Amy is now in the 408 area versus her defined 310 area code. This starts an endless loop. To avoid the loop, be sure that the CSS on the gateway doesn't contain partitions that contain route patterns matching the DID range pointing to the same gateway. The gateway's AAR calling search space should allow calls made to OffNet destinations other than the DID ranges assigned to the same gateway. For instance, Gateway A handling DID range 408-555-10XX should be configured with an AAR calling search space containing patterns allowing calls to any OffNet destination (for example, XXX-XXX-XXXX) but should block any calls made to Gateway A's DID range (for example, it should block calls to 408-555-10XX). This is to avoid the potential routing loop of extension mobility users located outside the branch.

TIP   It is critical to assign calling search spaces to gateways that allow only internal numbers. Failure to do so results in routing loops that eat up all the resources on your PSTN gateways.

Use Dial Plan Features to Prevent Toll Fraud

Toll fraud is a serious issue for anyone administering a phone system. The fraudulent use of corporate telecommunications networks can be costly for any organization. It's essential that you take all necessary precautions to prevent your company or organization from becoming a victim.

This section provides a series of steps that should be taken to help prevent toll fraud. The best practices described here are by no means a complete and exhaustive guide to preventing all toll fraud, but rather a set of quick and easy configuration tasks that may be implemented to prevent the most common attempts at toll fraud. Because toll fraud is becoming so prevalent, continually monitor the call detail records (CDR) of your CallManager servers to identify potential toll fraud exploits not thwarted by the configurations presented in this section. Apply the information you learn in this section to create configurations that thwart newly discovered toll fraud.

The basic preventive measures covered in this section are

- Use the dial plan to eliminate toll fraud
- Restrict auto-registered IP phones
- Use calling search spaces to restrict calls
- Block common fraudulent area codes using a single partition

Use the Dial Plan to Eliminate Toll Fraud

As explained earlier, partitions and calling search spaces allow you to specify the dialed patterns that may be reached by a specific calling device. More importantly, they can be used to restrict specific route patterns or destinations from being reached by a particular calling device. The point is that in many cases it's more effective to deny access to certain destinations than to try to include all the allowed destinations. Simply exclude the forbidden destinations in the allowed list. Exploitation of loose restrictions such as these makes toll fraud possible. Therefore, you should carefully consider the partitions and calling search spaces assigned to the devices in your network that have potential access to the PSTN. In some cases you should specifically restrict access to certain destinations, as explained in the following sections.

Restrict Auto-Registered IP Phones

Auto-registration, when used correctly, can be convenient because it allows IP phones not previously entered into the CallManager database to be automatically registered to CallManager. A potential problem with auto-registered phones is that they could be mistakenly authorized for long distance or international calls, which could result in fraudulent use. You can avoid this risk by assigning appropriate partitions and calling search spaces to the auto-registered phones. Perform the following tasks to assign the appropriate partitions and CSSs:

- Create partitions such as AutoPhones_PT, HelpDesk_PT, TAPS_PT, and 911_PT.

- Create a CSS such as AutoPhones_CSS, and add the HelpDesk_PT, TAPS_PT, and 911_PT partitions to this CSS so that auto-registered phones can call only other auto-registered phones, the help desk, the TAPS server, and 911.

- For the device pool used by auto-registered phones, set the CSS for auto-registration to **AutoPhones_CSS**.

- On the Cisco CallManager Configuration page (**System > Cisco CallManager**), enter the directory number range to be used for auto-registration, and select **AutoPhones_PT** as the partition.

- Create or confirm the existence of the 9.911 and 911 route patterns, and add them to the 911_PT partition.

These tasks help protect auto-registered phones from being used for unauthorized calls. Fraudulent activity can be minimized by using auto-registration, the Bulk Administration Tool (BAT), and the Tool for Auto-Registered Phones Support (TAPS). In combination, they quickly register new IP phones with defined settings. Nevertheless, during the interval between auto-registration and final phone configuration via TAPS, following these procedures prevents these phones from being used to make unauthorized outbound calls.

Use Calling Search Spaces to Restrict Calls

Use calling search spaces to restrict calls in combination with other features: call forwarding, voice mail, applications, and gateways.

Restrict Call Forward All Calling Search Spaces

The call forwarding feature on IP phones can be used to rob your company or organization of the cost of long distance charges. For example, employees could forward their IP phones to their home phone number and then have family members in another state or country call the company's toll-free number, enter the employee extension, and be forwarded to the home number, all at the company's expense. Also, employees could forward their IP phones to long distance or international numbers, and then from home call their own phones to connect to the numbers they had previously set as the call forward destinations, again at the company's expense.

You can prevent this type of toll fraud by using partitions and calling search spaces. On the Directory Number Configuration page for each directory number, assign a CSS to the Call Forward All field. For the general populace, consider restricting the call forward all CSS to OnNet numbers. For specific other users, such as managers, executives, and so on, use a CSS that also allows OffNet numbers.

You can do this using the following sample guidelines:

- Create a CSS such as CFA_OffNet_CSS, and add partitions that contain internal, local, and long distance numbers.
- Create a CSS such as CFA_OnNet_CSS, and add partitions that contain only internal destinations.
- Assign the appropriate CSS for the Call Forward All field for each user's directory number.

This example assumes that you have already separated internal, local, long distance, and international route patterns into internal, local, long distance, and international partitions.

TIP   You can update the Call Forward All CSS by using BAT to update the CSS (Line). To do this, select **Configure > Phones > Update Lines**, and run a query for CSS (Line)s that use the <None> CSS. Then update the CSS fields that relate to the forwarding feature. If you want to implement the previously described strategy, you update the CSS (Line) to the OnNet CSS for all phones and then manually in CallManager Administration update each manager or executive phone to the OffNet CSS.

Restrict Voice Mail Calling Search Spaces

Some voice mail systems give users the option of being transferred, which could allow those users to dial long distance or international numbers. You can prevent this type of toll fraud by using partitions and calling search spaces.

NOTE Although the voice mail system might let you disable call transfers from the voice mail system itself, you should restrict the calling rights of the voice mail system on the CallManager side as well.

There are two common situations in which this vulnerability should be addressed. The first pertains to a voice mail system that has specific voice mail ports configured in CallManager Administration, as is the case with Cisco Unity. The second scenario involves the connection to a third-party voice mail system, such as using FXS gateways. In either case, the basic approach is the same.

When you add Cisco Unity to CallManager, each configured voice mail port must be assigned a CSS. This CSS determines what destinations can be reached from the actual voice mail application. It should at least include internal destinations so that the Unity AutoAttendant functions properly. In the most secure implementation—which prevents users from successfully transferring to external destinations—the CSS assigned to the voice mail ports would include only internal destinations.

For deployments involving third-party voice mail systems interfaced to FXS gateways, a similar type of CSS should be applied. To provide maximum protection, the FXS ports of the gateway connected to the voice mail system should be assigned a CSS that includes only partitions with internal phone number extensions. Such an assignment thwarts transfers to external destinations from the third-party voice mail system.

TIP Assuming that you follow the naming best practice discussed in the section "Use Descriptive Names for All Configuration Items," you can update the CSS for all voice mail ports by using BAT. To do this, select **Configure > Phones > Update Phones**, and run a query for the description that matches your voice mail ports prefix, such as **VM_**.

Restrict Application Calling Search Spaces

Using other standalone applications such as Cisco Customer Response Solutions or Personal Assistant opens the possibility of abuse by users who exploit the rules within the applications themselves. For instance, a user could configure a rule in Personal Assistant that directs calls from a relative in Europe to the user's home phone in the United States. Although Personal Assistant can be helpful in allowing user-defined, rules-based call routing, it can also be abused if not properly configured. The same applies to the Customer Response Solutions application or any other standalone application integrated with CallManager that can make and direct calls. The best way to prevent such abuse is to ensure that only authorized users have access to the various applications in your network. Most of these applications have detailed administration guides available within the product and on

Cisco.com that provide guidelines for the correct configuration of partitions and calling search spaces to prevent misuse of the application. Consult the relevant guides for further details.

Restrict Gateway Calling Search Spaces

Gateways provide the connection between the IP telephony network and the PSTN. Gateways are an obvious target for toll fraud exploits, the most common of which is hairpinning. *Hairpinning* occurs when a call comes into a gateway on one port/timeslot and exits the gateway on another port/timeslot. In most cases, hairpinning is undesirable because calls entering the gateway from external callers should be directed to destinations internal to the IP telephony network. Therefore, to prevent outside callers from successfully hairpinning to external destinations, the CSS assigned to the gateway ports should include only internal partitions.

Block Common Fraudulent Area Codes Using a Single Partition

Several area codes are often used to host premium rate (fee-based) number services that should typically be blocked by CallManager. However, you might have a legitimate need to reach a phone number within one of these countries. If so, you could simply allow calls to that area code or, preferably, create explicit route patterns that allow calls only to the specific numbers you need to reach. Table 7-5 lists many of the area codes you should consider blocking, along with the pattern you configure to block calls to the specified area code. Note that the pattern supplied is for calls originating from the NANP.

NOTE   This is not a complete and exhaustive list of possible fraudulent area codes.

Table 7-5   *Common Area Codes to Block*

Country	Area Code	Blocked Route Pattern for NANP
Anguilla	264	9.1264XXXXXXX
Antigua and Barbuda	268	9.1268XXXXXXX
Bahamas	242	9.1242XXXXXXX
Barbados	246	9.1246XXXXXXX
Bermuda	441	9.1441XXXXXXX
British Virgin Islands	284	9.1284XXXXXXX

continues

Table 7-5 *Common Area Codes to Block (Continued)*

Country	Area Code	Blocked Route Pattern for NANP
Cayman Islands	345	9.1345XXXXXXX
Dominica	767	9.1767XXXXXXX
Dominican Republic	809	9.1809XXXXXXX
Grenada	473	9.1473XXXXXXX
Jamaica	876	9.1876XXXXXXX
Montserrat	664	9.1664XXXXXXX
Puerto Rico	787	9.1787XXXXXXX
Some conference numbers	700	9.1700XXXXXXX
St. Kitts and Nevis	869	9.1869XXXXXXX
St. Lucia	758	9.1758XXXXXXX
St. Vincent and the Grenadines	784	9.1784XXXXXXX
Toll charge area code	900	9.1900XXXXXXX
Toll charge area code	976	9.1976XXXXXXX
Trinidad and Tobago	868	9.1868XXXXXXX
Turks and Caicos Islands	649	9.1649XXXXXXX
U.S. Virgin Islands	340	9.1340XXXXXXX

TIP   You can learn more about toll fraud, including a fraud scheme involving conference numbers using the 700 area code, at http://www.claypro.com/CTF/GATEWAY.html.

The best way to implement area code blocking in CallManager is to create a separate route pattern for each area code you want to block and select the **Block this pattern** option on the Route Pattern/Hunt Pilot Configuration page (**Route Plan > Route Pattern/Hunt Pilot**). Then place these route patterns in a specific partition such as Fraud_Prevention_PT and include it in every CSS in the system.

If you are using line-based calling search spaces, another way to implement area code blocking is to use translation patterns that are set to block. Place the translation patterns in a partition that is part of every possible line-based CSS. This results in universal blocking.

Yet another option is to use the @ wildcard and create a route filter specifying an area code in each clause (for example, **Area-Code==900**) and combining multiple clauses in a single route filter until you reach the 1024-character limit. Keep adding route filters until all the area codes are configured. Then simply apply each route filter to a 9.@ route pattern and select the **Block this pattern** option. As with the previous option, you should place these route patterns in a specific partition such as Fraud_Prevention_PT and include it in every CSS.

Configure Explicit External Route Patterns

Configure explicit route patterns rather than patterns using macros such as 9.@. So many patterns are represented in the 9.@ pattern that troubleshooting and provisioning become much more difficult. You'll find you have to use lots of route filters to achieve options such as seven-digit dialing and area code-based routing. Explicit patterns such as 9.555XXXX and 9.972555XXXX are much easier to provision and are more descriptive (you can immediately understand what the pattern provides just by looking at it).

Accommodate PBX Requirements for Prepended Digits by Using the Prefix Digits (Outgoing Calls) Field

If you have a gateway that sends calls through a Private Branch Exchange (PBX) that requires prepended digits, you must add the digits in the Route/Hunt List Detail Configuration page, shown in Figure 7-14 (**Route Plan > Route/Hunt > Route/Hunt List**). In the Called Party Transformations area, enter the necessary digits in the Prefix Digits (Outgoing Calls) field.

Figure 7-14 *Route/Hunt List Detail Configuration*

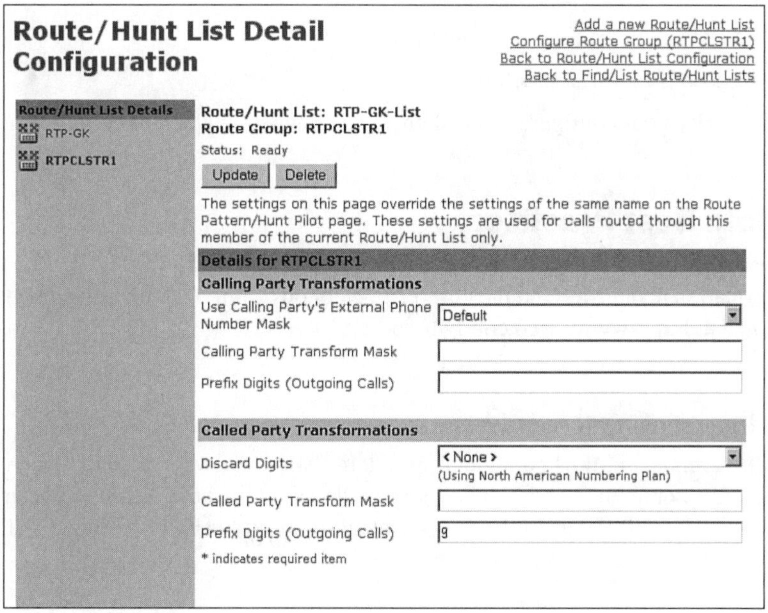

Use the Cisco Dialed Number Analyzer to Test Your Configuration

The Cisco Dialed Number Analyzer (DNA) helps you test a dial plan. After you enter a number such as the five-digit extension 51000, DNA analyzes the dialed digits and shows the path that the call would take if everything is registered and working properly. This analysis helps you verify that the dial plan has been configured correctly, which is particularly useful when you add CTI, IP Manager Assistant (IPMA), and so on, to the system. You can also use the DNA results to troubleshoot dial plan configuration, identify problems (if any), and tune the dial plan before it's deployed.

Best Practices for Configuring Features

This section provides best practices for configuring the various telephony features, such as Music on Hold, extension mobility, intercom, IPMA, and more.

The following topics are covered:

- Music on Hold best practices.
- Use local DSPs for conferencing at remote sites.
- Deploy video as needed.
- Extension mobility best practices.
- Configure intercom and group intercom.
- Manipulate outbound caller ID according to policy.
- Alter internal caller ID on a per-line basis.
- Configure system and group speed dials.
- Get more lines for fewer buttons.
- Cisco IPMA best practices.
- Verify your configuration and physical connection when using CMI.

Music on Hold Best Practices

The following sections provide best practices for Music on Hold (MOH). You can find more information about MOH in the Cisco IP Telephony Solution Reference Network Design, located at http://www.cisco.com/go/srnd.

Prevent MOH from Playing to Conferences

For systems with MOH configured, problems can occur when a conference participant places the conference on hold; doing so could cause the hold music to stream to the conference. CallManager release 4.x protects against this by providing a CallManager service parameter, Suppress MOH to Conference Bridge, which by default prevents music from streaming to conferences. Do not change this default value. This service parameter applies only to CallManager-hosted conferences; it does not apply to Cisco Conference Connection or Cisco MeetingPlace conferences.

In addition to using the service parameter, you can address this problem by using either of the following methods:

- Disable MOH (the least-desirable solution to the problem).

- Place the H.323 gateway used for Cisco MeetingPlace or Cisco Conference Connection integration in a device pool that has an MRGL that does not have an active MOH source. Because the called party determines the MOH stream, no stream plays.

TIP   In Cisco MeetingPlace, users can mute the hold music before going on hold during a conference by pressing **#5**. Users press **#5** again to unmute the phone.

Use MRGLs to Ensure Tone on Hold Rather than MOH (if Desired)

Just as you use MRGLs to ensure that MOH is available to phones, you can use them to prevent music from playing during hold. CallManager substitutes tone on hold instead. Just be sure that the MRGL is configured so that phones cannot reach a valid MOH source. Also be sure that all MOH resources are in a media resource group (MRG). If they aren't, they become part of the default MRGL that is available to all devices.

Use Cisco IOS SRST Functionality to Provide Multicast MOH in a WAN Environment Rather Than Putting an MOH Server at a Remote Site

Multicast MOH provides a few advantages, such as the ability to service many MOH streams at a remote site using a single stream. The tree-like nature of IP multicast lets a single stream be sent over the WAN even though many users might be putting calls on hold. Without the multicast capability, you would either have to put an MOH server onsite and make it part of the cluster—which would have to conform to the clustering over the WAN guidelines—or you would have to put multiple streams on the WAN.

The Cisco IOS SRST functionality allows for local multicast streaming using the router Flash as the source. For more information, see the Configuring MOH from Flash Files section in the Cisco SRST V3.0: Configuring Additional Call Features documentation at the following link. You can also refer to Chapter 2 for more information about SRST.

http://www.cisco.com/en/US/products/sw/iosswrel/ps5012
/products_feature_guide_ chapter09186a0080181322.html#1336408

Configure a Continuously Running MOH Stream

Many organizations prefer to have a continuously running MOH stream because they're used to plugging CD players or radio stations into the PBX. These live sources provide a continuous stream, which means that callers put on hold always hear something different.

In general with MOH, when any user in the system is put on hold, a dynamic conference bridge is created that consists of the hold source and the user on hold. When any other user is placed on hold, that user joins the bridge, if it exists. This means that if any call is on hold in the entire system, the music always plays continuously without starting from the beginning.

You can achieve the same condition—continuously running hold music—regardless of whether someone is already on hold in the system. This is possible because the continuous playback that happens as a result of the Multicast stream keeps the dynamic conference up all the time. Follow these steps:

Step 1 Enable Multicast MOH on the server.

Step 2 Enable Multicast MOH on the source.

NOTE   Do not enable Multicast MOH on the MRG.

You do not enable Multicast on the MRG because you still want the user to receive MOH via Unicast delivery. This works because the source and server are configured as Multicast.

This configuration doesn't require any Multicast configuration on the network. No actual Multicasting occurs.

Use Local DSPs for Conferencing at Remote Sites

Design, provision, and use the digital signal processors (DSP) available at the remote site rather than using DSPs from the central site when possible. If you intend to use hardware DSPs at the central site for conferencing and you're using the G.729a codec, you do not need to provision transcoders because transcoding is done by the hardware conference resource. The software-based conference resource does not provide this capability. In this case, you need to configure hardware transcoders.

For more information, refer to the following link or search Cisco.com for "Cisco conferencing and transcoding for voice gateway routers":

http://www.cisco.com/en/US/products/sw/iosswrel/ps1839
/products_feature_guide 09186a0080110bc5.html

Deploy Video as Needed

CallManager release 4.0 supports desktop video through an inexpensive solution called Cisco VT Advantage. Some users, executives, or entire companies want the option of desktop video. See Chapter 1 for more information about determining which features should be deployed to the various user classes. VT Advantage is integrated with CallManager, allowing simple configuration in CallManager Administration and integration with your existing video-capable Cisco IP Phone models (such as 7960, 7970, and so on). After configuration, attach a VT Advantage camera to your PC or IP phone and video is ready to go. Users simply go off-hook on their existing IP phones and make the call. The video pops up on their PC screen. See the Appendix, "CallManager 4.0 New Feature Description," for more information.

Extension Mobility Best Practices

Extension mobility allows users to temporarily access their Cisco IP Phone configuration, such as line appearances, services, and speed dials, from other Cisco IP Phones. In fact, users don't need to have actual IP phones assigned to them—instead, they have device profiles that can be accessed from any phone. With extension mobility, several employees can share office space on a rotational basis instead of having individual offices. This approach proves useful in environments such as sales offices and consulting firms where employees do not routinely conduct business in the same place or keep the same hours every day.

Provide Users with a Device Profile Rather Than a Specific Device

When rolling out extension mobility, be aware that many users get confused because it's not clear to them that a device profile is different from an actual device. The best method of deploying extension mobility is to simply give your users a device profile and not assign a specific physical phone to them.

Then explain to users that the device profile gives them a single point of administration for speed dial entries, fast dials, IP phone services, and more. It requires your users to log in to use a phone, but it also simplifies things for them by allowing them to use any phone.

TIP   Be sure your users know that although they can log into any phone that supports IP phone services (and that has the extension mobility services configured on it), unless the phone matches the model type configured in their device profiles, they might not have the exact same configuration. For example, suppose the user's device type is a 7960, and the six buttons are configured with one line and five speed dials. If the user logs into a 7940, one line and only the first speed dial appear because the 7940 has only two buttons.

Force Automatic Logout When a User Logs in to Another Phone

You can prevent extension mobility users from logging into more than one phone by setting the Extension Mobility service parameter Multiple Login Behavior to Auto Logout (**Service > Service Parameters > Extension Mobility**). Doing so automatically logs users out of the first device they logged into when they log into a second device. Setting this parameter handles the situation that occurs when a user moves from one area to another and forgets to log out on the first phone. For example, if John works in the San Jose office for part of the day and moves to the San Francisco office for the remainder of the day, when he logs in to the second phone in San Francisco, the San Jose phone automatically logs out.

Allowing multiple logins can enable toll fraud for unauthorized users who discover a phone that is still logged in. To avoid such situations, use Auto Logout to ensure that users can log into a single device only.

Customize Extension Mobility with AVVID XML Layer Scripts

If you want to effect custom actions for extension mobility, such as forcing logout at a certain time during the workday, write a custom script using the AVVID XML Layer (AXL) Application Programming Interface (API). See the section "Use the AXL SOAP API to Write Custom Scripts That Interact with the CallManager Database" for more information.

Use the Global Timer to Force Logout

You can configure an auto-logout timer, which forces a logout after a certain amount of time. This is generally set to 8 to 10 hours, depending on your organization's definition of a normal workday. Most of the time, users log in when they arrive for work, so eight hours is a good rule of thumb, but your environment might be different. The key is getting the phone logged out so that it is ready for use by the next user and is not subject to misuse for an extended period of time. Set the global timer using a combination of the Enforce Maximum Login Time and Maximum Login Time service parameters, discussed in Chapter 8.

Configure Intercom and Group Intercom

Intercom is a feature typically enabled between two phones, such as those belonging to a boss and his or her assistant. Using intercom, the caller may initiate a conversation by pressing a button on his or her phone that instantly connects to the recipient's speakerphone. CallManager offers the flexibility of configuring intercom a few different ways—using PLAR or speed dials—depending on how strictly you want to control the intercom pairings within your network. The following sections describe the methods of implementing intercom. Read through each intercom option to determine the best implementation option for your organization:

- Using PLAR extensions

- Using speed dial buttons
- Using speed dial buttons and the Speed Dial Await Further Digits service parameter
  (to implement group intercom)

NOTE	Auto-mute is not available with intercom. This means that it is possible to silently monitor an office if you intercom in before the manager or assistant arrives.

Implementing Intercom Using PLAR Extensions

Intercom can be deployed in a fashion similar to PLAR (discussed in this chapter), with a few notable differences. Intercom is usually established between two internal extensions, whereas PLAR can involve an external destination. Intercom also does not give the called party the option of not answering the call. You configure intercom in nearly the same way as PLAR between two internal extensions, and you enable auto-answer on the destination directory number(s).

If you want to statically determine every intercom pairing, you configure it much like PLAR. The only difference is that you enable auto-answer to the speakerphone of the destination directory number, as shown in Figure 7-15. The benefits of this approach are that your users have to press only a single button to initiate the intercom session, and every aspect of the configuration is under administrative control. The drawback is that it requires more configuration on your part because you must create a separate intercom extension on the IP phones and a unique partition, CSS, and translation pattern for *every* intercom destination in your network.

The following task list provides a configuration example for two IP phones implementing intercom between extension 21111 on IP phone A and extension 23333 on IP phone B. Bidirectional intercom is configured so that either side can initiate the intercom session to the other.

Step 1   Create two new partitions, such as Intercom_To_21111_PT and Intercom_To_23333_PT.

Step 2   Create a new CSS, such as Intercom_To_21111_CSS, and add only the Intercom_To_21111_PT partition.

Step 3   Create another new CSS, such as Intercom_To_23333_CSS, and add only the Intercom_To_23333_PT partition.

Step 4   Create a new translation pattern. Leave the Translation Pattern field blank, select Intercom_To_21111_PT as the partition, and assign a CSS that has access to the partition that contains the destination 21111.

Figure 7-15 *Intercom Example Using PLAR Extensions*

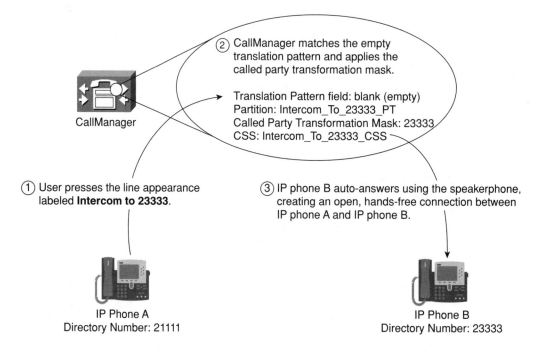

Step 5 Enter the destination number **21111** in the Called Party Transformation Mask field of the translation pattern.

Step 6 Create another new translation pattern. Leave the Translation Pattern field blank, select Intercom_To_23333_PT as the partition, and assign a CSS that has access to the partition that contains the destination 23333.

Step 7 Enter the destination number **23333** in the Called Party Transformation Mask field of the translation pattern.

Step 8 On IP phone A, assign the calling search space Intercom_To_23333_CSS to the directory number 21111, and enable **Auto Answer with Speakerphone**. Then enter **Intercom to 23333** in the Line Text Label field, and reset the phone for the changes to take effect.

Step 9 On IP phone B, assign the calling search space Intercom_To_21111_CSS to the directory number 23333, and enable **Auto Answer with Speakerphone**. Then enter **Intercom to 21111** in the Line Text Label field and reset the phone for the changes to take effect.

NOTE	The CSS you configure on the PLAR line must be unique to the line. If any other lines in addition to the PLAR line can access the CSS, everyone with that CSS will call it when they go off-hook.

With this configuration, the user of either IP phone can press his or her respective intercom line appearance. The corresponding IP phone auto-answers using the speakerphone, and the intercom session is established.

NOTE	To CallManager, establishing an intercom communication between two parties is the same thing as a call. Because of this, the intercom call is handled according to the phone's call state at the time of the intercom call's initiation. For example, if the target phone of an intercom call has a connected call in progress on another line, then call waiting, call forward all, or call forward no answer treatment is applied to the intercom call, depending on the call's condition. Be sure to keep the Forward No Answer field on the line blank because if the phone is in use, you do not want intercom calls going to voice mail.

Implementing Intercom Using Speed Dial Buttons

You can implement intercom in CallManager using speed dial buttons configured to dial auto-answering extensions. Use this method if you do not want such strict control over the intercom pairings. You simply need to configure separate line appearances for intercom extensions for the desired IP phones and enable those lines to auto-answer to the speakerphone (**Device > Phone >** *find and select the necessary phones > click the link to a new directory number*). Then individual users can configure their own speed dials to these intercom extensions. With this approach, you could easily enable an intercom extension on every IP phone. If your network consisted of five-digit extensions in the form of 2XXXX, you could create all intercom extensions in the form of 3XXXX. Keeping the same last four digits as the regular extension would allow users to easily intercom their intended parties. The users could configure speed dial buttons to their most-used intercom extensions and name them accordingly. The benefits of this approach are the dynamic nature of the intercom pairings and the reduction of CallManager configuration required to implement intercom. The drawback of this approach is the lack of administrative control because users are free to edit their own speed dials. Because of this, the speed dial button method is not recommended for emergency or security intercom because the users could possibly delete or incorrectly configure the emergency speed dial.

Implementing Group Intercom Using the Speed Dial Await Further Digits Service Parameter

You can implement group intercom by using speed dial prefixes. In fact, this is the best method if you want the intercom pairings to be dynamic so that a group of users with intercom extensions can receive intercom sessions from multiple users. A good example of this is a pool of administrative assistants working for several executives. Each assistant's IP phone can have an additional directory number configured to auto-answer to the speakerphone. For example, you could assign extension 27771 to Assistant 1, extension 27772 to Assistant 2, and extension 27773 to Assistant 3. Each executive could then configure a speed dial to the intercom directory number prefix of 2777, press that speed dial button, and then press 1, 2, or 3 to complete the intercom call to the desired assistant. To enable the appending of digits to what essentially becomes a speed dial prefix, you must set the CallManager service parameter Speed Dial Await Further Digits to True (**Service > Service Parameters > Cisco CallManager**). Using this method, the executives need to use only a single speed dial button for all intercom calls, freeing the other speed dials for other destinations. You can also restrict the directory numbers allowed to call the assistants' intercom lines by putting the intercom directory numbers in a partition that is available only to the executives.

Manipulate Outbound Caller ID According to Policy

Depending on the policy for your organization or company, you might want to manipulate the caller ID of your outbound calls or disable caller ID altogether, perhaps by displaying the main company number for all calls or by sending the caller ID of individual DID numbers. The following sections describe how to manipulate caller ID to accommodate these policies on a global and per-call level.

Blocking Caller ID on Outbound Calls

You can configure CallManager to block the sending of caller ID information for each outbound call. This is most easily done on the gateway connected to the PSTN. Because this gateway is the last device encountered by outbound calls destined for the PSTN, it has final authority regarding the sending of caller ID. To disable the presentation of caller ID for all outbound calls, change the Calling Line ID Presentation field to Restricted on the Gateway Configuration page (**Device > Gateway**), as shown in Figure 7-16. Be aware that if you set presentation to Restricted, CallManager still sends the calling party number information, but the far-end device does not display the phone number. Most such devices display "Private" instead of showing the number. This is different from not sending a calling party at all, which results in the far end showing "Unknown" as the calling number.

Figure 7-16 *Gateway Configuration Page Showing the Calling Line ID Presentation and Caller ID DN Fields*

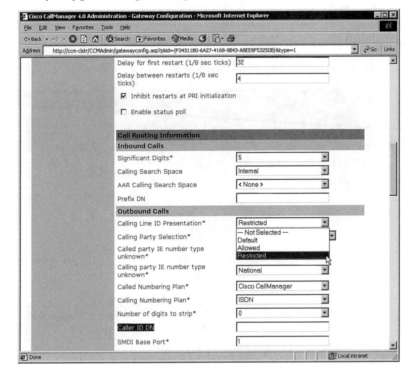

Changing Outbound Caller ID to the Main Number

You can configure all outbound calls with a caller ID of the main company directory number. This is most easily done on the gateway connected to the PSTN. Because this gateway is the last device encountered by outbound calls destined for the PSTN, it has final authority regarding the sending of caller ID. To change the caller ID to the company's main number for all outbound calls, enter the main company number in the Caller ID DN field on the Gateway Configuration page (**Device > Gateway**), shown in Figure 7-16.

Enabling Outbound Caller ID for Extensions Connected to the Same Exchange

You can configure CallManager to send as the caller ID the extension number that's making each outbound call. You enable this on the Route/Hunt List Detail Configuration page of the route list used by the external route pattern (**Route Plan > Route/Hunt > Route/Hunt List**). On the Route/Hunt List Detail Configuration page, shown in Figure 7-17, enter the appropriate Calling Party Transform Mask. This mask should consist of the local prefix followed by the number of wildcards equal to the number of digits in your phone directory numbers. For example, if your network uses four-digit extensions, and your company has been assigned the DID range 408-555-0000 through 408-555-9999, your Calling Party Transform Mask would be 408555XXXX. Then you must ensure that you did not override this setting in the actual gateway configuration by instructing it to block outbound caller ID or replace it with the main company number for all calls.

Figure 7-17 *Route/Hunt List Detail Configuration Page*

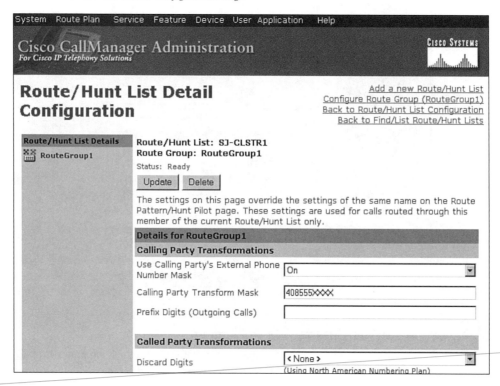

Enabling Outbound Caller ID for Extensions Connected to Different Exchanges

If you have phones in areas serviced by multiple central office exchanges, you cannot configure a single caller ID mask for all phones. Instead, you must configure each directory number with its respective external phone number mask so that you can specify the correct NPA-NXX information on a per-line basis. Configuring the external phone number mask on the primary line also causes the IP phone to display the entire number in the top bar of the phone's display. Next, you must go to the Route/Hunt List Detail Configuration page of the route list used by the external route pattern and set the Use Calling Party's External Phone Number Mask to On. Doing so allows the configured per-line caller ID to be passed to the PSTN.

Blocking Outbound Caller ID on a Per-Call Basis

You can configure CallManager to block outbound caller ID on a per-call basis by using a translation pattern with the Calling Line ID Presentation and Calling Name Presentation fields set to Restricted. Do not provide outside dial tone in the translation pattern. The actual translation pattern could be something like *679 (assuming that your access code is 9). Then, configure explicit route patterns such as *679[2-9][2-9]XXXXX for seven-digit dialing, *6791XXXXXXXXXX for 10-digit dialing, and *679011! for international dialing. Indicate Caller ID Block in the Description field for the route patterns.

NOTE   It would be easier to configure the route pattern *679.@, but be aware of the implications (see the earlier section "Use the 9.@ Route Pattern with Great Care").

With this configuration, users can begin a call with *67 (followed by the usual 9 and the number), which would block their caller IDs. There are a multitude of other options whereby you can apply this feature only to local seven-digit numbers or only to local and long distance numbers, all depending on how you define the route pattern. Just be sure that the translation pattern is in a partition accessible by the users and is assigned a CSS that can reach the call's intended destination.

TIP   The ability to block caller ID on a per-call basis is required by law in some states and is being considered in others. Be sure to check your state's requirements to ensure that you are compliant and are offering this valuable functionality to employees who need it, such as battered spouses, students, and others.

Alter Internal Caller ID on a Per-Line Basis

A particular user within your network might need to have his or her caller ID changed when calling internal destinations only. An example is an executive who wants her assistant's caller ID information displayed whenever the executive makes an internal call. To do this, you need to create a unique partition just for this purpose and create a CSS that contains only this partition. Then create a translation pattern to match all the internal extensions, and place it in the unique partition. The CSS assigned to the translation pattern must be able to reach all internal extensions. It's important to enter the assistant's caller ID as the Calling Party Transform Mask. After you assign the CSS that contains only the translation pattern to the executive's extension, all the executive's internal calls match the translation pattern and have the caller ID replaced with that of the assistant.

The following task list provides a configuration example for changing the caller ID from the executive's extension of 20000 to the assistant's extension of 20001 for all internal calls. This example assumes that all internal extensions are in the form 2XXXX.

Step 1 Create a new partition, such as Exec_Hide_CLID_PT.

Step 2 Create a new CSS such as Exec_Hide_CLID_CSS, and add only the Exec_Hide_CLID_PT partition to it.

Step 3 Create a new translation pattern of 2XXXX, select Exec_Hide_CLID_PT as the partition, and assign a CSS that has access to the internal extensions.

Step 4 Enter the assistant's directory number, 20001, in the Calling Party Transform Mask field of the translation pattern.

Step 5 Assign the CSS Exec_Hide_CLID_CSS to the executive's directory number, 20000, on the IP phone, and reset the phone for the change to take effect.

Configure System and Group Speed Dials

For users' convenience, you might want to create systemwide speed dials for important or commonly dialed destinations such as emergency or security numbers, the cafeteria, the IT group or other technical support, taxi service, local take-out, or delivery or catering restaurants. Creating system speed dials is simple using translation patterns. Choose a range of unused numbers in your dialing plan, reserve them for system speed dial use, and create a partition called SYS_SPEED. Place the translations in the partition, and assign that partition to all the desired calling search spaces.

You can easily create group speed dials this way as well. For example, suppose the manager of the Finance department wants to create a set of speed dials for his or her whole group. The following steps are required:

Step 1 Create a partition called SPEED_GROUP_FINANCE.

Step 2 Copy an existing CSS and name it FINANCE_CSS.

Step 3 Add the SPEED_GROUP_FINANCE partition to the FINANCE_CSS CSS.

Step 4 Add translation patterns to the SPEED_GROUP_FINANCE partition.

See the sidebar "Understanding the Important Role of Calling Search Spaces" earlier in this chapter for more information.

Get More Lines for Fewer Buttons

One of the more powerful new features available in CallManager release 4.0 is the ability to have multiple calls per line appearance. With the multiple calls per line capability, you also get related features such as call join, direct transfer, immediate divert, and more, which are discussed in the Appendix.

Multiple calls per line is basically an extension of the traditional call waiting feature. Whereas before release 4.0 you could have one call active and another call ringing or on hold on the same line, now you can have up to 200 inbound or outbound calls on a single line appearance.

This capability eliminates the need for extra line buttons or Cisco IP Phone 7914 Expansion Modules strictly for line appearance use. Be sure to consider your use cases (discussed in Chapter 1) to determine which users need multiple calls per line and how many allowable calls to configure.

Configure multiple calls per line on the Directory Number Configuration page in CallManager Administration (**Device > Phone >** *find and select a phone* **>** *select a line*).

Examine the following sections to learn more about the multiple calls per line feature:

- Configure per-line no answer ring duration
- Check the busy trigger
- Understand call stacking (the behavior of multiple calls per line, the busy trigger, and no answer ring duration)
- Manage the settings for one assistant or a pool of assistants
- Think of the buttons on the phone as line/feature buttons

Configure Per-Line No Answer Ring Duration

With CallManager release 4.0, you can configure—on a per-line basis—how long a call rings before being forwarded to the call forward no answer (CFNA) destination. You can configure the No Answer Ring Duration in the Call Forward and Pickup Settings area of the Directory Number Configuration page in CallManager Administration, as shown in Figure 7-18.

The ability to configure the duration on a per-line basis is handy when you're also configuring items such as IPMA and direct intercom, which is described in the section "Implementing Intercom Using PLAR Extensions."

Figure 7-18 *Directory Number Configuration Page in CallManager Administration*

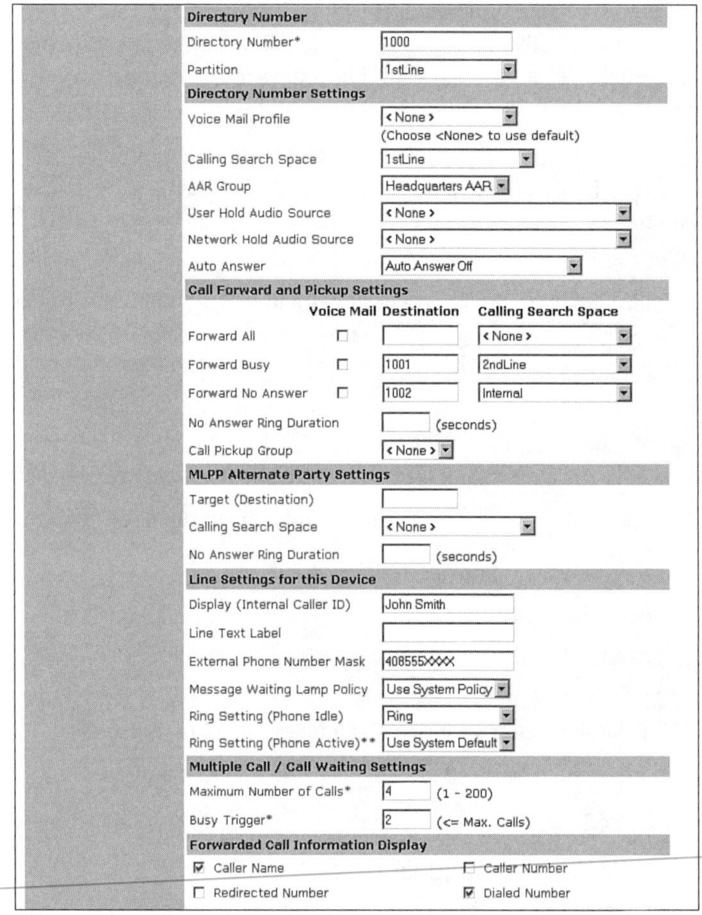

Check the Busy Trigger

When you configure multiple calls per line, you can also configure a busy trigger that determines the number of inbound calls that can be present on a single line before any subsequent calls are sent to the call forward busy destination. The default busy trigger is 2, which matches the behavior users had before the capability of up to 200 calls per line was added. When multiple calls per line are configured and the number of calls present on a line is less than the Busy Trigger value, and an inbound call is presented to the line, the line rings for the duration configured in the No Answer Ring Duration field. As soon as the time specified elapses, the call is forwarded to the call Forward No Answer destination. The default value for the No Answer Ring Duration field is 12 seconds, which is controlled by the Forward No Answer Timer service parameter (**Service > Service Parameter > Cisco CallManager**).

Understand Call Stacking (the Behavior of Multiple Calls Per Line, the Busy Trigger, and No Answer Ring Duration)

The Maximum Number of Calls and Busy Trigger fields on the Directory Number Configuration page in CallManager Administration establish the depth of inbound and outbound calls that can be stacked on a given line at the same time, as shown in Figure 7-19.

Figure 7-19 *Multiple Calls Per Line Configuration*

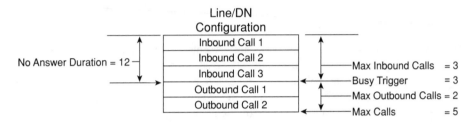

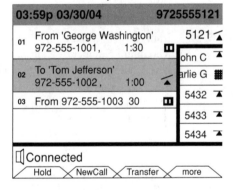

Remote In Use status on selected call indicates no operations other than barge/cBarge may be performed on the selected call.

Privacy disabled on this IP Phone by default, allowing barge operation from other phones.

In Figure 7-19, the Maximum Number of Calls for the line is 5, and the Busy Trigger is 3. With this configuration, the first inbound call is presented to the line, and the call information is displayed on the phone. The call sequence number for that line is displayed as well. This call sequence number is displayed on all lines that share the same directory number, as Fred and Barney do. If the user answers this first call, the line state changes to indicate that the call is connected. If a second inbound call is received, the new call information is displayed, along with that call's sequence number. After it's answered, the second call is connected, and all other calls on this line are in a state other than connected (such as hold, ring-in, ring-out, or dial-out states).

With two calls active (one on Fred's phone and one on Barney's phone), two additional calls arrive for the same line. The third call is allowed to ring through to the line, but when the fourth inbound call arrives, CallManager determines that the number of inbound calls is equal to the busy trigger value and immediately forwards the fourth call to the call forward busy target directory number. The fourth call never actually makes it to the line, so no call information is displayed.

No matter how many inbound calls are presented to the line, the user can still place and manage some number of outbound calls in addition to the inbound calls. In this example, where three calls are present on the line, up to two outbound calls are possible. The number of outbound calls that are allowed per line when calls are present on the line is equal to the Maximum Number of Calls minus the number of calls that are present on the line. For example, if the Maximum Number of Calls is 10 and there are no inbound calls, the user can place and manage up to 10 outbound calls. If the user has seven inbound calls present on the line, he or she could place up to three outbound calls.

NOTE   In the case of a shared line on which two or more devices have different settings for the Maximum Number of Calls and Busy Trigger fields, some calls might be presented to one phone but not the other. For example, if the Maximum Number of Calls is set to 2 on Phone A and to 4 on Phone B, when the third call is presented to the shared line, only Phone B sees it even if one of Phone A's calls is disconnected while the third call is still active on Phone B.

NOTE   An IP phone migrated to CallManager release 4.0 from release 3.x is automatically configured with a maximum of two calls. If call waiting was enabled via the Call Waiting Enabled service parameter, the migrated phone would be configured with a Busy Trigger of 2. If call waiting was disabled, the Busy Trigger would be 1. If call waiting was set to Use System Default, either 1 or 2 would be applied to the phone, depending on the service parameter setting.

Managing the Settings for One Assistant or a Pool of Assistants

The default values for the multiple calls per line fields are adequate for normal operation. In the case of a manager-assistant scenario in which a single assistant handles a large call volume for multiple managers, you should adjust the Maximum Number of Calls and Busy Trigger values to achieve a balance of acceptable immediate call forwarding busy rate. For an assistant who must answer and distribute all but 1 percent of a single manager's inbound calls, a Maximum Number of Calls value of 10 and a Busy Trigger value of 6 for each manager line are recommended. For a pool of assistants responsible for managing multiple managers' calls, the assistant is typically trained to respond to a much higher call volume and therefore can more rapidly answer and distribute calls than might be the case for a single assistant-single manager setup. If you have a pool of assistants, you could configure a Maximum Number of Calls value of 16 and Busy Trigger value of 12 for each manager's line. These larger settings allow for the bursts of call volume associated with a pool of assistants servicing a single manager's call traffic during the day.

You should also adjust the No Answer Ring Duration field in consideration of the Busy Trigger field. If the Busy Trigger number is high, the No Answer Ring Duration value should be high as well, allowing more time for the assistant(s) to keep up with call volume. But take care not to set the No Answer Ring Duration too high, or you might encounter a high incidence of callers hanging up in frustration when the phone just rings and rings rather than being answered or forwarded to voice mail.

Think of the Buttons on the Phone as Line/Feature Buttons

Before the capability for multiple calls per line, the buttons on IP phones were closely tied to either line appearances or speed dials. If you had a Cisco IP Phone model 7960, which has six buttons, you had to give up some valuable line buttons for features such as speed dials, or purchase a Cisco IP Phone 7914 Expansion Module to get more lines and speed dials. And if you went with the less expensive Cisco IP Phone model 7940, you had only two buttons to choose from.

As of CallManager release 4.0, you have more options for the phone buttons. Fewer line buttons are needed because each line can accommodate up to 200 calls, which frees up your remaining buttons for features such as XML services (see the earlier section "Configure IP Phone Services on Line/Feature Buttons on the Phone") and speed dials.

Cisco IP Manager Assistant Best Practices

The following sections provide best practices for IPMA:

- Consider not using the IPMA Configuration Wizard
- Configure redundant servers and force failback
- Run IPMA on a dedicated server if you configure a large number of managers and assistants
- If the assistant's line is the primary line, use the primary line for voice mail
- Save directory numbers in proxy line mode by using a prefix character
- Interaction with Personal Assistant

Consider Not Using the IPMA Configuration Wizard

If you are configuring IPMA for the first time, you can use the wizard (**Service > Cisco IPMA Configuration Wizard**). The wizard is not an option if you have already configured IPMA on the server.

The IPMA Configuration Wizard creates calling search spaces and partitions related to the IPMA feature. You will likely have to modify these to fit with your naming conventions and ensure that whatever policies you have in place (for example, the ability to call long distance or international) are unaffected by the IPMA wizard changes. Make note of the new additions in your dial plan documents.

By creating the necessary calling search spaces and partitions yourself rather than using a wizard, you gain a good understanding of how the application works and how to better use it.

Configure Redundant Servers and Force Failback

IPMA supports redundancy through the Cisco IPMA service parameters (**Service > Service Parameters > Cisco IP Manager Assistant**) so that you can configure primary and backup servers. At any given time, only one server's IPMA service is running. When a failure is detected, the backup server takes over. You need to force failback to the primary server because IPMA does not fail back automatically when the primary server is back up. You can force failback by stopping the IPMA service on the backup server after the primary server has come back online.

Run IPMA on a Dedicated Server if You Configure a Large Number of Managers and Assistants

IPMA supports 1250 managers and 1250 assistants on a server. If you intend to support a number of managers approaching the maximum number, you should run IPMA on a dedicated server. It would be ideal to have a dedicated backup server as well in case the primary IPMA server fails.

If the Assistant's Line is the Primary Line, Use the Primary Line for Voice Mail

If you have configured IPMA for shared line mode with the assistant's line as the primary line, you should set the CallManager service parameter Always Use Prime Line for Voice Mail (**Service > Service Parameters > Cisco CallManager**) to True (it defaults to False). Do not set it to True if you have configured the manager's line as the primary line on the assistant's phone. Setting it to True causes the phone to automatically dial the voice mail system from the primary line when the assistant presses the **messages** button.

Save Directory Numbers in Proxy Line Mode by Using a Prefix Character

To preserve available directory numbers in the system, prefix the assistant's Proxy Line Number with a # or * character. For example, if the manager's number is 1000, the assistant's proxy line for DN 1000 could be configured as #1000 or *1000.

Interaction with Personal Assistant

You can configure the interaction between IPMA and Personal Assistant (PA) in two ways:

- PA intercepts incoming calls for a line, and then IPMA intercepts the calls that are routed to manager lines.

- IPMA intercepts incoming calls for a manager, and then if PA is active for the line IPMA routed the call to, PA rules are applied.

Configure PA to Intercept an Incoming Call and Then Forward It to IPMA

Use this configuration to first let PA handle all calls for Herb, a manager. For example, Herb might have a PA rule saying that from 8 a.m. to 5 p.m. Monday through Friday, calls should be directed to his work phone. If the work phone is not answered, calls should be sent to his cell phone. On other days and at other times, calls should be sent to his cell phone.

For a call that arrives at 9 a.m. Monday morning, PA forwards the call to Herb's work phone, where IPMA intercepts it and checks whether Herb has an online assistant. If an assistant is configured, IPMA sends the call to the assistant or to other destinations, depending on IPMA Divert All targets and filtering rules.

All calls flow through the IPMA route point. IPMA intercepts only calls that are intended for IPMA manager's lines. Consider the following partitions and calling search spaces:

- Partitions

  - **IPMA-Managers**—Assign this partition to manager lines that are administered for IPMA. These IPMA managers can be PA users also.

  - **IPMA-Route Point**—Assign this partition to lines on the IPMA route point used to intercept incoming calls to IPMA manager lines.

  - **PA**—Assign this partition to lines on CTI route points used by PA to intercept incoming calls to PA users.

  - **PA-Managed**—Assign this partition to lines for all users who want to use PA. The exception is that IPMA manager lines for managers who want to use PA still need to be assigned to the IPMA-Managers partition.

  - **Everyone**—Assign this partition to lines for users who do not want to use either IPMA or PA.

- Calling Search Spaces
  - **CSS-PA**—This is the CSS assigned to the PA interceptor route point and PA route point used for IVR functionality. This CSS contains the following partitions in the following order: IPMA-Route Point, PA-Managed, Everyone.
  - **IPMA Managers**—This is the CSS assigned to the IPMA route point and assistant proxy lines. This CSS contains the following partitions in the following order: IPMA-Managers, Everyone.
  - **CSS-IPMA-PA**—This is the CSS assigned to the translation patterns that are used when either IPMA or PA or both are down. This CSS contains the following partitions in the following order: IPMA-Managers, PA-Managed, Everyone.
  - **All_Calls**—This is the CSS assigned to all other lines, gateways, PBXs, and so on. This CSS contains the following partitions in the following order: PA, IPMA-Route Point, Everyone.

Refer to Table 7-6 for configuration details.

Table 7-6   *Configuring Devices for PA Forwarding to IPMA*

CTI Route Point	Partition	CSS
IPMA route point	IPMA-Route Point	IPMA-Managers
PA route point for interception	PA	CSS-PA
PA route point (used for IVR function)	Everyone	CSS-PA
Translation Pattern (for Example, 23XXX)		
The translation pattern should match both the PA and IPMA route point directory numbers. You can have multiple translation patterns if the directory numbers are different.	Everyone	CSS-IPMA-PA
Lines		
IPMA manager's lines (with or without PA support)	IPMA-Managers	All_Calls
Other users who want PA	PA-Managed	All_Calls
Users who do not want PA	Everyone	All_Calls
Media Ports (Skinny) for PA		
Media ports for PA	Everyone	All_Calls

Configure IPMA to Intercept an Incoming Call and Then Forward It to PA

Use this scenario to first let IPMA handle all calls for the managers. When a call arrives for the manager, IPMA applies the manager's filtering/DivAll rules first. Then IPMA sends the call to a destination number, which can be either the manager or the assistant's proxy line or another destination. If the destination number is a PA user's number, PA intercepts the call and applies any PA rules. All calls flow through the PA route point. PA intercepts only calls that are intended for PA users. An assistant or another target can be a PA user also.

Consider the following partitions and calling search spaces:

- Partitions

    - **IPMA-Managers**—Assign this partition to lines for IPMA managers who do not want to use PA.

    - **IPMA-Route Point**—Assign this partition to lines on the IPMA route point used to intercept incoming calls to IPMA manager lines.

    - **PA**—Assign this partition to lines on route points used by PA to intercept incoming calls to PA users.

    - **PA-Managed**—Assign this partition to lines for all users who want to use PA. Note that IPMA manager lines for managers who want to use PA should also be assigned to this partition.

    - **Everyone**—Assign this partition to lines for users who do not want to use either IPMA or PA.

- Calling Search Spaces

    - **IPMA Managers**—This is the CSS assigned to the IPMA route point and assistant proxy lines. This CSS contains the following partitions in the following order: PA, IPMA-Managers, Everyone.

    - **CSS-PA**—This is the CSS assigned to the PA interceptor route point and PA route point used for IVR functionality. This CSS contains the following partitions in the following order: PA-Managed, Everyone.

    - **CSS-IPMA-PA**—This is the CSS assigned to the translation patterns that are used when either IPMA or PA or both are down. This CSS contains the following partitions in the following order: IPMA-Managers, PA-Managed, Everyone.

    - **All_Calls**—This is the CSS assigned to all other lines, gateways, PBXs, and so on. This CSS contains the following partitions in the following order: IPMA-Route Point, PA, Everyone.

Refer to Table 7-7 for configuration details.

Table 7-7 *Configuring Devices for IPMA Forwarding to PA*

CTI Route Point	Partition	CSS
IPMA route point	IPMA-Route Point	IPMA-Managers
PA route point for interception	PA	CSS-PA
PA route point (used for IVR function)	Everyone	CSS-PA
Translation Pattern (for Example, 23XXX)		
The translation pattern should match both the PA and IPMA route point directory numbers. You can have multiple translation patterns if the directory numbers are different.	Everyone	CSS-IPMA-PA
Phones		
IPMA manager's phone (with or without PA support)	IPMA-Managers	All_Calls
IPMA manager's phone (with PA support)	PA-Managed	All_Calls
All other users who want PA	PA-Managed	All_Calls
All other users who do not want PA	Everyone	All_Calls
Media Ports (Skinny) for PA		
Media ports for PA	Everyone	All_Calls

Verify Your Configuration and Physical Connection When Using CMI

When using CMI to connect your legacy voice mail system to CallManager, make sure the configuration of the following five fields in CMI matches the physical connection to the voice mail server:

- Baud rate
- Data bits
- Parity
- Serial port
- Stop bits

Also, double-check that the cable is plugged into the same port on the server that is configured in CMI and the voice mail system. It sounds basic, but double-checking these simple things can solve common problems before they occur. To confirm settings, connect the serial cable between CallManager and a PC running Hyperterminal or another terminal emulation program, and match the settings. Place test calls to confirm that simple message desk interface (SMDI) is transmitted by the CMI service.

Two frequent misconfigurations can occur with CMI:

- The Voice Mail Partition service parameter (**Service > Service Parameters >** *select a server* **> Cisco Messaging Interface**) is not configured to match the partition of the corresponding route pattern.

  Both the CMI pilot number and the route pattern must use the same pattern and be in the same partition for CMI to intercept the call information and generate the appropriate SMDI message.

- The Message Waiting Indicator Calling Search Space service parameter must be configured as a colon-separated list of partitions.

  This parameter should not contain the name of a CSS, as the name implies. It must contain a colon-separated list of valid destination partitions for MWI.

Tools and Application Best Practices

This section provides best practices for tools such as tracing and applications such as the Bulk Administration Tool:

- Use the Trace Collection Tool for convenient trace collection.
- Use the AXL SOAP API to write custom scripts that interact with the CallManager database.
- Bulk Administration Tool best practices.
- Cisco IP SoftPhone/Communicator best practices.
- Attendant Console best practices.
- Provide personalized call distribution via Cisco Personal Assistant (with or without speech recognition).
- Use Directory.asp and Cisco WebDialer to initiate calls from a web page.

Use the Trace Collection Tool for Convenient Trace Collection

Use the Cisco CallManager Trace Collection tool, a plugin provided in CallManager Administration (**Application > Install Plugins**), to collect trace information for any CallManager service in the cluster and the time and date of the trace for that service. By entering the Publisher's IP address in the Trace Collection Tool, you can collect traces for all servers in the cluster just by checking checkboxes for the services and applications you want to trace. The Tool collects, zips, and saves the chosen files to a location you specify, making it easy to access the information or send it the Cisco Technical Assistance Center (TAC) if needed.

NOTE   Running the Trace Collection Tool can cause performance degradation on CallManager; because of this, use the tool for troubleshooting only as needed.

Use the AXL SOAP API to Write Custom Scripts That Interact with the CallManager Database

Use the AXL Simple Object Access Protocol (SOAP) API to perform custom actions against the CallManager database. Anything that resides in the database can be customized using AXL scripts, such as phones, directory numbers, translation patterns, voice mail ports, and much more. The possibilities are nearly limitless. Consider the following uses of custom scripts:

- Write a script that allows you to simultaneously reset all devices in the system (normally you can reset all devices only by resetting all device pools).

- Write a script that logs out specific extension mobility (EM) users, specific groups of EM users, or all EM users at a specified time, such 7:00 or 8:00 p.m. Because extension mobility only allows you to specify the length of time a user can stay logged in, you can't be certain that phones will be automatically logged out by the end of the business day (for example, if someone logged in after returning from lunch). By forcing a logout at a certain time of day for some or all users, you can keep unauthorized personnel from making long distance calls.

Acquire the AXL SOAP API through the Developer Support Central page at the following link:

http://www.cisco.com/pcgi-bin/dev_support/access_level/product_support

Click the **Log in now** link, log in, and then in the Voice Technology/AVVID list box, select **AXL SOAP API**.

Use the Bulk Administration Tool

The Bulk Administration Tool (BAT) allows you to configure a large number of phones, users, managers/assistants, user device profiles, VG200 gateways, Catalyst 6000 FXS analog interface modules, and TAPS. BAT is widely known for performing bulk add operations, but it does much more. BAT is the most efficient means of adding, updating, and deleting a large number of users, devices, and device settings. Be sure to learn how to use this tool, and employ it as often as possible for your CallManager configuration work.

Although it might seem straightforward to simply load the BAT template and enter your data manually, there are many ways of making the process easier and more accurate. The following sections provide information to help make your work with BAT more efficient or productive.

The Best Way to Add Devices and Users to CallManager

Use BAT. It lets you add huge numbers of devices and users quickly and easily instead of adding them one by one in CallManager Administration.

BAT also provides a combined function of adding phones and users all in one CSV file. For new systems in which you are adding phones and users, choose the combined version to save time.

Validate the CSV File

BAT provides a Validate button when you are inserting or updating CSV files. Be sure to click the Validate button to allow BAT to ensure that CSV data has the proper values and is in the proper format. Validated files ensure zero or very few errors during bulk configurations. You can view the validation results by clicking the View Latest Log File Now link, located next to the Validate button.

Use Your Existing Spreadsheet Data

Every installation should have a cut-sheet or project plan document that has the names, extensions, office locations, and usernames of the people moving or being added to the system. This is most often stored in an Excel spreadsheet. Because BAT also uses Excel, you can copy and paste from your existing data.

From the Publisher, copy the BAT.xlt file from C:\CiscoWebs\BAT\ExcelTemplate to a local machine. Choose the proper tab in the BAT.xlt template for your bulk-add operation (phones, phones and users, and so on), and save the .xlt file with a new name. Then copy and paste the relevant columns from your existing project plan spreadsheet into the BAT.xlt form.

Convert Spreadsheet Data to a BAT-Acceptable Format

Sometimes your existing data isn't in the required format for BAT. For example, names are often stored with first and last name together or separated with a comma, and phone numbers are listed with area codes. You need to convert any data in your project plan spreadsheet that does not match the format BAT expects before pasting the data into BAT.xlt. Table 7-8 lists some Excel formulas to help you convert data.

Table 7-8 *Commonly Used Excel Formulas for Converting Data*

Original Data (Cell A1 Assumed)	Formula	Result
John Smith	=LEFT(A1,(SEARCH(" ",A1,1))-1)	John
Burrell Smith	=RIGHT(A1,LEN(A1)-SEARCH(" ",A1))	Smith
Smith, John	=RIGHT(A1,LEN(A1)-SEARCH(" ",A1))	John
Smith, John	=LEFT(A1,(SEARCH(",",A1,1))-1)	Smith
Smith,John	=RIGHT(A1,LEN(A1)-SEARCH(",",A1))	John
Smith,John	=LEFT(A1,(SEARCH(",",A1,1))-1)	Smith
408-555-1122	=RIGHT(A1,SEARCH("-????",A1))	1122
408.555.1122	=RIGHT(A1,SEARCH(".????",A1))	1122
408-555-1122	=SEARCH("",A1,7)&RIGHT(A1,SEARCH("-????",A1))	51122
408.555.1122	=SEARCH("",A1,7)&RIGHT(A1,SEARCH(".????",A1))	51122

Use Standard Calling Party Names

Use a standard convention for the calling party name, such as last name first (Smith John), first then last name (John Smith), or comma-separated last name then first name (Smith,John). Be sure to set a standard naming convention, and stick with it. Be sure that as soon as you import your data with BAT, all administrators are trained to use the standard display name. Table 7-9 shows some Excel formulas for deriving common calling party names.

Table 7-9   *Excel Formulas for Deriving Calling Party Names*

Original Data (Cell A1 Assumed	Formula	Result
John Smith	=UPPER(A1)	JOHN SMITH
John Smith	=RIGHT(A1,LEN(A1)-SEARCH(" ",A1))& ", " &LEFT(A1,1) & "."	Smith, J.
John Smith	=RIGHT(A1,LEN(A1)-SEARCH(" ",A1))&", "&LEFT(A1,(SEARCH(" ",A1))-1)	Smith, John

Use a Barcode Scanner with Keyboard Input

All Cisco IP Phones ship in individual boxes that display the phone's MAC address on the outside of the box. This allows you to open a group box of five phones, extract each individual phone box, write the name of the end user on the box, and then use a barcode scanner with keyboard connector to scan the MAC address directly into the BAT spreadsheet. Doing so saves time and increases accuracy when compared with manually entering MAC addresses into the spreadsheet.

TIP   You can use any scanner with a PS2 or USB connection, such as the handheld scanners available at the Barcoding website at the following link:

http://www.barcoding.com/barcode_scanning.shtml

Use BAT to Update Partitions on Lines So That You Never Use the <None> Partition

If your existing installation does not conform to the best practice of never using the <None> partition, you can easily change all uses of the <None> partition by using BAT. BAT allows you to search for phones based on directory number and then change any parameter, including the line partition (**Configure > Phones > Update Lines**). For example, you could use 3XXX on the primary line and 4XXX on the secondary line. Searching for all directory numbers starting with 3 and then changing the line partition to LINE_PT would follow the best practice, as shown in Figure 7-20.

TIP   Click the View Query Result button to see the results of your query before performing the action to ensure you get the right result.

Figure 7-20 *BAT Steps 1 and 2 for Updating Lines to Use a Partition Other Than <None>*

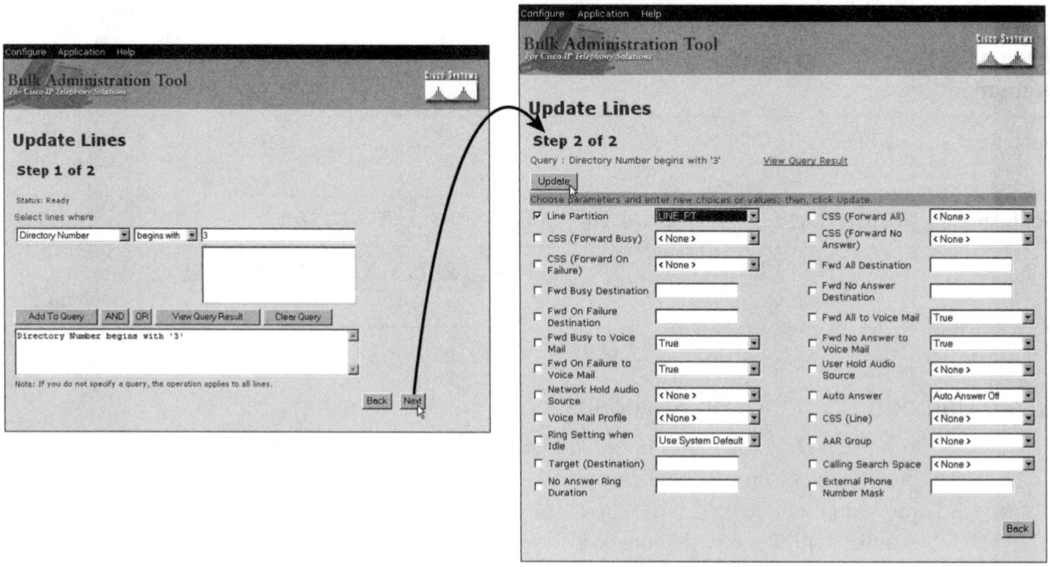

Run a Query in BAT to Generate a List of Unassigned DNs

Use BAT to generate a list of orphan directory numbers that are not assigned to any device. Follow these steps:

Step 1 In BAT, click **Configure > Phones**.

Step 2 Click **Update Lines** and then click **Next**.

Step 3 In the **Select lines where** field, choose **Unassigned DN**.

Step 4 Click **View Query Result**.

Cisco IP SoftPhone/Communicator Best Practices

The following sections provide best practices for Cisco IP software-based phone applications:

- Use Cisco IP Communicator as the preferred software-based phone model unless collaboration is needed.

- Use G.711 for best audio quality or G.729 in a limited-bandwidth environment to save on bandwidth and achieve better voice quality because of less packet loss.

- Advise users that dialup with SoftPhone or Communicator might result in poor audio quality, especially over IP networks that do not have QoS measures configured.

- Test the headset for audio quality.

- Stay local to ensure available bandwidth for your SoftPhone/Communicator.

Use Cisco IP Communicator as the Preferred Software-Based Phone Model Unless Collaboration Is Needed

Cisco IP SoftPhone is a CTI-based application that can initiate and operate collaborative application sessions, a feature not yet available on Cisco IP Communicator.

Cisco IP Communicator is a SoftPhone version that uses Skinny Client Control Protocol (SCCP) signaling and the Cisco IP Phone 7970G user interface, as shown in Figure 7-21. Communicator provides increased scalability (about a four-fold improvement in call processing server resource consumption). It also offers reduced client image size and inheritance of features associated with existing hardware IP phones.

Figure 7-21 *Cisco IP Communicator Interface*

Use G.729 for Best Audio Quality in a Limited-Bandwidth Environment

G.711 provides better audio quality than G.729, but to conserve bandwidth in a limited-bandwidth environment such as a virtual private network (VPN) over the Internet, configure SoftPhone or Communicator to force G.729 codec selection for every call. You can do this through individual device settings by the region specified in the device pool (**System > Device Pool**).

Advise Users That Dialup with SoftPhone or Communicator Might Result in Poor Audio Performance, and Ensure That QoS Is Provided When Possible

Dialup modem connections to the corporate network are usually too slow to support acceptable audio performance, even when low-bandwidth codecs are forced. Because of this, you should warn users that the audio quality might be severely degraded when using SoftPhone or Communicator via dialup.

Users also might have poor audio over broadband connections if any part of the voice path is expected to traverse IP networks without quality of service (QoS) measures configured.

Test the Headset for Audio Quality

The headset you choose contributes to the audio quality. The biggest complaint about headset quality—a pervasive, annoying hum—is usually lodged by the far-end party rather than the near-end party. If your end users report that the people they're talking to while using SoftPhone or Communicator complain of a hum, recommend that the end user try a different headset. Cisco has not yet provided a list of approved headsets, but practical tests have shown than 90 percent of headsets tested work equally well, regardless of cost. Perform some testing with your headset choice(s) before rolling out headsets or recommendations to the end-user community.

The Cisco site http://cisco.getheadsets.com lists and describes headsets approved for use with Cisco IP Phone models 7960 and 7940.

Stay Local to Ensure Available Bandwidth for Your SoftPhone/Communicator

Both Cisco IP SoftPhone and Communicator can automatically detect whether the PC is connecting to the network over a VPN or is behind a NAT boundary. This makes it easier for the user to move from one network to another without having to know specifics of local network configuration. However, moving around the network raises an important consideration for CAC.

Locations-based CAC assumes that endpoints such as SoftPhone/Communicator remain within the location configured in the CallManager database. All calls to and from the endpoint are allowed or disallowed based on the bandwidth available for voice at the instant the call is set up. But CallManager has no dynamic awareness of the location of mobile users such as those who use SoftPhone or Communicator. If a user moves from one CallManager location to another, CallManager still assumes that a call directed to or from that user's SoftPhone/Communicator is traversing the WAN of the statically configured location for that endpoint. The result is that bandwidth can become oversubscribed and thereby produce poor-quality audio during the call. Because of this, it's best to advise mobile users to use SoftPhone/Communicator in their home location only.

Attendant Console Best Practices

The following sections provide best practices for Cisco CallManager Attendant Console (AC).

Don't Configure Personal Lines on the Attendant Console Phone; Supply a Second Phone Instead

You can prevent a receptionist from making personal calls on a secondary line on the IP phone that is associated with Attendant Console by not configuring additional non-AC-related lines. Teach the users that this phone is for application use only, not general use. Provide a second IP phone for personal calls if necessary. Especially if you experience high turnover of receptionists, the frustration factor can be great when an inexperienced receptionist is faced with quickly putting a personal call on hold to catch a business call ringing on a different line on the same phone.

If you can't provide a second IP phone and you want to configure a second line that is not associated with AC (which can be beneficial if the receptionist has to place business-related calls), be sure you do not route calls to both the first *and* second lines because receptionists can handle only one line at a time. Make sure the second line is not associated in the pilot point.

Put the Pilot Point of the Attendant Console Number Behind a Translation Pattern

Putting the AC pilot point number behind a translation pattern allows you to change the number and click **Update** to keep a receptionist in business while you troubleshoot a problem with Attendant Console or the configuration. For example, if a problem with the Attendant Console application or the Attendant's PC occurs, you can change the translation pattern to point to a DN on the attendant's phone and keep calls flowing. Functionality such as knowing phone status might be lost, but calls can still be handled. When the Attendant Console application problem or PC problem has been resolved, the translation pattern can be changed back.

Provide Personalized Call Distribution via Cisco Personal Assistant (with or Without Speech Recognition)

Because CallManager's hunt list/hunt pilot capability (described in the Appendix) is administered exclusively through the system administrator, users who need to manage routing of their own calls should use Cisco Personal Assistant (PA). PA, a Cisco Java Telephony API (JTAPI) application sold separately from CallManager, allows users to distribute calls to OnNet and OffNet numbers based on phone state (connected or idle, for example), time of day, who's calling them, and more.

Users can configure rules in PA and divert calls to voice mail, cell phone, and other destinations based on the preconfigured rules. You can also provide a speech recognition-enabled automated dialer, which lets users interact with PA using voice commands—a particularly handy feature for mobile executives.

NOTE   PA relies on the local language being supported and on the dial plan used by CallManager. Although users within the NANP should have no trouble, you should expect some challenges if you're using an international dial plan (non-NANP).

Use Directory.asp and Cisco WebDialer to Initiate Calls from a Web Page

You can deploy a web page that allows users to access the directory function online rather than through their IP phone. This functionality is provided by directory.asp and is available at http://*CMServer*/ccmuser/directory.asp and is only enabled to use WebDialer. Dialing from a directory web page saves users the hassle of pressing multiple digits to spell out parts of the first and last name of a user they want to call. Non-English-speaking users might not want to or might not be able to use the English alphabet printed on some Cisco IP Phone keypads, so they need an alternative method to use the directories feature. Cisco WebDialer provides this alternative method.

WebDialer allows users to access the WebDialer web page and enter a partial or complete first name, last name, directory number, or user ID and press **Enter** or click **Submit**. A list of matching entries is returned. When the user clicks a name, a phone call to that person is automatically initiated from the user's associated IP phone.

Summary

This chapter provided best practices related to CallManager, IP phones, gateways, and other IP Telephony components such as BAT, extension mobility, IPMA, and more. By considering these best practices for use in your deployment, you can achieve a total IP Telephony solution that is easier for you to maintain and more user-friendly for your users.

## CHAPTER 8

Managing Services and Parameters

In this chapter you'll learn about the services that can run in a Cisco CallManager cluster and some of the associated parameters, how to tune them, and best practices to achieve sound configurations. Because each service provides a portion of CallManager functionality, the overall CallManager deployment can be affected when individual services are manipulated incorrectly. Make note of settings before any changes are made to the system, and make minimal changes at any given time so that it's easier to understand the behavior the changes cause to the system as a whole. Each service is detailed in this chapter in terms of its function, the system's need for the service, issues that might arise with the basic configuration of the service, and noteworthy parameters. This chapter brings to your attention selected parameters that are considered especially useful or important, so not all services include a discussion of related parameters. The goal of this chapter is to help you make informed decisions about how to manipulate each of the services in the CallManager system and be aware of those important parameters.

For more information about services, refer to the documentation on the Voice Products page at the following link, or you also can search the help contents and index in CallManager Administration (**Help > Contents and Index**):

http://www.cisco.com/univercd/cc/td/doc/product/ipvoice.htm

Service parameters are like the control knobs and levers behind the curtain in the *Wizard of Oz*. They're the devices you and Cisco support engineers use to manipulate the cluster or server in a behind-the-scenes sort of way. The vast majority of parameters should be kept at their default values, and many should not be changed unless a Cisco support engineer instructs you to do so. But there are several service parameters you might find useful to adjust in your deployment to gain more system resources or change system functionality.

Individual services are added as features to CallManager, and parameters are added frequently. Be sure to check the documentation online in CallManager Administration (**Service > Service Parameters >** *select a server* **>** *select a service* **>** *click on a service parameter name to launch the help text*), or check the following link for the latest information about these and other new service and enterprise parameters:

http://www.cisco.com/univercd/cc/td/doc/product/voice/c_callmg/index.htm

In a single CallManager server deployment, you need to run all the services that are necessary for basic call processing functionality plus any desired specialty functions on the same server. In multiple-server CallManager cluster deployments, particular services might run on select machines, but not all. Depending on the size of your deployment, you might have servers dedicated to single tasks such as Trivial File Transfer Protocol (TFTP service) or call processing (CallManager service). Keep in mind that every service that is running consumes memory on the server. Enable only those services your deployment needs on any server to avoid unnecessarily using memory. Although the service load typically is not large, it can still be a contributing factor to performance degradation.

Refer to Tables 8-3 through 8-6, shown later, for recommendations on the services to run on the various servers you might have, depending on the size of the deployment. These tables provide generic recommendations only; your needs might vary, and you might have more or fewer servers to distribute your services across.

NOTE   CallManager Serviceability segregates the services in the Control Center and Service Activation pages by NT (or core) services and Tomcat web services.

Tomcat services are aimed at user productivity and are serviced by a coresident web server. You can think of all Tomcat services as user-enhancing web services. All Tomcat services depend on the Cisco CTIManager service for call initiation, answer, or manipulation. With Tomcat services, users directly interact with the servlets after authenticating interactively via a variety of interfaces including the web, phones with XML capabilities, and PC-based applications. Users and their applications directly access a specific server as configured in the application. Running Tomcat web services only on the Publisher is common because frequently they depend on writing to the Publisher for their functionality, as is the case for Extension Mobility.

The following services are discussed in this chapter in the order shown in the Control Center and Service Activation pages in CallManager Serviceability:

- Cisco CallManager
- Cisco TFTP
- Cisco Messaging Interface
- Cisco IP Voice Media Streaming App
- Cisco CTIManager
- Cisco Telephony Call Dispatcher
- Cisco MOH Audio Translator
- Cisco RIS Data Collector
- Cisco Database Layer Monitor

- Cisco CDR Insert
- Cisco CTL Provider
- Cisco Extended Functions
- Cisco Serviceability Reporter
- Cisco WebDialer (Tomcat)
- Cisco IP Manager Assistant (Tomcat)
- Cisco Extension Mobility (Tomcat)

About Services

As you will see throughout this chapter, many services depend on one another for operation. Table 8-1 summarizes the dependencies among services.

Read the table starting with the leftmost column, and check each row to see, for each service, what other services are required or are optional. Services that must be running are marked with a D (dependent), and services that can be running but are not required are marked with O. For example, the Cisco CTIManager service requires that the CallManager service and the Cisco Database Layer Monitor service be running. In addition, Cisco Real-Time Information Server (RIS) Data Collector can be running, but it does not directly affect CTIManager.

Table 8-1 *Service Dependencies*

Services in the First Column Are Dependent On:															
	CallManager	TFTP	CMI	IP Voice Media Streaming	CTIManager	TCD	MOH Audio Translator	RIS Data Collector	Database Layer Monitor	CDR Insert	CTL Provider	Extended Functions	Serviceability Reporter	WebDialer	IP Manager Assistant	Extension Mobility
CallManager	D								D							
TFTP		D							D							
CMI	D		D					D	D							
IP Voice Media Streaming App	D	D		D					D							

continues

Table 8-1   *Service Dependencies (Continued)*

Services in the First Column Are Dependent On:	CallManager	TFTP	CMI	IP Voice Media Streaming	CTIManager	TCD	MOH Audio Translator	RIS Data Collector	Database Layer Monitor	CDR Insert	CTL Provider	Extended Functions	Serviceability Reporter	WebDialer	IP Manager Assistant	Extension Mobility
CTIManager	D				D			O	D							
TCD	D				D			D	D							
MOH Audio Translator	D	D		O				D	D							
RIS Data Collector	D							D	D							
Database Layer Monitor									D							
CDR Insert	D								D							
CTL Provider	D								D							
Extended Functions	D							D	D			D				
Serviceability Reporter	D								D							
WebDialer	D								D							
IP Manager Assistant	D								D							
Extension Mobility	D							D	D							

Services on a CallManager server are either mandatory or optional. Table 8-2 describes them.

- **Mandatory**—These services must be running on one or more servers in the cluster.
- **Optional**—These services support optionally deployed features such as MOH, extension mobility, WebDialer, IPMA, and more. Generally, you should run optional services on at least two servers to provide redundancy. There are a few exceptions, as noted in Table 8-2.

Depending on the number of devices a service needs to support, you might want to run a particular service on a dedicated server. A *dedicated server* means that the primary resources for the entire server are devoted to a single service. Likely candidates for dedicated servers in a large deployment include TFTP and the IP Voice Media Streaming App, among others. In the case of the IP Voice Media Streaming App, you can further dedicate resources by running only MOH, software conferencing, or software MTP on a particular server. In all cases, other services also run on a dedicated server, such as the RIS Data Collector and Cisco Database Layer Monitor, but the other services that run on a dedicated server provide supporting functions required by the dedicated services and do not consume a large amount of server resources. A good example is a dedicated TFTP server. On a dedicated TFTP server, you would run the Cisco TFTP service, but you would also run RIS Data Collector and Cisco Database Layer Monitor. RIS Data Collector and Cisco Database Layer Monitor services would consume minimal resources, leaving the majority of the resources to the TFTP service. Without the Database Layer Monitor service running, the dedicated TFTP server would not be able to properly receive database change notifications or perform a database failover in the case of a Publisher failure. Without the RIS Data Collector service, some management information would be unavailable, but end users would not be affected.

Table 8-2   *Mandatory and Optional Services*

Service	Description
Cisco CallManager	Mandatory. There is a limit of eight instances of the Cisco CallManager service per cluster.
Cisco TFTP	Mandatory. A separate server within a cluster can be dedicated to primarily running just this service.
Cisco Messaging Interface	Optional. Needed only for an SMDI voice mail interface. Run this service on two servers to achieve redundancy where the Y-cable (data splitter) is connected to the voice mail system.
Cisco IP Voice Media Streaming App	Optional. Needed only for MTP, software audio conferencing, and MOH audio source; each function can be enabled exclusively. Run this service on servers that are also running the Cisco CallManager service unless you are running this service on a dedicated server. Run as many instances of this service as you need to accommodate the number of resources required by your deployment. Be sure to consider the impact this service will have on call processing. If there is a heavy call processing load on a particular server, run this service on a backup server or other CallManager server with a lighter load.

continues

Table 8-2   *Mandatory and Optional Services (Continued)*

Service	Description
Cisco CTIManager	Optional. Needed only for TAPI or JTAPI applications. If you are not running any CTI applications, you do not need to run this service. For small deployments, run this service on servers that are also running the Cisco CallManager service. This service typically does not need to run on a dedicated TFTP server or dedicated Publisher. Run as many instances of this service as you need to accommodate the number of CTI applications in your deployment. Be sure to consider the impact this service will have on call processing. If a particular server has a heavy call processing load, run this service on a backup server or other CallManager server with a lighter load.
Cisco Telephony Call Dispatcher	Optional. Needed only for Cisco CallManager Attendant Console (AC); if you are not using AC, you do not need to run this service. Must be running on all servers where CallManager is activated.
Cisco MOH Audio Translator	Optional. Needed to translate audio files to a format that CallManager understands. Run this service on only one server in the cluster. Run this service on a server that is also running Cisco TFTP service.
Cisco RIS Data Collector	Mandatory. Run this service on all servers.
Cisco Database Layer Monitor	Mandatory. This service must be running on all servers.
Cisco CDR Insert	Optional. Needed if CDRs are enabled and are configured via the CDR Format enterprise parameter to be inserted into the CDR database (not saved as flat files). Run this service on the Publisher.
Cisco CTL Provider	Optional. Needed only if you have enabled security-related enterprise parameters (Device Security Mode and Cluster Security Mode). If you have not enabled security, you do not need to run this service. This service allows for media and signaling encryption of voice packets. Run this service on all servers where the Cisco CallManager and Cisco TFTP services run.
Cisco Extended Functions	Optional. Provides support for CallManager features such as call back and Quality Reporting Tool (QRT). Run this service on one or more servers that run the Cisco RIS Data Collector.

Table 8-2   *Mandatory and Optional Services (Continued)*

Service	Description
Cisco Serviceability Reporter	Optional. Generates reports once a day based on information collected by the RIS Data Collector service. Run this service on the Publisher server only.
Cisco WebDialer	Optional. Needed only for the WebDialer application. If you are not using WebDialer, you do not need to run this service. You should typically activate this service on one server per cluster, but you can run it on a second server for redundancy.
Cisco IP Manager Assistant	Optional. Needed only for the Cisco IP Manager Assistant application. If you are not using IPMA, you do not need to run this service. Run this service on two servers to achieve redundancy. Run this service on servers that are also running the Cisco CallManager service. Be sure to consider the impact this service will have on call processing. If a particular server has a heavy call processing load, run this service on a backup server or other CallManager server with a lighter load.
Cisco Extension Mobility	Optional. Needed only for the extension mobility application. If you are not using extension mobility, you do not need to run this service. Run this service on two servers to achieve redundancy. Run this service on servers that are also running the Cisco CallManager service. Be sure to consider the impact this service will have on call processing. If a particular server has a heavy call processing load, run this service on a backup server or another CallManager server with a lighter load.

Tables 8-3 through 8-6 offer general recommendations for the services that should be running on the various servers in a cluster based on the size of the deployment. These tables represent generic recommendations only; your needs might vary. Refer to the Solution Reference Network Design (SRND) guides on Cisco.com for recommendations on how many servers you should have based on your deployment size. The following recommendations are based on the highest-performance servers available as of CallManager release 4.0: Cisco MCS-7845. The following recommendations take into consideration general device weights and dial plan weights; hence, the largest deployment recommendation is for 20,000 users. Be sure to read more about device weights and dial plan weights in the IP Telephony SRND at http://www.cisco.com/go/srnd.

Refer to Table 8-2 to decide which servers to run optional services on. For optional services that should run on only one CallManager server in the cluster, decide between the Publisher and a Subscriber server by taking into consideration the call processing load on each server. Run the optional service on the server with the lightest load (the most available resources). To achieve redundancy, you need to activate the optional services on both servers.

Table 8-3 *Service Recommendations for a System with 500 Users*

Service	Publisher Server	Subscriber Server
Cisco CallManager	Activated	Activated
Cisco TFTP	Activated	Optional
Cisco Messaging Interface	Optional	Optional
Cisco IP Voice Media Streaming App	Optional	Optional
Cisco CTIManager	Optional	Optional
Cisco Telephony Call Dispatcher	Optional	Optional
Cisco MOH Audio Translator	Optional	Deactivated
Cisco RIS Data Collector	Activated	Activated
Cisco Database Layer Monitor	Activated	Activated
Cisco CDR Insert	Optional	Deactivated
Cisco CTL Provider	Optional	Optional
Cisco Extended Functions	Optional	Optional
Cisco Serviceability Reporter	Optional	Optional
Cisco WebDialer	Optional	Optional
Cisco IP Manager Assistant	Optional	Optional
Cisco Extension Mobility	Optional	Optional

Table 8-4 *Service Recommendations for a System with 1500 Users*

Service	Publisher Server	Subscriber Server	Subscriber Server
Cisco CallManager	Deactivated	Activated	Activated
Cisco TFTP	Activated	Optional	Deactivated
Cisco Messaging Interface	Deactivated	Optional	Optional
Cisco IP Voice Media Streaming App	Deactivated	Optional	Optional

Table 8-4   *Service Recommendations for a System with 1500 Users (Continued)*

Service	Publisher Server	Subscriber Server	Subscriber Server
Cisco CTIManager	Deactivated	Optional	Optional
Cisco Telephony Call Dispatcher	Deactivated	Optional	Optional
Cisco MOH Audio Translator	Optional	Deactivated	Deactivated
Cisco RIS Data Collector	Activated	Activated	Activated
Cisco Database Layer Monitor	Activated	Activated	Activated
Cisco CDR Insert	Optional	Deactivated	Deactivated
Cisco CTL Provider	Optional	Optional	Optional
Cisco Extended Functions	Deactivated	Optional	Optional
Cisco Serviceability Reporter	Optional	Deactivated	Deactivated
Cisco WebDialer	Deactivated	Optional	Deactivated
Cisco IP Manager Assistant	Deactivated	Optional	Optional
Cisco Extension Mobility	Deactivated	Optional	Deactivated

Table 8-5 assumes that the Cisco IP Voice Media Streaming App service is used for MOH only and that hardware resources on the network such as an NM-HDV-FARM are being used as conference resources.

Table 8-5   *Service Recommendations for a System with 10,000 Users*

Service	Publisher Server	TFTP Server	TFTP Server	Subscriber Server	Subscriber Server	Subscriber Server	Subscriber Server
Cisco CallManager	Deactivated	Deactivated	Deactivated	Activated	Activated	Activated	Activated
Cisco TFTP	Deactivated	Activated	Activated	Deactivated	Deactivated	Deactivated	Deactivated

continues

Table 8-5 *Service Recommendations for a System with 10,000 Users (Continued)*

Cisco Messaging Interface	Deactivated	Deactivated	Deactivated	Optional	Deactivated	Deactivated	Deactivated
Service	**Publisher Server**	**TFTP Server**	**TFTP Server**	**Subscriber Server**	**Subscriber Server**	**Subscriber Server**	**Subscriber Server**
Cisco IP Voice Media Streaming App	Deactivated	Deactivated	Deactivated	Optional	Optional	Optional	Optional
Cisco CTIManager	Deactivated	Deactivated	Deactivated	Optional	Optional	Optional	Optional
Cisco Telephony Call Dispatcher	Deactivated	Deactivated	Deactivated	Optional	Optional	Optional	Optional
Cisco MOH Audio Translator	Deactivated	Optional	Optional	Deactivated	Deactivated	Deactivated	Deactivated
Cisco RIS Data Collector	Activated	Activated	Activated	Activated	Activated	Activated	Activated
Cisco Database Layer Monitor	Activated	Activated	Activated	Activated	Activated	Activated	Activated
Cisco CDR Insert	Optional	Deactivated	Deactivated	Deactivated	Deactivated	Deactivated	Deactivated
Cisco CTL Provider	Optional	Optional	Optional	Optional	Optional	Optional	Optional
Cisco Extended Functions	Deactivated	Deactivated	Deactivated	Optional	Optional	Optional	Optional
Cisco Serviceability Reporter	Optional	Deactivated	Deactivated	Deactivated	Deactivated	Deactivated	Deactivated
Cisco WebDialer	Deactivated	Deactivated	Deactivated	Optional	Optional	Deactivated	Deactivated
Cisco IP Manager Assistant	Deactivated	Deactivated	Deactivated	Optional	Optional	Deactivated	Deactivated

Table 8-5   *Service Recommendations for a System with 10,000 Users (Continued)*

Cisco Extension Mobility	Deactivated	Deactivated	Deactivated	Optional	Optional	Deactivated	Deactivated

Table 8-6 assumes that the Cisco IP Voice Media Streaming App service is used for MOH only and that hardware resources on the network such as the NM-HDV-FARM are being used as conference resources. A second TFTP server is optional, but it helps to divide the deployment in half to make phone upgrades go faster and to have a redundant failover.

Table 8-6   *Service Recommendations for a System with 20,000 Users*

Service	TFTP Server	TFTP Server	Publisher Server	Subscriber Server	Subscriber Server	Subscriber Server	Subscriber Server	Subscriber Server	Subscriber Server	Subscriber Server	Subscriber Server
Cisco CallManager	Deactivated	Deactivated	Deactivated	Activated	Activated	Activated	Activated	Activated	Activated	Activated	Activated
Cisco TFTP	Activated	Activated	Deactivated	Deactivated	Deactivated	Deactivated	Deactivated	Deactivated	Deactivated	Deactivated	Deactivated
Cisco Messaging	Deactivated	Deactivated	Deactivated	Optional	Deactivated	Deactivated	Optional	Deactivated	Deactivated	Deactivated	Deactivated

continues

Table 8-6 *Service Recommendations for a System with 20,000 Users (Continued)*

Cisco MOH Audio Translator	Cisco Telephony Call Dispatcher	Cisco CTIManager	Service	Cisco IP Voice Media Streaming App
Optional	Deactivated	Deactivated	TFTP Server	Deactivated
Optional	Deactivated	Deactivated	TFTP Server	Deactivated
Deactivated	Deactivated	Deactivated	Publisher Server	Deactivated
Deactivated	Optional	Optional	Subscriber Server	Optional
Deactivated	Optional	Optional	Subscriber Server	Optional
Deactivated	Optional	Optional	Subscriber Server	Optional
Deactivated	Optional	Optional	Subscriber Server	Optional
Deactivated	Optional	Optional	Subscriber Server	Optional
Deactivated	Optional	Optional	Subscriber Server	Optional
Deactivated	Optional	Optional	Subscriber Server	Optional
Deactivated	Optional	Optional	Subscriber Server	Optional

Table 8-6   *Service Recommendations for a System with 20,000 Users (Continued)*

Cisco Extended Functions	Cisco CTL Provider	Cisco CDR Insert	Service	Cisco Database Layer Monitor	Cisco RIS Data Collector
Deactivated	Optional	Deactivated	TFTP Server	Activated	Activated
Deactivated	Optional	Deactivated	TFTP Server	Activated	Activated
Deactivated	Optional	Optional	Publisher Server	Activated	Activated
Optional	Optional	Deactivated	Subscriber Server	Activated	Activated
Optional	Optional	Deactivated	Subscriber Server	Activated	Activated
Optional	Optional	Deactivated	Subscriber Server	Activated	Activated
Optional	Optional	Deactivated	Subscriber Server	Activated	Activated
Optional	Optional	Deactivated	Subscriber Server	Activated	Activated
Optional	Optional	Deactivated	Subscriber Server	Activated	Activated
Optional	Optional	Deactivated	Subscriber Server	Activated	Activated
Optional	Optional	Deactivated	Subscriber Server	Activated	Activated

continues

Table 8-6   *Service Recommendations for a System with 20,000 Users (Continued)*

Cisco Extension Mobility	Cisco IP Manager Assistant	Service	Cisco WebDialer	Cisco Serviceability Reporter
Deactivated	Deactivated	TFTP Server	Deactivated	Deactivated
Deactivated	Deactivated	TFTP Server	Deactivated	Deactivated
Deactivated	Deactivated	Publisher Server	Deactivated	Optional
Optional	Optional	Subscriber Server	Optional	Deactivated
Optional	Optional	Subscriber Server	Optional	Deactivated
Deactivated	Deactivated	Subscriber Server	Deactivated	Deactivated
Deactivated	Deactivated	Subscriber Server	Deactivated	Deactivated
Deactivated	Deactivated	Subscriber Server	Optional	Deactivated
Deactivated	Deactivated	Subscriber Server	Deactivated	Deactivated
Deactivated	Deactivated	Subscriber Server	Deactivated	Deactivated
Deactivated	Deactivated	Subscriber Server	Deactivated	Deactivated

The following sections provide general information about working with services:

- How to change or display the status of services
- How to start/stop and activate/deactivate services
- How to restart services

- How to document the system and limit the number of changes made at any one time

Changing or Displaying the Status of Services

Use the Control Center in CallManager Serviceability, shown in Figure 8-1, to display or change the status of CallManager-related services (**Tools > Control Center**).

Each service shown in Figure 8-1 can be started or stopped through this interactive page. You can activate or deactivate a service in the Service Activation page, which is available by clicking the **Service Activation** link in the upper-right corner.

Figure 8-1   *Control Center*

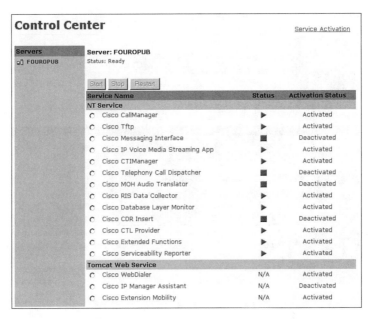

Starting/Stopping and Activating/Deactivating Services in CallManager Serviceability

In CallManager Serviceability, the Control Center (**Tools > Control Center**) allows you to start and stop services, and Service Activation (**Tools > Service Activation**) allows activation and deactivation of services. You can disable services through the Windows Services administrative tool, but it's highly recommended that you perform those actions via these two CallManager Serviceability pages instead.

The problem with disabling or enabling a service from the Windows Services tool is that the CallManager database configuration for that service will be out of sync with the service activation status. For example, you might manually enable a service that is not configured in the database, so the service won't be able to start. Also, the Service Activation page automatically checks the service status and warns you to correct the problem if you've made an out of sync change via the Services administrative tool.

TIP   Service Activation tells you exactly what services need to be running on the same server. When you select a service for which other required services are not already running, a popup dialog appears, indicating the other services that also need to be activated. For example, Figure 8-2 shows the services that are required to be running for the Cisco IP Voice Media Streaming App service.

Figure 8-2   *Popup Dialog Showing Required Services*

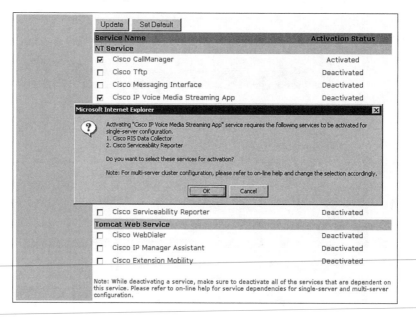

Restarting Services

Table 8-7 shows the conditions that necessitate a restart because of major or minor configuration changes. Restart a service in the Control Center by selecting the service(s) and clicking the **Restart** button. Restarting a service is very disruptive and should be done only during nonproduction hours when possible. For example, restarting the CallManager service causes all IP phones and gateways that are currently registered to that CallManager service to fail over to their secondary CallManager service. Starting and stopping a CallManager service causes other installed applications (such as conference bridge or

Cisco Messaging Interface) that are homed to that CallManager to restart as well, potentially causing interrupted voice services.

Table 8-7   *Conditions That Necessitate a CallManager Service Restart*

Condition	Potential Need for Change
Change IP address on the Server Configuration page (**System > Server**)	DNS update or new dedicated address assignment.
Change auto-registration partition to a value other than the <None> default (**System > Cisco CallManager**)	Start new devices in a restricted partition or dedicated partition for security.
Change auto-registration external phone number mask to a value other than the blank default (**System > Cisco CallManager**)	Single number appearance to external callers or addition of digits to internal dial plan.
Condition	**Potential Need for Change**
Changes to TCP port settings for phones, digital or analog gateways, and Media Gateway Control Protocol (MGCP) gateways from the default (**System > Cisco CallManager**)	Conflict with existing network service or security implementation.
Some service parameter changes (**Service > Service Parameters**)	General configuration changes. If a device or service requires a restart, you are notified after you click **Update** on the Service Parameters Configuration page.

Document the System Before Making Changes, and Limit the Number of Changes Made at One Time

It's a good idea, before making any modifications, to document the specific services that are activated, running, deactivated, or stopped. This information is useful if you need to roll back any changes. Also consider limiting the number of changes you make to service parameters at any one time. In case unexpected results occur because of the changes, making only a small number of parameter changes helps when troubleshooting. Having documentation showing what was changed makes reversing the changes to get back to a known working configuration much simpler.

About Service Parameters

The following sections provide general information about enterprise and service parameters:

- Distinguishing clusterwide parameters
- Using Advanced parameters
- Waiting until nonproduction hours to change parameters that require a restart
- Knowing which enterprise parameters require you to restart all devices
- Checking parameter settings for all servers

Distinguishing Clusterwide Parameters

You can identify clusterwide service parameters by the heading, which conveniently includes the word "Clusterwide." This means that the setting in the service parameter applies to all devices or CallManager servers or gateways and so on in the entire cluster. Often, the same setting can be specified at the device level. For example, the Built In Bridge field on the Phone Configuration page in Cisco CallManager Administration has a matching clusterwide service parameter called Built-in Bridge Enable. When you specify a value other than Default in the Built In Bridge field on the Phone Configuration page, the device uses the value you specified (in this example, On or Off) and overrides—for that device only—the clusterwide setting in the Service Parameters Configuration page. For all other devices that use Default (in some cases the value is called Use System Default), the determination is made by the service parameter. This allows you to configure the general availability of some features and then override it for select devices.

Understanding Advanced Parameters

The Service Parameters Configuration page (**Service > Service Parameters** > *select a server* > *select a service*) in CallManager Administration displays the basic parameters for the selected service. Some services also have Advanced parameters. Access the complete set of parameters by clicking the **Advanced** button. CallManager Administration segregates the parameters this way because the parameters that appear in the Advanced section are usually best left at their default values. However, there are times when network congestion, your deployment specifics, or other issues might prompt you to adjust an Advanced parameter. As a general warning, it's best to leave the Advanced parameters at their default value unless you know for sure what you're doing.

Wait Until Nonproduction Hours to Change Parameters That Require a Restart

There are ways to determine if the parameter you want to tweak requires you to restart the service. The easiest way is to click the parameter name to display the help text, which indicates if a restart of the service or device is required. A second notification occurs after you make a change to a parameter and click **Update**. If a restart is required, a popup dialog advises you to restart the service or device for the change to take effect. You can make the change and later perform the restart during nonproduction hours, as long as you realize that the change doesn't take effect until you restart the service or device. If you choose not to make the change, you must go back to the service parameter and manually reverse the change. There's no undo after you click Update.

Beware of Enterprise Parameters That Require a Restart of All Devices

A few enterprise parameters (**System > Enterprise Parameters**) require you to restart every device on all nodes for the change to take effect. Unless you're willing to write a custom AVVID XML Layer (AXL) script to do so (see Chapter 7, "Configuring CallManager and IP Telephony Components"), there's no easy way to restart all devices at once across a CallManager cluster, and this action is naturally extremely disruptive. Therefore, you should definitely wait for nonproduction hours to make the change. You can reset all devices in the cluster by using the Reset Devices button for every device pool in the system (**System > Device Pools**) or by resetting each device type on the Device Defaults Configuration page (**System > Device Defaults**). Also, the Bulk Administration Tool (BAT) allows you to bulk-reset phones and some gateway models. The enterprise parameters that require a restart of all devices are

- Default Network Locale
- MLPP Domain Identifier
- MLPP Indication Status
- MLPP Preemption Setting

Checking Parameter Settings for All Servers

From the Service Parameters Configuration page (**Service > Service Parameters**), you can click the link in the upper-right corner for **Parameters for All servers**. This handy link shows you the values specified for each parameter on every server.

Check for Out of Sync Parameters

After you have clicked the link for **Parameters for All servers**, additional links appear in the upper-right corner. The link to **Out of Sync Parameters for All Servers** displays the parameters that have different values set on different servers in the same cluster, as shown in Figure 8-3. No parameters should be out of sync between nodes in the cluster, so it's a good idea to periodically check for any out of sync parameters and correct them as needed.

Figure 8-3 *Out of Sync Parameters*

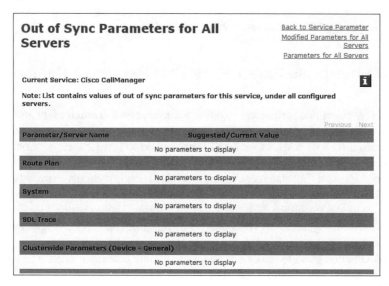

Cisco CallManager Service and Related Parameters

The heart and soul of the system is CallManager. Call processing and phone registration occur only when the CallManager service is running. This service can fail to start because of a service password or account change, incorrect installation or upgrade, or the inability to look up the machine's given name via DNS to an IP address. (In fact, it's a best practice to always use IP addresses instead of host names.) The Cisco Database Layer Monitor Service must be running for the CallManager service to operate.

A single CallManager cluster can have a maximum of eight servers running the CallManager service. If you are using dedicated servers for specific tasks, such as a music on hold (MOH) server solely for streaming audio or a dedicated TFTP server to provide phone images and configurations, you might not need to run the CallManager service on such dedicated servers. Refer to Tables 8-3 through 8-6 for recommendations.

The following sections discuss CallManager service parameters.

Collect CDR Data for Billing Purposes and Troubleshooting

For you to collect call detail record (CDR) information for troubleshooting or billing, call detail records must be enabled. Three service parameters enable CDR data collection:

- **CDR Enabled Flag**—Enables the collection of call detail records.

- **Call Diagnostics Enabled**—Enables the collection of call management records.
- **Log Calls with Zero Duration Flag**—Enables the collection of CDRs for calls that never connected or that lasted for less than 1 second.

These parameters are disabled by default, so you need to enable each or minimally set the CDR Enabled Flag if you want to collect CDR data for billing purposes. You should set the Call Diagnostics Enabled parameter to True if you want to use CDR Data for troubleshooting voice quality problems. Another parameter, Max CDR Records, determines the maximum number of CDRs to be collected. By default, this parameter is set to 1.5 million records, which represents about 400 MB worth of data.

To learn more about CDR data collection and managing these and other service parameters related to CDR data collection, read Chapter 11, "Administering Call Detail Records."

TIP   One potential issue with enabling CDRs is disk space. Make sure you have enough free disk space to save the number of CDRs you need and that you have configured alarms to monitor disk space and alert you when disk space is low.

Customize Data for CCM Traces and Cisco Dialed Number Analyzer

You can customize CCM trace data and the level of detail provided by the Cisco Dialed Number Analyzer (DNA) by using some or all of the following service parameters.

Digit Analysis Complexity

This parameter determines whether detailed digit analysis information is included in the trace output and Cisco DNA. If you want to see translation pattern and alternative pattern match information, set this parameter to TranslationAndAlternatePatternAnalysis. The default is StandardAnalysis, which does not show pattern transformations.

Status Enquiry Poll Flag

One function of this parameter is to determine whether CCM trace files will include the channel status for MGCP primary rate interface/channel-associated signaling (PRI/CAS) and analog gateways, the Precedence status of channels for MGCP devices, and Multilevel Precedence and Preemption (MLPP) information for the devices that support MLPP. The default is False, but if you want this information to appear in CCM trace files, set this parameter to True.

TIP   PRI gateways can set this flag on the Gateway Configuration page in CallManager
Administration (**Device > Gateway**). Select the **Enable status poll** checkbox in the
Interface Information area.

Locations Trace Details Enabled

This parameter determines whether additional details, such as the current state of all
locations whenever bandwidth is allocated or released, are collected in the CCM trace.
CCM traces do not collect this additional information by default, so if you want this
information to be included, set this parameter to True.

Managing System Performance

Some service parameters help you manage system performance. In most cases, the default
values satisfy basic needs. However, depending on your network, you might want to tweak
some of these parameters.

Maximum Phone Fallback Queue Depth

This parameter controls the number of phone registration requests that a CallManager
server accepts during fallback. After fallback has occurred and the higher-priority
CallManager server has come back online, this parameter protects phones that are currently
registered to a lower-priority CallManager from unregistering from a working
CallManager, just to be placed in a waiting queue for a higher-priority CallManager. If the
phones cannot register quickly, users might not hear a dial tone while the phone waits to
register to the higher-priority CallManager. It's a good idea to leave this parameter at its
default value of 10 phones. A small number ensures that users won't likely go off-hook and
discover they have lost dial tone.

Maximum Number of Registered Devices

This parameter controls how many devices are allowed to register with the CallManager
server. Any devices beyond the value configured in this parameter are rejected. If
registrations are being rejected, one troubleshooting step is to check this parameter to
ensure that it is set to the appropriate number of allowable registrations, depending on
server capacity and the number of devices in the system. The default is 5000; you might
need to increase this value for a high-end server such as the MCS 7845, which can handle
more than the default 5000 devices.

Parameters You Should Ignore

You can safely ignore a number of parameters until a Cisco support engineer asks you to change them. Most parameters in the Advanced section fall into this category. You should never change the signal distribution layer (SDL) parameters without guidance from Cisco, which is good because there's no documentation (including this book) to teach you what the different values mean.

Parameters You Should Notice

It's a good idea to be aware of the parameters described in the following sections. You should understand what they do and how they interact with the system.

T301 Timer (Alerting Timeout)

This parameter determines how long CallManager waits to receive the Alerting message. The value in this parameter should always be greater than the values in certain other parameters, such as Forward No Answer Timer and Auto Answer Timer. Basically, you want this timer to always expire last. If the value in this parameter is lower than the other parameters, which means that this timer expires before one of the others, calls are not forwarded or auto-answered, and the caller receives a busy signal.

T302 Timer (Interdigit Timeout)

This parameter represents an interdigit timer, which restarts with each new digit dialed after the first digit. The timeout for the first digit dialed is controlled by the Offhook to First Digit Timer parameter, discussed in the following section. For IP phones, CallManager routes the call using the digits it has collected up to the point when this timer expires. This is also an ISDN timer that controls the interdigit timer for inbound calls with overlap sending. When this timer expires, CallManager tries to route the call using the numbers it has received up to the point when the timer expired.

Offhook to First Digit Timer (First Digit Timeout)

This parameter specifies how long CallManager waits for a user to dial the first digit. For example, suppose a user goes off-hook and then realizes she needs to get the number she wants to dial. CallManager waits 15 seconds by default for the user to dial the first digit. If no digits are dialed before this timer expires, the user hears a reorder tone. After the first digit is dialed, the T302 Timer controls how long CallManager waits to receive additional digits.

Forward Maximum Hop Count

This parameter determines how many times CallManager forwards a call. The default is 12, but you should consider lowering it if possible to minimize resource consumption during errant routing configurations. In previous CallManager releases, 12 hops might have been needed to ensure access to voice mail, but now that voice mail uses a hunt pattern, the number of forwarding hops you should need is reduced.

Forward No Answer Timer

This parameter allows you to control how long a phone rings before rolling to voice mail or another destination specified for Call Forward No Answer (CFNA). The default value is 12 seconds, but you can specify any number of seconds in the range 1 to 300. Make certain that the value in this parameter is less than the value in the T301 Timer parameter; otherwise, callers hear a reorder tone rather than being forwarded to the CFNA destination.

As of CallManager release 4.0, no answer ring duration can be configured on a per-line basis. You can read more about this in Chapter 7.

Max Forward Hops to DN

This parameter is designed to prevent forwarding loops from occurring. It controls how many times CallManager forwards the same call to the same directory number (DN). For example, suppose Phone A is forwarded to Phone B, and Phone B is forwarded to Phone A. When a call arrives for Phone A, it's forwarded to Phone B, and then back to A, and then back to B, and so on until the number of forwards in this parameter is exhausted. The default is 12 hops to the same DN, but you can set this parameter much lower. Also, you are allowed the option of 0, which disables loop prevention. You should never use 0 unless instructed to by a Cisco support engineer for troubleshooting purposes.

Statistics Enabled

This parameter determines whether performance statistics used by Microsoft Performance (PerfMon) and the Real-Time Monitoring Tool (RTMT) in CallManager Serviceability are generated. This parameter is enabled by default, so ideally you don't need to change anything unless you want to disable statistics generation (which is not advised).

Automated Alternate Routing Enable

This parameter determines whether to use automated alternate routing (AAR) when the system does not have enough bandwidth. This parameter is disabled by default, so if you want to use AAR, set this parameter to True. AAR functionality is detailed in Chapter 2, "Planning Centralized Call Processing Deployments."

Check the Display Text for Translated Parameters

CallManager provides a string of text for the Out of Bandwidth Text and AAR Network Congestion Re-routing Text parameters by default. The strings are translated into the foreign languages that CallManager supports. But for a non-U.S. locale, you might prefer to word these messages differently, so you should check the default text that is displayed for the following parameters:

- **Out of Bandwidth Text**—Up to 23 characters; the default is "Not Enough Bandwidth".
- **AAR Network Congestion Re-routing Text**—Up to 31 characters; the default is "Network Congestion.Rerouting".

Specify Unknown Caller ID Text if It Is Not Passed from the PSTN

If you want specific text to be displayed when a call is received without a calling party number, you need to keep the Unknown Caller ID Flag set to True (it's enabled by default) and specify text in the Unknown Caller ID Text parameter. You do not need to specify anything in this parameter if you want to use the text sent by the Public Switched Telephone Network (PSTN) for unknown numbers.

If Secondary Lines Are Shared, Use the Primary Line

For situations in which a second line is shared or owned by someone else, a user might want to always go off-hook on the first line and then, when the second (shared) line is desired, manually select it. The service parameter Always Use Prime Line ensures that the user doesn't inadvertently answer a call on the shared line.

For example, suppose a busy assistant is scheduling a conference on the web, fielding an instant message, and talking to another employee. The phone rings. The assistant reaches for the phone without looking and picks up the handset to answer the call. As it turns out, the ringing call was on the second line, and the manager, who was waiting in her office for the call, now has to wait a little longer while the assistant transfers the call to the manager. In the same situation, if the Always Use Prime Line parameter were set to True, the busy assistant would have heard a dial tone on the idle primary line rather than intercepting the call on the secondary line inadvertently. The downside, of course, is that anytime the assistant wants to answer the shared line, he has to select the secondary line manually.

If Secondary Lines Are Shared, Use the Primary Line for Voice Mail Access

For situations in which a second line is shared or owned by someone else, users might want to always go off-hook on the primary line when they press the **messages** button. When set to True, the service parameter Always Use Prime Line for Voice Mail ensures that the phone always dials the voice messaging system from the primary line when the **messages** button is pressed. The default is False.

The Many Uses of Speed Dial Await Further Digits

Speed Dial Await Further Digits is a handy parameter that allows you to use speed dial buttons as access codes or feature enablers. For example, if a multiple digit prefix or code is required for users to access an outside line or place a certain type of call, you can configure the necessary prefix as a speed dial button, assign it to phones via the softkey template, and then instruct users to press the speed dial button followed by the remaining digits to be dialed.

You can also use this parameter to enable features such as intercom (see Chapter 7 for instructions) and entering account codes. CallManager extends the call as soon as a route pattern match is made based on the speed dial digits plus the digits dialed by the user. If there are multiple potential matches, CallManager waits for the T302 Timer to expire (15 seconds by default) before routing the call based on the digits dialed so far. (In the case of potential matches, CallManager routes the call using closest-match routing. See the Cisco documentation or the Cisco Press book *Cisco CallManager Fundamentals* for more information.)

Take B-Channels Out of Service for Troubleshooting or Maintenance

The service parameters Change B-Channel Maintenance Status 1 through 5 allow you to take B-channels out of service for up to five MGCP gateways without disrupting calls or waiting until nonproduction hours. Use value 1, which takes the B-channel out of service only when there are no active calls. When you update the service parameters, it takes up to 2.5 seconds for the change to take effect on the endpoints. This parameter applies to MGCP gateways only, and for it to work, all MGCP gateways must have the **Enable status poll** check box selected. You can select this check box on the Gateway Configuration page in CallManager Administration (**Device > Gateway**). It's best to update this checkbox when you first configure the gateway and leave it checked all the time because you have to restart the gateway for the Enable status poll change to take effect.

You can confirm that the channel has been taken out of service by checking the value of the appropriate Channel Status counter in the Cisco MGCP PRI Device object in PerfMon or RTMT. The counter should reflect a value of 1.

Here are a few things to note about these parameters:

- You cannot take the D-channel or framing channel out of service, even if you set these parameters to try to do so; the value in this parameter has no effect on the D-channel or framing channels on an MGCP gateway.

- Only five gateways can be affected by these parameters at any one time. So if you set five gateways with these parameters, and then you set five more gateways, the original five are returned to service when you set the subsequent five.

- If your plan is to use these parameters to achieve a fractional PRI service from your telephone company, your plan will work. The settings remain even after CallManager and/or the gateways are reset. Just be sure that the service parameters are not modified, or you will lose the fractional PRI for the affected gateway.

WARNING   CallManager sends a SERVICE message to the ISDN network indicating a change in the channel's status only for the NI2, DMS100, and DMS250 protocols. When the channel comes back in service because of a configuration change in CallManager, the ISDN switch is notified of the status change. NI2 support was first added in CallManager release 4.0(1)sr1.

However, for all other PRI protocols, CallManager currently does not support the sending of SERVICE messages to signify changes to channel status. The result is that you can mark the channel out of service internally, but if the ISDN switch sends a SETUP message asking for an exclusive channel that is marked out of service in CallManager, CallManager responds with a RELEASE_COMPLETE message saying "No circuit/channel available." The ISDN switch continues trying to connect to the channel, and after repeated failed attempts, it marks the channel out of service internally on its side.

Assume you put the channel back in service on the CallManager side. The ISDN switch does not know this because CallManager does not send a SERVICE message indicating the in-service status. The problem is that the ISDN switch does not send any calls requesting that channel because it believes it to be faulty. The only way you can begin to receive calls on that channel again is if CallManager sends a call to the ISDN switch requesting that channel. The ISDN switch returns a RELEASE_COMPLETE message with a cause of "No circuit/channel available," and in response, CallManager initiates a RESTART procedure.

However, note that when using a protocol other than NI2, DMS100, or DMS250, if you change the channel status via these parameters on a PRI gateway that is being used only for incoming calls (meaning that CallManager does not route any outbound traffic to this PRI), you could have a problem. The ISDN switch might be trying to route calls to the gateway repeatedly while you have marked all the channels out of service, eventually causing the ISDN switch to internally mark all the channels out of service. Because CallManager will never send any outbound calls to this PRI after you have brought the channels back into service, the channels will never come back into service until the entire PRI is restarted so that RESTART procedures can take place upon initialization.

Refer to the help text for the Change B-Channel Maintenance Status parameters for detailed instructions.

Enable Distinctive Rings for OnNet and OffNet Calls

Three parameters—MGCP Network Location OffNet, MGCP Network Location OffNet for E1 and T1, and H323 Network Location OffNet—allow you to specify a distinctive ring that tells users whether the call is internal or external. When these parameters are enabled, a single ring indicates an internal (OnNet) call, and a double ring indicates an external (OffNet) call. The default for the MGCP Network Location OffNet and H323 Network Location OffNet parameters is False. Therefore, if you want to enable distinctive rings for calls that come in through H.323 or analog MGCP gateways, set this parameter to True. The default for the MGCP Network Location OffNet for E1 and T1 parameter is True, so distinctive rings are enabled by default for calls that come in on a digital MGCP gateway.

Distinguish National Numbers and Prepend a Digit String So That Users Can Return Calls from the Missed Calls List in the Directory

If you use MGCP gateways and need overlap sending support, you need a way to manipulate the calling PSTN number so that the calling number displays correctly as an international or national number in the Missed Calls directory on Cisco IP Phones. Incorrect routing could cause calls that were supposed to go to business numbers in another country to end up at local residences. Three service parameters—National Number Prefix, International Number Prefix, and Subscriber Number Prefix—allow you to prepend a digit string to international, national, and subscriber calls so that the numbers display properly in the Missed Calls directory. This means that, for example, when a user dials from the Missed Calls directory, the call is extended to the desired number rather than being routed as a national number instead of an international one.

These three service parameters make it easy for you to allow convenient and accurate dialing from the Missed Calls list. Simply prepend the necessary digit string for external access. For example, in the North American Numbering Plan (NANP), you can specify 9011 for the International Number Prefix. When a user presses the Dial softkey, the international call is successfully placed (assuming that you use a digit to access an outside line, such as the 9 in this example).

These parameters work well in non-NANP countries. The successful use of these parameters in the NANP depends on the PSTN delivering the correct numbering plan and type for the call in the calling party information element. Also, the call must come in on a PRI gateway to get this information.

Enable FastStart with Centralized Call Processing

Latency problems can occur with H.323 when you use centralized call processing. Enabling FastStart usually eliminates *voice clipping*, which occurs when someone answers the phone and the first second or two of conversation is cut off. If users are reporting that callers can't hear them say hello, consider enabling FastStart by setting the H323 FastStart Inbound parameter to True (it is set to False by default). This allows the signaling to begin immediately between the gateway and CallManager when a call is received inbound on the gateway.

You should enable this parameter for H.323 intercluster trunks or devices to a remote site if delays of 100 ms or greater are occurring on inbound calls.

This parameter affects inbound calls only; as of release 4.0, outbound FastStart is not supported. In the next minor CallManager release (for example, 4.1), outbound FastStart will be supported, and the service parameter will be removed in favor of configuring FastStart settings on a per-device basis on the Gateway Configuration page.

In conjunction, proper queuing over the WAN, as discussed in Chapter 2, can greatly reduce call setup times.

Customize Call Park

Two parameters allow you to customize call park interaction. The Call Park Display Timer parameter determines how long the number at which the call has been parked appears on the IP phone. The default is 10 seconds, but you can specify any number of seconds in the range 0 to 100. It might seem as if 0 seconds would be a poor choice if you want users to be able to see the number at which the call is parked. In fact, 0 means that the parked number is displayed until it is overwritten by another message of equal or higher priority, which could be a matter of seconds or hours or days. For this reason, 0 is not a recommended value.

The Call Park Reversion Timer parameter determines how long a call remains parked without being retrieved. When this timer expires, the call is returned to the user who parked it. The default is 60 seconds, but you might need to increase this number. To help determine the appropriate number of seconds, consider how your users will use this feature. (This could be a question you ask when interviewing users to help determine user classes, as discussed in Chapter 1, "Planning the CallManager Installation.") If users plan to park calls so that they can leave their cubicles and walk to a nearby conference room to retrieve calls in private, you should walk around your office building gauging how long it would take people to comfortably accomplish this.

Play a Tone on Barge, Join, and Conference

The Party Entrance Tone parameter alerts users when a party joins or exits a call that has two or more parties. This behavior applies to Barge, cBarge, Conference, Join, and Meet-

Me conference and is enabled by default. If you do not want a tone to alert users that someone has joined or departed a conversation or conference, you should set this parameter to False. Be sure to check local regulations before disabling the tone; in some areas, the party entrance tone is a legal requirement.

Prevent Hold Music from Streaming to a Conference

New to CallManager release 4.0, the Suppress MOH to Conference Bridge parameter prevents conference participants from hearing the hold music when a conference participant places the conference on hold. The default value for this parameter is True. Leave this parameter at the default value to prevent hold music from being played to conferences.

Your Hardware and Software Determine the Number of Conference Participants

Two parameters—Maximum Ad Hoc Conference and Maximum MeetMe Conference Unicast—determine the maximum number of participants in a conference of the specified type. Determine how many ports you have on your conferencing device, and then set these parameters according to the number of ports. If you specify a value higher than the actual number of conferencing ports on your hardware or software, participants are denied access to conferences when all available ports are used. Therefore, setting the parameter to 24 doesn't enable 24 ports if your hardware supplies only 16. The default for both these parameters is 4. If you have hardware or software that supports more than four ports, increase this value.

Check the documentation for your hardware or software conference bridge solution to determine the maximum number of conference participants the hardware or software can support. New gateways and new blades are introduced frequently, each with their own limits, so the documentation that ships with your gateway or blade is your best source of information.

Use Silence Suppression if Needed

Three parameters determine whether silence suppression is used: Silence Suppression, Silence Suppression for Gateways, and Strip G.729 Annex B (Silence Suppression) from Capabilities. Silence suppression can be disturbing to users because often the user thinks the other party has hung up because of the lack of random background noises, even with sidetone provided. The default for the silence suppression parameters is False, so to use silence suppression, set these parameters to True. Ensure that IOS-based gateways are also appropriately configured for silence suppression when they are part of the voice path.

Choose a Dial Tone

CallManager allows you to have different dial tones for OnNet and OffNet calls. For example, say you use the access code 9 to reach an external line. When a user goes off-hook, you might want one dial tone to play. When the user dials 9, a different dial tone with a higher pitch plays, alerting the user that he or she has accessed an outside line. The parameter Always Use Inside Dial Tone determines the dial tone behavior. The default means that different dial tones are heard. If you want the same dial tone used regardless of whether the call is OnNet or OffNet, set this parameter to True.

Change Your Preferred Packet Size if Needed

The parameters Preferred G711 Millisecond Packet Size, Preferred G723 Millisecond Packet Size, Preferred G729 Millisecond Packet Size, and Preferred GSM EFR Millisecond Packet Size control the sampling rate for the specific codecs. Depending on your WAN deployment, you might need to adjust these default values. For example, in an ATM Frame Relay deployment, the G.729 codec uses a 20 ms sampling rate by default, which is poor for an ATM network. Changing to a 30 ms sampling period saves 7 kbps per call by making more efficient use of the ATM cell size.

Cisco TFTP Service

The TFTP service builds configuration files and transfers those configurations on demand, along with binary image files and ring tones to devices on the network. TFTP also moves MOH files from the MOH Audio Translator service to CallManager servers running the IP Voice Media Streaming App service. Every IP phone in the deployment relies on the TFTP service, along with the CallManager-based gateways, for their binary image file and configuration file to operate. Requests for these files can reach the TFTP service only from devices that have passed their power-up diagnostics and either have a statically configured IP address or have successfully obtained that information via Dynamic Host Configuration Protocol (DHCP).

Certainly you should have the TFTP service run on at least two members of a CallManager cluster for redundancy when the DHCP server can support an Option 150 array, as detailed in the next section. Large deployments might have a dedicated TFTP server to achieve greater scalability and redundancy, as discussed in the section "Cisco CallManager Service and Related Parameters."

Providing Redundancy and Selecting the TFTP Server via DHCP

Typically a DHCP deployment occurs along with a CallManager deployment to dynamically furnish the IP address and network settings to all the phones. These settings can also be manually entered into each phone. One of these settings within the DHCP reply needs to be the name or address of the TFTP server. After the phone has the correct network settings, it can download a configuration file from the TFTP server and continue registering with a CallManager based on the information contained in the configuration file. The Cisco TFTP service depends on the Cisco Database Layer Monitor service.

You can use DHCP Option 150 to tell the device the TFTP server's location. Up to two TFTP server entries can be listed through an array or list. This way, a primary TFTP server can be identified, along with an additional backup TFTP server in the same cluster. Keep the Cisco TFTP service running because stopping the service can cause problems with the phone binary image version compatibility in the long term when CallManager itself gets upgraded or in the short term when phone configuration changes occur. Problems can occur immediately if you're using the extension mobility feature and the TFTP service is not running.

TIP When a CallManager cluster grows beyond 2500 phones, Cisco recommends establishing a dedicated TFTP server to enhance scalability. This dedicated server can be used for other CallManager housekeeping items such as MOH translation. For a dedicated server, adjust the Maximum Serving Count parameter (**Service > Service Parameter >** *select the TFTP server >* **Cisco TFTP > Advanced**) to allow up to 5000 simultaneous TFTP sessions.

In a large cluster scenario, to drop CPU utilization for all members of a cluster as well as to provide better response in loading phones, dedicate a server to handling just TFTP requests for binary images and configuration files. The dedicated TFTP server gets update information via the Cisco Database Layer Monitor service and re-creates files as needed to stay synchronized like any other member of the cluster. Use this dedicated server as the primary TFTP server, and have the Publisher listed as the secondary TFTP server in an Option 150 array. However, this is not always practical for smaller deployments. In that case, have at least two servers provide TFTP service for the network, again by using the DHCP Option 150 array, but in this scenario, configure the DHCP scope or zone to alternate between the two servers to achieve both load balancing and redundancy.

If you can make multiple choices when attempting to locate a TFTP server in the network, the devices follow a certain order. Devices that get their configuration and image data via TFTP are phones such as the Cisco IP Phone model 7960 and gateways such as the Catalyst WS-x6608. During the device's boot sequence, as detailed in the following list, a manually configured TFTP address on a device always gets preference, while an answer to a ciscocm1.*xyzdomain.com* DNS resolution is favored over a DHCP entry, and so on. It's important to understand how the TFTP server is located because it ultimately affects the device's ability to load an image and configuration file. Without these files, the device will not be operational.

The following list outlines the order of precedence from first chosen to last used for the entry of TFTP devices:

1 **Manually entered TFTP server address**—Configured manually on the gateway or phone.

2 **Successful ciscocm1 DNS address resolution**—A received domain entry in the DHCP reply formats this to ciscocm1 *xyzdomain.com* for the *xyzdomain.com* domain.

3 **DHCP Server/Next Server IP Address receipt (siaddr in the DHCP header of the reply packet)**—The available parameter or forced field in select DHCP servers. Use only a dotted-decimal IP address.

4 **DHCP Option 150 entry in the Reply, Custom Field**—The device attempts to contact the first entry received, and then the second. Dotted-decimal IP addresses only. *Recommended.*

5 **Optional Server Host Name (sname in the DHCP header)**—The available parameter in select DHCP server implementations. Use only a DNS name.

6 **DHCP Option 066 entry in the Reply, Boot Server**—Can be either a dotted-decimal IP address or DNS name entry.

TIP   List two different TFTP servers and provide a layer of redundancy to the device boot process as a best practice. Always use an array or list for the Option 150 DHCP parameter to achieve this. Alternate the order of the entries in the array for each zone or scope of the DHCP server to achieve partial balancing of TFTP services as well as redundancy.

Filling anything other than an Option 150 array with different TFTP server addresses does not provide redundancy—only management confusion. When using any DHCP server that fills the siaddr header field, dual Option 150 entries are never used because of the precedence order. Therefore, it's important to understand the capabilities of the chosen DHCP server as well as to test redundancy scenarios for proper operation beforehand.

Cisco Messaging Interface Service and Related Parameters

Cisco Messaging Interface (CMI) facilitates messaging for calls that are destined for a voice mail system using simplified message desk interface (SMDI) integration. An asynchronous serial connection directly ties one of the COM ports on the Publisher server to the attached legacy voice mail system. This serial connection runs at 9600 baud by default and allows CallManager to communicate with the legacy system by telling it which port on that system CallManager has sent a call to, along with redirect reasons and port information. This interface also allows the legacy system to communicate back to

CallManager the status of the message waiting indicator (MWI) for a particular phone extension-to-mailbox association. For operation, this service depends on the CallManager service and the Cisco Database Layer Monitor service.

TIP   It can take up to five minutes for configuration changes made to this service to take effect. To make changes occur immediately, stop and then restart this service after changes have been made.

Unless a CallManager server has a serial cable interconnecting it to a legacy voice mail system, running CMI consumes memory and CPU cycles for no reason. Do not use CMI if you are using Cisco Unity or a Cisco VG248 with an SMDI interface because the SMDI messaging proxies through the Cisco VG248 and CallManager does not even know that an SMDI link exists.

During the failure of an SMDI link, either physically because of cabling issues or logically because of CMI service, calls destined for the messaging system receive a generic greeting. Because no information about the call is delivered to the voice mail server, there's no way for the messaging system to handle the call. As a best practice when employing SMDI integration, achieve redundancy when two CallManager servers are physically available to be cabled via a data splitter to the messaging system. The data splitter allows one CallManager server to act as the primary and the other to act as a backup. This topic is covered in the CallManager 4.0 System Guide in the topic "SMDI Voice Mail Integration" at the following link:

> http://www.cisco.com/univercd/cc/td/doc/product/voice/c_callmg/4_0/sys_ad/ 4_0_1/ccmsys/a06smdi.htm

The following sections discuss some of the Cisco Messaging Interface service parameters.

Do Not Configure CMI Parameters if You Use Cisco Unity or Integrate Legacy Voice Mail Using SMDI on a Cisco VG248

CMI service parameters are used only for legacy voice mail systems that are connected to the COM port on the CallManager server for SMDI integration. You do not need to configure any CMI parameters or activate the CMI service if you are using Cisco Unity for your voice messaging or integrating with a legacy voice mail system using SMDI on a Cisco VG248.

Specify a CallManager Name and a Backup CallManager Name

If you are using a legacy voice mail application that connects to the COM port on the CallManager server for SMDI integration, you need to select the primary CallManager server and, if applicable, the backup CallManager server. No default values are provided, so you must complete these parameters to properly configure CMI.

Specify the MWI Calling Search Space

If you are using a legacy voice mail application that connects to the COM port on the CallManager server for SMDI integration, you need to specify the list of partitions in order of priority. CallManager searches through the list for the directory number that has been specified for MWI On and Off operations. To specify more than one partition, use colons to separate each partition in the list (for example, Partition1:Partition2:Partition3).

Change the Serial Port Parameter if You Use COM2

If you are using a legacy voice mail application that connects to the COM port on the CallManager server for SMDI integration and you use COM2, you need to update the Serial Port parameter. It defaults to COM1.

Specify the Voice Mail Directory Number and Voice Mail Partition

If you are using a legacy voice mail application such as Octel, you need to specify the directory number (DN) on the voice messaging system that CMI monitors to intercept calls destined for the voice messaging system. Enter this value in the Voice Mail DN parameter. Also, in the Voice Mail Partition parameter, enter the partition in which the voice mail DN resides. No default values are provided for these parameters.

Do Not Enter a Trailing Space in Edit Fields

Sometimes by habit or when typing fast, you can accidentally include a space at the end of a word or number, such as "1000 " when the value should actually be "1000". Parameters that use edit fields, such as Voice Mail DN, fail if the value entered is not exact, so be careful when you type.

Cisco IP Voice Media Streaming App Service

This service encompasses much more than its name reveals. Although the IP Voice Media Streaming App service does involve media streaming, it includes many functions, including media termination points (MTP), audio conferencing, MOH, and Annunciator (ANN). The real purpose of running this service is to create a messaging path between CallManager and the RTP packet driver that streams these services. This service depends on the Cisco Database Layer Monitor service for change notification and access to the Publisher/local database. It also depends on the Cisco TFTP service to retrieve a copy of the audio source files; the TFTP service does not need to be running on the same server. Audio conferencing provided by the IP Voice Media Streaming App service supports G.711 (automatic μ-law and A-law) and Wideband. The MOH codec streams can be G.711 μ-law or A-law, G.729a, or Wideband. Software MTP supports G.711 μ-law or A-law and Wideband. Annunciator, new in CallManager release 4.0, provides recorded audio versus simple tones to indicate incorrectly dialed numbers and other system messages. Also in CallManager release 4.0, the IP Voice Media Streaming App provides DTMF relay for SIP trunks. The software MTP provided by this service is required for SIP trunks to do DTMF, so the IP Voice Media Streaming App service must be configured and running on at least one server in the cluster for SIP trunks to receive digits.

The IP Voice Media Streaming App service can tax the server CPU resources and LAN bandwidth because it services potentially hundreds of streams. To allow greater scaling, consider running this service on a dedicated server. The dedicated MOH server would run only the IP Voice Media Streaming App service along with the Cisco Database Layer Monitor service. It's preferable to use dedicated hardware to host MTP, convert audio streams or transcoding, and host audio conferencing services, thereby freeing up CallManager resources on the other servers.

If simple tone on hold with no conferencing, Annunciator, software MTP, or MOH satisfies the requirements, the IP Voice Media Streaming App service can be stopped, though this is an unlikely scenario. When hardware-based resources exist on the network, the IP Voice Media Streaming App service potentially can be stopped, but doing so means that only hardware-based resources are available to the network. Sourcing MOH at multiple locations or conferencing calls nearly always requires that this service be enabled. Have this service running on all machines in a cluster other than the Publisher when possible, except servers already under a heavy call processing load.

MOH relies on the media resource group (MRG) and media resource group list (MRGL) to associate media resources to a device. When no conferencing resources are available, the IP phone displays "No Conference Bridge Available." This message lets the user know that the system cannot support conferencing at this time.

Cisco CTIManager Service

The Computer Telephony Integration Manager (CTIManager) provides call setup and manipulation from a standard Telephony Application Programming Interface (TAPI) or Java Telephony Application Programming Interface (JTAPI). Applications that use TAPI/JTAPI include those listed here and many others:

- Cisco IP Contact Center (IPCC) Express for call center functionality
- Cisco IP Interactive Voice Response (IVR) for menu-based call interaction
- Cisco Conference Connection (CCC) for scheduled conferencing
- Cisco IP SoftPhone for software-based phone-on-the-PC communications

Many Cisco-certified third-party applications use CTIManager for their functionality as well.

To operate, the Cisco CTIManager service depends on the Cisco Database Layer Monitor service. If any coresident applications such as IVR run on the same server in a single-server environment, the CTIManager service must be running. Not all software-based phone clients necessitate TAPI or JTAPI, so choosing a Skinny-based software phone such as Cisco IP Communicator can alleviate the need to run this service.

You can run this service on one or more CallManager servers in a cluster. Coresident applications need not necessarily home their TAPI/JTAPI connections in a one-to-one fashion to the same server they are running on. They may indeed home to a central CallManager running the CTIManager service. Redundancy can be achieved if the TAPI or JTAPI application supports that functionality. You can read more about CTIManager in the CallManager 4.0 System Guide under Computer Telephony Integration at the following link:

> http://www.cisco.com/univercd/cc/td/doc/product/voice/c_callmg/4_0/sys_ad/
> 4_0_1/ccmsys/a08cti.htm

Other seemingly unrelated services such as the Telephony Call Dispatcher and other tools such as the Tool for Auto-Registered Phones Support (TAPS) rely directly on the Cisco CTIManager service to be operational. In general, any CallManager deployment outside of a simple call processing environment requires CTIManager because of the need for TAPI/JTAPI interaction.

Cisco Telephony Call Dispatcher Service

The Cisco Telephony Call Dispatcher (TCD) service provides back-end communication of login, line state status, and directory services to Cisco CallManager Attendant Console clients. It also provides pilot points and hunt groups to the system. The TCD service allows you to configure queuing parameters such as queue size and hold time (in seconds). It also provides call routing based on four call distribution algorithms:

- **Linear**—For each new call, this algorithm tests the availability of hunt group members one member at a time, beginning at the top of the ordered list of hunt group members. When a member is idle, the call is distributed to that member.
- **Longest idle**—For each new call, a simultaneous test of all hunt group members is made for the duration since a call was last disconnected from that member. The member with the longest idle duration is selected, and the call is distributed to that member.

- **Circular**—The relative position of the last distributed call within a hunt group is remembered. When new calls are extended, the first tested member is the one to which the last call was distributed. Also, if the last member is busy, the call is distributed to the first member of the group.

- **Broadcast**—A call is extended to all members marked as idle simultaneously.

Operator console functionality is enabled on any PC that is attached to the network when you run this service in conjunction with the Cisco CallManager Attendant Console application. You can download the Attendant Console application from the Install Plugins page in CallManager Administration (**Application > Install Plugins**). Limited call queuing and call routing hunt group scenarios can be implemented; they depend on this service to operate. TCD depends on the CTIManager, Cisco Database Layer Monitor, and Cisco RIS Data Collector services.

Cisco MOH Audio Translator Service and Related Parameter

The primary function of this service is to translate audio files that have been placed in the C:\Program Files\Cisco\MOH\DropMOHAudioSourceFilesHere directory into the multiple codecs supported by the Cisco IP Voice Media Streaming App service. The MOH Audio Translator can translate .wav, .mp3, and other file formats recognized by the Microsoft DirectShow filters. The Cisco IP Voice Media Streaming App service depends on the MOH Audio Translator service to create correctly formatted audio files that it can use as MOH source files without further manipulation.

The MOH Audio Translator service can immediately consume 100 percent of the CPU processing power. This spike in CPU usage can be mitigated only by *not* placing source files in the C:\Program Files\Cisco\MOH\DropMOHAudioSourceFilesHere directory during peak load times. Run the MOH Audio Translator service only on a single CallManager server and at a time when creating or updating new audio files will not interfere with call processing, such as during low-usage times.

As a best practice, use a dedicated server to run the MOH Audio Translator service and the TFTP service for large deployments, or run this service only on a lightly loaded server for smaller deployments. Because this service directly stores audio source files in folders on the server that is running the Cisco TFTP service, the MOH Audio Translator service requires that the Cisco TFTP service and Cisco Database Layer Monitor service be running.

Typically, converting MOH audio files is an infrequent task. The potential impact on call processing is never worth the risk of having this service run on all servers all the time. Small audio files convert within a second or so, but accidental or malicious large file conversions can have a systemwide impact. This service can be stopped and then started only when it is needed to convert new MOH audio files.

Increase/Decrease the MOH Volume

The Default MOH Volume Level parameter allows you to tweak the volume level that is used when the Cisco MOH Audio Translator service converts audio source files. If users complain that the hold music is too loud, you can reduce the volume level lower than the default of –24 decibels. Changes to this parameter automatically take effect within 60 seconds and affect only audio files that are processed after the change has taken effect.

TIP   There's no way to force reprocessing of existing MOH files after this parameter is changed. To have the files processed using the new volume level, you need to drag and drop them into the C:\Program Files\Cisco\MOH\DropMOHAudioSourceFilesHere directory and make sure the service is running.

Cisco RIS Data Collector Service and Related Parameters

The RIS Data Collector service communicates CallManager statistics and status information to the Simple Network Management Protocol (SNMP) agent on the CallManager server. It also provides the status of registered phones and gateways along with their IP addresses. Cisco recommends having all CallManager servers in a cluster run the RIS Data Collector service. Doing so is certainly a best practice.

SNMP queries alone necessitate the operation of this service, and CallManager Serviceability and CallManager Administration require it to be running on all CallManager servers in a cluster to allow systemwide serviceability and administration. The Cisco RIS Data Collector service depends on the Cisco Database Layer Monitor service.

The following sections discuss Cisco RIS Data Collector service parameters.

Schedule RIS Cleanup Time of Day for Nonproduction Hours

The RIS Data Collector parameter, RIS Cleanup Time of Day, determines when the RIS service performs housekeeping, which includes deleting old, unregistered device information and closed provider, closed device, or closed line information from CTIManager. The default is 22:00 or 10:00 p.m., which should be acceptable if you run an organization that has 8:00 a.m. to 5:00 p.m. business hours. However, you might need to change the default value of this parameter if you have a three-shift business that runs 24 hours a day or if you have other production hours that conflict with a 10:00 p.m. cleanup. In those cases, determine a time of day when call volume is the lowest, and schedule RIS cleanup during that period.

Leave the Data Collection Enabled Parameter at the Default Setting to Collect Systemwide Statistics

The RIS Data Collector parameter Data Collection Enabled determines whether real-time performance, alarm, and system information for the cluster is collected. This parameter is set to True (enabled) by default. If you want to use PerfMon and the RTMT in CallManager Serviceability, this parameter needs to remain enabled.

Use the Default Data Collection Polling Rate

This parameter controls the polling rate in each preconfigured monitoring window in the RTMT. The default is 30 seconds, but you can specify a polling rate in the range of 15 to 300 seconds. Shortening this interval can affect the system's performance, so it's best to leave it at the default value.

Use Redundancy for RIS Data Collector

Two parameters, Primary Collector and Failover Collector, allow you to specify the primary and backup RIS Data Collector servers. If no server is specified in the Failover Collector parameter and the primary Data Collector fails, RIS does not collect clusterwide, real-time performance, alarm, and system information until the Primary Collector is restored. For redundancy, it's best to specify the primary and backup Data Collectors.

Cisco Database Layer Monitor Service and a Related Parameter

The Database Layer Monitor service both provides database exchange between CallManager cluster members and moves CDR data from Subscribers to the master CDR database on the Publisher. All other services depend on this service. The Cisco Database Layer Monitor service continually monitors the Publisher's status to determine when to go to read-only failover database mode. It provides a robust mechanism for all additions, retrievals, and deletions of SQL database items common to a cluster. The service locally stores CDR data during Publisher outages and forwards it when the Publisher is restored. In addition, when the service reaches the maximum CDR record count, it deletes the oldest CDRs. Because this service must be running on all servers in a CallManager cluster, it cannot be deactivated.

Control the Number of CDRs in the CDR Database

The Max CDR Records parameter in the Cisco Database Layer Monitor service controls the number of CDRs in the CDR database. The default is 1.5 million records, which is about

400 MB of data. See the earlier section "Collect CDR Data for Billing Purposes and Troubleshooting" for more information about CDR parameters. See Chapter 11 for more information about other CDR parameters.

Cisco CDR Insert Service

The Cisco CDR Insert service picks up the transported CDRs and places them in the central CDR database. Run this service only on the machine that contains the CDR database. The Database Layer Monitor service moves the CDR data to the Publisher. If you are not interested in CDR information and have not enabled CDRs, you do not need to run the CDR Insert service on any server.

Cisco CTL Provider Service

The Cisco Certificate Trust List (CTL) Provider service, introduced in CallManager release 4.0, handles authentication and certificate requests from the Cisco CTL Client plugin and creates the CTL file. When you use the new security features in CallManager, this service must be running on all the CallManager and TFTP servers.

A new security USB token device provides certificates issued by a Cisco Certificate Authority. To upload the new crypto tokens from the USB device into the CTL File, you must download the Cisco CTL Client plugin, shown in Figure 8-4, from the CallManager server (**Application > Install Plugins**) and run it from a machine that has a USB port. The CTL Client connects to the CTL Provider Service on each CallManager node, creates and uploads the CTL file to the CTL provider service, and sets the enterprise parameter Cluster Security Mode. See the later section "Choose Your Default System Security" for more information.

A phone that supports security requests a CTL file from the TFTP server. Specifically, the phone requests a list of the public keys and certificates to begin the trust relationships before requesting the digitally signed TFTP configuration file and registering with CallManager.

The CTL plugin needs to be run at the following times:

- Initially after the cluster is set up and stable
- On every addition or removal of a security token, CallManager, Certificate Authority Proxy Function (CAPF), or TFTP server in that cluster
- When a CallManager name or IP address changes
- During the restoration of a CallManager server

Figure 8-4 *Cisco CTL Client*

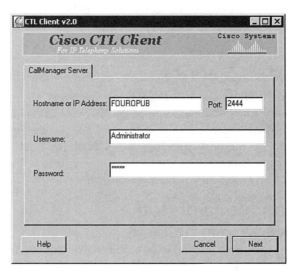

Cisco Extended Functions Service and a Related Parameter

The Cisco Extended Functions service supports select CallManager functionality, including the call back feature and the Quality Reporting Tool (QRT). The Cisco Database Layer Monitor service must be running for Extended Function features to operate.

Call back allows users to press the CallBack softkey to receive notification when a previously called busy or no answer extension becomes available. QRT allows users to automatically log audio quality problems that occur during an active call by pressing the QRT softkey on the phone. The QRT reporting and tracking of streaming statistics such as jitter are done via the RIS Data Collector service. To use either call back or QRT for phones homed to a CallManager server, the Extended Functions service must be running on the same server.

TIP   The server with the lowest IP address in a cluster that has multiple servers running the Extended Functions service becomes the active provider of this service to the cluster. This provides resiliency and redundancy. Graceful failover to a new server can take up to 2 minutes. Use the RTMT to actively check the current server status.

Change the Call Back Sound Using the Audio File Name Parameter if Desired

The Audio File Name parameter in the Cisco Extended Functions service determines which sound is played to Cisco IP Phone users for call back notification. The default audio file provides a twinkle-like sound. You can replace it with another sound of your choosing, so long as it's a 64-kbps audio μ-law file and is saved to the path C:\Program Files\ Cisco\TFTPPath.

Cisco Serviceability Reporter Service

New to CallManager release 4.0, this service generates five reports daily: Device Statistics, Server Statistics, Service Statistics, Call Activities, and Alert. Each report is a summary of predefined variables on the system, such as number of phones registered on a server, number of H.323 gateways in a cluster, hard disk usage, CPU usage, system alerts with severity, and so on, logically separated by the five report types. In a single CallManager server environment or in a multiple-server cluster, this service runs only on the Publisher at the time specified by the RTMT Report Generation Time parameter, once a day. No redundancy is supported for this service. If the Publisher is offline at the scheduled time, no reports are generated for the day.

The RTMT and CDR Analysis and Reporting (CAR) are two other plugins that are part of the CallManager Serviceability tool kit. Serviceability Reporter is the report generation service for RTMT.

You can adjust the relevant parameters as follows:

- By default, the RTMT Report Generation Time parameter runs the Serviceability Reporter service at 12:30 a.m. (30 minutes past midnight). Other services, such as the Backup and Restore System (BARS), CDR deletion, and so on, also run during these off hours. Ensure that no conflicts occur by spacing the start times for each appropriately.

- The other service parameter, RTMT Report Deletion Age, determines the number of days any generated report remains on the server before deletion. The default is seven days. Leaving this at such a low value helps keep the amount of disk space usage to a minimum. You can view generated reports from Cisco CallManager Serviceability by selecting **Tools > Serviceability Reports Archive**.

Cisco WebDialer Service

WebDialer allows PC-based URL linking of information to initiate dialing on an associated IP phone (basically, click-to-dial service). This provides a signaling bridge between the web link and the phone via CallManager. A corporate web-based directory is an implementation example. The user can access the company directory on the web, search for a coworker, and initiate a call to that user just by clicking the phone number link. The same mechanisms can be applied to any website with phone number or contact information. WebDialer provides a Simple Object Access Protocol (SOAP) interface that allows end-user or third-party applications to create plugins, such as a Microsoft Outlook address book add-in. WebDialer is an optional service. It is installed automatically during CallManager installation, but you need to activate it in the Service Activation page in CallManager Serviceability (**Tools > Service Activation**).

WebDialer depends on the Cisco Database Layer Monitor service and the CTIManager service for operation. Refer to the WebDialer documentation in the CallManager 4.0 Features and Services Guide on Cisco.com at

> http://www.cisco.com/univercd/cc/td/doc/product/voice/c_callmg/4_0/sys_ad/
> 4_0_1/ccmfeat/fswbdlr.htm

Cisco IP Manager Assistant Service

Cisco IP Manager Assistant (IPMA) lets managers and assistants work together more efficiently. It provides features such as do not disturb, immediate divert, transfer to voice mail, assistant watch, and divert all calls. In addition, IPMA provides the capability to create complex rules for screening a manager's calls and sending them to the configured assistant, the intended manager, or any other phone. IPMA provides a desktop client for the assistants, which they use to monitor their managers' calls and feature status, as well as handle calls on their own phones. When no managers or assistants are relying on IPMA, there is no need to run this service.

See Chapter 7 for IPMA best practices.

Cisco Extension Mobility Service and Related Parameters

Extension mobility allows users to temporarily access their Cisco IP Phone configuration, including their line appearances and speed dials, from other Cisco IP Phones via a simple login on the phone itself. This feature is highly prized in virtual desk assignments, mobile worker areas, and other areas with phones that do not have a single-user assignment.

Cisco Extension Mobility depends on the CallManager service and the Cisco Database Layer Monitor service for operation. Extension Mobility runs as a Tomcat Web Service, eliminating the JTAPI interface dependencies in earlier CallManager releases.

Scalability might be a concern for extremely large deployments that have thousands of users logging in and out at the same time and a need for all applicable phones to belong to the same CallManager cluster. For mobile or temporary telephone users, this is an extremely useful service to have deployed and running.

The following sections provide login best practices for Cisco Extension Mobility service parameters. Chapter 7 provides additional best practices relating to the extension mobility feature.

Enforce a Maximum Login Time for Extension Mobility

For greater toll fraud security, consider enforcing a maximum login time for extension mobility. The Enforce Maximum Login Time parameter defaults to False (no limit). Change it to True if you want users to be automatically logged out after a specified amount of time.

The default for the Maximum Login Time parameter is eight hours. Choose a time limit that represents an actual workday, such as 8, 10, or 12 hours. Logging out phones after a specified time period is useful to help protect against toll fraud. For example, suppose your usual workday is 8:00 a.m. to 5:00 p.m., so you set the Maximum Login Time parameter to 9 hours. As the name suggests, the login timer starts based on when login occurs. So if a user has a dental appointment one morning and does not arrive at work and log in until 1:00 p.m., the phone does not automatically log out at 5:00 p.m. as expected, but instead logs out at 10:00 p.m. If the purpose is to have all phones logged out before the building's cleaning crew arrives (so that no unauthorized personnel can use the phones for toll calls), the service parameters alone will not protect you. In such a case, you would need to teach users to log out when they leave, or write a custom AXL script that automatically logs out users at a specified time (see Chapter 7).

Allow a Single Login Only

The parameter Multiple Login Behavior allows you to specify whether users can log in to multiple devices. Allowing multiple logins can potentially allow toll fraud or can simply be a nuisance for anyone near the second phone. For example, a user could log in from home, work a few hours, and then leave to go into the office but forget to log out. When the employee arrives at work and logs into the work phone, the home phone is still logged in. This means that when the employee gets a call at work, the home office phone rings too, which could be confusing or annoying for the family members. Likewise, leaving the company phone at home logged in could allow family members to use it to place personal calls at the company's expense. To avoid such situations, choose Auto Logout to ensure that users are automatically logged out of the first device when they log into another device.

Configure Extension Mobility So That Phones Remember the Last User Logged In

Although it's not as secure or private, for employee convenience, consider allowing the phone to remember the last user who logged into that device. In many cases, the same employee logs into the same phone day after day. The parameter Remember the Last User Logged In defaults to False, so if you want phones to automatically display the username of the last user who logged in, set this parameter to True. Users still have to enter their PINs; this parameter just determines whether the username field is automatically populated.

General Enterprise Parameters

Enterprise parameters specify the default settings that apply to all devices and services clusterwide. Generally, the default values are sufficient, but some exceptions are described in the following sections.

To learn more about managing enterprise parameters specifically related to CDR data collection, see Chapter 11.

Speed Up Your Page Loads or Increase the Number of Items That Are Displayed

Unfortunately, you can't have both. Two enterprise parameters control the maximum number of items that appear, which directly affects the loading speed for certain CallManager Administration and Bulk Administration Tool (BAT) pages. The Max List Box Items parameter controls how many items are displayed in a list box on pages such as Partition, Calling Search Space, and Voice Mail Profile. If you specify a higher number (the maximum is 9999), more items are displayed so that you don't have to click the lookup (...) button as often, but the page loads more slowly. You can see the lookup button on the Calling Search Space and AAR Calling Search Space fields in Figure 8-5. The Max Lookup Items parameter controls how many items are displayed when you click the lookup button for a list box. If you choose a higher number (the maximum is 99999), more items display directly to the browser window, resulting in faster searches, but the page takes longer to load. You can choose a lower number for both these parameters if you want the pages to load more quickly.

Enable Dependency Records

You can use dependency records to determine which records in the database use other records. For example, you can determine whether any devices are using a specific device pool by clicking the link to Dependency Records on the Device Pool Configuration page.

If you want to use the dependency records feature provided in CallManager Administration, you need to set the Enable Dependency Records parameter to True. It is False by default because running a list of dependent records causes a spike in CPU usage and can affect system performance. To avoid possible performance issues, display dependency records only during off-peak hours.

Figure 8-5   *Example of a Lookup Button When Adding a New Phone*

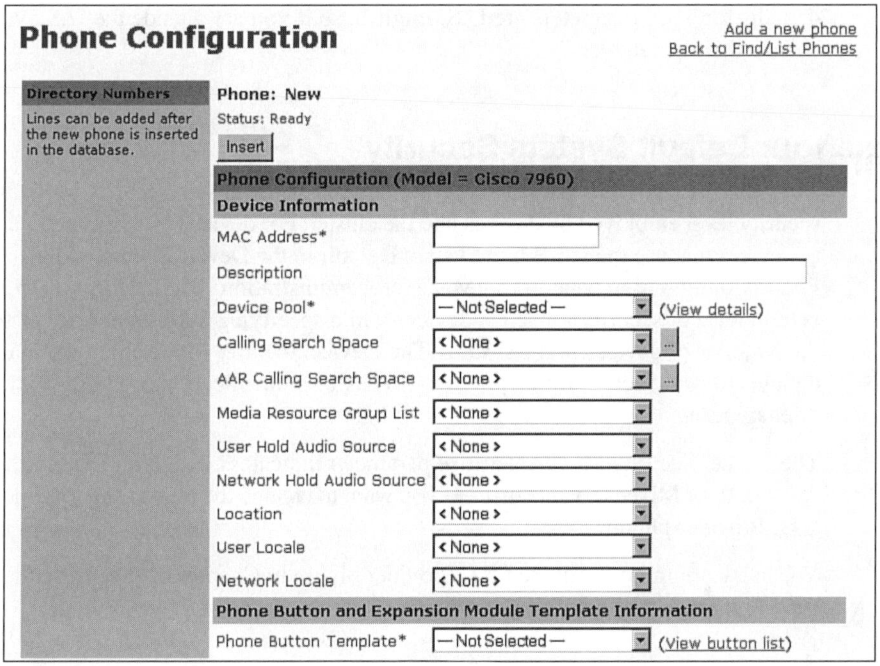

Let Users Customize Ring Tones

The enterprise parameter Show Ring Settings determines whether users can change their IP phone's ring setting via the Cisco CallManager User Options web page. If you set this parameter to True (it's set to False by default), users can decide between the options Ring Normally, Ring Once, Flash Only, and Do Nothing when the line is idle, and Beep Only when the phone is in use.

Make Sure That NT Users Have Access to CDR Paths

The CDR UNC Path parameter designates the universal naming convention (UNC) path that points to a read/write NT share for CDR file collection. Make sure that SQLSvc and CCMCDR NT users have read/write access to the path. Also, the Local CDR Path parameter, which specifies the local path used by CallManager to write CDR files, must allow read/write access for CCMServiceRW and SQLSvc NT users.

Choose Your Locale

Two enterprise parameters allow you to choose the network and user locales for your country. The Default Network Locale parameter ensures that tones and cadences used by devices such as gateways match the tones and cadences required by your country or region. Likewise, the Default User Locale ensures that prompts appear in the chosen language. The defaults for both parameters are U.S. English, so if you are outside the U.S., you should change these parameters.

Choose Your Default System Security

Two enterprise parameters, Device Security Mode and Cluster Security Mode, specify the security level employed by devices and the cluster. For devices, the parameter applies only to devices that use the value Use System Default in the Device Security Mode field on the Phone Configuration page in CallManager Administration. This allows you to specify a certain level of security for select devices while specifying a different level of security for the majority of devices in the system. The Device Security Mode enterprise parameter defaults to Non Secure, which provides no device authentication, signaling authentication, or encryption.

The Cluster Security Mode enterprise parameter indicates either Non Secure (the default, a value of 0) or Mixed (a value of 1). If you want to change the cluster security mode, run the CTL Provider plugin.

You can learn more about the CTL Provider plugin in Chapter 6, "Securing the Environment."

Summary

This chapter highlighted many of the service parameters whose default settings you might want to change, depending on your needs. It also provided recommendations for how to set some of the more useful parameters, and for what services you might want to run on the various servers based on the size of your deployment.

By reading through the description of each service presented in this chapter, you should understand that not every service needs to be run on every server. Many of these services perform important core functions, others provide optional features, and nearly all of them depend on other services to operate. Finding the appropriate mix of services might require some testing in your environment. Tuning CallManager-related services optimizes CPU performance on the server by better than 7 percent, but overly aggressive service deactivation might affect the function of features your organization uses.

## CHAPTER 9

Using Multilevel Administration

By regulating the privileges of a selected group of users and limiting the configuration functions that users can perform, multilevel administration (MLA) provides multiple levels of security to Cisco CallManager Administration and Cisco CallManager Serviceability. MLA provides these levels of security through the use of functional groups and user groups.

NOTE   MLA provides security by limiting access to specific pages in CallManager Administration and CallManager Serviceability based on login credentials. To learn how to protect those login credentials from being stolen or improperly accessed, read Chapter 6.

For different user groups, each functional group can be configured with different access levels (No Access, Read Only Access, and Full Access). MLA also provides audit logs of user logins and access and modifications to Cisco CallManager configuration data.

A *functional group* includes a collection of CallManager system administration functions. Two types of functional groups exist: standard functional groups, which are the default functional groups, and custom functional groups. All standard functional groups are created at installation. You cannot modify or delete them. In general, standard functional groups are built around the menu structure in CallManager Administration. For example, the Standard Feature functional group provides Full Access to all the menu items on the Feature menu: Call Park, Call Pickup, Cisco IP Phone Services, Meet-Me Number/Pattern, and Voice Mail (including the cascading menu items). You could create a custom functional group if you wanted a user to have access to some but not all of the menu items on the Feature menu.

A *user group* is a collection of CallManager users who are grouped for the purpose of assigning an access privilege level to the group members. Some default user groups are created at the time of installation, but those groups have no members initially. The CallManager *super user,* a user with Full Access to user group configuration, should add users to these groups and set the access rights for the user groups. The super user can configure additional user groups as needed and also delete any default user group except the SuperUserGroup.

This chapter provides information on how the MLA feature of CallManager release 4.0 differs from previous releases. This chapter also deals with password and login issues and best practices for MLA.

Table 9-1 details the standard user and functional group mapping.

Table 9-1 *Standard User and Functional Group Mapping*

Standard User Group	Standard Functional Group	Permission
GatewayAdministration	Feature	Read Only
	Gateway	Full Access
	Phone	Read Only
	Plugin	Read Only
	RoutePlan	Full Access
	Service	Read Only
	Service Management	Read Only
	Serviceability	Read Only
	System	Read Only
	User Management	Read Only
	User Privilege Management	Read Only
PhoneAdministration	Feature	Read Only
	Gateway	Read Only
	Phone	Full Access
	Plugin	Read Only
	RoutePlan	Read Only
	Service	Read Only
	Service Management	No Access
	Serviceability	Read Only
	System	ReadOnly
	User Management	Full Access
	User Privilege Management	Read Only
ReadOnly	Feature	Read Only
	Gateway	Read Only
	Phone	Read Only

Table 9-1   *Standard User and Functional Group Mapping (Continued)*

Standard User Group	Standard Functional Group	Permission
ReadOnly (Cont'd)	Plugin	Read Only
	RoutePlan	Read Only
	Service	Read Only
	Service Management	Read Only
	Serviceability	Read Only
	System	Read Only
	User Management	Read Only
	User Privilege Management	Read Only
ServerMaintenance	Feature	Full Access
	Gateway	Read Only
	Phone	Read Only
	Plugin	Full Access
	RoutePlan	Read Only
	Service	Full Access
	Service Management	Full Access
	Serviceability	Read Only
	System	Full Access
	User Management	Read Only
	User Privilege Management	Read Only
ServerMonitoring	Feature	Read Only
	Gateway	Read Only
	Phone	Read Only
	Plugin	Read Only
	RoutePlan	Read Only
	Service	Read Only

continues

Table 9-1 *Standard User and Functional Group Mapping (Continued)*

Standard User Group	Standard Functional Group	Permission
ServerMonitoring (Cont'd)	Service Management	Read Only
	Serviceability	Full Access
	System	Read Only
	User Management	Read Only
	User Privilege Management	Read Only
SuperUserGroup represents a named user group that always has Full Access permission to all named functional groups. You cannot delete this user group. You can add users to and delete users from this group. CCMAdministrator always represents a super user, even though CCMAdministrator might not be a member of the SuperUserGroup.	Feature	Full Access
	Gateway	Full Access
	Phone	Full Access
	Plugin	Full Access
	RoutePlan	Full Access
	Service	Full Access
	Service Management	Full Access
	Serviceability	Full Access
	System	Full Access
	User Management	Full Access
	User Privilege Management	Full Access

Changes from the Previous Release

In CallManager releases 3.2.x and 3.3.x, MLA was packaged as a separate product with a standalone installation, a separate SQL database, and its own interfaces to connect to the CallManager database and directory. In CallManager release 4.x, MLA is installed as part of CallManager and uses the CallManager database. Login authentication is based on Internet Information Server (IIS) basic authentication (no encryption), and an Internet Service API (ISAPI) filter authenticates the directory users. (The ISAPI filter provides a means to extend IIS with a custom program—in this case, MLA.)

The CallManager installation process handles MLA upgrade, replication, and database migration from CallManager releases 3.2 and 3.3.

Enabled Versus Disabled

In CallManager release 4.x the MLA features are disabled by default unless CallManager is upgraded from a previous release that had MLA installed. To enable MLA, you must set the MLA parameter Enable MultiLevelAdmin to **True** (**User > Access Rights > Configure MLA Parameters**).

Password Issues

MLA uses the Lightweight Directory Access Protocol (LDAP) user CCMAdministrator, which is created during CallManager installation as the super user. CCMAdministrator is the account that is required for logging into CallManager Administration and CallManager Serviceability the first time after CallManager installation and before other LDAP users are configured to use MLA.

The CCMAdministrator password change option in the User menu of CallManager Administration has been removed in release 4.x because MLA uses the CCMAdministrator LDAP user account.

MLA allows CCMAdministrator (and only CCMAdministrator) to log in even when the directory is down by authenticating against the password in the Registry. You are prompted to set a password for CCMAdministrator when MLA is enabled from the MLA Enterprise Parameter Configuration page regardless of the directory used.

In CallManager 4.x, you can change the CCMAdministrator password two ways: either in the MLA Enterprise Parameter Configuration page (**User > Access Rights > Configure MLA Parameters**) or via the CallManager Password Changer by running CCMPWDChanger.exe under C:\DCDSrvr\Bin.

NOTE	To make the password fields appear on the Configure MLA Parameters page, toggle the **EnableMLA** field from True to False and back to True again (without clicking Update).

If you are upgrading to release 4.x from a previous release in which MLA was enabled, MLA is enabled by default in release 4.x, and the existing password for MLA CCMAdministrator is preserved.

Integrated Database

Previously, MLA was required to be configured on one or more Subscriber servers for failover. However, with CallManager release 4.x, MLA is automatically configured on all Subscribers. Because MLA data is stored in the CallManager database, MLA data gets replicated along with the rest of the CallManager configuration information.

Simplified Upgrade, Backup, and Restore

Previously, for every CallManager patch or upgrade, a corresponding MLA patch or upgrade was required. Also, backup and restore operations had to be performed manually on every CallManager server. With CallManager release 4.x, this is no longer necessary; the standard CallManager processes implement all upgrades, backups, and restores.

Centralized Log Files

All MLA log files are saved to C:\Program Files\Cisco\Trace\MLA. MLA log files were previously saved to the \debug and \logs directories under C:\Ciscowebs\MLA. As of release 4.x, however, all log files are maintained in a central location.

MLA generates four application logs:

- ISAPIFilter*XXXXXX*.txt is a debug log generated by the MLA ISAPI filter. This log file captures login details and may provide useful information when you troubleshoot login problems for CallManager Administration or CallManager Serviceability.

- Permissions*XXXXXX*.txt is a debug log generated by the User Permissions API that is used by CallManager Administration and the Real-Time Monitoring Tool. This log file shows user and permissions information that might be useful when you're trying to resolve a problem such as a user having Read Only Access when he or she should have Full Access.

- DirAndUI*XX*.log is a debug log generated by the MLA LDAP component and MLA CallManager Administration pages.

TIP	You can increase the amount of information provided in this log file by setting the Debug Trace level to **Debug** (**User > Access Rights > Configure MLA Parameters**).

- Access*XX*.log is an audit (access) and login log generated by MLA. This log contains users' login attempts and records the actions performed on CallManager Administration pages.

Enable MLA for Added Security

In CallManager release 4.*x,* MLA is disabled by default unless CallManager is upgraded from a previous release that had MLA installed. For added security, enable MLA by setting the MLA parameter Enable MultiLevelAdmin to True (**User > Access Rights > Configure MLA Parameters**). If this parameter is set to True, MLA uses the LDAP directory for authentication; otherwise, NT authentication is used.

After installing and enabling MLA, you must log in as CCMAdministrator. The NT administrator login no longer works.

Log in as CCMAdministrator the first time you try to add users to user groups and to set up access privileges for user groups to functional groups. The password for CCMAdministrator is set to a default for DC Directory and has to be set after installation in Active Directory and Netscape Directory. You can use the existing user groups and functional groups or create custom groups and assign privileges. After you have done so, any directory user with appropriate privileges who belongs to a user group can log in to CallManager Administration and CallManager Serviceability pages.

No MLA Access When the Publisher Is Down

When the Publisher server is down, CallManager does not allow configuration changes. Assuming that you have appropriate privileges, you can still access the CallManager Administration and Serviceability pages to view the current configuration, check trace or parameter settings, and so on, but no configuration changes are accepted. When the Publisher is down, if you attempt to configure anything, such as devices, users, user groups, or functional groups, an error message appears, indicating that the primary database is down and that no updates can be performed.

Enable Tracing for MLA

Turn on trace logs to help troubleshoot MLA. Trace logs are useful when you encounter a problem in MLA, such as being unable to create a user group or functional group, or if you are encountering incorrect privileges, such as Full Access when the user group is configured for Read Only Access.

The MLA trace logs file size limit is 2 MB. When that limit is reached, a new consecutively numbered log file is created. Log files are overwritten in round-robin fashion.

MLA tracing is disabled by default. To enable tracing, set the Debug Level field to **Trace** or **Debug** (**User > Access Rights > Configure MLA Parameters**). Trace generates information useful for tracking down a problem in MLA, whereas Debug generates the more detailed information used by Cisco engineers to debug the MLA component.

The MLA trace and debug log files are saved to C:\Program Files\Cisco\Trace\MLA.

Monitor the Access Log for Malicious Login Attempts

MLA generates a log with a record of login and access/change attempts. The log provides a record of attempts to access or modify any database component through CallManager Administration and CallManager Serviceability. It details the date, time, username, type of access attempted, the menu that was accessed, the web page from which the change was made, and the success or failure status of the update. You should periodically check the log files to confirm that permissions are being enforced and to trigger any cleanup of personnel permissions that might be needed. Regular checks of the access log help you identify repeated login attempts, which could indicate that unknown individuals are attempting to gain access to the system for malicious purposes.

Unfortunately, the log file does not show you exactly what was changed, only the page on which the change was made. So if someone accessed the Gateway Configuration page and deleted a port, the log file would show that the Gateway Configuration page was accessed, by whom, and at what time, but not what gateway was affected or which port was deleted. Figure 9-1 shows an MLA Access log file.

To collect information in the Access log file, set the MLA enterprise parameter Debug Level to Trace (**User > Access Rights > Configure MLA Parameters**). You can view MLA log files at C:\Program Files\Cisco\Trace\MLA. The filename is Access*XX*.log, where *XX* represents the log number.

Check the Privileges Report

If users complain that they don't have the correct access privileges, check the privileges report to confirm that the users are listed as members of a user group for the page they are attempting to access. MLA provides detailed error messages that tell users why access was denied. (For example, perhaps he or she isn't part of the user group or isn't allowed access to the requested page.)

You can run a privileges report by selecting **User > Access Rights > Assign Privileges to User Group** and then clicking the link to **View Privileges Report** in the upper-right corner.

Figure 9-1 *Sample Access Log File*

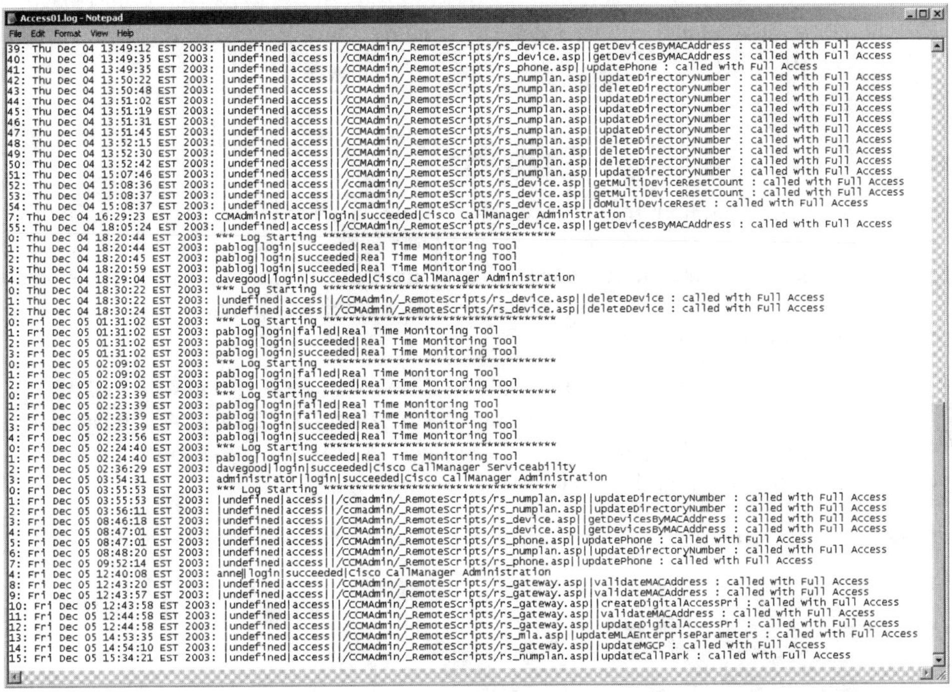

```
39: Thu Dec 04 13:49:12 EST 2003: |undefined|access||/CCMAdmin/_RemoteScripts/rs_device.asp||getDevicesByMACAddress : called with Full Access
40: Thu Dec 04 13:49:35 EST 2003: |undefined|access||/CCMAdmin/_RemoteScripts/rs_device.asp||getDevicesByMACAddress : called with Full Access
41: Thu Dec 04 13:49:35 EST 2003: |undefined|access||/CCMAdmin/_RemoteScripts/rs_phone.asp||updatePhone : called with Full Access
42: Thu Dec 04 13:50:22 EST 2003: |undefined|access||/CCMAdmin/_RemoteScripts/rs_numplan.asp||updateDirectoryNumber : called with Full Access
43: Thu Dec 04 13:50:48 EST 2003: |undefined|access||/CCMAdmin/_RemoteScripts/rs_numplan.asp||deleteDirectoryNumber : called with Full Access
44: Thu Dec 04 13:51:02 EST 2003: |undefined|access||/CCMAdmin/_RemoteScripts/rs_numplan.asp||updateDirectoryNumber : called with Full Access
45: Thu Dec 04 13:51:19 EST 2003: |undefined|access||/CCMAdmin/_RemoteScripts/rs_numplan.asp||updateDirectoryNumber : called with Full Access
46: Thu Dec 04 13:51:31 EST 2003: |undefined|access||/CCMAdmin/_RemoteScripts/rs_numplan.asp||updateDirectoryNumber : called with Full Access
47: Thu Dec 04 13:51:45 EST 2003: |undefined|access||/CCMAdmin/_RemoteScripts/rs_numplan.asp||updateDirectoryNumber : called with Full Access
48: Thu Dec 04 13:52:15 EST 2003: |undefined|access||/CCMAdmin/_RemoteScripts/rs_numplan.asp||deleteDirectoryNumber : called with Full Access
49: Thu Dec 04 13:52:30 EST 2003: |undefined|access||/CCMAdmin/_RemoteScripts/rs_numplan.asp||deleteDirectoryNumber : called with Full Access
50: Thu Dec 04 13:52:42 EST 2003: |undefined|access||/CCMAdmin/_RemoteScripts/rs_numplan.asp||deleteDirectoryNumber : called with Full Access
51: Thu Dec 04 15:07:46 EST 2003: |undefined|access||/CCMAdmin/_RemoteScripts/rs_numplan.asp||updateDirectoryNumber : called with Full Access
52: Thu Dec 04 15:08:36 EST 2003: |undefined|access||/ccmadmin/_RemoteScripts/rs_device.asp||getMultiDeviceResetCount : called with Full Access
53: Thu Dec 04 15:08:37 EST 2003: |undefined|access||/ccmadmin/_RemoteScripts/rs_device.asp||getMultiDeviceResetCount : called with Full Access
54: Thu Dec 04 15:08:37 EST 2003: |undefined|access||/ccmadmin/_RemoteScripts/rs_device.asp||doMultiDeviceReset : called with Full Access
7: Thu Dec 04 16:29:23 EST 2003: CCMAdministrator|login|succeeded|Cisco CallManager Administration
55: Thu Dec 04 18:05:24 EST 2003: |undefined|access||/CCMAdmin/_RemoteScripts/rs_device.asp||getDevicesByMACAddress : called with Full Access
0: Thu Dec 04 18:20:44 EST 2003: *** Log Starting ****************************************
1: Thu Dec 04 18:20:44 EST 2003: pablog|login|succeeded|Real Time Monitoring Tool
2: Thu Dec 04 18:20:45 EST 2003: pablog|login|succeeded|Real Time Monitoring Tool
3: Thu Dec 04 18:20:59 EST 2003: pablog|login|succeeded|Real Time Monitoring Tool
4: Thu Dec 04 18:29:04 EST 2003: davegood|login|succeeded|Cisco CallManager Administration
0: Thu Dec 04 18:30:22 EST 2003: *** Log Starting ****************************************
1: Thu Dec 04 18:30:22 EST 2003: |undefined|access||/CCMAdmin/_RemoteScripts/rs_device.asp||deleteDevice : called with Full Access
2: Thu Dec 04 18:30:24 EST 2003: |undefined|access||/CCMAdmin/_RemoteScripts/rs_device.asp||deleteDevice : called with Full Access
0: Fri Dec 05 01:31:02 EST 2003: *** Log Starting ****************************************
1: Fri Dec 05 01:31:02 EST 2003: pablog|login|failed|Real Time Monitoring Tool
2: Fri Dec 05 01:31:02 EST 2003: pablog|login|succeeded|Real Time Monitoring Tool
3: Fri Dec 05 01:31:02 EST 2003: pablog|login|succeeded|Real Time Monitoring Tool
0: Fri Dec 05 02:09:02 EST 2003: *** Log Starting ****************************************
1: Fri Dec 05 02:09:02 EST 2003: pablog|login|failed|Real Time Monitoring Tool
2: Fri Dec 05 02:09:02 EST 2003: pablog|login|succeeded|Real Time Monitoring Tool
0: Fri Dec 05 02:23:39 EST 2003: *** Log Starting ****************************************
1: Fri Dec 05 02:23:39 EST 2003: pablog|login|failed|Real Time Monitoring Tool
2: Fri Dec 05 02:23:39 EST 2003: pablog|login|failed|Real Time Monitoring Tool
3: Fri Dec 05 02:23:39 EST 2003: pablog|login|succeeded|Real Time Monitoring Tool
4: Fri Dec 05 02:23:56 EST 2003: pablog|login|succeeded|Real Time Monitoring Tool
0: Fri Dec 05 02:24:40 EST 2003: *** Log Starting ****************************************
1: Fri Dec 05 02:24:40 EST 2003: pablog|login|succeeded|Real Time Monitoring Tool
2: Fri Dec 05 02:36:29 EST 2003: davegood|login|succeeded|Cisco CallManager Serviceability
3: Fri Dec 05 03:54:31 EST 2003: administrator|login|succeeded|Cisco CallManager Administration
0: Fri Dec 05 03:55:53 EST 2003: *** Log Starting ****************************************
1: Fri Dec 05 03:55:53 EST 2003: |undefined|access||/ccmadmin/_RemoteScripts/rs_numplan.asp||updateDirectoryNumber : called with Full Access
2: Fri Dec 05 03:56:11 EST 2003: |undefined|access||/ccmadmin/_RemoteScripts/rs_numplan.asp||updateDirectoryNumber : called with Full Access
3: Fri Dec 05 08:46:18 EST 2003: |undefined|access||/CCMAdmin/_RemoteScripts/rs_device.asp||getDevicesByMACAddress : called with Full Access
4: Fri Dec 05 08:47:01 EST 2003: |undefined|access||/CCMAdmin/_RemoteScripts/rs_device.asp||getDevicesByMACAddress : called with Full Access
5: Fri Dec 05 08:47:01 EST 2003: |undefined|access||/CCMAdmin/_RemoteScripts/rs_phone.asp||updatePhone : called with Full Access
6: Fri Dec 05 08:48:20 EST 2003: |undefined|access||/CCMAdmin/_RemoteScripts/rs_numplan.asp||updateDirectoryNumber : called with Full Access
7: Fri Dec 05 09:52:14 EST 2003: |undefined|access||/CCMAdmin/_RemoteScripts/rs_phone.asp||updatePhone : called with Full Access
4: Fri Dec 05 12:40:08 EST 2003: anne||login|succeeded|Cisco CallManager Administration
8: Fri Dec 05 12:43:20 EST 2003: |undefined|access||/CCMAdmin/_RemoteScripts/rs_gateway.asp||validateMACAddress : called with Full Access
9: Fri Dec 05 12:43:57 EST 2003: |undefined|access||/CCMAdmin/_RemoteScripts/rs_gateway.asp||validateMACAddress : called with Full Access
10: Fri Dec 05 12:43:58 EST 2003: |undefined|access||/CCMAdmin/_RemoteScripts/rs_gateway.asp||createDigitalAccessPri : called with Full Access
11: Fri Dec 05 12:44:58 EST 2003: |undefined|access||/CCMAdmin/_RemoteScripts/rs_gateway.asp||validateMACAddress : called with Full Access
12: Fri Dec 05 12:44:58 EST 2003: |undefined|access||/CCMAdmin/_RemoteScripts/rs_gateway.asp||updateDigitalAccessPri : called with Full Access
13: Fri Dec 05 14:53:35 EST 2003: |undefined|access||/CCMAdmin/_RemoteScripts/rs_mla.asp||updateMLAEnterpriseParameters : called with Full Access
14: Fri Dec 05 14:54:10 EST 2003: |undefined|access||/CCMAdmin/_RemoteScripts/rs_gateway.asp||updateMGCP : called with Full Access
15: Fri Dec 05 15:34:21 EST 2003: |undefined|access||/CCMAdmin/_RemoteScripts/rs_numplan.asp||updateCallPark : called with Full Access
```

Create User-Specific Accounts

Create an account for each person who accesses the system. Accounts allow you to monitor each user's activity and provide some accountability along with an audit trail of users accessing the system. Allowing multiple users to log in as the CCMAdministrator reduces your ability to track the user who made a change. If users persist in logging in as the CCMAdministrator, you might be able to track the login to a machine. For more information, see the later section "Use the IIS Log File to Trace a CCMAdministrator Login to a Machine."

Create Custom Functional Groups

Many default functional groups are created for you during installation (see Table 9-1). However, you might want to create custom groups that provide specific functionality, such as an IP Phone Services functional group. For example, a company might employ service developers who write IP phone services. A custom functional group could be created to allow access to only the Cisco IP Phone Services pages in CallManager Administration. Access to these pages would allow the service developer to add phone services to CallManager and in turn make the new service(s) available to users.

To create a custom functional group, select **User > Access Rights > Functional Group**, name the group, and select the checkboxes that correlate to parts of CallManager Administration and CallManager Serviceability that users of this functional group can access.

Create Custom User Groups

Several default user groups are created during installation (see Table 9-1). However, you might want to create custom groups that provide specific access to each part of a functional group. Continuing the IP Phone Services functional group example from the preceding section, you would want to add a custom user group that provides access to the IP Phone Services functional group.

IP Phone Services developers should be included in a user group with Full Access privileges for the Cisco IP Phone Services pages in CallManager Administration and No Access to any other part of the CallManager system. Figure 9-2 shows the user group and group privileges for this example.

Figure 9-2   *User Group and Group Privileges for the Custom User Group*

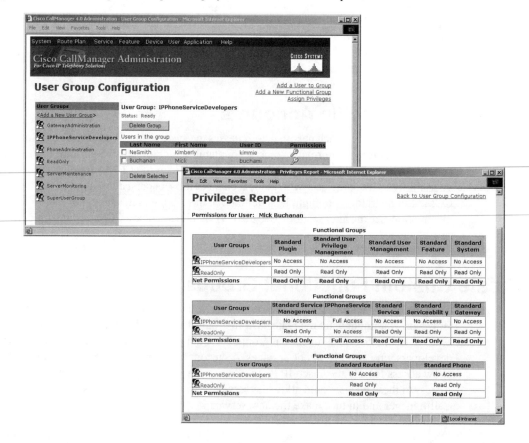

To create a custom user group, select **User > Access Rights > User Group**, name the group, and then add users. You can check a user's permissions by clicking the key icon to the far right of the username. Figure 9-2 shows the Privileges Report that appears when you click the key icon.

Assign Group Privileges

For each user group you create, you set the privileges for each functional group. For example, in the previous example of IP Phone Services developers, you would assign Full Access permission to the IPPhoneServiceDevelopers functional group and No Access to all other functional groups.

Manage Overlapping Permissions

In some cases, user or functional groups have overlapping permissions. For example, a user might belong to multiple user groups and have Read Only Access in one user group for a particular function but Full Access for the same function in a different user group. Similarly, the same CallManager Administration web pages might appear in more than one functional group and have conflicting privileges. In those cases, the functional group's or user's access level is determined by the setting in the **Effective Access Privileges** fields on the MLA Enterprise Parameter Configuration page (**User > Access Rights > Configure MLA Parameters**). The choices are **Maximum** and **Minimum**:

- **Maximum**—The maximum or most permissive privilege of all the overlapping user or functional groups is allowed.

- **Minimum**—The minimum or most restrictive privilege of all the overlapping user or functional groups is allowed.

For example, suppose Mick Buchanan belongs to several user groups. Figure 9-3 shows the permission levels he would have if the **Effective Access Privileges for Overlapping User Groups** field were set to **Minimum**. Notice that Mick would have No Access to any functional group in the system.

Figure 9-3 *Minimum Access for Overlapping User Groups*

Privileges Report

Back to User Group Configuration

Permissions for User: Mick Buchanan

Functional Groups

User Groups	Standard Plugin	Standard User Privilege Management	Standard User Management	Standard Feature	Standard System
IPPhoneServiceDevelopers	No Access	No Access	No Access	No Access	No Access
PhoneAdministration	Read Only	Read Only	Full Access	Read Only	Read Only
ReadOnly	Read Only	Read Only	Read Only	Read Only	Read Only
Net Permissions	No Access	No Access	No Access	No Access	No Access

Functional Groups

User Groups	Standard Service Management	IPPhoneServices	Standard Service	Standard Serviceability	Standard Gateway
IPPhoneServiceDevelopers	No Access	Full Access	No Access	No Access	No Access
PhoneAdministration	Read Only	No Access	Read Only	Read Only	Read Only
ReadOnly	Read Only	No Access	Read Only	Read Only	Read Only
Net Permissions	No Access	No Access	No Access	No Access	No Access

Functional Groups

User Groups	Standard RoutePlan	Standard Phone
IPPhoneServiceDevelopers	No Access	No Access
PhoneAdministration	Read Only	Full Access
ReadOnly	Read Only	Read Only
Net Permissions	No Access	No Access

In contrast, Figure 9-4 shows the permissions levels Mick would have if the **Effective Access Privileges for Overlapping User Groups** field were set to **Maximum**. Notice that he would have Full Access to the Standard User Management, IPPhoneServices (a custom functional group), and Standard Phone functional groups and Read Only Access to all other groups.

Keep an Eye on Your System

At a specific interval, such as weekly or biweekly, check the logins to identify changes that need to be made to user levels or access. The Access file provides details on who accessed the various CallManager Administration and CallManager Serviceability pages. In particular, you should look for people who are accessing pages they no longer need to access, such as users to whom you gave temporary access, or users who have left the company or changed job duties and no longer require the same level of access.

Figure 9-4   *Maximum Access for Overlapping User Groups*

| System | Route Plan | Service | Feature | Device | User | Application | Help |

Cisco CallManager Administration
For Cisco IP Telephony Solutions

CISCO SYSTEMS

Privileges Report

Back to User Group Configuration

Permissions for User: Mick Buchanan

Functional Groups

User Groups	Standard Plugin	Standard User Privilege Management	Standard User Management	Standard Feature	IPPhoneServices
IPPhoneServiceDevelopers	No Access	No Access	No Access	No Access	Full Access
PhoneAdministration	Read Only	Read Only	Full Access	Read Only	No Access
ReadOnly	Read Only	Read Only	Read Only	Read Only	No Access
Net Permissions	Read Only	Read Only	Full Access	Read Only	Full Access

Functional Groups

User Groups	Standard System	Standard Service Management	Standard Service	Standard Serviceabilit y	Standard Gateway
IPPhoneServiceDevelopers	No Access	No Access	No Access	No Access	No Access
PhoneAdministration	Read Only	Read Only	Read Only	Read Only	Read Only
ReadOnly	Read Only	Read Only	Read Only	Read Only	Read Only
Net Permissions	Read Only	Read Only	Read Only	Read Only	Read Only

Functional Groups

User Groups	Standard RoutePlan	Standard Phone
IPPhoneServiceDevelopers	No Access	No Access
PhoneAdministration	Read Only	Full Access
ReadOnly	Read Only	Read Only
Net Permissions	Read Only	Full Access

Use the IIS Log File to Trace a CCMAdministrator Login to a Machine

Consider periodically checking the MLA Access log file to see if CCMAdministrator has
been logged on. Creating user-specific accounts is recommended so that the number of
people logging in as the CCMAdministrator is zero or, at the very least, a small number.
Searching for CCMAdministrator shows both failed logins and successful logins. Repeated
failed access attempts can alert you to someone who is trying to compromise an account (or
potentially just someone who has forgotten his or her password). If you suspect malicious
activity and you need to trace the attempts back to a user (or at least a machine the user
might own), you can determine the machine's identity by matching the timestamp of the
login attempt and the web page name with the IP address provided in the IIS log file.

To work back to the identity of the host where the login attempt came from, search the
IIS log file at C:\WINNT\system32\LogFiles\W3SVC1\ex*daymonyear*.log. (For example,
ex020204.log stands for an activity that occurred on February 2, 2004.) In the IIS log file,
you will find a record of the same page loads as recorded in Access*XX*.log as well as the
originating source IP address.

In the IIS file you can see the source IP address, such as 10.10.10.192. Having an IP address gives you a place to start looking for the person who logged in. If the IP address reflects a Windows machine, the command **nbtstat -a** *ip address* returns the machine name and also the logged-on user if he or she is running the Messenger service:

```
C:\>nbtstat -a 10.10.10.192

Local Area Connection:
Node IpAddress: [10.44.189.249] Scope Id: []
        NetBIOS Remote Machine Name Table
      Name                Type            Status
   ---------------------------------------------
   JDOE-W2K1     <00>  UNIQUE      Registered
   APAC          <00>  GROUP       Registered
   JDOE-W2K1     <20>  UNIQUE      Registered
   JDOE-W2K1     <03>  UNIQUE      Registered
   JDOE-W2K1$    <03>  UNIQUE      Registered
   JDOE          <03>  UNIQUE      Registered
```

Get to Know Your Company's Human Resources Managers

What process is currently in place at your company or organization to notify you when an employee quits or changes job duties? For most organizations, the number of administrators is small, and you might know everyone who accesses the system, which makes keeping up with personnel changes easy. However, if you have divided administration duties among many users and many user groups, it's possible to overlook personnel changes that could affect user access. If this possibility applies to your system, you should work with the HR department in your organization to determine whether you can be notified when an employee leaves the company or goes on a leave of absence. You can then search in CallManager Administration for the affected user and view his or her permissions to ensure that the appropriate access is provided (or revoked).

Maintain the Tightest Security Possible

Security takes many forms: preventing unauthorized access, protecting the integrity of your database, and providing the highest level of privacy to your users. Use MLA to restrict personnel access to your database and sensitive user information, such as phone forwarding when private numbers might be in use, services the users have subscribed to, and so on. Be sure that only administrators who need to access phone configuration pages are allowed to do so.

NOTE	Refer to Chapter 6, "Securing the Environment," for detailed security information.

Always Close the Web Browser

After accessing CallManager Administration or CallManager Serviceability, teach all administrators to close the web browser to ensure that no unauthorized user can access the system. If the browser is left open and the session times out, all pages are still accessible without login. This is because IIS uses the previously logged-in user's ID and password and does not prompt for new authentication credentials when the page browser is left open and a page is accessed again. IIS does not clear the session cookie, but instead keeps appending new cookies to the original session. This problem persists even when the web server/IISAdmin is restarted. To ensure that no one can access the web pages, all administrators should close the browser window when it is not in use.

TIP   The web browser times out after a specified amount of time has passed, forcing you to log in again. You can increase/decrease the timeout value by adjusting the **Connection Timeout** value in the properties for the Default Web Site (CallManager Administration) in IIS (**Start > Programs > Administrative Tools > Internet Information Services**).

Turn off IIS on Subscribers

You can provide an additional level of security by turning off IIS on CallManager servers that do not need web access, such as Subscriber servers. It's always a good idea to turn off unnecessary services. Turning off IIS protects unauthorized users from accessing CallManager in a distributed architecture. You can turn off IIS by opening the Internet Services Manager and stopping the Default Web Site.

Be Careful When Assigning Full Access

MLA configuration can be tricky if you are using the default groups but do not fully understand the default settings. For example, if you have an administrator who handles everything phone-related, you will probably give her access to the Standard Phone functional group. Because IP Phone Services are an important aspect of phone management, you might assume that your phone administrator can add or update IP phone subscriptions. However, default access to that area of CallManager Administration is provided only in the Standard Feature functional group. Study the permissions listed in Table 9-1 if you plan to use the standard functional and user groups provided by MLA.

Do Not Save Passwords in the Password List

Web browsers allow you to save your password in a list of passwords, as shown in Figure 9-5. Saving the password allows the username and password to be automatically populated for you when you access the same page again. Do not save passwords in a list.

Figure 9-5 *Password List Checkbox*

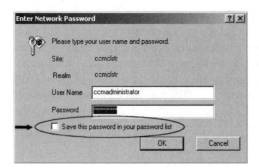

Conduct Periodic Security Audits

Perform security audits on a regular basis, perhaps weekly or monthly, depending on the size of your system and the number of authorized administrators. You can perform a security audit by checking the Access log files to see who is doing what based on his or her user ID. Figure 9-1, shown earlier, provides an example of an Access log file.

Summary

MLA controls the access users have to CallManager Administration and CallManager Serviceability. You can create detailed levels of access based on job function to ensure that only administrators who need to access certain areas of CallManager Administration and CallManager Serviceability are allowed to do so. Use MLA to safeguard your CallManager database as well as provide a level of privacy for your users by giving only administrators who need to access personal information the ability to do so, such as the Phone Configuration pages or CallManager Serviceability.

## CHAPTER 10

Mastering Directory Integration

This chapter covers the main design principles for integrating Cisco CallManager with a corporate Lightweight Directory Access Protocol (LDAP) directory. It also summarizes design considerations for providing Cisco IP Telephony endpoints, such as Cisco IP Phones and Cisco IP SoftPhone, with access to a corporate LDAP directory. The main topics are as follows:

- Directory access versus directory integration
- Directory access for Cisco IP Telephony endpoints
- Directory integration for CallManager
- Best practices for directory integration

Directory Access Versus Directory Integration

The following definitions and distinctions apply throughout this chapter:

- **Directory access** refers to the ability of Cisco IP Telephony endpoints, such as Cisco IP Phones and Cisco IP SoftPhone, to access a corporate LDAP directory.

- **Directory integration** refers to the ability of an application, such as CallManager, to store its user-related information in a centralized corporate LDAP directory instead of using its own embedded directory.

Figure 10-1 illustrates directory access as it is defined in this chapter. In this example, the access is provided to a Cisco IP Phone. The client application performs a user search against an LDAP directory, such as the corporate directory of an enterprise, and receives a number of matching entries. One entry can then be selected and used to dial the corresponding person from the Cisco IP Phone.

Note that directory access as defined here involves only read operations on the directory and does not require you to make any directory schema extensions or other configuration changes.

Figure 10-1 *Directory Access for Cisco IP Telephony Endpoints*

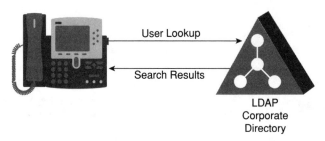

In contrast, directory integration of several applications with a corporate directory means that these applications actually store their user-related information in a centralized directory instead of using their own, separate, embedded directories. Figure 10-2 shows an example of directory integration as it is defined in this chapter.

Figure 10-2 *Directory Integration for Cisco IP Telephony Applications*

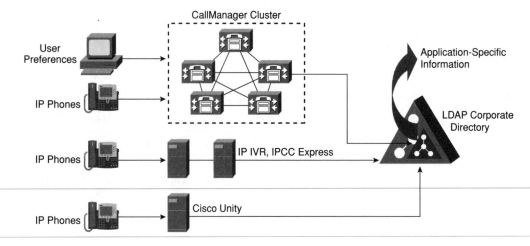

Note that directory integration involves read and write operations on the directory, so it requires you to make schema extensions and other configuration changes to your corporate LDAP directory.

By default, CallManager stores user information (such as devices controlled by the user, personal address book entries, and so on) in an embedded LDAP directory. However, CallManager can also be integrated with a corporate LDAP directory, which is normally used to store general employee information such as e-mail address, office address, and job title. In those cases, CallManager no longer uses its own embedded directory but stores its application-specific user information in the corporate directory.

NOTE   As of CallManager release 3.1, directory integration is supported for Microsoft Active Directory (AD) 2000 and Netscape Directory Server release 4.*x*. Support for iPlanet/Sun Directory Server 5.1 was added in CallManager release 3.3(2).

Integrating applications such as CallManager with a corporate directory also has the following implications, which go beyond simply providing directory access to endpoints:

- The directory schema must be extended to store the application-specific user attributes in the corporate directory. This operation is not trivial and requires good knowledge of the directory structure.

- The applications must be able to contact the directory at all times, and the directory must provide adequate response times. Availability of the directory service can affect application functionality.

- Additional load is introduced on the directory in terms of both data storage and read/write queries. Careful planning and sizing are recommended to avoid oversubscription of the servers when any new service or application is introduced.

Although directory integration across applications has numerous advantages, it's important to understand all its implications and to verify the business needs of each specific deployment.

Directory Access for IP Telephony Endpoints

The guidelines contained in this section apply regardless of whether CallManager and other IP Telephony applications have been integrated into a corporate directory. The end-user perception in both cases is the same, because the differences affect only how applications store their user information and how such information is kept consistent across the network.

The following sections summarize how to configure corporate directory access to any LDAP v3-compliant directory server for XML-capable phones such Cisco IP Phone models 7940, 7960, and so on.

NOTE   As of release 1.2, Cisco IP SoftPhone has a built-in mechanism to access and search LDAP directories, as does the Cisco IP Communicator. Refer to the product documentation for details on how to configure this feature.

XML-capable Cisco IP Phones (such as models 7940, 7960, and so on) can search a corporate LDAP directory when a user presses the **directories** button on the phone. The IP Phones use HTTP to send requests to a web server. The responses from the web server must contain some specific XML objects that the phone can interpret and display. In the case of a corporate directory search, the web server operates as a proxy by receiving the request from the phone and translating it into an LDAP request, which is in turn sent to the corporate directory server. After being encapsulated in the appropriate XML objects, the response is interpreted and sent back to the phone.

Figure 10-3 illustrates this mechanism in a deployment in which CallManager has not been integrated with the corporate directory. Note that in this scenario, CallManager is not involved in the message exchange.

Figure 10-3 *Message Exchange for Cisco IP Phone Corporate Directory Access Without Directory Integration*

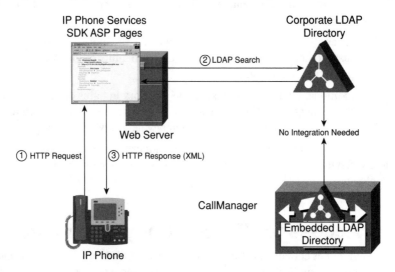

The proxy function provided by the web server can be configured using the Cisco IP Phone Services Software Development Kit (SDK) version 2.0 or later, which includes the Cisco LDAP Search COM server. You can download the latest Cisco IP Phone Services SDK from Developer Support Central at

http://www.cisco.com/pcgi-bin/dev_support/access_level/product_support

Click the **Log in now** link, log in, and then select **CallManager - IP phone Services SDK** from the **Voice Technology/AVVID** list box.

Follow these steps to configure directory access for IP Phones:

Step 1   Install the Cisco IP Phone Services SDK on a web server running Microsoft Internet Information Server (IIS). This server *must* be distinct from any CallManager server, but it can be an existing web server on the corporate network. (Refer to the SDK product documentation for more details on the installation procedure.)

Step 2 Using the documentation provided with the SDK, create active server pages (ASP) to interface with the LDAP Search COM object. Sample ASPs are provided with the SDK, but you can write your own if you need a higher level of customization. If you're using release 3.3 of the IP Phone Services SDK, place the sample ldapsearch.asp page in an IIS virtual directory, and then edit the file to point to your corporate LDAP directory server. You can do this by setting the following parameters:

- **s.server**—Set this to the LDAP server name or IP address (for example, ldap.vse.lab).

- **s.port**—Set this to the port used for LDAP requests on your LDAP server (the standard port is 389).

- **s.base**—Set this to the search base for LDAP lookups. This search base should include all users who must be returned from a lookup (for example, cn=Users, dc=vse, dc=lab).

- **s.AuthName**—If your LDAP server requires authentication for lookups, set this to the distinguished name for a user who has permissions to search the subtree specified in the search base (for example, cn=CCMDirMgr, ou=System Accounts, cn=Users, dc=vse, dc=lab).

- **s.AuthPasswd**—If your LDAP server requires authentication for lookups, set this to the password for a user who has permissions to search the subtree specified in the search base.

Step 3 In the Enterprise Parameter Configuration page in Cisco CallManager Administration (**System > Enterprise Parameters**), edit the **URL Directories** field, as shown in Figure 10-4. Set this field to the URL leading to the ldapsearch.asp file on the web server you previously set up.

Figure 10-4 *Configuring the Enterprise Parameters on CallManager to Enable Directory Access*

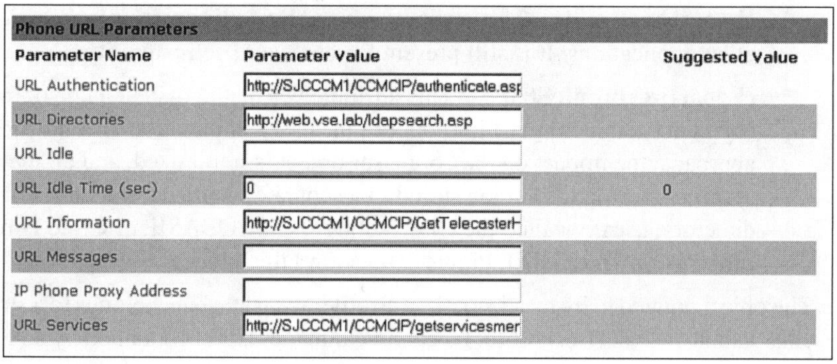

Phone URL Parameters		
Parameter Name	**Parameter Value**	**Suggested Value**
URL Authentication	http://SJCCCM1/CCMCIP/authenticate.asp	
URL Directories	http://web.vse.lab/ldapsearch.asp	
URL Idle		
URL Idle Time (sec)	0	0
URL Information	http://SJCCCM1/CCMCIP/GetTelecaster+	
URL Messages		
IP Phone Proxy Address		
URL Services	http://SJCCCM1/CCMCIP/getservicesmer	

Step 4   Reset the IP Phones to have the changes take effect.

Here are some final remarks on directory access for IP Phones:

- All LDAPv3-compliant directories are supported.

- CallManager user preferences (speed dials, call forward all, Personal Address Book) are not integrated with the corporate LDAP directory. Therefore, users have a separate login and password to access the Cisco CallManager User Options web page.

Directory Integration for CallManager

CallManager uses an embedded Microsoft SQL database to store system and device configuration data, such as dial plan information, phone and gateway configuration, and media resource utilization. It also uses an embedded LDAP directory to store user and application profiles, such as devices controlled by a user, computer telephony integration (CTI) user parameters, and Personal Address Book entries.

Both the SQL database and the LDAP directory run on every CallManager server within a cluster, and replication agreements are automatically set up between servers. The Publisher server contains the master copy of both the SQL database and the LDAP directory, and it handles replication to all Subscriber servers, which contain read-only copies of both repositories.

To store application-specific information in an LDAP directory, CallManager adopts an approach that is valid both when using the embedded directory and when integrating with a corporate directory.

Because different directory vendors typically use different User object models with several additional, nonstandard attributes, CallManager uses only the standard LDAPv3 core attributes from the User object. The User object is then augmented with an auxiliary class, ciscoocUser, which contains three attributes:

- **ciscoatGUID**—This attribute is used to uniquely identify a user within the directory.

- **ciscoatUserProfile**—This attribute is used by earlier versions of CallManager and other applications. It is still present for backward compatibility.

- **ciscoatUserProfileString**—This attribute is a distinguished name pointer to another object in the directory, which contains the user's application-specific profile. With this approach, the impact on the core User object is minimized, and all the application-specific information can be stored in a separate organizational unit (OU) within the directory, usually called the Cisco subtree, CISCOBASE, or Cisco Directory Information Tree (DIT). Figure 10-5 shows this process.

The object pointed to by the ciscoatUserProfileString attribute belongs to a structural object class called ciscoocUserProfile. Its canonical name (CN) is obtained by concatenating the core User object's username (SAMAccountName by default with Active Directory) with the suffix **-profile** and the globally unique identifier (GUID) provided by the ciscoatGUID attribute. The main purpose of this object is to store some specific details for the user, including the user's locale, any Cisco IP Manager Assistant (IPMA) assistants for the user, and pointers to various specific profile objects for all Cisco applications that integrate with the directory. (This is done through the multiple-valued attribute ciscoatAppProfile.) The application profile used by CallManager belongs to the auxiliary class called ciscoCCNocAppProfile. Its CN is obtained by adding the suffix **-CCNprofile**, followed by the GUID, to the core user's CN. This is where CallManager stores the user's extension mobility PIN, the list of devices controlled by this user, information on whether this user is permitted to use CTI applications, and so on. Figure 10-6 depicts the relationship between these two profile objects.

Figure 10-5 *Cisco Approach to Storing Application-Specific User Information in the Directory*

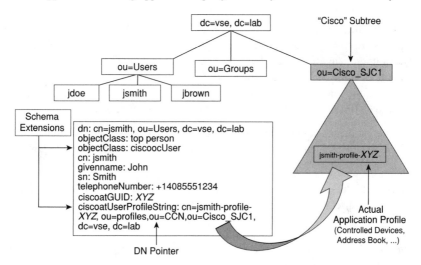

Figure 10-6 *Relationship Between Cisco Application Profiles*

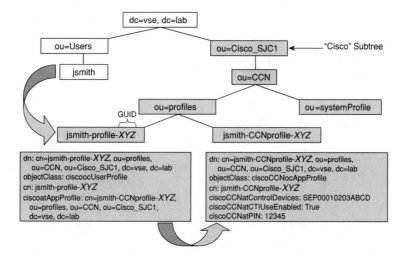

Run the Cisco Customer Directory Configuration Plugin

To integrate CallManager with an external LDAP directory, run the Cisco Customer Directory Configuration Plugin, which is bundled with CallManager (**Applications > Install Plugins**). This plugin serves three main purposes:

- It extends the corporate directory schema to accommodate the application-specific objects and attributes.

- It populates the "Cisco" subtree with the configuration objects needed by CallManager.

- It configures CallManager to use the corporate directory and disables its embedded directory.

Usually, running the plugin locally on CallManager carries out the schema update. However, starting with CallManager release 4.0, a new option exists to create the LDAP Data Interchange Format (LDIF) files so that the schema update can be carried out directly on the Schema Master using the LDIF files. This allows different groups of people to perform the relevant parts of the work and reduces the need to update over the network where CallManager is not local to the Schema Master server.

For recommendations on how to best configure the plugin, see the later sections "Preparing the Directory for Integration" and "Integrating CallManager with the Directory."

After the plugin has been run, CallManager effectively uses the corporate directory to store user preferences. If the Cisco IP Telephony endpoints have also been enabled to access the corporate directory, as described in the preceding section, the resulting scenario is that shown in Figure 10-7.

Figure 10-7 *Message Exchange for Cisco IP Phone Corporate Directory Access When CallManager Is Integrated with the Corporate Directory*

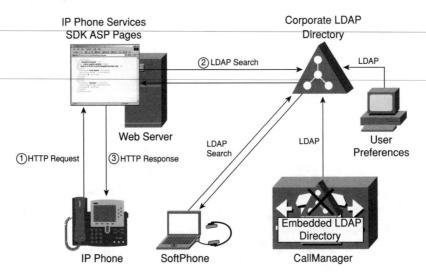

Adding CallManager Servers to a Domain

It's important to understand that there is a substantial difference between adding the CallManager servers to a Microsoft Windows domain and integrating CallManager with an external directory.

Although these operations do not exclude each other, they are completely independent and have different implications:

- Adding CallManager servers to a Microsoft Windows Active Directory domain could cause domain policies to be applied to the Windows 2000 Server operating system, and the addition affects only the management of the CallManager server itself.

- Integrating CallManager with an external directory (such as Microsoft Active Directory or Netscape Directory Server) causes CallManager to store all its user information and preferences in that directory, but it does not affect management of the CallManager server itself.

It's possible to add CallManager servers to a domain, but you should be careful to avoid applying domain policies to the server that could interfere with its normal operation. Also note that you must remove the server from the domain before performing each CallManager upgrade.

Best Practices for Directory Integration

The directory integration process involves several components and services in your network and therefore should be carefully planned and implemented. This section is organized as follows:

- Planning the directory integration
- Preparing the directory for integration
- Integrating CallManager with the directory
- Maintaining the directory integration

NOTE   Because the majority of known CallManager integrations are performed with Microsoft Active Directory (AD), this chapter focuses on best practices for AD. However, most recommendations and best practices mentioned in this section also apply to the other directory product supported by CallManager, Sun/iPlanet Netscape Directory Server.

Planning the Directory Integration

Because the directory is an enterprise-wide resource that is used by a potentially wide number of applications and end users, it's essential to plan the integration carefully to minimize the impact on all other applications.

TIP   Before starting the integration, ensure that your organization's directory team is involved in the planning, design, and implementation phases.

As mentioned earlier in this chapter, integrating CallManager and other applications with an external directory involves extending the directory schema. Schema extension is a delicate operation. For example, in the case of Microsoft Windows 2000 Active Directory, schema changes cannot be undone. You should take the following precautions to avoid damaging the directory:

- Review the planned schema changes with your organization's directory team. This should be part of your organization's change control procedures.

- Create a replica of the production directory in a lab setup, and test the integration against it.

- Back up the production directory, both data as well as schema, before integration, and make sure a workable back-out plan exists to enable successful restoration of the data and schema if it becomes necessary.

- Plan and perform the schema extension during off-peak hours to minimize the impact on other applications and end users.

If reading the preceding list causes you concern, you should know that the schema extension rarely causes problems that would require it to be backed out of. However, no matter how safe an operation is known to be, there is no need to increase risk by skipping precautions that would enable speady recovery from unplanned events.

Another important consideration is that as soon as the voice applications have been integrated with the directory, they rely on it for their correct operation, and inability to reach the directory server can negatively affect the voice system.

For example, if the directory suddenly becomes unavailable, end users cannot log into the Cisco CallManager User Options web page and configure their preferences; extension mobility users, Attendant Console operators, and IPCC Express agents cannot log in or out; and the dial-by-name function is unavailable.

To avoid these problems, you should design your directory infrastructure so that it is highly available to all Cisco voice applications. You can use different methods to achieve this high availability:

- Leverage the directory replication mechanism to place a directory server or servers in the same location as the Cisco voice applications.

- Use a server load-balancing mechanism (such as Cisco IOS software server load balancing [SLB]) to provide server redundancy in a specific campus/data center and to ensure that local servers are accessed by preference.

- Use DNS-resolvable domain names instead of specific domain controller host names when configuring the directory plugin.

A potential issue with using Domain Name System (DNS) concerning redundancy is that the first name returned by DNS might be the name of a server that is not as local to CallManager as others returned later in the response. Also, if your DNS server has the round-robin feature enabled, by design it rotates the order in which addresses are returned in the response. Depending on mechanisms such as client-side DNS cache timeout, along with other possible clients querying for the same domain in the interim, CallManager could run two consecutive operations against two different domain controllers (DC). In addition to the locality problem already mentioned, using DNS redundancy could keep objects created in the first operation from being found by a search on a different DC by a later query if the directory has not replicated in the meantime. Therefore, before choosing to use DNS to make the implementation redundant, be sure that these issues do not affect your deployment.

Also note that DNS is needed for proper LDAP referral; CallManager must be able to resolve the host names of any of the DCs returned in an LDAP referral.

NOTE   Although Microsoft Windows 2000 DNS has the concept of returning local resources first (called LocalNetPriority), it is based on inspecting the requesting client's classful IP address. Therefore, it is of limited use in subnetted networks. Microsoft Knowledge Base article 177883 documents this feature (see http://support.microsoft.com/). If you are not using Windows 2000 DNS, you should check to see what features in your chosen implementation might alleviate some of these issues.

These recommendations are based on the assumptions that CallManager is set to use DNS and that it is the same DNS infrastructure used by your Active Directory.

Preparing the Directory for Integration

With Microsoft Windows 2000 Active Directory, the domain controllers have to be set to allow schema changes. This needs to be carried out only on the domain controller that acts as the Schema Master (the location where change takes place). This is fully documented in Microsoft Knowledge Base article 285172, which you can find at http://support.microsoft.com.

If you are integrating CallManager with the Microsoft Windows 2000 Active Directory, and if Microsoft Exchange 2000 needs to coexist in the same forest, you need to perform an additional preparation step.

CallManager uses the labeled URI attribute specified by the iNetOrgPerson class as defined in RFC 2798. Microsoft currently defines this attribute differently for Exchange 2000, which causes a naming clash with the CallManager schema. The problem is documented in Microsoft Knowledge Base article 314649 (available from http://support.microsoft.com). The iNetOrgPerson kit mentioned can be obtained from

> http://msdn.microsoft.com/library/en-us/dnactdir/html/inetopkit.asp

WARNING   Remember to back up your directory before extending the schema. Make sure you have tested the restore mechanism you intend to use *before* you need it.

To extend the directory schema for CallManager, run the Cisco Customer Directory Configuration plugin from the Publisher server for the cluster (**Application > Install Plugins**), and follow these steps:

Step 1   Choose the directory type that matches your corporate directory, **Microsoft Active Directory** or **Netscape Directory Server**, and click **Next**.

Step 2   Select the **Custom** setup type and click **Next**. Note that the Express setup type is appropriate only for integration with a standalone domain used exclusively for CallManager and other Cisco voice applications. You should never use it when integrating with an existing domain.

Step 3   Select only the **Install Schema on the Schema Master** option. Uncheck all the other options, as shown in Figure 10-8. Click **Next**.

Figure 10-8   *Choosing the Setup Type in the Cisco Customer Directory Configuration Plugin*

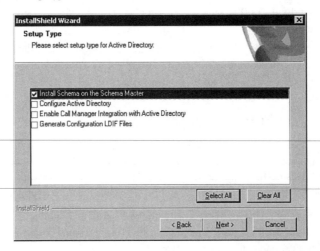

Step 4   Specify the host name of the Schema Master for your Active Directory forest and the port number to access it (port 389 is the default port for LDAP). Click **Next**. Try to ensure that the Schema Master server is relatively local to CallManager or that a high-speed connection exists

between them. If this is not possible, consider creating just the LDIF files with the plugin and using those directly to update the schema on the Schema Master.

Step 5   Provide the credentials (distinguished name and password) for a user who is a member of the Schema Admins group in Active Directory. These credentials are used only for the schema extension, not for normal CallManager operation. Enter the root domain of your AD forest in the Domain Name field. Click **Next**.

Step 6   Review the configuration, and click **Finish**.

NOTE   If you have a large AD forest or a complex topology, schema changes might take some time to propagate to all domains and all domain controllers in the forest. Allow enough time for this to happen before continuing with the preparation process, or force replication if required.

As soon as the schema has been extended, you need to decide where to create the "Cisco" OUs (that is, the subtrees) that will be used by the CallManager clusters and the other Cisco voice applications. There must be one OU for each CallManager cluster to be integrated.

For a single domain AD or Netscape directory server deployment, placement is not critical. The OU can effectively be placed anywhere in the tree.

In a multiple-domain AD forest, the root domain is often kept free of users and resources and is used as a placeholder domain, so the "Cisco" subtrees would typically reside in the child domains. In this type of multiple-domain topology, domains can be created based on geographic boundaries. Therefore, it is unlikely that every location has a local domain controller for each domain. To reduce replication traffic across the network, domain controllers are usually placed only where needed. With this in mind, it's best to try to place the Cisco OU for a given cluster in the domain containing the majority of users serviced by that cluster. Figure 10-9 shows a multiple-domain, single-tree AD forest in which the "Cisco" OUs for two CallManager clusters have been created in the two respective child domains—emea.vse.lab and amer.vse.lab.

In this example, each cluster services the corresponding geography in a centralized call processing model, ensuring that its user data stored in AD is also local. This saves having to retrieve the information from a DC that is probably nonlocal and reduces the number of LDAP referrals required to find the relevant information in a search.

Figure 10-9 *Multiple-Domain, Single-Tree AD Forest*

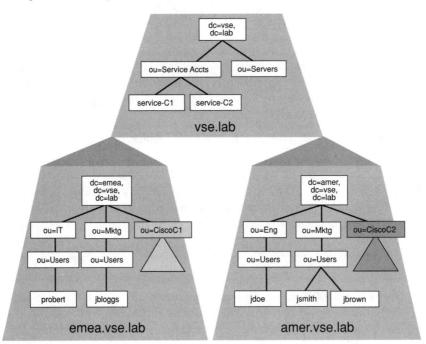

It is typically not recommended to have a CallManager cluster service users who exist in different domains. This is because response times while user data is being retrieved might be less than optimal if domain controllers for all included domains are not local. However, this scenario should not be a common one, because the reasons for creating a multiple-domain AD would likely be the same reasons for needing multiple clusters—namely, geography, bandwidth, or organizational structure.

It should also be noted that clusters spanning trees within an AD forest are currently unsupported, because they do not have a contiguous namespace, which is a requirement for LDAP referrals. A cluster can exist within a domain or a single tree, even in a multiple-tree forest (as described previously), but all the users for a specific cluster must be contained in the same namespace, as shown in Figure 10-10.

The preceding paragraphs implicitly introduce another concept used by CallManager when integrating with a directory: the User Search Base. The User Search Base refers to the root of the subtree used by CallManager to search for users who can potentially be associated with devices within the cluster. The next section discusses how to set this parameter.

You should create a special user account that CallManager and the other Cisco voice applications use to access and manage the directory. There should be one account per CallManager cluster, because this allows each account to be granted specific permissions

Figure 10-10 *CallManager Clusters Must Be Contained Within a Tree (Contiguous Namespace)*

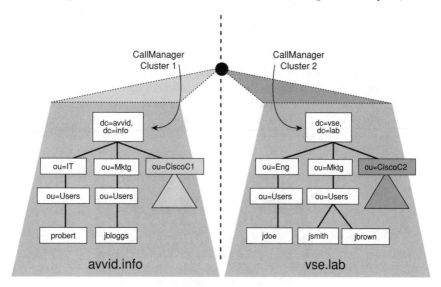

only when needed and allows for easier administration on a per-cluster basis without the risk of affecting other parts of the enterprise. In the examples in this chapter, this account is called the CCM Directory Manager. The name you choose for this user account might be different.

Each CCM Directory Manager account should be granted at least the following permissions within your directory:

- **Read/Write/Create all child objects/Delete all child objects** privileges on the respective "Cisco" OU subtrees. The rights must be set to apply to **This object and all child objects** for both the object and the properties. In AD, this can be set using the advanced options for security within Active Directory Users and Computers (ADUC). The default is to apply only to the object, so this needs to be changed to apply to child objects also.

- **Read** privileges on all the OUs contained at and below the User Search Base. This can be done just at the User Search Base level as long as inheritance is not blocked lower in the tree.

- **Read/Write** privileges on the ciscoatGUID, ciscoatUserProfile, and ciscoatUserProfileString attributes for all User objects contained below the User Search Base. In AD, this can be done using the advanced options for security within ADUC.

TIP   In AD, to set the permissions for the ciscoatGUID, ciscoatUserProfile, and ciscoatUserProfileString attributes for all User objects within the User Search Base, select the **CCM Directory Manager** user from the Advanced security window for the OU at the root of the User Search Base (in this chapter, the user is called **CCM Directory Manager** but your naming may be different). Then, click **View/Edit** and go to the **Properties** tab of the new window, as shown in Figure 10-11. From the **Apply onto** drop-down menu, select **User objects**, and then scroll down to the ciscoatGUID, ciscoatUserProfile, and ciscoatProfileString attributes. Allow **Write** permissions to all of them.

Figure 10-11 *Setting Permissions for the User Account in Active Directory*

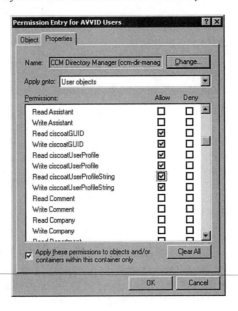

TIP   While creating the CCM Directory Manager account, set the **Password never expires** option. When the password needs to be changed, run the CCMPwdChanger utility from CallManager to change the password. This method updates the password in AD, updates the registry in CallManager, and updates directory initialization files. To access the CCM Password Changer tool, open a DOS window (**Start > Run >** *type* **cmd**), enter **CCMPwdChanger**, and press **Enter**.

Integrating CallManager with the Directory

After you have prepared the directory as described in the preceding section, you can start performing the actual integration by running the Cisco Customer Directory Configuration plugin again.

The two key concepts you need to consider at this point are the User Search Base and the User Creation Base.

The User Search Base parameter was introduced in the preceding section. It represents the root of the subtree used by CallManager for all user searches.

The User Creation Base parameter tells CallManager where to create the three system accounts needed by some applications and the features bundled with it:

- **CCM Administrator** (used by multilevels of administration [MLA])
- **CCM SysUser** (used by CallBack and extension mobility)
- **IPMA SysUser** (used by Cisco IP Manager Assistant)

The User Creation Base *must* be contained within the User Search Base, because CallManager needs to be able to search for the system account users before authenticating them.

To choose where to set the User Search Base, you need to look at where the users serviced by the cluster are located, and set the User Search Base to the lowest point in the tree containing all domains with users serviced by CallManager. Remember, the lower you set the User Search Base, the better response times and performance you achieve, because you do not have to follow a large number of referrals, potentially across slow WAN links, to get to remote domain controllers. Also, user data not needed by the cluster does not have to be parsed in the search.

In a single-domain AD forest (or standalone Netscape Directory), set the User Search Base to the lowest OU that contains all potential users for the CallManager cluster (for example, ou=AVVID Users, dc=vse, dc=lab). This might even be the root of the domain (for example, dc=vse, dc=lab, or o=avvid.lab) if users are spread across a set of OUs directly under this.

In a multiple-domain AD forest, try to keep the users for a specific CallManager cluster within a single domain, and follow the guidelines described previously. If this is not possible and users are spread across multiple domains, set the User Search Base to the lowest point in the tree containing all domains with users serviced by CallManager. In structures in which child domains serviced are under the top-level domain, the User Search Base must be set at the root of the entire AD forest. In all cases, though, try to ensure that a domain controller for each domain serviced is collocated with CallManager, or that the network is sufficiently resilient and fast to allow remote searches with no greater performance degradation than occurs with local searches.

NOTE	Although the User Creation Base must exist within the User Search Base, take care to ensure that no Active Directory user policies that are in force are applied to the system accounts created there. A simple way to do this is to put them in a sub-OU and block inheritance of the Group Policy Object (GPO) to that OU.

When integrating multiple CallManager clusters with the same AD domain (or standalone Netscape Directory), you can share the system accounts across clusters by specifying the same User Creation Base, as shown in Figure 10-12.

Figure 10-12 *Setting the User Search Base and User Creation Base in a Single-AD Domain*

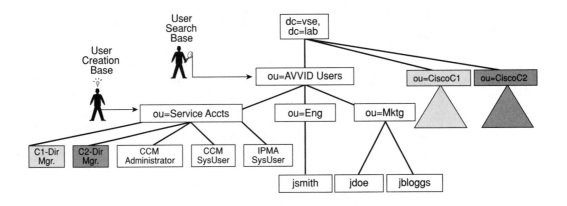

When integrating multiple CallManager clusters with different AD domains within a forest, we recommend that you define a different User Creation Base for each cluster, setting it to an OU within the relevant domain, as shown in Figure 10-13.

TIP	You can prevent system and service accounts from appearing in CallManager Administration by adding the string **CiscoPrivateUser** to the user's Description field. The CCM Administrator, CCM SysUser, and IPMA SysUser accounts have this field set by default, but the description can be safely added to the CCM Directory Manager account as well. Use Microsoft ADSIEdit (Active Directory Service Interfaces, available as a part of the Windows 2000 Support Tools) or any other LDAP tool to update the Description field.

After you have decided how to set the User Search Base and User Creation Base, you can follow these steps to run the Cisco Customer Directory Configuration plugin again (**Applications > Install Plugins**) on the CallManager Publisher server within your cluster:

Step 1   Choose the directory type that matches your corporate directory—
Microsoft Active Directory or **Netscape Directory Server**—and click **Next**.

Figure 10-13   *Setting the User Search Base and User Creation Base in a Multiple-Cluster, Multiple-Domain Forest*

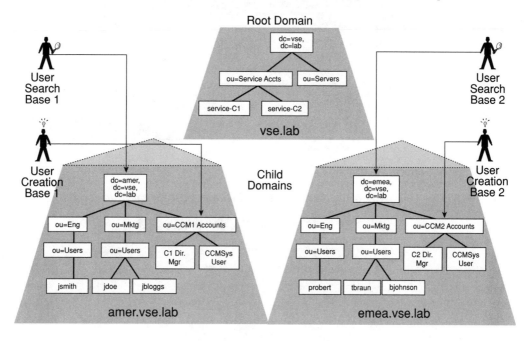

Step 2   Select the **Custom** setup type, and click **Next**.

Step 3   Select the **Configure Active Directory** and the **Enable CallManager Integration with Active Directory** options, and uncheck all other options (see Figure 10-14). Click **Next**.

Step 4   Specify the host name of a domain controller located within the same LAN as CallManager, or use the domain name if you are using DNS and all domain controllers for this domain are located in the same LAN as CallManager (see Figure 10-15). Click **Next**. Refer to the "Planning the Directory Integration" section for more details on how to provide high availability for the directory integration.

Figure 10-14   *Choosing the Setup Type in the Cisco Customer Directory Configuration Plugin*

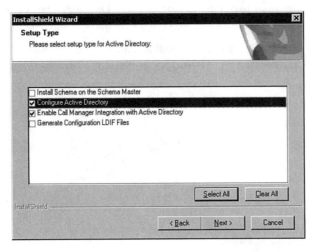

Figure 10-15   *Specifying Server Information in the Cisco Customer Directory Configuration Plugin*

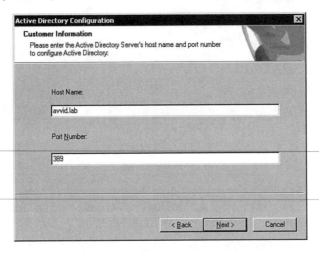

Step 5   Complete the fields in the Customer Information window (see Figure
10-16) according to the recommendations in this and the preceding section:

— **Directory Administrator DN**—Set this field to the DN of the
CCM Directory Manager user described in the preceding section.

— **Cisco Directory Configuration DN**—Set this field to the "Cisco"
OU described in the preceding section.

- **User Search Base**—Set this field to the User Search Base described earlier in this section.

- **User Creation Base**—Set this field to the User Creation Base described earlier in this section.

- **Domain Name**—Set this field to the domain name of the directory with which you are integrating.

- **User Search Attribute**—Set this field to the attribute that you want CallManager to use to identify users and to name application profiles (the default for AD is sAMAccountName).

Figure 10-16 *Specifying Customer Information in the Cisco Customer Directory Configuration Plugin*

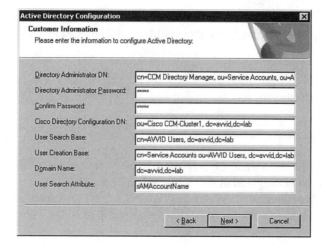

Step 6 Click **Next**.

Step 7 Verify the configuration, and click **Next**.

Step 8 Restart the server.

After completing these steps on the Publisher server, you need to set the passwords for the three system accounts. To do so, either use the CCMPwdChanger tool bundled with CallManager (open a DOS window [**Start > Run >** *type* **cmd**], enter **CCMPwdChanger**, and press **Enter**) or your corporate directory's interface (for example, ADUC in the case of Active Directory). We recommend that you set the password policy for these users so that their passwords never expire and are not set to change on first logon. This is also one of the reasons to avoid having any GPOs in use applied to these accounts.

If you enforce an expiration policy, CallManager will stop working when the password expires and there will be no warning to alert you that the problem is an expired password. If you have policies that require password changes every three months for example, you should run the CCMPwdChanger tool every three months.

You can now run the Cisco Customer Directory Configuration plugin on every Subscriber server within the CallManager cluster and follow these steps:

Step 1 Provide the credentials to authenticate to the Publisher server, and click **Next**.

Step 2 Choose the directory type that matches your corporate directory— **Microsoft Active Directory** or **Netscape Directory Server**—and click **Next**.

Step 3 Specify the host name of a domain controller or use the domain name if you are using DNS (these fields should be filled in automatically), and click **Next**.

Step 4 Verify the configuration, and click **Next**.

Step 5 Restart the server.

NOTE   When you perform the integration, no data migration occurs between the CallManager embedded directory and the corporate directory. If you want to migrate users and profiles that you had configured in the embedded directory, Cisco has developed some migration scripts that can help you in this task. To obtain these, contact your Cisco account team or channel partner. Note that the scripts are provided as is and without support.

Maintaining the Directory Integration

After CallManager has been integrated with an external directory, the user and password management procedures and policies should be set accordingly.

Use the corporate directory's interface (or supported API) for the following administrative operations:

- Adding a user
- Removing a user
- Setting and changing the core user attributes (such as display name, department, address, and password)

Conversely, use CallManager Administration for the following administrative operations:

- Configuring CallManager-specific user attributes (such as PIN and user locale)
- Associating a user with a device (such as an IP phone or a CTI port)

NOTE	By default, you cannot use CallManager Administration to add or remove users. You also cannot modify any of their core user attributes, such as name and phone number. If you want to enable adding and removing users in CallManager Administration, you can modify the UMDirectoryConfiguration.ini file on the CallManager servers, as described in the "Installing the Cisco Customer Directory Configuration Plugin for Cisco CallManager Release 4.0(1)" document, available on Cisco.com at the following link (login to Cisco.com is required):

http://www.cisco.com/en/US/partner/products/sw/voicesw/ps556/
products_installation_and_configuration_guide09186a00801ed28e.html

This functionality, provided for your convenience, does not replace your existing user/ directory management tools. Be aware that this functionality is limited; Cisco expects that you typically will add or delete users by using other available tools.

If CallManager is integrated with Active Directory, you will still not be able to set or modify user passwords through CallManager Administration because Active Directory does not allow passwords to be set via clear-text LDAP. You can use either the CCMPwdChanger tool bundled with CallManager to change directory passwords in a secure fashion, or the management interface provided by the directory vendor.

Even after modifying the UMDirectoryConfiguration.ini file on CallManager, you still have to give the CCM Directory Manager account sufficient permissions to create and delete users in AD.

When integrating multiple CallManager clusters with the same directory, keep in mind that you cannot associate the same user with devices in different clusters. Each user must be associated with a single, specific CallManager cluster at any point in time. (You can, of course, move users from one cluster to another by simply disassociating them from devices in the first cluster and associating them to devices in the second cluster.)

For user-initiated password changes and setting of preferences, instruct your users to do the following:

- Use the directory application's interface to change their passwords. In the case of Microsoft Active Directory, this is done through users' Windows workstations or by the administrator using the management tools.

- Use the Cisco CallManager User Options web page to change PINs and CallManager preferences (such as speed dials and call forward all numbers).

NOTE	Although the Cisco CallManager User Options web page allows users to change their passwords even after integration with AD, this is not the recommended procedure. Users probably won't realize that they are changing their Windows passwords at the same time. Also, the communication between the client workstation and the CallManager server uses HTTP, so the password would travel across the network in clear text. You can remove the **Change your Password** option from the Cisco CallManager User Options web page by simply removing the relevant code from the ASP.

As far as adds, moves, and changes are concerned, be aware that the following operations are *not supported* when CallManager is integrated with the directory:

- Changing a user's username (in the case of AD, this is the sAMAccountName)
- Moving a user from one OU to another
- Moving or renaming the "Cisco" OU

However, to work around these restrictions, the user's CallManager-specific attributes can be deleted manually (such as the profile in the "Cisco" OU and the data in the ciscoatGUID, ciscoatUserProfile, and ciscoatUserProfileString attributes for the user in question). Then the user can be renamed or moved using the directory management tools before being re-added as a CallManager subscriber. Although it's more cumbersome, this procedure preserves the file ownership and security principles belonging to the user in the directory application.

CallManager Upgrades

Because the schema might change with every major CallManager release, you should run the Cisco Customer Directory Integration plugin after every upgrade.

Also note that if you have integrated multiple CallManager clusters with the same directory, you need to extend the schema only once. If the clusters are running different CallManager releases, you should extend the schema from within the cluster that is running the most recent release.

Summary

This chapter covered best practices on how to integrate CallManager with a corporate directory, as well as how to provide the IP phones with directory access. Special attention was given to integration with Microsoft Active Directory, in terms of both planning and implementation.

## CHAPTER 11

Administering Call Detail Records

Call detail records (CDR) and call management records (CMR) are golden nuggets of data to be mined by both you and applications that manage CDR data. Cisco CallManager provides an application, the CDR Analysis and Reporting tool, that uses *CDR data* (both CDRs and CMRs) to show the system's health by tracking things such as gateway load, top talkers, call quality across the whole CallManager deployment, and much more. Each CDR comprises a single call leg or voice path. For each record, a range of data points related to the call and to the underlying network is captured and stored within the SQL database running on the Publisher.

The Publisher keeps all the CDR data for the entire cluster in its CDR database that is then used by applications that generate reports based on the CDR data. When a user makes a call from a device associated with a Subscriber, the CDR data for that call writes locally to a file on that Subscriber (as specified in Table 11-3 under CDR UNC Path).

As part of its duties, the Cisco Database Layer Monitor service regularly (as configured in the CDR File Time Interval parameter) moves the flat file from a staging location on the Subscriber to the Publisher. A companion service, Cisco CDR Insert, runs only on a cluster's Publisher. The CDR Insert service picks up those files from the common directory share and periodically inserts those records into the CDR database. This is the mechanism by which CDR data is combined in a CallManager cluster.

This chapter discusses the following:

- CDR-related service and enterprise parameters
- The format and functionality of CDR data in CallManager
- Search and export operations that can be executed manually
- Enabling Network Time Protocol
- Converting Epoch time and IP addresses to a human-readable format
- The CDR Analysis and Reporting (CAR) tool
- Third-party applications that process CDR data

NOTE	This chapter highlights the features and functions of CDR data in CallManager release 4.0. CallManager release 3.3 mirrors CallManager 4.0 functionality, although the settings in CallManager Administration differ slightly and there are new fields within the records. CAR was formerly named ART (Administrative Reporting Tool); some directory, URL, and other structures still refer to ART.

You can learn much more about the creation, use, storage, and maintenance of CDR data in Chapter 7 of the Cisco Press book *Cisco CallManager Fundamentals* (ISBN: 1-58705-008-0).

Use CDR Data for Accounting/Billing or Troubleshooting

Call detail records are typically used for billing purposes for an individual, department, business unit, or entire corporation. CDR data, which includes both CDRs and CMRs, contains information that provides a good view into past events and can be used for much more than billing. Additional uses include troubleshooting or evaluating such big-picture items as gateway or voice mail port utilization, and such detailed events as excess jitter and poor voice quality during a specific call. CDRs hold much of the call setup data when audio paths are established and store that data in a time-stamped record within a line of an SQL database or flat file. Combine CDR information with CMRs, which provide call diagnostic information such as jitter and latency, and you can learn much more about the network health at the time of a call. The CDR and CMR fields in Table 11-4 give you an idea of the vast amount of information that the collective CDR data contains.

Use the information provided by CDR data for time-based troubleshooting by using the CAR tool, third-party packages, or by searching the records manually. You can research general complaints about a specific location receiving poor voice quality during a certain time period by searching CDR data based on parameters such as extension, IP address, time, and so on, and then verify your search results against past time periods, or possibly start tracking against future events. Using CDR data for trends often helps you find the common denominator to a problem that is difficult to track due to the number of variables to uncover.

Enable CDR Data Collection

CDR data collection is not enabled by default, so to allow gathering of this information you must first enable the service parameters relating to CDRs. Collecting CDR data affects the system's overall processing horsepower, uses disk space, and is used by only some deployments. Staying within design guidelines helps you ensure proper processor availability to enable CDR collection. Review the recommended guidelines in the Solution Reference Network Design guide on Cisco.com (http://www.cisco.com/go/srnd or search Cisco.com for "SRND").

You must enable CDR and CMR collection on all servers in the CallManager cluster to gather systemwide information. In both single-server and CallManager cluster environments, the Publisher holds all CDR data. Subscribers in a cluster send their CDR data to the Publisher individually.

Enable the parameters specified in Table 11-1.

Table 11-1   *Enabling CDR Service Parameters*

Parameter	Action	Additional Information
CDR Enabled Flag	Set to True to enable the collection of CDRs.	Enable this for every server on which you want to collect CDRs (**Service > Service Parameters >** *select a server >* **Cisco CallManager**).
Call Diagnostics Enabled	Set to True to enable the collection of CMRs.	This is a clusterwide parameter, so you need to enable it on one server only for it to take effect for all servers in the cluster (**Service > Service Parameters >** *select a server >* **Cisco CallManager**).
Log Calls with Zero Duration Flag	Set to True to enable the collection of CDRs for calls that never connected or that lasted for less than 1 second.	Enable this for every server on which you want to collect zero-duration CDRs (**Service > Service Parameters >** *select a server >* **Cisco CallManager**).
Cisco CDR Insert Service	Run the CDR Insert Service to combine CDR data into one database.	CAR cannot generate reports without CDR data. The Cisco CDR Insert service aggregates CDR information clusterwide (**CallManager Serviceability > Tools > Control Center**).

Limit the Number of CDR and CMR Entries

Limiting the number of entries in the CDR database is important because data collection and export are processor-intensive and can cause performance degradation on CallManager. Limit the entries through the use of the three service parameters discussed in Table 11-2 (**Service > Service Parameters >** *select a server >* **Cisco Database Layer Monitor**).

Table 11-2 *Limiting the Size of the CDR Database*

Parameter	Description	Additional Information
Max CDR Records	Determines the maximum number of records the CDR database can contain after records are purged as specified by the Maintenance Time parameter. The default of 1.5 million records is appropriate for most deployments, but if you export frequently this value can be reduced.	You can change the default value to reduce or increase the number of records stored in the CDR database. Setting this to a low number with a high amount of daily CDR activity causes excessive purging of old CDR data.
Maintenance Time	Determines when old CDR data is purged to remain under the value specified in the Max CDR Records parameter. Leave this parameter at the default value unless midnight conflicts with peak usage time for this CallManager or with other processor-intensive activities.	Other events can potentially compete for CPU resources at the default time for this parameter, such as backups of the system and CallManager Serviceability report generation. Make certain that the start times of all three activities—backups, Serviceability report generation, and purging CDR data—occur consecutively rather than simultaneously and during off-peak usage times for this CallManager.
Maintenance Window	Specifies how many hours will be allowed to purge the old CDR data from the database to keep the number of records in the CDR database below the value specified in the Max CDR Records value. Leave this parameter set to the default of 2.	If the number of records collected daily is significantly larger than the Max CDR Records setting, deletion takes some time and CPU resources.

Configure CDR Enterprise Parameters

CallManager clusters house all CDR data on the Publisher. Every Subscriber needs to be able to reach a common network directory share to replicate data to the Publisher. The section "Resolving NetBIOS and WINS Issues" in Chapter 4 makes suggestions on maintaining and keeping reachability between Publishers and Subscribers. Also, Chapter 17 of the Cisco Press book *Troubleshooting Cisco IP Telephony,* by Giralt, Hallmark, and Smith, covers many of the replication issues that can occur.

Table 11-3 breaks down the CDR-related enterprise parameters, the behaviors their settings change, and caveats.

Table 11-3 *Cisco CDR Enterprise Parameters*

Enterprise Parameter	Behavior and Recommended Setting
CDR File Time Interval	Specifies the number of minutes of CDR information in each CDR file as set by the Local CDR Path parameter. Leave this parameter at the default of 1 minute to minimize the risk of losing data.
CDR Format	CDRs can start as flat files and may be either inserted into the database and deleted, or not inserted and saved. Leave this parameter at the default to have all CDR information flowing to the Publisher be put into a common cluster CDR database.
CDR UNC Path	Specifies the network path to a Publisher share point for CDRs in a cluster. All members of a single cluster must use the same share point and have NetBIOS reachability to it. Changing this from the default causes CAR not to function, so leave this parameter at the default value if you want to use CAR.
Cluster ID	Defines the string that uniquely identifies the cluster name in the CDR. Leave this parameter at the default value (specified during CallManager installation) unless you're interleaving multicluster CDR data into a single CDR database with a differing Cluster ID.
Local CDR Path	Specifies the staging location for export to the CDR UNC Path directory or the final CDR flat file storage directory, depending on the value specified in the CDR Format parameter. Leave this at the default because the Cisco Backup and Restore System (BARS) expects the default path.
Off Cluster CDR Connection String	When using a third-party billing or reporting application, it might be best to host the CDR database on a separate machine. The Off Cluster CDR Connection String allows an Open Database Connectivity (ODBC)-capable host to receive CDR data directly. When a value exists, data cannot be replicated and is sent only to the specified location. When this parameter is set at a value other than the default, CAR does not have CDR data to pull from and does not function. Leave this parameter at the default unless you're using a third-party application that must receive CDR data via ODBC.

Enable Network Time Synchronization on All CallManagers and Update the Configuration File if Needed

The CallManager installation process installs and enables the Network Time Protocol (NTP) service within Windows, but the associated configuration file needs to be configured. Having a common clock to accurately time-stamp all CDR events clusterwide is critical for synchronizing a CDR to an event that may span several devices. IOS routers, dedicated hosts, or even a remote Internet NTP service can serve as an NTP server for the network. For more detailed time information, go to the following link:

http://www.boulder.nist.gov/timefreq/service/its.htm

The NTP service can be found under **Start > Programs > Administrative Tools > Services** on the CallManager server. It should be Started and set for Automatic startup, as shown in Figure 11-1.

Figure 11-1 *NTP in the Services Window*

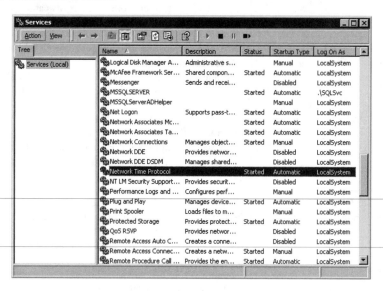

The default configuration file points to the fictitious NTP server shown in Example 11-1.

Example 11-1 *NTP Configuration File* C:\WINNT\ntp.conf

```
server 127.127.1.1              # Set Local Clock to Authoritative Time Source
fudge 127.127.1.1 stratum 5     # Resets Stratum from default 3 to 5
driftfile %windir%\ntp.drift    # path for drift file
```

You can find the sample configuration file for NTP in C:\WINNT\ntp.conf. Make a copy of it and paste it to C:\WINNT\Sytem32\Drivers\etc. Then open the configuration file in C:\WINNT\Sytem32\Drivers\etc and modify it using Notepad or Wordpad. Change the first line to reflect the IP address of the preferred NTP server. Configure a backup NTP server as well in the second line of the file, as shown in Example 11-2.

Example 11-2 *Modified NTP Configuration File Placed in* C:\WINNT\Sytem32\Drivers\etc\ntp.conf

```
server 17.254.0.26
server 132.163.4.101
driftfile %windir%\ntp.drift
```

Save the file when you have finished modifying it. Restart the NTP service to have it read the changes you made to the configuration file, otherwise synchronization will not occur until the next restart of the system. The synchronization takes a few minutes to complete.

Make sure the time zone and local time are within 1000 seconds (16.67 minutes) of matching the server designated within the NTP configuration file or synchronization with the NTP server will not occur. You can verify NTP operation by manually moving the time on the CallManager server back 5 minutes (double-click the time in the system tray) from a reference time such as the atomic clock or your watch, restarting NTP, and verifying resynchronization on CallManager after a few minutes.

TIP   Search for "atomic clock real-time" on Google.com to find a list of websites that provide accurate time synchronized to the atomic clock.

Learn how to synchronize the time on CatOS and Cisco IOS software devices in Chapter 3 of the book *Troubleshooting Cisco IP Telephony* (ISBN: 1-58705-075-7).

Understanding the Call Detail Record Format

CallManager release 4.0 contains 66 CDR fields and 18 CMR fields in each record. This is a substantial amount of information to process, especially when you consider that multiple entries can exist in the CDR database for any call that has been transferred, conferenced, or diverted in some fashion.

NOTE   Only devices that use Skinny Client Control Protocol (SCCP) or Media Gateway Control Protocol (MGCP) for call signaling generate CMR data. For each completed call, up to two CMRs can be entered—one from each endpoint in the conversation. If only one endpoint in the call signals via SCCP or MGCP, only one record is entered. CDR data is retained for every call, capturing the essential billing and network data elements listed in Table 11-4.

Table 11-4 shows all the fields in the CDRs and CMRs for CallManager release 4.0. The fields in Table 11-4 are listed in the order in which they appear in the actual CDR or CMR. When the database format changes, it affects not only utilities developed at Cisco, but also all third-party tools that use the CDR data. In Table 11-4, **New** indicates a new field in CallManager release 4.0, and **Common** indicates a field that is common to both CDRs and CMRs.

Table 11-4   *CDR and CMR Fields*

New or Common	CDR or CMR Field	Additional Information
CDR Fields		
Common	cdrRecordType	
Common	globalCallID_callManagerId	
Common	globalCallID_callId	See Table 11-13.
	origLegCallIdentifier	
	dateTimeOrigination	See Table 11-13.
	origNodeId	
	origSpan	
	origIpAddr	See Table 11-13.
New	origIPport	See Table 11-5.
	callingPartyNumber	See Table 11-13.
	origCause_location	
New	origCause_value	See Table 11-5. See Table 11-13.
	origMediaTransportAddress_IP	
	origMediaTransportAddress_Port	
	origMediaCap_payloadCapability	
	origMediaCap_maxFramesPerPacket	
	origMediaCap_g723BitRate	
	destLegIdentifier	
	destNodeId	

Table 11-4   *CDR and CMR Fields (Continued)*

New or Common	CDR or CMR Field	Additional Information
CDR Fields *(Continued)*		
	destSpan	
	destIpAddr	See Table 11-13.
New	destIpPort	See Table 11-5.
	originalCalledPartyNumber	See Table 11-13.
	finalCalledPartyNumber	See Table 11-13.
	destCause_location	
New	destCause_value	See Tables 11-5 and 11-13.
	destMediaTransportAddress_IP	
	destMediaTransportAddress_Port	
	destMediaCap_payloadCapability	
	destMediaCap_maxFramesPerPacket	
	destMediaCap_g723BitRate	
	dateTimeConnect	See Table 11-13.
	dateTimeDisconnect	See Table 11-13.
	lastRedirectDn	
Common	pkid	
	originalCalledPartyNumberPartition	See Table 11-13.
	callingPartyNumberPartition	See Table 11-13.
	finalCalledPartyNumberPartition	See Table 11-13.
	lastRedirectDnPartition	See Table 11-13.
	duration	
	origDeviceName	

continues

Table 11-4 *CDR and CMR Fields (Continued)*

New or Common	CDR or CMR Field	Additional Information
CDR Fields *(Continued)*		
	destDeviceName	
New	origCalledPartyRedirectReason	See Table 11-5.
New	lastRedirectRedirectReason	See Table 11-5.
	destConversationId	
	origCallTerminationOnBehalfOf	
	destCallTerminationOnBehalfOf	
New	origCalledPartyRedirectOnBehalfOf	See Table 11-5.
New	lastRedirectRedirectOnBehalfOf	See Table 11-5.
Common	globalCallId_ClusterID	
	joinOnBehalfOf	
New	origPrecedenceLevel	See Table 11-5.
New	origVideoCap_Codec	See Table 11-5.
New	origVideoCap_Bandwidth	See Table 11-5.
New	origVideoCap_Resolution	See Table 11-5.
New	origVideoTransportAddress_IP	See Table 11-5.
New	origVideoTransportAddress_Port	See Table 11-5.
New	destPrecedenceLevel	See Table 11-5.
New	destVideoCap_Codec	See Table 11-5.
New	destVideoCap_Bandwidth	See Table 11-5.
New	destVideoCap_Resolution	See Table 11-5.
New	destVideoTransportAddress_IP	See Table 11-5.
New	destVideoTransportAddress_Port	See Table 11-5.
New	comment	See Table 11-5.
New	callingPartyLoginUserID	See Table 11-5.

Table 11-4 *CDR and CMR Fields (Continued)*

New or Common	CDR or CMR Field	Additional Information
CDR Fields *(Continued)*		
New	finalCalledPartyLoginUserID	See Table 11-5.
CMR Fields		
Common	cdrRecordType	
Common	globalCallID_callManagerId	
	nodeId	
Common	globalCallID_callId	See Table 11-13.
	directoryNum	
	callIdentifier	
	dateTimeStamp	See Table 11-13.
	numberPacketsSent	
	numberOctetsSent	
	numberPacketsReceived	
	numberOctetsReceived	
	numberPacketsLost	
	jitter	
	latency	
Common	pkid	
	directoryNumPartition	See Table 11-13.
	deviceName	
Common	globalCallId_ClusterID	
origIpPort	Positive integer	The IP port number of the origIpAddr IP address. This field is reserved for future use and is not currently used.

New CDR Fields in CallManager Release 4.0

Table 11-5 details the CDR fields that are new to CallManager release 4.0, or existing fields that have new values associated with them.

Table 11-5 *CDR Field Updates for CallManager 4.0*

Field Name	Type	Definition
origIpPort	Positive integer	The IP port number of the origIpAddr IP address. This field is reserved for future use and is not currently used.
destIpPort	Positive integer	The IP port number of the destIpAddr IP address. This field is reserved for future use and is not currently used.
origCause_value	0 to 128	The value indicates the reason the call was cleared by the originating party. See Tables 11-6 through 11-8 for redefined and new cause codes.
destCause_value	0 to 128	The value indicates the reason the call was cleared by the destination party. See Tables 11-6 through 11-8 for redefined and new case codes.
origPrecedenceLevel	0 to 4	The precedence level of an MLPP originating call leg. See Table 11-9 for new precedence value type values.
destPrecedenceLevel	0 to 4	The precedence level of an MLPP destination call leg. See Table 11-9 for new precedence value type values.
origVideoCap_Codec	100 to 102	The codec type of the originating party video stream. See Table 11-10 for new codec values.
destVideoCap_Codec	100 to 102	The codec type of the terminating party video stream. See Table 11-10 for new codec values.
origVideoCap_Bandwidth destVideoCap_Bandwidth	Positive integer	Bandwidth is measured in kilobits per second.

Table 11-5   *CDR Field Updates for CallManager 4.0 (Continued)*

Field Name	Type	Definition
destVideoCap_Resolution destVideoCap_Resolution	1 to 5	The stream's video resolution. See Table 11-11 for new video resolution values.
origVideoTransportAddress_IP	Integer	The IP address of the originator of the video call.
destVideoTransportAddress_IP	Integer	The IP address of the terminator of the video call.
origVideoTransportAddress_Port	Positive integer	The video RTP port number of theorigVideoTransportAddress_IP IP address.
destVideoTransportAddress_Port	Positive integer	The video RTP port number of the destVideoTransportAddress_ IP IP address.
origCalledPartyRedirectedOnBehalfOf	Integer	The original called party's reason for redirection. New On Behalf Of codes: 14—Immediate Divert 15—Barge
lastRedirectRedirectOnBehalfOf	Integer	The last redirected party's reason for redirection. New On Behalf Of codes: 14—Immediate Divert 15—Barge
comment	Text string, up to 256 characters	This new flexible field allows up to 256 characters of text to be added to the CDR to specify details about the call. Text can be added without corrupting the database or file structure. For example, for the field used to flag malicious calls, the following text can be added: Comment—CallFlag: MALICIOUS_TRACEME

continues

Table 11-5 *CDR Field Updates for CallManager 4.0 (Continued)*

Field Name	Type	Definition
origCalledPartyRedirectReason	Integer	The redirect reason for the original redirect. See Table 11-12 for new redirect reason codes.
lastRedirectRedirectReason	Integer	The redirect reason for the last redirect. See Table 11-12 for new redirect reason codes.
callingPartyLoginUserID	Text string, up to 250 characters	This new field captures the calling user's login ID, up to 250 characters.
finalCalledPartyLoginUserID	Text string, up to 250 characters	This new field captures the final called user's login ID, up to 250 characters.

Table 11-6 describes how MLPP makes use of existing cause codes. These values are used in the origCause_value and destCause_value fields.

Table 11-6 *New MLPP Usage of Existing Cause Codes*

Value	Cause	Description
8	Preemption	The call was preempted. The circuit is not reserved for reuse by another call.
9	Preemption	The call was preempted. The circuit is reserved for reuse by another call.
46	Precedence call blocked	The called user is busy with a call of equal or higher precedence level, or no preemptable circuit with a call of lower precedence level is available.
50	Requested facility not subscribed	CallManager never generates this value natively. If received from another network, CallManager transmits this value when applicable.

Table 11-7 describes the new MLPP cause codes used in the origCause_value and destCause_value fields.

Table 11-7 *New MLPP Cause Codes*

Value	Cause	Description
122	Precedence level exceeded	The precedence level is exceeded.
123	Device not preemptable	The device cannot be preempted for a higher precedence call.

Table 11-7 *New MLPP Cause Codes (Continued)*

Value	Cause	Description
129	Precedence out of bandwidth	No more bandwidth for precedence.

Table 11-8 describes the new conferencing cause codes used in the origCause_value and destCause_value fields.

Table 11-8 *New Conference Cause Codes*

Value	Cause	Description
124	Conference full	No more available resources for joining the conference.
128	Conference drop any party	Indicates when a call was dropped from a conference by pressing softkeys associated with the drop any party/drop last party capabilities.

Table 11-9 describes the new MLPP precedence value type values used in the origPrecedenceLevel, destPrecedenceLevel, and origCause_value fields.

Table 11-9 *New Precedence Values*

Precedence Level	Precedence Name
0	FLASH OVERRIDE
1	FLASH
2	IMMEDIATE
3	PRIORITY
4	ROUTINE

Table 11-10 describes the new codec values used in the origVideoCap_Codec and destVideoCap_Codec fields.

Table 11-10 *New Codec Values*

Value	Description
100	H.261
101	H.263
102	Cisco VT Advantage

Table 11-11 describes the new video resolution values used in the origVideoCap_Resolution and destVideoCap_Resolution fields.

Table 11-11 *New Video Resolution Values*

Value	Description
1	Sub-Quarter Common Interface Format (SQCIF)
2	Quarter Common Interface Format (QCIF)
3	Common Interface Format (CIF)
4	CIF4
5	CIF16

Table 11-12 describes the new redirect reason codes used in the OrigCalledPartyRedirectReason and lastCalledPartyRedirectReason fields.

Table 11-12 *New Redirect Reason Code Values*

Value	Description
0	No Reason
1	Call Forward Busy
2	Call Forward No Answer
4	Call Transfer
5	Call Pickup
7	Call Park
8	Call Park Pickup
9	CPE Out of Order
10	Call Forward
11	Call Park Reversion
15	Call Forward Unconditional
18	Call Deflection
34	Blind Transfer
50	Call Immediate Divert
66	Call Forward Alternate Party

Table 11-12 *New Redirect Reason Code Values (Continued)*

Value	Description
82	Call Forward on Failure
98	Conference
114	Barge

Frequently Searched CDR Fields

Table 11-13 describes several of the fields in CDR data that you should understand well. These field names appear in every record. You should become familiar with the information these fields provide, because they uniquely identify a single CDR record. Extension numbers can match differing CallManager partitions, so it's important to know what other fields help identify a record.

Table 11-13 *Pertinent Information for Select CMR and CDR Fields*

CMR/CDR Fields	Description
globalCallID_callId	The unique identifier for this call record. The CallManager server sequentially assigns this identifier when the phone goes off-hook or the gateway signals an incoming call. The callId is not inserted into the CDR until a call finishes. Some callIds might never be inserted into the CDR because of conference joins overwriting the callId, and so on. The callId can restart at 1 because of upgrades and therefore becomes nonunique.
callingPartyNumber originalCalledPartyNumber finalCalledPartyNumber	These three fields capture the number that was originally dialed and the number that was finally called. All dialed numbers are subject to modification by translation patterns and other transformations that manipulate the original dialed number. Gateway digit manipulation is not saved in the CDR because of local processing on the gateway.
originalCalledPartyNumberPartition callingPartyNumberPartition finalCalledPartyNumberPartition lastRedirectDnPartition directoryNumPartition	When you use CallManager partitions, a single CallManager can have duplicate matching extension numbers, and therefore so does the CDR data. These fields identify the partition information. Use both extension and partition information to accurately identify the endpoint.

continues

Table 11-13 *Pertinent Information for Select CMR and CDR Fields (Continued)*

CMR/CDR Fields	Description
dateTimeOrigination dateTimeConnect dateTimeDisconnect dateTimeStamp	As calls originate, terminate, and are recorded, it's naturally important to capture the time the event occurred. These fields provide that data using timestamps written in Universal Coordinated Time (UTC), which is the number of seconds since January 1, 1970 GMT, or simply Epoch time. See the later section "Convert Epoch Time to Human-Readable Time Using the CDR Time Converter Utility." It discusses a nifty tool that converts UTC to a human-readable format.
origCause_value destCause_value	When a call ends, a decimal call clearing cause code (per ITU Q.850) is used to identify the reason. More information about cause codes is provided in Table 11-14. CallManager determines the cause code for OnNet calls. The remote switch sends cause codes for OffNet calls.
origIpAddr destIpAddr	These fields capture the originating and destination IP addresses. An IP address is saved in the CDR as a signed integer, although it is originally an unsigned value. See the section "Converting a 32-Bit Signed Integer Value to an IP Address" for more information on how to convert this value to dotted-decimal notation.

ITU Q.850 Cause Codes Table

When a call ends for whatever reason, there is an associated cause. This can be for a "normal call clearing" cause code 16, or for another reason, such as a "call rejected" cause code 21. The decimal call clearing cause codes listed in Table 11-14 are per ITU Q.850 unless otherwise noted. CallManager determines the value for OnNet calls; the remote switch sends CallManager the cause code for OffNet calls.

Table 11-14 *ITU Cause Codes with Cisco Extensions*

Code	Cause
0	No error
1	Unallocated (unassigned) number
2	No route to specified transit network (national)
3	No route to destination

Table 11-14 *ITU Cause Codes with Cisco Extensions (Continued)*

Code	Cause
4	Send special information tone
5	Misdialed trunk prefix (national)
6	Channel unacceptable
7	Call awarded and being delivered in an established channel
8	Preemption
9	Preemption with circuit reserved for reuse
16	Normal call clearing
17	User busy
18	No user responding
19	No answer from user (user alerted)
20	Subscriber absent
21	Call rejected
22	Number changed
26	Nonselected user clearing
27	Destination out of order
28	Invalid number format (address incomplete)
29	Facility rejected
30	Response to STATUS ENQUIRY
31	Normal, unspecified
34	No circuit/channel available
38	Network out of order
39	Permanent frame mode connection out of service
40	Permanent frame mode connection operational
41	Temporary failure
42	Switching equipment congestion

continues

Table 11-14 *ITU Cause Codes with Cisco Extensions (Continued)*

Code	Cause
43	Access information discarded
44	Requested circuit/channel not available
46	Precedence call blocked
47	Resource unavailable, unspecified
49	Quality of service not available
50	Requested facility not subscribed
53	Service operation violated
54	Incoming calls barred
55	Incoming calls barred within Closed User Group (CUG)
57	Bearer capability not authorized
58	Bearer capability not presently available
62	Inconsistency in designated outgoing access information and subscriber class
63	Service or option not available, unspecified
65	Bearer capability not implemented
66	Channel type not implemented
69	Requested facility not implemented
70	Only restricted digital information bearer capability available (national use)
79	Service or option not implemented, unspecified
81	Invalid call reference value
82	Identified channel does not exist
83	A suspended call exists, but this call identity does not
84	Call identity in use
85	No call suspended
86	Call having the requested call identity has been cleared
87	User not a member of CUG

Table 11-14 *ITU Cause Codes with Cisco Extensions (Continued)*

Code	Cause
88	Incompatible destination
90	Destination number missing and DC not subscribed, or nonexistent CUG
91	Invalid transit network selection (national use)
95	Invalid message, unspecified
96	Mandatory information element is missing
97	Message type is nonexistent or not implemented
98	Message is incompatible with the call state, or the message type is nonexistent or not implemented
99	An information element or parameter does not exist or is not implemented
100	Invalid information element contents
101	Message is incompatible with the call state
102	Call was terminated when a timer expired and a recovery routine was executed to recover from the error
103	Parameter nonexistent or not implemented—passed on (national use)
110	Message with unrecognized parameter discarded
111	Protocol error, unspecified
122	Precedence level exceeded (Cisco-specific code)
123	Device not preemptable (Cisco-specific code)
124	Conference full (Cisco-specific code)
125	Out of bandwidth (Cisco-specific code)
126	Call split (Cisco-specific code). Used when a call terminates during a transfer operation because it was split off and terminated (was not part of the final transferred call). This can help determine which calls were terminated as part of a feature operation.
127	Interworking, unspecified (Cisco-specific code)
128	Drop any party or drop the last party (Cisco-specific code)
129	Precedence out of bandwidth (Cisco-specific code)

Understanding CDR Data Through Call Examples

Table 11-4 provided a complete list of CDR and CMR field values; the following examples highlight just a few of those fields. You can find a complete listing of cause codes in Table 11-14. The pertinent records are shown in tables to increase legibility and to highlight the correlation between CDR and CMR data.

NOTE Records are listed in the order of activity completion, which means that call legs from different parties might be intertwined. This occurs because invoking supplementary features, such as conferencing and consultation transfer, results in additional CDRs being generated and added to the CDR database.

Understanding CDRs: An Example of a Normal Call

An average IP phone-to-IP phone conversation generates a single CDR and two CMRs. In Table 11-15, which depicts a typical call across the WAN, notice that the originalCalledPartyNumber value matches the finalCalledPartyNumber. This means that the call was not diverted in any way and reached the phone number that was dialed directly. When a call is diverted or forwarded in some fashion, the finalCalledPartyNumber changes. Also notice that the caller disconnected first and caused the origCause_value to be saved as 16, which indicates normal call clearing (see Table 11-14). If the called extension hangs up first, the cause codes reverse.

Table 11-15 *Normal Call CDR and CMR Values*

CDR Fields	CDR Value	CMR 1 Entry	CMR 2 Entry
globalCallID_callId	3	3	3
callingPartyNumber	1003		
callingPartyNumberPartition	Sales		
originalCalledPartyNumber	1001		
originalCalledPartyNumberPartition	Engineering		
finalCalledPartyNumber	1001		
origCause_value	16		
destCause_value	0		

Table 11-15 *Normal Call CDR and CMR Values (Continued)*

CDR Fields	CDR Value	CMR 1 Entry	CMR 2 Entry
duration (in seconds)	70		
CMR Fields			
directoryNum		1003	1001
numberPacketsSent		3488	3474
numberPacketsReceived		3474	3488
numberPacketsLost		0	0
Jitter		26	28
Latency		48	49

Establish Baseline Jitter and Latency Characteristics

Jitter and latency values are unique to every network connection. In general, you want low latency and stable jitter, but the actual values differ for each endpoint on each different deployment, so there is no one universal baseline to strive for. To determine an appropriate baseline for your system, note what typical values (latency, jitter) are for the LAN and WAN when things are operating normally, and use those as a reference point when examining suspicious values in the CDR data.

Table 11-15 showed jitter and latency values for a sample WAN connection. Calls placed across a WAN have very different latency characteristics than those made across a LAN. Establishing a good baseline for both WAN and LAN calls is key to being able to judge what is good or bad when looking at CMRs. Incorrect deployment of quality of service (QoS) parameters on network devices such as routers and switches causes jitter and latency values to fluctuate wildly from call to call or during a single call. These fluctuations are typically at their worst during peak network usage in the mornings and afternoons.

TIP   CMRs are generated after a call is completed. Pressing the **i** or **?** button on the IP Phone twice in quick succession during an active call provides a real-time view of call statistics such as jitter and lost packets. You can also see this information by selecting **CallManager Administration > Device > Phone > Find** and clicking the phone's IP address. This takes you to the phone's internal web page.

Understanding CDRs: An Example of an Unsuccessful Call

The call shown in Table 11-16 was redirected to a voice mail port (see the finalCalledPartyNumber field value). No ports were available to take the call, which resulted in cause code 17 (user busy). This same example might have a cause code of 41 (network failure) if the ports to the voice mail system were not registered to CallManager. Notice the call's zero-second duration. CallManager logs failed calls regardless of the setting in the Log Calls with Zero Duration Flag service parameter (described in Table 11-1). In other cases, such as busy resources on a remote time-division multiplexing (TDM) switch or Public Switched Telephone Network (PSTN) line, the call clears normally and results in a zero duration. In that case, if the Log Calls with Zero Duration Flag parameter is not enabled, the information is not logged in the CDR. Unless CallManager is enabled to log CDRs with zero duration, no record exists of unique events such as remote switch clearing. Because there's no call set up in this example, there's no CMR data to capture.

Table 11-16 *Unsuccessful Call CDR and CMR Values*

CDR Fields	CDR Value	CMR 1 Entry	CMR 2 Entry
globalCallID_callId	4		
callingPartyNumber	1001		
callingPartyNumberPartition	Engineering		
originalCalledPartyNumber	1003		
originalCalledPartyNumberPartition	Sales		
finalCalledPartyNumber	1999		
origCause_value	0		
destCause_value	17		
duration (in seconds)	0		
CMR Fields			
directoryNum		—	—
numberPacketsSent		—	—
numberPacketsReceived		—	—
numberPacketsLost		—	—
jitter		—	—
latency		—	—

Search the CDR SQL Database

For a quick query on a known value, use the SQL query builder in the Enterprise Manager. In the following example, the CDR database searches for any calls originating from extension 1003. This same technique can be used to search for any known value in any of the fields. You can use this technique to trace dialed digit patterns from an extension along with the time they occurred to obtain a cause code value and verify the real cause of a failed call. Users often dial incorrectly, dial a nonworking number, or encounter a busy gateway and think there is something wrong with their phones because the call wouldn't go through. By examining the cause code, you can determine the real cause of the problem. In a troubleshooting scenario, use the data from the extension to verify or baseline voice quality problems of jitter or latency given a particular dialed number. The CDR data within the database can be useful given a single known parameter for a particular CDR or CMR field.

To SQL search, follow this procedure on the console of the CallManager Publisher or via remote session:

Step 1 Start Enterprise Manager by clicking **Start > Programs > Microsoft SQL Server > Enterprise Manager**.

Step 2 Click the **+** next to **Microsoft SQL Servers**.

Step 3 Click the **+** next to **SQL Server Group**.

Step 4 Click the **+** next to **(local)** server.

Step 5 Click the **+** next to the **Databases** folder.

Step 6 Click the **+** next to the **CDR** database.

Step 7 Click **Tables**.

Step 8 Right-click **CallDetailRecord** and select **Open Table > Query**. The Query window opens.

Step 9 In the CallDetailRecord window, check the field to be searched (**CallingPartyNumber**), as shown in Figure 11-2.

Step 10 In the Criteria cell for the field specified in Step 9, enter the value you want to search for (**1003**).

Query Builder does all the SQL language formatting in the middle pane.

Step 11 Click the **!** icon at the top of the window to run the query.

You now have the matches to the query in the lower portion of the window.

Figure 11-2 *SQL Database Search with Enterprise Manager*

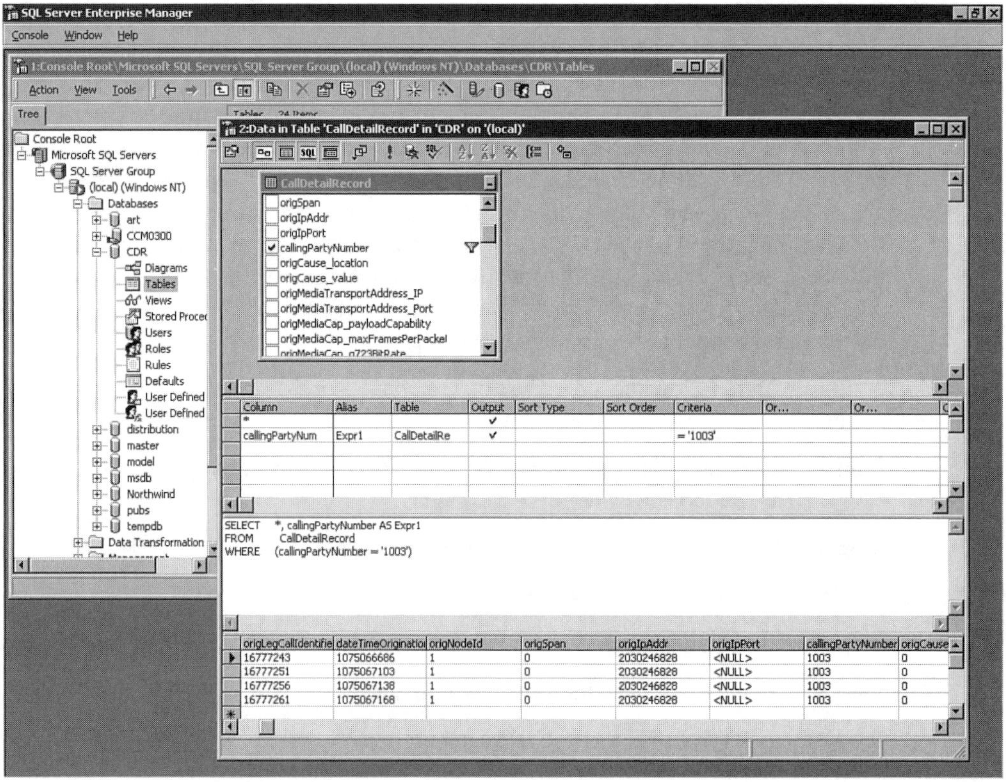

Export CDR Data for Further Analysis

You can use the export functionality in the SQL Enterprise Manager to create an Excel-compatible file. The exported file can be used for meaningful searching, graphing, or troubleshooting. It then can be transported and used without immediate access to the Publisher. When you export, CDR data is accessible in a flat file without changing the enterprise parameter CDR Format to export a flat file.

WARNING   Exporting data can be a CPU-intensive process, especially when thousands or even millions of records must be manipulated. Use caution when deciding the time of day for CDR exporting. Use tools such as the Real-Time Monitoring Tool or Microsoft Performance to monitor the CallManager load.

To export CDR data from the SQL database, follow this procedure on the Publisher or via a remote session:

Step 1 Start Enterprise Manager by clicking **Start > Programs > Microsoft SQL Server > Enterprise Manager**.

Step 2 Click the **+** next to **Microsoft SQL Servers**.

Step 3 Click the **+** next to **SQL Server Group**.

Step 4 Click the **+** next to **(local)** server.

Step 5 Click the **+** next to the **Databases** folder.

Step 6 Click the **+** next to the **CDR** database. Click **Tables**.

Step 7 Right-click **CallDetailRecord** and choose **All Tasks > Export Data**.

Step 8 When the wizard window opens, click **Next**.

Step 9 All source settings have been populated because of the prior steps. Click **Next**.

Step 10 In the Destination box, choose **Microsoft Excel**, and enter a filename and path of your choosing. Click **Next**.

Step 11 Click the button **Copy table(s) and view(s) from the source database**. Click **Next**.

Step 12 Choose the **CallDetailRecord** and **CallDetailRecordDiagnostic** sources. Click **Next**.

Step 13 Choose a run time for a time period when the system is least used. Click **Next**.

Step 14 Click **Finish**. The result is a handy Excel file with separate tabs for the CDRs and CMRs.

Convert Epoch Time to Human-Readable Time Using the CDR Time Converter Utility

Time stamps are written in UTC in the CDR, not in a human-readable form. UTC is the number of seconds that have passed since January 1, 1970 GMT, or simply Epoch time. The Cisco Press book *Troubleshooting Cisco IP Telephony* introduced the CDR Time Converter Utility. Check the book's website on Cisco Press for a free, downloadable file containing this tool (**http://www.ciscopress.com/1587050757 > Downloads**). Check the site regularly, because you might find updates to this tool.

WARNING This is not an officially supported tool. If you download, install, or use it, you do so at your own risk. Cisco Systems is not responsible for correcting problems that might arise as a result of your using this unsupported tool.

Figure 11-3 shows a sample run of the CDR Time Converter Utility with the UTC integer 1056851136 taken from a CDR's dateTimeOrigination field. The multiple time zone output displayed in the utility makes it easy to discern the time of the event in relation to local time.

Figure 11-3 *UNIX Epoch Time Converter Utility*

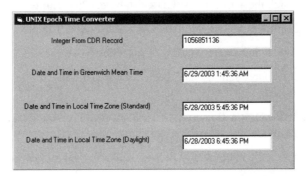

Convert a 32-Bit Signed Integer Value to an IP Address

CallManager saves IP address information in the CDR as a 32-bit signed integer value. Converting that signed value can be tricky, but with a scientific calculator it becomes fairly easy to convert the number to the familiar dotted-decimal notation.

Change the standard Windows calculator (**Start > Programs > Accessories > Calculator**) to Scientific (**View > Scientific**), and follow this procedure:

Step 1 Click the **Dec** button to input a decimal value.

Step 2 Enter the signed integer (for example, **-1744626772**).

Step 3 Convert to hexadecimal by clicking the **Hex** button (**FFFFFFFF98031BAC**).

Step 4 Keep only the last eight values, and dot the pairs (**98.03.1B.AC**).

Step 5 Reverse the hexadecimal bytes by swapping the number pairs front-to-back (**AC.1B.03.98**).

Step 6   Enter the pairs one at a time into the calculator while still in hexadecimal mode (AC).

Step 7   Click the **Dec** button to reveal 8 bits of the IP address in decimal (172).

Step 8   Click the **Hex** button to return to hexadecimal mode.

Step 9   Repeat Steps 6 through 8 until you achieve full address conversion (172.27.3.152).

TIP   When searching CDR entries for a specific IP address, you can use this method to translate the address in question into a signed integer.

Using Microsoft Excel Formulas to Convert UTC and IP Addresses

After the CDR has been exported from the CDR database into a file compatible with Microsoft Excel (see the earlier section "Export CDR Data for Further Analysis"), changing the display of the time or IP address into a human-readable format can be automated with a formula. After you have exported a CDR into an Excel file, open the spreadsheet and add a row at the top. The following steps show you how to convert the dateTimeOrigination and origIpAddr fields:

Step 1   Set up the cell that will display the value to be of the "date" type. In Excel, select **Format > Cells**, and chose the date display format you prefer.

Step 2   Insert the following formula into the cell. Replace **E3** with the field in the spreadsheet that you want to convert to human-readable form:

=**E3**/86400+DATE(1970,1,1)

The time is displayed in Greenwich Mean Time (GMT).

The following steps show you how to convert an IP address to human-readable format. After you have exported a CDR into an Excel file, open the spreadsheet, add a row at the top, and follow these steps:

Step 1   Install or verify that the optional Analysis ToolPak package has been installed (check for the Analysis ToolPak under **Tools > Add-Ins**). Without the optional ToolPak installed, the formula does not operate. You can install the Analysis ToolPak from the Microsoft Office Suite installations CDs or check the Microsoft Office\Office\ Library\Analysis directory.

Step 2 Insert the following long formula into the cell to display the value as an IP address. Replace all four instances of H3 with the field in the spreadsheet that you want to convert to a human-readable form:

=CONCATENATE(HEX2DEC(MID((DEC2HEX(ABS(**H3**),8)),7,2)),".".",HEX2DEC(MID((DEC2HEX(ABS(**H3**),8)),5,2)),".",HEX2DEC(MID((DEC2HEX(ABS(**H3**),8)),3,2)),".",HEX2DEC(MID((DEC2HEX(ABS(**H3**),8)),1,2)))

The IP address is displayed in dotted-decimal format.

Using the CAR Tool

CDR Analysis and Reporting (CAR), an application bundled with CallManager and installed via plugin (**Application > Install Plugins > CDR Analysis and Reporting**), is a powerful tool for use by system administrators, managers, and end users to run reports on CDR data. This plugin needs to be installed only for use on Publisher, because it ties directly to the CDR database. CallManager documentation effectively explains CAR's installation and functionality, so the focus in this section is on detailing potential pitfalls in the installation process and highlighting a few of the reports that can be generated.

CAR can be a CPU-intensive application. Because it runs on the Publisher, you should run reports at off-peak usage hours; by default, report generation is set for midnight. Other events also might be running during those off-hours, including CDR deletion, so you should make sure that reports run not just during low CPU usage times but also before any records might be deleted. CDR deletion is covered in Table 11-2.

System administrators, managers, and individual users can access CAR by logging on to http://*CallManagerNameOrIPAddress*/art/Logon.jsp. If you want to provide access to CAR for managers and users, be sure to make the CAR URL known to them. System administrators can also access CAR by selecting **Programs > Cisco CallManager 4.0 > Cisco Service Configuration > Tools > CDR Analysis and Reporting**. Which reports each group of users can access is determined by the user information in the directory (**User > Global Directory**). For example, managers can access individual, department, and Top *N* usage reports; individual users can access their own call billing and quality of service reports only. System administrators can access all reporting and configuration functions in CAR.

Configure CDR Load Settings for Times When CallManager Resources Are Most Available (Midnight Daily by Default)

After the settings in Table 11-1 have been established to start collecting CDR data, ensure that the CAR Load settings correspond to times when CallManager is under the lightest load (preferably nonproduction hours). The CAR Load settings determine how frequently

CAR receives new data from the CDR database. Figure 11-4 shows the CDR Load page with the default values (**System > Scheduler > CDR Load**). By default, CAR loads CDRs every 24 hours at midnight. If you specify a different time, you need to restart the CAR Scheduler service for the change to take effect immediately (**System > Control Center**); if you do not restart, the change takes effect at midnight.

Figure 11-4 *CDR Load Page in CAR*

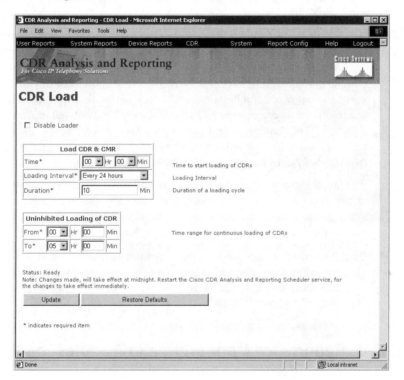

| WARNING | Loading CDR data into CAR can be a CPU-intensive process, especially when thousands or even millions of records must be manipulated. Use caution when deciding the interval, duration, and time of day to run the CDR loading process. Other events such as backups and CDR deletion can potentially load the system at the same time. Make sure that the times you choose to run these three activities do not unnecessarily load the CallManager system. Use tools such as the Real-Time Monitoring Tool (**CallManager Serviceability > Tools > Real-Time Monitoring Tool**) or Microsoft Performance (**Start > Programs > Administrative Tools > Performance**) to monitor CallManager load. |

Avoid Common Installation Pitfalls

Installing CAR is a relatively straightforward process, but certain pitfalls exist:

- During installation, you are prompted to enter the CallManager password phrase. Although the installation would continue without it, the resulting reports produced by CAR will have no data, because database reads cannot occur unless you enter the correct password phrase. Be sure to provide the same password phrase you used when installing CallManager.

- After the basic installation finishes, the only tricky part is getting the administration rights correct. When CAR starts the first time, a unique, one-time username/password combination must be entered to gain temporary administrative rights so that permissions to current CallManager users can be set for subsequent logins. The initial username/password combination works only for the first login after installation. Therefore, be sure that other users have already been entered into the CallManager database (**CallManager Administration > User > Add a New User**), and set permissions for the appropriate user(s) in CAR before exiting CAR for the first time (**System > System Parameters > Admin Rights**).

  The initial login combination is username **admin** and password **admin**. Be sure to configure access rights for additional users during your first CAR session. After the administrators have been chosen from the **Admin Rights** tab and set via the **Update** button, the initial password combination no longer functions.

- Configure dial plan information, gateway information, and mail server parameters. Gateway parameter information is needed for any gateway-related report, so at least complete those settings after logging into CAR with a valid administrative user chosen for CAR.

Standard CAR Reports for Monitoring and Troubleshooting

The following is a summary of reports that CAR can generate:

- Billing (Individual/Department)
- Top *N* (Charge/Duration/# of Calls)
- IPMA (Manager/Assistant Usage)
- CTI Application User
- Cisco IP Phone Services
- Quality of Service (Detail/Summary/Gateway/Call Type)
- Traffic Information (Extension/Summary)
- Malicious Call Details

- Precedence Call Summary
- System Overview
- CDR Errors
- Gateway (Detail/Summary/Utilization)
- Route Plan (Route and Line Group, Route/Hunt List, Route Pattern/Hunt Pilot Utilization)
- Conference Bridge (Details/Utilization)
- Voice Messaging Utilization

In addition to these reports, you can use CAR to perform CDR searches and exports of the CDR database. Also, you can schedule automatic report generation. Reports can be output in comma-separated file format (*.csv), which can be imported into Microsoft Excel. Reports can be exported to Adobe Acrobat (*.pdf) for later review. Restrictions exist on the number of records in the report by type: 5000 records for an Acrobat file and 20,000 records for a comma-separated file format.

Examine Weekly and Monthly Utilization Reports

Reports such as Gateway Utilization and Voice Messaging Utilization, which are discussed next, provide a view into the current usage of your CallManager deployment and help you plan load sharing across a CallManager system. This is useful information that helps you make informed decisions about gateway or voice mail additions or upgrades. This can be taken further for conferencing resources, overall traffic, precedence calling, and so forth. Running an automatic monthly system overview gives you insight into the overall CallManager operation. Tracking more specific components of the system is especially useful when you're tracing or troubleshooting issues.

Run Weekly Gateway Utilization Reports to Monitor Usage on Gateways That Connect to the PSTN

The gateway utilization report provides an excellent estimate of trunk port utilization. The report can be run by the hour of the day, day of the week, or day of the month for a specified time period. This report can be run for a single gateway or for all selected gateways. The route pattern can be specified, so busy gateways can be further identified by the called number. Even the specific gateway model can be specified.

Gateways connect to the PSTN and provide access to the outside world. Line charges associated with the PSTN make tracking gateways the single most important point in a deployment to control ongoing costs. You should run the Gateway Utilization report weekly on gateways that connect to the PSTN to establish which gateways in which locations are most utilized, and to determine which dial patterns are most common. Reports like this can be generated weekly and automatically mailed in Acrobat format to a specific user or internal mail alias (**Report Config > Automatic Generation/Alert**). Configure mail account settings under **System > System Parameters > Mail Parameters**.

Run Weekly Voice Messaging Utilization Reports to Check for Oversubscription

The Voice Messaging Utilization report provides multiple views of the amount of use in a given hour, day of the week, or day of the month for a specific time period. Additional parameters include the specific dialed number and the virtual messaging port.

Busy voice messaging ports can lead to intermittent message waiting indicators (MWI) and, more importantly, calls not being answered by the messaging system. Reports like this can help you determine when you need to add more voice messaging ports. You can set CAR to generate the Voice Messaging Utilization report weekly and automatically mail it in Acrobat format to a specific user (**Report Config > Automatic Generation/Alert**).

Track Individual Usage Patterns via CAR

You can track users by charge information, number of calls placed, and duration of calls and use these reports to identify individuals who do the bulk of the work, or who are potentially abusing the system. Managers can run reports about their employees' usage and track the QoS on those calls. Even end users can track their own billing information with a valid CallManager login and device association through CAR. For the calls to have a cost value associated with them, you need to provide call configuration details for call duration, time of day, and voice quality variables (**Report Config > Rating Engine > Duration** and **Time of Day** and **Voice Quality**).

Figure 11-5 shows a simple CDR search by user extension of extension 1003. Media information is displayed, along with a link to dump the entire contents of each specific record.

Track Quality of Service via CAR

Quality of service tracking is without a doubt one of the highlights of CAR. Service tracking can be as granular as creating a QoS report for a single user or can be broadened to list the percentage of all calls that meet a predetermined set of QoS specifications. You can also run a systemwide report on all calls that grades the call quality and graphs the results. The Define Quality of Service page (**Report Config > Define QoS**), shown in Figure 11-6, allows you to set the parameters for the systemwide report. The other reports use an introductory screen to get the parameters. As discussed earlier, you should tune these QoS parameters for typical calls on your network, because each network has a different baseline.

Figure 11-5 *CDR Analysis and Reporting Search by User Extension*

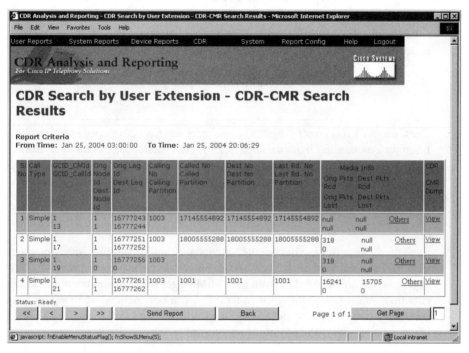

Figure 11-6 *CDR Analysis and Reporting QoS Definitions*

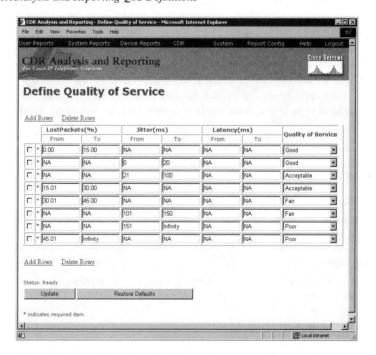

Third-Party CDR Applications

The Cisco AVVID Partner Program tests interoperability between Cisco networking solutions and third-party applications to ensure a high measure of success when deploying both. Table 11-17 lists the call accounting and billing participants in the AVVID Partner Program as of early 2004. You can check the AVVID Partner Program home page on Cisco.com for the latest list of partners participating in the program.

TIP   The Cisco AVVID Partner Program has partners that have developed interoperable packages for unified messaging, IP phone applications, call centers, voice endpoints, and much more, in addition to the call accounting and billing discussed in this chapter. Go to http://www.cisco.com/go/partners, and follow the links to the Cisco AVVID Partner Program for more information.

Each third-party package has unique functionality and capabilities, many of which overlap with the features of other packages listed. Some select packages support the ability to aggregate not only CDR data from the CallManager environment but also additional CDR data from an existing TDM voice system. This can be beneficial when you're attempting to correlate new IP telephony deployment data with shared trunk usage on a legacy PBX, or when you're showing the potential lack of trunk usage because of the newfound benefits of IP telephony.

Keep in mind that the CallManager version number is very much tied to the third-party solution. Multiple factors, including the format of the database, must match between the third-party and CallManager systems for a successful integration. When CallManager adds new fields, the third-party application must be able to process the new data. See Table 11-5 earlier in the chapter for the most recent set of changes in CallManager release 4.0(1). If you're interested in learning more about the solutions discussed in Table 11-17, you should contact the appropriate companies directly to ensure that the versions you're planning to deploy have been tested and do indeed interoperate with the version of CallManager you're running.

Table 11-17 *CDR Partners in the AVVID Partner Program*

Product	Company
CommView Call accounting and billing; real-time analysis for endpoints, trunks, fraud, or departments	**@Comm** http://www.atcomm.com
AlwinPro Call accounting and billing, telecommunication cost inspection and analysis	**aurenz** http://www.aurenz.com

Table 11-17 *CDR Partners in the AVVID Partner Program (Continued)*

Product	Company
Avotus Enterprise/Professional Call accounting and billing, CDR and CMR data processing, copies CDR data to the local database	**Avotus** http://www.avotus.com/cisco
ECLIPSE III Call accounting and billing, managed service specialty, response reporting	**Data Track** http://www.dtrack.com
Infortel for Windows Call accounting and billing, law firm and lodging specialty, web interface, auto scheduler	**ISI** http://www.isi-info.com
MEIPS Call accounting and billing, CDR and CMR data processing, web-based, cross-VPN billing	**MIND CTI** http://www.mindcti.com
TABS.IT Call accounting and billing for IP telephony, calling card, cell phone, and pagers	**MTS IntegraTRAK** http://www.mtsint.com
Sigma-5 Call accounting and billing for single or multitenant, trend analysis, volume billing	**NEVOTEK** http://www.nevotek.com
Revolution Shadow with Winlink Call accounting and billing, alarm monitoring and logging, unlimited database size, charge-back	**RSI** http://www.telecost.com
Soft-ex Telephony Manager Call accounting and billing, CDR and CMR data processing, combined QoS charts/reports	**Soft-ex Communications** http://www.soft-ex.net
Tiger 2020 Pro Call accounting and billing, hacking and malicious call tracing, alarm on exceptions	**Tiger Communications** http://www.tigercomms.com
eCAS Call accounting and billing outsourced or in-house, web-based, search, system alarms	**Veramark** http://www.veramark.com

Summary

This chapter went into detail on how to use and translate CDR data generated in the CallManager cluster for tracing individual calls or for tracking an entire deployment. Many aspects of CDR functionality were covered:

- Enabling the collection of CDR data
- Setting service parameters to tune the system
- Exporting data from the CDR database
- Installing and using the CAR tool

Because the CDR capabilities native to CallManager might not satisfy your particular requirements, additional applications from other vendors have been identified. Third-party applications offer a myriad of choices. The AVVID Partner Program offers reassurance that the choice you make has seen some level of interoperability testing and can be deployed with confidence.

Use CDR data as an additional tool in your bag of troubleshooting tricks. Although CDR information might not locate the exact cause of a specific problem, it often can be used to tie a general symptom to a specific network issue. CDR data can be used to uncover these types of events and more:

- Down or oversubscribed gateway
- Voice mail port exhaustion
- Lack of proper QoS settings in a router or switch
- Poor dial plan design

All this goes a long way beyond the traditional use of billing data.

## CHAPTER 12

Managing and Monitoring the System

This chapter discusses the various management and monitoring tools available in a Cisco CallManager environment and how they should be configured and used to best maintain the system's health.

CallManager offers tight integration with Windows operating system (OS) monitoring tools such as the Event Viewer and Microsoft Performance (formerly known as Performance Monitor). In addition, CallManager provides the tools necessary to create a management environment outside the Windows OS through the use of syslog, Simple Network Management Protocol (SNMP), and the Real-Time Monitoring Tool, discussed in Chapter 13, "Using Real-Time Monitoring Tool."

This chapter explains the different management and monitoring facilities available in a Cisco IP Telephony environment so that you can devise a methodology that suits your environment.

This chapter covers the following management tools:

- Authentication, Authorization, and Accounting (AAA)
- Syslog
- Windows event subsystem (Event Viewer)
- SNMP
- Microsoft Performance
- Serviceability Reports Archive
- CallManager trace facility
- Windows Terminal Services
- Virtual Network Computing (VNC)

Because every installation is different, it's impossible to paint a picture of the perfect management environment. Any attempt at creating a fixed set of rules would serve only certain installations. By the end of this chapter, you will have a real sense of what's possible, and you'll understand how to fit the various tools into your particular implementation.

It's also worth noting that there's a fine line between management, monitoring, and troubleshooting. Although the facilities covered in this chapter address some aspects of troubleshooting, that is not the main focus of this chapter. For the definitive guide to Cisco IP Telephony troubleshooting, pick up a copy of *Troubleshooting Cisco IP Telephony* from Cisco Press (ISBN 1-58705-075-7).

Choosing the Best Overall Methodology

There are several ways to get the most out of managing the system:

* Host-based monitoring
* Tool-based monitoring
* Collecting only what you need
* Using what you have

Host-Based Monitoring

The host-based monitoring methodology focuses on tools available in the operating system for monitoring and management. Administrators manually check the various servers for events and performance information or have automated processes send the information to the administration team through e-mail.

Tools such as the Windows Event Viewer, Microsoft Performance, Windows Terminal Services, HP Insight Manager, and IBM Director are common in this type of environment. If you work in an organization that often uses these tools, CallManager fits right into this model, because its processes all leverage the Windows Event Viewer and expose numerous Microsoft Performance objects.

If you're running a simple two-machine CallManager cluster, managing the servers within the telecommunications staff, or working in a small organization, the host-based monitoring methodology is probably a good fit. CallManager can be configured to send all events and alarms to the Windows Event Viewer, providing a central repository of all events.

However, if a server management team is managing CallManager in a midsized or large organization, host-based monitoring is generally a poor method of management and monitoring and is unlikely to fit with the existing management scheme. Most large organizations have a Network Operations Center (NOC) with syslog servers and SNMP monitoring stations, and those tools are more applicable.

Tool-Based Monitoring

Most midsized or large organizations tend to rely on a couple of management tools to manage their networks, such as HP Openview, CiscoWorks, Tivoli, or Spectrum. These tools use standards-based protocols for their operation, such as syslog, SNMP, RADIUS, and TACACS+.

CallManager is also at home in these environments. Simply point your management tool to the addresses of the CallManager servers and IOS gateways, and you can monitor them. To make your experience more fruitful, however, it's important to follow the detailed configuration information presented later in this chapter.

Collect Only What You Need

The conventional wisdom is that more is better. Some organizations have so many tools collecting so much information that they are awash in data. However, as some of your college professors might have told you, "Data isn't information; it's just data." Leaving every logging level at the most detailed, enabling every SNMP trap, and generating every syslog message won't help you as much as you think.

In fact, the only upside of having all this information is that if you need to do a postmortem on a problem, you will probably have the information you need. The issue with having that much information is finding what you need when you need it. In addition, the primary purpose of monitoring and management is to *avert* disaster—not react to it after it happens.

The best practice is to log only what you need. Perhaps in the beginning of a deployment, having logging levels set to very detailed is good, but as soon as the environment is stable, it's important to scale back the amount of management data the system generates.

Use What You Have

Most organizations try to fit CallManager into their existing management systems, which is probably the best approach. CallManager provides all the facilities necessary to fit into just about any environment. You should not put any unapproved agents on the CallManager servers, such as backup agents, Tivoli agents, and Microsoft Operations Manager agents.

WARNING   NetIQ Vivinet agents, HP Openview agents, and Integrated Research Prognosis are supported on earlier CallManager servers, such as 3.x, however, these tools must be approved by Cisco for each new major release of CallManager. Be sure to check with your software provider before installing any software on the CallManager servers.

Make Monitoring a Daily Process

It's critical to establish a daily process that telecom administrators or the NOC must use to ensure the system's health. The problem with most forms of management is that few organizations actually examine—on a regular basis—the data gathered in daily monitoring.

Systems all over the network could be generating log files, performance data, and statistics, but it takes a procedure and a commitment to analysis to ensure that the data is made useful.

Use the information in this chapter to decide what you want to log, and then assign someone to monitor and interpret the data. Most systems can put the data right at an administrator's fingertips. For example, syslog and Event Viewer data can be delivered via e-mail, real-time alerts can be delivered via pager, and SNMP utilization reports can be delivered via e-mail and the web. It's just a matter of interpreting the data to discover the system's overall health.

Configuring Authentication, Authorization, and Accounting on Cisco IOS Gateways

This section covers Authentication, Authorization, and Accounting (AAA) functions of Cisco IOS as they relate to voice services. Most IP Telephony networks use Cisco routers for gateway services somewhere in the network. Hence, AAA is relevant and should be considered a requirement.

Although the network is converged, many telecom and IT departments are not. Often, the routers containing the voice interfaces are actually managed by data support staff, because those routers might already be supplying the data service at a particular site. This presents a big problem for voice support people who need to gather statistics or troubleshoot voice features and cards in these devices. Most router administrators do not want lots of people accessing their devices.

AAA addresses these concerns. All Cisco routers employ an AAA feature set that allows the router administrator to delegate, authorize, and track access to the devices by different support personnel.

This section is not intended to be a complete guide to AAA. However, it tells you where the technology applies in the overall voice management infrastructure and how best to deploy it. There's a good possibility that your data networking equipment is already AAA-enabled.

TIP Ask your network administrators if they have Cisco Secure Access Control Server (ACS). If they do, they can provide you with a URL and a login ID. In addition, they can set up ACS by using the instructions in this chapter. Furthermore, they can provide you with read-only access to authentication and accounting records on the Cisco Secure ACS server should you need them to audit an IOS gateway problem. If you are setting up Cisco Secure

ACS yourself, you should read the Secure ACS for Windows Server documentation, found at the following link:

http://www.cisco.com/univercd/cc/td/doc/product/access/acs_soft/csacs4nt/acs32/index.htm

Choose the Right AAA Protocol

The two main AAA protocols are Remote Authentication Dial-In User Service (RADIUS) and Terminal Access Controller Access Control System Plus (TACACS+). Both have been around for quite some time, and they share many of the same conventions. They are simply protocols that allow a device such as a router to send AAA requests to a central server to validate credentials and establish access to resources. Each protocol defines a set of attribute/value pairs used in various AAA activities.

Which protocol you use most likely depends on what your organization is already running. As mentioned, it's best to leverage what's already in place. In the absence of a standard, use TACACS+. All Cisco devices support it, and it provides more robust features than RADIUS offers.

Configure Cisco Secure ACS to Talk to CallManager's DC Directory

This section assumes that you have Cisco Secure ACS up and running. If you are not using Cisco Secure ACS or TACACS+, refer to your product's user manual to authenticate against a standard Lightweight Directory Access Protocol (LDAP). The following steps will surely be of help, even in a non-Cisco RADIUS-based environment such as Funk Software's Steel Belted RADIUS.

NOTE   The goal of using the DC Directory is to maintain a single name and password that voice personnel use to access CallManager and the associated Cisco IOS gateways. Using AAA is the only way to provide this functionality. The entire configuration shown in the following sections was done using Cisco Secure ACS version 3.2. If you are using a lower version, it's highly recommended that you upgrade to 3.2.

To maintain a single sign-on between multilevel administration-enabled CallManager systems and Cisco IOS gateways, Cisco Secure ACS needs to be configured to authenticate against the DC Directory running on CallManager. If you are running an Active Directory environment for CallManager Administration, this can be configured as well. For the purposes of illustration, a DC Directory implementation is detailed next. Systems that are not running MLA simply use the Windows password rather than DC Directory accounts for system management, so this procedure does not apply.

To set up ACS to communicate with DC Directory, follow these steps:

Step 1 Browse to the Cisco Secure ACS Admin page, and log in.

Step 2 Click **External User Databases**.

Step 3 Click **Database Configuration**.

Step 4 Click **Generic LDAP**.

Step 5 Click **Create New Configuration**.

Step 6 Choose the name you just created, and click **Configure** in the **External User Database Configuration** box.

Step 7 The **Domain Filtering** box should remain at the default.

Step 8 The **Common LDAP Configuration** box should be configured as shown in Figure 12-1.

Figure 12-1 *FACS Generic LDAP Configuration*

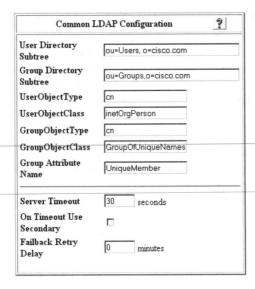

Step 9 The **Primary LDAP Server** should be configured as shown in Figure 12-2, except you should enter your own CallManager Publisher's IP address.

Figure 12-2 *ACS Primary LDAP Server Configuration*

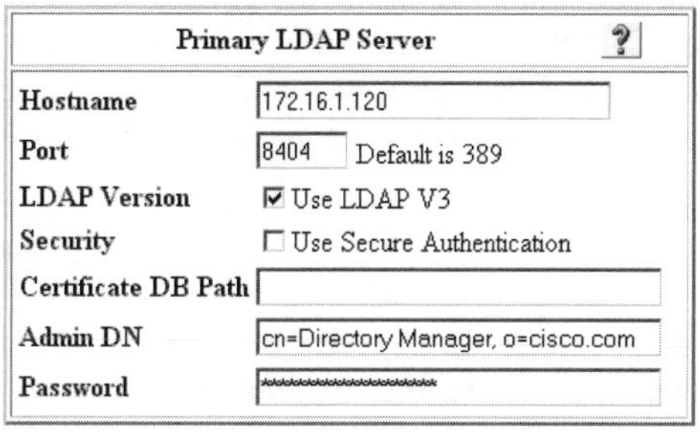

Primary LDAP Server	?
Hostname	172.16.1.120
Port	8404 Default is 389
LDAP Version	☑ Use LDAP V3
Security	☐ Use Secure Authentication
Certificate DB Path	
Admin DN	cn=Directory Manager, o=cisco.com
Password	*************

Baseline AAA Configuration

To enable AAA, the following IOS commands are necessary. In the following commands, replace *ip_address* with the IP address of the TACACS+ or RADIUS server and *private_key* with the private key configured in the TACACS+ or RADIUS server.

```
aaa new-model
```

For TACACS+:

```
tacacs-server host ip_address
tacacs-server key private_key
```

For RADIUS:

```
radius-server host ip_address
radius-server key private_key
```

These commands are the prerequisite for all AAA-related commands that follow.

NOTE   Although all configurations listed in the next sections use IOS, Catalyst 6500 switches are often used in IP Telephony implementations. For instructions on how to configure AAA and syslog on Catalyst 6500 devices, see the "Configuring TACACS+, RADIUS, and Kerberos on Cisco Catalyst Switches" document at the following link or by searching Cisco.com for "Configuring TACACS+ RADIUS Kerberos Catalyst.":

http://www.cisco.com/en/US/tech/tk583/tk642/technologies_tech_note09186a00800
94ea 4.shtml

Configure Authentication to Limit and Track Access

By default, Cisco routers use a simple password scheme and do not require usernames. A level 0 password and a level 15 "enable" password are local to the device. This is generally not very secure and cannot be logged.

By configuring AAA authentication and pointing to an authentication server, such as Cisco Secure ACS, you can control access to the gateway device using the CallManager DC Directory, Active Directory, Windows Domain, or SecurID password. Using external databases minimizes the number of passwords that a user must remember. This chapter focuses on the use of the built-in CallManager DC Directory as configured in the preceding section.

TACACS+ Configuration

In the following commands, replace *ip_address* with the IP address of the TACACS+ or RADIUS server and *private_key* with the private key configured in the TACACS+ or RADIUS server. Example 12-1 shows the minimum TACACS+ configuration.

Example 12-1 *Minimum TACACS+ Configuration*

```
tacacs-server host ip_address
tacacs-server key private_key
aaa new-model
aaa authentication login GATEWAY group tacacs+ local
line vty 0 4
    login authentication GATEWAY
```

This configuration tells the router in question to use the TACACS+ protocol to authenticate users requesting access to log in to the system through the Telnet interface. The **local** parameter at the end of the fourth line signifies that if the TACACS+ server isn't available, a password stored locally on the router should be used. It's *critical* that you provide this failsafe mechanism.

RADIUS Configuration

Example 12-2 shows the minimum RADIUS configuration. In the following commands, replace *ip_address* with the IP address of the RADIUS server and *secret_passphrase* with the secret password phrase configured in the RADIUS server.

Example 12-2 *Minimum RADIUS Configuration*

```
radius-server host ip_address
radius-server key secret_passphrase
aaa new-model
aaa authentication login GATEWAY group radius local
line vty 0 4
    login authentication GATEWAY
```

This configuration is essentially the same as TACACS+, except that the RADIUS protocol is used. Using **debug** commands on the router, you can see that requests are made to the server when a login is attempted, as shown in Example 12-3.

Example 12-3 debug radius *Output Displays Requests Made to the Server During Login Attempts*

```
voice-gw2#debug radius
Radius protocol debugging is on
Radius protocol brief debugging is off
Radius protocol verbose debugging is off
Radius packet hex dump debugging is off
Radius packet protocol debugging is on
Radius packet retransmission debugging is off
Radius server fail-over debugging is off
voice-gw2#debug aaa authentication
AAA Authentication debugging is on
*Mar  1 00:57:13.379: AAA/AUTHEN/LOGIN (00000010): Pick method list 'RADIUS'
*Mar  1 00:57:13.379: RADIUS/ENCODE(00000010): ask "Username: "
*Mar  1 00:57:13.383: RADIUS/ENCODE(00000010): send packet; GET_USER
*Mar  1 00:57:15.082: RADIUS/ENCODE(00000010): ask "Password: "
*Mar  1 00:57:15.082: RADIUS/ENCODE(00000010): send packet; GET_PASSWORD
*Mar  1 00:57:16.320: RADIUS(00000010): sending
*Mar  1 00:57:16.320: RADIUS(00000010): Send Access-Request to 172.16.1.238:1645
   id 11, len 76
*Mar  1 00:57:16.320: RADIUS:  authenticator 31 01 B4 C7 B8 1E A9 CE - 14 B4 67
   59 5C 36 04 63
*Mar  1 00:57:16.320: RADIUS:  User-Name         [1]   7   "sully"
*Mar  1 00:57:16.320: RADIUS:  User-Password     [2]   18  *
*Mar  1 00:57:16.324: RADIUS:  NAS-Port          [5]   6   67

*Mar  1 00:57:16.324: RADIUS:  NAS-Port-Type     [61]  6   Virtual
        [5]
*Mar  1 00:57:16.324: RADIUS:  Calling-Station-Id [31]  13  "172.16.1.16"
*Mar  1 00:57:16.324: RADIUS:  NAS-IP-Address    [4]   6   172.16.1.234

*Mar  1 00:57:16.536: RADIUS: Received from id 21645/11 172.16.1.238:1645,
   Access-Accept, len 57
```

As you can see from Example 12-3, the user authentication request was passed to the RADIUS server and accepted. This example does not show that the Cisco Secure ACS Server running the RADIUS protocol actually passed the credentials supplied by the user to the CallManager DC Directory.

Configure Authorization to Limit Allowable Commands

Although authentication controls who has access to a device, authorization controls what that person can do after being logged in. This is extremely important, because you might have networking administrators who don't want the telecom staff to configure the data-specific configuration tasks, and vice versa. Cisco Secure ACS allows specific voice-related commands to be authorized for specific groups of individuals, as demonstrated in Example 12-4.

Example 12-4 *Configuring Authorization to Limit Allowable Commands*

```
aaa authorization commands 1 GATEWAY group tacacs+ local
aaa authorization commands 15 GATEWAY group tacacs+ local
line vty 0 4
 password 7 110A1016141D
 authorization commands 1 GATEWAY
 authorization commands 15 GATEWAY
 login authentication GATEWAY
```

To configure Cisco Secure ACS to authorize only certain commands, follow this procedure:

Step 1   Step 1.Click **Shared Profile Components**.

Step 2   Click **Shell Command Authorization Sets**.

Step 3   Click **Add**.

Step 4   In the **Name** field, enter **VoiceCommands**.

Step 5   Click the **Deny for the Unmatched Commands** button.

Step 6   In the box above the grayed out Add Command button, enter **show**.

Step 7   In the box to the right, enter the following lines:

```
permit call
permit dialplan
permit dial-peer
permit controllers
permit ephone
permit ephone-dn
permit gateway
```

```
                    permit h323
                    permit mgcp
                    permit num-exp
                    permit tdm
                    permit translation-rule
                    permit voice
                    permit voip
```

Step 8   Click **Submit**.

To establish a group for all voice administrators, follow these steps:

Step 1   Click **Group Setup**.

Step 2   Select any unused group from the drop-down box.

Step 3   Click **Rename**.

Step 4   Enter **VoiceAdmins**, and click **Submit**.

Step 5   Click **Edit Settings**.

Step 6   Scroll to the heading **Shell Command Authorization Set**.

Step 7   Select **VoiceCommands**.

Step 8   Click **Submit and Restart**.

If you attempt to log in as any user in the voice administrators group and try to enter commands that are not in the allowed list, you are denied authorization, as shown in Example 12-5.

Example 12-5 *Denial of Command Authorization*

```
Username: sully
Password:


voice-gw2>show ip route
Command authorization failed.


voice-gw2>show ip eigrp neighbors
Command authorization failed.


voice-gw2>show voice port summary
                                        IN      OUT
PORT      CH   SIG-TYPE    ADMIN OPER STATUS   STATUS   EC
========= == ============ ===== ==== ======== ======== ==
1/0/0     -- fxo-ls       up    dorm idle     on-hook  y
```

Example 12-5 *Denial of Command Authorization (Continued)*

```
1/0/1    --  fxo-ls    up    dorm idle     on-hook  y
1/1/0    --  fxs-ls    up    dorm on-hook  idle     y
1/1/1    --  fxs-ls    up    dorm on-hook  idle     y
```

As you can see, a voice-related command that was in the allowed commands list provides output, whereas the disallowed commands are denied.

Configure Accounting to Track Issued Commands

Being able to track administration activity on your Cisco IOS gateways is extremely important for auditing and troubleshooting. Without knowing what someone has done on the device and when it was done, troubleshooting becomes much more difficult.

From a security perspective, it's important to know if someone is reconfiguring your gateways and if he or she is doing it at an inappropriate time. Example 12-6 shows the IOS configuration to track administration activity.

Example 12-6 *Configuring a Gateway to Track Issued Administration Commands*

```
aaa accounting commands 0 GATEWAY start-stop group tacacs+
aaa accounting commands 1 GATEWAY start-stop group tacacs+
aaa accounting commands 15 GATEWAY start-stop group tacacs+
line vty 0 4
 password 7 110A1016141D
 authorization commands 1 GATEWAY
 authorization commands 15 GATEWAY
 accounting commands 0 GATEWAY
 accounting commands 1 GATEWAY
 accounting commands 15 GATEWAY
 login authentication GATEWAY
```

By default, Cisco Secure ACS doesn't track TACACS+ or RADIUS accounting or administration. To enable it, perform the following tasks:

Step 1   Click **System Configuration**.

Step 2   Click **Logging**.

Step 3   Click **CSV TACACS+ Accounting**.

Step 4   Check the **Log to CSV TACACS+ Accounting report** box.

Step 5   Click **Submit**.

Step 6   Click **CSV TACACS+ Administration**.

Step 7   Check the **Log to CSV TACACS+ Administration report** box.

Step 8   Click **Submit**.

To double-check that logging is working, Telnet to an IOS gateway and issue some commands. From there, follow these steps:

Step 1   Click **Reports and Activity**.

Step 2   Click **TACACS+ Administration**.

Step 3   Click **TACACS+ Administration active.csv**.

At this point, you should see a screen similar to Figure 12-3.

Figure 12-3   *TACACS+ Command Accounting Data in ACS*

Tacacs+ Administration active.csv									
Date ↓	Time	User-Name	Group-Name	cmd	priv-lvl	service	NAS-Portname	task id	NAS-IP-Address
08/30/2003	18:17:53	sully	VoiceAdmins	exit <cr>	0	shell	tty67	114	172.16.1.234
08/30/2003	18:17:41	scollora	Default Group	show privilege <cr>	1	shell	tty66	110	172.16.1.234
08/30/2003	18:17:08	sully	VoiceAdmins	enable <cr>	0	shell	tty67	113	172.16.1.234
08/30/2003	18:16:59	sully	VoiceAdmins	show controllers <cr>	1	shell	tty67	112	172.16.1.234
08/30/2003	18:16:44	scollora	Default Group	exit <cr>	0	shell	tty67	103	172.16.1.234
08/30/2003	18:15:57	scollora	Default Group	show <cr>	0	shell	tty66	107	172.16.1.234
08/30/2003	18:11:25	sully	VoiceAdmins	exit <cr>	0	shell	tty68	108	172.16.1.234
08/30/2003	18:11:16	sully	VoiceAdmins	enable <cr>	0	shell	tty68	106	172.16.1.234
08/30/2003	18:11:01	scollora	Default Group	write terminal <cr>	15	shell	tty66	93	172.16.1.234

Using Syslog to Monitor the System

This section covers the configuration and use of the syslog facility to isolate problems and monitor both the IOS gateway environment and CallManager.

The following sections describe syslog's basic operation. Syslog is an event-logging facility that reports system-level events. The syslog application operates through the use of facilities, severities, a common message format, clients, and servers.

Facilities

Syslog facilities comprise a number of reporting events. You can think of a syslog facility as a type of pipe through which different sources report events to a syslog server. The syslog server can be configured to handle events sent using a given facility in different ways. For example, you might want CallManager events to be placed in one file and Cisco IOS router events in another. You can configure the router to use a different syslog facility to facilitate this.

Severities

Syslog has eight levels of severity, as listed Table 12-1. Detailed explanations for the severities can be found in the Berkeley Software Distribution (BSD) syslog protocol in RFC 3164. You can find all RFCs online at http://www.isi.edu/in-notes/rfc*xxxx*.txt, where *xxxx* is the RFC number.

Table 12-1 *Syslog Severity Codes*

Numeric Code	Severity
0	Emergency: system is unusable
1	Alert: action must be taken immediately
2	Critical: critical conditions
3	Error: error conditions
4	Warning: warning conditions
5	Notice: normal but significant
6	Informational: informational messages
7	Debug: debug-level messages

Just as with facilities, the server can be configured to handle events with a certain severity in unique ways. For example, events with a severity of Emergency might spawn a process that generates a page to designated personnel's pagers, whereas Debug messages can simply be logged to a file. Event severities are most often hard-coded into applications themselves and generally cannot be configured.

Syslog Message Format

Although RFC 3164 defines the BSD syslog format, not every application and server conforms to the exact message format defined in the RFC. However, any given syslog message can be broken down and must contain some key information. For example, consider the following syslog message:

```
Aug 23 13:39:43 scollora-vpn 35: 20:12:18: %SYS-5-CONFIG_I: Configured from
   console by vty0 (172.16.1.16)
```

Let's break down this message by fields:

- **Aug 23 13:39:43**—The local date and time the message was received by the syslog server, based on the syslog server clock.

- **scollora-vpn**—The name of the host generating the message, as listed in the hosts database of the server or in DNS.

- **35**—The sequential numeric identifier inserted by the server. This number increments by 1 for each message generated by the server.

- **20:12:18**—The time on the device generating the message. CallManager, however, puts the time in this format: 22:24:14.653 UTC.

- **%SYS-5-CONFIG_I**—This field has three parts:

  - **SYS**—Generally the name of the application generating the message. For example, CCM_CALLMANAGER, CCM_TFTP, and CCM_TCD are just a few of the facility codes used by CallManager. In this case, SYS stands for system.

  - **5**—The message's severity, as discussed in Table 12-1. The possible values are 0 to 7.

  - **CONFIG_I**—The subapplication (or mnemonic) to SYS in this example. You can think of it as a CONFIG event in the SYS application.

- **Configured from console by vty0 (172.16.1.16)**—The event's actual text. This varies for every message and contains the information the software designer deemed pertinent.

Watch the Syslog Data Every Day

Part of the daily monitoring of the system should include a review of the syslog data from the day before. The importance of daily monitoring cannot be understated. This is a 10-minute process that can save a great deal of time and could alert you to potential problems before end users start complaining about them. CiscoWorks 24-hour reports contain all the syslog events generated from the day before. The later section "Use the CiscoWorks Syslog Service if Available" covers CiscoWorks in detail.

Determine the Right Logging Severity

The age-old question is how much do you log? There is no real best practice for this. It depends on disk space, processor load, and how much data you can parse.

Many administrators start by enabling debug-level severity logging, only to find that the staff can neither work through that much data nor draw any conclusions from it. One of the more useful things you could learn from Debug syslog messages is that a large number of phones are unregistering from CallManager. This could signify a server problem or a network failure. If you get a torrent of unregister messages, you know something's very wrong. However, other tools, such as the Real-Time Monitoring Tool (RTMT), generate notifications much more quickly than someone combing through a syslog file.

NOTE   Syslog information is generally not used for real-time reporting but rather as an event correlation tool. It is also used as a general health-checking mechanism through the use of daily monitoring of syslog events. It can be useful during troubleshooting as well, because it's generally a central repository for all events.

As a general recommendation, set the severity to Warning. By default, syslog reports events with the setting you've chosen and anything more severe. In other words, selecting Warning produces Emergency, Alert, Critical, and Error messages to the syslog server. This gives you enough information to start with, and then you can change the severity on a given server if needed during troubleshooting. The RTMT, which is covered in Chapter 13, "Using Real-Time Monitoring Tool," can be used to provide alerts via e-mail, whereas syslog is just a collection of information to be viewed later. Here's a good example of a way to correlate the tools discussed so far: A problem is reported, stating that for the past two hours, users have been unable to call certain numbers on the PSTN. Your search through the syslog data for your devices reveals a configuration change on an IOS gateway about 2 hours ago. From there, you can look at the TACACS+ Administration Activity Report on Cisco Secure ACS and determine who made the change and what changes were made.

Enable and Configure the CallManager Serviceability Alarm Subsystem for Syslog

To take advantage of syslog, you must enable it on the CallManager Serviceability Alarm Configuration page (**Alarm > Configuration >** *select a server* **> Cisco CallManager**), as shown in Figure 12-4.

Check the box for **Syslog Trace**, and change the **Alarm Event Level** to the desired setting. Then enter the IP address or host name of your syslog server, and click **Update**. If you do not specify a server name, all syslog messages are sent to localhost.

Figure 12-4 *CallManager Alarm Configuration Screen*

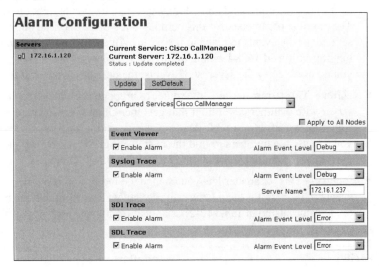

To apply this configuration to all the nodes in the cluster, check the **Apply to All Nodes** checkbox. In most cases, checking this checkbox is the desired setting unless you are troubleshooting a specific server.

Configure IOS Gateways for Syslog

To configure your Cisco routers for logging, enter the commands shown in Example 12-7. In the following commands, replace *syslog_level* with the numeric code that correlates to the severity level as shown in Table 12-1, replace *interface* with the router interface you want to be the source of syslog packets, and replace *ip_address_of_syslog_server* with the—you guessed it—IP address of the syslog server.

Example 12-7 *Cisco IOS Syslog Configuration*

```
logging trap syslog_level
logging source-interface interface
logging ip_address_of_syslog_server
```

Here are some of the command options you might include:

- **buffered**—In most instances, you want to buffer the messages at the router itself before sending them to the server. Buffering allows the administrator to troubleshoot directly on the console without having to look at the syslog server data. When used in conjunction with AAA as previously mentioned, buffering can be a powerful monitoring and troubleshooting tool. The router administrator can allow the telecom staff to use the command **show logging** to see the events right on the router console. The possible parameters for this command are the size of the buffer in bytes and the severity of the events to place in the buffer. An example of this command is **logging buffered 16384**, where the size is 16384 bytes and no severity is specified. If you do not specify the severity of events, the default is level 7, debugging.

- **count**—This parameter tells the router to prepend each message sent to the syslog server with a numeric identifier that gets incremented by 1 with every message. Counting is useful for troubleshooting when tracking a particular device in a large file; you can use the numbers to find the next event generated by any particular device. Turn on this feature by issuing the **logging count** command.

- **facility**—This parameter lets you change the facility used by the router to report events. The default is **local7**, the same as CallManager, but this can be modified to any of the values listed in Table 12-2. Change it from local7 only if you absolutely have to.

Table 12-2 *Syslog Facilities*

Facility	Description
auth	Authorization system
cron	Cron/at facility
daemon	System daemons
kern	Kernel
local0	Local use
local1	Local use
local2	Local use
local3	Local use
local4	Local use
local5	Local use
local6	Local use
local7	Local use
lpr	Line printer system
mail	Mail system
news	USENET news

Table 12-2 *Syslog Facilities (Continued)*

Facility	Description
sys10	System use
sys11	System use
sys12	System use
sys13	System use
sys14	System use
sys9	System use
syslog	Syslog itself
user	User process
uucp	UNIX-to-UNIX copy system

- **origin-id**—This parameter adds the hostname, IP address, or a custom text string to the syslog message. For example, entering **logging origin-id hostname** results in the following entry in the syslog file:

    ```
    Aug 25 09:32:57 voice-gw 62: Voice-GW: 2d16h: %SYS-5-CONFIG_I: Configured
        from console by vty1 (172.16.1.16)
    ```

    As you can see, the router inserts **62: Voice-GW**. You can also see that the particular syslog server in use prepends all messages with the date and the hostname of the system sending the message—in this case,
    Aug 25 09:32:57 voice-gw.

- **rate-limit**—This parameter keeps the server from being overloaded. In some cases, as when a port is flapping, the number of messages generated can be substantial. Also, when set to Debug level, syslog can be quite chatty. The setting you use depends on the number of devices sending data to your syslog server and the server's processor and disk speed. A sample command is **logging rate-limit 100**.

Configure a Linux-Based Syslog Server if Your Network Doesn't Have a Server

This section covers how to configure a Linux-based syslog server. These configurations were done on Red Hat 6.0, but other Linux implementations should be similar, if not exactly the same. Linux has the advantage of being low-cost, and it doesn't require fast hardware. The flip side is that you need someone who understands Linux to administer it. This might seem like a substantial amount of work, but it's actually quite simple to create a syslog server from a default Linux server.

The configuration of the syslog server allows you to assign different log files to different facility types. CallManager uses the facility **local7** when generating its messages.

Follow this generic procedure:

Step 1 Add the router or CallManager server names and IP addresses to DNS or /etc/hosts.

Step 2 Add the ability for syslog to receive events from remote hosts.

Step 3 Add the list of permitted hosts to the syslog command line.

Step 4 Edit the syslog configuration file to log events to a file.

If you're using a Linux-based syslog server, you need to edit the following files:

- /etc/hosts (if you're not using DNS)
- /etc/syslog.conf
- /etc/rc.d/init.d/syslog

Example 12-8 is a snippet of /etc/hosts from a Linux server running syslog. The highlighted section contains the hosts that need to be added to the system. If you use domain name service (DNS) and CallManager(s), and the gateways in use are listed in the DNS, this step is unnecessary.

Example 12-8 *Add Hosts to Your* /etc/hosts *File*

```
127.0.0.1                localhost localhost.localdomain
172.16.1.237             linux1.collora.com linux1
172.16.1.120             ccm1.collora.com ccm1
172.16.1.254             voice-gw.collora.com voice-gw
172.16.1.234             voice-gw2.collora.com voice-gw2
```

Example 12-9 is a snippet from the /etc/syslog.conf file, which contains the log files used for the various facilities mentioned earlier. CallManager uses **local7** as its facility. The asterisk (*) indicates all severities.

Example 12-9 *Editing Your* syslog.conf *File*

```
#/etc/syslog.conf
# Save boot messages also to boot.log
local7.*                                          /var/log/ccm1.log
local6.*                                          /var/log/local6.log
```

Linux systems do not allow remote hosts to send messages to the syslog service by default. The file in Example 12-10 is /etc/rc.d/init.d/syslog, which the system uses to start the syslog service every time the machine is booted. It's mandatory to add the **-r** parameter shown in Example 12-10, as well as the **-l** and the list of hosts with permission to send messages to the server. If this change isn't made, messages will not be placed in the log file.

Example 12-10 *Edit Your /etc/rc.d/init.d/syslog File to Allow Hosts to Send Messages*

```
# See how we were called.
case "$1" in
  start)
        echo -n "Starting system logger: "
        # we don't want the MARK ticks
        daemon syslogd -m 0 -r -l ccm1,voice-gw,voice-gw2
        echo
        echo -n "Starting kernel logger: "
        daemon klogd
        echo
        touch /var/lock/subsys/syslog
        ;;
```

After you have modified /etc/rc.d/init.d/syslog, to make your changes take effect, you must execute the command shown in Example 12-11, which restarts the syslog process. Example 12-11 shows the command and the output.

Example 12-11 *Restarting the Syslog Daemon*

```
[root@linux1 /etc]#/etc/rc.d/init.d/syslog restart
Shutting down kernel logger:                         [  OK  ]
Shutting down system logger:                         [  OK  ]
Starting system logger:                              [  OK  ]
Starting kernel logger:                              [  OK  ]
```

Example 12-12 shows some sample output from the /var/log/ccm1.log file generated by syslog. The lines are long and contain detailed information. The first three messages are generated by CallManager, but the highlighted message is generated by a Cisco router.

Example 12-12 *Example CallManager and IOS Router Syslog Output*

```
Aug 23 13:31:50 ccm1 313: Aug 23 20:32:25.421 UTC : %CCM_CALLMANAGER-CALLMANAGER
-6-StationAlarm: Station alarm. TCP ProcessID:1.100.117.58 Device Text:25: Name=
SEP003094C26716 Load=4.0(0.3) Last=Initialized Param1:2048 Param2:134287532 App
ID:Cisco CallManager Cluster ID:CCM1-Cluster Node ID:172.16.1.120

Aug 23 13:31:50 ccm1 314: Aug 23 20:32:25.436 UTC : %CCM_CALLMANAGER-CALLMANAGER
-6-DeviceRegistered: Device registered. Device name.:SEP003094C26716 Device IP
address.:172.16.1.8 Device type. [Optional]:7 Performance monitor object type:2
Device description [Optional].:Auto 2000 Load ID. [Optional]:P00304000003
Associated directory numbers. [Optional].:2000 App ID:Cisco CallManager Cluster
ID:CCM1
-Cluster Node ID:172.16.1.120

Aug 23 13:31:50 ccm1 315: Aug 23 20:32:25.483 UTC : %CCM_CALLMANAGER-CALLMANAGER
-6-DeviceDnInformation: Device DN information. Device Name:SEP003094C26716
Device type. [Optional]:7 Station Desc:Auto 2000 Station Dn:2000, App ID:Cisco
CallManager Cluster ID:CCM1-Cluster Node ID:172.16.1.120

Aug 23 13:39:43 voice-gw 35: 20:12:18: %SYS-5-CONFIG_I: Configured from console
by vty0 (172.16.1.16)
```

Use the CiscoWorks Syslog Service if Available

You might already have a CiscoWorks server on the network that manages all Cisco devices on the network. Cisco IOS gateways and CallManager can be also be set up in this tool.

CiscoWorks has a syslog server and analyzer built in, which means that rather than using a Linux-based syslog server, you can leverage functionality that provides advantages over basic syslog, such as the ability to create custom reports based on device and severity. For more information, see the Syslog Analysis document on the CiscoWorks Resource Manager Essentials web page at the following link or by searching Cisco.com for "CiscoWorks Resource Manager Essentials":

> http://www.cisco.com/en/US/products/sw/cscowork/ps2073/products_user_guide_
> chapter09186a008007fed6.html

CiscoWorks also allows the use of a separate server to receive syslog messages and send them to CiscoWorks. This is called the Remote Syslog Analyzer Collector (RSAC). You can find the installation guide at http://www.cisco.com/en/US/products/sw/cscowork/ps2073/products_installation_guide_chapter09186a008017b341.html or search Cisco.com for

"Installing the Remote Syslog Analyzer Collector." The RSAC also provides filtering capabilities that download from the central CiscoWorks server. The real purpose of the RSAC is to allow the CiscoWorks server to scale. Whether you need it depends on the size of your network and the number of syslog events your systems generate. If your CiscoWorks server starts to slow down considerably and your disk fills up quickly, it's probably best to use RSAC. It's hard to provide exact guidelines because every environment uses different hardware and memory for CiscoWorks.

To enable the use of the CiscoWorks syslog facility, refer to the earlier section "Enable and Configure the CallManager Serviceability Alarm Subsystem for Syslog." Use the IP address of the CiscoWorks host or the RSAC host, depending on what you're using.

As soon as data starts flowing to the CiscoWorks server, you can use the CiscoWorks web interface to sort syslog information and provide custom views. A sample report is shown in Figure 12-5.

Figure 12-5 *CiscoWorks Sample Syslog Report*

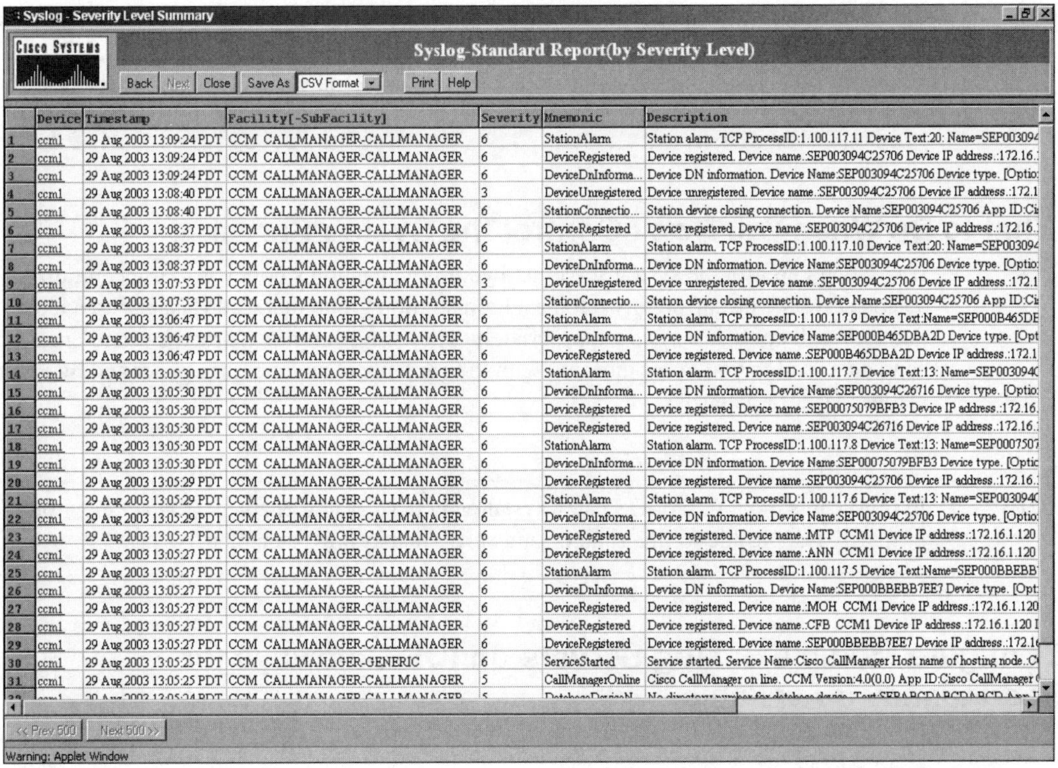

CiscoWorks also allows you to specify certain actions based on various syslog events. You configure these by browsing to the CiscoWorks web interface, logging in, and following this procedure:

Step 1 Click **Resource Manager Essentials > Administration > Syslog Analysis > Define Automated Action**.

Step 2 Click **Add**.

Step 3 Provide a name for the Action, such as **Page Staff**.

Step 4 Check the **Enable Action** box.

Step 5 Scroll to the desired message type, and click **Add**.

Step 6 In the **Command Line** box, enter the full pathname (or browse) to the file that you want to execute on receipt of the matching syslog message(s).

NOTE Most network management teams have preconfigured executable files you can use. This is common in the data networking world. Most NMS packages, such as Spectrum, HP Openview, and Tivoli, come with executables that can send e-mail to a pager. Check with your NOC.

What to Do When You Don't Control the Syslog Server

If you don't control the syslog server and your organization's policy is to use centralized syslog servers, you can simply tell the administration group that CallManager uses local7, and they will configure syslog appropriately. They can configure a process called cron to send an e-mail to you every morning with the contents of any message generated by CallManager or gateways.

NOTE In most cases, your Cisco IOS gateways already have syslog enabled. Contact the group primarily responsible for the routers, and verify that syslog is enabled.

Configure Multiple Syslog Servers on IOS Gateways for Redundancy if Available

Cisco routers support the reporting of events to more than one syslog server as shown in the highlighted portion of Example 12-13.

Example 12-13 *Adding a Second Syslog Server*

```
logging trap debugging
logging origin-id hostname
logging source-interface FastEthernet0/0
logging 172.16.1.237
logging 172.16.1.238
```

When multiple hosts have been configured, all messages simultaneously go to both syslog servers listed.

Unfortunately, since CallManager doesn't support the ability to send alerts to multiple syslog servers, you must choose one and configure it in the Alarm Configuration page in CallManager Serviceability (**Alarm > Configuration**). It's important to set up, configure, and maintain your syslog server to provide maximum availability. Any messages sent by CallManager when the syslog server is unavailable will be lost.

Use a Syslog Analyzer if You Can

Using a syslog analyzer is highly recommended. Analyzers break down the contents of a syslog file into more digestible parts, giving you a broader view of what's happening on CallManager and IOS gateways.

In addition, analyzers allow you to sort and change the view of the information. In its purest form, a syslog file is simply a list of events. For example, the analyzer lets you sort by date, severity, or server. Many packages offer preconfigured reports and let you define your own. They also offer additional functionality such as paging and e-mail notification.

One such analyzer is SyslogAnalyzer from eIQ Networks. More information can be found on the eIQ website: http://www.eiqnetworks.com/products/systemanalytics.shtml. The eIQ product supports both syslog and the Windows event subsystem, which is discussed in the next section.

Check the Windows Event Subsystem (Event Viewer)

Just as syslog was the original logging facility for UNIX-based systems, the Windows event subsystem and the associated Event Viewer came with Windows NT 3.x when it shipped from Microsoft in the early 1990s. Windows applications such as CallManager generate events to the subsystem, which in turn get divided into categories and presented in the Viewer.

The Event Viewer data is available only to administrators who have privileged access and require login to the Windows OS. There are cases in which Event Viewer data can prove valuable, such as when low-level application events keep processes from running or starting.

If you want to have a single place to log all events and you don't want to check both the Event Viewer and syslog, you can consolidate everything in the Event Viewer. To do this, you have to configure CallManager Serviceability not to use syslog at all. You do that by disabling syslog and making sure that the Event Viewer is enabled in the Alarm Configuration page in CallManager Serviceability (**Alarm > Configuration >** *click the server* **>** *click the service* **>** *uncheck the* **Enable Alarm** *checkbox under* **Syslog Trace**). After you have disabled syslog, all alarms are delivered only to the Event Viewer.

WARNING   Even though all four facilities can be enabled in the Alarm Configuration, CallManager reports alarms only to the facilities specified in the Routing List of each alarm definition (**Alarm > Definition**).

Figure 12-6 shows an alarm that went to Event Viewer after the preceding configuration steps were followed.

Figure 12-6   *Event Viewer Message Indicating Phone Status*

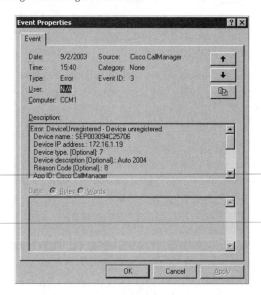

Syslog Versus Windows Event Viewer

In some cases, the Windows administration team at your organization treats CallManager servers as Windows servers and does not want to grant you access to the Windows OS itself—access that is necessary to view Event Viewer information.

A CallManager feature called multiple levels of administration (MLA) allows you to administer the system without requiring access to the Microsoft Windows OS. Many organizations have strict policies on local administrator access to Windows servers. Using syslog rather than Event Viewer adheres to those policies while providing real-time feedback from CallManager. The key is that there is still some data that you cannot see without full access to the Windows OS and the Event Viewer.

However, using syslog unifies the location of all events across the system of CallManager servers and gateways. This is a big advantage, especially when coupled with an analyzer, as mentioned previously in this chapter.

Using SNMP Where Possible

SNMP is a standards-based mechanism used to query devices for statistics. It also provides a facility called a *trap* to inform a network management station if certain faults occur.

Traps are designated using a set of identifiers contained in a Management Information Base (MIB). A *MIB* is a text file saved in a standard format that can be read by all SNMP management applications. MIBs can generally be downloaded from the vendors' websites. You can download the Cisco MIBs by browsing to http://www.cisco.com/go/mibs or to ftp:/ /ftp.cisco.com/pub/mibs/supportlists/callmanager/callmanager-supportlist.html for CallManager-specific MIBs.

SNMP relies on a set of passwords called *community strings* that define the capabilities of any particular entity. In general, entities can poll a device by using a community string associated with read-only access. Conversely, management stations can set attributes using a read-write community string.

Enable SNMP Support on CallManager

CallManager supports SNMP in a few different and important ways. The first is the ability for a CallManager server, as well as an IOS gateway, to appear on a standards-based SNMP management console such as HP Openview or Castle Rock Computing SNMPc. Many organizations have a 24/7 NOC always looking at the network using SNMP polling. When CallManager generates traps, the NOC is notified. NOC engineers can start the troubleshooting process by correlating the SNMP traps seen on the management console with other events on the network. Tools such as HP Openview give you a holistic view of the network that makes it easy to see the various devices that could be causing a particular problem.

SNMP is implemented on CallManager servers through the use of two Windows services called the SNMP Service and SNMP Trap Service. You need to configure these services to integrate into your management environment. Do the following:

Step 1   Click **Start > Programs > Administrative Tools > Services**.

Step 2   Double-click **SNMP Service**.

Step 3 On the **General** tab, change the **Startup Type** to **Automatic**.

Step 4 Click **Start** if the service is not already started.

Step 5 Make sure that the Cisco RIS Data Collector has been activated and is running by checking the Service Activation page in CallManager Serviceability (**Tools > Service Activation**).

The CallManager SNMP Agent requires RIS Data Collector to be activated, and populating the CISCO-CCM-MIB requires the RIS Data Collector to be started. You can start CallManager-related services in the Control Center in CallManager Serviceability (**Tools > Control Center**).

Choose Complex Community Strings

Do not use simple community strings that can be subject to dictionary attacks. Simple strings can lead to certain disaster if you are hacked. In fact, many organizations choose not to implement SNMP on their networks because of potential security vulnerabilities. If properly implemented, however, SNMP provides an excellent level of real-time information about the system in a secure fashion. The community strings should be a complex set of characters that have no pattern or linguistic order. (Figure 12-7 in the next section shows some examples of complex community strings.)

NOTE SNMP community strings are set during installation, but SNMP is not enabled by default. You must open the Services panel of Windows 2000 Administrative Tools and start the service (**Start > Programs > Administrative Tools > Services > SNMP Service**).

Open the SNMP Service Properties window to set the community strings:

Step 1 Click **Start > Programs > Administrative Tools > Services**.

Step 2 Double-click **SNMP Service**.

Step 3 On the **General** tab, change the Startup Type to **Automatic**.

Step 4 Click **Start** if the service is not already started.

Step 5 Click the **Security** tab.

Step 6 Click **Add**.

Step 7 Select **READ ONLY** from the Community rights list.

Step 8 Enter the desired community name, and click **Add**.

Step 9 Click **Add**.

Step 10 Select **READ-WRITE** from the **Community rights** list.

Step 11 Enter the desired community string, and click **Add**.

Step 12 Click **OK** or continue to the next section for instructions on how to limit the number of allowable hosts.

Limit Allowable Hosts

Few hosts in the network actually run any kind of SNMP software. They are limited to network management stations that generally have fixed IP addresses. Figure 12-7 shows a sample configuration for complex community strings and an allowed host.

Figure 12-7 *CallManager SNMP Service Configuration with Complex Community Strings*

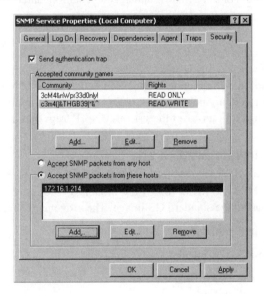

Perform the following tasks in the Security tab of the SNMP Service Properties window (**Start > Programs > Administrative Tools > Services** > *double-click* **SNMP Service** > *click the* **Security** *tab*).

Step 1 Click the **Accept SNMP packets from these hosts** button.

Step 2 Click **Add**.

Step 3 Enter the IP address of the host, and click **Add**.

Step 4 Repeat Steps 2 and 3 to add more hosts if necessary.

Step 5 Click **OK**.

Configure Trap Destinations

When traps occur, CallManager must know where to send them. You configure a trap destination through the SNMP Service with the following procedure:

Step 1   Click **Start > Programs > Administrative Tools > Services**.

Step 2   Double-click **SNMP Service**.

Step 3   Click the **Traps** tab.

Step 4   Enter the Community name, and click **Add to list**.

Step 5   In the **Trap destinations** box, click **Add**.

Step 6   In the **SNMP Service Configuration** popup window, enter the IP address of your SNMP management station, and click **Add**.

Step 7   Click **OK**.

Monitor for Traps

It's important that you monitor your SNMP console for traps generated by devices in the CallManager system, including call processing servers, application servers, and gateways. The following sections cover the various SNMP traps that are triggered.

HP Insight Agents Generate SNMP Traps

On all Media Convergence Servers (MCS) with the H designation, as well as older MCS-7825-1133 and MCS-7835-1266 models, Cisco installs and enables HP Insight Agents as part of the standard OS image. These agents include

- HP Insight Foundation Agents
- HP Insight NIC Agents
- HP Insight Server Agents
- HP Insight Storage Agents
- HP Insight Event Notifier

For more information about these HP Insight Agents, see the following links:

ftp://ftp.compaq.com/pub/products/servers/management/imaug.pdf

http://h18004.www1.hp.com/products/servers/management/cim7-intermediate.html

You can learn more about SNMP traps generated by the agents at the following link:

ftp://ftp.compaq.com/pub/products/servers/management/Agevents.pdf.

In addition to generating traps, the HP Insight Agents can be queried to gather server information. You can find the MIBs containing the object IDs in the \CNMS\MIBS directory on the HP Management CD that's included with every MCS H-designated server, as well as HP-branded Proliant servers.

Users with a large contingent of HP/Compaq servers can manage the CallManager servers using Compaq Insight Agents.

Traps in CISCO-CCM-MIB

By default, all traps are enabled with the exception of the ccmPhoneStatusUpdate and ccmPhoneFailed traps.

The following sections define traps in CISCO-CCM-MIB.

ccmCallManagerFailed Trap

The ccmCallManagerFailed notification signifies that the CallManager process detects a failure in one of its critical subsystems. It can also be detected from a heartbeat/event-monitoring process.

ccmPhoneFailed Trap

If ccmPhoneFailedTable has at least one entry, the ccmPhoneFailed notification generates at the interval specified in ccmPhoneFailedAlarmInterval. The ccmPhoneFailed trap is not enabled by default. To enable it, issue an SNMP set for the ccmPhoneFailedAlarmInterval object in seconds. After this is set, the CCM SNMP extension agent checks the ccmPhoneFailedTable for entries. If an entry exists, it triggers a trap at the interval specified in ccmPhoneFailedAlarmInterval as long as ccmPhoneFailedTable has at least one entry. The value stored in ccmPhoneFailedStorePeriod is the length of time in seconds that each entry in ccmPhoneFailedTable is stored. (The minimum and default is 1800.) In addition to knowing which phone's registration failed, you also have to do an SNMP get on ccmPhoneFailedTable.

ccmPhoneStatusUpdate Trap

If ccmPhoneStatusUpdateTable has at least one entry, the ccmPhoneStatusUpdate notification generates at the interval specified in ccmPhoneStatusUpdateAlarmInterv. The ccmPhoneStatusUpdate trap is not enabled by default in the MIB. To enable it, issue an SNMP set for the ccmPhoneStatusUpdateAlarmInterv object in seconds. After this is set, the CCM SNMP extension agent checks ccmPhoneStatusUpdateTable for entries. If an entry exists, it triggers a trap at the interval specified in ccmPhoneStatusUpdateAlarmInterv as long as ccmPhoneStatusUpdateTable has at least one entry. The value stored in ccmPhoneStatusUpdateStorePeriod is the length of time in seconds that each entry in ccmPhoneStatusUpdateTable is stored (the minimum and default is 1800). In addition to knowing which phone's status has changed, you have to do an SNMP get on ccmPhoneStatusUpdateTable, as shown in Figure 12-8.

ccmGatewayFailed Trap

The ccmGatewayFailed notification indicates that at least one gateway has attempted to register or communicate with CallManager and failed.

Figure 12-8 *SNMPc Management Console with Alarms and MIB Information for ccmPhoneStatusUpdate Trap*

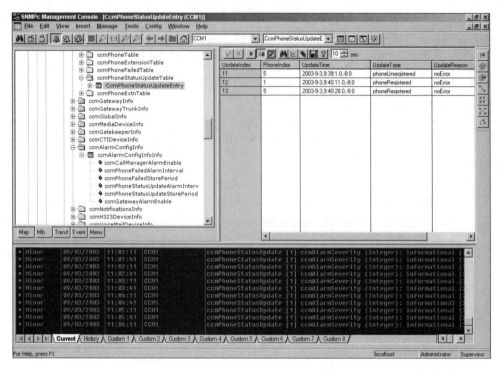

ccmMediaResourceListExhausted Trap

The ccmMediaResourceListExhausted notification indicates that CallManager has run out of the specified type of resource.

ccmRouteListExhausted Trap

The ccmRouteListExhausted notification indicates that CallManager could not find an available route in the specified route list.

ccmGatewayLayer2Change Trap

The ccmGatewayLayer2Change notification is sent when the D-channel/layer 2 of an interface in a Skinny gateway that has registered with CallManager changes state.

ccmQualityReport Trap

The ccmQualityReport notification is sent when a user presses the Quality Reporting Tool (QRT) softkey and submits a report.

ccmMaliciousCall Trap

The ccmMaliciousCall notification indicates that a user has triggered malicious call tracing by pressing the MCID softkey.

CCM Alarm Facility Traps

The following is a list of traps generated by the CallManager Serviceability Alarm Facility:

- **DeviceRegisteredAlarm**—This alarm indicates that a device successfully registered with CallManager. Assume that the device is in service.

- **DeviceUnregisteredAlarm**—This alarm indicates that a device that previously registered with CallManager has unregistered. This alarm may be issued as part of a normal unregistration event or for another reason, such as loss of KeepAlive messages.

- **DeviceTransientAlarm**—This alarm indicates that a connection was established and immediately dropped before completing registration. Incomplete registration might indicate that a device is rehoming in the middle of registration. The alarm could also indicate a device misconfiguration, a database error, or an illegal/unknown device trying to attempt a connection.

- **CallManagerFailure**—This alarm indicates that a failure occurred in the CallManager system.

- **MediaResourceListExhausted**—This alarm indicates that an available resource could not be found, as indicated by the device type in the specified media route list.

- **RouteListExhausted**—This alarm indicates that an available route could not be found in the specified route list.

- **DChannelISV**—This alarm indicates that the specified D-channel has gone into service.

- **DChannelOOS**—This alarm indicates that the specified D-channel has gone out of service.

- **MaliciousCall**—This alarm indicates that a malicious call has been detected in CallManager and that the Malicious Call Identification (MCID) feature has been invoked.

- **QRTRequest** (from the Cisco Extended Functions service)—This alarm indicates that a user has experienced a problem with a phone and has submitted a problem report by pressing the QRT softkey.

Use Microsoft Performance for Real-Time Data If It Fits Your Current Model

Microsoft bundles an application called Microsoft Performance (generally known as PerfMon) with Windows 2000. Windows applications, such as CallManager, expose various objects to PerfMon to provide visibility into application health.

Each server running CallManager maintains its own set of performance objects. Each server must be monitored individually.

Microsoft Performance does have a facility for generating alarms and logging information to disk, but the configuration must be replicated on every server, which can be a tedious process. PerfMon can also be configured on a central server, but you must change the PerfMon service user from Local System to a user with appropriate access rights on all the servers in question. This process is familiar to Microsoft-centric organizations. For organizations whose voice staff monitors the systems, it makes much more sense to access performance objects through the Real-Time Monitoring Tool, which is discussed in detail in Chapter 13.

TIP   Although using PerfMon as the main gauge of application health isn't the best practice, it can be useful in certain situations. For example, when you're troubleshooting specific problems, such as lack of bandwidth when using locations-based call admission control, it can sometimes be faster to launch either VNC or Terminal Services and view the PerfMon counter than to watch it in RTMT because of faster updates.

Check the Serviceability Reports Archive Every Day

The Serviceability Reports Archive (SRA) is a page in CallManager Serviceability (**Tools > Serviceability Reports Archive**) that shows the reports generated by the Cisco Serviceability Reporter service. The Serviceability Reporter takes the data collected by the Real-Time Information Service Data Collector (RISDC) and generates .PDF files that contain various reports.

Change Service Parameters if Applicable

Two service parameters control when the reports are generated and purged:

- RTMT Report Generation Time specifies the number of minutes after midnight (00:00hrs) when the RTMT reports are generated.
- RTMT Report Deletion Age is how many days elapse before reports are deleted.

The Acrobat files are stored in C:\CiscoWebs\Service\RTMTReports. Most reports are in the 50 to 150 KB range in terms of file size, so don't be afraid to increase the deletion time.

Check the CallManager Trace Facility Configuration and Log Files

The following sections describe best practices for the CallManager trace facility and how they relate to the overall management of the system. For an in-depth discussion of the trace facility, refer to *Troubleshooting Cisco IP Telephony: A Cisco AVVID Solution* from Cisco Press (ISBN 1-58705-075-7).

Don't Allow Files to Become Too Large

When configuring the trace facility in CallManager, it's important to avoid letting the files become too large. A file size of 250 to 500 KB is optimal when you'll be doing extensive troubleshooting across WAN links.

When files are larger than 500 KB, and you're accessing the server across a WAN link, VNC and Terminal Services can be used to view the log files on the server itself; however, you often have to send log files to the Cisco Technical Assistance Center (TAC) for analysis. In this case, having smaller files is helpful. The flip side is that there might be valuable data in more files, and you might have to search for it a little more diligently. Overall, it's best to leave the trace levels at the default and then change them when a potential problem arises. You must balance disk space against the potential problem of overwriting files on busy systems.

In many large environments, it's good to use a dedicated server to receive trace information if you're keeping the trace levels high. Using a dedicated server allows you to keep the log files for a much longer period of time. It also allows you to gather more detailed traces.

Another distinct advantage is the ability to integrate the trace server into your enterprise backup system. CallManager doesn't support the addition of backup agents such as Veritas, Legato, and Arcserve. However, placing the backup agent on the dedicated trace server lets you keep traces and back them up in case they're needed later. In many cases, trace files from the weeks before a problem occurred can be used to troubleshoot a current problem.

Simply find a Microsoft share point on the network and mount the drive from the CallManager system. From that point forward, set up the Trace facility to put files in that location (**CallManager Serviceability > Trace > Configuration**).

WARNING   When using a dedicated trace server, it's best to create a Windows user for the sole purpose of mounting the share. Be sure to lock down the user's security settings so that person can access the share and nothing else. Ensure that the Windows policy does not allow the user to log in locally. This keeps you safe in case the user account is compromised in any way.

If your CallManager servers do not participate in a Windows domain, be sure that the username that is used to mount the share exists on both systems and that the passwords are synchronized. This is important should CallManager or the trace server be rebooted. The share will automatically reconnect.

Using Windows Terminal Services

Terminal Services is an indispensable tool when running a CallManager system. It provides a way of getting local console access to any CallManager server from any location. This section describes how and when to use Terminal Services to manage and monitor the system.

Downloading the Remote Desktop Client

For all non-Windows XP operating systems, Microsoft's Remote Desktop Client can be downloaded from the following link:

http://www.microsoft.com/windowsxp/pro/downloads/rdclientdl.asp

For XP, go to

http://www.microsoft.com/windowsxp/pro/downloads/rdwebconn.asp

Even Macintosh users can connect via Terminal Services by using the client located at

http://www.microsoft.com/mac/downloads.aspx?pid=download&location=/mac/DOWNLOAD/MISC/RDC.xml&secid=80&ssid=9&flgnosysreq=True

When to Use Terminal Services

The best uses for Terminal Services are

- **Checking service activation at the OS level**—After an upgrade or patch, it's useful to make sure that the various CallManager services have actually started (**Start > Administrative Tools > Services**) and are not hung.

NOTE   To start or stop services, use the Control Center in CallManager Serviceability rather than the Windows Services administration.

- **Looking at CCM trace files locally**—In the midst of troubleshooting, you often are accessing CallManager over a slow link. Mounting the c$ file system and looking at the traces generally takes much longer than launching Terminal Services and looking at them locally.

Upgrades Are Not Supported via Terminal Services

Never try to upgrade or patch CallManager servers by using Terminal Services. This is not supported by TAC and cannot even be assured to work. Performing remote upgrades and patches requires the use of VNC, which is covered in the next section.

WARNING   If you perform upgrades and patches via Terminal Services, there is no guarantee that your system will continue to function.

Potential Security Implications of Terminal Services

Leaving Terminal Services enabled on the system can potentially open the system to anyone with network access and the Remote Desktop Connection software. Although a potential intruder would still need a username and password to log in, it's important to add more security to this tool.

Terminal Services listens on TCP port 3389. There are a few things you can do to enable more security:

- **Add access control lists (ACLs) to the network that allow only certain administrative subnets to access the servers on port 3389**—This method definitely makes the system more secure; however, it keeps you from accessing the servers from all over the network. For example, if you happen to be away from your desk but you're still attached to the network, you are denied access. Chapter 6, "Securing the Environment," provides more information about ACLs.

- **Use Cisco Lock-and-Key security**—Lock-and-Key security allows you to define an ACL that takes effect only when a user logs into a router and enters a valid name and password. In addition, Lock-and-Key can be configured to close the hole after a certain amount of time. This way, any valid administrator can open a temporary hole in the ACL that allows access for a short duration.

  You can find more information on configuring Lock-and-Key at or by searching Cisco.com for "Configuring Lock-and-Key Security":

  > http://www.cisco.com/en/US/products/sw/iosswrel/ps1835/products_
  > configuration_guide_chapter09186a00800ca7c2.html

- **Combine Lock-and-Key with AAA and dynamic passwords**—Lock-and-Key security entails using Telnet to access a router and providing a name and password that result in temporary access. If you use AAA on that router in combination with Cisco Secure ACS and a one-time password server such as SofToken or SecurID, you have a much higher level of security. (Using a router in combination with Cisco Secure ACS is discussed at the beginning of this chapter.)

In this scenario, you Telnet to the router and are prompted with a USERNAME prompt. After you enter the username, you see a PASSCODE prompt. At this point you enter the dynamic password generated by your token generator. The router takes the combination of username and dynamic passcode and sends it to ACS, which then sends it to the token server. If— and only if— there's a match, the temporary hole is opened. The advantage is that the token generator changes the password every so many seconds, and it's hard, if not impossible, to hack.

You can find more information on AAA in the SC: Part 1: Authentication, Authorization, and Accounting (AAA) documentation at the following link:

http://www.cisco.com/univercd/cc/td/doc/product/software/ios122/122cgcr/
fsecur_c/fsaaa/index.htm

You can learn more about ACS in the Cisco Secure ACS 3.2 for Windows Server documentation at the following link:

http://www.cisco.com/univercd/cc/td/doc/product/access/acs_soft/
csacs4nt/acs32/index.htm

You can find more information about one-time passwords in the Token Server User Databases section of the CiscoSecure User Database documentation at the following link:

http://www.cisco.com/univercd/cc/td/doc/product/access/acs_soft/
csacs4nt/acs32/user/d.htm#44000

For AAA configuration information, see the earlier section "Baseline AAA Configuration." For more information on CallManager security, see Chapter 6.

Using VNC

This section discusses how to use VNC to perform upgrades and troubleshoot. VNC is the only method of remote upgrades supported by Cisco. Terminal Services should never be used for patching or upgrading.

Install and Use VNC

VNC is included free of charge with CallManager and is located in the C:\utils directory. It serves the same purpose as Terminal Services; however, it works at a lower level of the OS, enabling support for remote installation of upgrades and patches because it provides an actual console session. VNC is a remote-control package, which means that by default your cursor movements appear on the server's screen as well as the client PC's screen.

VNC has two components—the viewer and the server. To install the server component on the CallManager server, go to the directory C:\utils\VNC\ and double-click **vnc-3.3.7_x86_win32.exe**. After the installer has finished, restart your machine. VNC will be running as a Windows service.

To install the VNC client, simply copy vncviewer.exe from C:\utils\VNC\vnc_x86_win32\vncviewer onto your PC. The easiest way to do this is to mount the hidden c$ share that is enabled by default in Windows. To do this, use the following procedure on the client onto which you want to install VNC:

Step 1   Click **Start > Run**.

Step 2   Enter **cmd** and press **Enter**.

Step 3   Enter **net use j: **CallManagerIPaddress**\c$ /user:administrator**.

Step 4   Enter the password when prompted.

Step 5   Enter **j:**.

Step 6   Enter **cd \utils\VNC\vnc_x86_win32\vncviewer**.

Step 7   Enter **copy vncviewer.exe** *directory* where *directory* is the directory into which you want to install VNC.

After adding a shortcut to VNC Viewer to your desktop, double-click it to launch VNC Viewer. Enter the server's IP address and the password.

Close VNC After Initiating Upgrades

When using VNC for upgrades, be sure to close VNC after initiating your upgrade. VNC consumes considerable CPU load that can cause your upgrades to take much longer than expected. Because VNC is like being at the console, you can start the upgrade, close VNC on your desktop, and check in on it later by relaunching it.

Summary

Cisco IP Telephony environments offer a wide array of facilities that allow administrators to track, manage, and monitor the system. The information contained in this chapter supplies you with the tools needed to run the system on a daily basis and have a clear view of what's happening on the various devices throughout the system.

## CHAPTER 13

Using Real-Time Monitoring Tool

The Real-Time Monitoring Tool (RTMT) is a management application bundled with Cisco CallManager. It's installed from the Install Plugins page in CallManager Administration (**Application > Install Plugins**). RTMT is a cluster-specific application that provides real-time information only; it does not provide historical information. To manage multiple clusters, you can use Cisco's IP Telephony Environment Monitor (ITEM), an application that can be purchased separately from Cisco and that provides more extensive management and monitoring. In addition, ITEM reaches more extensively into the network, covering the routing and switching infrastructure as well as telephony components. You can learn more about ITEM at the following link or by searching Cisco.com for "ITEM":

> http://www.cisco.com/en/US/products/sw/cscowork/ps2433/index.html

RTMT uses performance objects, which are comprised of counters, to display the state of the CallManager environment. The same performance objects are used in RTMT and Microsoft Performance, discussed in Chapter 12, "Managing and Monitoring the System."

Configuring RTMT

In keeping with the goals of this book, the intention of this chapter is to point out best practices for using these tools, not to repeat information you can find in the documentation. That being said, by far the best practice is to actually *use the tool*.

Be Aware of Changes to RTMT

With the release of CallManager 4.0, RTMT's interface has been overhauled to provide information in a friendlier and more useable format. In addition, log data is generated in comma-separated value (CSV) format and is accessed by the new Serviceability Reporter tool (mentioned later in this chapter).

RTMT has also moved the function of alerting from a client-side Java application to a server-side process. Version 3.x required a client PC running RTMT to generate alerts. Also, if two machines were running RTMT, they would both issue alerts, which might be configured differently and cause confusion. In RTMT 4.0, this is no longer the case. You simply load the application from the Plugins page and set your alerts and thresholds. You can close the application if you don't need a real-time display for monitoring.

<table>
<tr><td>**WARNING**</td><td>If more than one machine is running the RTMT client, and a user makes a change, the change dynamically shows on every other client's RTMT instance. The changes are made to the server, which then updates all the clients. The back-end service is not locked by a single user, so all users with the proper rights can make changes that might overwrite changes made by others. Be careful when running RTMT in this scenario.</td></tr>
</table>

Changes from Earlier Releases

Some drastic changes in RTMT 4.0 might throw you off if you've used the tool in the past. The first is that the attribute tabs shown in Figure 13-1 cannot be modified. In previous versions of RTMT, you could choose from a list of attributes and drag them onto the workspace and configure thresholds and alerts. In RTMT 4.0, you cannot modify the groups of attributes because they are preconfigured. In addition, each group of attributes comes with a preconfigured set of alerts (see Table 13-1 later in this chapter).

Figure 13-1 *RTMT Attribute Tabs*

<table>
<tr><td>**NOTE**</td><td>To set alerts on individual attributes, you need to use the Perfmon attribute group, drag the components onto the workspace, and set the thresholds in the same manner as RTMT in CallManager 3.x. For more information, see the later section "Configure Microsoft Performance Counters and Set Alerts."</td></tr>
</table>

Decide What to Monitor

It's important to decide what information you want to gather and monitor, who will receive alerts about that information, and what should be done when an alert is received.

Sometimes alarms go off and no one is there to see them. Just as with syslog and Simple Network Management Protocol (SNMP), discussed in Chapter 12, if no one is reading the reports, potential disaster cannot be averted, and valuable information for capacity planning goes unnoticed. Be sure to decide who will monitor the system (covered in the next section) and the course of action when an alarm sounds.

Decide Who Monitors What

When configuring alerts in RTMT, it's important to ensure that the right alerts go to the right people. In many large organizations, one group, such as the Network Operations Center (NOC), monitors the servers, and the telecom department monitors the telephony components, such as gateways and media resources. If this is the case in your organization, and if the person reading alerts cannot react quickly and effectively, don't configure all alerts to go to a single in-box. Instead, use an alias that several people subscribe to, or configure multiple alert recipients.

NOTE   Generally, the e-mail addresses used for alerts go directly to text pagers. As of CallManager release 4.0, RTMT doesn't have a native paging interface.

For example, when configuring the target of the CriticalServiceDown alert, in addition to alerting the NOC, it's a good idea to send that alert to someone who is familiar with the workings of Windows 2000 services. Similarly, it wouldn't make sense to send a RouteListExhausted alert to a server manager. Configure a single alert box only if a single NOC team is managing everything and the NOC team forwards the alerts to the right team.

In addition, when configuring alerts, it's important to configure non-user-specific mailboxes such as "Telephony Administrator" because staff members tend to move departments and employees leave the company. Therefore, rather than sending alerts to a specific individual, teach the people who are responsible for receiving alerts to check the appropriate mailbox.

Monitor Media Resources Closely

In larger, centralized cluster environments, having ample media resources available without grossly overprovisioning can be a real challenge. One of RTMT's best assets is the ability to see when media resources are exhausted. Be sure to set alerts that allow you to be proactive. You can set performance counters to alert you when resources start to get scarce.

The preconfigured alert MediaListExhausted is a reactive alert that sends a signal when a media resource group list (MRGL) has no more available resources. You can set the ResourceAvailable counter in the Cisco HW Conference Bridge Device object to trigger the alert. Set an alert that triggers when only 5 percent of the resources are left. To provide a highly granular representation of the media resources, you need to do this for every server in the cluster to which media resources are registered.

NOTE   All performance objects in RTMT are configured per server. If you want to monitor the same objects on all servers, you must configure each one separately.

Monitor Trunk Utilization Closely

Large centralized environments usually include many gateways. You can watch trunk utilization counters to help prevent accidental overprovisioning of trunks (this usually occurs when administrators are trying reduce the possibility of busy signals). Smaller organizations have the opposite problem: While trying to keep recurring circuit costs down, they often underprovision.

Setting thresholds on these values for each individual gateway gives you the information you need to trunk appropriately. Thresholds are set with the performance counters in RTMT. For example, if eight FXO ports are provisioned on a gateway, a good alert to set would be for six active calls. If you never trigger an alert, you know you are overprovisioned and can potentially scale back. In large networks, this can save a lot of money. In addition, it's a good idea to check the gateway utilization using the Serviceability Reports Archive (discussed in more detail later in this chapter).

Some important counters to watch are in the Cisco MGCP objects, as well as the PRI, T1, FXO, and FXS PortsActive and PortsInService counters in the CallManager object. Set your thresholds to fit the environment. Be aware that these counters are not available for H.323 gateways, but other counters for H.323 are provided in the Cisco H323 object.

Change the Polling Interval if Needed

The polling rate in each preconfigured monitoring window is fixed; the default polling value is 30 seconds. If you require information in shorter intervals, you can lower this poll interval, but doing so is not recommended. The collection rate of the back-end Real-Time Information Server Data Collector (RISDC) is changed through the RIS Data Collector service parameter Data Collection Polling Rate (**Service > Service Parameters** > *select a server* > **Cisco RIS Data Collector**). For more information on service parameters, see Chapter 8, "Managing Services and Parameters." A shorter polling interval provides quicker statistics updates, but you need to balance the benefit of that information against the adverse effect on server performance.

Modify Preconfigured Alerts if Needed

RTMT 4.0 provides a preconfigured set of alerts. These alerts are not to be confused with the CallManager Serviceability Alarm Facility discussed in Chapter 12. There are two kinds of alerts: preconfigured and user-defined. Both can be modified, but the main difference is that you cannot delete preconfigured alerts, only disable them.

Table 13-1 lists the preconfigured alerts in RTMT. The names are self-explanatory. Most of the preconfigured alerts can be mapped to a particular screen in RTMT. The value of knowing what the mappings are is that if you notice that the counters in a particular screen are continually spiking, you can configure the associated alert by clicking **Alert >
Set Alert/Properties** from the appropriate RTMT screen.

Table 13-1   *Mapping of RTMT 4.0 Preconfigured Alerts to RTMT Screens*

RTMT Screen	Related Alert
Summary > Summary	CallProcessingNodeCpuPegging
	NonCallProcessingNodeCpuPegging
	LowAvailableMemory
	RouteListExhausted
	MediaListExhausted
	NumberOfRegisteredPhonesDropped
	MgcpDChannelOutOfService
Server > CPU&Memory	CallProcessingNodeCpuPegging
	NonCallProcessingNodeCpuPegging
	LowAvailableMemory
Server > Disk Usage	LowAvailableDiskSpace
Server > Critical Services	CriticalServiceDown
CallProcess > Call Activity	—
Call Process > Gateway Activity	RouteListExhausted
	MgcpDChannelOutofService
Call Process > Trunk Activity	—
Call Process > SDL Queue	—
Service > Cisco TFTP	LowTFTPServerHeartbeatRate
Service > Directory Server	DirectoryConnectionFailed
	DirectoryReplicationFailed

continues

Table 13-1 *Mapping of RTMT 4.0 Preconfigured Alerts to RTMT Screens (Continued)*

RTMT Screen	Related Alert
Service > Heartbeat	LowCallManagerHeartbeatRate LowTFTPServerHearbeatRate LowTcdServerHeartbeatRate
Device > Device Summary	NumberOfRegisteredPhonesDropped NumberOfRegisteredGatewaysDecreased NumberOfRegisteredGatewaysIncreased NumberOfRegisteredMediaDevicesDecreased NumberOfRegisteredMediaDevicesIncreased
Device > Device Search	—
CTI > CTI Manager	—
CTI > CTI Search	—
Perfmon	No preconfigured alerts; all alerts are custom

The following list describes each preconfigured alert in alphabetical order and its significance, as well as its possible triggering conditions. Four alerts (CodeRedEntry, CodeYellowEntry, ExcessiveVoiceQualityReports, and MaliciousCallTrace) that do not map to a screen in RTMT are also described.

- **CallProcessingNodeCpuPegging**—This alert means that a node in the cluster that services phones is experiencing high CPU load for a sustained period of time. Check to see if dial tone is delayed when the phone goes off-hook. If you experience delayed dial tone, the high CPU load is affecting your service levels. Use either Virtual Network Computing (VNC) or Remote Desktop Connection to log onto the machine, and use the Windows Task Manager to check every service's CPU utilization. It's important to note the service and open a priority 2 (P2) case with the Cisco Technical Assistance Center (TAC) that indicates a degraded, but working, state. You can also check each process's CPU utilization by selecting **Server > CPU&Memory** in RTMT, which shows the process and percentage of CPU utilization in a format similar to that supplied by the Windows Task Manager.

- **CodeRedEntry**—Although not associated with any particular RTMT screen, this alert indicates that CallManager has restarted itself. On receiving this alert, check the Windows Event Log to understand why the restart occurred.

- **CodeYellowEntry**—Although not associated with any particular RTMT screen, this alert means that CallManager has started to reject calls because of high load. When this alert gets triggered, it's important to look at the system's CPU load and begin troubleshooting.

- **CriticalServiceDown**—An alert is issued when any of the following services go down:
    - Cisco Extended Functions (CallBackService.exe)
    - Cisco CallManager (ccm.exe)
    - Cisco CDR Insert (InsertCDR.exe)
    - Cisco CTIManager (CTIManager.exe)
    - Cisco Database layer Monitor (AuPair.exe)
    - Cisco IP Voice Media Streaming App (Ipvmsapp.exe)
    - Cisco Messaging Interface (CiscoMessagingInterface.exe)
    - Cisco MOH Audio Translator (AudioTranslator.exe)
    - Cisco RIS Data Collector (RISDC.exe)
    - Cisco Telephony Call Dispatcher (TcdSrv.exe)
    - Cisco TFTP (ctftp.exe)
    - Cisco Tomcat (jk_nt_service.exe Cisco Tomcat)

    In addition, the following NT services are monitored:

    - DC Directory Server (DCX500.exe)
    - World Wide Web Publishing Service (inetinfo.exe)
    - MSSQLServer (sqlservr.exe)
    - SQLServerAgent (sqlagent.exe)
    - SNMP Service (snmp.exe)

- **DirectoryConnectionFailed**—This alert indicates a problem with CallManager accessing the directory. If CallManager cannot access the directory, several applications might fail, including IPCC Express, the Cisco CallManager User Options web page, extension mobility, and software-based IP phones such as SoftPhone and Communicator. When you get this alert, it's a good idea to cross-check it with the CriticalServiceDown alert to see if the Directory service has stopped.

- **DirectoryReplicationFailed**—This alert is important because it represents a fundamental problem in communication and process between a cluster's nodes. This alert often gets triggered during the upgrade process if consistent passwords are not used or if pieces of the cluster are not upgraded in the proper order.

- **ExcessiveVoiceQualityReports**—Although not associated with any particular RTMT screen, this alert is triggered when the QRT softkey is pressed ten times in one hour (by default) by any combination of users (not just the same user). You can configure the number of QRT softkey presses and the time period in which they occur. When you receive this alert, take the information contained in the alert and begin troubleshooting.

- **LowCallManagerHeartbeatRate**—This alert indicates that the CallManager process is not generating and/or responding to heartbeat requests in a timely manner. If the heartbeat rate slows down significantly, this indicates a problem with the Cisco CallManager service; the service might be going down.

- **LowAvailableDiskSpace**—This is a critical alert to watch for because low disk space can cause directory-related functions to cease. These include but are not limited to access to the Cisco CallManager User Options web page, IPCC Express, and IP interactive voice response (IVR). It also can cause serious database problems that make adding phones and making changes problematic.

- **LowAvailableMemory**—CallManager is optimized to run from memory. Given this fact, in large deployments the system can run low on memory if not designed properly. It's also quite possible that your requirements push CallManager's overall design limits. Software bugs can also affect memory availability, so this alarm is quite important.

  If you encounter this alarm, call TAC and open a case. If TAC advises you that the problem is not related to a bug or memory leak, you should revisit your cluster's design and move resources to another server.

- **LowTcdServerHeartbeatRate**—This alert indicates that the Cisco Telephony Call Dispatcher (TCD) process is not generating and/or responding to heartbeat requests in a timely manner. If the heartbeat rate slows down significantly, this indicates a problem with the TCD service; the service might be going down.

- **LowTFTPServerHeartbeatRate**—This alert indicates that the TFTP process is not generating and/or responding to heartbeat requests in a timely manner. If the heartbeat rate slows down significantly, this indicates a problem with the Cisco TFTP service; the service might be going down.

- **MaliciousCallTrace**—Although not associated with any particular RTMT screen, this alert is triggered when a malicious call trace alarm is received from CallManager. When you receive this alert, you should collect the information contained in the alert, contact the party making the report, and work according to your malicious call policy.

- **MediaListExhausted**—This alert indicates that a conference or transcoding resource has been exhausted. When this happens, check to see if enough conferencing digital signal processors (DSP) are allocated on any Cisco Catalyst 6608 cards or Communication Media Modules (CMM) in your network. It's very possible that as you add users to the network, more conferencing resources will be needed.

NOTE   MediaListExhausted is a critical alert in centralized call processing environments that require conferencing and transcoding resources at the core (central site). If this alert triggers, it potentially means that users cannot initiate conference calls or receive voice mail if your voice mail service is G.711-only, such as an Octel or SMDI connection.

- **MgcpDChannelOutOfService**—This counter's triggering should prompt an immediate check of cabling between your minimum point of entry (MPOE) and the extended demarcation point. If the cabling is good, it's a good idea to call your service provider and open a help case.

  You should also check to see if the D-channel is *flapping* (going up and down). If the counter fluctuates between 1 and 0, you should call your service provider and open a help case.

- **NonCallProcessingNodeCpuPegging**—This alert could indicate that a system has processes that are hanging or that a certain process is using all the CPU on the server. When this alarm triggers, be sure to check the Windows Task Manager on the system, and be ready to end the process or reboot the system. You can also check each process's CPU utilization by selecting **Server > CPU&Memory** in RTMT, which shows the process and percentage of CPU utilization in a format similar to that supplied by the Task Manager.

- **NumberOfRegisteredGatewaysDecreased**—This is a key statistic to monitor because it can indicate a problem with inbound and outbound Public Switched Telephone Network (PSTN) calls. When the number of registered gateways decreases, either a device has crashed, or a network connectivity problem exists between CallManager and a gateway. Depending on the size of the organization, this can have a major impact.

- **NumberOfRegisteredGatewaysIncreased**—This alert might trigger when a gateway that has failed comes back online, or if gateways are added to the system. It's important to inform your NOC when you intend to add devices and gateways to the CallManager environment to ensure that the NOC team doesn't spend time troubleshooting problems that don't exist.

- **NumberOfRegisteredMediaDevicesDecreased**—This alert generally indicates some kind of device failure. If you have media resources in a Catalyst switch or Cisco router, and that device experiences a problem, this alert triggers. When you receive this alert, it's best to contact the network administration team. If all alerts go to a central NOC, it's a simple exercise to correlate the errors. Depending on how you've set up MRGLs in CallManager Administration, it's possible that users will not be able to use conference or cBarge features during the outage. This alert also triggers when devices are taken out of service for maintenance.

- **NumberOfRegisteredMediaDevicesIncreased**—This alert indicates that either failed devices have been restored to service or that resources have been added to the network. This is more of an information alert.

- **NumberOfRegisteredPhonesDropped**—A drop in the number of registered phones could indicate a network failure. Although it's true that the network management center should be aware of any outage, a low-to-medium number in this alert could indicate the failure of an edge switch, whereas a large number could indicate a distribution layer switch outage.

- **RouteListExhausted**—When a route list is exhausted, you might not have enough gateway resources available to service your traffic patterns. If this alert triggers once or twice, generally this is not a cause for concern. However, if this alert starts triggering many times per day, it's time to add more gateway resources. Given that adding resources can't happen overnight because of telephone company and equipment delivery lead times, it's important to continuously check the T1ChannelsActive or PRIChannelsActive counters in the Cisco CallManager object to ensure that you do not have an upward trend. Alternatively, you can configure the alert properties to trigger the alert only if route lists are exhausted a certain number of times in a certain amount of time.

Configure Perfmon Counters and Set Alerts

Although most of the relevant information is reflected in other application tabs in RTMT, some applications such as McAfee NetShield create performance counters that can be set to trigger alerts. You can monitor these in the Perfmon tab in RTMT.

Setting Threshold Triggers on Counters

Performance counters are the only way to set threshold triggers on a per-device basis for media resources and gateway ports. Although preconfigured alerts trigger when certain conditions are met, performance monitoring is the only way to set a threshold on a particular counter. For example, if you've installed a remote site with four Foreign Exchange Office (FXO) ports, and you want to keep a close eye on the ports, only RTMT's Perfmon facility provides a way of setting a threshold of, for example, four ports to trigger an alert. By setting this alert, you know you're actually hitting the ceiling. If a fifth call is attempted, the RouteListExhausted alert triggers, but by then it's too late. If you know you're hitting four quite often, you'll probably be able to provision more trunks before service is negatively affected.

Use Device Search to Quickly Find Device Status

Although CallManager Administration lets you perform searches based on static properties such as directory number and description, there are many cases when you might need to find a number of devices that match a certain criterion. The Device Search feature in RTMT provides a mechanism to identify the following:

- Unregistered phones/gateways
- Phones/gateways registered to a certain CallManager
- Phones/gateways in a certain IP subnet
- Phones that match a certain directory number pattern
- Phones whose registration has been rejected

Use the **Device Search** icon on the **Device** tab. Double-click any type of device, and the search boxes appear. Simply add the search criteria on each page of the search window, as shown in Figure 13-2. The results of your query are displayed in tabular format.

Figure 13-2 *Searching for Unregistered Phones in RTMT*

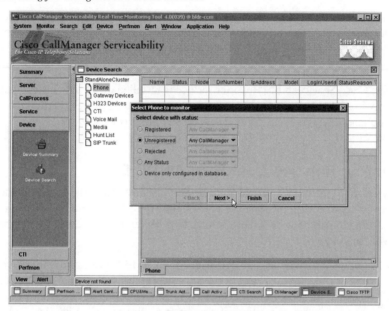

The kind of search information specified in this list can be critical when you're cleaning up after an installation or migration. It's often important to know if phone registrations are being rejected or phones are not registering properly.

Use the Serviceability Reports Archive

The RISDC service gathers predefined statistics (explained in the following sections) at a rate set in the RIS Data Collector service parameter Data Collection Polling Rate (**Service > Service Parameters** > *select a server* > **Cisco RIS Data Collector**).

Each evening, the Cisco Serviceability Reporter service creates five preconfigured reports using the data collected by RISDC: Alert, Server, Service, Call, and Device. These reports are saved as Adobe Acrobat files. You can access them through the Serviceability Reports Archive in CallManager Serviceability (**Tools > Serviceability Reports Archive**). Each is a summary report consisting of charts that display the statistics for that particular report.

NOTE	A report is not generated unless data is available for all the charts in the report. If there are no log files for the generation of a particular type of report, other than the Alert Report, an error message is logged in the ErrorLog file, saying that no report was generated because no log files were available.
	If no Alert Log files exist, a blank report is generated that says no alerts were generated for the day.

The Cisco Serviceability Reporter service is installed on all the cluster's nodes. It is active only in the Publisher, where reports are generated, and failover is not supported. Should the Publisher fail, reports are not created on any Subscriber servers.

Create Custom Reports from Raw RISDC Data

Sometimes the reports provided in the Serviceability Reports Archive do not provide the necessary historical information you require. To aggregate multiple days/months of information, the raw data must be saved off-server and processed by programs such as Microsoft Excel.

Each of the preconfigured objects listed in Table 13-1 belongs to the devices, services, servers, or call activities category. Each category uses a separate log file contained in the C:\Program Files\Common Files\Cisco\Logs\RTMTLogger directory. Alert details and performance counters are logged into separate files as well. Log files are in standard CSV format and can be read natively by Microsoft Performance (**Start > Programs > Administrative Tools > Performance**).

New log files are created every day at 00:00 hours (midnight) on the local system. New logs for devices, services, servers, and calls are created when the time zone is changed, when a new node is added to the cluster, or during failover/fallback scenarios. The first column of all these logs contains the time zone information and the number of minutes from Greenwich mean time (GMT). A sample first column header is (PDH-CSV 4.0)(Indian Standard Time)(–330).

TIP	Be sure to change the Cisco Serviceability Reporter service parameter RTMT Report Deletion Age (**Service > Service Parameters > Cisco Serviceability Reporter**) to keep logs for a longer period of time. The maximum is 30 days. When you do this, be sure to keep an eye on disk space utilization. You can always move the files off-server to save space.

Alert Log Format

The Alert Log uses a combination of file and memory storage. When the service is started or restarted, the last 30 minutes of alert data is loaded into memory from the log files of every node in the cluster. On RTMT startup, all logs that occurred in the last 30 minutes are shown in the RTMT Alert Central log history. The Alert Log is periodically updated, and new logs are inserted into the log history window. When the number of logs reaches 100, RTMT removes the oldest 40 logs.

The filename format of the Alert Log is AlertLog_*MM_DD_YYYY_hh_mm*.csv where *MM* represents the two-digit month, *DD* represents the two-digit day, *YYYY* represents the four-digit year, *hh* represents the two-digit hour, and *mm* represents the two-digit minutes. For example, AlertLog_10_12_2004_10_36.csv indicates a log file that was saved on October 12, 2004, at 10:36 a.m. This date format applies to all of the log files including Server Log, Service Log, Call Log, Device Log, and Perfmon Log.

The Alert Log has the following attributes:

- Time Stamp
- Alert Name
- Node ID
- Alert Message
- Monitored Object Name
- Severity
- PollValue
- Action

The first line of each log file is the header. Details of each alert are written in comma-separated format on a single line. The sample format of the Alert Log is as follows:

Header:

```
"Time Stamp","Alert Name","Node ID","Alert Message","Monitored Object Name",
"Severity","PollValue","Action"
```

Data:

```
"1046434186","LowTcdServerHeartbeatRate","CISCART253","\n\nAt 17:39:46 on
02/28/2003 on node CISCART253.\nTcd Server heartbeat rate below 24 beats per
minute.\nCurrent heartbeat rate is 0 beats per minute.",,"4","0",
```

Server Log Format

The server data is held in memory and is written to disk every 5 minutes regardless of the polling interval. The data is logged into the file as a single record, and the memory is cleared. Table 13-2 shows the counters that are logged.

Table 13-2   *Server Log Counter Description*

Counter	Description
cpuUsage	Average of all the values collected in the last 5 minutes.
MemoryInUse	Average of all the values collected in the last 5 minutes.
DiskSpaceInUse	Average of all the values collected in the last 5 minutes.

Log files are in standard CSV format and can be read natively by Microsoft Performance (**Start > Programs > Administrative Tools > Performance**).

The filename format of the Server Log is ServerLog_*MM_DD_YYYY_hh_mm*.csv.

The first line of each log file is the header. The sample format of the Server Log for a single node is as follows:

Header:

```
"(PDH-CSV 4.0)(India Standard Time)(-330)","\\Node1\Server\%CPU Utilization",
"\\Node1\Server\%Memory Utilization","\\Node1\Server\%Hard Disk Usage of the
largest partition"
```

Data:

```
"05/02/2003 00:00:00","7.400000","32.000000","12.000000"
"05/02/2003 00:05:00","6.300000","32.000000","12.000000"
```

Service Log Format

The service data is held in memory and is written to disk every 5 minutes regardless of the polling interval. The data is logged into the file as a single record, and the memory is cleared. Table 13-3 shows the counters that are logged.

Table 13-3   *Service Log Counter Description*

Counter	Calculation	Description
ctiOpenDevices	Average	Values collected in the last 5 minutes.
ctiLines	Average	Values collected in the last 5 minutes.
ctiConnections	Average	Values collected in the last 5 minutes.
ctiActiveCMLinks	Average	Values collected in the last 5 minutes.
tftpRequests	Cumulative	The difference between the last collected value and the first collected value in the last 5 minutes.
tftpAbortedRequests	Cumulative	The difference between the last collected value and the first collected value in the last 5 minutes.

Log files are in standard CSV format and can be read natively by Microsoft Performance (**Start > Programs > Administrative Tools > Performance**).

The filename format of the Service Log is ServiceLog_*MM_DD_YYYY_hh_mm*.csv.

The first line of each log file is the header. The sample format of the Service Log for a single node is as follows:

Header:

```
"(PDH-CSV 4.0)(India Standard Time)(-330)","\\Node1\Service\Number of Open CTI
Devices","\\Node1\Service\Number of CTI Lines","\\Node1\Service\Number of CTI
Connections","\\Node1\Service\Number of Active CTI Links","\\Node1\Service\Number
of TFTP Requests","\\Node1\Service\Number of Aborted TFTP Requests"
```

Data:

```
"05/02/2003 00:00:00","2.000000","2.000000","2.000000","1.000000","1.000000",
"0.000000"
"05/02/2003 00:05:00","2.000000","2.000000","2.000000","1.000000","1.000000",
"0.000000"
```

Call Log Format

The call data is held in memory and is written to disk every 5 minutes regardless of the polling interval. The data is logged into the file as a single record, and the memory is cleared. Table 13-4 shows the counters that are logged.

Table 13-4   *Call Log Counter Description*

Counter	Calculation	Description
cmCallsAttempted	Cumulative	The difference between the last collected value and the first collected value in the last 5 minutes.
cmCallsCompleted	Cumulative	The difference between the last collected value and the first collected value in the last 5 minutes.
cmCallsInProgress	Average	Values collected in the last 5 minutes.
gwMGCP_FXS_CallsCompleted	Cumulative	The difference between the last collected value and the first collected value in the last 5 minutes.
gwMGCP_FXO_CallsCompleted	Cumulative	The difference between the last collected value and the first collected value in the last 5 minutes.

continues

Table 13-4 *Call Log Counter Description (Continued)*

Counter	Calculation	Description
gwMGCP_PRI_CallsCompleted	Cumulative	The difference between the last collected value and the first collected value in the last 5 minutes.
gwMGCP_T1_CAS_CallsCompleted	Cumulative	The difference between the last collected value and the first collected value in the last 5 minutes.
gwH323_CallsAttempted	Cumulative	The difference between the last collected value and the first collected value in the last 5 minutes.
gwH323_CallsInProgress	Average	Values collected in the last 5 minutes.
gwH323_CallsCompleted	Cumulative	The difference between the last collected value and the first collected value in the last 5 minutes.
trunkH323_CallsAttempted	Cumulative	The difference between the last collected value and the first collected value in the last 5 minutes.
trunkH323_CallsInProgress	Average	Values collected in the last 5 minutes.
trunkH323_CallsCompleted	Cumulative	The difference between the last collected value and the first collected value in the last 5 minutes.
trunkSIP_CallsAttempted	Cumulative	The difference between the last collected value and the first collected value in the last 5 minutes.
trunkSIP_CallsInProgress	Average	Values collected in the last 5 minutes.
trunkSIP_CallsCompleted	Cumulative	The difference between the last collected value and the first collected value in the last 5 minutes.
gwMGCP_FXS_PortsInService	Average	Values collected in the last 5 minutes.
gwMGCP_FXO_PortsInService	Average	Values collected in the last 5 minutes.
gwMGCP_PRI_SpansInService	Average	Values collected in the last 5 minutes.
gwMGCP_T1_CAS_SpansInService	Average	Values collected in the last 5 minutes.
gwMGCP_FXS_ActivePorts	Average	Values collected in the last 5 minutes.

Table 13-4   *Call Log Counter Description (Continued)*

Counter	Calculation	Description
gwMGCP_FXO_ActivePorts	Average	Values collected in the last 5 minutes.
gwMGCP_PRI_ActiveChannels	Average	Values collected in the last 5 minutes.
gwMGCP_T1_CAS_ActiveChannels	Average	Values collected in the last 5 minutes.

Log files are in standard CSV format and can be read natively by Microsoft Performance (**Start > Programs > Administrative Tools > Performance**).

The filename format of the Call Log is CallLog_*MM_DD_YYYY_hh_mm*.csv.

The first line of each log file is the header. The sample format of the Call Log for a single node is as follows:

Header:

```
"(PDH-CSV 4.0)(India Standard Time)(-330)","\\Node1\Call\Number of CallManager
Calls Attempted","\\Node1\Call\Number of CallManager Calls Completed","\\Node1\
Call\Number of CallManager Calls In-Progress","\\Node1\Call\Number of Gateway
MGCP FXS Calls Completed","\\Node1\Call\Number of Gateway MGCP FXO Calls
Completed","\\Node1\Call\Number of Gateway MGCP PRI Calls Completed","\\Node1\
Call\Number of Gateway MGCP T1 CAS Calls Completed","\\Node1\Call\Number of
Gateway H323 Calls Attempted","\\Node1\Call\Number of Gateway H323 Calls
Inprogress","\\Node1\Call\Number of Gateway H323 Calls Completed","\\Node1\Call\
Number of Gateway MGCP FXS Ports In-Service","\\Node1\Call\Number of Gateway MGCP
FXO Ports In-Service","\\Node1\Call\Number of Gateway MGCP PRI Spans
In-Service","\\Node1\Call\Number of Gateway MGCP T1 CAS Spans In-Service","
\\Node1\Call\Number of Gateway MGCP FXS ActivePorts","\\Node1\Call\Number of
Gateway MGCP FXO ActivePorts","\\Node1\Call\Number of Gateway MGCP PRI
ActiveChannels","\\Node1\Call\Number of Gateway MGCP T1 CAS ActiveChannels","
\\Node1\Call\Number of Trunk H323 Calls Attempted","\\Node1\Call\Number of Trunk
H323 Calls Inprogress","\\Node1\Call\Number of Trunk H323 Calls Completed","
\\Node1\Call\Number of Trunk SIP Calls Attempted","\\Node1\Call\Number of Trunk
SIP Calls Inprogress","\\Node1\Call\Number of Trunk SIP Calls Completed"
```

Data:

```
"05/02/2003 0:00:00","4","3","1","2","1","0","0","2","1","0","1","1","0","0","1",
"1","2","1","0", "0","0","0","0","0"

"05/02/2003 0:05:00","3","2","0","1","1","0","0","1","1","0","1","1","0","0","1",
"1","2","1","0", "2","0","0","0","0"
```

Device Log Format

The device data is held in memory and is written to disk every 5 minutes regardless of the polling interval. The data is logged into the file as a single record, and the memory is cleared. Table 13-5 shows the counters that are logged.

Table 13-5 *Device Log Counter Description*

Counter	Description
gatewayDevicesFXS	Average of all the values collected in the last 5 minutes.
gatewayDevicesFXO	Average of all the values collected in the last 5 minutes.
gatewayDevicesPRI	Average of all the values collected in the last 5 minutes.
gatewayDevicesT1	Average of all the values collected in the last 5 minutes.
gatewayDevicesH323	Average of all the values collected in the last 5 minutes.
phone	Average of all the values collected in the last 5 minutes.

Log files are in standard CSV format and can be read natively by Microsoft Performance (**Start > Programs > Administrative Tools > Performance**).

The filename format of the Device Log is DeviceLog_*MM_DD_YYYY_hh_mm*.csv.

The first line of each log file is the header. The sample format of the Device Log for a single node is as follows:

Header:

```
"(PDH-CSV 4.0)(India Standard Time)(-330)","\\Node1\Device\Number of FXS Device",
"\\Node1\Device\Number of FXO Device","\\Node1\Device\Number of PRI Device",
"\\Node1\Device\Number of T1 Device","\\Node1\Device\Number of H323 Device",
"\\Node1\Device\Number of Phones","\\Node1\Device\Number of H323 Trunk Devices",
"\\Node1\Device\Number of SIP Trunk Devices"
```

Data:

```
"05/02/2003 00:00:00","3","2","3","2","2","7","1","1"
"05/02/2003 00:05:00","2","2","3","2","2","6","1","1"
```

Perfmon Log Format

The Perfmon data is logged whenever the LogPerfmon API is called. The file log is compatible with the Microsoft Performance CSV format and can be opened using Microsoft Performance for analysis (**Start > Programs > Administrative Tools > Performance**).

When new counters are added, the header is changed to accommodate the new counters and the values are logged correspondingly. When data is unavailable for an existing counter (added to the header already), blank values are inserted in the file. If the character length of the new counters added is greater than 2000, the new file is generated with all the counters.

The filename format of the Perfmon Log is
PerfmonLog_*NodeName_MM_DD_YYYY_hh_mm*.csv.

Following is the list of performance counters that are logged. All the following counters are
under the Cisco CallManager System Performance object:

- At the system level:
  - QueueSignalsPresent 1-High
  - QueueSignalsPresent 2-Normal
  - QueueSignalsPresent 3-Low
  - QueueSignalsPresent 4-Lowest
  - QueueSignalsProcessed 1-High
  - QueueSignalsProcessed 2-Normal
  - QueueSignalsProcessed 3-Low
  - QueueSignalsProcessed 4-Lowest
- For each process running on the system:
  - Process\% Processor Time
  - Process\ID Process
  - Process\Private Bytes
  - Process\Virtual Bytes

Summary

RTMT is a robust application for reporting alarms that allow you to act on real-time events.
The keys to successfully using this tool are

- Know what data are important to you.
- Make sure that the people receiving alerts can act on them.
- Configure alerts that signal potential problems.

As a rule of thumb, the most important things to monitor on a frequent basis are

- Gateway utilization
- Media resource utilization
- CPU and disk utilization
- Critical server process status

In addition to RTMT, the Serviceability Reporter provides historical data that is useful for
planning purposes. Leverage this data to plan future rollouts and to optimize your current
deployment. The data is provided in flat CSV files and can be manipulated to provide data
in the format that is the most useful to you.

CallManager 4.0 New Feature Description

This appendix briefly describes the new features in Cisco CallManager release 4.0. It is not a substitute for formal product documentation, but you can use it as a digest to help you understand, in abbreviated form, the capabilities of the new features.

Do not use the information in this appendix to design systems or to respond to a Request for Proposal (RFP) or Request for Information (RFI). You should consult the appropriate Cisco Systems design guides and product description documents for that purpose.

CallManager Release 4.0(1) Feature List

The following list summarizes the new features added to CallManager for the 4.0(1) release:

- Multilevel Precedence and Preemption
- Annunciator
- Q.SIG enhancements
- Session Initiation Protocol (SIP) trunk signaling interface support
- Desktop video telephony
- Multiple calls per line appearance
- Call join
- Call barge enhancements
- Privacy enhancements
- Immediate call divert to voice mail
- Dropping any party from an Ad Hoc conference
- Assigning a Uniform Resource Locator (URL) to any line button
- Display of configurable call forward information
- Direct transfer of selected calls
- IP Manager Assistant enhancements
- Conferencing infrastructure enhancements

- Hunt group enhancements
- Malicious call identification
- Published Application Programming Interface (API) enhancements
- Bulk Administration Tool (BAT) enhancements
- Management and monitoring enhancements
- Multilevel Administration enhancements
- Cisco CallManager Attendant Console enhancements
- Security enhancements

Multilevel Precedence and Preemption

Multilevel Precedence and Preemption (MLPP) is a military-unique feature designed to give individuals who are assigned critical job responsibilities a special priority calling function. At critical events, these users may initiate calls that preempt existing calls of lower priority. In the context of the original military and government users of MLPP, five levels of precedence granularity allow a "Missiles are inbound!" call to critical personnel to interrupt less-important calls. Although this feature was designed for use in military environments, it applies to emergency services and related scenarios in non-military environments.

Do Not Use MLPP to Provide Class of Service Restrictions

MLPP is not well-suited to providing class of service restriction capabilities to users who merely want preferred call routing during normal operations. For example, an executive who requires dedicated outbound calling service to eliminate busy trunk conditions is best served by a reserved trunk channel rather than MLPP. An executive who has the ability to preempt a valid emergency call could open the organization to a lawsuit. Accordingly, for reserved trunk service, use the components of the CallManager dial plan, such as partitions, route patterns, and calling search spaces, rather than MLPP.

MLPP service is extended within two scenarios—phone-to-phone calls on the same network and phone-through-trunk (VoIP gateway) calls to another MLPP-capable network. You associate users with a precedence value according to their job function and configure MLPP using a variety of route patterns, partitions, and calling search spaces. To initiate an MLPP call, the user dials a specific set of digits followed by the phone number. For example, *11-51000 where *11 indicates an MLPP call and the target destination is extension 51000. User authentication as a precedence caller is configured through the application of a calling search space (CSS) to lines on IP phones. Therefore, a precedence value is only indirectly associated with a specific user through his or her IP phone. If any other person places a precedence call from that phone, authentication to make the call is automatically implied. An artifact of original MLPP conceptual design, strict user authentication is not provided for MLPP calls.

Extension mobility can provide a level of user authentication. When the MLPP line/partition/CSS is a part of the extension mobility user template, the privileged calling is only available when the user is logged into the phone and can be disabled when the user logs out or is timed out of extension mobility.

When a number with a precedence value is entered, CallManager determines whether the call will be directed to an MLPP-capable station device (IP phone) or through a voice over IP (VoIP) gateway to a separate MLPP-capable network. Higher precedence calls to busy stations or through fully subscribed gateways alert the target user's phone and preempt the connected, lower-precedence call. To avoid abuse and misuse, configuring MLPP on a system requires the training and discipline of all members who are accorded MLPP precedence call privileges. MLPP calls are specially marked in call detail records (CDR) along with the call's precedence number.

MLPP can be employed within LANs for CallManager systems. Precedence VoIP calls across low-bandwidth IP WANs requiring call admission control (CAC) are not allowed. The original MLPP specification, drafted by the U.S. Department of Defense (DoD) in the 1960s and 1970s, does not take into account the availability of VoIP over WANs. Therefore, CAC mechanisms are not considered in the original specification and cannot be implemented today. DoD architects are in the process of including a provision for VoIP calls over low-bandwidth WANs in future specifications. If an MLPP call is rejected due to locations-based CAC, it will not properly preempt an existing low-priority call.

Until future specifications are available, calls between two LANs require the two domains to be interconnected by MLPP-capable VoIP gateways with a time-division multiplexing (TDM) trunk.

Cisco IP Phone models 7905, 7912, 7940, and 7960 can initiate precedence calls. Destination IP phones for MLPP calls are restricted to Cisco IP Phones 7905, 7910, 7912, 7940, 7960, and 7970. MLPP-capable gateways for the initial introduction of MLPP include the Catalyst 6608 T1-PRI and T1-CAS gateway blades, controlled through Media Gateway Control Protocol (MGCP). MLPP support for selected Cisco 27*xx*, 36*xx*, and 37*xx* series routers with T1-PRI and T1-CAS configured voice interface cards (VIC) controlled through MGCP is anticipated shortly after the release of CallManager release 4.0. Check the MLPP section in the Cisco CallManager Features and Services Guides for an updated list of supported devices:

http://www.cisco.com/univercd/cc/td/doc/product/voice/c_callmg/index.htm

Precedence Calls Between Selected IP Phones in the Same Cluster

Station-to-station precedence calls require acknowledging the destination user before the media connection. When a call is extended to the destination IP Phone and the line is busy with a lower-precedence call, the target user and the user on the phone to which the target user was originally connected are first notified with a unique audible tone and visual display. At the same time, the connected call in progress to the target phone is immediately disconnected. The target user's "acknowledgment" is the physical hanging up of the phone. After the hangup is detected, CallManager connects the higher-precedence call to the target phone. The displays of both the originating and target user's phones continue indicating the call's precedence level. Additional rules for alternative MLPP call routing in the event of nonacknowledgment are implemented in release 4.0 and conform to the MLPP specification. The configuration of an alternative party target directory number (DN) is separate from that of the normal call forward no answer or call forward busy target DN.

Precedence Calls from an IP Phone to a Phone on a Connected MLPP-Capable Network

A precedence call that is extended through a trunk to another network requires CallManager to determine whether the trunk resource is fully utilized. If one channel is idle, the call is automatically extended through the trunk to the destination device. CallManager specially marks the call as a precedence call on that trunk gateway. Furthermore, CallManager signals the precedence call's attached MLPP-capable network. That network then extends the precedence call to the endpoint, notifying the destination user and connected party as described previously. After the precedence notification is presented and the destination call processing server acknowledges the precedence call by disconnecting the preempted call, the two networks connect the media path between the two phones.

During the call setup, if the trunk gateway or trunk group is fully utilized—which means that none of the voice channels are idle and all other route groups are busy as well—CallManager selects a call in progress through that gateway that has a lower precedence value. After it is selected, the original connected parties are audibly notified of the pending precedence call and the call is automatically terminated. Immediately thereafter, CallManager reserves the idle gateway channel and interacts with the connected network to connect media between the originating and destination endpoints.

Q.SIG Enhancements

Q.SIG is a signaling protocol designed to allow feature transparency between two or more interconnected PBXs. CallManager can interconnect to a PBX using Q.SIG. CallManager supports the following ISO-based Q.SIG enhancements:

- Call transfer—A call between endpoints on two separate Q.SIG-enabled PBXs or CallManager servers can be transferred from one of the endpoints. When transferred, the Connected Name ID (COND), Calling Name ID (CNID), Connected Line ID (COLD), and Calling Line ID (CLID) are dynamically updated during the alerting phase as well as when the call is ultimately connected between the two parties.

- Call forward busy, call forward no answer, call forward all—A call to an endpoint from one Q.SIG-enabled CallManager/PBX to another can be forwarded on one of three conditions (line is idle and ring-no-answer timeout expires, line is busy and the Call Forward Busy trigger value is exceeded on the line, and unconditional) at the target endpoint. When forwarded, the COND, COLD, CNID, and CLID are dynamically updated during the alerting phase as well as when the call is ultimately connected between the two parties to reflect the called party's ID.

- Message waiting indication (MWI)—A single voice messaging system can serve users on two Q.SIG-enabled CallManager servers/PBXs. A voice message left in the mailbox of a user will have a message waiting indication delivered to the user's phone regardless of the CallManager/PBX to which the voice mail system or phone is registered. CallManager and the PBX interact to deliver the appropriate MWI message (MWI-ON or MWI-OFF) to the user's phone.

Annunciator

An *annunciator* is a network device that streams media to connected users under special conditions. Annunciator provides voice prompts for special situations. MLPP is one feature that employs annunciator voice prompts. Annunciator supports G.711, G.729, and Cisco wideband audio streaming. Some of the announcements streamed by annunciator include

- Unauthorized precedence announcement (UPA)

- Blocked precedence announcement (BPA)

- Precedence access limitation announcement (PALA)

- Busy not equipped announcement (BNEA)

- Your call cannot be completed as dialed

Session Initiation Protocol (SIP) Trunk Signaling Interface

CallManager 4.0 supports SIP logical trunks (see RFC 3261 for details). SIP trunks support the following capabilities:

- Intercluster communications through a SIP logical trunk connection.

- Communications between a CallManager cluster and a network of SIP-enabled devices through interaction with Cisco SIP Proxy Server (CSPS).

- Bidirectional delivery of line and name identification services on the initial call—CLID, COLD, CNID, and COND.

- After initial call setup, support for supplementary services such as transfer, forward, hold/resume, and Ad Hoc conference are supported when initiated from any CallManager-controlled endpoint (such as Skinny Client Control Protocol (SCCP, or simply, Skinny) phone, SoftPhone, JTAPI application). If the feature is initiated from a SIP endpoint (a SIP phone on the logically connected network) the supplementary services are not allowed.

- Bidirectional, in-band (RFC 2833-compliant devices) to out-of-band (CallManager devices and applications) dual-tone multifrequency (DTMF) signaling translation between CallManager-controlled devices and SIP network devices.

- Configuration of multiple SIP logical trunks.

- SIP trunks have been interoperability tested to support G.711 pass-through fax to compatible gateways; endpoints abstracted by Cisco SIP Proxy Server, which include Cisco SIP-enabled IP Phones including the ATA-186/8, Cisco IP Phones 7905, 7912, 7940, 7960, Cisco SIP-enabled VoIP gateways; Microsoft Messenger; and other CallManager clusters of the same version.

Desktop Video Telephony

Desktop video telephony, as opposed to conference-based video, places the tools of video and collaborative communications on the desk of individual users. Desktop video endpoints that are dedicated to a single individual are combined with shared video conferencing systems to provide a more complete video solution to the enterprise.

Because desktop video is integrated with CallManager, features your users are accustomed to using on their phone calls are also available during video calls, such as hold and transfer. Also, existing H.323 videoconferencing systems are interoperable with the desktop video solution. Calls can be connected to any other H.323 endpoint whether the endpoint is configured in CallManager Administration or whether it is accessible through an H.323 gatekeeper.

CallManager release 4.0 incorporates video enhancements to H.323 and SCCP signaling and call processing within CallManager. In addition, signaling, configuration, and management and monitoring support for the following new Cisco SCCP-controlled, voice-video IP phones is provided in release 4.0:

- Cisco VT Advantage desktop video client application —Targeted for completion in mid-2004. You can learn more about VT Advantage in the following section.

- Third-party SCCP-controlled video endpoints

- Far-end camera control between SCCP-controlled, video-capable endpoints and compatible H.323 video-capable endpoints

CallManager release 4.0 supports the following Cisco IP/VC H.323 video products:

- Cisco video gateways—Models 3510, 3520, and 3540 video gateways provide for video call access to H.320 video endpoints from OnNet desktop video stations.

— Selected H.323 video endpoint support. Several third-party H.323 endpoints have been tested and certified for configuration as H.323 video endpoints within CallManager Administration, including VCON ViGo, Polycom 512 and Polycom ViaVideo. Configuration of these endpoints within CallManager Administration is an alternative to allowing the devices to register to a separate H.323 gatekeeper.

— CAC and call-by-call automated codec selection (regions) for video and voice. Call-by-call call admission control has been adapted within CallManager to account for bandwidth requests when a video call is set up from a desktop video endpoint. Both H.323 gatekeeper-controlled CAC and locations-based CAC have been adapted to allow or reject video calls based upon available bandwidth across a constrained bandwidth WAN. Further, the regions configuration within CallManager Administration has been adapted to recognize a video endpoint's native video codec capabilities. CallManager recognizes audio codec advertisement from G.728 and G.722.1 capable audio and video endpoints as well as H.263 and high-resolution proprietary video codecs. For example, the Cisco VT Advantage supports both an H.263 codec and a proprietary higher-resolution, higher-bandwidth video codec. Per-device bandwidth utilization policy and voice-video fallback policy are assignable per device to allow differentiated service to different user classes.

— Unified administration of voice and video components. A principal benefit of incorporating video within CallManager is the ability to provision video endpoints directly within CallManager Administration. A unified database implies a common dial plan, common user policies, and common monitoring and diagnostics among all voice and video endpoints. Among the monitoring and diagnostics enhancements that have been added are new video-related performance counters and Simple Network Management Protocol (SNMP) traps. CDRs and CDR Analysis and Reporting (CAR) tool have also been enhanced to present video bandwidth usage.

• Call control and the Cisco IP Phone Services interface APIs are video-aware. The IP Phone Services interface allows the development of multicast receive and transmit video applications.

Cisco VT Advantage

The Cisco VT Advantage solution includes a Cisco USB camera, video software that installs to a PC or laptop, and a VT Advantage-enabled Cisco IP Phone — including the phone firmware to enable video on supported IP Phone models you already own. The camera/software combination provides video encoding and decoding and video Real-Time Transport Protocol (RTP) path termination. The IP phone provides the voice path and the user interface for placing calls and using phone features such as hold, conference, extension mobility, and so on. Figure 1 shows the streaming relationship between endpoints.

Users can configure their video solutions to initially autotransmit or mute video for outbound calls. They can also configure their video solutions to autoanswer inbound calls with video active if the calling device is transmitting video. To establish a video session, the user first places a voice call. If the called endpoint is also video capable (such as another VT Advantage, a Skinny-controlled IP video phone, an H.323 endpoint capable of H.263 video encoding, or an H.323 video gateway), CallManager automatically establishes an audio RTP path and separate video RTP path (assuming the called endpoint's user has configured his or her system for autoanswer in video mode). Once the video session is established, the user can invoke the usual telephony features on the phone, such as transfer. For example, when the user transfers the call by pressing the **Transf** . . . softkey, both the voice and video RTP streams are redirected to the party to which the video call was transferred. If the destination party is not video capable, CallManager automatically stops the video component and the call continues as an audio-only call. If the same call is then transferred back to a video-capable endpoint, CallManager reinstates video as well as voice RTP paths and the video session is up again.

The ovals encircling the RTP streams in Figure A-3 indicate the following:

- A call from a VT Advantage to another VT Advantage has voice and video as separate RTP streams in the same call.

- A call from a VT Advantage to an H.323 endpoint has both RTP streams terminating on the H.323 endpoint.

- A call from a VT Advantage to a SCCP video endpoint like Tandberg also has voice and video terminating on the same device, on the Tandberg in this case.

- A call from a VT Advantage to another VT Advantage has voice and video separately terminating on the respective user's PC and phone combination.

- A call from a VT Advantage to an IP phone only has a single RTP stream—the voice stream between the two phones; there is no video stream.

Configure Cisco-Approved H.323 Video Endpoints in CallManager Administration Instead of Using a Gatekeeper

If you are already using H.323 video endpoints, you can choose between two configuration options so that the endpoints can interoperate with other Cisco AVVID video endpoints:

- **Configuration Option 1**—Connect the H.323 video endpoints to the CallManager cluster through an H.323 gatekeeper. This configuration has the advantage of maintaining existing configuration and requiring little additional system administration training.

- **Configuration Option 2**—Configure the H.323 video endpoints in CallManager Administration. This approach provides the advantage that the dial plan for all voice and video devices is configured within a single database. Also, locations-based CAC is applied to calls originating from or destined to these endpoints through a low-bandwidth WAN.

In general, it's best to configure Cisco-approved H.323 video endpoints in CallManager Administration. Configure all nonapproved H.323 video endpoints on a separate H.323 video network and connect this network to CallManager through a gatekeeper, as described in Configuration Option 1

Figure 1   *Video Endpoint Streaming*

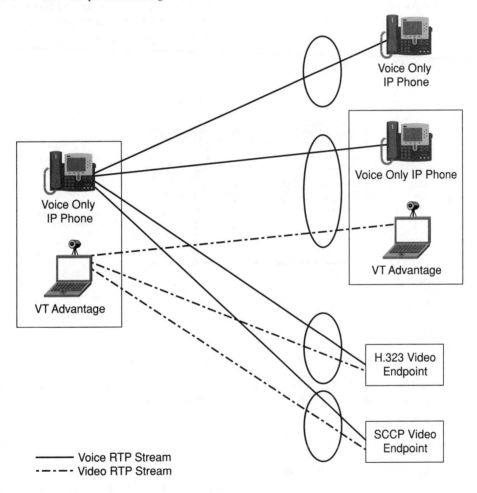

TIP   You can determine if your H.323 video endpoints are Cisco-approved by accessing the AVVID Application Portal at http://www.cisco.com/pcgi-bin/ecoa/Search and selecting **IP Videoconferencing and Networking** in Step 1 and **Videoconferencing Clients** in Step 2. When you click **Submit**, a table of Cisco-approved vendors appears, and the approved products are listed in the Partner Product and Cisco Product columns of the table.

Multiple Calls Per Line Appearance

CallManager 4.0 supports up to 200 calls per line appearance (the previous maximum was two calls per line appearance). You can specify the settings for the maximum number of calls, busy trigger, and no answer ring duration for each line on the Directory Number Configuration page in CallManager Administration (**Device > Phone >** *select a phone > click a line number*). Information about each call, including call state, call ID information, call duration, and a unique call number, is provided for each call on a single line appearance. Figure 2 illustrates multiple calls on a single line appearance.

Figure 2   *Three Active Calls on a Single Line Appearance*

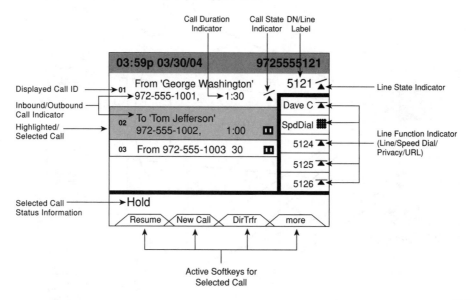

See Chapter 7, "Configuring CallManager and IP Telephony Components," for more information about the multiple calls per line appearance feature.

Call Join (Join)

The call join feature allows users to bridge multiple calls that are present on a single line; cross-line joins are not supported except for IP Manager Assistant (IPMA). Call join differs from an Ad Hoc conference call in that a join bridges calls that are already in progress on the user's phone, whether they are connected or on hold. The user selects two or more calls in progress on the same line by scrolling and selecting the calls with the Select softkey and then pressing the Join softkey. If the user presses the Join softkey without previously selecting two calls, CallManager automatically selects the last two active calls and joins them.

After the calls are joined, CallManager treats the call like an Ad Hoc conference. The invoking user becomes a party on the conference and can leave the conference at any time, and the conference remains in progress. And as with other Ad Hoc conferences, as soon as the invoking user leaves the joined conference, no other party may drop or add parties to the joined conference.

Call join operations initiated from the IPMA Assistant Console can be across lines. Practically, this allows a call on one manager's proxy line to be joined to a call at another manager's proxy line.

NOTE   Users are unable to join an existing call into an existing conference (no Ad Hoc conference chaining).

Barge Enhancements (cBarge)

CallManager release 3.2 introduced the barge feature, which was activated by the Barge softkey. It allowed a user to enter into a three-party conference with a call in progress between two callers. The result of the barge operation is that the target IP phone mixes together three audio streams to create the conference.

CallManager release 4.0 introduces the conference barge feature, which is activated by the cBarge softkey. It creates a multiple party conference with the target callers using a network digital signal processor (DSP) conferencing resource rather than using the IP phone to mix the audio streams. Improvements in cBarge functionality over the earlier barge feature include the following:

- The target of the barge can hang up without disconnecting all three parties on the call.
- G.711 or G.729 is supported.
- The conference can have a maximum of six parties. Up to four barges may be conducted on a single call, resulting in an Ad Hoc conference of as many as six parties.
- When the last two parties are in barge, the network conference resource is released and the call reverts to a two-party call.

TIP   Normally an individual user's phone is configured for either Barge or cBarge. Configuring both features on the same phone is impractical and might confuse the user.

Privacy Enhancements (Privacy)

Privacy, in its original implementation in CallManager release 3.2, when enabled via service parameter, prevented users who shared a DN with other users from barging into their calls. CallManager release 4.0 enhances privacy through two means. First, privacy can be applied on a per-phone basis. Second, privacy is extended to include the ability to restrict the display of call information to other users whose IP phone lines share a common DN.

Privacy is enabled by default. To disable it, you can set the clusterwide CallManager service parameter Privacy Setting to False (**Service > Service Parameter**). However, this can be overridden on a per-device basis in the Phone Configuration page in CallManager Administration.

Enhancements to the privacy feature include the following:

* Privacy can be assigned to a line/feature button on a device. The user toggles the Privacy button to enable/disable the privacy feature (an icon shows the current privacy state).

* When privacy is enabled or disabled on an IP phone, it affects the behavior of all lines on the configured device.

* When privacy is enabled, no other users on other phones that share a line appearance can barge into a call on the privacy-enabled phone. When privacy is disabled and the user on the privacy-disabled IP phone answers or places a call, the real-time call information is displayed on any IP phone lines that share a common DN.

* Privacy does not affect the call history (missed, placed, or received) display on phones with shared line appearances. If privacy is enabled on IP Phone A, and a user at Phone A places a call on a shared line appearance, the real-time call information is not displayed on the other phones. However, the placed call history shows call information on the other phones.

Immediate Divert to Voice Mail (iDivert)

The immediate divert feature, activated by the iDivert softkey, allows a user, such as an administrative assistant, to immediately divert a call to voice mail. The primary target of transfers in an administrative assistant environment is the manager's voice mail. This feature can be applied to any IP phone that can accept programmable softkeys.

When an active call is in progress and the user presses the iDivert softkey, the call is immediately transferred to the voice mail profile target for the associated line.

After the call is diverted to voice mail, the original called party number is delivered to the voice mail pilot. The voice mail system can use this number to immediately divert the call to the associated mailbox of the original called party without the invoking user having to enter the voice mailbox number.

NOTE   The immediate divert feature is not supported for inbound calls extended through a Q.SIG trunk.

Drop Any Party from Ad Hoc Conference (Drop)

CallManager release 4.0 allows Ad Hoc conference controllers to drop any party from the conference. This is an improvement over earlier functionality, which allowed only the last party to be dropped with a press of the RmLstC softkey. To drop a party from the current conference, the conference controller presses the Drop softkey. A dialog appears on the phone's display, showing a list of all parties on the conference and their calling information. The controller scrolls to highlight the target party and then presses the Drop softkey again to drop the party. This feature can be applied to any IP phone that can accept programmable softkeys.

All participants in the Ad Hoc conference can display a list of conference participants if their IP phones have display capabilities that allow it; only the conference controller can drop a party.

Assign a URL to a Line/Feature Button (Service URL)

You can assign a URL to a line/feature button so that users can invoke an IP phone service at the touch of a button. Normally, IP phone services such as extension mobility login/logout services, MyFastDials, and other services such as weather lookup were available only by pressing the **settings** button and then selecting the desired phone service. Now you can configure the URL for a phone service on a line/feature button on an XML-capable IP phone such as Cisco IP Phone models 7960, 7940, or 7970. When the user presses the associated line/feature button, the URL is accessed, and, in the case of XML services, the service is invoked.

Display of Configurable Call Forward Information

Cisco IP Phone models 7940, 7960, and 7970 and Cisco IP Communicator can display forwarded call information. For calls transferred or forwarded from attendants or administrative assistants, this information was lost to the destination user in previous CallManager releases. CallManager release 4.0 allows you to configure, on a per-line basis, the call forward information that appears on the phone.

The following information can be enabled or disabled for display on an IP phone line at ringing (call alerting) and connected states. This information is displayed on all lines in the case of shared DNs. If none of the following information is enabled, only call duration is displayed.

- Original dialed number
- Redirected (last) dialed number
- Calling line ID (when available)
- Calling name ID (when available)

Direct Transfer (DirTrfr)

Direct transfer is similar to call join in that the user can conference together calls that are already in progress; unlike call join, a maximum of two calls can be joined. Furthermore, after the two calls are joined, the user who joined the calls is immediately dropped from the call and his or her IP phone no longer displays the joined call information. The resulting joined call cannot be retrieved after the direct transfer operation is invoked. Direct transfer can be assigned to any IP phone that can support softkeys.

To perform a direct transfer, the user scrolls to the two calls from the same line appearance that are already in progress (connected or on hold on the IP phone), presses the **Select** softkey for each call to select it, and then presses the **DirTrfr** softkey. The two selected calls are joined immediately and directly between the two selected endpoints without a conference resource. If the initiating user does not select two calls, the last two handled calls are automatically selected. The following exceptions apply:

- When invoked on IPMA Assistant Console, the selected calls can be on different line appearances.
- Direct transfer of two joined or conferenced calls is not supported.

IPMA Enhancements

The IPMA application consists of the administrative assistant's IP phone, the Assistant Console PC application, the manager's IP phone, and the IPMA server application. Calls directed to the manager's DN are handled according to IPMA logic and manager/assistant configuration. The purpose of the application is to provide both managers and assistants with tools to effectively manage calls. IPMA normally is configured for one assistant and one manager, but it can support one assistant and multiple managers. IPMA provides redundancy in the event that the primary Assistant Console is either out of service or unattended.

CallManager release 4.0 introduces feature enhancements to the manager's IP phone and the administrative assistant's Assistant Console application. These new enhancements are outlined in the following list:

- Support for common directory number (shared lines) between primary line appearance on the manager's phone and the associated line appearance on the Assistant Console/IP phone.

- Two IPMA server configuration modes are available within a cluster. When configured for one mode or the other, the configuration affects the operation of all managers and assistants in that cluster. The two configuration modes are call filtering mode and shared line mode:

  — Call filtering mode refers to the original operational mode of IPMA in which the Assistant Console is configured with a manager proxy line. This proxy line is a line appearance that represents the manager's line. Inbound calls are filtered (tested) for calling line ID information during call alerting against a preconfigured filtering list of calling line IDs (CLID). If a match is found for the test, the call is routed to either the manager's primary line or the manager's proxy line on the assistant's IP phone. The manager's proxy line on the assistant's IP phone is not configured with the common DN of the manager's IP phone primary line. In this mode, barge and privacy features are not offered between the manager and assistant.

  — Shared line mode refers to the configuration in which the manager's line and an assistant's line share a common DN. The conditional call filtering feature is unavailable in this mode. When configured in shared line mode, calls to the manager's DN alert at both IP phones simultaneously. In this mode, the call filtering feature of the call filtering mode is unavailable for the manager's line, but barge and privacy between the manager and assistant are available.

- New features that can be invoked at the manager's IP phone, the assistant's IP phone and the Assistant Console application include the following:

  — Multiple calls per line appearance

  — Call join on same-line calls and across multiple lines

  — Enhanced call barge (Barge and cBarge) for shared line mode only

  — Enhanced privacy for shared line mode only

  — Add/drop any party to/from Ad Hoc conference

  — Direct transfer on same-line calls and across multiple lines

  — Configurable call forward information display

- Common directory number support for multiple lines on the same device (manager phone, assistant phone, and Assistant Console) is not supported. Therefore, call rollover from one line to another as configured in CallManager release 3.3 and earlier is not supported in IPMA. Note that support for multiple calls per line appearance effectively removes the need to support multiple line appearances on the same phone with common DNs.

Conferencing Infrastructure Enhancements

Conferencing infrastructure describes the underlying media transport platforms required to mix voice or video media in a multiple party conference. Underlying CallManager infrastructure enhancements are described in the following list. The system administrator benefits from the increased unification of the system configuration. The user benefits from the increased feature transparency and quicker system performance.

- The Cisco Conference Connection (CCC) conferencing engine has been ported from its architecture as a standalone conference server with an H.323 signaling interface between CallManager and CCC. The CCC conferencing engine has been ported to an architecture that is founded on interaction based on Computer Telephony Integration (CTI) with CallManager's call control. With this release, CallManager handles all call control, provisioning, and resource management through a nonpublic API. All call processing is handled by CallManager.

- Support for voice and video Ad Hoc conferencing is offered.

You can learn more about Cisco Conference Connection at the following link or search Cisco.com for "Cisco Conference Connection":

http://www.cisco.com/en/US/products/sw/voicesw/ps752/index.html

Hunt Group Enhancements

CallManager release 4.0 provides hunt list functionality to achieve general, high-performance call distribution that works in conjunction with route filters and route lists to direct calls to specific devices and to include, exclude, or modify specific digit patterns. Previously, only Cisco CallManager Attendant Console was capable of using a scalable hunt list solution via the Telephony Call Dispatcher (TCD) service. While TCD is still used for Attendant Console and is enhanced to provide true queuing in CallManager release 4.x, hunt lists are now provided in CallManager for calls that do not require queuing and are not associated with an Attendant Console.

Hunt lists are composed of one or more ordered line groups or ordered route groups. A hunt pilot number is associated with each hunt list. The hunt pilot represents an explicit route pattern configured in CallManager Administration, and when dialed, the pilot number initiates the associated hunt list's call distribution process. Line groups are composed of an ordered list of phone DN/partition pairs. Assigning a route group to a hunt list allows distribution of calls to both physical (VoIP gateway) and logical (signaling) trunks.

Hunt group call distribution logic selections include support for two existing hunt group logic selections—linear and longest idle—and support for two additional hunt group logic selections—broadcast and circular.

Hunt groups allow you to associate any four distribution logic types to any line group— linear (also called top-down), circular, broadcast, and longest idle. The logic types can build upon one another as well (longest idle hunt first, then broadcast ring second, and so on). Linear, circular, and longest idle can be assigned to route groups. Broadcast logic allows simultaneous call distribution to multiple directory numbers. See Figure 3 for a view of call sequencing. The numbers indicate the order that the DNs receive the call, depending on which hunt logic is employed. For example, if longest idle logic is used, 4007 receives the call initially and if it does not answer, then 4006 receives the call, and so on. In broadcast logic, all available DNs receive the call simultaneously. Busy DNs are not included in the hunt distribution.

Figure 3   *Hunt Group Logic*

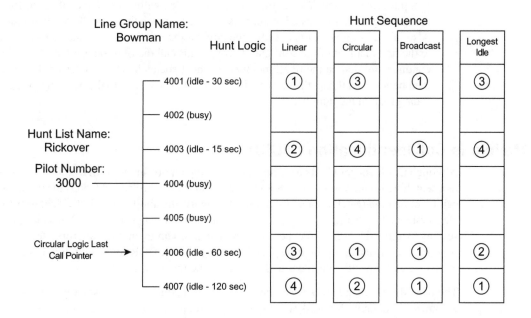

The following list details the different types of call distribution logic selections: linear, longest idle, broadcast, and circular:

- **Linear** (also supported by TCD)—For each new call, this hunt logic tests the availability of hunt group members one member at a time, beginning at the top of the ordered list of hunt group members. When a member is idle, the call is distributed to that member. This logic statistically overworks the top members of the ordered hunt group.

- **Longest idle** (also supported by TCD)—For each new call, a simultaneous test of all hunt group members is made for the duration since a call was last disconnected from that member. The member with the longest idle duration is selected, and the call is distributed to that member. Of the four available hunt group logics, this logic is the fairest in that the average calls per hunt group member per unit of time that is given to similar call lengths is more equal among the members than with the other hunt logic types.

- **Broadcast**—Distribution of calls within any line group that is configured for broadcast distribution logic is such that a call is extended to all members marked as idle. All members marked as idle alert simultaneously or nearly so.

- **Circular**—The relative position of the last distributed call within a line group or route group is remembered. When new calls are extended within a group configured for circular logic, the first tested member is the one to which the last call was distributed. Also, if the last member is not idle, the circular distribution logic distributes the call to the first member of the configured group. This call distribution availability testing continues for that call until all members of the associated group are tested. If not all members are available, the call distributor distributes the call to the next line group or route group in the hunt list.

Malicious Call Identification (MCID)

Although CallManager CDRs and third-party billing reports are tools that enable after-the-fact searching for the source of malicious calls, CallManager release 4.0 adds the malicious call identification (MCID) capability. MCID supports the ability of an individual user to alert system administrators immediately when a malicious call is received. You configure a softkey to allow the user who experiences a malicious call to alert the appropriate personnel. CallManager provides special markings on the CDR for a call tagged as a malicious call. Specific attributes and caveats of the feature are as follows.

The new MCID feature softkey can be applied to IP phones to which softkeys can be assigned. By default, this softkey is not configured on any softkey template.

When a malicious call is received at the target phone, the user presses the MCID softkey. CallManager responds by issuing an immediate alert via e-page or e-mail to the system administrator. The target and content of the e-mail or e-page notification can be preconfigured. The user who pressed the MCID softkey hears a confirmation tone and the originating caller's CLID and CNID (if available) are displayed to the invoking party's IP phone. When the call is completed, a unique "malicious call ID" marker is associated with the CDR entry.

MCID event details can be diverted to syslog, RTMT, or SNMP for further action by those services. The CAR tool can be used to post-process the CDRs and report malicious call activity. Third-party CDR analyzers can provide the same post-event reports.

Published API Enhancements

CallManager's suite of configuration, management and monitoring, services, and call control APIs is extended and expanded in CallManager release 4.0. The following sections describe these enhancements.

Java Telephony API/Telephony API Enhancements

Telephony API (TAPI) and Java Telephony API (JTAPI) have been enhanced to provide support for autoinstalled infrastructure and media termination at the application server. Additional enhancements have occurred in the areas of login, SNMP, and performance monitoring. The following sections describe these improvements.

Autoinstallation Infrastructure Enhancements

CallManager provides a facility for applications to download compatible TAPI and JTAPI service providers for this and all CallManager releases going forward. Applications must be modified to take advantage of this capability.

Media Termination at the Route Point

This enhancement allows applications that terminate media, such as IP interactive voice response (IVR), to answer calls at the application server without configuring separate CTI ports for each required IVR channel. The benefit to users is twofold: more scalable media termination applications and a more scalable number of CTI applications per cluster.

Calls terminated at the CTI route point may have the following operations performed on them:

- Answer call
- Have multiple active calls per CTI route point
- Redirect (forward)
- Hold/resume
- Terminate call

Logon Services Enhancements

Support is provided for underlying architectural changes to allow a common directory login interface among all applications, including Personal Assistant, extension mobility, IPMA, and more. In earlier CallManager releases, the lack of an API for common login services dictated the need for a directory login method that was unique for every application that required user login. The benefit to users of the login service enhancements is the potential for more consistent user login transactions among applications. The benefit to system administrators is the potential for a common user login provisioning interface among all applications.

SNMP Enhancements

Additional Management Information Base (MIB) objects related to new devices and services are provided. You can see the latest MIBs at the Network Management Software Download Center at

http://www.cisco.com/public/sw-center/netmgmt/cmtk/mibs.shtml

Performance Monitoring Enhancements

New performance counters have been added for Attendant Console, CTI interfaces, IPMA, TFTP service, server platform performance, and security. You can see the new objects and counters in RTMT or PerfMon.

Bulk Administration Tool (BAT) Enhancements

BAT allows you to add, update, and delete large quantities of configuration information, such as phone, users, and much more. Some of the specific attributes and caveats for the BAT enhancements are as follows:

- Support is provided for more flexible comma-separated value file format.
- Broadened support for the Export Utility. The Export Utility operates on clusters with common CallManager releases; it does not work between release 3.3 and release 4.0 CallManager databases.
- Support for bulk configuration of new IP Phone device types and new line attributes:
  - Support for IP Phone 7970, IP Communicator
  - MLPP settings
  - URL assignment to the line button
  - Configurable call forwarding information per line

Management and Monitoring Enhancements

CallManager release 4.0 provides new management and monitoring tools, extensions of existing tools, and closer integration with CiscoWorks 2000 modules. Some of the specific attributes of the management and monitoring tool enhancements are as follows:

- New SNMP MIBs and new performance objects and counters are included for new devices and services:

  — Support for new devices and attribute extensions—annunciator, hunt groups, shared lines, video, SIP trunk, and conferencing infrastructure

  — Support for new services—security services counters

  — Support for new SNMP traps

  — Syslog events for MCID occurrences

  — Quality Reporting Tool (QRT) notification

- CDR and CAR—Support for new features and devices, such as video, MLPP, TCD enhancements, malicious call identifiers, and shared lines.

- QRT enhancements—Support for e-mail and e-page that is initiated from an IP phone.

- RTMT enhancements

  — Remote RTMT client—Operates when RTMT service is down. Allows operation of RTMT service remotely from a CallManager server.

  — Preconfigured, frequently used performance objects and counters.

- Troubleshooting enhancements—new support allows the Cisco Technical Assistance Center (TAC) to more efficiently consult with its customers who have TAC cases to gather troubleshooting and diagnostics information:

  — Trace setup administrative interface—Includes preconfigured trace setups for the most frequently requested traces

  — Park—Identifies lists of assigned call park numbers.

  — Pickup groups—Identifies pickup group membership.

  — Meet-Me conference DNs—Identifies assigned Meet-Me conference DNs.

Multilevel Administration (MLA) Enhancements

MLA allows you to provide segregated, authenticated access to CallManager Administration and CallManager Serviceability web pages. Originally delivered with CallManager release 3.2 and backward-compatible with release 3.1, MLA allows the system administrator superuser to create user groups and functional (web page) groups and associate levels of access between the two pairs of groups. MLA therefore controls selective access to CallManager database configuration to users who authenticate through a user logon process. MLA is enhanced in CallManager release 4.0 through an integrated installation script. Whereas in previous versions of CallManager MLA was an add-on application, overlaid on CallManager Administration and the CallManager database, installation of MLA with release 4.0 is now achieved as part of the base CallManager installation. Another enhancement is that MLA is enabled/disabled via the use of an MLA parameter (**User Access Rights > Configure MLA Parameters**).

See Chapter 9, "Using Multilevel Administration," for more information.

Cisco CallManager Attendant Console Enhancements

Cisco CallManager Attendant Console feature enhancements derive from new CTI enhancements. The new features and capabilities are summarized as follows:

- Support for native call queuing on a busy hunt group
- Support for multiple calls per line
- Support for shared lines

You can learn more about these enhancements in the Cisco CallManager Attendant Console documentation at

http://www.cisco.com/univercd/cc/td/doc/product/voice/attendnt/call_att/index.htm

Security Enhancements

The primary security enhancement in CallManager 4.0 is the addition of device authentication, signaling privacy, and media privacy for selected IP Phones (Cisco IP Phone models 7940G, 7960G, and 7970G).

Each of these IP Phones has an embedded certificate. CallManager 4.0 has a new certificate service founded upon a private key. When these security features are enabled in CallManager, before the IP Phone is allowed to register to CallManager, the phone establishes a trust relationship with its CallManager. Once established, the IP Phone is allowed to register to CallManager. This process is referred to as *device-to-CallManager authentication*.

Signaling privacy refers to the encryption of all call control SCCP traffic between the IP Phones and their active CallManager. The encryption is to AES-128 encryption standard.

Media privacy refers to the encryption of all media (voice Real-Time Transport Protocol) packets passed between two security-enabled IP Phones.

The security enhancements also provide a means by which the user is notified as to the security state of the voice conversation in progress. If the phone has security capabilities but is connected to an endpoint that does not have security capabilities, the security icon on the phone indicates that the voice call is nonsecure. If the call is encrypted, the icon reflects secure status.

You can learn more about security enhancements in Chapter 6, "Securing the Environment."

Other Enhancements and Caveats

The following enhancements have been added in CallManager release 4.0:

- The maximum length of a dialed digit string has been extended from 24 to 30 characters. This extension provides the benefit of enhanced support for a simple authorization codes workaround through dialed digit string extensions.

- Phone settings on an upstream phone switch port are displayed through the IP phone web page with the benefit of a more accessible view of switch port settings for diagnostics. The link is accessible by browsing to the IP phone's IP address, for example: http://1.2.3.4.

- CAR has enhanced ability to track capacity utilization by individual stream for media processing devices such as transcoders, gateways, and conference bridges. This provides more realistic presentation of capacity utilization statistics for selected devices.

- Enhanced overlap sending—Explicit configuration is allowed on a per-route pattern basis.

You should note the following caveats:

- CallManager 4.0 is not supported on some Cisco Media Convergence Servers, including MCS7820, MCS7822, and MCS-7830 class servers.

- Configuration and operation with security capabilities enabled (device/firmware image/configuration file authentication, signaling integrity, and media encryption) reduces the performance of CallManager servers, TFTP servers, and application servers. Users can enable or disable these functions to balance the relative need for security and performance.

This glossary lists terms and acronyms that are applicable to this book. You can find additional information at

http://www.cisco.com/univercd/cc/td/doc/product/voice/evbugl4.htm

NUMBERS AND SYMBOLS

24/7. A time frame referring to 24 hours a day, 7 days a week.

9-1-1. A service in North America in which phone users can dial the digits 911 and reach an emergency operator who can dispatch police, fire, or medical assistance as appropriate. This service is sometimes called *basic 9-1-1* because the emergency operator might not have access to the callback phone number or the caller's location. Indeed, the call might not even reach the appropriate emergency call center based on the caller's location.

E9-1-1 (Enhanced 9-1-1). An emergency communications service in North America in which phone users can dial the digits 911 and reach an appropriate emergency call center based on the caller's location. The location information and the callback phone number are displayed to the emergency operator. Residential subscribers typically receive this service from their phone service providers. Organizations that manage their own private phone switch must make special arrangements to provide this lifesaving service to ensure that their users are protected.

µ-law. A North American standard for converting analog data into digital form using pulse code modulation.

A

AAA. Authentication, authorization, and accounting. A group of Cisco IOS software features that allows devices to authenticate users, authorize what actions they can perform, and keep track of all actions on the device.

AAR. Automated Alternate Routing. A CallManager feature that automatically reroutes calls when not enough WAN bandwidth is available. Works in conjunction with locations-based call admission control.

ABR. Available bit rate. An ATM permanent virtual circuit (PVC) type that does not have a specific bit rate assigned to it.

ACD. Automatic call distributor. A device that handles incoming calls used for call answering and automated routing.

ACELP. Algebraic Code Excited Linear Prediction. An algorithm used to compress human voice before it is transmitted over a packet network.

ACL. Access control list. A feature in Cisco IOS software that allows and denies access to network resources based on criteria such as IP address, TCP or UDP port number, or QoS marking.

acoustic echo. A form of echo that occurs when the acoustic energy from a device such as a handset, headset, or speakerphone enters the microphone of the same device.

ACS. Access control server. A server that provides authentication, authorization, and accounting functions to network devices.

AD. Active Directory. A Windows 2000 LDAP directory service.

adapter teaming. A way for a Cisco Media Convergence Server to have two connections to the network to provide continuous connectivity in the event of network switch failure.

ad hoc. Improvised or impromptu.

Ad Hoc conference. A type of conference in the CallManager system that requires a user (called the conference controller) to include conference attendees by calling them individually. See also *Meet-Me conference*.

ADUC. Active Directory Users and Computers. A tool used to provision users and groups in Windows 2000 environments.

AIM. Advanced Integration Module. A variety of modules available for Cisco IOS software routers and voice gateways that provide additional functionality such as voice DSP resources.

A-law. A European standard for converting analog data into digital form using pulse code modulation.

algorithmic delay. The look-ahead delay that occurs when a coder (such as G.729) tries to compress a block of audio. The coder looks at the subsequent audio block to make the calculation for the current sample. This means that the current sample must be delayed by the amount of the look-ahead time before being compressed. G.729 has an algorithmic delay of 5 ms, and G.723.1 has an algorithmic delay of 7.5 ms.

Alpha cluster. A complete, working CallManager environment that is used by a small group of people as the test bed for the rest of the company.

ANI. Automatic number identification; also known as calling party number. A service that provides the phone number of an incoming call.

Annunciator (ANN). A service that lets CallManager play prerecorded announcements and tones to Cisco IP Phones, gateways, and other configurable devices. Can be used to tell callers why a call failed or was not preempted and to play tones for some transferred calls and conferences.

ANSI. American National Standards Institute. A private, nonprofit organization that administers and coordinates the U.S. voluntary standardization and conformity assessment system. See http://www.ansi.org.

API. Application programming interface. Usually a set of libraries with accompanying header files that application programmers can use in their programs to interact with a third-party application.

ARP. Address Resolution Protocol. Allows a device on an IP network to obtain the layer 2 address (MAC address) of a device on its local subnet using that device's IP address.

ASCII. American Standard Code for Information Interchange. A code for representing English characters as numbers, with each letter assigned a number from 0 to 127. Directory numbers in CCM trace files are represented in ASCII.

ASIC. Application-specific integrated circuit. A chip designed for a particular application.

ASN.1. Abstract Syntax Notation. Used to encode messages in various protocols, including H.225 and H.245.

ASP. Active Server Page. A web page that uses ActiveX scripting to dynamically control the web page's content. Cisco CallManager Administration relies on Active Server Pages.

ATM. Asynchronous Transfer Mode. The international standard for cell relay in which multiple service types (such as voice, video, or data) are conveyed in fixed-length (53-byte) cells.

AXL. AVVID XML Layer. The AXL API provides a mechanism for inserting, retrieving, updating, and removing data from the database using an XML SOAP interface. This allows a programmer to access data using XML and to receive the data in XML form instead of using a binary library or DLL.

B

backup server. A server that copies information from servers targeted for backup to the medium used for backing up, such as a DAT drive.

backup target. The server containing the data to be backed up, or the server to which backed-up data is restored.

bandwidth. A measurement of the amount of data per unit of time that a communications interface can send or receive.

BARS. Cisco Backup and Restore System. BARS backs up and restores CallManager and application server data.

BAT. Bulk Administration Tool. A web-based tool bundled with CallManager that allows you to add, update, or delete large numbers of users, devices, and more in the CallManager database.

Bc. Committed burst rate. On Frame Relay permanent virtual circuits (PVCs), the maximum bit rate to which data can burst over the committed information rate (CIR).

B-channel. Bearer channel. A fundamental component of ISDN interfaces. It carries 64 kbps in both directions, is circuit-switched, and can carry either voice or data.

BIOS. Basic input/output system. Built-in software on a computer that controls a PC motherboard's interaction with various components such as keyboard, mouse, display screen, disk drives, and more.

bit mask. A string of bits that each represent a particular trace setting. Commonly used in SDL tracing.

blind transfer. A form of transfer whereby the user redirects a call to another extension without speaking to the party where the call is being redirected. See also *consultation transfer*.

BPDU. Bridge Protocol Data Unit. Used by LAN switches participating in Spanning Tree Protocol to discover the network topology to ensure a loop-free bridged network.

BRI. Basic Rate Interface. The basic ISDN configuration consisting of two B-channels that can each carry voice or data at a rate of 64 kbps and one D-channel that carries call control information at a rate of 16 kbps.

C

CA. Certification authority. Used to create digital certificates for use in securing applications by providing a guarantee of identity.

call admission control (CAC). A CallManager feature that ensures that voice QoS is maintained across constricted WAN links and automatically diverts calls to alternative PSTN routes when WAN bandwidth is unavailable. The two types of CAC are locations-based and gatekeeper. CAC is used in situations where a limited amount of bandwidth exists between telephony endpoints such as phones and gateways.

calling search space. An ordered list of partitions used by CallManager digit analysis to decide which endpoint to extend a call to.

call leg ID. Call leg identifier. A value appearing in CCM traces and CDRs, unique among all CallManager nodes in a cluster, that identifies each participant in a call.

CallManager. A Cisco AVVID IP Telephony service whose primary function is to control and route calls to and from voice-enabled IP devices.

CAM table. Content Addressable Memory table. A table maintained by layer 2 network switches that maps a MAC address to the port where the MAC address was learned.

CAPF. Certificate Authority Proxy Function. A service that acts on behalf of a security-enabled Cisco IP Phone to request a certificate from a certificate authority using the Simple Certificate Enrollment Protocol (SCEP).

CAR. CDR Analysis and Reporting. A web-based tool bundled with CallManager Serviceability that helps you analyze the raw data that comprises the CDR database and create reports based on your search criteria.

CAS. Channel-associated signaling. See *robbed-bit signaling*.

CatOS. Cisco Catalyst operating system. The operating system that runs on Catalyst 4000, 5000, and 6000 series LAN switches.

cBarge. Conference barge. A CallManager feature introduced in release 4.0 that creates a multiple party conference with the target callers using a network DSP conferencing resource rather than using the IP phone to mix the audio streams.

CBL. Color block logic. The ability of a LAN switch with VLAN support to block all packets on a particular VLAN from entering or exiting a particular port while allowing traffic for other VLANs to pass.

CBR. Constant bit rate. An Asynchronous Transfer Mode (ATM) permanent virtual circuit (PVC) type that provides a guaranteed constant rate of transmission. CBR is most often used in circuit emulation applications.

CB-WFQ. Class-based weighted fair queuing. Allows you to define traffic classes that are based on certain match criteria, such as access control lists, input interface names, protocols, and QoS labels.

CCAPI. Call control application programming interface. The call routing engine in Cisco IOS software voice gateways.

CCC. Cisco Conference Connection. A Meet-Me audio conference server that integrates with CallManager.

CCM. An abbreviation of Cisco CallManager.

CCMAdmin. A shortened term and part of the URL for Cisco CallManager Administration. See *Cisco CallManager Administration*.

CCMPWDchanger. A CallManager utility that is used to change passwords. Access it by entering **CCMPwdChanger** at a DOS prompt.

CCMUser. A shortened term and part of the URL for the Cisco CallManager User Options web page. See *Cisco CallManager User Options*.

CDCC. Call-Dependent Call Control. A CDCC process is created inside CallManager for every instance of a call.

CDP. Cisco Discovery Protocol. A device-discovery protocol that runs on most Cisco-manufactured equipment. It lets a device advertise its existence to other devices and receive information about other devices in the network.

CDR. Call detail record. A record that CallManager logs after a call completes to permit billing or auditing of system use.

CDR Analysis and Reporting Tool. See *CAR*.

CDR data. The grouping of CDRs and CMRs.

central office (CO). A telecommunications office centralized in a specific locality to handle the telephone service for that locality. Abbreviated as CO.

CER. Cisco Emergency Responder. A Cisco product that dynamically addresses the need to identify the location of 911 callers in an emergency. No administration is required when phones and/or people move from one location to another.

CFA. Call forward all. Forwards all calls to a designated number.

CFB. Call forward busy. Forwards calls to a designated number when the called number is busy.

CFF. Call forward on failure. Forwards calls to a designated number when an application that controls the called number fails. This feature is offered only for CTI ports and CTI route points.

CFNA. Call forward no answer. Forwards calls to a designated number when the called number does not answer.

CGI. Common gateway interface. A standard method of interacting with a web server for requests and responses.

CHAP. Challenge Handshake Protocol. A system for determining if a user has the correct password without openly revealing that password. CHAP does not itself prevent unauthorized access; it merely identifies the remote end. The router or access server then determines whether that user is given access.

CIA. Confidentiality, integrity, availability.

CID. Call ID.

CIP. Cisco IP Phone. A full-feature telephone that provides voice communication over an IP network.

CIPT. Cisco IP Telephony. A software and hardware product suite offering an IP alternative to traditional PBXs. Includes CallManager, Cisco IP Phones, gateways, and server software enabling voice and data over an existing LAN or WAN infrastructure.

CIR. Committed information rate. The amount of bandwidth a service provider guarantees over a Frame Relay network without dropping or marking packets as discard eligible (DE).

Cisco AVVID IP Telephony. The IP Telephony feature of the Cisco Architecture for Voice, Video, and Integrated Data.

Cisco CallManager Administration. The web-based interface to CallManager. CallManager Administration allows you to add, update, or delete users, devices, and the system configuration for CallManager.

Cisco CallManager node. See *Cisco CallManager server.*

Cisco CallManager server. A Cisco-certified Windows 2000 server that runs CallManager software.

Cisco CallManager User Options. A website that users can access to make changes to their IP phone's configuration, including setting or canceling call forward all designations, managing speed dials, managing IP phone service subscriptions, and more.

CiscoWorks. Network management tools that allow you to easily access and manage the advanced capabilities of Cisco AVVID.

CLI. Command-line interface. A way of interacting with a device that provides a text-based, iterative interface rather than a graphical user interface to enter commands.

CLID. Calling Line ID. Information about the billing telephone number from which a call originated. The CLID value might be the entire phone number, the area code, or the area code plus the local exchange. Also known as caller ID.

closest-match routing. A call routing feature whereby CallManager matches the dialed number that has the most explicit route pattern match. The most explicit match is selected based on the number of possible matches that could occur for a given pattern.

CM. An abbreviation of CallManager.

CMI. Cisco Messaging Interface. A service that allows a CallManager cluster to integrate with third-party voice mail systems using the SMDI protocol.

CMM. Communications Media Module. A module for the Catalyst 6500 series that provides digital and analog telephony connections and media resources such as conferencing and transcoding.

CMR. Call management record (also known as a diagnostic record). A record that CallManager logs that provides information about the media session on which a device participated.

CN. Canonical name. See *CNAME*.

CNAME. Canonical name. A record created on a DNS server that serves as an alias for another DNS address. For example, a CNAME entry can be created for Cisco.com that points to the DNS record Cisco.com.

CNID. Calling Name ID.

CO. See *central office*.

codec. Coder-decoder. A media-encoding scheme by which an end device encodes speech or visual information into a digital representation for transmission across a media connection and decodes the digital representation into speech or visual information for playback by the recipient.

coder delay. The time taken by the DSP to compress a block of PCM samples. Because different coders work in different ways, this delay varies with processor speed and the voice codec used. Also known as processing delay. A form of fixed delay.

COLD. Connected Line ID.

comfort noise. A small amount of quiet noise during a phone conversation, usually characterized as a slight hiss on the line. Comfort noise makes users feel like there is still someone on the other end of the line, even when no one is speaking.

community string. A password that allows an SNMP application to access specific resources and data on an SNMP-enabled device such as a router or switch.

COND. Connected Name ID.

conference controller. The user who calls the first conference attendee (in the case of Ad Hoc conferencing) or who establishes the Meet-Me conference number.

consultation transfer. A form of transfer whereby the user discusses the redirected call with the intended recipient before completing the transfer operation.

CoR. Class of restriction. A Cisco IOS software feature that provides the ability to deny certain call attempts based on who originates the call.

core. The central site in a centralized call processing deployment.

CoS. Class of service. Any form of layer 2 quality of service marking. For Ethernet, this is typically 802.1p priority bits.

CPU. Central processing unit. The chip or chips inside a computer that execute the instructions that permit applications to function.

CRA. Cisco Customer Response Applications. See *CRS*.

CRL. Certificate Revocation List. Used to revoke a digital certificate when the owner of the certificate no longer wants the certificate to be valid, such as if the private key is compromised by a hacker. When a device presents a digital certificate, the authenticating party checks this list to ensure that the certificate is still valid.

CRS. Cisco Customer Response Solutions. A suite of CTI-based applications, including IP AA, IP IVR, and IP ICD. Formerly known as *CRA*.

cRTP. Compressed RTP or RTP Header Compression. A method of compressing IP, UDP, and RTP headers over low-speed point-to-point connections to reduce the amount of bandwidth consumed by an audio and/or video call. Defined in RFC 2508.

CSA. Cisco Security Agent. A Cisco software application that provides threat protection for servers and desktop computers by identifying and preventing malicious behavior. The Cisco Security Agent aggregates and extends multiple endpoint security functions by providing host intrusion prevention, distributed firewall capabilities, malicious mobile code protection, operating system integrity assurance, and audit log consolidation.

CS-ACELP. Conjugate Structure Algebraic Code Excited Linear Prediction. An algorithm used to compress human voice before it's transmitted over a packet network.

CSPS. Cisco SIP Proxy Server. A Cisco product that provides Session Initiation Protocol (SIP) proxy functionality and provisioning interface.

CSRC. Computer Security Resource Center. One of eight divisions within NIST's Information Technology Laboratory. Learn more at http://csrc.nist.gov/mission.html.

CSS. See *calling search space*.

CSV. Comma-separated value. A type of file in which commas are used to separate individual fields of a complex data record and new lines indicate the end of an individual record.

CTI. Computer telephony integration. A set of protocols that allow a call processing engine such as CallManager to integrate with third-party applications. TAPI and JTAPI are examples of CTI protocols.

CTL. Certificate Trust List. A file used by a security-enabled endpoint to receive public key information for the servers and system administration identities that the endpoint is permitted to communicate with securely.

CUG. Closed User Group. A restricted group of users on an ISDN network. Members of a specific CUG can communicate among themselves but not with users outside the group.

cutover. The act of switching from one phone system to another.

D

DAT. Digital audio tape. A format for recording music or computer data on magnetic tape.

dB. Decibel. A unit of measurement in sound.

DBL. Database layer. A set of software components that provide a programming interface to the SQL database containing all the CallManager configuration information.

DC. Domain controller. A Windows server that houses all information about user and machine accounts and that provides authentication in a Windows domain.

D-channel. Data-channel. In an ISDN interface, the D-channel is used to carry control signals and customer call data in a packet-switched mode. In a BRI, the D-channel runs at 16 kbps. In a PRI, the D-channel runs at 64 kbps.

DDI. Digit discard instruction. A form of called-number transformation that, with one exception, works only when used with the @ wildcard (the exception is the PreDot DDI).

dejitter buffer. A feature on any VoIP endpoint that transforms variable delay into a fixed delay by holding the first sample received for a period of time before playing it.

delay. A voice quality issue. The amount of time it takes the sound from a talker's mouth to reach the far-end listener's ear.

DHCP. Dynamic Host Configuration Protocol. A network service whose primary purpose is to automatically assign IP addresses to new devices that connect to the network or existing devices that reconnect to the network.

DID. Direct inward dial. A type of central office trunk that provides additional routing information on incoming calls. DID allows trunk calls to be routed directly to a specific directory number instead of being routed to a common attendant.

DIT. Directory information tree. A directory component that contains information about network objects such as users, applications, and more.

DN. Directory number. The numerical address assigned to an endpoint, such as a phone, gateway port, or route point within an enterprise.

DNA. Cisco Dialed Number Analyzer. A Cisco software tool that allows you to test and analyze a CallManager dial plan configuration.

DNIS. Digital Number Identification Service (also known as the called party number). The digits for the phone number being dialed.

DNS. Domain Name System. A network service whose primary function is to convert fully qualified domain names (textual) into numerical IP addresses and vice versa.

DOD. Direct outward dialing. A service that permits a device in the enterprise to place calls directly to the public network.

DOS. Denial of service. In a voice security context, denial of service basically means you lose dial tone, specific voice features, access to outside phone lines for OffNet calling, access to voice mail, and so on.

DRAM. Dynamic RAM. A general pool of memory accessible and addressable by an operating system.

DSCP. Differentiated Services Code Point, or DiffServ CodePoint. A marker in the header of each IP packet that prompts network routers and switches to apply differentiated grades of service to various packet streams.

DSP. Digital signal processor. A specialized type of CPU used for computationally intensive tasks. CallManager uses DSP resources to process voice streams. For example, DSPs are used to transcode voice and join multiple streams into a conference.

DSP farm. An IP endpoint with a large number of DSP resources for providing services such as conferencing and transcoding.

DTMF. Dual-Tone Multifrequency. A common tone-signaling method used by touchtone phones in which two pure frequencies are superimposed.

DTP. Dynamic Trunking Protocol. Provides the ability to negotiate the trunking method with the other device.

E

E1. A digital trunk specification that permits the transfer of 2.048 Mbps of information.

E.164 address. A fully qualified numerical address for a device attached to a national network. The ITU-T specification E.164 defines the framework in which nations manage their national numbering plans.

E&M. Ear and Mouth. A trunking arrangement generally used for two-way switch-to-switch or switch-to-network connections.

EAP. Extensible Authentication Protocol. An authentication protocol that supports various authentication methods, including public key authentication, one-time passwords, certificates, and more.

echo canceller. A device or system that reduces or eliminates echoes in voice transmission systems.

EIA/TIA. Electronics Industries Alliance/Telecommunications Industry Association. A group that specifies electrical transmission standards. See http://www.eia.org and http://www.tiaonline.org.

EIGRP. Enhanced Interior Gateway Routing Protocol. An advanced version of IGRP developed by Cisco. A routing protocol that provides superior convergence properties and operating efficiency. It combines the advantages of link state protocols with those of distance vector protocols.

enbloc sending. A method of sending a call setup in which the complete called party number is sent as part of the setup message.

endpoint. A device or software application that provides real-time, two-way communication for users.

ER. See *CER*.

ESF. Extended Superframe. A framing protocol used on T1 circuits in which 24 frames, each containing 1 framing bit and 24 timeslots of 8 bits apiece, are grouped into a superframe. See also *robbed-bit signaling*.

Ethernet. A LAN architecture that uses a bus or star topology and supports data transfer rates of 10 Mbps. CallManager uses a newer version of Ethernet called 100BASE-T or Fast Ethernet, which supports data transfer rates of 100 Mbps. See also *Fast Ethernet* and *Gigabit Ethernet*.

ETSI. European Telecommunications Standards Institute. An independent, nonprofit organization whose mission is to produce telecommunications standards. See http://www.etsi.org.

Event Viewer. A Windows OS tool that allows you to monitor and manage system, security, and application events and errors on your system.

extension mobility. A CallManager feature that allows a user to log in to any extension mobility-enabled IP Phone. After a user logs in, the IP Phone downloads all the information related to the device profile, in effect becoming the user's personalized phone, including line number, calling search spaces, speed dials, and services.

F

failback. The process whereby devices in a Cisco IP Telephony network register themselves to their primary CallManager node when it becomes available after a failover to a backup CallManager node. See also *fallback*.

failover. The process whereby devices in a Cisco IP Telephony network register themselves to a backup CallManager node if they lose their connection to their primary CallManager. Phones open a connection to the backup CallManager at the same time they register to the primary CallManager so that they can failover faster.

fallback. The process of offering a call to a less-desirable route after all desirable routes have been exhausted. In the context of CallManager priority, fallback occurs when the higher-priority server comes back online and devices begin registering to the higher-priority server from a lower-priority server.

FAQ. Frequently asked question.

fast busy. See *reorder tone*.

Fast Ethernet. A LAN architecture that supports data transfer rates of 100 Mbps. See also *Ethernet* and *Gigabit Ethernet*.

feature inventory. A document that details the phone features in use at a particular site.

FIFO. First-in, first-out.

firewall. A computer system placed at the junction between a private computer network and other computer networks. It is designed to protect systems of a private network from users in the other networks.

fixed delay. A delay in a call that is constant for every call regardless of varying network conditions. See also *coder delay, packetization delay, propagation delay,* and *serialization delay.*

flash cut. A clean break from one phone system to the other.

FLP. Fast Link Pulse. A burst of 100BASE-T link test pulses that encapsulate auto-negotiation information for identifying the speed and mode at which a device operates.

forwarding loop. A condition caused when calls are routed back and forth between two endpoints in an endless loop.

fractional PRI. A T1 or E1 PRI in which only a fraction of the B-channels are provisioned to carry voice or data traffic. The remaining B-channels are unused. As of release 4.0, CallManager does not officially support fractional PRIs.

full-mesh. A network topology in which all devices are physically or logically connected to each other.

functional group. A grouping in MLA that includes a collection of CallManager system administration functions. Two types of functional groups exist: standard functional groups and custom functional groups.

FXO. Foreign Exchange Office. A VoIP gateway providing analog access to the central office's line termination.

FXS. Foreign Exchange Station. A VoIP gateway providing analog access to a POTS station.

G–H

G.711. A simple codec used to encode voice communications that requires 64 kbps bandwidth.

G.723. A codec used to encode voice communications that requires either 5.3 or 6.3 kbps bandwidth.

G.729. A codec used to encode voice communications that requires 8 kbps bandwidth.

GARP. Gratuitous ARP. A packet broadcast by an IP endpoint that contains the IP endpoint's TCP/IP address so that duplicate addresses can be prevented.

gatekeeper CAC. Uses an H.323 gatekeeper to control the number of calls between multiple CallManager clusters. See also *call admission control (CAC)*.

Gb. Gigabit.

Gigabit Ethernet. A LAN architecture that supports data transfer rates of 1 Gbps (1000 Mbps). See also *Ethernet* and *Fast Ethernet*.

GMT. Greenwich Mean Time. See *UTC*.

GPO. Group Policy Object. A collection of settings that define a system's look and feel for a specified group of users.

green field. A new installation with no prior IP telephony.

GSM. Global system for mobile communications. The codec used to compress voice samples on GSM cellular phones.

GUID. Globally unique identifier. CallManager uses the GUID internally to identify various components such as phones and gateways. CallManager assigns GUIDs at the time of entry into the database. The end user does not see GUIDs.

H.323. A recommendation from ITU-T that contains a complex set of protocols designed to facilitate media communication sessions over an IP network.

hairpinning. See *tromboning*.

HDSM. High-Density Service Module. A wider interface form factor available in some Cisco voice routers.

HDV. High-Density Voice Module. The HDV series of modules provides the Cisco 2600, 3600, and 3700 series with digital and analog voice connectivity.

held party. The party who is placed on hold.

hexadecimal (hex). Refers to the base-16 number system, which consists of 16 unique symbols: the numbers 0 to 9 and the letters A to F. IP addresses in CCM trace files are sometimes represented in hex.

holding party. The party who initiates a hold action.

HSRP. Hot Standby Router Protocol. A Cisco-proprietary protocol used to increase the availability of default gateways used by end hosts.

HTTP. Hypertext Transfer Protocol. A simple, stateless request/response protocol that is used at the application level.

hub. An Ethernet device that repeats Ethernet packets accepted on one port and transmits them on all other ports of the hub.

hybrid. A telephony device that converts two-wire analog circuits to four-wire analog circuits.

I

ICCP. Intracluster Control Protocol. A signaling protocol used by CallManager servers to communicate runtime data.

ICMP. Internet Control Message Protocol. A protocol that supports packets containing error, control, and informational messages.

iDivert. Immediate divert. A softkey introduced in CallManager release 4.0 that lets a user immediately divert a call to voice mail.

IE. Information element. Carries a specific piece of information within a Q.931 or H.225 message.

IE. See *Internet Explorer*.

IEEE. Institute of Electrical and Electronics Engineers. A professional organization whose activities include the development of communications and network standards.

IETF. Internet Engineering Task Force. The main standards organization for the Internet.

IIS. Internet Information Server. A Microsoft service designed to permit users to create and manage Internet services such as web servers.

in-band. The exchange of call control information on the same channel as the telephone call or data transmission.

inside dial tone. The initial dial tone provided when a user goes off-hook on an IP phone.

intercluster trunk. A virtual trunk connecting CallManager clusters. An intercluster trunk uses the H.323 protocol to communicate between CallManager clusters.

interdigit timeout. The number of seconds CallManager delays routing a call if an immediate pattern match is not made when a user dials a phone number. Interdigit timeout is controlled by the CallManager service parameter T302 Timer.

Internet Explorer. Microsoft's version of a web browser.

IP. Internet Protocol. A layer 3 protocol used by one computer to communicate packets of information to another computer on a network.

IP AA. IP Auto Attendant. An application designed to distribute calls by automated means. Part of CRA/CRS.

IPCC. IP Contact Center. A group of applications that create an IP-based call center.

IP ICD. IP Integrated Contact Distribution. A voice application that provides call center functionality by queuing and delivering calls to agents. Part of CRA/CRS.

IP IVR. IP Interactive Voice Response. A voice application that provides a telephone user interface and that can retrieve data and redirect calls. Part of CRA/CRS.

IPMA. Cisco IP Manager Assistant. A CallManager feature that facilitates call management for managers and assistants.

IP Telephony. The implementation of telephony over a data network using the IP layer 3 protocol.

IP/VC. Cisco IP videoconferencing. Enables videoconferencing over IP networks.

ISDN. Integrated Services Digital Network. An international communications standard for sending voice, video, and data over digital telephone lines.

ISP. Internet service provider. A company that provides Internet access to other companies and individuals.

IT. Information technology. A group concerned with all aspects of managing and processing information, especially within a large organization or company.

ITEM. Cisco IP Telephony Environment Monitor. A suite of applications and tools that continuously evaluate and report the operational health of your Cisco IP Telephony implementation.

ITU. International Telecommunication Union. The telecommunications agency of the United Nations, established to provide worldwide standard communications practices and procedures.

ITU-T. ITU Telecommunications Standardization Sector. The telecommunications standardization sector of ITU. An international body that develops worldwide standards for telecommunications technologies. See also *ITU*.

IXC. Interexchange carrier, or long distance company. A company whose chief responsibility is to interconnect local exchange carriers.

J–K

jitter. The difference in time between a packet's expected arrival time and the time the packet actually arrives. Also called variable delay.

JTAPI. Java Telephony Application Programming Interface. A CTI protocol that allows applications to use CallManager's call control functionality.

kbps. Kilobits per second.

KVM. Keyboard, video, mouse. Generally used when talking about KVM switch boxes that allow a single keyboard, monitor, and mouse to be used for multiple systems.

L

LAN. Local-area network. A high-speed, low-error data network covering a relatively small geographic area (up to a few thousand meters). LANs connect workstations, peripherals, terminals, and other devices in a single building or other geographically limited area. LAN standards specify cabling and signaling at the OSI model's physical and data link layers. Ethernet, Fast Ethernet, and Gigabit Ethernet are widely used LAN technologies.

LCD. Liquid crystal display. A type of display used in Cisco IP Phones, laptops, and flat panel displays.

LDAP. Lightweight Directory Access Protocol. A protocol that defines a programming interface that can be used to access computer-based directories. LDAP directories are a specialized form of database that are often used to hold user information in large organizations. CallManager uses an LDAP directory to store user information.

LDIF. LDAP Data Interchange Format. A data file format used to represent data contained in an LDAP directory. Can be used to import and export data to and from an LDAP directory.

legacy. Using established, possibly outdated, methods.

LFI. Link fragmentation and interleaving. Used on WAN links with a speed of 768 kbps and below to facilitate the transmission of large data frames combined with voice without voice quality degradation.

line appearance. A logical entity on a phone or gateway that can terminate calls. Often associated with a particular button on a phone. Line appearances have addresses called directory numbers (DN).

listener echo. A form of echo in which one party in the call hears the other person's words repeated.

LLQ. Low Latency Queuing. A queuing mechanism used on Cisco IOS software routers to facilitate a dedicated priority queue for voice applications while still providing Class-Based Weighted Fair Queuing for other traffic classes.

locations-based CAC. A feature in CallManager that limits the number of calls between devices registered to a single CallManager cluster. See *call admission control (CAC)*.

logical channel. A network pathway that carries a streaming data connection between two endpoints.

M

MAC address. Media Access Control address. A hardware address that uniquely identifies a device.

MAN. Metropolitan-area network. A network that spans a metropolitan area. Generally, a MAN spans a larger geographic area than a LAN but a smaller geographic area than a WAN.

mask. A CallManager call routing feature that provides specific number presentation and digit manipulation. Masks format a calling or called party number in a specific way.

MB. Megabyte.

MBSA. Microsoft Baseline Security Analyzer. A Microsoft product that identifies common security misconfigurations.

MCID. Malicious caller identification. A feature introduced in CallManager release 4.0 that, when invoked by the phone user via the **MCID** softkey, alerts the system administrator to a malicious call.

MCM. Cisco Multimedia Conference Manager. The feature set of Cisco IOS software that provides H.323 gatekeeper functionality.

MCS. Media Convergence Server. A Cisco certified server that comes preinstalled with the components that comprise Cisco AVVID IP Telephony.

MCU. Multipoint Conference Unit. A device in an H.323 network that combines multiple video streams to provide multiple party conference capabilities.

media resource. A network device that terminates a media stream to provide a service to IP telephony endpoints, such as IP phones and voice gateways.

MeetingPlace. A Cisco conferencing solution that includes voice and web conferencing capabilities.

Meet-Me conference. A type of conference that allows attendees to dial into the conference after a user (called the conference controller) has created the conference. See also *Ad Hoc conference*.

MFT. Multi-Flex Trunk. Interface cards for Cisco IOS software voice gateways and routers used to terminate a T1 or E1 connection.

MGCP. Media Gateway Control Protocol. A UDP-based, plain-text, master/slave protocol whereby a call agent—in this case, CallManager—controls the function of a particular gateway. Messages are sent as ASCII-encoded text.

MGCP package. A grouping of the events and signals supported by a particular type of MGCP endpoint.

MIB. Management information base. A database of network management information that is used and maintained by a network management protocol such as SNMP or CMIP. The value of a MIB object can be changed or retrieved using SNMP or CMIP commands, usually through a network management system. MIB objects are organized in a tree structure that includes public (standard) and private (proprietary) branches. The latest Cisco MIBs are available at http://www.cisco.com/public/sw-center/netmgmt/cmtk/mibs.shtml.

MLA. Multilevel administration. A security feature in CallManager Administration that regulates the privileges of a selected group of users and limits the configuration functions users can perform.

MLP. Multilink Point-to-Point Protocol. A method of splitting, recombining, and sequencing datagrams across multiple logical data links. MLP allows packets to be fragmented and the fragments to be sent at the same time over multiple point-to-point links to the same remote address.

MLPP. Multilevel precedence and preemption. A feature designed to give individuals assigned critical job responsibilities a special priority calling function.

MOH. Music on Hold. A CallManager feature that allows users to place OnNet and OffNet users on hold with music streamed from a preconfigured source.

most-significant bit. The first bit of a binary number.

MPLS. Multiprotocol Label Switching. Integrates a label-swapping framework with network layer routing. The basic idea involves assigning short, fixed-length labels to packets at the ingress to an MPLS cloud. Throughout the interior of the MPLS domain, the labels attached to packets are used to make forwarding decisions (usually without recourse to the original packet headers).

MPOE. Minimum point of entry. The first point at which telecommunications facilities are provided by the phone company to a customer.

MRG. Media resource group. A logical grouping of media servers in CallManager Administration that can be used to provide geographically specific, class of service, or class of user access to a set of media resources.

MRGL. Media resource group list. A list in CallManager Administration that consists of prioritized MRGs. An application can select required media resources from the available ones according to the priority order defined in the MRGL.

ms or msec. Millisecond.

MTBF. Mean time between failures. The average time, in hours, that a device functions before failing.

MTP. Media termination point. A device that terminates a media stream for the purpose of allowing the stream to be redirected.

Multicast. A type of streaming that allows multiple users to use the same audio source stream to provide Music on Hold.

MWI. Message waiting indicator. An audible or visual alert that alerts the user to the presence of a new voice mail message.

N

NANP. North American Numbering Plan. The default numbering plan that ships with CallManager. It applies to the U.S. and Canada.

NAT. Network Address Translation. A mechanism for conserving registered IP addresses in large networks and simplifying IP addressing management tasks. As its name implies, Cisco IOS software NAT translates IP addresses within private internal networks to "legal" IP addresses for transport over public external networks (such as the Internet). Incoming traffic is translated back for delivery within the inside network.

NBAR. Network-Based Application Recognition. A Cisco IOS software feature that allows traffic to be classified by name to be used in ACLs to provide QoS or security.

network hold. A type of hold operation in which the user invokes a feature operation such as transfer, conference, or call park that requires CallManager to place the call on hold while performing the feature operation. See also *user hold*.

NFAS. Network Facility Associated Signaling. The capability for the telephone company to provision multiple PRI lines using a single D-channel for signaling.

NIST. National Institute of Standards and Technology. A nonregulatory federal agency within the U.S. Commerce Department's Technology Administration. See http://www.nist.gov.

NM. Network module. A module that can be inserted into a Cisco 2600, 3600, or 3700 series router that provides additional capabilities and/or ports such as Fast Ethernet and serial ports.

NMS. Network management system. A system responsible for managing at least part of a network.

NOC. Network operations center. A place from where network management functions are administered. Typically staffed 24/7 with access to all network devices.

no-way audio. A voice-quality problem in which no audio is heard on both sides of a conversation, even though the participants are speaking.

NPA *NXX*. Numbering Plan Area. A phone number's area code and exchange code. *N* represents any digit 2 through 9, and *X* represents any digit 0 through 9.

NTP. Network Time Protocol. An Internet standard protocol (built on top of TCP/IP) that ensures accurate synchronization to the millisecond of computer clock times in a network of computers.

O

ODBC. Open Database Connectivity. A Microsoft standard for access to database tables by distributed applications.

off-hook. Literally, the action of removing the handset from the hookswitch. In modern telephony, this term indicates that the phone is no longer in the idle state. On Cisco IP Phones, off-hook can be accomplished in many ways, not limited to the following: lifting the handset, pressing the **Speaker** button, and pressing the **Answer** or **NewCall** softkeys.

OffNet. A term applied to calls between the enterprise and another telephone network (generally the PSTN).

one-way audio. A voice-quality problem in which one side of the conversation cannot hear the other.

on-hook. Literally, the action of returning the handset to the hookswitch. In modern telephony, this term indicates that the phone has returned to the idle state. On Cisco IP Phones, on-hook can be accomplished in many ways, not limited to the following: returning the handset to the cradle, pressing the **Speaker** button, and pressing the **EndCall** softkey.

OnNet. A term applied to calls that are placed and received within the same enterprise.

OOB. See *out-of-band*.

open trees. A general auto attendant greeting on a voice mail system.

OS. Operating system. Software running on a hardware platform that gives other applications access to the resources (such as processor, memory, and network interfaces) that the hardware platform provides.

OSI. Open System Interconnection. An ISO standard for worldwide communications that defines a networking framework for implementing protocols in seven layers.

OSPF. Open Shortest Path First. An RFC-standard link-state dynamic routing protocol that uses link cost as its metric.

OU. Organizational unit. A single branch of an LDAP directory tree.

out-of-band. The exchange of call control information on a different channel than the telephone call or data transmission.

outside dial tone. For OffNet calls, the dial tone (sometimes called the secondary dial tone) provided when a user goes off-hook and dials an access code on an IP phone.

overlap receiving. Allows the PSTN to send a setup message with only part of the called party number.

overlap sending. Allows CallManager to send a setup message to the PSTN with only part of the called party number.

P

PA. Personal Assistant. An application that works with CallManager. It is designed to permit a user to customize call forwarding behavior based on who is calling and to locate a user given multiple possible destinations.

packetization delay. The time taken to fill a packet payload with encoded/compressed speech and to add the various IP/UDP/RTP headers. A form of fixed delay.

PACL. Port ACL. An access control list defined to a port.

parser. A program that breaks an input stream into syntactic elements. Cisco IP Phones have an XML parser that breaks out individual element values for the phone's firmware.

partition. A group of directory numbers and route patterns used to divide a route plan into subsets.

PAT. Port Address Translation. A feature that lets you address hosts on a LAN with inside local addresses and filter them through one globally routable IP address.

PBX. Private branch exchange. A small phone system located at a customer site. The PBX is used to supplement or replace functionality that might normally be provided by a central office.

PC. Personal computer.

PCM. Pulse code modulation. A sampling technique for digitizing analog signals, especially audio signals.

PDLM. Packet Description Language Module. Contains a series of defining characteristics that allow the router to identify particular applications in use on the network. Used by the Cisco IOS software NBAR feature to describe an application.

PerfMon. Microsoft Performance. An administrative tool provided by the Windows 2000 operating system used to monitor a variety of performance objects.

performance object. A set of counters reported by a process or application running on the system that can be monitored using PerfMon or RTMT.

PKI. Public-Key Infrastructure. The combination of software, encryption technologies, and services that allows enterprises to protect the security of their communications and business transactions on the Internet without the need for shared secret keys.

PKS. Public-Key Cryptography Standards. Specifications produced by RSA Laboratories in cooperation with secure systems developers worldwide for the purpose of accelerating the deployment of public-key cryptography. See http://www.rsasecurity.com.

PLAR. Private line automatic ringdown. A call routing feature whereby a phone immediately places a call to a specified destination when taken off-hook.

playout delay. Also known as jitter buffer size. The amount of time packets are stored in the jitter buffer before being played out to the listener.

POTS. Plain old telephone service. Generally used to refer to the PSTN.

POTS dial peer. Defines the characteristics of a traditional telephony network connection on a Cisco IOS software voice gateway. The POTS dial peer maps a dial string to a specific voice port on the local gateway. Normally, the voice port connects the gateway to the local PSTN, a PBX, or an analog telephone.

power cycle. To reset a device by interrupting and restoring power to it.

PPP. Point-to-Point Protocol. A link layer encapsulation method for dialup or dedicated circuits. PPP is designed to work with several network layer protocols, such as IP, IPX, and AppleTalk.

pps. Packets per second.

PQ. Priority queue. A packet queue in an IOS router that is serviced whenever packets are present regardless of the status of any other queue for the given port.

PRI. Primary Rate Interface. A type of ISDN service designed for large organizations. Includes B-channels (bearer channels) for voice or data and one D-channel (data channel) for signaling. PRI is composed of 23 B-channels in North America and 30 B-channels in Europe.

propagation delay. The amount of time it takes for a single bit of data to get from one side of a digital connection to the other. A form of fixed delay.

PSAP. Public Safety Answering Point. A physical location where 911 emergency telephone calls are received and then are routed to the proper emergency services. Used in CIPT in conjunction with Cisco ER.

PSTN. Public Switched Telephone Network. The international phone system.

Publisher. The master database in a CallManager cluster.

PUT. Cisco Product Upgrade Tool. A web-based tool available to Cisco customers to request upgrades to CallManager and other products. The PUT can be found at http://www.cisco.com/upgrade (login required).

PVC. Permanent virtual circuit. A virtual circuit that is permanently available. Usually refers to a virtual connection through a service provider's Frame Relay or ATM network.

PVDM. Packet Voice/Data Module. A module that provides one or more DSPs to some Cisco routers.

PVLAN. Private virtual local-area network. Provides layer 2 isolation between ports within the same PVLAN by placing devices in one of three types of ports in the PVLAN: promiscuous, isolated, or community. A promiscuous port can communicate with all interfaces within a PVLAN. Traffic from an isolated port is forwarded only to promiscuous ports in the PVLAN. Community ports communicate among themselves and with promiscuous ports in the PVLAN.

Q–R

Q.931. An ITU-T specification that defines the layer 3 messages used on an ISDN circuit's D-channel.

QoS. Quality of service. A distributed multimedia system's traffic-management mechanisms that permit it to guarantee the transmission of coherent information. Such mechanisms include traffic classification, traffic prioritization, bandwidth management, and admissions control.

QRT. Quality Reporting Tool. A tool in CallManager that allows phone users to report voice quality and other problems by pressing the **QRT** softkey on their phones.

Q.Sig. A unified international corporate network signaling standard supported by CallManager.

RADIUS. Remote Authentication Dial-In User Service. A standards-based protocol for AAA. See also *AAA*.

RAID. Redundant array of independent disks. A group of hard drives that provides redundancy and/or increased performance by operating as a single logical entity.

RAS. Registration, Admission, and Status. A portion of the H.323 specification that defines a gatekeeper's operation.

RDNIS. Redirected dial number ID service (also called the redirecting party number or the original called party number). Typically used to convey information about the original called party to a voice mail system.

reorder tone. A fast, cyclical tone that CallManager uses to indicate a problem during call establishment. Commonly called fast busy.

reset. A command that causes a device to completely power-cycle and begin the registration process again as if it had just been plugged in.

restart. A command that tells a device to unregister and then reregister with CallManager.

RFC. Request for Comments. A series of notes about the Internet dating from 1969.

ringback. The tone heard at the calling party's end when the called party's phone rings.

RIS. Real-Time Information Server. A Cisco facility that stores real-time information such as device IP address and registration status.

RISDC. RIS Data Collector. A CallManager service that collects runtime data from the CallManager services in the cluster and distributes that data to other RISDC services in the cluster.

RNAR. Ring no answer reversion. A CallManager line group setting that specifies the time, in seconds, after which CallManager distributes a call to the next available or idle member of this line group or to the next line group or route group if the call is not answered and if the first hunt option, *Try next member; then, try next group in Hunt List*, is selected.

robbed-bit signaling. Also known as channel-associated signaling (CAS), this is called robbed-bit signaling because some bits from each T1 speech bearer channel are "robbed" and used for signaling. On a T1 with Superframe (SF) framing, these are called the A and B bits, whereas a T1 with Extended Superframe (ESF) framing has A, B, C, and D bits. A gateway uses these bits to indicate on-hook, off-hook, and ringing.

rollout. The method you use to enter phones into CallManager Administration and distribute the phones to users' desks.

round-robin. A cyclic method of traversing a finite number of items where each item is used one at a time from first to last. When the last item has been used, the items are reused starting from the first item in the list. So in the case of overwriting files in round-robin fashion, when File1 is completely written, File2 is written next. When File2 is completely written, File3 is written next, and so on. Assuming a case of four available files, when File4 is written, File1 is overwritten next.

route filter. A call routing feature used with numbering plans when using the @ wildcard.

route pattern. A CallManager call routing feature that represents one or more strings of dialed digits used to route a call to a particular destination.

RSA. Rivest-Shamir-Adelman. An algorithm used to generate 2048-bit binary number sequences.

rsh. Remote shell. A protocol used to establish a remote terminal session to a Cisco IOS software device.

RSVP. Resource Reservation Protocol. An Internet protocol that supports the reservation of resources across an IP network.

RTCP. Real-Time Control Protocol. The control protocol that works in conjunction with RTP. RTCP control packets are periodically transmitted by each participant in an RTP session to all other participants. Feedback of information to the application can be used to control performance and for diagnostic purposes.

RTMT. Real-Time Monitoring Tool. A web-based application bundled with CallManager Serviceability that provides up-to-the-second information about the state of a CallManager cluster.

RTP. Real-Time Transport Protocol. An Internet-standard protocol for the transport of real-time data, including audio and video. See also *cRTP*.

S

sa. System administrator. The superuser account for Microsoft SQL server when using mixed-mode authentication.

SABME. Set Asynchronous Balanced Mode Extended. Messages used at layer 2 of ISDN to establish a link.

SCCP. See *Skinny protocol*.

SDI. System Diagnostic Interface. SDI trace files are also called CCM trace files. Contain information about the operation of CallManager, including Skinny, H.323, and MGCP messages; digit analysis results; and other diagnostic messages.

SDK. Software Development Kit. A set of programming interfaces and documentation provided to programmers seeking to interface with a given operating system, application, or other product.

SDL. Signal Distribution Layer. An application framework that provides all the components required to implement a state-machine-based application. It provides for creation of state machines and the interprocessor communication of signals between those state machines.

Specification and Description Language. An ITU-T language defined in specification Z.100 that describes a notation for state-machine-based systems.

SDP. Session Description Protocol. Describes multimedia sessions for the purposes of session announcement, session invitation, and other forms of multimedia session initiation. CallManager uses SDP to describe sessions to MGCP and SIP devices. Defined in RFC 2327.

secondary line. Any line appearance on a station other than the primary.

serialization delay. The delay required to clock an IP packet out a network interface. It is directly related to the clock rate on the interface. A form of fixed delay.

server clustering. A group, or cluster, of servers work together to provide the overall system functionality.

service parameters. Settings on CallManager that take effect on a servicewide and sometimes clusterwide basis.

SF. Superframe. A framing protocol used on T1 circuits in which 12 frames, each containing 1 framing bit and 24 timeslots of 8 bits apiece, are grouped into a superframe. See also *robbed-bit signaling*.

SGCP. See *Skinny gateway protocol*.

sidetone. Occurs in almost every telephone device when some of the transmit signal is fed back into the earpiece so that the user can hear himself or herself speaking.

silence suppression. See *VAD*.

SIP. Session Initiation Protocol. A signaling protocol that initiates call setup, routing, authentication, and other feature messages to endpoints within an IP domain. SIP is used in CallManager, some phones, and gateways.

Skinny client. A client, such as a Cisco IP Phone, that uses the Skinny protocol.

Skinny gateway protocol. Skinny Gateway Control Protocol. A now-obsolete protocol used by legacy gateway devices to communicate with CallManager.

Skinny protocol. Skinny Client Control Protocol. A protocol used by devices to communicate with CallManager. Commonly referred to as Skinny.

SLA. Service level agreement. A contract between a service provider and a customer that defines the levels of service to which the service provider will be held.

SLB. Server load balancing. Used to get more even usage out of servers and networks.

sniffer. A packet-capture tool that lets you see exactly what is happening on the network at any given time.

SMDI. Simplified Message Desk Interface. An RS-232 protocol that can be used to integrate a voice mail system with a PBX. CallManager provides an interface to voice mail systems via the Cisco Messaging Interface (CMI) service.

SNMP. Simple Network Management Protocol. A protocol designed to permit monitoring and management of devices on a computer network.

SNMP trap. An alert in SNMP. Traps are network packets that contain data relating to the system component that sent the trap.

SOAP. Simple Object Access Protocol. A protocol that defines a method for applications to communicate with each other over an IP network independent of the platform.

softkey. A context-sensitive digital display button on the bottom row of the display on some Cisco IP Phone models, including the 7940, 7960, and 7970.

SPAN. Switch Port Analyzer. A Cisco Catalyst feature that sends a copy of packets destined for one or more ports to another port where a network analyzer can be connected to monitor the network traffic.

SQL. Structured Query Language. A standard language defined to permit reading from and writing to databases.

SRA. Serviceability Reports Archive. A page in CallManager Serviceability that displays the reports generated by the Cisco Serviceability Reporter service.

SRND. Solution Reference Network Design. Documents that supply design guidance to implement an overall network architecture. Available at http://www.cisco.com/go/srnd.

SRST. Survivable Remote Site Telephony. A software feature available in Cisco IOS software that lets a router at a remote branch assume basic call processing responsibilities if phones at a remote site are unable to contact the central CallManager.

SRTP. Secure Real-Time Transport Protocol. A protocol that provides privacy, message authentication, replay protection, and implicit header authentication while providing high throughput and low packet expansion. See also *RTP*.

SSAPI. Supplementary Services Application Programming Interface. A messaging interface provided by CallManager to allow the CMI service to light message waiting indicators and to allow the Cisco Database Layer Monitor service to issue change notification commands.

ssh. Secure Shell. An application and protocol that provides secure replacement for the suite of Berkeley r-tools, such as rsh, rlogin, and rcp. (Cisco IOS software supports rlogin.) This protocol secures the sessions using standard cryptographic mechanisms. The application can be used much like the Berkeley rexec and rsh tools.

SSL. Secure Sockets Layer. A protocol developed by Netscape to encrypt and transmit documents over an IP network such that confidentiality of the information is ensured.

station. Any device that gives the user a direct interface to a voice network.

StationD. A Skinny message sent from CallManager to an IP phone.

StationInit. A Skinny message sent from an IP phone to CallManager.

STP. Spanning Tree Protocol. A link-management protocol that is part of the IEEE 802.1 standard for media access control bridges used to prevent layer 2 bridge loops.

stream. A one-way, active media session connected through a simplex (one-direction) logical channel from one device to another.

subnet. A portion of a network that shares a common address component. On TCP/IP networks, subnets are defined as all devices whose IP addresses have the same prefix.

Subscriber. One or more duplicate databases serving the CallManager system. Subscriber databases are updated with information from the Publisher database.

subscriber. A user of a (usually public) telephone network.

superuser. An account with superuser access has full control over the operating system and is allowed to access all system resources.

switchback. The process whereby devices unregister with one CallManager node and reregister with a higher-priority CallManager node. See *failback*.

switchover. A process whereby a secondary call agent assumes control of the call signaling and media control for a call that earlier was controlled by a different call agent. See *failover*.

syslog. An event logging facility that reports system-level events.

T

T1 CAS. T1 channel-associated signaling. A dedicated phone connection supporting data rates of 1.544 Mbps using channel-associated signaling.

T1 PRI. T1 primary rate interface. A dedicated phone connection supporting data rates of 1.544 Mbps using an ISDN primary rate interface.

TAC. Cisco Technical Assistance Center. The well-regarded place to call for support on any Cisco product.

TACACS+. Terminal Access Controller Access Control System+. A Cisco-proprietary protocol for authentication, authorization, and accounting. See also *AAA*.

talker echo. A form of echo in which one party in the call hears himself or herself echoed.

TAPI. Telephony Application Programming Interface. An API for providing telephone services to applications running on the Microsoft Windows operating system.

TAPS. Tool for Auto-Registered Phones Support. A feature used in concert with BAT to allow an IP Phone to be installed without the presence a system administrator.

TCD. Telephony Call Dispatcher. The server component of Cisco CallManager Attendant Console. TCD keeps track of line states for all the IP phones in the cluster. It is responsible for accepting calls on pilot points and dispatching the calls to agents that are online using the Attendant Console.

TCP. Transmission Control Protocol. A connection-oriented transport layer protocol that provides for the reliable, end-to-end, ordered delivery of IP packets.

TCP handle. A unique value in a CCM trace file that identifies a specific Skinny client registered to a specific CallManager server.

TDM. Time-division multiplexing. A method of transporting information for multiple endpoints across a single interface that relies on assigning each endpoint a specific window of time when it has exclusive access to the interface.

TFTP. Trivial File Transfer Protocol. A User Datagram Protocol (UDP)-based protocol that permits the transmission of files between network devices.

TIA. Telecommunications Industry Association. An organization that represents providers of communications products globally.

tie-line. A dedicated circuit linking two communication devices, such as two PBXs or a CallManager to a PBX.

time stamp. The date and time listed at the beginning of a line in a debug or trace file that tells you the exact time when the event listed in the debug or trace occurred.

TLS. Transport Layer Security. Provides a secure transport path as per RFC 2712.

TLV. Type, Length, and Value. Blocks of information that are sent within Cisco Discovery Protocol (CDP) packets to identify attached devices.

token reject. A Skinny message sent by CallManager to an IP phone in response to a token request when it is too busy to accept a registration.

token request. A Skinny message sent by an IP phone to its primary CallManager before a failback to ensure that the primary CallManager can service the registration request.

transactional replication. A form of database replication. A method of replicating data from a master copy (Publisher) of the database to servers that carry a copy (Subscriber) of the same data. An initial snapshot of the database is taken when the Subscriber first needs to replicate the database data, but from that point on, only database changes are replicated.

transcoder. A hardware device that allows devices with incompatible codecs to communicate with each other.

transformation. See *mask*.

translation pattern. A CallManager call routing feature that allows you to take an originally dialed number and change all or part of the calling and/or called number into another number. A translation pattern transforms the calling and called party numbers through the use of calling and called party transformations that are configured as part of the translation pattern.

trap. See *SNMP trap*.

tromboning. Also called hairpinning. A call comes in a gateway and is forwarded back out another channel on that (or a different) gateway, with the end result being that two channels are tied up. So named because the result is like a trombone's U shape.

TSV. Tab-separated value. A file format in which a record's individual data fields are separated by a tab character and records are separated by new lines.

TTY. Text telephony device, also known as Telephony Device for the Deaf (TDD). Allows hearing- or speech-impaired individuals to communicate over standard phone lines via a terminal-type device.

U

UDP. User Datagram Protocol. A connectionless protocol that, like TCP, runs on top of IP networks.

UNC. Universal naming convention. Allows network paths to be specified much as a web page makes use of the Uniform Resource Locator (URL) format. A network location of a file may be simply referenced as *\\fileserver\networkshare\file.txt*.

Unicast. A type of streaming that uses a separate source stream for each user or connection. Users connect to a specific device or stream.

UPS. Uninterruptible power supply. A device that provides power to an electronic device in the event of a power outage. A continuous online UPS is one in which the load is continually drawing power through the batteries, battery charger, and inverter, not directly from the AC supply.

URL. Uniform Resource Locator. Allows a common naming format and is the basis for locating resources on the Internet. Both the protocol and the location are identified within a URL as http://*webserver/file.txt*.

USB. Universal Serial Bus. Allows many types of peripheral devices to be connected to a PC or server. Devices include mouse, keyboard, identification scanning devices, and more.

user class. A set of users with equivalent requirements and skills.

user group. A grouping in MLA that includes a collection of CallManager users that are grouped for the purpose of assigning an access privilege level to the members of the user group.

user hold. A type of hold operation whereby the user presses the **Hold** softkey to put a call on hold. See also *network hold*.

User-User IE. An IE that carries H.323-specific information such as signaling IP addresses. The User-User IE is coded in a format called ASN.1.

UTC. Universal Coordinated Time. Starts with hour 0 in Greenwich, England. Each global time zone is either positively or negatively referenced. For example, the Pacific time zone is a negative 8 reference (–8) from UTC.

UTP. Unshielded twisted-pair. The cable type that interconnects 10/100/ 1000BASE-T devices as per the IEEE 802.3 standard.

UUIE. See *User-User IE*.

V

V3PN. Voice and video virtual private network. Relies on multiple technologies to create an encrypted connection that can carry time and/or sensitive information across a public network.

VACL. VLAN access control list. Allows or denies traffic between two VLANs that are either bridged or routed, much like traditional Access ACLs, but without the physical interface.

VAD. Voice activity detection (also called silence suppression). A CallManager feature that detects when there is silence in a conversation. With VAD enabled, the endpoint stops sending voice packets filled with silence when a party is not speaking and instead indicates to the far end that there is a silent period. Substantial bandwidth savings can be achieved by enabling VAD, although some voice-quality issues might arise.

variable delay. See *jitter*.

VBR. Variable bit rate. An Asynchronous Transfer Mode (ATM) permanent virtual circuit (PVC) type that provides a variable rate of transmission. Specifies that the speed will change over time as compared to a fixed rate such as CBR.

VIC. Voice interface card. Provides physical layer connectivity to a wide array of voice interface types for the Cisco modular series routers such as the Cisco 2600 series.

VLAN. Virtual local-area network. A group of devices on one or more LANs that are configured so that they can communicate as if they were attached to the same wire, when in fact they're located on a number of different LAN segments. Because VLANs are based on logical instead of physical connections, they are extremely flexible. See also *LAN*.

VMPS. VLAN Membership Policy Service. Allows switched Ethernet ports to be assigned automatically to a designated VLAN based on MAC address.

VNC. Virtual Network Computing. A remote display system that allows you to view a remote desktop environment.

VoIP. Voice over IP. The process of routing voice communications over a network running Internet Protocol.

VPQ. VMPS Query Protocol.

VRRP. Virtual Router Redundancy Protocol. Allows two independent routers that share common connectivity to provide redundant routing capabilities to each other.

VTP. VLAN Trunking Protocol. Provides a mechanism for multiple VLANs to be placed on a single interface and be transported or "trunked" to another capable device.

vty. Virtual terminal. A terminal session created with a Cisco IOS software device over the network as opposed to via the console port. Protocols such as Telnet, rsh, and ssh can be used to establish a vty session.

VWIC. Voice/WAN Interface Card. Provides physical layer connectivity to a wide array of voice or WAN interface types for the Cisco modular series routers such as the Cisco 2600 series.

W–X

WAN. Wide-area network. A data communications network that serves users across a broad geographic area and often uses transmission devices provided by common carriers.

war room. A dedicated conference room during IP telephony deployments where support staff can work together to field questions and modify the deployment.

web server. A server machine that provides dynamic or static content using HTTP.

WFQ. Weighted Fair Queuing. A variation on the class-based queuing (CBQ) technique used in routers. WFQ queues traffic according to traffic class definition, guaranteeing each queue some portion of the total available bandwidth. WFQ goes further to portion out available bandwidth on the basis of individual information flows according to message parameters.

wink. When the terminating side of a gateway using CAS is ready to receive the digits, it goes off-hook for approximately 200 ms and then goes back on-hook.

WINS. Windows Internet Name Service. An integral part of any established Microsoft network. Provides NetBIOS name-to-IP address resolution much as DNS provides domain name-to-IP address resolution.

XML. Extensible markup language. The universal format for structured documents and data on the web.

Numerics

A

G-H

M

N

O

Q

DISCUSS
NETWORKING PRODUCTS AND TECHNOLOGIES WITH CISCO EXPERTS AND NETWORKING PROFESSIONALS WORLDWIDE

VISIT NETWORKING PROFESSIONALS
A CISCO ONLINE COMMUNITY
WWW.CISCO.COM/GO/DISCUSS

CISCO SYSTEMS

THIS IS THE POWER OF THE NETWORK. now.

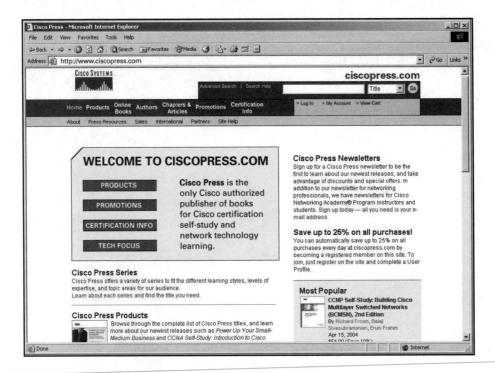
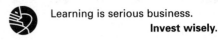

IP Telephony Unveiled

Kevin Brown

1-58720-075-9 • Available Now

This book explains four key points to help you successfully implement your IP telephony strategy:

- IP telephony works today. This is not new, unproven technology. Thousands of customers have implemented IP telephony successfully. So can you.

- Expect to save money. IP telephony may well cost your organization money-initially. But the business impact and post-installation process improvements give you a significant and rapid return on your investment.

- It's more than voice over IP. You'll understand the difference between voice over IP (VoIP) and IP telephony and what that means for your business. This is critical. They are not the same. It's more than a dial tone. There are potential business-impacting applications within your own organization. IP Telephony Unveiled helps you recognize these applications.

The emerging IP telephony market is fraught with misunderstandings and misinformation. IP telephony can impact a company's business model in tremendous ways. It can open new revenue streams, enhance profitability, drive new levels of customer and employee satisfaction, and be a key enabler in a company's strategy to differentiate itself competitively-but only if you're aware of these benefits.

IP Telephony Unveiled is written for all those responsible for corporate strategies for revenue generation, cost containment, and customer satisfaction. *IP Telephony Unveiled* uncovers the value behind this technology, which helps you see past what might appear to be only a new telephone system, to understand the strategic enabler laying dormant in many companies' networks. Through this book, you will understand the real benefits of an IP telephony strategy and get assistance in developing this strategy inside your organization.

This volume is in the Network Business Series offered by Cisco Press. Books in this series provide IT executives, decision makers, and networking professionals with pertinent information on today's most important technologies and business strategies.

CCIE Security

The Road to IP Telephony: How Cisco Systems Migrated from PBX to IP Telephony

Stephanie L. Carhee

1-58720-088-0 • Available Now

There is no better path to the successful implementation of a new technology than to follow in the experienced footsteps of an organization that has already been there. *The Road to IP Telephony* tells you how Cisco Systems successfully moved its own organization to a converged, enterprise-wide network. You will learn the implementation and operational processes, what worked, what didn't work, and how to develop your own successful methodology. After presenting this topic to hundreds of Cisco customers, including Fortune 500 companies, Stephanie Carhee consistently encountered the same question, "If I decide to move to IP Telephony, where do I begin and what can I do to ensure that I do it right the first time?" Although the needs of every enterprise are different, some things are universal; planning, communication, teamwork, and understanding your user's requirements are as important as technical expertise. The Road to IP Telephony shares with you everything you need to know about managing your deployment. It starts with where to begin, including what needs to be addressed before you even begin the planning process, to building your project team. Key best practices are also offered to help you set the project's pace and schedule, get your users on board, identify a migration strategy, develop a services and support strategy, and work toward the final PBX decommission.

"Cisco IT wants to share its implementation experience with Cisco customers and partners to aide in the deployment practices of new Cisco technologies. While conducting our own company-wide cutover, we learned a great deal about what to do and what not to do. This book shares our experiences."
-Brad Boston, Senior Vice President and Chief Information Officer, Cisco Systems, Inc.

This volume is in the Network Business Series offered by Cisco Press. Books in this series provide IT executives, decision makers, and networking professionals with pertinent information on today's most important technologies and business strategies.

Voice over IP Fundamentals

Jonathan Davidson (Editor), James Peters, and Brian Gracely

1-57870-168-6 • Available Now

A systematic approach to understanding the basics of voice over IP

- Understand the basics of PSTN services and IP signaling protocols, including SS7
- Learn how VoIP can run the same applications as the existing telephony system, but in a more cost-efficient and scalable manner
- Delve into such VoIP topics as jitter, latency, packet loss, codecs, quality of service tools, and mean opinion scores
- Learn about the functional components involved in using Cisco gateways to deploy VoIP networks

Voice over IP (VoIP), which integrates voice and data transmission, is quickly becoming an important factor in network communications. It promises lower operational costs, greater flexibility, and a variety of enhanced applications. *Voice over IP Fundamentals* provides a thorough introduction to this new technology to help experts in both the data and telephone industries plan for the new networks.

You will learn how the telephony infrastructure was built and how it works today, the major concepts concerning voice and data networking, transmission of voice over data, and IP signaling protocols used to interwork with current telephony systems. The authors cover various benefits and applications of VoIP and how to ensure good voice quality in your network.

This book is part of the Networking Technology Series from Cisco Press, which offers networking professionals valuable information for constructing efficient networks, understanding new technologies, and building successful careers.

Learning is serious business. **Invest wisely.**

Cisco Press
Learning is serious business.
Invest wisely.

Cisco CallManager Fundamentals

Anne Smith, John Alexander, Chris Pearce, and Delon Whetten

1-58705-008-0 • Available Now

Exposes the inner workings of CallManager to help you maximize your Cisco IP Telephony solution

- Learn how to deploy and manage a CallManager solution
- Understand how CallManager processes information through detailed architectural examples and descriptions
- Understand the components that make up CallManager call routing through the use of basic to advanced examples that solve enterprise call routing problems
- Learn detailed information about North American and international dial plans, trunk and station devices, media resources, managing and monitoring CallManager, and call detail records

Cisco CallManager Fundamentals provides examples and reference information about CallManager, the call processing component of the Cisco AVVID (Architecture for Voice, Video, and Integrated Data) IP Telephony solution. *Cisco CallManager Fundamentals* uses examples and architectural descriptions to explain how CallManager processes calls. This book details the inner workings of CallManager so that those responsible for designing and maintaining a voice over IP (VoIP) solution from Cisco Systems can understand the role each component plays and how they interrelate. You'll learn detailed information about hardware and software components, call routing, media processing, system management and monitoring, and call detail records. The authors, all members of the CallManager group at Cisco Systems, also provide a list of features and Cisco solutions that integrate with CallManager. This book is the perfect resource to supplement your understanding of CallManager.

Deploying Cisco Voice over IP Solutions

Jonathan Davidson, Editor

1-58705-030-7 • Available Now

Deploying Cisco Voice over IP Solutions provides networking professionals the knowledge, advice, and insight necessary to design and deploy voice over IP (VoIP) networks that meet customers' needs for scalability, services, and security. Beginning with an introduction to the important preliminary design elements that need to be considered before implementing VoIP, *Deploying Cisco Voice over IP Solutions* also demonstrates the basic tasks involved in designing an effective service provider-based VoIP network. You'll conclude with design and implementation guidelines for some of the more popular and widely requested VoIP services, such as prepaid services, fax services, and virtual private networks (VPNs).

This book is a collaboration of Cisco Systems CCIE engineers, technical marketing engineers, and systems engineers. You'll find design experience from people who have designed some of the world's largest VoIP networks.

Cisco Press Solutions

Troubleshooting Cisco IP Telephony
Paul Giralt, Addis Hallmark, and Anne Smith

1-58705-075-7 • Available Now

Reveals the methodology you need to resolve complex problems in an IP telephony network

- Master troubleshooting techniques and methodologies for all parts of a Cisco IP Telephony solution-Cisco CallManager, IP phones, gateways, applications, and more
- Learn how to investigate and resolve voice quality problems, including delayed audio, choppy or garbled audio, static and noise, one-way or no-way audio, and echo
- Read about the variety of trouble-shooting tools at your disposal and how and when to use them based on the problem type
- Discover the potential causes of common problems and how to efficiently troubleshoot them to resolution
- Learn how to identify and resolve gateway problems by breaking the components into logical groups and following a methodical troubleshooting approach
- Use best practices recommendations to build a stronger IP telephony deployment and avoid common mistakes

IP telephony represents the future of telecommunications: a converged data and voice infrastructure boasting greater flexibility and more cost-effective scalability than traditional telephony. The ability to troubleshoot an IP telephony environment and the underlying network infrastructure is vitally important, just as it is in any complex system.

Troubleshooting Cisco IP Telephony teaches the troubleshooting skills necessary to identify and resolve problems in an IP telephony solution. This book provides comprehensive coverage of all parts of a Cisco IP Telephony (CIPT) solution, including CallManager, IP phones, gateways, analog devices, database and directory replication, call routing, voice mail, applications, network infrastructure, and more. You'll learn how to read trace files, determine when to turn on tracing and Cisco IOS Software voice debugging, and how to troubleshoot voice quality issues.